ADVANCED PROGRAMMING USING VISUAL BASIC .NET

ADVANCED PROGRAMMING USING VISUAL BASIC .NET

Julia Case Bradley
Mt. San Antonio College

Anita C. Millspaugh
Mt. San Antonio College

Boston   Burr Ridge, IL   Dubuque, IA   Madison, WI   New York   San Francisco   St. Louis
Bangkok   Bogotá   Caracas   Kuala Lumpur   Lisbon   London   Madrid   Mexico City
Milan   Montreal   New Delhi   Santiago   Seoul   Singapore   Sydney   Taipei   Toronto

The McGraw·Hill Companies

 Irwin

ADVANCED PROGRAMMING USING VISUAL BASIC .NET

Published by McGraw-Hill/Irwin, a business unit of The McGraw-Hill Companies, Inc., 1221 Avenue of
the Americas, New York, NY, 10020. Copyright © 2003 by The McGraw-Hill Companies, Inc. All rights
reserved. No part of this publication may be reproduced or distributed in any form or by any means, or
stored in a database or retrieval system, without the prior written consent of The McGraw-Hill Companies,
Inc., including, but not limited to, in any network or other electronic storage or transmission, or broadcast
for distance learning.

Some ancillaries, including electronic and print components, may not be available to customers outside the
United States.

This book is printed on acid-free paper.

domestic   3 4 5 6 7 8 9 0 QPD/QPD 0 9 8 7 6 5 4
international   1 2 3 4 5 6 7 8 9 0 QPD/QPD 0 9 8 7 6 5 4 3

ISBN 0-07-251239-3

Sponsoring editor: *Steve Schuetz*
Developmental editor: *Craig S. Leonard*
Marketing manager: *Greta Kleinert*
Media producer: *Greg Bates*
Senior project manager: *Jean Lou Hess*
Senior production supervisor: *Rose Hepburn*
Coordinator freelance design: *Artemio Ortiz Jr.*
Senior supplement producer: *Rose M. Range*
Senior digital content specialist: *Brian Nacik*
Cover design: *Artemio Ortiz Jr.*
Interior design: *Artemio Ortiz Jr.*
Typeface: *11/13 Bodoni*
Compositor: *GAC Indianapolis*
Printer: *Quebecor World Dubuque Inc.*

Library of Congress Cataloging-in-Publication Data

Bradley, Julia Case.
    Advanced programming using Visual Basic.NET / Julia Case Bradley, Anita C. Milspaugh.
        p. cm.
    ISBN 0-07-251239-3 (alk. paper) -- ISBN 0-07-115143-5 (international : alk. paper)
    1. Microsoft Visual BASIC. 2. BASIC (Computer program language) 3. Microsoft
.NET. I. Millspaugh, A. C. (Anita C.) II. Title.

QA76.76.B3 B73 2003
005.2'768--dc21

                                                    2002041070

INTERNATIONAL EDITION ISBN 0-07-115143-5

Copyright © 2003. Exclusive rights by The McGraw-Hill Companies, Inc. for manufacture and export. This
book cannot be re-exported from the country to which it is sold by McGraw-Hill.

The International Edition is not available in North America.

www.mhhe.com

PREFACE

Visual Basic (VB) has become the most popular programming language for several reasons. VB is easy to learn, which makes it an excellent tool for understanding programming concepts. In addition, it has evolved into such a powerful and popular product that skilled Visual Basic programmers are in demand in the job market.

Visual Basic .NET, the latest version of VB, is practically a new language. Microsoft has completely rewritten the language to be fully object-oriented, compatible with many other languages using the new .NET Framework. This book incorporates the object-oriented concepts throughout, as well as the new syntax and terminology of the language.

Visual Basic .NET is designed to allow the programmer to develop applications that run under Windows and/or in a Web browser without the complexity generally associated with programming.

About This Text

This textbook is intended for use in an advanced programming course, which assumes completion of an introductory course. The text incorporates the basic concepts of programming, problem solving, and programming logic, as well as the design techniques of an object-oriented language.

Approach

Chapter topics are presented in a sequence that allows the programmer to learn how to deal with a visual interface while acquiring important programming skills such as accessing and updating data in a relational database, developing applications for the Web and for mobile devices, and adding browser-based Help files to an application.

The chapters may be used in various sequences to accommodate the needs of the course, as well as a shorter quarter system or a semester-long course.

Changes in This Edition

This edition is a complete rewrite of the previous edition. It presents material in a sequence designed for teaching students and does not attempt to cover all topics for certification exams.

Many topics from the introductory course are presented in greater detail and demand more from the students. Many other advanced topics are presented, including displaying and updating relational databases, Web services, data structures, user controls, Help files, and the Mobile Internet Toolkit.

Features of This Text

Hands-On Programming Examples

These complete programming exercises guide students through the process of planning, writing, and executing Visual Basic programs.

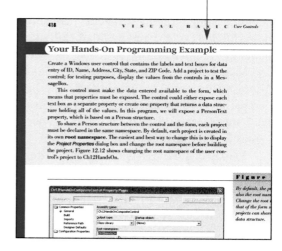

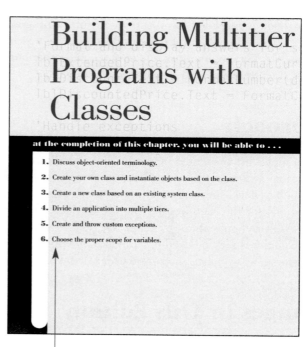

Learning Objectives

These specific objectives tell students what will be covered in the chapter and what they will be able to do after completing the chapter.

Feedback 2.2

1. What is the purpose of property procedures?
2. Why should the property variables of a class be declared as Priva[te]
3. You want to create a new class called Student that inherits from P[erson]. Properties required to create an instance of the class are Last[Name], FirstName, and BirthDate. Write a parameterized constructor f[or the] class.
4. Write the statement(s) to create an instance of the Student class d[efined] in the previous question. Supply the arguments for the paramet[erized] constructor.
5. An error occurs in a class written for the business tier. Explain how to handle the error condition and how the user should be notified.

for your project. The
with a Buttons collec-
with "tlb" for the pre-
[pr]operty of the toolbar.
[A]dd button for the But-
[ton]BarButton Collection

✓ TIP

Add a ToolTip component and set the ToolTip text property for your toolbar buttons so that text descriptions pop up for your users. ■

Feedback Questions

The Feedback Questions give students time to reflect on the current topic and to evaluate their understanding of the details.

TIPs

Tips in the margins help students avoid potential trouble spots in their programs and encourage them to develop good programming habits from the start.

Programming Exercises

The programming exercises test students' understanding of the programming skills covered in the chapter.

Case Studies

The Case Studies provide continuing-theme exercises that may be used throughout the course.

V I S U A L   B A S I C   *Web Forms Database*

Case Studies

Claytor's Cottages

1. Modify the Web application for the Chapter 6 case study. Add a page that displays the guest information in a data grid that allows for sorting by last name and by last visit date. Include pagination. Modify the room pages to include the information from the database.

(You created the page with static text in Chapter 6; now it's time to connect it to a data source.)
2. Modify the project to use a separate data tier component.

Christian's Car Rentals

1. Modify the Web application for the Chapter 6 Car Rental case study. Add a Web page that contains a list of the vehicles by manufacturer and model. When the user selects an item from the list, display the details for that car on a separate page. Include a Select button that transfers control to a Billing page. The Billing page should include the daily rate for the vehicle and rental terms. It also must collect customer information:

name, address, city, state, ZIP, credit card type (from a drop-down list), account number, and a phone number.
Allow navigation across all pages and maintain all values entered by the user.
2. Modify the project to use a separate data tier component.

Programming Exercises

2.1 Tricia's Travels: You can add to your Exercise 1.3 or just create the main form.

Presentation Tier

Main Form—Monthly Specials
Include text boxes for the customer name, phone number, number traveling, departure date, return date, and credit card number. Include a list box for the destinations: Caribbean, Mediterranean, and Alaska. Include radio buttons for 7-day or 14-day packages and a check box for first class. Validate that the user has made an entry for all fields.

Summary Form
Display the total price.

Business Tier

Calculate the amount due based on the following schedule:

Days	Destination	Standard price	First-class price
7	Caribbean	3250	5000
14	Caribbean	6000	9000
7	Mediterranean	4250	7999
14	Mediterranean	7999	11999
7	Alaska	3300	5250
14	Alaska	7200	10500

2.2 Kenna's Kandles offers candles in various shapes, scents, and colors. Write an MDI project that contains a Main form, an About form, and a Summary form using a separate tier for the business rules.

Presentation Tier

Main Form

- Text boxes for customer information (name and credit card number).
- Text box for quantity.
- Radio buttons or list box for candle style (tea light, votive, or pillar).

Chapter Organization

Each chapter begins with identifiable objectives and a brief overview. Numerous coding examples as well as hands-on projects with guidance for the coding appear throughout. Thought-provoking feedback questions give students time to reflect on the current topic and to evaluate their understanding of the details. The end-of-chapter items include a chapter review, questions, programming exercises, and two case studies. The case studies provide a continuing-theme exercise that may be used throughout the course. The in-chapter programs are included on the student CD, allowing the student to test and modify existing code. Of course, it is also important to develop a complete application from scratch to really learn the programming techniques.

Chapter 1, "Visual Studio .NET," discusses the features of the Visual Studio IDE and the .NET Framework. Applications demonstrate how to display data from the AssemblyInfo.vb file. MDI projects, toolbars, and status bars are reviewed.

Chapter 2, "Building Multitier Programs with Classes," reviews object-oriented terminology, creating classes, and instantiating objects. Creating and throwing exceptions from the business tier is introduced.

Chapter 3, "Windows Database Applications," explains the relationship of datasets, tables, rows, and constraints. Database applications use the SQLServerClient data provider to display information in grids, combo boxes, and labels.

Chapter 4, "Windows Database Using Related Tables," explores the types of table relationships. The chapter discusses how to retrieve and display the parent row for a selected child row and also an array of child rows for a selected parent row.

Chapter 5, "Windows Database Updates," uses the form's binding context to navigate records. Updates are performed on a grid and for bound controls on a form. Updating related tables is also covered.

Chapter 6, "Using Web Forms—ASP.NET," discusses the concepts of Web-based applications and the files that make up a Web project. Hyperlinks and link buttons allow navigation from one Web page to another while maintaining the state (data values).

Chapter 7, "Web Forms Database," introduces the data reader as an alternative to the data adapter. Pagination for a DataGrid is demonstrated. The DataList control displays data using data-bound template fields. The concept of multitier applications is applied to a Web project.

Chapter 8, "Related Database Tables and Updates in Web Forms," covers the techniques for displaying data from related tables on Web Forms. Updating database records provides an opportunity to introduce writing and executing SQL statements directly to a database.

Chapter 9, "Web Services," discusses the concepts of Web services. Examples for Web services include calculations and data access.

Chapter 10, "Writing Database Reports Using Crystal Reports," uses many reporting features, such as numeric functions, grouping, sorting, and special fields. Both Windows applications and Web applications are covered.

Chapter 11, "Using Collections," discusses types of collections including stacks, queues, dictionaries, hash tables, sorted lists, and array lists. The chapter demonstrates adding and manipulating objects in the Items collection of a list box.

Chapter 12, "User Controls," creates Windows user controls and Web controls. The techniques for raising an event and writing code in the form to handle the event are covered.

Chapter 13, "Creating Help Files," creates the necessary files to set up HTML Help and uses HTML Help Workshop to create a Help file.

Chapter 14, "Looking Ahead," demonstrates how to install and use the Microsoft Mobile Internet Toolkit. The steps for localizing an application and using threads are also covered.

The Appendices offer important additional material. Appendix A holds the answers to all Feedback questions. Appendix B is an extensive review of VB .NET topics generally covered in an introductory course. Appendix C gives step-by-step instructions for installing MSDE (the SQL Server desktop version), and Appendix D is a primer for writing SQL statements. Appendix E contains many helpful tips and shortcuts for mastering the Visual Studio environment.

Resources for Instructors

Instructor's Manual   The Instructor's Manual is available on CD-ROM or on the book's Web site. It contains the following features:

- Objectives with built-in summaries for each chapter.

- Teaching suggestions.

- Answers to the Review Questions from the back of each chapter.

- Chapter topics covered in the Programming Exercises.

Testbank   The Testbank provides questions that cover the terminology and concepts found in each chapter. The test questions appear in the form of true/false and multiple-choice questions.

Diploma by Brownstone   Diploma is the most flexible, powerful, and easy-to-use computer-based testing system available for higher education. The Diploma system allows instructors to create an exam as a printed version, as a LAN-based online version, or as an Internet version. Diploma also includes grade book features, which automate the entire testing process.

PowerPoint Presentation   The PowerPoint presentation follows the outline of the Instructor's Manual and gives instructors a resource for presenting the text material to a classroom.

Figures from the Book   All of the illustrations, screenshots, and tables are available electronically for use in presentations, transparencies, or handouts.

Online Learning Center   (www.mhhe.com/cit/program/bradley/advanced vbnet) Designed to provide a wide variety of learning opportunities for students, the Web site includes additional Case Studies, Self-Quizzes for students, down-loadable data files, and other great resources for both instructors and students.

Digital Solutions to Help You Manage Your Course

PageOut   PageOut is our Course Website Development Center that offers a syllabus page, URL, McGraw-Hill Online Learning Center content, online exercises and quizzes, gradebook, discussion board, and an area for student Web pages.

Available free with any McGraw-Hill/Irwin product, PageOut requires no prior knowledge of HTML, no long hours of coding, and a way for course coordinators and professors to provide a full-course Web site. PageOut offers a series of templates—simply fill them with your course information and click on one of 16 designs. The process takes under an hour and leaves you with a professionally designed Web site. We'll even get you started with sample Web sites, or enter your syllabus for you! PageOut is so straightforward and intuitive, it's little wonder that more than 12,000 college professors are using it. For more information, visit the PageOut Web site at www.pageout.net.

The Online Learning Center can be delivered through any of these platforms:

McGraw-Hill Learning Architecture (TopClass)

Blackboard.com

Ecollege.com (formerly Real Education)

WebCT (a product of Universal Learning Technology)

McGraw-Hill has partnerships with WebCT and Blackboard to make it even easier to take your course online. Now you can have McGraw-Hill content delivered through the leading Internet-based learning tool for higher education. At McGraw-Hill, we have the following service agreements with WebCT and Blackboard:

Instructor Advantage   Instructor Advantage is a special level of service McGraw-Hill offers in conjunction with WebCT designed to help you get up and running with your new course. A team of specialists will be immediately available to ensure everything runs smoothly through the life of your adoption.

Instructor Advantage Plus   Qualified McGraw-Hill adopters will be eligible for an even higher level of service. A certified WebCT or Blackboard specialist will provide a full day of on-site training for you and your staff. You will then have unlimited e-mail and phone support through the life of your adoption. Contact your local McGraw-Hill representative for more details.

Acknowledgments

We would like to express our appreciation to the many people who have contributed to the successful completion of this text. Most especially, we thank the students at Mt. San Antonio College and Theresa Berry who helped class-test the material and who greatly influenced the manuscript.

Many people have worked very hard to design and produce this text. We would like to thank our editors, Steve Schuetz and Craig Leonard, and the publisher, George Werthman. Our thanks also to the many people who produced this text including Jean Lou Hess and Artemio Ortiz.

We greatly appreciate Theresa Berry and Robert Price for their thorough technical reviews, constructive criticism, and many valuable suggestions. Wesley Davis provided a great contribution by writing the exercise solutions. And most importantly, we are grateful to Dennis and Richard for their support and understanding through the long days and busy phone lines.

The Authors

We have had fun teaching and writing about Visual Basic. We hope that this feeling is evident as you read this book and that you will enjoy learning or teaching this outstanding programming language.

Both of us have taught courses in beginning and advanced Visual Basic for several years at Mt. San Antonio College. We have also taught Visual Basic at the National Computer Educator's Institute at the University of Central Oklahoma.

Julia Bradley developed the Faculty Computing Center at Mt. San Antonio College and acted as director during the first year of operation. Anita Millspaugh served as the department chair of Computer Information Systems for several years.

Julia Case Bradley

Anita C. Millspaugh

TO THE STUDENT

Welcome to the exciting new features of Visual Basic .NET. You have probably already learned that the best way to learn how to program is to actually sit at a computer and code, change things, and test it again. Stepping through existing code is also a great tool in learning new techniques. With that in mind, we have included all of the code from the examples within the chapters on your student CD. Please feel free to load the programs, change things, and test it again.

But . . . if you really want to learn how it works, it is critical that you create a blank project and try the techniques yourself. If you run into a problem, take a look at the sample and compare properties and code.

There are several tools in this text to help you on your way.

- Each chapter begins with a list of topics and ends with a summary. Combine these for a thumbnail review of the chapter. Understanding the terminology is an important part of learning any new language, which is also true with programming languages.

- A list of key terms is at the end of each chapter. Each of those terms is in boldface within the chapter. There is also a glossary at the end of the text where you can look up the definition of the terms.

- Test yourself with the feedback questions as you work through each section of a chapter. The review questions at the end of the chapter can test your understanding of the topics.

- Tips are included to give suggestions in situations where you may run into problems caused by the version of software installed/not installed or with settings.

- Make sure to check out the appendices, which hold a wealth of support material.

J.C.B.

A.C.M.

Student Data Files

The student data files are located on the CD-ROM that accompanies the text and also on the text's Web site. The following table lists the student data files:

Readme.txt

Access Database Files—*folder*

  Access files that can be used in place of the SQL Server files;
    for the in-chapter examples and programming exercises.

    RnRBooks.mdb

    Northwind.mdb

    Pubs.mdb

    Cottages.mdb

    Cars.mdb

SQL Server Files—*folder*

  SQL Server files for the programming exercises.

    InstallingSQLServerFiles.txt

     Instructions for installing the SQL Server files in MSDE.

    RnRBooks.mdf

    Cottages.mdf

    Cars.mdf

Graphics—*folder*

  Graphics for HTML pages in Chapter 13 and for About forms in
  various chapters.

    ReadingAndRefreshment.gif

    RnR.gif

    RnRLogo.gif

    RnRLogo.jpg

Ch13SBS—*folder*

  Ch13SBSHelp—*folder*

    Project files for the in-chapter step-by-step exercise

  HTML—*folder*

    HTML files for the in-chapter step-by-step exercise

CONTENTS

1

Visual Studio .NET

at the completion of this chapter, you will be able to . . .

1. Distinguish the features of the Visual Studio IDE versus the .NET Framework.

2. Identify and understand the purpose of each of the files listed in the Solution Explorer.

3. Understand what happens at compile time.

4. Display data from the assembly attributes in AssemblyInfo.vb.

5. Recognize features from the VB6 compatibility library and why you should avoid them.

6. Create an MDI project with a parent form, child forms, a toolbar, status bar, context menu, and ToolTips.

Microsoft has revolutionized the programming for Windows applications and has become a bigger player in the development of Web applications with the introduction of the .NET Framework and Visual Studio .NET. These new products introduce significant changes into program development for Visual Basic. Not only does .NET bring true object-orientation to the language, it also provides great advances in the ease of developing projects for cross-platform compatibility.

Two major parts of .NET are the Microsoft .NET Framework Software Development Kit (SDK) and the Visual Studio Integrated Development Environment (IDE). The IDE is used to develop programs while the Framework runs the programs.

The .NET Framework

The **.NET Framework** provides a platform for developing and running applications and XML Web Services written in multiple languages on multiple platforms. The Framework is composed of the common language runtime, class libraries, and ASP.NET—a component-based version of active server pages (ASP).

Common Language Runtime

The **common language runtime (CLR)** is an environment that manages execution of code. It provides services for tasks such as integrating components developed in different languages, handling errors across languages, handling security, and managing the storage and destruction of objects.

Any code that is compiled to run in the CLR is called ***managed code***. The managed code automatically contains **metadata**, which means *data that describe data*. A common language runtime portable executable (PE) file contains the metadata along with the code. The metadata include data types, members, references, and information needed to load classes and to call methods from a class.

The CLR also manages data storage. Objects that are no longer being used are automatically removed from memory by the garbage collector component of the CLR. When you allow the runtime to handle the garbage collection of objects, the data are referred to as ***managed data***. Although you *can* manage the memory of your data, it is usually better to let the runtime handle it.

Your code can be integrated with classes and methods of managed code written in other programming languages. The CLR has standards for data types allowing you to pass an instance of one of your classes to a method created in a different language. Although we will not be doing any cross-language programming in this text, you should be aware of this powerful feature.

Class Library

All of the classes and interfaces that are a part of the .NET language are stored in a library known as the **.NET Framework class library**. The library is divided into sections or groups known as *namespaces*. You should be familiar with some of the common namespaces such as *System* and *System.Drawing*. Each namespace contains classes, structures, enumerations, delegates, and/or inter-

Table 1.1

Namespace	Contents
System	Base classes and fundamental classes for data types, events, and event handlers.
System.Collections	Definitions of collections of objects such as lists, queues, and dictionaries.
System.Data	ADO.NET architecture.
System.Drawing	GDI+ graphics.
System.IO	Types for reading and writing data streams and files.
System.Security	Base classes for permissions.
System.Threading	Classes for multithreaded programming.
System.Web.Services	Classes for building and using Web Services.
System.Windows.Forms	Classes for creating graphical components for programs that execute in the Windows operating system.
System.XML	Support for XML processing. XML is a standard for transferring data.

Selected namespaces from the .NET class library

faces that you can use in your programs. Table 1.1 shows some of the namespaces in the .NET Framework class library.

The classes in the library comply with published standards known as the **Common Language Specification (CLS)**. The CLS specifies how a language that interacts with the CLR should behave. If you want your programs to interact with programs and components written in other languages, you should make sure that they are CLS-compliant. The rules for CLS compliance can be found in the .NET Framework Developer's Guide under the heading "What Is the Common Language Specification?"

Types

The .NET documentation uses the general term *types* to refer to the classes, structures, enumerations, delegates, interfaces, and data types in the library, as well as any that you define. You can think of a type as any element that you can use in the As clause of a declaration:

```
Dim AnyName As SomeType
```

Value Types versus Reference Types

When you declare a variable, it may be considered a **value type** or a **reference type**. The difference between the two determines how the runtime will treat the variables when you assign one variable to another. For example, if you assign one integer variable to another, you have two memory locations with the same value:

```
intSecondValue = intFirstValue
```

However, if you assign one reference type to another, you have two variables
that point to the same object in memory:

```
frmSecondForm = frmFirstForm      'Assign reference for first form to second form
```

Any changes that you make to either variable are made to the one object in
memory to which both variables refer. In previous versions of VB, reference
types were called *object variables*. However, VB .NET reference types include
more types than the object variables of VB 6.

```
'Value types
Dim intFirstValue As Integer = 10
Dim intSecondValue As Integer
intSecondValue = intFirstValue
intFirstValue = 5
Debug.WriteLine("intFirstValue = " & intFirstValue.ToString() & _
  "; intSecondValue = " & intSecondValue.ToString())

'Reference types
Dim frmFirstForm As New Form1()
Dim frmSecondForm As Form1
frmSecondForm = frmFirstForm      'Assign reference for first form to second form
frmSecondForm.Text = "Second Form Caption"
frmFirstForm.Text = "New Caption for First Form"
'What is the Text property of frmFirstForm? Of frmSecondForm?
Debug.WriteLine("frmFirstForm = " & frmFirstForm.Text & _
  "; frmSecondForm = " & frmSecondForm.Text)
```

All numeric data types are value types. Reference types include class types, arrays (even if the individual elements are numeric), and strings. A value type
always holds a value; when you declare a new variable of a value type, the
variable is always initialized, either to a value that you supply or to the default value. A reference type may or may not hold a value; you can use the
IsNothing function to determine whether the variable refers to an actual
object.

Compiling to Intermediate Language

The program code that you write is referred to as *source code*. The compiler
translates your code into **Microsoft intermediate language (MSIL)** or
sometimes referred to as just *IL*. MSIL is a platform-independent set of instructions that is combined with the metadata to form a file called a *portable executable* (PE) file, which has an .exe or .dll extension. When your program runs,
the MSIL is converted to the native code of the specific machine using a just-
in-time (JIT) compiler, which is part of the CLR (Figure 1.1).

Figure 1.1

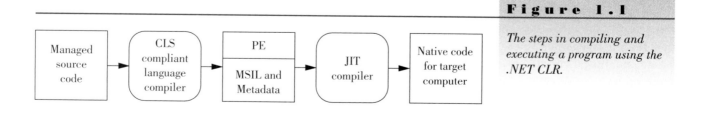

The steps in compiling and executing a program using the .NET CLR.

Assemblies

An **assembly** is a basic unit of code that may be a single PE file or multiple files. Each of your applications will be contained in a single assembly, which is the smallest deployable piece of code. An assembly has an **assembly manifest** that contains metadata about the version, a table describing all of the files needed by the assembly, and an "assembly reference list" that specifies all of the external files needed, such as DLLs created by someone else. An assembly is similar to an exe or a dll file written in earlier versions of Visual Basic—it contains all of the necessary information to run the application or component.

Recall that the .NET Framework class library is not one big file but rather a collection of files. The classes are stored in many files with the extension .dll and referred to as *DLLs* (for dynamic link libraries). Each of the DLLs in the class library is one assembly. As your program begins execution, only the needed assemblies are loaded into memory. When you want to use a type that is not already referenced, you must add a reference to the DLL (assembly).

Attributes

Attributes are tags containing information about parts of a program such as types or methods. The system defines many attributes of your assembly, such as the name, version, culture, and security. The attributes are part of the metadata in a .NET assembly. The process of examining the metadata in an assembly's attributes is called *reflection*.

Later in this chapter you will learn to retrieve and use the custom attributes in a project's AssemblyInfo file.

References Collection

A **reference object** is used to connect a Visual Basic project to external components. The two types of reference objects are assemblies and COM objects. A reference to another project is an assembly reference and is called *a project-to-project reference*. COM objects are components written in previous versions of VB or other non-CLS-compliant languages.

ASP.NET

Another big part of the .NET world is the improvement in Web development. ASP.NET is the newest version of **Active Server Pages (ASP)**. It is a Web development environment that can compile applications written in any .NET-compatible language including Visual Basic. This means that the benefits of the common language runtime and managed code are available for developing Web applications. ASP.NET makes Web development easier by providing the same debugging support for Web Forms and Web Services as for Windows applications.

You will begin working with ASP.NET in Chapter 6. Chapters 7 and 8 cover accessing databases from ASP.NET, which is a common technique for displaying data on a Web site.

Feedback 1.1

1. What is meant by the term *.NET Framework*?
2. What is the meaning and function of each of these terms?
   a. CLR   b. CLS   c. MSIL   d. PE

Visual Studio .NET

Although you could write your programs in any editor and then use the SDK to compile them, Visual Studio provides an environment to make your development task easier. You should already be familiar with the various windows in the environment as well as the basic debugging capabilities. For a review of the VS IDE, see Appendix E. This section introduces you to more details about the parts of a project.

Solution Explorer Files

Take a look at the files in the Solution Explorer for a Windows application (Figure 1.2). The files that you start with depend on the type of the project. When you click on the *Show All Files* button, you can see the hidden files and folders. You can see the References collection, the bin folder, the obj folder, the AssemblyInfo.vb file, the Form1.vb file, and the Form1.resx file. Expand each of the nodes to see more details. Notice that the obj folder contains a temporary PE folder. All of your compiled exe files are stored in the bin folder when you compile a project.

The Bin Folder

When your program compiles without errors—a clean compile—the resulting .exe or .dll file is stored in the bin folder. Notice in Figure 1.2 that the bin

Figure 1.2

Click the Show All Files *button to see all of the files and folders in the Solution Explorer.*

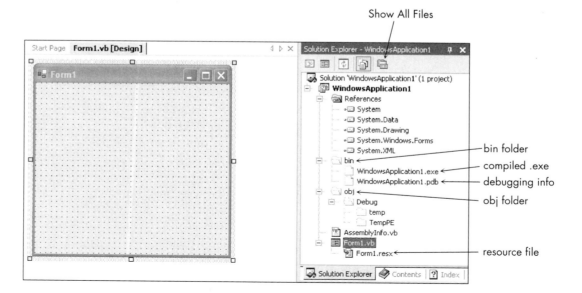

folder holds an .exe file and a .pdb file. The .exe or .dll file is the executable, which is used to run your program. The .pdb file holds debugging information. If you are distributing your application, you only need to distribute the .exe or .dll file, not the .pdb file.

If your program accesses the Application.StartupPath property, perhaps to store or retrieve a saved text file, the StartupPath points to the bin folder.

References

In the References folder you can see a list of System libraries (DLLs) such as System, System.Data, System.Drawing, System.Windows.Forms, and System.XML. You can add a reference by right-clicking on the References folder and selecting *Add Reference* from the context menu. You may need to add a reference if you want to refer to objects in another assembly or components written in a different language.

The Form's .resx File

Each form in your project has a resource file with a .resx extension and the same name as the form file. For example, Form1.vb has a Form1.resx file, which you can see in the Solution Explorer when you click on the *Show All Files* button. If you rename your form file in the Solution Explorer, the .resx file is automatically renamed to match. At times you can get into trouble if you have already compiled the program and the file is not automatically renamed, or if a new .resx file is created by the IDE. You can safely delete any extra .resx files if their names do not match any forms in the project.

The .resx file is mostly text in XML format, which you can open and view in the IDE. Any graphic elements that you add to the form, such as a Picture-Box's Image property or a Form's Icon property, are also stored in the .resx file in text that represents the binary graphic file. It's the .resx file that supplies the graphics to the form at compile time.

AssemblyInfo.vb

Each project has an *AssemblyInfo.vb* file that contains many attributes with information about your application. This is the standard file that is generated by default:

```
Imports System.Reflection
Imports System.Runtime.InteropServices

'General Information about an assembly is controlled through the following
'set of attributes. Change these attribute values to modify the information
'associated with an assembly.

'Review the values of the assembly attributes

<Assembly: AssemblyTitle("")>
<Assembly: AssemblyDescription("")>
<Assembly: AssemblyCompany("")>
<Assembly: AssemblyProduct("")>
<Assembly: AssemblyCopyright("")>
<Assembly: AssemblyTrademark("")>
<Assembly: CLSCompliant(True)>
```

```
'The following GUID is for the ID of the typelib if this project is exposed to COM
<Assembly: Guid("919A14A8-2540-4EDA-BAB6-9183818A0774")>

'Version information for an assembly consists of the following four values:
'
'    Major Version
'    Minor Version
'    Build Number
'    Revision
'
'You can specify all the values or you can default the Build and Revision Numbers
'by using the '*' as shown below:
<Assembly: AssemblyVersion("1.0.*")>
```

Notice the attributes for the version, the company, the product, the copyright, and the trademark. You can give these attributes values at design time and retrieve them at run time. You might want to retrieve and display the attribute values on a splash screen or an About form.

For the version attribute, you can enter any value you wish. By default, Visual Studio sets the version to "1.0.*", which means that you want the compiler to automatically increment the version. For example, increment from 1.0.1 to 1.0.2 and then 1.0.3.

Viewing a Project's Attributes After you enter custom attributes in the AssemblyInfo.vb file and compile your project, you can view the attributes in Windows Explorer. Point to the filename in the project's bin folder, either an .exe or .dll file, right-click, and choose *Properties* from the context menu. Display the *Version* tab to see the attributes (Figure 1.3). In Windows XP it's even easier: Point to the filename and pause; the attributes pop up automatically.

F i g u r e   1 . 3

Display the application's attributes in Windows Explorer.

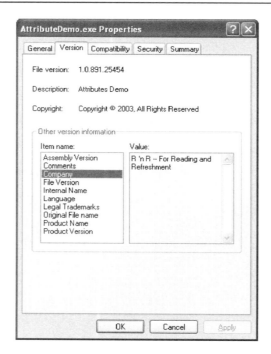

Retrieving Attributes To retrieve assembly attributes in a VB program, you should first import the System.Reflection namespace. Then you can declare an **Assembly object**. Note that *Assembly* is a reserved word; you must use brackets around the word to use *Assembly* as a class name, but the editor adds the brackets for you in a Dim statement.

```
'VB program code
Imports System.Reflection        'Place this statement before the class header

'Declare the variable and instantiate it in a procedure
Dim asmInfo As [Assembly]
'Retrieve the assembly information for this project
asmInfo = [Assembly].Load("ProjectName") 'Where ProjectName is the name of this project
```

Note that ProjectName is actually the name of your assembly, which by default is the same as the name of your project. But if you rename your project, the assembly name does not automatically change to the new name. You can change the project's assembly name in the *Project Properties* dialog box.

You can display the FullName property of an assembly, which gives information about the version:

```
lblInfo.Text = asmInfo.FullName
```

The preceding line of code produces this string: "ProjectName, Version = 1.0.891.19636, Culture = neutral, PublicKeyToken = null"

Retrieving Custom Attributes Most of the attributes in the AssemblyInfo.vb file are considered custom attributes. You can retrieve attributes such as Title and Description by setting up an array of objects and using the GetCustomAttributes method of the Attribute object.

```
Dim objAttributes() As Object                     'Declare an array of objects
objAttributes = asmInfo.GetCustomAttributes(False) 'Argument is ignored. Use true or false
```

To display an array element, you must declare an object of the correct attribute class and assign the corresponding array element to the new object. For example, to retrieve the Product attribute, you declare an AssemblyProductAttribute object.

```
Dim atrProduct As AssemblyProductAttribute
atrProduct = CType(objAssembly(n), AssemblyProductAttribute)
```

You can find the complete list of attribute types in MSDN under "System.Reflection." This is a partial list of some of the more useful attributes:

AssemblyCompanyAttribute
AssemblyCopyrightAttribute
AssemblyDescriptionAttribute
AssemblyProductAttribute
AssemblyTitleAttribute

AssemblyTrademarkAttribute
AssemblyVersionAttribute

If `Option Strict` is on, you must convert the array element to an object of
the appropriate type. And the sequence of items in the array can vary, so you
must check the type of each array element to determine its attribute type. Use
a `For Each` loop and a `Select Case` to retrieve the attributes you want.

```
Dim objItem As Object
'Convert from object to desired types
'Need Select Case because order of attributes in array varies
For Each objItem In objAttributes
    Select Case objItem.GetType.ToString()
        Case "System.Reflection.AssemblyTitleAttribute"
            atrTitle = CType(objItem, AssemblyTitleAttribute)
            lblTitle.Text = atrTitle.Title.ToString()
        Case "System.Reflection.AssemblyCompanyAttribute"
            atrCompany = CType(objItem, AssemblyCompanyAttribute)
            lblCompany.Text = atrCompany.Company.ToString()
        Case "System.Reflection.AssemblyProductAttribute"
            atrProduct = CType(objItem, AssemblyProductAttribute)
            lblProduct.Text = "We Sell: " & atrProduct.Product.ToString()
        Case "System.Reflection.AssemblyCopyrightAttribute"
            atrCopyright = CType(objItem, AssemblyCopyrightAttribute)
            lblCopyright.Text = atrCopyright.Copyright.ToString()
    End Select
Next
```

Test It Now it's time to try implementing some of these techniques by writing a
program that displays attributes from the AssemblyInfo.vb file on a form.

Open a new Project in Visual Basic and open the default AssemblyInfo.vb
file. Modify the code by inserting the following text:

```
<Assembly: AssemblyTitle("Attributes Demo")>
<Assembly: AssemblyDescription("Displays info from the AssemblyInfo.vb")>
<Assembly: AssemblyCompany("R 'n R - For Reading and Refreshment")>
<Assembly: AssemblyProduct("Books and Drinks")>
<Assembly: AssemblyCopyright("Copyright © 2003, All Rights Reserved")>
```

You can also change the Trademark information if you wish.

On the form add labels for Full Name, Title, Description, Company, Product, and Copyright. Write the code to assign values to the labels in the
Form_Load event procedure.

```
'Project:       Attributes
'Programmer:    Bradley/Millspaugh
'Date:          January 2003
'Description:   Retrieve and display assembly attribute data

Option Strict On
Imports System.Reflection

Public Class frmMain
    Inherits System.Windows.Forms.Form
```

```vb
Private Sub frmMain_Load(ByVal sender As System.Object, _
    ByVal e As System.EventArgs) Handles MyBase.Load
        'Display attribute information
        Dim objAttributes() As Object
        Dim asmInfo As [Assembly]
        Dim atrTitle As AssemblyTitleAttribute
        Dim atrCompany As AssemblyCompanyAttribute
        Dim atrProduct As AssemblyProductAttribute
        Dim atrCopyright As AssemblyCopyrightAttribute

        asmInfo = [Assembly].Load("AttributeDemo")
        lblFullName.Text = "Assembly FullName:" & asmInfo.FullName
        objAttributes = asmInfo.GetCustomAttributes(False)
        Dim objItem As Object
        'Convert from object to desired types
        'Need Select Case because order of attributes in array varies
        For Each objItem In objAttributes
            Select Case objItem.GetType.ToString()
                Case "System.Reflection.AssemblyTitleAttribute"
                    atrTitle = CType(objItem, AssemblyTitleAttribute)
                    lblTitle.Text = atrTitle.Title.ToString()
                Case "System.Reflection.AssemblyCompanyAttribute"
                    atrCompany = CType(objItem, AssemblyCompanyAttribute)
                    lblCompany.Text = atrCompany.Company.ToString()
                Case "System.Reflection.AssemblyProductAttribute"
                    atrProduct = CType(objItem, AssemblyProductAttribute)
                    lblProduct.Text = "We Sell:" & atrProduct.Product.ToString()
                Case "System.Reflection.AssemblyCopyrightAttribute"
                    atrCopyright = CType(objItem, AssemblyCopyrightAttribute)
                    lblCopyright.Text = atrCopyright.Copyright.ToString()
            End Select
        Next
    End Sub
```

Web Assembly Files

Web projects also contain the AssemblyInfo.vb file. You can use the same techniques to display the attribute information on a Web Form.

```vb
'Project:      WebAttributes
'Programmer:   Bradley/Millspaugh
'Date:         January 2003
'Description   Retrieve and display assembly attribute data

Option Strict On
Imports System.Reflection

Public Class WebForm1
    Inherits System.Web.UI.Page
    Protected WithEvents lblTrademark As System.Web.UI.WebControls.Label

    Private Sub Page_Load(ByVal sender As System.Object, _
        ByVal e As System.EventArgs) Handles MyBase.Load
        'Access assembly information

        Dim objAttributes() As Object
        Dim asmInfo As [Assembly]
```

```
     Dim atrTrademark As AssemblyTrademarkAttribute
     Dim objItem As Object

     asmInfo = [Assembly].Load("WebAttributes")
     objAttributes = asmInfo.GetCustomAttributes(True)
     'Convert from object to the desired type
     'Need Select Case because order in array varies
     For Each objItem In objAttributes
         Select Case objItem.GetType.ToString()
             Case "System.Reflection.AssemblyTrademarkAttribute"
                 atrTrademark = CType(objItem, AssemblyTrademarkAttribute)
                 lblTrademark.Text = atrTrademark.Trademark.ToString()
         End Select
     Next
 End Sub
```

Deploying Applications

Most of this text is devoted to writing and testing applications using the VS IDE. However, once you get an application tested and ready for use, you will want to deploy it and run it on another computer. To run a .NET Windows application, the target computer must have the .NET Framework or the .NET Framework Redistributable installed. The Redistributable file is available on the Components CD of VS.NET in the DotNetFramework folder as dotnetfx.exe, and a free download on Microsoft's Web site. It is available for Windows 98, ME, NT, 2000, and XP. Notice that you can run .NET applications on Windows 98 and ME, even though the VS .NET IDE does not run on those operating systems.

You can choose from two methods for deploying your applications: (*1*) XCopy deployment or (*2*) Windows Installer technology. Microsoft Windows Installer is a separate application that ships with Windows and creates .msi files.

XCopy deployment gets its name from the old DOS XCOPY command, which copied all files in the current folder and all subfolders. Although you *can* use the XCOPY command for copying files, XCopy deployment in .NET simply means that you copy the necessary files from the development machine to the target machine.

Deploying a compiled Windows application can be as easy as copying the .exe file from the bin folder to another computer. However, deploying a Web application is a little more complicated because more than one file is needed to run an application.

To copy a Web application for deployment, you can manually copy the files you need or use the *Project / Copy Project* command (which appears on the menu only for Web projects). The files that you need to copy are at least *.aspx, global.asax, web.config, *.dll from the bin folder, and any images used by the application. If you use the *Project / Copy Project* command, all necessary files are copied to the destination that you choose. If you copy the project to a new folder in Inewpub/wwwroot on the host machine, the virtual directory is created for you. But if you copy to another location or move the project to another machine, you must set up the virtual directory in IIS. See Appendix E for help with setting up a virtual directory.

You can run a copied (deployed) project by typing its URL into the browser. For example, if you use *Project / Copy Project* to copy a Web project to a folder named RnrCustomers and a startup page of Main.aspx to Inetpub/wwwroot, type this URL into the browser:

```
http://localhost/RnrCustomers/Main.aspx
```

Feedback 1.2

Write the statements necessary to retrieve and display the copyright attribute in a label called lblCopyright.

Helpful Hints for .NET

Some of the new features of .NET can be handy for enhancing your projects. You have control over the form such as setting a default font and specifying the minimum and maximum sizes of the form.

Default Font

You can set a default font for your form, which applies to all controls on the form that do not have a font specifically assigned. You can set the form's Font property at design time or run time, either before or after adding controls to the form. As long as you don't set the Font property for an individual control, it will use the form's font. To change the form's default font in code, you can include a line similar to this one, generally in the Form_Load event procedure.

```
Me.Font = New Font("Arial", 14, FontStyle.Underline)
```

Form Size

.NET allows you to set a minimum and/or maximum size for your form. Your user can resize only within the limits that you allow. You can set the Minimum-Size and MaximumSize properties at design time or in code.

```
Me.MinimumSize = New Size(200,200)
Me.MaximumSize = New Size(500,500)
```

VB6 Compatibility Library

When Microsoft upgraded VB from version 6 to .NET, they removed many features, so that VB code would be consistent for all CLR languages. Then they gave you a way to access many of the obsolete VB 6 features: the VB6 compatibility library. If you try to open a VB 6 application in VS .NET, the Upgrade

Wizard opens and attempts to convert your program from VB 6 to VB .NET. After the conversion you can look through your code and see that the wizard incorporated many features of the VB6 compatibility library and likely inserted some comments about statements that couldn't be converted. The code looks bad, is inefficient, and may not run in future versions of VB. This statement comes directly from the MSDN Help files that accompany Visual Studio:

> **Caution**   *Functions in the Visual Basic 6.0 Compatibility library are provided only for use by the upgrading tools. Although it is possible to use this library when writing new code, there is no guarantee that it will be supported in future versions of Visual Basic.*

So, although you can use the old functions, it is not a good idea to do so. One example is the MsgBox function from VB 6. Although the Upgrade Wizard will keep the MsgBox statements, you should always use the new MessageBox object.

If you want to make sure that you are not using any features of the VB6 compatibility library, check the *References* node of the Solution Explorer and the *Imports* node in the *Project Properties* dialog box. If you find *Microsoft. VisualBasic.Compatibility* listed, delete it and see what error messages are generated.

Many professionals agree that the Upgrade Wizard causes more problems than it solves and should be avoided.

Review Topics

This section is intended as a review for the chapter hands-on exercise that follows. You will create an MDI (multiple document interface) project with parent and child forms, a toolbar, and a status bar.

MDI

This short section is intended as a quick review of MDI in VB .NET. For a more in-depth review of MDI parent forms and child forms, see Appendix B.

- You can make any form into a parent form by setting its IsMdiContainer property to True. You can do this at design time.

- Make a form into a child form by setting its MdiParent property to the parent form. You must do this in code.

```
Dim frmChildOne As New frmChildOne()
frmChildOne.MdiParent = Me
frmChildOne.Show()
```

- A project can have multiple parent forms, multiple child forms, and forms that are independent. You may want to consider independent forms for such tasks as a splash form.

- When you close a parent form, all of its children also close.

- A child cannot wander outside of its parent's area.

The Window Menu

A parent form should have a *Window* menu to list the open child windows and to allow the user to arrange multiple child windows. For an example, look at the *Window* menu in Word; you will see a list of the open documents as well as options for arranging the windows.

To make a menu show a list of the open child windows, set the MdiList property to True for the mnuWindow object.

Example

Window	(mnuWindow)
Tile Horizontal	(mnuWindowHorizontal)
Tile Vertical	(mnuWindowVertical)
Cascade	(mnuWindowCascade)

Layout Options

When several child windows are open, they may be arranged in several different layouts: tiled vertically, tiled horizontally, or cascaded. The type of alignment is set as an argument of the **LayoutMdi method.**

```
Me.LayoutMdi(MdiLayout.TileVertical)
Me.LayoutMdi(MdiLayout.TileHorizontal)
Me.LayoutMdi(MdiLayout.Cascade)
```

Redisplaying Child Windows

In some applications, such as a word processor, you may allow the user to open multiple child windows of the same type. In other applications, you want to allow only one child form of a particular type. For example, if your application has a Summary window that the user can display by selecting a menu option, he or she may select the option multiple times. The first time, you must instantiate the form, but the next time you should just activate the existing form, which brings it to the top of any other open child forms.

You can check for the existence of a child form by using the parent form's MdiChildren property, which is a collection of all open child forms that belong to the parent.

```
'Determine if form already exists
Dim frmTest As Form
Dim blnFound As Boolean = False

'Does form already exist?
For Each frmTest In Me.MdiChildren
    With frmTest
        If .Name = "frmSummary" Then
            .Activate()        'Activate previous instance
            blnFound = True
        End If
    End With
Next
If Not blnFound Then
    Dim frmSummaryInstance As New frmSummary()
    With frmSummaryInstance
        .MdiParent = Me
        .Show()
    End With
End if
```

Image Lists

Use an ImageList component to store the images for toolbars and other controls. The component appears in the component tray and should have a prefix of "ils."

To add images to the image list, select the Images collection Build button from the Properties window. Use the *Add* button in the Image Collection Editor to add each image to the collection. An index is automatically assigned to each image in the collection. When you assign the images to your toolbar buttons, you will see the index and a preview of each image.

Toolbars

Use the Toolbar icon in the toolbox to create a Toolbar object for your project. The toolbar itself does not have any buttons. You add those with a Buttons collection in the Properties window. Name your Toolbar object with "tlb" for the prefix; assign your image list component to the ImageList property of the toolbar.

To add buttons to the toolbar, simply click on the Build button for the Buttons collection and select the *Add* button from the ToolBarButton Collection Editor. When you drop down the list for the ImageIndex property, the index and images from the image list appear.

Add a ToolTip component and set the ToolTip Text property for your toolbar buttons so that text descriptions pop up for your users. ∎

Coding a Toolbar

A Toolbar component has one ButtonClick event that occurs when the user clicks on any of the buttons. Use the procedure's event arguments to determine which button was clicked. Assuming that the toolbar is named tlbParent, you can find the index of the selected button with tlbParent.Buttons.IndexOf(e.Button)

You can use the index of the selected button in a Select Case statement to send the user to the appropriate procedure.

```
Private Sub tlbParent_ButtonClick(ByVal sender As System.Object, _
    ByVal e As System.Windows.Forms.ToolBarButtonClickEventArgs) _
    Handles tlbParent.ButtonClick
    'Execute appropriate procedure for the button clicked

    Select Case tlbParent.Buttons.IndexOf(e.Button)
        Case 0
            mnuDisplayChildOne_Click(sender, e)
        Case 1
            mnuDisplayChildTwo_Click(sender, e)
    End Select

End Sub
```

Status Bars

A status bar is usually located at the bottom of a form to display information such as date, time, or status of the Cap Lock or Num Lock key. If you want a status bar on your form, you need to take two steps: add a StatusBar control to your form and add StatusBarPanel objects to the status bar. Add a StatusBar control from the toolbox and name it using "sbr" as the prefix. By default, the ShowPanels property is set to False; change this to True.

Add StatusBarPanels to display the desired information by using the Panels collection. You may find that you need to adjust the panel width to display the information completely.

Assign the value that you want to display to the Text property of the panel. You can either name the panels or refer to them by their index.

```
sbrParent.Panels(0).Text = Now.ToShortDateString()
```

Consider using the methods of the Now object for the date.

Context Menus

It's easy to add context menus (also called shortcut menus or popup menus) to a form or controls. Use the regular menu designer to create a menu; the top-level menu should have a name but a blank Text property. Assign the menu name to the ContextMenu property of the form and/or any controls on the form. The easiest way to code the context menu is to add its event to the `Handles` clause of the similar selection from the main menu.

☑**TIP**
━━━━━━━━━━━━━━
You can just refer to the Text property of the status bar if you intend to use only one panel. ■

Your Hands-On Programming Example ──────

Write an MDI project for R 'n R—For Reading and Refreshment. The project should have four forms: the Main form, the About form, the Payroll form, and the Summary form. The Payroll and Summary forms should have only a *Close* button. You will write code for the Payroll and Summary forms in Chapter 2.

The About form should display the company name and the copyright information from the assembly attributes.

Menu

<u>F</u>ile	<u>V</u>iew	<u>H</u>elp
E<u>x</u>it	<u>P</u>ayroll Form	<u>A</u>bout
	<u>S</u>ummary	

Include a toolbar with buttons to display each of the forms: Payroll, Summary, and About. Each button should display an appropriate ToolTip. Also allow the user to display any of the forms from a context menu.

Display the current date in the status bar.

Planning the Project

Sketch the four forms for the application (Figure 1.4). Your users must sign off
the sketches as meeting their needs before you begin programming.

Figure 1.4

Sketch the forms for the R 'n R Payroll project: a. Main form (parent); b. Payroll form; c. Summary form; and d. About form.

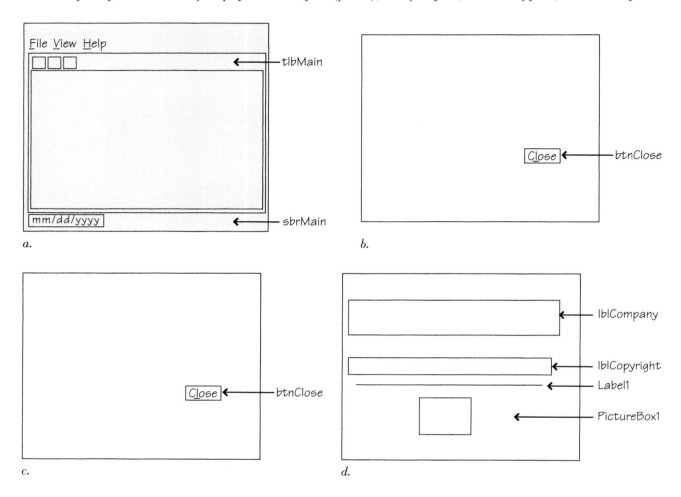

Plan the Objects, Properties, and Methods

Determine the objects and property settings for the forms and controls. Figure
1.5 shows the diagram of the program classes.

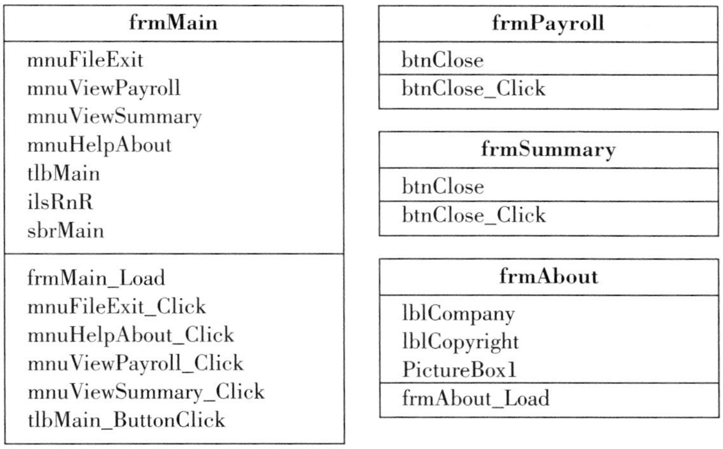

Figure1.5

The class diagram for the hands-on programming example.

frmMain
mnuFileExit
mnuViewPayroll
mnuViewSummary
mnuHelpAbout
tlbMain
ilsRnR
sbrMain
frmMain_Load
mnuFileExit_Click
mnuHelpAbout_Click
mnuViewPayroll_Click
mnuViewSummary_Click
tlbMain_ButtonClick

frmPayroll
btnClose
btnClose_Click

frmSummary
btnClose
btnClose_Click

frmAbout
lblCompany
lblCopyright
PictureBox1
frmAbout_Load

frmMain

Object	Property	Setting
frmMain	Text	R 'n R For Reading and Refreshment
	IsMdiContainer	True
mnuFileExit	Text	E&xit
mnuViewPayroll	Text	&Payroll Form
mnuViewSummary	Text	&Summary
mnuHelpAbout	Text	&About
tlbMain	Buttons collection	View Payroll
		View Summary
		View About
	ImageList	ilsRnR
ilsRnR	Images collection	Images for 3 buttons
sbrMain	Panels collection	Add 1 panel for the date

Procedure	Actions—Pseudocode
frmMain_Load	Retrieve the date for the status bar.
mnuFileExit_Click	Close the form.
mnuHelpAbout_Click	Create an instance of the About form.
	Set the MdiParent property.
	Show the form.
mnuViewPayroll_Click	Create an instance of the Payroll form.
	Set the MdiParent property.
	Show the form.
mnuViewSummary_Click	Create an instance of the Summary form.
	Set the MdiParent property.
	Show the form.
tlbMain_ButtonClick	Execute the corresponding menu item event procedure.

frmPayroll

Object	Property	Setting
frmPayroll	Text	Payroll
	WindowState	Maximized
btnClose	Text	&Close

Procedure	Actions—Pseudocode
btnClose_Click	Close the form.

frmSummary

Object	Property	Setting
frmSummary	Text	Payroll Summary
	WindowState	Maximized
btnClose	Text	&Close

Procedure	Actions—Pseudocode
btnClose_Click	Close the form.

frmAbout

Object	Property	Setting
frmAbout	FormBorderStyle	FixedDialog
	StartPosition	CenterParent
	Text	About This Application (Changes at run time.)
lblCompany	Text	(blank)
lblCopyright	Text	(blank)
Label1	Size	280,1 (one-pixel-wide line)
PictureBox1	Image	StudentData/Graphics/Books.gif
	SizeMode	StretchImage

Procedure	Actions—Pseudocode
frmAbout_Load	Retrieve the attributes and set up the labels.

Write the Project

Following the sketches in Figure 1.4, create the forms. Figure 1.6 shows the completed forms.

- Set the properties of each of the objects, as you have planned.
- Write the code for the forms. Working from the pseudocode, write each procedure.
- Modify the AssemblyInfo.vb file to hold the company attributes.
- When you complete the code, test each of the options. Make sure that all menu items work, the context menus work, and ToolTips appear for each button.

Figure 1.6

The forms for the R 'n R Payroll project: a. Main form (parent); b. Payroll form; c. Summary form; and d. About form.

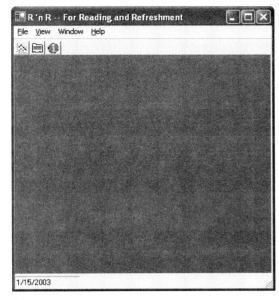

a.

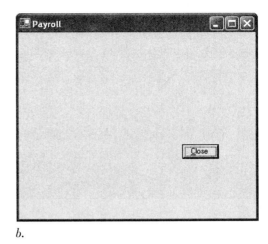

b.

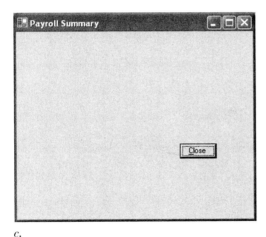

c.

d.

The Project Coding Solution

frmMain

```
'Project:      Ch01HandsOn
'Form:         frmMain
'Programmer:   Bradley/Millspaugh
'Date:         January 2003
'Description:  MDI Parent form; contains the menu and displays
'              the various forms.

Option Strict On

Public Class frmMain
    Inherits System.Windows.Forms.Form
```

```vb
    Private Sub mnuFileExit_Click(ByVal sender As System.Object, _
      ByVal e As System.EventArgs) Handles mnuFileExit.Click
        'Close all forms

        Me.Close()
    End Sub

    Private Sub mnuHelpAbout_Click(ByVal sender As System.Object, _
      ByVal e As System.EventArgs) Handles mnuHelpAbout.Click, mnuAbout.Click
        'Display the About box
        Dim blnFormExists As Boolean = False

        blnFormExists = CheckFormExistence("frmAbout")
        If Not blnFormExists Then
            Dim frmAboutInstance As New frmAbout()
            With frmAboutInstance
                .MdiParent = Me
                .Show()
            End With
        End If
    End Sub

    Private Sub mnuViewPayroll_Click(ByVal sender As System.Object, _
      ByVal e As System.EventArgs) Handles mnuViewPayroll.Click, mnuPayroll.Click
        Display the Payroll form
        Dim blnFormExists As Boolean = False

        blnFormExists = CheckFormExistence("frmPayroll")
        If Not blnFormExists Then
            Dim frmPayrollInstance As New frmPayroll()
            With frmPayrollInstance
                .MdiParent = Me
                .Show()
            End With
        End If
    End Sub

    Private Sub mnuViewSummary_Click(ByVal sender As System.Object, _
      ByVal e As System.EventArgs) Handles mnuViewSummary.Click, mnuSummary.Click
        'Display the Summary form
        Dim blnFormExists As Boolean = False

        blnFormExists = CheckFormExistence("frmSummary")
        If Not blnFormExists Then
            Dim frmSummaryInstance As New frmSummary()
            With frmSummaryInstance
                .MdiParent = Me
                .Show()
            End With
        End If
    End Sub

    Private Sub tlbMain_ButtonClick(ByVal sender As System.Object, _
      ByVal e As System.Windows.Forms.ToolBarButtonClickEventArgs) _
      Handles tlbMain.ButtonClick
        'Execute the appropriate event procedure

        Select Case tlbMain.Buttons.IndexOf(e.Button)
            Case 0
                mnuViewPayroll_Click(sender, e)
```

```
                Case 1
                    mnuViewSummary_Click(sender, e)
                Case 2
                    mnuHelpAbout_Click(sender, e)
            End Select
        End Sub

        Private Sub frmMain_Load(ByVal sender As System.Object, _
          ByVal e As System.EventArgs) Handles MyBase.Load
            'Get the date for the status bar

            sbrMain.Panels(0).Text = Now.ToShortDateString
        End Sub

        Private Function CheckFormExistence(ByVal strFormName As String) As Boolean
            'Determine if form already exists
            Dim frmTest As Form
            Dim blnFound As Boolean = False

            'Does form already exist?
            For Each frmTest In Me.MdiChildren
                With frmTest
                    If .Name = strFormName Then
                        .Activate()                    'Activate previous instance
                        blnFound = True
                    End If
                End With
            Next
            Return blnFound
        End Function
End Class
```

frmPayroll

```
'Project:       Ch01HandsOn
'Module         Payroll Form
'Programmer     Bradley/Millspaugh
'Date           January 2003
'Description:   User interface for the payroll information.

Option Strict On

Public Class frmPayroll
    Inherits System.Windows.Forms.Form

    Private Sub btnClose_Click(ByVal sender As System.Object, _
      ByVal e As System.EventArgs) Handles btnClose.Click
        'Close this form and return to the parent form

        Me.Close()
    End Sub
End Class
```

frmSummary

```
'Project:       Ch01HandsOn
'Module         Summary Form
'Programmer     Bradley/Millspaugh
'Date           January 2003
'Description:   User interface to display the payroll summary information.
```

```
Public Class frmSummary
    Inherits System.Windows.Forms.Form

    Private Sub btnClose_Click(ByVal sender As System.Object, _
      ByVal e As System.EventArgs) Handles btnClose.Click
        'Close this form

        Me.Close()
    End Sub
End Class
```

frmAbout

```
'Project:        Ch01HandsOn
'Form:           frmAbout
'Programmer:     Bradley/Millspaugh
'Date:           January 2003
'Description:    Display information about the application from the attributes
'                in the AssemblyInfo.vb file.

Option Strict On

Imports System.Reflection

Public Class frmAbout
    Inherits System.Windows.Forms.Form

    Private Sub frmAbout_Load(ByVal sender As System.Object, _
      ByVal e As System.EventArgs) Handles MyBase.Load
        'Load the labels from AssemblyInfo.vb
        'Display attribute information
        Dim objAttributes() As Object
        Dim asmInfo As [Assembly]
        Dim atrCompany As AssemblyCompanyAttribute
        Dim atrCopyright As AssemblyCopyrightAttribute
        Dim atrTitle As AssemblyTitleAttribute

        asmInfo = [Assembly].Load("Ch01HandsOn")
        objAttributes = asmInfo.GetCustomAttributes(False)
        Dim objItem As Object
        'Convert from object to desired types
        'Need Select Case because order of attributes in array varies
        For Each objItem In objAttributes
            Select Case objItem.GetType.ToString()
                Case "System.Reflection.AssemblyTitleAttribute"
                    atrTitle = CType(objItem, AssemblyTitleAttribute)
                    Me.Text = "About" & atrTitle.Title.ToString()
                Case "System.Reflection.AssemblyCompanyAttribute"
                    atrCompany = CType(objItem, AssemblyCompanyAttribute)
                    lblCompany.Text = atrCompany.Company.ToString()
                Case "System.Reflection.AssemblyCopyrightAttribute"
                    atrCopyright = CType(objItem, AssemblyCopyrightAttribute)
                    lblCopyright.Text = atrCopyright.Copyright.ToString()
            End Select
        Next

    End Sub
End Class
```

AssemblyInfo.vb Modify the attributes:

```
<Assembly: AssemblyTitle("R 'n R Payroll")>
<Assembly: AssemblyDescription("MDI User Interface")>
<Assembly: AssemblyCompany("R 'n R -- For Reading and Refreshment")>
<Assembly: AssemblyProduct("Books and Drinks")>
<Assembly: AssemblyCopyright("Copyright 2003 - All Rights Reserved")>
```

Summary

1. The .NET Framework SDK contains the class libraries, the common language runtime, and ASP.NET.
2. Managed code is compiled to run in the common language runtime.
3. A portable executable file contains intermediate language (managed code) and metadata.
4. Metadata store information about the methods, classes, and types for the run-time PE file.
5. The .NET Framework is composed of a set of classes stored in the class library. The classes are organized into a hierarchy of namespaces.
6. The CLR treats value types and reference types differently. Each value type variable has the value stored in the variable's memory location and is always initialized. A reference type variable holds a pointer to an actual object and may be equal to Nothing if not assigned.
7. The compiler produces MSIL (Microsoft Intermediate Language), a platform-independent set of instructions.
8. An assembly is the smallest deployable unit of code, which contains one or more .exe or .dll files and a manifest that describes the assembly.
9. The AssemblyInfo.vb file holds attributes, which are tags that contain information about the assembly. Both Windows applications and Web pages can access the attribute information at run time.
10. A Reference object connects Visual Basic to external components, either assemblies or COM objects.
11. Web development is done using ASP.NET.
12. A compiled program becomes an .exe or .dll file in the bin folder of the project. The .resx file holds resources for the form, including any graphics.
13. You can retrieve and display the attributes from AssemblyInfo.vb at run time in a Windows or a Web application.
14. You can deploy a Windows application by copying the .exe file to another location. For a Web application, more files are needed. Use the *Copy Project* menu item to copy all needed files.
15. Setting the Font property of a form sets the default font for all controls on the form that do not have a specific font assigned.
16. Forms can have a minimum size and/or a maximum size.
17. It is not advised to use the VB6 compatibility library.

Key Terms

Active Server Pages (ASP)   *5*
assembly   *5*
assembly manifest   *5*
Assembly object   *9*
attributes   *5*
common language runtime
  (CLR)   *2*
Common Language Specification
  (CLS)   *3*
LayoutMdi method   *15*
managed code   *2*

managed data   *2*
metadata   *2*
Microsoft intermediate language
  (MSIL)   *4*
.NET Framework   *2*
.NET Framework class
  library   *2*
reference object   *5*
reference type   *3*
value type   *3*

Review Questions

1. Differentiate between the Framework and Visual Studio.
2. Explain the following:
     a. CRL
     b. CLS
     c. PE
     d. MSIL
     e. ASP.NET
3. Explain the relationship between the common language runtime and managed code.
4. What is the purpose of compiling to an intermediate language?
5. What is the difference between a value type and a reference type?
6. What is an assembly? What does an assembly contain?
7. What are attributes? Give three examples.
8. What is ASP.NET and what is its purpose?
9. Where can you find a project's compiled version? What else might you find in that same location?
10. Explain how to display the attributes in AssemblyInfo.vb on a form at run time.
11. How can you deploy Windows applications? Web applications?
12. How can you set the default font for all controls on a form?
13. Why should you avoid the functions in the VB6 compatibility library?
14. What is an MDI application? How many parent forms can be in a single MDI application?

Programming Exercises

1.1   Create a Web project that displays the company, title, and copyright information from the attributes on the page. Make up your own information and modify the attributes file.
1.2   Create a Windows application that displays the company, title, and copyright information from the attributes on the form. Make up your own information and modify the attributes file.

1.3   Create a multiple form project for Tricia's Travels that contains a Main form and an About form. The main form will have a menu that contains the following:

Menu

File   *Help*

Exit   *About*

Change the default font of the main form to a font of your choice. Make the About form show the company and copyright information from the attributes. Make up your own values and modify the attribute file.

Case Studies

Claytor's Cottages

Create a project for Claytor's Cottages, a small bed and breakfast. Use an MDI form with a menu, a toolbar, and a status bar.

The About form should be a child form and contain at least your name, copyright, and company name, taken from the attributes.

Create child forms for each option (Guests, Rooms, Reservations) that simply have the title bar caption indicating the form purpose and a Close button to return to the main form. *Note:* These forms will be modified in later chapters.

Menu

File	*Edit*	*Window*	*Help*
Exit	*Guests*	Tile *Horizontal*	*About*
	Rooms	Tile *Vertical*	
	Charges	*Cascade*	

Select the window list option that allows the open forms to display on the *Window* menu.

Toolbar

Include three buttons to open each of the child forms. Place ToolTips on each button.

Guests
Rooms
Charges

Status Bar

Include the date and the time of day at the right side of the toolbar. Leave a panel for text messages to the left side.

Context Menu

Create a context menu on the parent form that has options to display the Guests, Rooms, and Charges forms.

Standards

- Use standard prefixes for naming variables, objects, and procedures.

- Menu items and controls must have keyboard access. Use standard selections when appropriate.

- Use a maximized window state for the main form.

- Set the form's Icon property to an appropriate icon.

Christian's Car Rentals

Create a project for Christian's Car Rentals. The project should contain an MDI Main form with a menu, a toolbar, and a status bar.

The About form should be a child form and contain at least your name, copyright, and company name, taken from the attributes.

Create child forms for each option (Customers, Vehicles, and Rentals) that simply have the title bar caption indicating the form purpose and a Close button to return to the main form. *Note:* These forms will be modified in later chapters.

Menu

File	Edit	Window	Help
Exit	Customers	Tile Horizontal	About
	Vehicles	Tile Vertical	
	Rentals	Cascade	

Include keyboard shortcuts for all menu options, following standards where applicable. Select the window list option that allows the open forms to display on the *Window* menu.

Toolbar

Place three buttons on the toolbar, one to display each of the child forms. Use any icon that you wish for each of the buttons and include ToolTips for each.

Customers
Vehicles
Rentals

Status Bar

Include the date in a panel at the right end of the toolbar. Leave a panel for text messages at the left end.

Context Menu

Create a context menu on the parent form that has options to display the Customers, Vehicles, and Rentals forms.

Standards

• Use standard prefixes for naming variables, objects, and procedures.

• Menu items and controls must have keyboard access. Use standard selections when appropriate.

• Use a maximized window state for the main form.

• Set the form's Icon property to an appropriate icon.

2

Building Multitier Programs with Classes

1. Discuss object-oriented terminology.

2. Create your own class and instantiate objects based on the class.

3. Create a new class based on an existing system class.

4. Divide an application into multiple tiers.

5. Create and throw custom exceptions.

6. Choose the proper scope for variables.

At this point in your programming career you should be comfortable with using objects, methods, and properties. You have already learned most of the basics of programming including decisions, loops, and arrays. Now it is time to start writing your programs in styles appropriate for larger production projects.

Most programming tasks are done in teams. Many developers may work on different portions of the code and all of the code must work together. One of the key concepts of object-oriented programming (OOP) is that of using building blocks. You must now break your programs into blocks, or, using the proper term, classes.

This chapter reviews object-oriented programming concepts and techniques for breaking your program into multiple tiers with multiple classes. Depending on how much of your first course was spent on OOP, you may find that much of this chapter is review.

Object-Oriented Programming

Visual Basic .NET is an object-oriented language and all programming uses the OOP approach. If you learned to program in a previous version of VB, you *used* objects, but you were shielded from most of the nitty-gritty of *creating* objects. But in VB .NET you will find that everything you do is based on classes. Each form is a class, which must be instantiated before it can be used. Even variables of the basic data types are objects, with properties and methods.

OOP Terminology

The key features of object-oriented programming are abstraction, encapsulation, inheritance, and polymorphism.

Abstraction

Abstraction means to create a model of an object, for the purpose of determining the characteristics (properties) and the behaviors (methods) of the object. For example, a Customer object is an abstract representation of a real customer, and a Product object is an abstract version of a real product. You need to use abstraction when planning an object-oriented program to determine the classes that you need and the necessary properties and methods. It is helpful to think of objects generically; that is, what are the characteristics of a typical product, rather than a specific product.

Encapsulation

Encapsulation refers to the combination of characteristics of an object along with its behaviors. You have one "package" that holds the definition of all properties, methods, and events.

Encapsulation is sometimes referred to as data hiding. Each object keeps its data (properties) and procedures (methods) hidden. Through use of the `Public` and `Private` keywords, an object can "expose" only those data elements and procedures that it wishes to allow the outside world to see.

You can witness encapsulation by looking at any Windows program. The form is actually a class. All of the methods and events that you code are enclosed within the `Class` and `End Class` statements. The public variables that you place in your code are actually properties of that specific form class.

Inheritance

Inheritance is the ability to create a new class from an existing class. You can add enhancements to an existing class without modifying the original. When you create a new class that inherits from an existing class, you can add or change class variables and methods. For example, each of the forms that you create is inherited from, or derived from, the existing Form class. The original class is known as the **base class**, **superclass**, or **parent class**. The inherited class is called a **subclass,** a **derived class**, or a **child class**. Of course, a new class can inherit from a subclass—that subclass becomes a superclass as well as a subclass.

Look closely at the first line of code for a form:

```
Public Class frmMain
    Inherits System.Windows.Forms.Form
```

Inherited classes should always have an "is a" relationship with the base class. In the form example, the new frmMain "is a" Form (Figure 2.1). You could create a new Customer class that inherits from a Person class; a customer "is a" person. But you should not create a new SalesOrder class that inherits from Person; a sales order is *not* a person.

Figure 2.1

A derived or inherited class has an "is a" relationship with its base class.

The real purpose of inheritance is **reusability**. You may need to reuse or obtain the functionality from one class of object when you have another similar situation. The new frmMain class that you create has all of the characteristics and actions of the base class, System.Windows.Forms.Form. From there you can add the functionality for your own new form.

You can create your own hierarchy of classes. You place the code you want to be common in a base class. You then create other classes, the derived classes or subclasses, which can call the shared functions. This concept is very helpful if you have features that are similar in two classes. Rather than writing two classes that are almost identical, you can create a base class that contains the similar procedures.

Sometimes you create a class specifically to use as a base for derived classes. You cannot instantiate objects from an **abstract class**, only inherit new classes from it. Some of the methods in the base class may not even contain any code but are there as placeholders, forcing any derived classes to have methods with the defined names. A derived class with a method named the same as a method in the base class is said to **override** the method in the base class. Overriding allows an inherited class to take different actions from the identically named method in the base class.

An example of reusing classes could be a Person class, where you might have properties for name, address, and phone number. The Person class can be a base class, from which you derive an Employee class, a Customer class, or a Student class (Figure 2.2). The derived classes could call procedures from the base class and contain any additional procedures that are unique to the derived class. In inheritance, typically the classes go from the general to the more specific. You can add functionality to an inherited class. You can also change or delete a function by overriding a method from the base class.

F i g u r e   2 . 2

Multiple subclasses can inherit from a single base class.

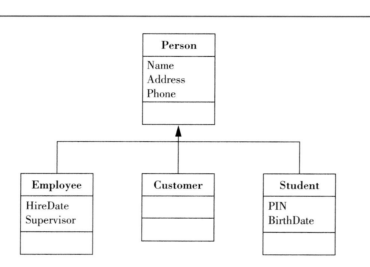

Polymorphism

The term ***polymorphism*** actually means the ability to take on many shapes or forms. As applied to OOP, polymorphism refers to method names having identical names but having different implementations, depending on the situation. For example, radio buttons, check boxes, and list boxes each has a `Select` method. In each case, the `Select` method operates appropriately for its class.

When a derived class overrides a method of its base class, both methods have the same name. But in each case, the actions performed are appropriate for the class. For example, a Person class might have a `Print` method that prints an address label with name and address information. But the `Print` method of the Employee class, which overrides the `Print` method of the Person class, might display the employee's information, including hire date and supervisor name, on the screen.

Polymorphism also allows a single class to have more than one method with the same name but a different argument list. When the overloaded method is called, the argument type determines which version of the method to use. Each of the identically named methods performs its tasks in a slightly different way from the other methods.

Reusable Objects

A big advantage of object-oriented programming over traditional programming is the ability to reuse objects. When you create a new class by writing a class module, you can then use that class in multiple projects. Each object that you create from the class has its own set of properties. This process works just like the built-in VB controls you have been using all along. For example, you can create two PictureBox objects: picOne and picTwo. Each has its own Visible property and Image property, which will probably be set differently than for the other.

The building-block concept can streamline programming. Consider a large corporation such as Microsoft, with many different programming teams. Perhaps one team develops the Word product and another team works on Excel. What happened when the Word team decided to incorporate formulas in tables? Do you think they wrote all new code to process the formulas? Likewise, there was a point when the Excel team added spell checking to worksheets. Do you think that they had to rewrite the spell-checking code? Obviously it makes more sense to have a spell-checking object that can be used by any application and a calculation object that processes formulas in any application where needed.

Developing applications should be like building objects with Lego™ blocks. The blocks all fit together and can be used to build many different things.

Multitier Applications

A common use of classes is to create applications in multiple "tiers" or layers. Each of the functions of a **multitier application** can be coded in a separate component and the components may be stored and run on different machines.

One of the most popular approaches is a three-tier application. The tiers in this model are presentation tier, business tier, and data tier (Figure 2.3). You may also hear the term "n-tier" application, which is an expansion of the three-tier model. The middle tier, which contains all of the business logic or **business rules**, may be written in multiple classes that can be stored and run from multiple locations.

Figure 2.3

The three-tier model for application design.

Presentation Tier	Business Tier	Data Tier
User Interface Forms, controls, menus	Business Objects Validation Calculations Business logic Business rules	Data Retrieval Data storage

In a multitier application, the goal is to create components that can be combined and replaced. If one part of an application needs to change, such as a redesign of the user interface or a new database format, the other components do not need to be replaced. A developer can simply "plug in" a new user interface and continue using the rest of the components of the application.

The **presentation tier** refers to the user interface, which in a Windows application is the form. Consider that in the future the user interface could be completely redesigned or even converted to a Web page.

The **business tier** is a class or classes that handle the data. This layer can include validation to enforce business rules as well as the calculations. If the validation and calculations are built into the form, then modifying the user interface may require a complete rewrite of a working application.

The **data tier** includes retrieving and storing the data in a database. Occasionally an organization will decide to change database vendors or need to retrieve data from several different sources. The data tier retrieves the data and passes the results to the business tier, or takes data from the business tier and writes them in the appropriate location.

Programmers must plan ahead for reusability in today's environment. You may develop the business tier for a Windows application. Later the company may decide to deliver the application via the Web or a mobile device, such as a cell phone or palm device. The user interface must change but the processing shouldn't have to change. If you develop your application with classes that perform the business logic, you can develop an application for one interface and easily move it to another platform.

Feedback 2.1

1. Name at least three types of operations that belong in the business tier.
2. List as many operations that you can think of that belong in the presentation tier.

Creating Classes

You most likely learned to create classes in your introductory course. It's time to review the techniques and to delve deeper into the concepts. If you are comfortable with creating new classes, writing property procedures including read-only properties, and using a parameterized constructor, you may want to skip over the next few sections and begin with "A Basic Business Class."

Designing Your Own Class

To design your own class, you need to analyze the characteristics and behaviors that your object needs. The characteristics (properties) are defined as variables, and the behaviors (methods) are sub procedures or function procedures.

Creating Properties in a Class

Inside your class you define variables, which are the properties of the class. Theoretically you could declare all variables as `Public` so that all other classes could set and retrieve their values. However, this approach violates the rules of encapsulation that require each object to be in charge of its own data. Remember that encapsulation is also called *data hiding*. To accomplish encapsulation, you will declare all variables in a class as `Private`. As a private variable, the value is available only to the procedures within the class, the same way that private module-level variables in a form are available only to procedures within the form's class.

When your program creates objects from your class, you will need to assign values to the properties. Because the properties are private variables, you will use special property procedures to pass the values to the class module and to return values from the class module.

Property Procedures

The way that your class allows its properties to be accessed is through **property procedures**. A property procedure may contain a Get to retrieve a property value and/or a Set to assign a value to the property. The name that you use for the Property procedure becomes the name of the property to the outside world. Create "friendly" property names that describe the property without using a prefix, such as LastName or EmployeeNumber.

The Property Procedure—General Form

```
Private ClassVariable As DataType    'Declared at the module level

[Public] Property PropertyName As DataType
    Get
        PropertyName = ClassVariable
        or
        Return ClassVariable
    End Get

    Set (ByVal Value As DataType)

        [statements, such as validation]
        ClassVariable = Value
    End Set
End Property
```

Property procedures are public by default, so you can omit the optional Public keyword. Get blocks are similar to function procedures in at least one respect: Somewhere inside the procedure, before the End Get, you must assign a return value to the procedure name or use a Return statement. The Set statement uses the **Value keyword** to refer to the incoming value for the property. The data type of the incoming value for a Set must match the type of the return value of the corresponding Get and the data type of the private property variable.

The Property Procedure—Example

```
Private mstrLastName As String      'Declared at the module level

Property LastName As String
    Get
        Return mstrLastName
        'Alternate version:
        'LastName = mstrLastName
    End Get

    Set(ByVal Value As String)
        mstrLastName = Value
    End Set
End Property
```

Remember, the private module-level variable holds the value of the property. The `Property Get` and `Set` retrieve the current value and assign a new value to the property.

Read-Only and Write-Only Properties

In some instances you may wish to set a value for a property that can only be retrieved by an object but not changed. To create a read-only property, use the **ReadOnly** modifier and write only the `Get` portion of the property procedure.

```
Private mdecPay As Decimal          'Declared at the module level

ReadOnly Property Pay() As Decimal  'Make the property read-only
    Get
        Return mdecPay
    End Get
End Property
```

A write-only property is one that can be set but not returned. Use the **WriteOnly** modifier and write only the `Set` portion of the property procedure.

```
Private mstrPassword As String    'Declared at the module level

WriteOnly Property Password(ByVal Value As String)    'Make the property write-only
    Set
        mstrPassword = Value
    End Set
End Property
```

Constructors and Destructors

A **constructor** is a method that automatically executes when an object is instantiated. A **destructor** is a method that automatically executes when an object is destroyed. In VB, the constructor must be a procedure named *New*. The destructor must be named *Dispose* and must override the `Dispose` method of the base class. You will generally write constructors for your classes, but usually not destructors. Most of the time the `Dispose` method of the base class handles the class destruction very well.

You create a constructor for your class by writing a `Sub New` procedure. The constructor executes automatically when you instantiate an object of the class. Because the constructor method executes before any other code in the class, the constructor is an ideal location for any initialization tasks that you need to do, such as opening a database connection.

The `Sub New` procedure must be Public, because the objects that you create must execute this method. Remember that the default is Public.

```
Sub New()
    'Constructor for class

    'Initialization statements
End sub
```

Overloading the Constructor

Recall that *overloading* means that two methods have the same name but a different list of arguments (the signature). You can create overloaded methods in your class by giving the same name to multiple procedures, each with a different argument list. The following example shows an empty constructor (one without arguments) and a constructor that passes arguments to the class.

```
'Constructors in the Payroll class

Sub New()
    'Constructor with empty argument list
End Sub

Sub New(ByVal decHours As Decimal, ByVal decRate As Decimal)
    'Constructor that passes arguments

    'Assign incoming values to properties
    mdecHours = decHours
    mdecRate = decRate
End Sub
```

Note: It isn't necessary to include the ByVal modifier to arguments, since ByVal is the default. However, the editor adds ByVal to the arguments if you leave it out.

A Parameterized Constructor

The term ***parameterized constructor*** refers to a constructor that requires arguments. This popular technique allows you to pass arguments/properties as you create the new object. In the preceding example, the Payroll class requires two decimal arguments: the hours and the rate. By instantiating the Payroll object in a Try/Catch block, you can catch any missing input value as well as any nonnumeric input.

```
'Code in the Form class to instantiate an object of the Payroll class
Try
    Dim payObject As New Payroll(CDec(txtHours.Text), CDec(txtRate.Text))
Catch Err As Exception
    MessageBox.Show("Enter the hours and rate.", "Payroll")
End Try
```

Assigning Arguments to Properties

As a further improvement to the Payroll parameterized constructor, we will use the property procedures to assign initial property values. Within the class module, use the Me keyword to refer to the current class. So Me.Hours refers to the Hours property of the current class. This technique is preferable to just assigning the passed argument to the module-level property variables, since validation is performed in the Property Set procedure.

```
'Improved constructor in the Payroll class
Sub New(ByVal decHours As Decimal, ByVal decRate As Decimal)
    'Assign properties

    Me.Hours = decHours
    Me.Rate = decRate
End Sub
```

When your class has both an empty constructor and a parameterized constructor, the program that creates the object can choose which method to use. For example, you could instantiate the Payroll object like this:

```
Dim payObject As New Payroll(CDec(txtHours.Text), CDec(txtRate.Text))
```

or like this:

```
Dim payObject As New Payroll
With payObject
    .Hours = CDec(txtHours.Text)
    .Rate = CDec(txtRate.Text)
End With
```

A Basic Business Class

The following example creates a very simplistic payroll application in two tiers (Figure 2.4). The application does not have a data tier, since it doesn't have any database element.

Figure 2.4

Create a nondatabase project in two tiers.

Presentation Tier	Business Tier
User Interface frmPayroll Controls Menus	**Business Objects** Validation Calculations Business logic Business rules

This first version of the payroll application inputs hours and rate from the user, validates for numeric data and some business rules, calculates the pay, and displays the pay on the form. We must analyze the tasks that belong in the presentation tier and those that belong in the business tier (Figure 2.5).

Figure 2.5

The form is the user interface; the validation and calculations are performed in the Payroll class, which is the business tier.

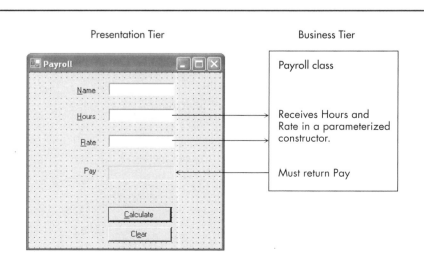

The Presentation Tier

The presentation tier, also called the *user interface*, must handle all communication with the user. The user enters input data and clicks the Calculate button. The result of the calculation and any error messages to the user must come from the presentation tier. Generally, validation for numeric input is handled in the form, but validation for business rules is handled in the business tier.

The Business Tier

Looking at Figure 2.5, you can see what should go in the class for the business tier. The class needs private property variables for Hours, Rate, and Pay. It also needs a parameterized constructor to pass the arguments, property procedures to validate and set the Hours and Rate, and a read-only property to allow the presentation tier (the form) to retrieve the calculated pay from the Payroll object.

The property procedures will include code to validate the input Hours and Rate for business rules. At this point, company policy is that the number of hours must be in the range 0–60 and the pay rate must be at least 6.25 and no more than 50. If the input values for Hours or Rate are outside of the acceptable range, the class will throw an exception that can be caught in the form's code. Remember that all user interaction, including any error messages, should occur in the presentation tier (the form).

Note: Throwing exceptions is covered in the section that follows the class code.

TIP

Use #Region and #End Region statements to create collapsible regions in code. ■

The Payroll Class

```
'Project:      Ch02Payroll
'Module:       Payroll Class
'Programmer:   Bradley/Millspaugh
'Date:         January 2003
'Description:  Business tier for payroll calculation: validates input data;
'                calculates pay.

Option Strict On

Public Class Payroll

#Region "Private fields"
    Private mdecHours As Decimal   'Hours property
    Private mdecRate As Decimal    'Rate property
    Private mdecPay As Decimal     'Pay property
    Private Const mdecMINIMUM_WAGE As Decimal = 6.25D
    Private Const mdecMAXIMUM_WAGE As Decimal = 50D
    Private Const mdecMINIMUM_HOURS As Decimal = 0D
    Private Const mdecMAXIMUM_HOURS As Decimal = 60D
#End Region
```

```
#Region "Methods"
    'Parameterized constructor
    Sub New(ByVal decHours As Decimal, ByVal decRate As Decimal)
        'Assign properties and calculate the pay

        Me.Hours = decHours
        Me.Rate = decRate
        FindPay()
    End Sub

    Private Sub FindPay()
        'Calculate the pay

        mdecPay = mdecHours * mdecRate
    End Sub

#End Region

#Region "Property Procedures"

    Public Property Hours() As Decimal
        Get
            Return mdecHours
        End Get
        Set(ByVal Value As Decimal)
            If Value >= mdecMINIMUM_HOURS And _
              Value <= mdecMAXIMUM_HOURS Then
                mdecHours = Value
            Else
                Throw New PayrollException( _
                  "Hours are outside of the acceptable range.", "Hours")
            End If
        End Set
    End Property

    Public Property Rate() As Decimal
        Get
            Return mdecRate
        End Get
        Set(ByVal Value As Decimal)
            If Value >= mdecMINIMUM_WAGE And _
              Value <= mdecMAXIMUM_WAGE Then
                mdecRate = Value
            Else
                Throw New PayrollException( _
                  "Pay rate is outside of the acceptable range.", "Rate")
            End If
        End Set
    End Property

    Public ReadOnly Property Pay() As Decimal
        Get
            Return mdecPay
        End Get
    End Property
#End Region

End Class
```

```
Public Class PayrollException
    Inherits System.ApplicationException

    Private mstrFieldInError As String

    Sub New(ByVal strMessage As String, ByVal strFieldInError As String)
        'Set the message for the new exception.
        MyBase.New(strMessage)
        mstrFieldInError = strFieldInError
    End Sub

    Public ReadOnly Property FieldInError() As String
        Get
            Return mstrFieldInError
        End Get
    End Property
End Class
```

Throwing and Catching Exceptions

The system throws an exception when an error occurs. Your program can catch
the exception and take some action, or even ignore the exception. Your own
class can also **throw an exception** to indicate that an error occurred, which
is the best way to pass an error message back to the user interface. You can enclose any code that could cause an exception in a Try/Catch block.

```
'Code in the form's class
Try
    Dim payObject As New Payroll(CDec(txtHours.Text), CDec(txtRate.Text))

Catch Err As PayrollException
    'Display a message to the user
    MessageBox.Show(Err.Message)
End Try
```

Note: If you are not familiar with structured exception handling using a
Try/Catch block, see Appendix B.

What Exception to Throw?

The .NET Framework has several exception classes that you can use, or you
can create your own new exception class that inherits from one of the existing
classes.

Microsoft recommends that you use the System.ApplicationException class
when you throw your own exceptions from application code. System.Applica-
tionException has the same properties and methods as the System.Exception
class, which is the generic system exception. All specific exceptions generated
by the CLR inherit from System.Exception.

When you want to throw a generic application exception, use the **Throw
statement** in this format:

```
Throw New ApplicationException("Error message to display.")
```

The message that you include becomes the Message property of the exception, which you can display when you catch the exception.

```
Catch Err As PayrollException
    'Display a message to the user
    MessageBox.Show(Err.Message)
```

Inheriting from ApplicationException

Sometimes you want to provide your exceptions with additional properties, beyond those included in the generic ApplicationException class. In our Payroll class, we want to be able to indicate which field is in error, so that the code in the form can set the focus and select the text in the field in error.

To customize an existing class, you must create a new class that inherits from the base class. Then you can add properties and methods to include the new capabilities. For our Payroll class, we will create a new PayrollException class that inherits from ApplicationException (Figure 2.6). Note that the new class can appear in the same file as the Payroll class.

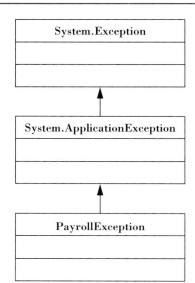

Figure 2.6

The new PayrollException class inherits from System.ApplicationException, which inherits from System.Exception.

When you make a new class inherit from an existing class, usually the first statement in the constructor is MyBase.New(). This executes the constructor of the base class. For our PayrollException class, you pass the error message as an argument to the base-class constructor:

```
MyBase.New(strMessage)
```

Here is the code for the new PayrollException class, which has a FieldInError property in addition to the inherited Message property:

```
Public Class PayrollException
    Inherits System.ApplicationException

    Private mstrFieldInError As String
```

```
'Constructor
Sub New(ByVal strMessage As String, ByVal strFieldInError As String)
    'Set the message for the new exception.

    MyBase.New(strMessage)
    mstrFieldInError = strFieldInError
End Sub

Public ReadOnly Property FieldInError() As String
    Get
        Return mstrFieldInError
    End Get
End Property
End Class
```

After you write the code for the custom PayrollException, you can throw the exception and include both arguments: the error message and the name of the field that caused the error. This code comes from the Property Set for the Rate property in the Payroll class. (The complete class was shown on pages 39–40).

```
Set(ByVal Value As Decimal)
    If Value >= mdecMINIMUM_WAGE And _
    Value <= mdecMAXIMUM_WAGE Then
        mdecRate = Value
    Else
        Throw New PayrollException("Pay rate is outside of the acceptable range.", "Rate")
    End If
End Set
```

The form contains the following code:

```
Private Sub btnCalculate_Click(ByVal sender As System.Object, _
  ByVal e As System.EventArgs) Handles btnCalculate.Click
    'Create a Payroll object to connect to the business tier.
    Try
        Dim payObject As New Payroll(CDec(txtHours.Text), CDec(txtRate.Text))
        lblPay.Text = FormatCurrency(payObject.Pay)
    Catch Err As PayrollException    'Catch exceptions from the Payroll class
        MessageBox.Show(Err.Message, "Payroll")
        Select Case Err.FieldInError
            Case "Hours"
                With txtHours
                    .SelectAll()
                    .Focus()
                End With
            Case "Rate"
                With txtRate
                    .SelectAll()
                    .Focus()
                End With
        End Select

    Catch       'Catch any generic exceptions from the CDec functions
        MessageBox.Show("Enter the hours and rate.", "Payroll")
        txtHours.Focus()
    End Try
End Sub
```

(See Ch02Payroll for the complete listing.)

Guidelines for Throwing Exceptions

When you throw exceptions, you should always include an error message. The message should be

- Descriptive.

- Grammatically correct, in a complete sentence with punctuation at the end.

Note: You can pass an exception that occurs in a component back up to the calling procedure by using the keyword Throw.

Modifying the Business Class

As business rules change, you can modify the business class or create a new class that inherits from the original class. You can usually add properties and methods to an existing class without harming any application that uses the class, but you should not change the behavior of existing properties and methods if any applications use the class.

In our Payroll example, we will expand the user interface to display a summary form. The summary form displays the number of employees processed, the total amount of pay, and the number of overtime hours. We must modify the Payroll class to calculate these values and return the values in read-only properties (Figure 2.7).

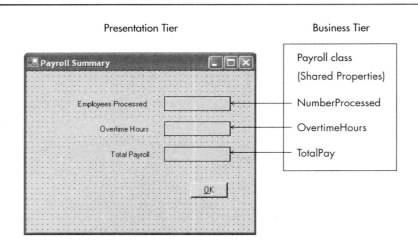

Figure 2.7

The new summary form displays summary information. The Payroll class must accumulate the summary figures in shared properties.

Instance Variables versus Shared Variables

Each new instance of the Payroll object has its own values for the hours, pay rate, and pay. These properties are called ***instance properties*** or ***instance variables***. But the properties we are adding now, such as the number of employees processed and the total pay amount, must accumulate totals for all instances of the class. These properties are called ***shared properties*** or ***shared variables***. Recall that properties are just the variables of a class, so the terms *properties* and *variables* can be used interchangeably.

The Payroll class requires three shared variables, one for each of the summary fields. As each instance of the Payroll class is created, the values are accumulated in the shared variables. In this way the values for employee two are added to the values for employee one, and so on.

```
'Payroll Class
'Shared properties declared at the module level

Private Shared mintNumberProcessed As Integer    'NumberProcessed shared property
Private Shared mdecTotalPay As Decimal           'TotalPay shared property
Private Shared mdecOvertimeHours As Decimal      'OvertimeHours shared property
```

Retrieving Shared Properties

The Shared keyword has a slightly different meaning when placed on a Public Get method. Any property procedures and methods declared as Shared are accessible by other classes without the necessity of instaniating an object of the class. Refer to a shared property or method directly by using the class name: Payroll.NumberProcessed.

```
Shared ReadOnly Property NumberProcessed() As Integer
    Get
        Return mintNumberProcessed
    End Get
End Property

Shared ReadOnly Property TotalPay() As Decimal
    Get
        Return mdecTotalPay
    End Get
End Property

Shared ReadOnly Property OvertimeHours() As Decimal
    Get
        Return mdecOvertimeHours
    End Get
End Property
```

The FindPay method must be modified to add to the summary fields and to calculate time-and-a-half for all employees that worked more than 40 hours. To aid the calculation, add two more named constants to the module-level declarations:

```
'Payroll class
'Additional module-level named constants
Private Const mdecREGULAR_HOURS As Decimal = 40D
Private Const mdecOVERTIME_RATE As Decimal = 1.5D

Private Sub FindPay()
    'Calculate the pay
    Dim decOvertimeHours As Decimal

    If mdecHours <= mdecREGULAR_HOURS Then      'No overtime
        mdecPay = mdecHours * mdecRate
        decOvertimeHours = 0D
    Else                                        'Overtime
        decOvertimeHours = mdecHours - mdecREGULAR_HOURS
        mdecPay = (mdecREGULAR_HOURS * mdecRate) + _
            (decOvertimeHours * mdecOVERTIME_RATE * mdecRate)
    End If
    mdecOvertimeHours += decOvertimeHours
    mdecTotalPay += mdecPay
End Sub
```

Following is the completed Payroll class that calculates and returns the shared properties:

```
'Project:       Ch02Payroll (Version2)
'Module:        Payroll Class
'Programmer:    Bradley/Millspaugh
'Date:          January 2003
'Description:   Business tier for payroll calculation; validates input data;
'               calculates pay and summary information.

Public Class Payroll

#Region "Private fields"
    'Instance variables
    Private mdecHours As Decimal    'Hours property
    Private mdecRate As Decimal     'Rate property
    Private mdecPay As Decimal      'Pay property

    'Shared variables
    Private Shared mintNumberProcessed As Integer   'NumberProcessed shared property
    Private Shared mdecTotalPay As Decimal          'TotalPay shared property
    Private Shared mdecOvertimeHours As Decimal     'OvertimeHours shared property

    'Named constants
    Private Const mdecMINIMUM_WAGE As Decimal = 6.25D
    Private Const mdecMAXIMUM_WAGE As Decimal = 50D
    Private Const mdecMINIMUM_HOURS As Decimal = 0D
    Private Const mdecMAXIMUM_HOURS As Decimal = 60D
    Private Const mdecREGULAR_HOURS As Decimal = 40D
    Private Const mdecOVERTIME_RATE As Decimal = 1.5D
#End Region

#Region "Methods"
    'Constructor
    Sub New(ByVal decHours As Decimal, ByVal decRate As Decimal)

        'Assign properties and calculate the pay

        Me.Hours = decHours
        Me.Rate = decRate
        FindPay()
    End Sub

    Private Sub FindPay()
        'Calculate the pay
        Dim decOvertimeHours As Decimal

        If mdecHours <= mdecREGULAR_HOURS Then     'No overtime
            mdecPay = mdecHours * mdecRate
            decOvertimeHours = 0D
        Else                                       'Overtime
            decOvertimeHours = mdecHours - mdecREGULAR_HOURS
            mdecPay = (mdecREGULAR_HOURS * mdecRate) + _
                (decOvertimeHours * mdecOVERTIME_RATE * mdecRate)
        End If
        mintNumberProcessed += 1
        mdecOvertimeHours += decOvertimeHours
        mdecTotalPay += mdecPay
    End Sub
#End Region
```

```vb
#Region "Property Procedures"

    Public Property Hours() As Decimal
        Get
            Return mdecHours
        End Get
        Set(ByVal Value As Decimal)
            If Value >= mdecMINIMUM_HOURS And _
               Value <= mdecMAXIMUM_HOURS Then
                mdecHours = Value
            Else
                Throw New PayrollException("Hours are outside of the acceptable _
                    range.", "Hours")
            End If
        End Set
    End Property

    Public Property Rate() As Decimal
        Get
            Return mdecRate
        End Get
        Set(ByVal Value As Decimal)
            If Value >= mdecMINIMUM_WAGE And _
               Value <= mdecMAXIMUM_WAGE Then
                mdecRate = Value
            Else
                Throw New PayrollException("Pay rate is outside of the acceptable _
                    range.", "Rate")
            End If
        End Set
    End Property

    ReadOnly Property Pay() As Decimal
        Get
            Return mdecPay
        End Get
    End Property

    Shared ReadOnly Property NumberProcessed() As Decimal
        Get
            Return mintNumberProcessed
        End Get
    End Property

    Shared ReadOnly Property TotalPay() As Decimal
        Get
            Return mdecTotalPay
        End Get
    End Property

    Shared ReadOnly Property OvertimeHours() As Decimal
        Get
            Return mdecOvertimeHours
        End Get
    End Property
#End Region

End Class
```

```
Public Class PayrollException
    Inherits System.ApplicationException

    Private mstrFieldInError As String

    Sub New(ByVal strMessage As String, ByVal strFieldInError As String)
        'Set the message for the new exception.

        MyBase.New(strMessage)
        mstrFieldInError = strFieldInError
    End Sub

    Public ReadOnly Property FieldInError() As String
        Get
            Return mstrFieldInError
        End Get
    End Property
End Class
```

Displaying the Summary Data

To display a second form from the main form, you must declare an instance of the form's class and show the form.

```
Dim frmSummaryInstance As New frmSummary()
frmSummaryInstance.Show()
```

You can choose from two techniques for filling the screen fields with the summary data:

1. Set the summary output from the Payroll form before showing the Summary form:

```
'In frmPayroll
Private Sub btnSummary_Click(ByVal sender As System.Object, _
  ByVal e As System.EventArgs) Handles btnSummary.Click
    'Create an instance of frmSummary and show it

    Dim frmSummaryInstance As New frmSummary()
    With frmSummaryInstance
        .lblCount.Text = mpayObject.NumberProcessed.ToString()
        .lblOvertime.Text = mpayObject.OvertimeHours.ToString()
        .lblTotalPay.Text = FormatCurrency(mpayObject.TotalPay)
        .Show()
    End With
```

2. In the Form_Activate procedure of the Summary form, retrieve the shared properties of the Payroll class and fill the labels.

```
'In frmSummary
Private Sub frmSummary_Activate(ByVal sender As Object, _
  ByVal e As System.EventArgs) Handles MyBase.Load
    'Retrieve the summary values each time the form displays

    lblCount.Text = Payroll.NumberProcessed.ToString()
    lblOvertime.Text = Payroll.OvertimeHours.ToString()
    lblTotalPay.Text = FormatCurrency(Payroll.TotalPay)
End Sub
```

Although both of these techniques work perfectly well, the second method is preferable for encapsulating the form's data. Each of the forms in the project can access the shared properties in the Payroll class, which is preferable to having frmPayroll access the controls on frmSummary.

Feedback 2.2

1. What is the purpose of property procedures?
2. Why should the property variables of a class be declared as Private?
3. You want to create a new class called Student that inherits from Person. Properties required to create an instance of the class are LastName, FirstName, and BirthDate. Write a parameterized constructor for the class.
4. Write the statement(s) to create an instance of the Student class defined in the previous question. Supply the arguments for the parameterized constructor.
5. An error occurs in a class written for the business tier. Explain how to handle the error condition and how the user should be notified.

Namespaces, Scope, and Accessibility

Visual Basic .NET introduced changes in scope and visibility of variables, constants, and classes. This section is intended as a review of declaring and using namespaces, scope, lifetime, and accessibility domains, such as Public, Private, Protected, and Friend.

Namespaces

Namespaces are used for grouping and referring to classes and structures. A name must be unique in any one namespace. You can think of namespaces like telephone area codes: a given phone number can exist only once in a single area, but that number may appear in many different area codes.

The classes in a namespace do not have to be in a single file. In fact, most of the classes in the .NET Framework are in the System namespace, which is stored in many files.

You can declare namespaces in your VB projects. In fact, by default each project has a namespace that matches the project name. If you display the *Project Properties* dialog box for any project, you will see an entry titled *Root Namespace*. However, if you change the project name in the Solution Explorer, the root namespace does not change automatically. Declare namespaces within your project using the Namespace/End Namespace construct:

```
Namespace RnRApplications
    'Classes and structures in the namespace can appear here
End Namespace
```

You can place the same Namespace statement in more than one project.

For most projects, there is no advantage in declaring a namespace. A company might choose to group applications by using namespaces.

Scope

The **scope** of a variable or constant refers to the area of the program that can "see" and reference it. For simplicity and clarity, we use the term *variable*, but each of the following examples applies to named constants as well as variables.

You determine the scope of a variable by the location of the declaration and the accessibility modifier (`Public` or `Private`). The choices for scope, from the widest to the narrowest, are namespace, module level, procedure level, and block level.

Namespace

Any variable, constant, class, or structure declared with the `Public` modifier has **namespace scope**. You can refer to the identifier anywhere within the namespace. Because each project is in its own namespace by default, generally *namespace scope* also means *project scope*. However, you can structure your own namespaces to contain multiple projects.

You usually need to declare classes and structures as Public, but not variables and constants. It is considered poor OOP programming to declare variables with namespace scope because it violates the rules of encapsulation. Each class should be in charge of its own data and share variables only by using `Property Let` and `Get` procedures.

Note: Earlier versions of VB, as well as many other programming languages, refer to variables that can be referenced from any location in a project as *global variables*. VB .NET has dropped this terminology.

Module Level

Module-level scope is sometimes also called *class-level* scope. A module-level variable is a Private variable that is declared inside any class, structure, or module, but outside of any sub procedure or function. By convention, you should declare module-level variables at the top of the class, but the variables can actually be declared anywhere inside the class that is outside of a procedure or function. Use "m" as the scoping prefix:

```
Private mdecTotal As Decimal
```

Note that if you leave off the accessibility modifier (`Public` or `Private`), and use `Dim` instead, the variable is Private by default.

In previous versions of Visual Basic, each file was called a module, so any variable declared as Private at the top of the file (not inside a sub procedure or function) was a module-level variable. The terminology carries through to VB .NET, even though the language now has a `Module/End Module` construct, which can contain miscellaneous procedures and functions that are not included in a class.

Procedure Level

Any variable that you declare inside a procedure or function, but not within a block, has **procedure-level scope**, also called *local scope*. You can reference the variable anywhere inside the procedure but not in other procedures. Procedure-level variables do not have a scoping prefix. Note that the `Public` keyword is not legal inside a procedure; all procedure-level variables are Private.

Block Level

If you declare a variable inside a code block, the variable has **block-level scope**. That is, the variable can be referenced only inside that block. Code blocks include

```
If/End If
While/End While
Do/Loop
For/Next
Select Case/End Select
Try/Catch/Finally/End Try
```

The blocks that are likely to cause confusion are the Try/Catch/ Finally/End Try. The Try is one block; each Catch is a separate block, and the Finally is a separate block. This means that you cannot declare a variable in the Try and reference it in the Catch or the Finally blocks. It also means that you can declare the same variable name for each Catch, since the scope of each is only that Catch block.

```
Try
    'Declare a block-level variable
    'Bad idea, since it cannot be referenced outside of this Try block
    Dim decAmount As Decimal = CDec(txtAmount.Text)
Catch Err As InvalidCastException
    'Err is a block-level variable valid only inside this Catch block
    MessageBox.Show(Err.Message, "Invalid Input Data")
Catch Err As Exception
    'Err is a block-level variable valid only inside this Catch block
    MessageBox.Show(Err.Message, "Unknown Error")
Finally
    'Any variable declared here is valid only inside this Finally block
End Try
```

When you instantiate objects, if there is any chance the creation will fail, you should create the new object inside a Try/Catch block. But if you declare the variable inside the Try block, the variable goes out of scope when the Try block completes. Therefore, most of the time you will declare the object variable at the module level or procedure level and instantiate the object inside the Try block.

```
'Declare the object variable at the module level of the Form class
Dim mpayObject As Payroll

Private Sub btnCalculate_Click(ByVal sender As System.Object, _
    ByVal e As System.EventArgs) Handles btnCalculate.Click
    'Create a Payroll object to connect to the business tier.

    Try
        'Instantiate the object in the Try block
        mpayObject = New Payroll(CDec(txtHours.Text), CDec(txtRate.Text))
```

Lifetime

The **lifetime** of a variable, including object variables, is as long as the variable remains in scope. The lifetime of a namespace-level variable is as long as the program is running. The lifetime of a module-level variable is as long as any reference to the class remains, which is generally as long as the program runs.

The lifetime of a procedure-level variable is one execution of the procedure. Each time the procedure is executed, a new variable is established and initialized. For this reason, you cannot use procedure-level variables to maintain running totals or counts unless you declare them with the `Static` keyword, which changes the lifetime of a procedure-level variable to the life of the class or module.

Accessibility Domains

You have already declared variables and classes with the `Public` and `Private` keywords. You can also use `Protected`, `Friend`, and `Protected Friend` (Table 2.1). Each of these keywords defines the **accessibility** of the variable or class.

Keyword	Description
`Public`	Accessible from anywhere in the program or from any other program that references this one.
`Private`	Accessible from anywhere inside this class.
`Protected`	Accessible from anywhere inside this class or in any class that inherits from this class.
`Friend`	Accessible from anywhere inside this program.
`Protected Friend`	A combination of `Protected` and `Friend`. Accessible from anywhere inside this program and in any class that inherits from this class, even though the derived class is in a different program.

Inheriting Variables and Methods

As you know, when you derive a new class from an existing class, all Public variables and methods are inherited, with the exception of the base class's constructors. (You must write the constructors for any inherited class.) In addition, any methods declared as Protected are also inherited.

Shadowing and Overriding Methods

An inherited class can have a method with the same name as a method in its base class. Depending on how it is declared, the new method may shadow or override the base class method.

Overriding To override a method in the base class, the method must be declared as **overridable**:

```
'Base Class
Public|Protected Overridable Sub DoSomething()
```

In the derived class, you must use the `Overrides` keyword:

```
'Derived Class
Overrides Sub DoSomething()
```

If the base-class method has more than one signature (overloaded methods), the override applies only to the base-class method with the identical signature. You must write separate methods to override each version (signature) of the base-class method.

Shadowing A method in a derived class can **shadow** a method in the base class. The new (shadowing) method replaces the base-class method in the derived class, but not in any new classes derived from that class. The shadowing method "hides" all signatures (overloaded methods) with the same name in the base class.

```
'Base Class
Public|Protected [Overridable] Sub DoSomething()
```

In the derived class, you can use the `Shadows` keyword:

```
'Derived Class
Shadows Sub DoSomething()
```

If you do not use either the `Overrides` or `Shadows` keyword, `Shadows` is assumed. And if you use the `Overrides` or `Shadows` keyword for one method of a group, you must include the keyword for all overridden or shadowed methods.

Passing Control Properties to a Component

So far in this chapter, all examples pass the Text property of text boxes to the business tier component. But often you need to pass data from check boxes, radio buttons, or list boxes. How you pass the data depends on how the properties are declared in the business class.

The examples in this section are based on a two-tier application to calculate prices for theater tickets (Figure 2.8). Seat prices vary by the section: General, Balcony, or Box Seats. Seniors and students receive a $5.00 discount from the ticket price.

Figure 2.8

In the user interface, the user makes selections in radio buttons and a check box, which must be used to set properties in the business tier component.

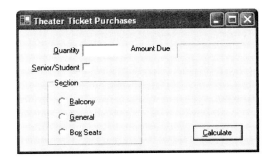

The business tier needs to know the section, the number of tickets, and whether a discount is to be given. Therefore, the constructor will receive three values:

```
Sub New(ByVal intQuantity As Integer, ByVal intSection As Integer, _
    ByVal blnDiscount As Boolean)
```

Notice that there are three values: the quantity, the section, and a boolean value for the discount. Passing the quantity is straightforward; you can convert the text box value to integer: `CInt(txtQuantity.Text)`. And you can easily pass the Checked property of a check box to a Boolean property:

```
Dim objTicket As New TicketPrice(CInt(txtQuantity.Text), intSection, chkDiscount.Checked)
```

Setting a property based on a selection in radio buttons or a list box presents an additional challenge, both in determining the best way to set up the property in the business tier component and in setting the correct value in the user interface. Notice that the Section property is declared as integer. Although you could set up the property as string, there is a real advantage in using integer—you can create an enumeration for the available choices.

Creating an Enumeration

Whenever you have a list of choices for a property, it's because someone set up an **enumeration** that lists the choices. For example, selecting `Color.Red`, `Color.Blue`, or `Color.Yellow`, is choosing one of the elements from the Color enumeration. When you choose one of the elements of the Color enumeration, the VB compiler actually substitutes the numeric value of the element. This saves you, the developer, of having to remember either the color names or the color numbers. You just type the name of the enumeration and a period, and the possible choices pop up in IntelliSense.

You can create your own enumeration, which is called an ***enum*** ("E-noom"). An enum is a list of named constants. The data type of the constants must be one of the integer types (integer, short, long, or byte). Whenever you create a reusable component class that has a list of possible choices for a property, consider setting up an enum.

The Enum Statement—General Form

```
Enum EnumName
    ConstantName1 [ConstantValue]
    ConstantName2 [ConstantValue]
    ...
End Enum
```

The Enum statement belongs at the namespace level or class level, which means that it cannot appear inside a procedure. By default, an Enum is public, but you can declare it to be private, friend, or protected, if you wish.

The Enum Statement—Examples

```
Public Enum SectionType
    General
    Balcony
    Box
End Enum

Enum ReportType
    BooksBySubject    1
    BooksByAuthor     2
End Enum

Enum EvenNumbers
    Two       2
    Four      4
    Six       6
    Eight     8
End Enum
```

When you don't assign a constant value to the element, VB automatically assigns the first element a value of zero, and each following element one greater than the last. So in the first of the examples above, *General* has a constant value of 0, *Balcony* has a value of 1, and *Box* has a value of 2.

In the business tier component for the program example, which you can see in Ch02EnumRadioButtons, the Section property is set up as an integer with an enum. In the CalculatePrice procedure, use the enum values in a `Select Case` to determine the correct constant to use for the price.

```
'Enum declared at the namespace level, above the class declaration
Public Enum SectionType
    General
    Balcony
    Box
End Enum

Public Class TicketPrice
    'Private variable for Section property
    Dim mintSection As Integer
'...Omitted code for class

    Private Sub CalculatePrice()
        'Determine the amount due
        Dim decPrice As Decimal

        Select Case mintSection
            Case SectionType.General
                decPrice = mdecGENERAL
            Case SectionType.Balcony
                decPrice = mdecBALCONY
            Case SectionType.Box
                decPrice = mdecBOX
        End Select
        If mblnDiscount Then
            decPrice -= mdecDISCOUNT
        End If
        mdecAmountDue = decPrice * mintQuantity
    End Sub
End Class
```

Use this code in the form's btnCalculate_Click event procedure to use the enum. Note that if you declare the enum inside the class in the business tier component, you must also specify the class name when using the enum (TicketPrice.SectionType.General).

```
Private Sub btnCalculate_Click(ByVal sender As System.Object, _
   ByVal e As System.EventArgs) Handles btnCalculate.Click
        'Find price by passing data input on the presentation tier
        'to the business tier using a TicketPrice object.
        Dim intSection As Integer

        'Determine the section from radio buttons
        If radBalcony.Checked Then
            intSection = SectionType.Balcony
        ElseIf radBox.Checked Then
            intSection = SectionType.Box
        Else
            intSection = SectionType.General     'Default to General
        End If

        Try
            Dim objTicket As New TicketPrice(CInt(txtQuantity.Text), _
              intSection, chkDiscount.Checked)
            lblAmount.Text = FormatCurrency(objTicket.AmountDue)
        Catch
            MessageBox.Show("Quantity must be numeric.", "Invalid Data")
        End Try
    End Sub
End Class
```

This example comes from Ch02EnumRadioButtons. To see an example of selecting from a combo box, rather than radio buttons, see Ch02EnumComboBox.

Garbage Collection

The .NET Framework destroys unused objects and reclaims memory in a process called *garbage collection*. The garbage collector runs periodically and destroys any objects and variables that no longer have any active reference. You have no way of knowing when the garbage collection will occur. In previous versions of VB, you were advised to set object variables to Nothing and to write Finalize procedures for your classes. For VB .NET, Microsoft recommends that you just allow object variables to go out of scope when you are finished with them.

► **Feedback 2.3**

Use this declaration to answer questions 1–4.

```
Dim intVariable As Integer
```

1. What is the scope of intVariable if it is declared inside a class but not inside a procedure?
2. What is its lifetime?
3. What is its accessibility?
4. If the class in which intVariable is declared is used as a base class for inheritance, will the derived class have access to the variable?

Your Hands-On Programming Example

R 'n R—For Reading and Refreshment needs an application to calculate payroll. Create a multiple-form project that includes an MDI parent form, a Payroll form, a Summary form, and an About form. The Payroll form, Summary form, and About form should be child forms of the parent form. If you worked the hands-on project for Chapter 1, you will now complete the Payroll and Summary forms.

The parent form should have the following menu:

File	View	Help
Exit	Payroll Form	About
	Summary	

This should be a multitier project, with the business rules and calculations in a class separate from the user interface.

Use attributes to display the company name and copyright information on the About form.

Make sure to validate the input data. Display a meaningful message to the user and select the field in error when the user enters bad data.

Include a toolbar and a status bar on the main form.

Planning the Project

Sketch the four forms for the application (Figure 2.9). Your users must sign off
the sketches as meeting their needs before you begin programming.

Sketch the forms for the R 'n R Payroll project: a. Main form (parent); b. Payroll form; c. Summary form; and d. About form.

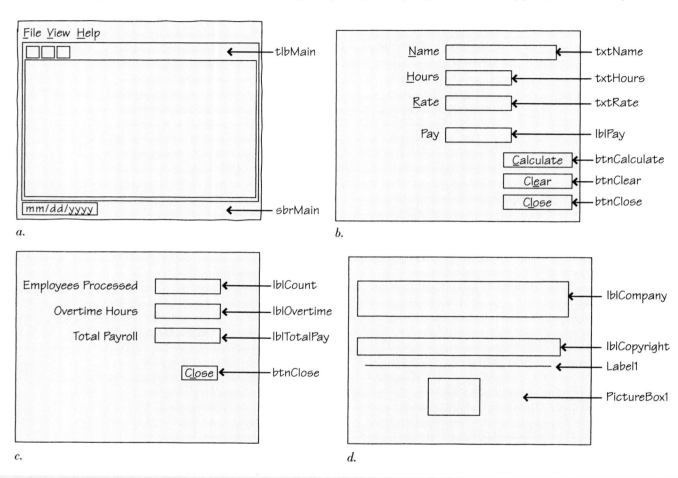

Plan the Objects, Properties, and Methods

Plan the classes for the two tiers. Determine the objects and property settings for the forms and controls and for the business tier. Figure 2.10 shows the diagram of the program classes.

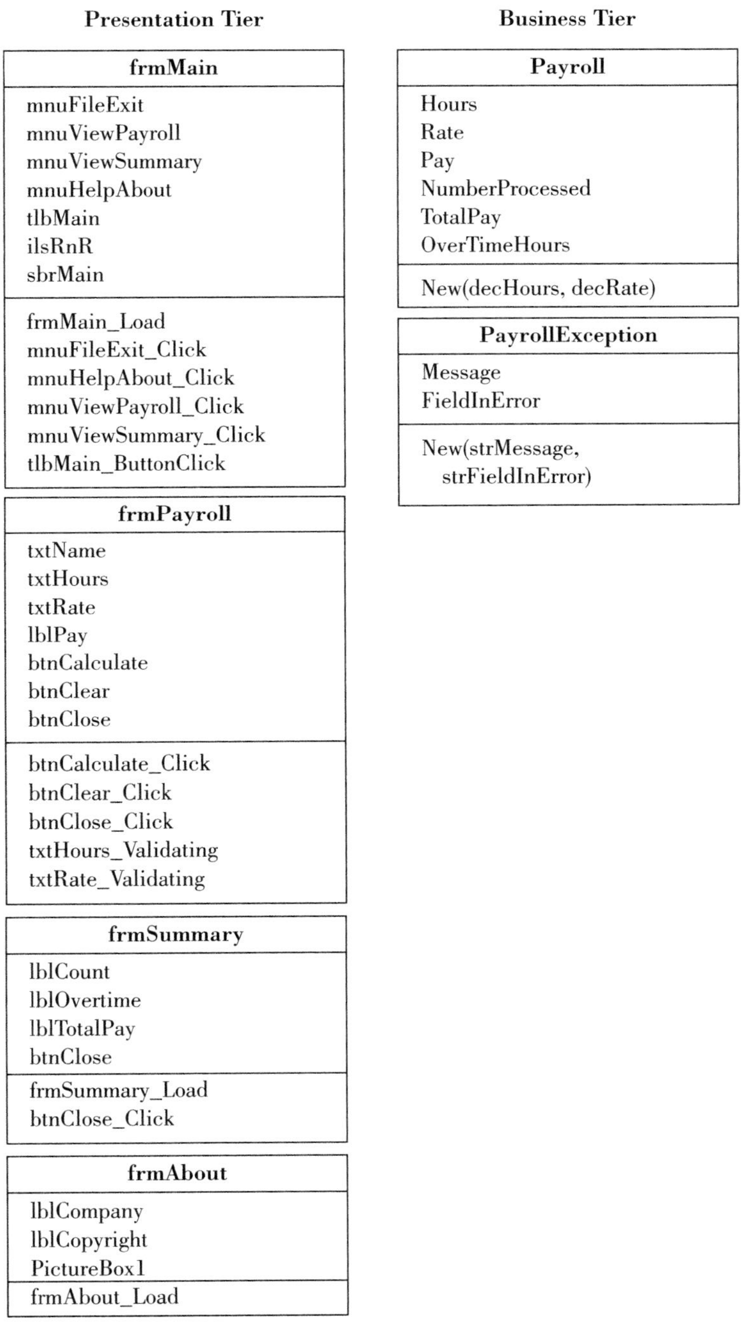

Figure 2.10

The class diagram for the hands-on programming example.

Presentation Tier

frmMain

mnuFileExit
mnuViewPayroll
mnuViewSummary
mnuHelpAbout
tlbMain
ilsRnR
sbrMain

frmMain_Load
mnuFileExit_Click
mnuHelpAbout_Click
mnuViewPayroll_Click
mnuViewSummary_Click
tlbMain_ButtonClick

frmPayroll

txtName
txtHours
txtRate
lblPay
btnCalculate
btnClear
btnClose

btnCalculate_Click
btnClear_Click
btnClose_Click
txtHours_Validating
txtRate_Validating

frmSummary

lblCount
lblOvertime
lblTotalPay
btnClose

frmSummary_Load
btnClose_Click

frmAbout

lblCompany
lblCopyright
PictureBox1

frmAbout_Load

Business Tier

Payroll

Hours
Rate
Pay
NumberProcessed
TotalPay
OverTimeHours

New(decHours, decRate)

PayrollException

Message
FieldInError

New(strMessage,
    strFieldInError)

Presentation Tier
frmMain

Object	Property	Setting
frmMain	Text IsMdiContainer	R 'n R For Reading and Refreshment True
mnuFileExit	Text	E&xit
mnuViewPayroll	Text	&Payroll Form
mnuViewSummary	Text	&Summary
mnuHelpAbout	Text	&About
tlbMain	Buttons collection ImageList	View Payroll View Summary View About ilsRnR
ilsRnR	Images collection	Images for 3 buttons
sbrMain	Panels collection	Add 1 panel for the date

Procedure	Actions—Pseudocode
frmMain_Load	Retrieve the date for the status bar.
mnuFileExit_Click	Close the form.
mnuHelpAbout_Click	Create an instance of the About form. Set the MdiParent property. Show the form.
mnuViewPayroll_Click	Create an instance of the Payroll form. Set the MdiParent property. Show the form.
mnuViewSummary_Click	Create an instance of the Summary form. Set the MdiParent property. Show the form.
tlbMain_ButtonClick	Execute the corresponding menu item event procedure.

frmPayroll

Object	Property	Setting
frmPayroll	AcceptButton	btnCalculate
	CancelButton	btnClear
	Text	Payroll
	WindowState	Maximized
Label1	Text	&Name
txtName	Text	(blank)
Label2	Text	&Hours
txtHours	Text	(blank)
Label3	Text	&Rate
txtRate	Text	(blank)
Label4	Text	Pay
lblPay	BorderStyle	Fixed3D
	Text	(blank)
btnCalculate	Text	&Calculate
btnClear	Text	Cl&ear
btnClose	Text	C&lose

Procedure	Actions—Pseudocode
btnCalculate_Click	Try Instantiate a Payroll object, passing the input values. Display the pay formatted in a label. Catch Display the error message. Select the field in error.
btnClear_Click	Clear all input fields on the screen. Set the focus in txtName.
btnClose_Click	Close the form.
txtHours_Validating	If not numeric Display a message box, allowing the user an option to cancel. If the user didn't cancel the operation Cancel the Validating event procedure. Select txtHours.
txtRate_Validating	If not numeric Display a message box, allowing the user an option to cancel. If the user didn't cancel the operation Cancel the Validating event procedure. Select txtRate.

frmSummary

Object	Property	Setting
frmSummary	AcceptButton	btnOK
	WindowState	Maximized
	Text	Payroll Summary
Label1	Text	Employees Processed
lblCount	BorderStyle	FixedSingle
	Text	(blank)
Label2	Text	Overtime Hours
lblOvertime	BorderStyle	FixedSingle
	Text	(blank)
Label3	Text	Total Payroll
lblTotalPay	BorderStyle	FixedSingle
	Text	(blank)
btnClose	Text	&Close

Procedure	Actions—Pseudocode
frmSummary_Load	Format and display the 3 summary properties in labels.
btnClose_Click	Close the form.

frmAbout

Object	Property	Setting
frmAbout	FormBorderStyle	FixedDialog
	StartPosition	CenterParent
	Text	About This Application (Changes at run time.)
lblCompany	Text	(blank)
lblCopyright	Text	(blank)
Label1	Size	280,1 (one-pixel-wide line)
PictureBox1	Image	StudentData/Graphics/Books.gif
	SizeMode	StretchImage

Procedure	Actions—Pseudocode
frmAbout_Load	Retrieve the attributes and set up the labels.

The Business Tier
Payroll Class

Properties	Data type	Property type	Accessibility
Hours	Decimal	Instance	Read / Write
Rate	Decimal	Instance	Read / Write
Pay	Decimal	Instance	Read Only
NumberProcessed	Decimal	Shared	Read Only
TotalPay	Decimal	Shared	Read Only
OverTimeHours	Decimal	Shared	Read Only

Methods

New(ByVal decHours As Decimal, ByVal decRate As Decimal) (Parameterized constructor)

Constants	Data type	Initial value
mdecMINIMUM_WAGE	Decimal	6.25D
mdecMAXIMUM_WAGE	Decimal	50D
mdecMINIMUM_HOURS	Decimal	0D
mdecMAXIMUM_HOURS	Decimal	60D
mdecREGULAR_HOURS	Decimal	40D
mdecOVERTIME_RATE	Decimal	1.5D

PayrollException Class

Properties	Data type	Property type	Accessibility
Message (inherited)	String	Instance	Read Only
FieldInError	String	Instance	Read Only

Methods

New(ByVal strMessage As String, ByVal strFieldInError As String)

Write the Project

Following the sketches in Figure 2.9, create the forms. Figure 2.11 shows the completed forms.

- Set the properties of each of the objects, as you have planned.

- Write the code for the business tier classes, referring to your planning document.

- Write the code for the forms. Working from the pseudocode, write each procedure.

- When you complete the code, use a variety of test data to thoroughly test the project.

Figure 2.11

The forms for the R 'n R Payroll project: a. Main form (parent); b. Payroll form; c. Summary form; and d. About form.

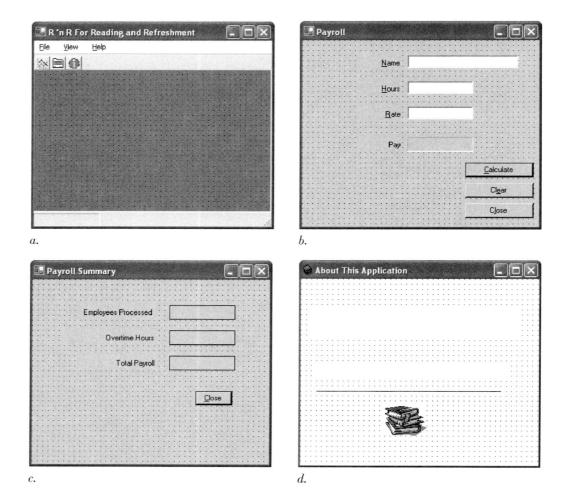

a.   b.

c.   d.

The Project Coding Solution

frmMain

```
'Project:      Ch02HandsOn
'Form:         frmMain
'Programmer:   Bradley/Millspaugh
'Date:         January 2003
'Description:  MDI Parent form; contains the menu and displays the various forms.

Option Strict On

Public Class frmMain
    Inherits System.Windows.Forms.Form

    Private Sub mnuFileExit_Click(ByVal sender As System.Object, _
      ByVal e As System.EventArgs) Handles mnuFileExit.Click
        'Use the Forms collection to close all forms

        Me.Close()
    End Sub
```

```vb
    Private Sub mnuHelpAbout_Click(ByVal sender As System.Object, _
      ByVal e As System.EventArgs) Handles mnuHelpAbout.Click, mnuAbout.Click
        'Display the About box

        Dim frmAboutInstance As New frmAbout()

        With frmAboutInstance
            .MdiParent = Me
            .Show()
        End With
    End Sub

    Private Sub mnuViewPayroll_Click(ByVal sender As System.Object, _
      ByVal e As System.EventArgs) Handles mnuViewPayroll.Click, mnuPayroll.Click
        'Create an instance of the payroll form

        Dim frmPayrollInstance As New frmPayroll()

        With frmPayrollInstance
            .MdiParent = Me
            .Show()
        End With
    End Sub

    Private Sub mnuViewSummary_Click(ByVal sender As System.Object, _
      ByVal e As System.EventArgs) Handles mnuViewSummary.Click, mnuSummary.Click
        'Display the Summary form

        Dim frmSummaryInstance As New frmSummary()

        With frmSummaryInstance
            .MdiParent = Me
            .Show()
        End With
    End Sub

    Private Sub tlbMain_ButtonClick(ByVal sender As System.Object, _
      ByVal e As System.Windows.Forms.ToolBarButtonClickEventArgs) _
      Handles tlbMain.  ButtonClick
        'Execute the appropriate event

        Select Case tlbMain.Buttons.IndexOf(e.Button)
            Case 0
                mnuViewPayroll_Click(sender, e)
            Case 1
                mnuViewSummary_Click(sender, e)
            Case 2
                mnuHelpAbout_Click(sender, e)
        End Select
    End Sub

    Private Sub frmMain_Load(ByVal sender As System.Object, _
      ByVal e As System.EventArgs) Handles MyBase.Load
        'Get the date for the status bar

        sbrMain.Panels(0).Text = Now.ToShortDateString()
    End Sub
End Class
```

frmPayroll

```
'Project:      Ch02HandsOn
'Module:       Payroll Form
'Programmer:   Bradley/Millspaugh
'Date:         January 2003
'Description:  User interface for the payroll application.
'              Provides data entry and validates for nonnumeric data.
'              Collects summary data.

Option Strict On

Public Class frmPayroll
    Inherits System.Windows.Forms.Form

    Dim mpayObject As Payroll

    Private Sub btnCalculate_Click(ByVal sender As System.Object, _
      ByVal e As System.EventArgs) Handles btnCalculate.Click
        'Create a Payroll object to connect to the business tier.

        Try
            mpayObject = New Payroll(CDec(txtHours.Text), CDec(txtRate.Text))
            lblPay.Text = FormatCurrency(mpayObject.Pay)

        Catch Err As PayrollException    'Catch exceptions from the Payroll class
            MessageBox.Show(Err.Message, "Payroll")
            Select Case Err.FieldInError
                Case "Hours"
                    With txtHours
                        .SelectAll()
                        .Focus()
                    End With
                Case "Rate"
                    With txtRate
                        .SelectAll()
                        .Focus()
                    End With
            End Select

        Catch Err As Exception    'Catch any generic exceptions from CDec functions
            MessageBox.Show("Enter the hours and rate.", "Payroll")
            txtHours.Focus()
        End Try
    End Sub

    Private Sub btnClear_Click(ByVal sender As System.Object, _
      ByVal e As System.EventArgs) Handles btnClear.Click
        'Clear the screen fields

        txtHours.Clear()
        txtRate.Clear()
        lblPay.Text = ""
        With txtName
            .Clear()
            .Focus()
        End With
    End Sub
```

```
        Private Sub btnClose_Click(ByVal sender As System.Object, _
            ByVal e As System.EventArgs) Handles btnClose.Click
            'Close this form and return to the parent form

            Me.Close()
        End Sub

        Private Sub txtHours_Validating(ByVal sender As Object, _
            ByVal e As System.ComponentModel.CancelEventArgs) Handles txtHours.Validating
            'Test hours for numeric

            Dim dgrButtonClicked As DialogResult

            If Not IsNumeric(txtHours.Text) Then
                'Give the user a way to cancel the validation
                dgrButtonClicked = MessageBox.Show( _
                  "Hours must be numeric.", "Hours", MessageBoxButtons.OKCancel)
                If dgrButtonClicked <> DialogResult.Cancel Then
                    e.Cancel = True
                    txtHours.SelectAll()
                End If
            End If
        End Sub

        Private Sub txtRate_Validating(ByVal sender As Object, _
            ByVal e As System.ComponentModel.CancelEventArgs) Handles txtRate.Validating
            'Test pay rate for numeric
            Dim dgrButtonClicked As DialogResult

            If Not IsNumeric(txtRate.Text) Then
                'Give the user a way to cancel the validation
                dgrButtonClicked = MessageBox.Show( _
                  "Pay rate must be numeric.", "Rate", MessageBoxButtons.OKCancel)
                If dgrButtonClicked <> DialogResult.Cancel Then
                    e.Cancel = True
                    txtRate.SelectAll()
                End If
            End If
        End Sub

End Class
```

frmSummary

```
'Project:      Ch02HandsOn
'Module:       Summary Form
'Programmer:   Bradley/Millspaugh
'Date:         January 2003
'Description:  User interface to display the payroll summary information.

Option Strict On

Public Class frmSummary
    Inherits System.Windows.Forms.Form

    Private Sub frmSummary_Load(ByVal sender As Object, _
        ByVal e As System.EventArgs) Handles MyBase.Load
        'Retrieve the summary values each time the form displays
```

```
                lblCount.Text = Payroll.NumberProcessed.ToString()

                lblOvertime.Text = Payroll.OvertimeHours.ToString()
                lblTotalPay.Text = FormatCurrency(Payroll.TotalPay)
            End Sub

            Private Sub btnClose_Click(ByVal sender As System.Object, _
                ByVal e As System.EventArgs) Handles btnClose.Click
                'Close this form

                Me.Close()
            End Sub
        End Class
```

frmAbout

```
'Project:       Ch02HandsOn
'Form:          frmAbout
'Programmer:    Bradley/Millspaugh
'Date:          January 2003
'Description:   Display information about the application from the attributes
'               in the AssemblyInfo.vb file.

Option Strict On

Imports System.Reflection

Public Class frmAbout
    Inherits System.Windows.Forms.Form

        Private Sub frmAbout_Load(ByVal sender As System.Object, _
            ByVal e As System.EventArgs) Handles MyBase.Load
        'Load the text boxes from AssemblyInfo.vb

        Dim objAssembly() As Object
        Dim myInfo As [Assembly]
        Dim myCopyright As AssemblyCopyrightAttribute
        Dim myCompany As AssemblyCompanyAttribute
        Dim myTitle As AssemblyTitleAttribute

        myInfo = [Assembly].Load("Ch02HandsOn")
        objAssembly = myInfo.GetCustomAttributes(True)
        Dim objItem As Object
        'Convert from object to desired types
        'Need select case because order in array changes
        For Each objItem In objAssembly
            Select Case objItem.GetType.ToString()
                Case "System.Reflection.AssemblyTitleAttribute"
                    myTitle = CType(objItem, AssemblyTitleAttribute)
                    Me.Text = "About " & myTitle.Title.ToString()
                Case "System.Reflection.AssemblyCompanyAttribute"
                    myCompany = CType(objItem, AssemblyCompanyAttribute)
                    lblCompany.Text = myCompany.Company.ToString()
                Case "System.Reflection.AssemblyCopyrightAttribute"
                    myCopyright = CType(objItem, AssemblyCopyrightAttribute)
                    lblCopyright.Text = myCopyright.Copyright.ToString()
            End Select
        Next
    End Sub
End Class
```

Payroll Class

```
'Project:       Ch02HandsOn
'Module:        Payroll Class
'Programmer:    Bradley/Millspaugh
'Date:          January 2003
'Description:   Business tier for payroll calculation; validates input data;
'                   calculates pay and summary information.

Option Strict On

Public Class Payroll

#Region "Private fields"
    'Instance variables
    Private mdecHours As Decimal      'Hours property
    Private mdecRate As Decimal       'Rate property
    Private mdecPay As Decimal        'Pay property

    'Shared variables
    Private Shared mintNumberProcessed As Integer     'NumberProcessed shared property
    Private Shared mdecTotalPay As Decimal            'TotalPay shared property
    Private Shared mdecOvertimeHours As Decimal       'OvertimeHours shared property

    'Named constants
    Private Const mdecMINIMUM_WAGE As Decimal = 6.25D
    Private Const mdecMAXIMUM_WAGE As Decimal = 50D
    Private Const mdecMINIMUM_HOURS As Decimal = 0D
    Private Const mdecMAXIMUM_HOURS As Decimal = 60D
    Private Const mdecREGULAR_HOURS As Decimal = 40D
    Private Const mdecOVERTIME_RATE As Decimal = 1.5D
#End Region

#Region "Methods"
    'Constructor
    Sub New(ByVal decHours As Decimal, ByVal decRate As Decimal)
        'Assign properties and calculate the pay

        Me.Hours = decHours
        Me.Rate = decRate
        FindPay()
        mintNumberProcessed += 1
    End Sub

    Private Sub FindPay()
        'Calculate the pay

        Dim decOvertimeHours As Decimal

        If mdecHours <= mdecREGULAR_HOURS Then   'No overtime
            mdecPay = mdecHours * mdecRate
            decOvertimeHours = 0D
        Else                                      'Overtime
            decOvertimeHours = mdecHours - mdecREGULAR_HOURS
            mdecPay = (mdecREGULAR_HOURS * mdecRate) + _
                (decOvertimeHours * mdecOVERTIME_RATE * mdecRate)
        End If
        mdecOvertimeHours += decOvertimeHours
        mdecTotalPay += mdecPay
    End Sub

#End Region
```

```vb
#Region "Property Procedures"

    Public Property Hours() As Decimal
        Get
            Return mdecHours
        End Get

        Set(ByVal Value As Decimal)
            If Value >= mdecMINIMUM_HOURS And _
              Value <= mdecMAXIMUM_HOURS Then
                mdecHours = Value
            Else
                Throw New PayrollException( _
                    "Hours are outside of the acceptable range.", "Hours")
            End If
        End Set
    End Property

    Public Property Rate() As Decimal
        Get
            Return mdecRate
        End Get

        Set(ByVal Value As Decimal)
            If Value > = mdecMINIMUM_WAGE And _
              Value <= mdecMAXIMUM_WAGE Then
                mdecRate = Value
            Else
                Throw New PayrollException( _
                    "Pay rate is outside of the acceptable range.", "Rate")
            End If
        End Set
    End Property

    ReadOnly Property Pay() As Decimal
        Get
            Return mdecPay
        End Get
    End Property

    Shared ReadOnly Property NumberProcessed() As Decimal
        Get
            Return mintNumberProcessed
        End Get
    End Property

    Shared ReadOnly Property TotalPay() As Decimal
        Get
            Return mdecTotalPay
        End Get
    End Property

    Shared ReadOnly Property OvertimeHours() As Decimal
        Get
            Return mdecOvertimeHours
        End Get
    End Property
#End Region

End Class
```

PayrollException Class

```
Public Class PayrollException
    Inherits System.ApplicationException

    Private mstrFieldInError As String

    Sub New(ByVal strMessage As String, ByVal strFieldInError As String)
        'Set the message for the new exception.

        MyBase.New(strMessage)
        mstrFieldInError = strFieldInError
    End Sub

    Public ReadOnly Property FieldInError() As String
        Get
            Return mstrFieldInError
        End Get
    End Property
End Class
```

Summary

1. In VB .NET everything is based on classes, which specify properties, methods, and events.
2. You can create a new class and use the class to create new objects.
3. Creating a new object is called *instantiating* the object; the object is called an *instance* of the class.
4. In OOP terminology, abstraction means to create a model of an object.
5. Encapsulation refers to the combination of the characteristics and behaviors of an item into a single class definition.
6. Inheritance provides a means to derive a new object class based on an existing class. The existing class is called a *base class*, *superclass*, or *parent class*. The inherited class is called a *subclass*, *derived class*, or *child class*.
7. An abstract class is a class designed strictly for inheritance; you cannot instantiate an object of the class but must derive new classes from the class.
8. Polymorphism allows different classes of objects to have similarly named methods that behave differently for that particular object.
9. One of the biggest advantages of object-oriented programming is that objects that you create for one application may be reused in other applications.
10. Multitier applications separate program functions into the presentation tier (the user interface), the business tier (the logic of calculations and validation), and the data tier (accessing stored data).
11. One advantage of using multitier development is that the business rules can be changed without changing the interface or the interface can be changed without changing the business tier.
12. The variables inside a class used to store the properties should be declared as Private, so that data values are accessible only by procedures within the class.

13. The way to make the properties of a class available to code outside the class is to use Property procedures. The `Get` portion returns the value of the property and the `Set` portion assigns a value to the property. Validation is often performed in the `Set` portion.

14. You can create read-only and write-only properties.

15. A constructor is a method that executes automatically when an object is created. In VB, the constructor must be named "New" and must be Public.

16. You can overload the `New` sub procedure to have more than one signature. A `New` sub procedure that requires arguments is called a *parameterized constructor*.

17. The public functions and sub procedures of a class module are its methods.

18. To instantiate an object of a class, you must use the `New` keyword on either the declaration statement or an assignment statement. The location of the `New` keyword determines when the object is created.

19. You can throw a generic ApplicationException or derive your own exception class from ApplicationException to customize an exception object.

20. Shared members (properties and methods) have one copy that can be used by all objects of the class, generally used for totals and counts. Instance members have one copy for each instance of the object. Declare shared members with the `Shared` keyword. You can reference Public shared members of a class without creating an instance of the class.

21. A namespace is an area used for grouping and referring to classes and structures.

22. The scope of variables, constants, and objects, from the greatest to the smallest: namespace, module level, procedure level, and block level.

23. The lifetime of a variable, constant, or object corresponds to its scope.

24. You can declare the accessibility of entities using the keywords `Public`, `Private`, `Protected`, `Friend`, and `Protected Friend`.

25. A subclass inherits all public and protected properties and methods of its base class, except for the constructor. An identically named method in a subclass will override or shadow the base-class method. Shadow is the default.

26. To override a method from a base class, the original method must be declared as overridable, and the new method must use the `Overrides` keyword.

27. A class that has a predefined set of possible values for a property should define the values in an enum. The enum structure can appear at the namespace or class level, and must define integer values.

28. The garbage collection feature periodically checks for unreferenced objects, destroys the object references, and releases resources.

K e y   T e r m s

abstract class *31*	child class *31*
abstraction *30*	constructor *36*
accessibility *52*	data tier *32*
base class *31*	derived class *31*
block-level scope *51*	destructor *36*
business rules *33*	encapsulation *30*
business tier *34*	enum *54*

Review Questions

1. Define abstraction, encapsulation, inheritance, and polymorphism.
2. What is an abstract class and how is it used?
3. Why should properties of a class be declared as private?
4. What are property procedures and what is their purpose?
5. Explain how to create a new class and instantiate an object from that class.
6. What is a constructor, how is it created, and when is it triggered?
7. What is a parameterized constructor?
8. How can you write methods for a new class?
9. What is a shared member? How is it created?
10. Explain the steps necessary to inherit a class from another class.
11. Differentiate between overriding and overloading.
12. What are the advantages of developing applications using multiple tiers?
13. Describe the steps necessary to perform validation in the business tier but display the message to the user in the presentation tier.
14. Explain the differences between a namespace-level variable and a module-level variable. How is each created and how is it used?
15. Explain the differences between a procedure-level variable and a block-level variable. How is each created and how is it used?
16. What is the lifetime of a procedure-level variable? A block-level variable? A module-level variable?
17. Explain the difference between overriding and shadowing methods.
18. What is the effect of using the Protected accessibility modifier? The Friend modifier?
19. What is the purpose of an enum? How is one created?
20. What is garbage collection? What does it do and when does it run?

Programming Exercises

2.1 Tricia's Travels: You can add to your Exercise 1.3 or just create the main form.

Presentation Tier

Main Form—Monthly Specials
Include text boxes for the customer name, phone number, number traveling, departure date, return date, and credit card number. Include a list box for the destinations: Caribbean, Mediterranean, and Alaska. Include radio buttons for 7-day or 14-day packages and a check box for first class. Validate that the user has made an entry for all fields.

Summary Form
Display the total price.

Business Tier

Calculate the amount due based on the following schedule:

Days	Destination	Standard price	First-class price
7	Caribbean	3250	5000
14	Caribbean	6000	9000
7	Mediterranean	4250	7999
14	Mediterranean	7999	11999
7	Alaska	3300	5250
14	Alaska	7200	10500

2.2 Kenna's Kandles offers candles in various shapes, scents, and colors. Write an MDI project that contains a Main form, an About form, and a Summary form using a separate tier for the business rules.

Presentation Tier

Main Form

- Text boxes for customer information (name and credit card number).

- Text box for quantity.

- Radio buttons or list box for candle style (tea light, votive, or pillar).

- Radio buttons or list box for color (Federal Blue, Sunflower Yellow, Christmas Red, and Lily White).

- Check box for Scented.

- Label for the price of the item.

Summary Form
Display the subtotal for all candles, the tax of 8 percent, a shipping fee of 3 percent, and the total due.

Business Tier

Calculate the price for each candle based on the options selected. The business tier should also accumulate the information for the total.

Style	Base price	Scented price (additional)
Tea Lights	5.75	0.75
Votives	7.50	1.25
Pillar	12.25	1.75

2.3 Create a project for maintaining a checkbook using multiple tiers.

Presentation Tier

Main Form
Use radio buttons or a drop-down list to indicate the transaction type: check, deposit, interest, or service charge. Allow the user to enter the amount in a text box for the amount and display the account balance in a label. Display a message box for insufficient funds, based on an appropriate exception generated by the business tier.

Summary Form
Display the total number and the total dollar amounts for deposits, checks, interest, and service charges.

Business Tier

Validate that the balance can cover a check. If not, throw an exception and deduct a service charge of $10; do not process the check. Make sure that input amounts are positive numbers. Process interest and deposits by adding to the balance and checks and service charges by reducing the balance.

Optional Extra

Create an MDI application that includes an About form, a toolbar, and a status bar.

2.4 Piecework workers are paid by the piece. Workers who produce a greater quantity of output are often paid at a higher rate.

Presentation Tier

The program should input the name and number of pieces (a required field) and calculate the pay. Include a *Calculate* button and a *Clear* button. You can include either a *Summary* button or menu item. The *Summary* option displays the total number of pieces, the total pay, and the average pay per person on a Summary form.

Business Tier

The number of pieces must be a positive number; throw an exception for negative numbers. Calculate the pay using this schedule:

Pieces completed	Price paid per piece for all pieces
1–199	.50
200–399	.55
400–599	.60
600 or more	.65

Accumulate and return the summary totals for number of pieces and total pay.

2.5 (Challenge) Add an inherited class to Exercise 2.4. This class calculates pay for senior workers, who are paid on a different scale. You must add a check box to the form for senior workers and use the inherited class for those workers.

Senior workers receive a base pay of $300 plus a per-piece pay using this schedule:

Pieces completed	Price paid per piece for all pieces
1–199	.20
200–399	.25
400–599	.30
600 –799	.35
800 or more	.40

Case Studies

Claytor's Cottages

Modify your Claytor's Cottages case study project from Chapter 1. Complete the Charges option using a presentation tier and a business tier.

Presentation Tier

The form should have a drop-down list or radio buttons for King, Queen, or Double. Include text boxes for entering the customer's name, phone number, the number of nights stayed, credit card type (use a list box for Visa, Mastercard, and American Express), and credit card number. Name, nights stayed, and credit card number are required fields. Use a check box for weekend or weekday rate and a check box for AARP or AAA members. Display the price in a label.

Business Tier

Throw an exception if the number of days is not greater than 0. Calculate the price using this table. Add a room tax of 7 percent. AAA and AARP customers receive a 10 percent discount rate.

Beds	Sun. through Thur. rate	Weekend rate (Fri. and Sat.)
King	95.00	105.00
Queen	85.00	95.00
Double	69.95	79.95

Optional extra: Enter the date of arrival and date of departure instead of the check boxes. You can use a calendar object or text boxes to obtain the dates. Use the methods of the DateTime structure to determine if the dates are weekdays or weekend. Increase the rates by 25 percent in May through September.

Christian's Car Rentals

Modify your Christian's Car Rentals project from Chapter 1. Code the Rentals form using a presentation tier and a business tier.

Presentation Tier

The presentation tier should include data entry for the size of car: Economy, Mid-size, or Luxury. Include text boxes for entering the renter's name, phone number, driver's license, credit card type, and credit card number. A group box should include the number of days rented, the beginning odometer reading, and the ending odometer reading.

Validate that the ending odometer reading is greater than the beginning odometer reading before allowing the data to be sent to the business tier. Make sure that an entry has been made for driver's license and number of days rented.

Business Tier

Validate that the number of days rented is greater than 0. There is no mileage charge if the number of miles does not exceed an average of 100 miles per day rented.

Rates

Car size	Daily rate	Mileage rate
Economy	26.95	.12
Mid-size	32.95	.15
Luxury	50.95	.20

Corporate and Insurance Accounts

Corporate accounts waive the mileage rate and have a 5 percent discount; insurance accounts have a 10 percent discount on the daily rate.

CHAPTER

3

Windows Database Applications

decDiscounted = decExtendedPrice - indecDiscount
decDiscountedPrice = decExtendedPrice - decDi
'Format and display answers for sale
lblExtendedPrice.Text = FormatCurrency(decExt
lblDiscountedPrice.Text = atNumber(decDiscount)
lblDiscountedPrice.Text = FormatCurrency(decD

'Handle exceptions

at the completion of this chapter, you will be able to . . .

1. Explain the relationship of datasets, tables, rows, and constraints.

2. Use MSDE to access SQL Server databases.

3. Set up connections to a database.

4. Create and display information from a DataSet object.

5. Bind a grid, a combo box, and labels to database fields.

6. Retrieve and display selected records on a form.

7. Write a multitier application, separating the data tier from the presentation tier.

In the previous chapter you created applications using a multitier design. In this chapter you will add the third tier—for accessing data. You will learn to use data adapters and datasets to display data from a database file. In Chapter 4 you will work with multiple related tables, and in Chapter 5 you will learn to update a database.

Visual Basic and Database Applications

Professional VB programmers spend the majority of their time on applications that involve databases. To be a good programmer, you will want to concentrate on the various methods of displaying and updating database information.

With VB you can create very simple database applications that require virtually no coding, all the way up to very powerful distributed applications that access and modify data on multiple large-scale servers. You can create programs that display and/or update data on a single stand-alone computer as well as multiuser networked databases. Although this text concentrates on Microsoft Data Engine (MSDE) databases, the techniques that you learn also extend to larger-scale databases, such as SQL Server, Oracle, Sybase, and DB2. You can also apply most of the techniques in this chapter to an Access database.

Universal Data Access

Microsoft's strategy for accessing data from multiple providers is called *Universal Data Access* (UDA). The goal of UDA is to be able to access any type of data from any application on any type of computer. The data could be from relational databases, text files, spreadsheets, email, or address books, and stored on a desktop computer, a local network, a mainframe, an intranet, or the Internet.

OLEDB

UDA is a concept; **OLEDB** is Microsoft's technology designed to implement that concept. In theory, any type of data source can be an OLEDB provider. All that is needed is the proper library routines that allow low-level access to the data, following OLEDB specifications. OLEDB is actually a standardized interface that allows the developer to refer to data from any source using the same set of programming tools, whether the data are stored in a database, a text file, or a spreadsheet.

Using OLEDB, a programmer need not be concerned with the syntax and intricacies of a particular data format. On top of OLEDB, Microsoft has created another layer, ADO.NET, to simplify the programming.

ADO.NET

ActiveX Data Objects (ADO) .NET is Microsoft's latest database object model. The goal of ADO.NET is to allow VB programmers to use a standard set of objects to refer to data from any source.

The common use of the Web and multiple platforms greatly changes the way in which data are handled. In the past it was common to connect to a database in a client/server format. The connection was kept open while the user browsed and/or updated the data, and data typing was not much of a concern. The .NET approach changes this to use disconnected datasets with common data representation (data types) from multiple sources. The .NET Framework is also tightly integrated with Extensible Markup Language (XML), an industry-standard format for storing and transferring data over multiple platforms.

A well-written multitier application that uses disconnected datasets provides for **flexibility** and **scalability**. A flexible application can adapt to changes in the database (the back end or data tier) or to the user interface (the front end or presentation tier). And a scalable application can handle increases in the number of users and the number of servers.

ADO.NET Components

ADO.NET has two major components: the DataSet object and the .NET data provider. The DataSet object holds the data and the provider manipulates the data using SQL statements or stored procedures.

Data Providers

The two managed providers that ship with the .NET Framework are **SQLClient** for SQL Server and **OleDbClient** for all other database formats. Microsoft has available for download an ODBC provider, and a provider for Oracle is in the works and may be available by the time you read this. The examples in this text all use the SQLClient provider.

DataSet Objects

A **DataSet object** holds a copy of the data in memory, disconnected from the data source. The DataSet object can be **populated** (filled) with data from many sources, including a SQL Server database, many other database formats such as Access or DB2, an XML stream, a simple text file, a spreadsheet, or even an array or a collection. Regardless of the source of the data, your code always handles a DataSet object in the same way.

A DataSet object can hold one or more **DataTable objects**. A **table** can be viewed like a spreadsheet—with rows and columns. Each **row** in a table represents the data for one item, person, or transaction and is called a **record**. Each **column** in a table is used to store a different element of data, such as an account number, a name, an address, or a numeric amount, and is called a **field**. You can think of the table in Figure 3.1 as consisting of rows and columns or of records and fields.

Figure 3.1

A table consists of rows (records) and columns (fields).

	AuID	LastName	FirstName	Phone	Address	City	State	Zip	
▶	172-32-1176	White	Johnson	408 496-7223	10932 Bigge	Menlo Park	CA	94025	
	213-46-8915	Green	Marjorie	415 986-7020	309 63rd St.	Oakland	CA	94618	
	238-95-7766	Carson	Cheryl	415 548-7723	589 Darwin L	Berkeley	CA	94705	
	267-41-2394	O'Leary	Michael	408 286-2428	22 Cleveland	San Jose	CA	95128	
	274-80-9391	Straight	Dean	415 834-2919	5420 College	Oakland	CA	94609	
	341-22-1782	Smith	Meander	913 843-0462	10 Mississipp	Lawrence	KS	66044	
	409-56-7008	Bennet	Abraham	415 658-9932	6223 Batema	Berkeley	CA	94705	
	427-17-2319	Dull	Ann	415 836-7128	3410 Blonde	Palo Alto	CA	94301	

Authors

Most tables use a **primary key field** (or combination of fields) to uniquely identify each record. The primary key field is often a number, such as employee number, account number, identification number, or Social Security number; or it may be a text field, such as last name, or a combination, such as last name and first name.

A relational database generally contains multiple tables and relationships between the tables. For example, an Employee table may have an Employee ID field and the Payroll table will also have an Employee ID field. The two tables are related by Employee ID. You can find the employee information for one payroll record by retrieving the record for the corresponding Employee ID. In this example, Employee ID is the primary key for the Employee table. The Employee ID field in the Payroll table is considered a **foreign key**—the field that links a Payroll record to its corresponding Employee record.

The DataSet Object Model

Each DataSet object contains information about the relationship of the Data-Table objects in the DataTable collection. The DataTable object has both DataRow and DataColumn collections. A single DataRow holds the actual data for one record. The DataRow object maintains the original values and any changed values. This information is used to determine which rows have changed during program execution.

A DataRelation object stores information about related tables, including which columns contain the primary keys and foreign keys that link the tables. This object also enforces referential integrity, which requires that changes in foreign key columns must match a corresponding primary key value. Figure 3.2 shows the object model of the DataSet object.

Figure 3.2

The DataSet Object Model.

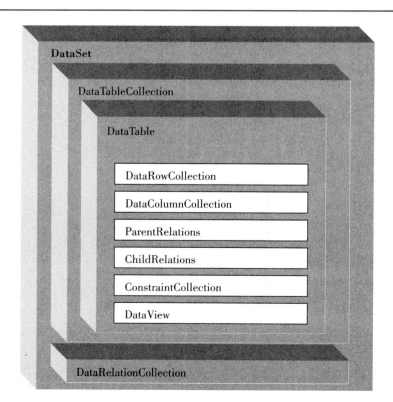

Data Provider Objects

A .NET data provider is a set of components designed for fast access and manipulation of data. The components include the Connection, Command, DataAdapter, and DataReader objects.

A **Connection object** is a link to a data source, which is a specific file and/or server. A **DataAdapter object** handles retrieving and updating the data in a DataSet object; it acts like a bridge to send the data back and forth between the data source and the disconnected DataSet. A **Command object** stores and executes SQL statements that can query the data, update the data, or run a stored procedure. The **DataReader object** is a high-performance, forward-only, read-only stream of data that bypasses the DataSet object to directly communicate with the database.

This chapter focuses on using DataAdapters to create DataSets. You should use a DataSet object, rather than a DataReader, when you want to

- Transfer data between tiers.

- Manipulate the data without an open connection.

- Relate data from multiple sources.

- Bind data to a Windows form.

Figure 3.3 shows the provider objects. Note that the terms *Connection*, *Command*, *DataAdapter*, and *DataReader* are used generically. There is actually a set of objects for each of the providers. For example, the SQL provider has an SQLConnection, SQLCommand, SQLDataAdapter, and SQL-DataReader. The OleDb provider has an OleDbConnection, OleDbCommand, OldDbDataAdapter, and OldDbDataReader.

Figure 3.3

The objects in a .NET data provider.

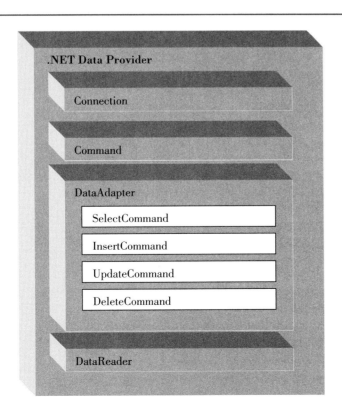

XML Data

XML is an industry-standard format for storing and transferring data. You can find the specifications for XML at http://www.w3.org/XML, which is the site for the World Wide Web Consortium (W3C).

You don't need to know any XML to write database applications in VB. The necessary XML is generated for you automatically, similar to the automatically generated VB code and HTML. However, a few facts about XML can help you understand what is happening in your programs.

Most proprietary database formats store data in binary, which cannot be accessed by other systems or pass through Internet firewalls. Data stored in XML is all text, identified by tags, similar to HTML tags. An XML file can be edited by any text editor program, such as Notepad.

If you have seen or written any HTML, you know that opening and closing tags define elements and attributes. For example, any text between <b> and </b> is rendered in bold by the browser.

```
<b>This text is bold.</b> <i>This is italic.</i>
```

The tags in XML are not predefined as they are in HTML. The tags can identify fields by name. For example, following are the first two records of a dataset called dsAuthors (refer to Figure 3.1), based on the Authors table in the Pubs SQL Server database, represented in XML. (Later in this chapter you will use the Pubs database for VB projects.)

```
<?xml version="1.0" standalone="yes"?>
<dsAuthors xmlns="dsAuthors.xsd">
    <authors>
        <au_id>172-32-1176</au_id>
        <au_lname>White</au_lname>
        <au_fname>Johnson</au_fname>
        <phone>408 496-7223</phone>
        <address>10932 Bigge Rd.</address>
        <city>Menlo Park</city>
        <state>CA</state>
        <zip>94025</zip>
        <contract>true</contract>
    </authors>
    <authors>
        <au_id>213-46-8915</au_id>
        <au_lname>Green</au_lname>
        <au_fname>Marjorie</au_fname>
        <phone>415 986-7020</phone>
        <address>309 63rd St. #411</address>
        <city>Oakland</city>
        <state>CA</state>
        <zip>94618</zip>
        <contract>true</contract>
    </authors>
</dsAuthors>
```

In addition to an XML data file, you usually also have an XML schema file. The schema describes the fields, data types, and any constraints, such as required fields. ADO.NET validates the data against the schema and checks for constraint violations. The schema also is defined with XML tags and can be viewed or edited in a text editor. You will be able to see the schema for your datasets in a VB project by viewing the .xsd file shown in the Solution Explorer. Here is a partial sample of the schema for the dsAuthors dataset.

```xml
<?xml version="1.0" standalone="yes"?>
<xs:schema id="dsAuthors" targetNamespace="dsAuthors.xsd"
    <xs:element name="authors">
        <xs:complexType>
            <xs:sequence>
                <xs:element name="au_id" type="xs:string" />
                <xs:element name="au_lname" type="xs:string" />
                <xs:element name="au_fname" type="xs:string" />
                <xs:element name="phone" type="xs:string" />
                <xs:element name="address" type="xs:string" minOccurs="0" />
                <xs:element name="city" type="xs:string" minOccurs="0" />
                <xs:element name="state" type="xs:string" minOccurs="0" />
                <xs:element name="zip" type="xs:string" minOccurs="0" />
                <xs:element name="contract" type="xs:boolean" />
            </xs:sequence>
        </xs:complexType>
    </xs:element>
    <xs:unique name="Constraint1" msdata:PrimaryKey="true">
        <xs:selector xpath=".//mstns:authors" />
        <xs:field xpath="mstns:au_id" />
    </xs:unique>
</xs:schema>
```

The format of XML data offers several advantages for programming. Because an XML schema provides for strong data typing, the various data types can be handled properly. ADO.NET can treat the XML data as objects, allowing the IntelliSense feature of the VS .NET environment to provide information for the programmer. In addition, data handling in XML and ADO.NET executes faster than in earlier forms of ADO.

Feedback 3.1

1. Assume that you have a data table that contains the names and phone numbers of your friends. Describe how the terms *row*, *column*, *record*, *field*, and *primary key field* apply to your table.
2. What is an advantage of transferring data as XML, rather than a proprietary format such as Access or SQL Server?

MSDE and SQL Server

Microsoft supports two products for designing and maintaining database files: Access and SQL Server. Microsoft Access uses the Jet Engine, which is designed for single-user databases or small networked databases with five or fewer users. SQL Server is designed for larger-scale databases that may support many users and require more robust security and reliability.

The exercises in this text are based on SQL Server databases. If you have SQL Server available, you can use that. Otherwise, you can use **Microsoft Data Engine (MSDE)**, the desktop or personal version of SQL Server, which is included with the .NET Framework. You can consider MSDE a "stripped down" version of SQL Server. It provides access to SQL Server database files and uses the same version of SQL as SQL Server. What MSDE is missing is the management and design tools of SQL Server.

You can install MSDE and the sample databases, so that your machine runs the MSDE server. After installation, the SQL Server Service Manager can run automatically when you start the computer. Before doing the projects in this chapter, check for the 🖥 icon in the notification area of the task bar, which indicates that the server is running. If you are using a school lab, likely the server is already installed. However, if you are using your own system, see Appendix C for help installing MSDE.

Note: SQL Server and SQL Server Service Manager are products from Microsoft. Do not confuse them with SQL, the industry-standard database query language, which is described on page 93 and in Appendix D.

Accessing Your Servers—Step-by-Step

With the SQL Server Service Manager running, your applications have easy access to data. You can look at the tables within the sample databases by simply expanding nodes in the Visual Studio Server Explorer. The first few steps of the following step-by-step example project will give you a feel for the power of the Server Explorer in the VS .NET IDE. You will use this project to create a database application later in this chapter.

Access Your SQL Server

STEP 1: Begin a New Project called *Ch03Employee* using the Windows Application template.

STEP 2: Display the Server Explorer window, if it isn't already showing. You may have to point to its icon if the window is hidden behind the toolbox, or select *Server Explorer* from the *View* menu (shortcut: Ctrl + Alt + S).

STEP 3: In the Server Explorer window, expand the *Servers* node.

STEP 4: After expanding the node for the local computer, you should see a node for *SQL Servers*. Expand that node to see the name(s) of your server(s).

STEP 5: If you have more than one server, select the one that ends with "\NETSDK". The NETSDK server is installed when you set up the sample databases that come with .NET, which you will need for the exercises in this text. (If you don't see the server and databases, see Appendix C for help installing the sample databases.)

STEP 6: Expand the *NETSDK* node to see a list of the available SQL Server databases.

View the Data

STEP 1: Expand the *pubs* node.

STEP 2: Expand the *Tables* node (Figure 3.4).

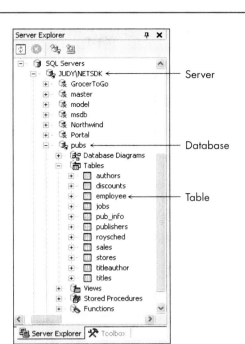

STEP 3: Right-click on *employee* and select *Retrieve Data From Table*.

Impressive? You can look at any of the tables or the views (results of queries) for any of the databases. Notice the other nodes: Database Diagrams, Stored Procedures, and Functions. A database diagram handles the relationship between tables.

Our next step is to get the data to the form.

Obtaining Data—Step-by-Step

Setting up data access in Visual Basic requires several steps. This list is an overview—each of the steps is further described in the sections that follow (see Figure 3.5).

- Set up a connection. A connection establishes a link to a data source, which is a specific file and/or server.

- Set up a data adapter. A data adapter handles retrieving and updating the data. In the programs in this chapter, the data adapter retrieves the records from the database and creates a DataSet object.

- Add controls to your form and set properties to bind the controls to the fields in the DataSet object.

- Write some VB code, primarily to fill the DataSet object.

Figure 3.5

Define a connection, a data adapter, and a dataset to display data in bound controls on a form.

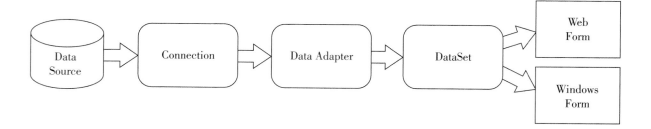

You can choose from several methods for setting up connections and data adapters. You can declare the components in code, visually add the components from the toolbox and set their properties, or use the easiest alternative: the Server Explorer. Simply select the table (or fields) that you want and drag to the form; the properly configured connection and adapter components are automatically added to the component tray.

Next you will use the easy way to add components to your Ch03Employee project.

Add a Data Adapter
STEP 1: Close the window showing the data preview.
STEP 2: Rename Form1 to *frmEmployee*, set the form's Text property to *Employees*, and set the project's startup object to *frmEmployee*.
STEP 3: In the Server Explorer, select the employee table in the pubs database and drag it to the form. Notice the new connection and data adapter components in the component tray.
STEP 4: Rename SqlDataAdapter1 as *daEmployee*.

If you don't see the properties for the data adapter, it is because more than one item is selected. Click on the form, then click on the adapter again. ■

Examine the Connection
STEP 1: Click on the connection component and rename it to *conPubs*.
STEP 2: Look at the properties. The database is set to pubs and the DataSource is your MSDE server.

Generate a DataSet object
STEP 1: Right-click on the daEmployee DataAdapter component in the component tray.
STEP 2: Select *Generate Dataset*.
STEP 3: Select *New dataset* and change the name to *dsEmployee*. Click *OK*.

SQL Server may be case sensitive depending on an option setting when the server was installed. ■

Note: After completing this step, you see a new item in the Solution Explorer: dsEmployee.xsd, which is the schema for the new DataSet. In the component tray, you see DsEmployee1, which is the instance of the new DataSet. You can think of dsEmployee as the class and DsEmployee1 as the object.

Display Data in a Grid

STEP 1: Select a DataGrid from the toolbox and add it to your form. You will want to widen the form and the grid to allow room to display the data.
STEP 2: Name the DataGrid *dgrEmployee*.
STEP 3: Set the DataSource property to *DsEmployee1*.
STEP 4: Set the DataMember to *employee*, which is the name of the table.

TIP

You can set the DataSource to the DataSet and table in one step, such as *DsEmployee1.employee*; then you do not have to set the DataMember. ∎

Write the Code

STEP 1: In the Form_Load event procedure, use the data adapter's Fill method to fill the dataset.

```
'Fill the dataset
daEmployee.Fill(DsEmployee1)
```

Run the Program

STEP 1: Run your program (Figure 3.6).
STEP 2: Stop the program and resize the grid, if necessary.

Not bad for a single line of code!

Figure 3.6

Display the DataSet in the DataGrid.

	emp_id	fname	minit	lname	job_id	job_lvl	pub_id	hire_date
▶	PMA42628M	Paolo	M	Accorti	13	35	0877	8/27/1992
	PSA89086M	Pedro	S	Afonso	14	89	1389	12/24/1990
	VPA30890F	Victoria	P	Ashworth	6	140	0877	9/13/1990
	H-B39728F	Helen		Bennett	12	35	0877	9/21/1989
	L-B31947F	Lesley		Brown	7	120	0877	2/13/1991
	F-C16315M	Francisco		Chang	4	227	9952	11/3/1990
	PTC11962M	Philip	T	Cramer	2	215	9952	11/11/1989
	A-C71970F	Aria		Cruz	10	87	1389	10/26/1991
	AMD15433F	Ann	M	Devon	3	200	9952	7/16/1991
	ARD36773F	Anabela	R	Domingues	8	100	0877	1/27/1993
	PHF38899M	Peter	H	Franken	10	75	0877	5/17/1992
	PXH22250M	Paul	X	Henriot	5	159	0877	8/19/1993

TIP

Click on a column header in a grid at run time to sort the data by the selected column. The grid's AllowSorting property must be set to True (the default). ∎

Displaying Data in Individual Fields

One of the most common ways to display data from any data source is to allow the user to select the desired record from a list. The list may hold the record keys or some other value, such as a person's name. Once the user has made a selection, you can retrieve the corresponding record and display the detail data on the form.

Populating Combo Boxes with Data

You can fill a list box or combo box with values from a database. List controls have the necessary properties to bind to a data source. To automatically fill a list box or combo box with data from a DataSet object (Figure 3.7), you must set two properties: the **DataSource** and **DisplayMember properties**. The DataSource connects to the dataset. The DisplayMember connects to the specific field name for the data that you want to display in the list.

F i g u r e   3 . 7

Allow users to select a value from a list. You can automatically fill the list by binding it to a field in a dataset.

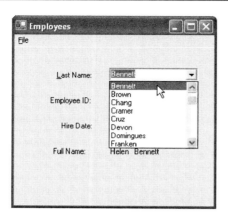

After you add a list control to a form that has a dataset defined, drop down the Properties list for the DataSource and select the dataset name. Then drop down the list for the DisplayMember property; it will show the field names in the dataset from which you can select. For example, for the combo box shown in Figure 3.7, the DataSource is set to DsEmployee1 (the data set) and the DisplayMember property is set to Employee.lname (the table and field name). That's all there is to it. When you run your program, the list automatically fills with the values from the selected field.

You must still use the Fill method for the dataset to load the list.

```
'Fill the dataset for the list box
daEmployee.Fill(DsEmployee1)
```

✅**TIP**

If you have duplicate entries in a list box, modify the SQL SELECT statement in the data adapter to include the keyword DISTINCT, such as SELECT DISTINCT Author FROM Books. ∎

DataViews—Sorting the Data for the ListBox

When you want to display data in alphabetical order in a list box, you can usually just set the Sorted property to True. Unfortunately this does not work when the list box is bound to a data source. The sorting must be done on the data.

ADO.NET offers a DataView object for changing the way data are viewed. One of the advantages of using a data view rather than a DataSet is the Sort property. You can think of a data view as a virtual table or a different way of looking at an existing table. Creating a DataView does not create a new table but allows you to display information in a manner different from the table on which it is based.

The easiest way to create a new DataView is to select its tool from the *Data* section of the toolbox (Figure 3.8). Assuming that you already have one or more DataSets defined, you can set the Table property of the new DataView component to an existing table and then set the Sort property to a field name.

Creating a Selection Project—Step-by-Step

The following step-by-step tutorial creates a new project that fills a combo box with values from a database field, allows the user to select the desired record, and retrieves and displays the detail data for the selected record. To display the fields in the combo box in alphabetic order, base the list on a data view rather than a data table. Refer to Figure 3.7 for the completed form.

Create a New Project
STEP 1: Open a new project called *Ch03List*.

STEP 2: Name the form *frmList* and set the Text property of the form to *Employees*. Set the project's startup object to *frmList*. In the *Project Properties* dialog box, *Build* tab, set *Option Strict On* (or add the statement to the form's code).

> *Note*: Setting Option Strict in the *Project Properties* dialog box does not add a visible line of code to a project, but does set the option on for all files in the project.

STEP 3: From Server Explorer, expand the employee table in pubs and select the *lname* (last name) field. Drag the field to the form, which sets up new connection and data adapter objects.

STEP 4: Name the components:
    SqlConnection1:   conPubs
    SqlDataAdapter: daLastName

STEP 5: Generate a new dataset called *dsLastName*, which will create the DsLastName1 object in the component tray.

Set Up the DataView
STEP 1: From the *Data* section in the toolbox, drag a DataView object to the component tray.

STEP 2: Name the DataView component *dvLastName*.

STEP 3: Set the Table property to *DsLastName1.employee*. Notice that a DataView is based on an existing table.

STEP 4: Set the Sort property to *lname*. Because there is no drop-down list of field names, you must know the exact spelling of the field name.

Add a Label and Combo Box

STEP 1: Select a combo box control from the *Windows Forms* section of the toolbox and add it to the form.
STEP 2: Name the control *cboLastName*.
STEP 3: Delete the Text property.
STEP 4: Set the DataSource property to *dvLastName*.
STEP 5: Set the DisplayMember property to *lname*.
STEP 6: Add a label to the left of the combo box; set the Text property to *Last Name*.
STEP 7: Code the Form_Load event procedure:

```
'Fill the dataset for the list box

daLastName.Fill(DsLastName1)
'Set the combo box for no current selection
cboLastName.SelectedIndex = -1
```

STEP 8: Run the program. The combo box should fill with the employee last names from the pubs database. Fortunately for this exercise, there are no duplicate last names. Later in this chapter, you will learn to handle both first and last names, as well as record keys.
STEP 9: Stop the program.

Creating a Parameterized Query

When you want your dataset to contain only selected record(s), you can modify the SQL SELECT statement used by the data adapter. Use a WHERE clause in an SQL query to specify which records to select, called the **criteria**.

Examples

```
SELECT Title, Author, ISBN FROM Books
    WHERE Title = "A Midsummer Night's Dream"

SELECT Name, AmountDue FROM OverdueAccounts
    WHERE AmountDue > 100

SELECT emp_id, lname, fname FROM employee
    WHERE lname = "Jones"
```

Usually you don't know until run time the value that you want to include in the WHERE clause. In that case, you can use a wildcard in place of the actual value and supply the value as a parameter in code. This type of query is called a **parameterized query**.

```
SELECT emp_id, fname, minit, lname, job_id, job_lvl, pub_id, hire_date FROM employee
    WHERE lname = @lname
```

The SQL SELECT statement is a property of the data adapter. You can either type the SELECT statement yourself or use the Query Builder to create it for you. Click on the data adapter and view its properties. By expanding the SelectCommand you can see the CommandText property. Click on the Build (...) button to display the Query Builder. For the lname field, type "=@lname" in the Criteria column (Figure 3.9). The Query Builder creates the correct SQL for you. Note that the Query Builder adds the optional parentheses around "(lname = @lname)" in the SQL statement, even when you leave them out.

In the SQL version used by SQL Server, the wildcard character is an "at sign" (@); in the SQL version used by Access, a question mark (?) is the wildcard character. ∎

F i g u r e   3 . 9

Add the parameter name in the Criteria column of the Query Builder.

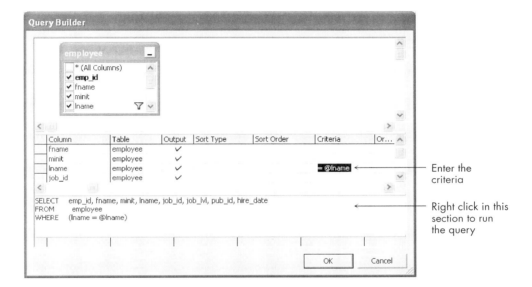

Structured Query Language (SQL) is a standard language for querying and updating data in a database. SQL SELECT statements select data from a database and return the values to the program. You can specify which fields from which table or tables, and select only certain records based on criteria.

When you use a parameterized query, you can allow the user to select an item from a combo or list box. After selecting the field, you would most likely display more information about the selected item in labels or text boxes.

If you have only a single field for selection, you can specify only the wildcard character (@) for the criteria (without the parentheses), rather than include the field name. Including the field name (@lname) makes the query a little clearer, however. ∎

Binding Individual Controls to Data Fields

You can connect (bind) individual controls to a single data field using the control's **DataBindings object**. For example, to bind a label or a text box to a dataset field, locate the control's DataBindings property at the top of the Properties list (above the Name property). Expand the DataBindings node to find the Text property; drop down the list to select the field that you want (Figure 3.10).

Figure 3.10

Bind a dataset field to a label by setting the label's DataBindings.Text property to the desired field.

Continuing the Selection Project Step-by-Step

Open your Ch03List project, if necessary, to add bound labels and modify the query. You will add a second data adapter to hold the employee records. Remember that the first data adapter (daLastName) generates a dataset that holds only the last names.

Add a Data Adapter and Dataset

STEP 1: Drag the employee table from pubs to the form, naming the data adapter *daEmployee*. Note that you must have the form open in design view to do this.

This data adapter uses the same connection as daLastName, which holds only the employee last names.

STEP 2: In the Properties window, expand the SelectCommand property and click on the entry for CommandText.

STEP 3: Click on the Build (...) button to open the Query Designer.

STEP 4: In the Criteria column for lname, type in "@lname". (Refer to Figure 3.9.)

STEP 5: Click elsewhere on the grid and view the modified SQL statement.
If a warning dialog box appears, click *Yes*.

STEP 6: Click *OK*.

STEP 7: Generate the dataset from daEmployee, calling it *dsEmployee*.

Add the Remaining Controls

STEP 1: Add labels for the employee id, hire date, and first name fields to the form (Figure 3.11).

TIP

If the form is not open but has a tab at the top of the Document window, you can drag a table from the Server Explorer to the form's tab, which opens its designer window. ■

Figure 3.11

Add labels to the form

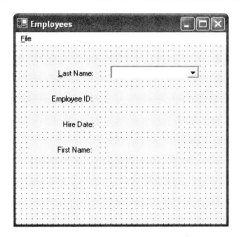

STEP 2: Name and set the Text properties of the labels as needed.

Name	Text
Label1	Employee ID
Label2	Hire Date
Label3	First Name
lblEmployeeID	(blank)
lblHireDate	(blank)
lblFirstName	(blank)

STEP 3: Select lblEmployeeID and locate the DataBindings at the top of the Properties window. Expand the DataBindings node and click on the Text property. Drop down the list of available choices (refer to Figure 3.10) and select *DsEmployee1*, *employee*, *emp_id*.

STEP 4: Set the DataBindings.Text value to the appropriate fields for lblHire-Date and lblFirstName.

Code the Combo Box Selection

STEP 1: Code the combo box SelectedIndexChanged event procedure.

```
'Get the record to match the selection

If cboLastName.SelectedIndex <> -1 Then
    DsEmployee1.Clear()
    daEmployee.SelectCommand.Parameters("@lname").Value = cboLastName.Text
    daEmployee.Fill(DsEmployee1)
End If
```

Test the Program

STEP 1: Run the program. Each time you select a new name from the list, the rest of the labels should fill with data (Figure 3.12).

STEP 2: To format the date, add the following line of code to the end of the SelectedIndexChanged event procedure:

```
lblHireDate.Text = FormatDateTime(CDate(lblHireDate.Text), DateFormat.ShortDate)
```

Adding an Expression to the DataSet Schema

Sometimes you need to use information from a database in a format other than how it is stored. You may need a calculated expression, such as a unit cost multiplied by a quantity on hand. Or you may wish to concatenate fields together such as first and last names. In fact, sometimes you need first name and then last name and other applications need last name followed by a comma and then the first name. If you create a new expression based on the fields in the table, you can bind the expression to one of the form's controls.

You create new expressions in the DataSet's schema. As you saw earlier in this chapter, each DataSet has an .xsd file in the Solution Explorer. You can open the .xsd file and view the DataSet schema as a table (Figure 3.13) or as XML (Figure 3.14). You can modify the schema in either view, but the easiest way is to use the table (the *DataSet* tab).

Figure 3.13

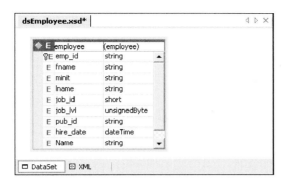

View the DataSet schema .xsd file as a table.

Figure 3.14

View the DataSet schema .xsd file as XML.

Adding an Expression—Step-by-Step

Next you will add an expression that creates a concatenated field for the name. You add expressions by adding an Element line to the schema table and setting the Element's Expression property.

Add a Name Field

STEP 1: Open your Ch03List project, if necessary.

STEP 2: Open your dsEmployee.xsd file from Solution Explorer. The table view (*DataSet* tab) should appear.

STEP 3: Scroll to the last line of the table (the line with the asterisk) and click on the first column. Select *E element* from the drop-down list (Figure 3.15).

Figure 3.15

Add a new element to the end of the DataSet schema.

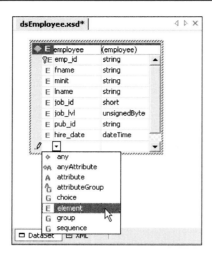

STEP 4: Type "Name" in the first column and make sure the second column is *string*.

STEP 5: Make sure the new Name element is selected. In the Properties window set the Expression property to

```
fname + '' + minit + '' + lname
```

Include one blank space between the single quotes to separate the data fields.

Notice that the concatenation operator in SQL is the plus sign (+), rather than VB's ampersand (&).

STEP 6: From the *Build* menu, select *Rebuild Solution*.

STEP 7: Change the Text property of Label3 from *First Name* to *Full Name*.

STEP 8: Change the Name property of the label that displays the name to lblName.

STEP 9: Set the Databindings.Text property of lblName to *Name* from *DsEmployee1*. You are binding the label to your new expression field.

Test the Project

STEP 1: Run the project. When you select a last name from the list, the entire name should appear in lblName (Figure 3.16).

Figure 3.16

The data for the selected record appear in the labels.

Using the ValueMember Property of Combo Boxes

The previous examples display the last name in the combo box and use the selected last name to find the corresponding record. This technique works great when no duplicates exist for the last name, or whatever field you are using for the selection. However, this method fails when there are duplicates.

The list box controls, ListBox and ComboBox, have a **ValueMember property** that you can use to solve this problem. The DisplayMember property determines the field to display in the list; the ValueMember property can hold the record's primary key or any other unique field value. When the user selects a name from the list, the ValueMember holds the corresponding key value. For example, you can assign the concatenated full name as the DisplayMember property and the primary key (emp_id in the Employee table) to the Value-Member property (Figure 3.17).

DisplayMember	ValueMember
FullName	**emp_id**
Accorti, Paolo M	PMA42628M
Afonso, Pedro S	PSA89086M
Ashworth, Victoria	PVPA30890F
Bennett, Helen	H-B39728F
Brown, Lesley	L-B31947F
Chang, Francisco	F-C16315M
Cramer, Philip T	PTC11962M
Cruz, Aria	A-C71970F

If you assign the record's key field to the ValueMember property and allow the user to select, the combo box SelectedValue property holds the ValueMember property that corresponds to the selected list item. Make the record key field the search parameter:

```
daEmployee.SelectCommand.Parameters("@emp_id").Value = cboNames.SelectedValue.ToString()
```

Moving a Database Project

If you create a database project on one computer and want to transfer to another computer for further development, the database connection string can be a problem. You can choose from several methods to solve this problem. The following two methods are the easiest. See Appendix E for instructions for using a dynamic property and the configuration file for connection strings.

- After you move the project, select the connection object in the designer, click on its ConnectionString property, and drop down the list for database connections on that computer. If the connection already exists, you can select it from the list; if it doesn't, click the *<new connection>* entry, set up a new connection, and select it.

- Before you move a project, make its connection string more generic, so that it can run on any computer that has the .NET sample database files installed. Select the connection object and change the ConnectionString property to this string, if you are using the pubs database:

```
"server=(local)\NetSDK;Trusted_Connection=yes;database=pubs".
```

Feedback 3.2

1. Explain the steps necessary to bind a label to a single field in a DataSet. Assume that the DataSet has already been generated.
2. How would you modify the SELECT statement if you want to find customers in a specific ZIP code?
3. List the steps to create an expression field combining the City, State, and ZIP fields.

Multiple Tiers

Now that you have worked with a DataSet object, the .NET data providers, and a DataView object, it's time to separate the project into multiple tiers. When possible, you should separate the database access from the user interface. For a multitier application, we will create a data component as a separate tier. The data component will contain the data connections, data adapters, and datasets, as well as methods to return the data to the presentation tier (Figure 3.18). When you have a well-constructed data tier, you can use the component in multiple projects with various user interfaces.

Figure 3.18

Good applications generally separate the user interface from the data access.

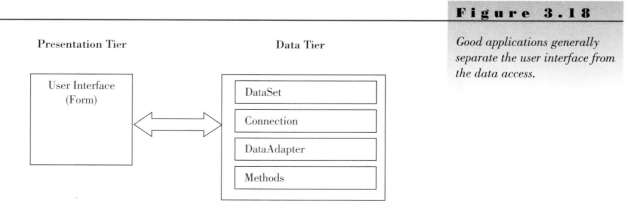

Creating a Data Tier—Step-by-Step

The following step-by-step tutorial recreates the Employee DataGrid project using a presentation tier and a data tier.

Create a New Project

STEP 1: Begin a new Windows Application project. Name the project *Ch03EmployeeTiers*.

STEP 2: Add a DataGrid to the form and name the grid *dgrEmployees*. Widen the form and the grid.

STEP 3: Name the form *frmEmployees* and change the Text property to *Employees*.

STEP 4: Set the project's startup object to *frmEmployees*.

Add a Component for the Data Tier

You need to add a new component for the data tier. Although you could just add a new class, a class does not provide a visual designer. The Component item *does* provide a visual designer, which allows you to drag tables and fields and visually create the connections, data adapters, and datasets.

STEP 1: From the *Project* menu choose *Add Component*. (Alternate method: Right-click the project name in the Solution Explorer and select *Add / Add New Item / Component Class*.)

STEP 2: Name the component *PubsData* in the Properties window and the file *PubsData.vb* in the Solution Explorer.

STEP 3: Drag the employee table from the pubs database to the Component Design window.

STEP 4: Name the data adapter *daEmployee* and the connection *conPubs*.

STEP 5: Generate the dataset and call it *dsEmployee*. Select *Add this dataset to the designer* and click *OK*.

TIP

To create the layout of a grid, create the data components on the form. Then cut and paste the data components on the data tier component. ∎

Code the Component

STEP 1: Display the code for your new component. Notice that the design template generated the lines

```
Public Class PubsData
    Inherits System.ComponentModel.Component
       ...

End Class
```

Your new component is a class that inherits from the Component class.

STEP 2: Write the getDataset method in the PubsData component. Notice that this method returns a DataSet object.

```
Public Function getDataset() As DataSet
    'Fill the dataset

    daEmployee.Fill(DsEmployee1)
    Return DsEmployee1
End Function
```

Code the Form

In the form, you must write code to retrieve the dataset and bind to the data grid. You cannot do this at design time, since the dataset is declared in the data tier component. You must declare an instance of the PubsData component (the data tier) and a DataSet object. Then you can call the getDataset method to retrieve the dataset from the data tier.

STEP 1: Switch to the form and code its Load event procedure.

```
Private Sub frmEmployees_Load(ByVal sender As System.Object, _
  ByVal e As System.EventArgs) Handles MyBase.Load

    Dim objEmployee As PubsData
    Dim dsEmployee As New DataSet()

    Try
        'Get the data from the data tier
        objEmployee = New PubsData()
        dsEmployee = objEmployee.getDataset()

        'Bind the dataset to the grid
        dgrEmployees.DataSource = dsEmployee
        dgrEmployees.DataMember = "employee"

    Catch err As Exception
        MessageBox.Show(err.Message)
    End Try
End Sub
```

STEP 2: Write the remarks at the top of both the form and component class.

Test the Project

STEP 1: Test the project. The data grid should fill with data, just as it did when the data access was in the form (refer to Figure 3.6).

Binding to Combo Boxes

Connecting to a combo box or list box from the data tier is similar to connecting to a grid. The data tier must have a method that returns a data view to fill the combo box. You set the combo box DataSource property to the data view and set the DisplayMember and ValueMember properties to the fields in the data view. When you perform data binding to a combo box in code, the SelectedIndexChanged event is triggered during the binding before you have any data. It's best to set up a module-level variable that indicates when the list has been initialized.

```
'Module-level declarations
Dim mblnListInitialized As Boolean = False

Private Sub frmList_Load(ByVal sender As System.Object, _
  ByVal e As System.EventArgs) Handles MyBase.Load
    'Load the combo box, bind the data fields, and retrieve the first record

    Dim objEmployee As EmployeeData    'Instance of data tier component
    Dim dvNames As DataView
```

```
Try
    'Get the data from the data tier
    objEmployee = New EmployeeData()
    dvNames = objEmployee.getNames()

    'Bind the data view to the combo box
    'Note that setting the binding triggers the SelectedIndexChanged event
    With cboName
        .DateSource = dvNames
        .DisplayMember = "FullName"
        .ValueMember = "emp_id"
        .SelectedIndex = -1
    End With
    mblnListInitialized = True

Catch err As Exception
    MessageBox.Show(err.Message)
End Try
End Sub
```

DataBindings for Multiple Tiers

When your project contains labels or text boxes that you want to bind to database fields, you need another technique for connecting to the data tier. Recall that you bind labels and text boxes using the DataBindings.Text property. Since the dataset is not declared in the form, you must set the DataBindings in code, using the `DataBindings.Add` method.

DataBindings.Add Method—General Form

```
ControlName.DataBindings.Add("text", DataSource, "FieldName")
```

The DataSource should be a table or data view; the FieldName is the name of the field from the database, enclosed in quotes.

DataBindings.Add Method—Examples

```
lblEmployeeID.DataBindings.Add("text", dsEmployee.Tables("employee"), "emp_id")
lblHireDate.DataBindings.Add("text", dsEmployee.Tables(0), "hire_date")
```

Notice that the DataSource in these examples refers to the Tables collection of a DataSet. You can reference an item from the collection using either an index or a string.

Location of Binding Code

In a multitier application you must write code to bind to individual fields. But where does the binding code appear? Once you bind the controls, they remain bound unless you actually remove the bindings. Depending on the logic of your program, you may want to bind the fields in the Form_Load event procedure or in another procedure. Note that you must have a dataset available before you can bind the fields. In the list-selection program, it works best to bind the fields in the SelectedIndexChanged event procedure, setting a boolean variable to indicate when the fields have been bound.

```
Static blnFieldsBound As Boolean = False    'Determines if form controls are bound

Try
    'Get the data matching the selected name from the data tier
    dsEmployee = objEmployee.getDataset(cboName.SelectedValue.ToString())

    If Not blnFieldsBound Then    'First time here must bind the data fields
        bindDataFields(dsEmployee)
        blnFieldsBound = True
    End If
'...Rest of code for the procedure follows
```

> ## Feedback 3.3

1. Where do you place the data connection and data adapter for a multi-tier project?
2. What return type is necessary for a function in the component class that fills a dataset from a data adapter?
3. Write the code to bind a first name label to a dataset called dsCustomers. Display the FirstName field in the Customer table.

Your Hands-On Programming Example

Create a list selection project similar to the Ch03List project but using multiple tiers. Display the full name in the combo box, concatenated as LastName, FirstName, MiddleInitial. When the user selects a name from the list, find the corresponding record by primary key (emp_id). Display the Employee ID, Job ID, Hire Date, First Name, Middle Initial, and Last Name in labels for the selected record.

Include a *File / Exit* menu item to terminate the program.

Planning the Project

Sketch a form (Figure 3.19) that your users sign off as meeting their needs.

Figure 3.19

A planning sketch for the hands-on programming example.

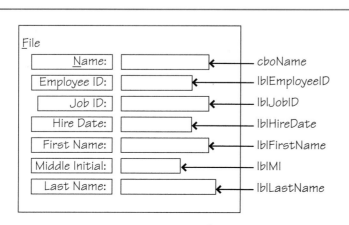

Plan the Objects, Properties, and Methods

Plan the two tiers. Determine the objects and property settings for the form and its controls and for the data tier component. Figure 3.20 shows a diagram of the components in the two tiers.

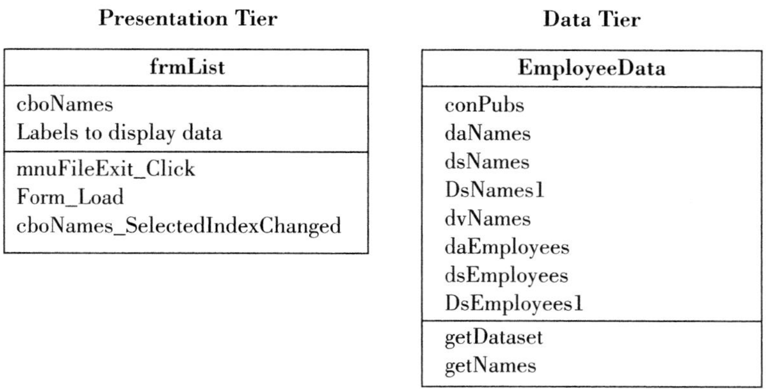

Figure 3.20

A diagram of the components in each tier for the hands-on programming example.

Presentation Tier

frmList
cboNames
Labels to display data
mnuFileExit_Click
Form_Load
cboNames_SelectedIndexChanged

Data Tier

EmployeeData
conPubs
daNames
dsNames
DsNames1
dvNames
daEmployees
dsEmployees
DsEmployees1
getDataset
getNames

Presentation Tier

Object	Property	Setting
frmList	Name	frmList
	Text	Employees
Label1	Text	& Name:
cboNames	Name	cboLastNames
	Text	(blank)
Label2	Text	Employee ID:
Label3	Text	Job ID:
Label4	Text	Hire Date:
Label5	Text	First Name:
Label6	Text	Middle Initial:
Label7	Text	Last Name:
lblEmployeeID	Name	lblEmployeeID
	Text	(blank)
lblJobID	Name	lblJobID
	Text	(blank)
lblHireDate	Name	lblHireDate
	Text	(blank)
lblFirstName	Name	lblFirstName
	Text	(blank)
lblMI	Name	lblMI
	Text	(blank)
lblLastName	Name	lblLastName
	Text	(blank)
mnuFileExit	Name	mnuFileExit
	Text	E&xit

Event procedures/Methods	Actions—Pseudocode
mnuFileExit_Click	Exit the project.
Form_Load	Instantiate the data tier.
	Retrieve the data view to fill the combo box.
	Set the combo box properties.
	Retrieve the first employee record from the dataset.
	Bind the labels to display the employee fields.
	Format the date field.
	Set switch to show that the list has been loaded.
cboNames_SelectedIndexChanged	If the list has been loaded
	Retrieve the data for the selected list item.
	Format the date.

Data Tier

Object	Property	Setting
Class	Name	EmployeeData
conPubs	Name	conPubs
daEmployee	Name	daEmployee
	Criteria	@emp_id
DsEmployee1	Name	DsEmployee1
daNames	Name	daName
DsNames1	Name	DsNames1
dvNames	Name	dvNames
	Table	DsNames1.employee
	Sort	lname

Methods	Actions—Pseudocode
getDataset	Create a dataset that holds the selected record.
	Return the dataset.
getNames	Fill the dataset holding the names.
	Return the data view.

Write the Project

Following the sketch in Figure 3.19, create the form. Figure 3.21 shows the completed form.

- Set the properties of each of the form objects, according to your plans.
- Create the data tier component, adding the objects from your plan.

- Write the methods for the data tier component, following the pseudocode.

- Write the code for the form. Working from the pseudocode, write each event procedure.

- When you complete the code, test the operation several times. Compare the screen output to the data tables to make sure that you are displaying the correct information.

Figure 3.21

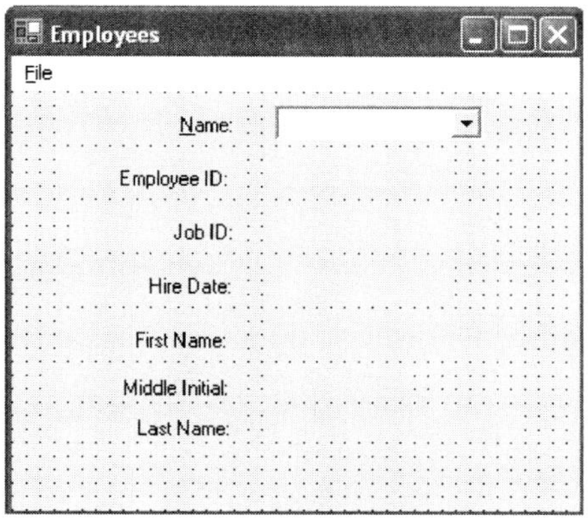

The completed form for the hands-on programming example.

The Project Coding Solution
The Form

```
'Project:        Ch03HandsOn
'Programmer:     Bradley/Millspaugh
'Date:           January 2003
'Description:    Displays a list of employee names; retrieves and
'                displays the rest of the data for the selected employee.
'                This module holds only the user interface. The database
'                access is performed by the data tier.

Option Strict On

Public Class frmList
    Inherits System.Windows.Forms.Form

    [Windows Form Designer generated code]

    Dim mobjEmployee As EmployeeData    'Instance of data tier component
    Dim mblnListInitialized As Boolean = False

    Private Sub frmList_Load(ByVal sender As System.Object, _
      ByVal e As System.EventArgs) Handles MyBase.Load
        'Load the combo box, bind the data fields, and retrieve the first record

        Dim dvNames As DataView
        Dim dsEmployee As DataSet

        Try
            'Get the data from the data tier
            mobjEmployee = New EmployeeData()
```

```
            dvNames = mobjEmployee.getNames

            dsEmployee = dataEmployee.getDataset(cboName.SelectedValue)

            'Bind the data view to the combo box
            'Note that setting the binding triggers the SelectedIndexChanged event
            With cboName
                .DataSource = dvNames
                .DisplayMember = "FullName"
                .ValueMember = "emp_id"
                .SelectedIndex = -1
            End With
            mblnListInitialized = True

        Catch err As Exception
            MessageBox.Show(err.Message)
        End Try
    End Sub

    Private Sub cboName_SelectedIndexChanged(ByVal sender As System.Object, _
      ByVal e As System.EventArgs) Handles cboName.SelectedIndexChanged
        'Get the record to match the selection

        Static blnFieldsBound As Boolean = False   'Determines if form controls are bound
        Dim dsEmployee As DataSet                  'Declare a dataset

        If mblnListInitialized Then          'Do not allow to happen as the form is loaded
            Try
                'Get the data matching the selected name from the data tier
                dsEmployee = mobjEmployee.getDataset(cboName.SelectedValue.ToString())
                If Not blnFieldsBound Then    'First time here must bind the data fields
                    bindDataFields(dsEmployee)
                    blnFieldsBound = True
                End If

                'Format the date
                lblHireDate.Text = FormatDateTime(CDate(lblHireDate.Text), _
                  DateFormat.ShortDate)

            Catch err As Exception
                MessageBox.Show(err.Message)
            End Try
        End If
    End Sub

    Private Sub bindDataFields(ByVal dsEmployee As DataSet)
        'Bind the data fields

        Try
            'Bind the dataset fields to the controls
            lblEmployeeID.DataBindings.Add("text", dsEmployee.Tables("employee"), "emp_id")
            lblJobID.DataBindings.Add("text", dsEmployee.Tables("employee"), "job_id")
            lblHireDate.DataBindings.Add("text", dsEmployee.Tables("employee"), "hire_date")
            lblFirstName.DataBindings.Add("text", dsEmployee.Tables("employee"), "fname")
            lblMI.DataBindings.Add("text", dsEmployee.Tables("employee"), "minit")
            lblLastName.DataBindings.Add("text", dsEmployee.Tables("employee"), "lname")

        Catch err As Exception
            MessageBox.Show(err.Message)
        End Try
    End Sub
```

```
    Private Sub mnuFileExit_Click(ByVal sender As System.Object, _
      ByVal e As System.EventArgs) Handles mnuFileExit.Click
        'End the program

        Me.Close()
    End Sub
End Class
```

The Data Tier

```
'Project:       Ch03HandsOn
'Programmer:    Bradley/Millspaugh
'Date:          January 2003
'Description:   Data tier to supply Employee data from the Pubs database.
'               Returns a DataSet and a DataView.

Option Strict On

Public Class EmployeeData
    Inherits System.ComponentModel.Component

    [Component Designer generated code]

    Public Function getDataset(ByVal strParameter As String) As DataSet
        'Fill the dataset

        DsEmployee1.Clear()
        daEmployee.SelectCommand.Parameters("@empID").Value = strParameter
        daEmployee.Fill(DsEmployee1)
        Return DsEmployee1
    End Function

    Public Function getNames() As DataView
        'Fill the dataset

        daNames.Fill(DsNames1)
        Return dvNames
    End Function
End Class
```

Summary

1. Data are accessible from many sources including databases, files, email, and spreadsheets.
2. OLEDB is Microsoft's technology for universal data access. Any type of data can be accessed using the proper OLEDB provider.
3. ADO.NET is the object model for referencing data in a .NET program. The two major components of ADO.NET are the DataSet object and the .NET providers.

4. The .NET Framework includes two managed providers for accessing data, SQLClient for SQL Server and MSDE, and OleDbClient for all other sources.

5. A DataSet can contain multiple DataTable objects, as well as relationships and constraints. Each table contains rows, columns, and fields.

6. A primary key uniquely identifies a record. When a primary key is included in a second table for linking purposes, it is called a foreign key in the second table.

7. The data provider contains Connection, Command, DataAdapter, and/or DataReader components.

8. XML is an industrywide standard for storing and transferring data in a text-based format with tags that identify the data fields. An XML file may also have a schema file that defines field names, data types, and constraints.

9. MSDE, which allows programming against SQL Server databases, is included with Visual Studio .NET.

10. When MSDE and the sample databases are installed, the Server Explorer displays all servers and the associated tables, views, and stored procedures.

11. To create a dataset you must set up a connection and a data adapter, generate the dataset, and fill the dataset.

12. To bind a dataset to a data grid, set the grid's DataSource property to the name of the dataset and the DataMember property to the name of the table.

13. A common way to allow the user to access data is to display a list box with a field for the user to select. You must set the list's DataSource and DisplayMember properties to automatically fill the list.

14. A data view can be used to sort the data allowing the table to be viewed in a different sequence. A data view is based on a data table.

15. In a parameterized query, the selection criteria are passed to the query at run time.

16. To bind individual controls, such as labels and text boxes, to database fields, set the DataBindings.Text property of the control.

17. Fields may be combined or calculated as expressions by adding fields to the XML schema.

18. The SQL statements are generated automatically by the data adapter but can also be modified by the programmer.

19. List boxes and combo boxes have a ValueMember property as well as a DisplayMember property. When the user selects an item from the list, the control's SelectedValue property holds the ValueMember that corresponds to the selected DisplayMember.

20. To create a separate data tier, add a Component to the project and define the connection, data adapter, and dataset in the new component. The dataset can be passed to the user interface (presentation tier) as needed.

K e y   T e r m s

ActiveX Data Objects (ADO)
  .NET   *80*
column   *81*
Command object   *83*

Connection object   *83*
criteria   *92*
DataAdapter object   *83*
DataBindings object   *93*

Review Questions

1. What is referred to by the following acronyms:
    a. ADO.NET
    b. XML
    c. UDA
2. Define the following terms: table, row, record, column, and field.
3. What is a primary key field? Why must it be unique? What is a foreign key?
4. What is MSDE? How is it used?
5. List and describe the steps to set up an application for accessing data and displaying the data in a grid.
6. How would you sort data before populating a list box?
7. Describe how you would combine the city, state, and ZIP code fields into a single field. Where would this step appear?
8. What type of item is added to a project to create a data tier?
9. What types of items should be added to the data tier?
10. How can a parameterized query value be accessed by the data tier?

Programming Exercises

For each of these programming exercises, write a multitier application with a presentation tier and a data tier component that provides the database access. Make sure to turn `Option Strict On`, either in each code module or on the *Project Properties* dialog box.

3.1 Use a grid control to display customer information from the Northwind database. Include the CustomerID, CompanyName, ContactName, Region, Phone, and Fax fields.

3.2 Display information from the Employees table in the Northwind database. Populate a drop-down list with the concatenated first and last names sorted in alphabetic order by last name. When a name is selected from the list, display the title, region, and extension in labels.

3.3 Create a project that displays information from the Products table in the Northwind database. Fill a drop-down list with the product name. When the user selects a product, find the record by ProductID and display these fields in labels: ProductID, UnitPrice, and UnitsInStock.

3.4   Display the Products table from the GrocerToGo database in a grid. Include ProductId, Name, Description, UnitPrice, ServingSize, and Servings.
Note: If an error message appears concerning the SQL UPDATE and DELETE commands, click *OK* to continue.

3.5   Display all of the fields in the publishers table in the pubs database. You may display all of the fields in a grid or use a list box for the pub_name in alphabetic order and display the rest of the fields in labels.

Case Studies

Claytor's Cottages

Modify your Claytor's Cottages case study project to make the *Edit / Guests* menu item show a Guest form. Display the guest names in a list box sorted in alphabetic order. When the user selects a guest name, display the fields from the Guest table in text boxes with the ReadOnly property set to True.

Christian's Car Rentals

Modify your Christian's Car Rentals project to implement the *Edit / Vehicles* menu item. Display the Vehicle table in a grid.

4

Windows Database Using Related Tables

1. Explain the types of table relationships.

2. Display related tables using a DataGrid.

3. Format the columns of a DataGrid control.

4. Retrieve and display the parent row for a selected child row.

5. Retrieve and display an array of child rows for a selected parent row.

6. Display database fields in bound and unbound controls.

7. Retrieve and display data from more than two related tables.

Now that you know some basics about data access, it's time to consider multiple tables in a dataset. This chapter examines techniques for establishing relationships among tables and extracting data from the tables.

Data Relationships

In relational databases, the data items are generally stored in multiple related tables. The primary table is called the **parent** or **master table** and the second table is the **child** or **detail table**. The relationships among two tables may be one-to-one (1:1), one-to-many (1:M), or many-to-many (M:N). Each table usually has a field or fields, called the *primary key,* that uniquely identify each record. When the primary key of one table is included as a field in a related table to link the two tables, that field is called a ***foreign key***. The foreign key is common to both tables.

One-to-Many Relationships

The most common type of relationship is **one-to-many:** one record in the parent table relates to one or more records in the child table. Examples include a customer with multiple orders, a department with multiple employees, or a student with multiple courses. In a one-to-many relationship, a row in the parent table can have many matching rows in the child table but a row in the child table has only one matching record in the parent.

Figure 4.1 shows a database diagram of a 1:M relationship, using the stores and sales tables of the pubs database. Figure 4.2 shows some sample data from the two tables. You can see that one store can have many sales but each sale has only one store.

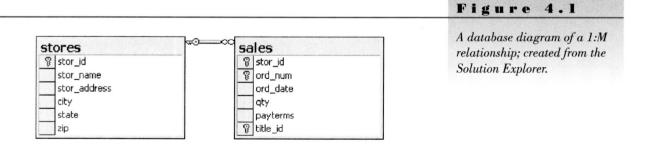

Many-to-Many Relationships

Another possible relationship is **many-to-many**. An example in the pubs database is titles and authors. One author can write many books and one book can have many authors. Most database management systems, including SQL Server and Access, cannot directly handle many-to-many relationships. Instead, a third table is needed to join the two tables. In the third table, called a ***junction table***, the primary key consists of the foreign keys from both tables. In pubs the junction table is called titleauthors and contains title_id and au_id columns.

Figure   4.2

A 1:M relationship exists between the stores and sales tables. One store may have many sales.

stores					
stor_id	**stor_name**	**stor_address**	**city**	**state**	**zip**
6380	Eric the Read Books	788 Catamaugus Ave.	Seattle	WA	98056
7066	Barnum's	567 Pasadena Ave.	Tustin	CA	92789
7067	News & Brews	577 First St.	Los Gatos	CA	96745
7131	Doc-U-Mat:Quality Laundry	24-A Avogadro Way	Remulade	WA	98014
7896	Fricative Bookshop	89 Madison St.	Fremont	CA	90019
8042	Bookbeat	679 Carson St.	Portland	OR	89076

sales					
stor_id	**ord_num**	**ord_date**	**qty**	**payterms**	**title_id**
6380	6871	9/14/1994	5	Net 60	BU1032
6380	722a	9/13/1994	3	Net 60	PS2091
7066	A2976	5/24/1993	50	Net 30	PC8888
7066	QA7442.3	9/13/1994	75	ON invoice	PS2091
7067	D4482	9/14/1994	10	Net 60	PS2091
7067	P2121	6/15/1992	40	Net 30	TC3218
7067	P2121	6/15/1992	20	Net 30	TC4203
7067	P2121	6/15/1992	20	Net 30	TC7777

Figure 4.3 shows the database diagram of a many-to-many relationship and Figure 4.4 shows some sample data from the three related tables. Verify from the figures that one author can have more than one book and one book can have more than one author. Notice that book BU1111 has two authors, and that Stearns MacFeather wrote two books.

Figure   4.3

A database diagram of a M:N relationship. The diagram was created in Access.

One-to-One Relationships

A **one-to-one relationship** is the least common. This type of relationship has one record in the parent matching one record in the child table. Usually the two tables can be combined, but may be kept separate for security reasons or because the child table contains short-term information. In the case of the publishers and pubs_info tables, the pubs_info table holds graphics that could complicate and slow down access to the publishers table. Figure 4.5 shows the database diagram of a 1:1 relationship.

Figure 4.4

A M:N relationship. The titleauthor table joins the titles and authors tables.

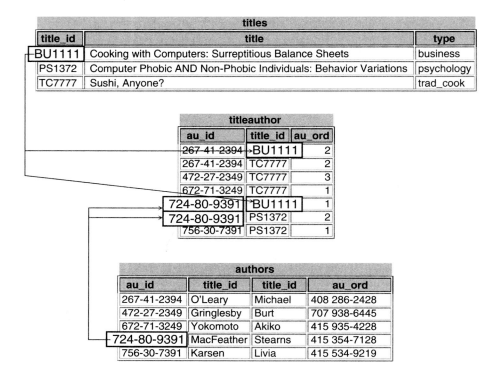

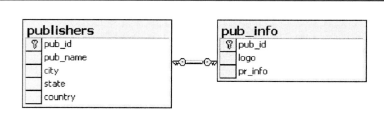

Figure 4.5

A database diagram of a 1:1 relationship.

Constraints

Relationships may also require the use of constraints. A **unique constraint** specifies that no duplicate entries are allowed in a column. **Foreign-key constraints** ensure that parent and child tables remain synchronized when records are deleted or changed. As an example, in the pubs database, if an author's ID is changed, the ID much be changed for all books written by that author. This concept, called *referential integrity*, can be enforced by the database management system by setting foreign-key constraints.

▶ **Feedback 4.1**

1. Give one example each of an appropriate situation to use 1:1, 1:M, and M:N relationships. Do not use the examples already given in the text.

Use this diagram from the Northwind database to answer the following questions:

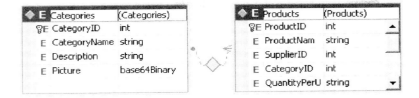

2. In this 1:M relationship, which table is the one and which is the many? Which field is used as the primary key and which is the foreign key in the relationship?
3. Which table is the parent and which is the child?

Related Tables in a Grid

You can use the DataGrid control to display related tables. And a dataset can hold multiple tables and their relationships. The next section shows you how to set up the dataset and DataGrid for multiple tables.

Creating a Dataset

One of the big advantages of the DataSet object in ADO.NET is that it can hold more than one table and the relationships between the tables. Before ADO.NET and datasets, you had to use an SQL JOIN statement to join multiple tables, which produces one row in the result set for every matching record; the columns in the parent table are repeated for every matching record in the child table. Using a dataset, each record appears only once and the data can be displayed hierarchically.

It's easy to create a dataset with more than one table and their relationships. You must create a data adapter for each table. Then when you generate the dataset, you specify that you want the dataset to include both (or all) tables. Figure 4.6 shows generating a dataset for the stores and sales tables of the pubs database.

Setting a Relationship

A **DataRelation object** describes the relationship between the tables. You can create a relationship using the XML schema. Open the XML schema (.xsd) file for the dataset. Right-click on the child table and select *Add / New Relation* or drag a Relation component from the toolbox. The *Edit Relation* dialog appears (Figure 4.7) showing a default name combining the two tables. You may want to change the name since the default is all lowercase. Make sure that your parent and child tables are set correctly and that the keys are correct. Click *OK*. Remember that the parent is always the "one side" of the one-to-many relationship.

Figure 4.6

To generate a dataset with related tables, check the boxes for both tables in the Generate Dataset dialog box.

Figure 4.7

Set up a relationship between tables in the Edit Relation dialog box.

TIP

If the OK button is disabled in the *Edit Relation* dialog box, the keys are not set correctly. Try dropping down the list on the child table. ∎

DataRelation objects perform two major functions: relating tables and setting up constraints. You have already added new relations in the schema of a dataset, but in those cases the keys were already specified. Often you must set up the keys before you can relate the tables.

Specifying the Parent, Child, and Foreign Key

When you add a relationship to a dataset's schema, it's important to get the parent/child relationship right. No matter how you think of the parent/child or master/detail relationship of the data you are working with, you must determine which table is the "one side" and which is the "many" in a one-to-many relationship. The "one side" should always be the parent and the "many side" should be the child.

The next two examples use the employee and jobs tables in the pubs database, which are related by job_id. Before you read on, can you determine which is the parent and which is the child? If you have any problem with this, ask yourself: Can one employee have more than one job (as the table is structured, not in real life)? Can one job title be assigned to more than one employee? Or another way to ask the same questions: Can one job_id appear more than once in the employee table? Can one job_id appear more than once in the jobs table? If the key field (the job_id in this case) can appear only once in a table, the field must be unique and is most likely the "one side" of the 1:M. If the field in question can appear multiple times in the table, the field is a foreign key and is the "many side" of the 1:M. Therefore, the jobs table is the parent and the employee table is the child, whether you are looking up the job from the employee or the employee(s) from the job title.

You can set up relationships in code or visually in the dataset's XML schema. As usual, we'll stick with the visual way. Figure 4.8 shows the completed relationship for the employee and jobs tables; notice the symbols that indicate the "one side" and the "many side."

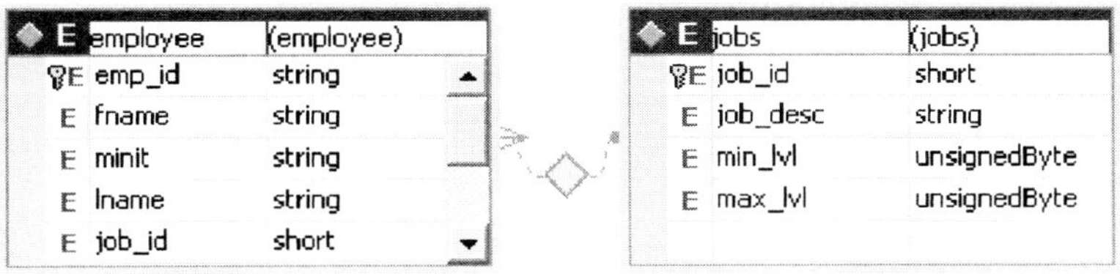

Figure 4.8

A 1:M relationship between the employee and jobs tables. Notice that jobs is the parent (the one) and employees is the child (the many).

To set up the relationship, right-click on one of the tables and select *Add / New Relation*. In the *EditRelations* dialog box, select the table for *Parent element* and the table for *Child element*. Notice that the name of the relation automatically changes when you change the parent and child selections. If you have chosen correctly, the key field and foreign key field should automatically show the field that joins the tables (Figure 4.9). (If the field names don't appear automatically, stop and reexamine your choice of parent and child. It's possible to add new keys and relate the tables differently in this dialog box, but make sure that you've specified correctly before doing this.)

After you create the relation, the schema displays the connection between the two tables (Figure 4.10). To delete the connection, you can select the gray diamond and press the Delete button. Right-click on the gray button to return to the *Edit Relations* dialog box.

Figure 4.9

Choose the parent table and the child table, which should automatically select the correct field to join the two tables and name the relation.

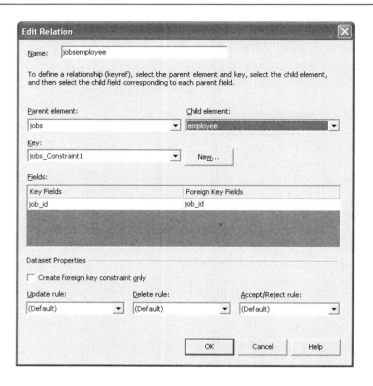

Figure 4.10

The schema shows the relationship. Right-click on the gray button to delete or edit the relation.

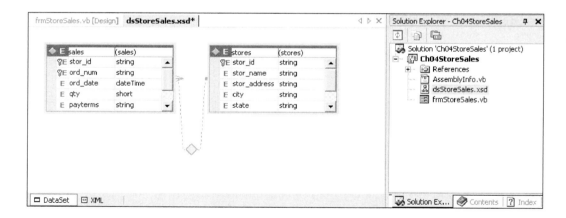

Using a DataGrid to Display Related Tables—Step-by-Step

The DataGrid control is specially designed to handle related records. The following step-by-step tutorial creates a dataset that holds the stores and sales tables and displays the dataset in a DataGrid. Figure 4.11 shows the completed grid. A plus (+) sign displays on a parent row. When the row is expanded, a link to the child table appears.

Figure 4.11

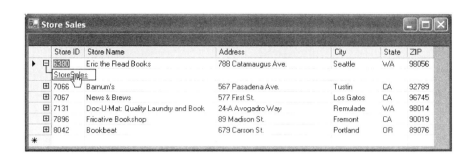

The completed grid that displays related tables. Click on a plus sign to display the child records for a parent record.

Begin a New Project

STEP 1: Begin a new Windows Application project called Ch04StoreSales.

STEP 2: Rename the form to *frmStoreSales*, set its Text property to *Store Sales*, and set the project's startup object to *frmStoreSales*.

Create the Dataset

STEP 1: In the Server Explorer, open the pubs database and drag the stores and sales tables to the form. A connection and two data adapters should appear.

STEP 2: Name the connection *conPubs*. Name the two data adapters *daStores* and *daSales*. If you don't know which adapter is which, you can look at the adapter's SelectCommand.CommandText property.

STEP 3: Right-click on daStores and select *Generate Dataset*. Name the dataset *dsStoreSales* and select both the sales and stores tables. Make sure that *Add this dataset to the designer* is checked and click *OK*. (Refer to Figure 4.6.) You should now have a DsStoreSales1 component in the component tray.

STEP 4: Double-click on dsStoreSales.xsd in the Solution Explorer to open the dataset's schema. Right-click on the stores table (the parent) and select *Add / New Relation*.

STEP 5: In the *Edit Relation* dialog box, set up the relation. Name the relation *StoreSales*. For the *Parent element*, select *stores*; for the *Child element*, select *sales*. The *Key Field* and *Foreign Key Field* should both be set to *stor_id*. The check box for *Create foreign key constraint* should be deselected (Figure 4.12). Click *OK*.

Set Up the DataGrid

STEP 1: Add a DataGrid to the form; name the grid *dgrStores*. Widen the form and grid to better display data. (Refer to Figure 4.11.)

STEP 2: Set the grid's DataSource to *DsStoreSales1* and the DataMember to the stores table. You may want to resize the form and/or grid after this step.

Write the Code

STEP 1: The only code required is to fill the dataset. You must execute the Fill method for each data adapter, naming the same dataset. This retrieves the data for both tables into the single dataset.

```
Private Sub frmStoreSales_Load(ByVal sender As System.Object, _
  ByVal e As System.EventArgs) Handles MyBase.Load
    'Fill the datasets

    daStores.Fill(DsStoreSales1)
    daSales.Fill(DsStoreSales1)
End Sub
```

Run the Program

STEP 1: Run the program. The grid should appear showing the parent rows
        (the stores) and plus signs indicating that child rows exist (Figure
        4.13).

STEP 2: Click on a plus sign for the first record. Then click on the StoreSales
        link that appears.

Figure 4.13

Click on the link to see the child rows for the parent row.

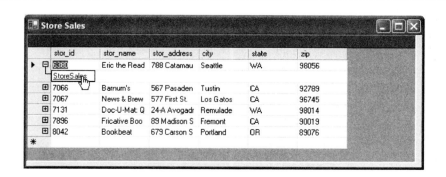

STEP 3: The child records for that parent now appear in the grid (Figure 4.14). Notice that the column headings have changed for the second table, and the parent record appears at the top of the grid with scroll arrows. You can turn off the display of the parent record using the button to the right of the Navigation button.

Figure 4.14

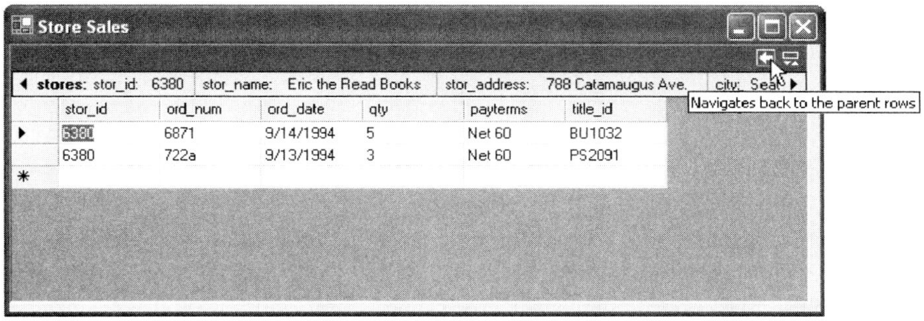

The parent row appears at the top and the child rows appear in the grid.

stor_id	ord_num	ord_date	qty	payterms	title_id
6380	6871	9/14/1994	5	Net 60	BU1032
6380	722a	9/13/1994	3	Net 60	PS2091

stores: stor_id: 6380 stor_name: Eric the Read Books stor_address: 788 Catamaugus Ave. city: Sea

Navigates back to the parent rows

STEP 4: You can resize the grid's columns by dragging the divider between column headings or double-click on the divider to resize to the largest data element or column heading. Click on a heading to sort by that column. In the next section you will learn to format the table columns at design time. If you haven't already done so, stop execution now.

Formatting a DataGrid

You can set the format of DataGrid columns by setting up table and column styles. Each DataGrid has a GridTableStylesCollection that holds one DataGridTableStyle for each table. A DataGridTableStyle holds a GridColumnStylesCollection that has an individual DataGridColumStyle for each column (Figure 4.15). When you link a table to a DataGrid, the styles are created automatically, using the defaults. In this section you will create your own styles to control the display of data in the grid.

Figure 4.15

The DataGrid control's style objects.

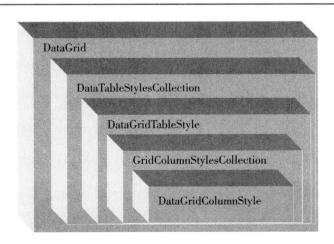

DataGrid / DataTableStylesCollection / DataGridTableStyle / GridColumnStylesCollection / DataGridColumnStyle

Create Table and Column Styles for the Stores Table

The next section formats the grid for the stores table. Figure 4.16 shows the completed grid.

Figure 4.16

The DataGrid with column formatting applied.

STEP 1: Select the DataGrid control and locate the TableStyles property, which is a collection. Click on the Build button to open the DataGridTableStyle Collection Editor.

STEP 2: Click on the *Add* button to add your first table style. Look through the available properties that you can set for formatting the whole table.

STEP 3: Select the MappingName property (under *Misc*) and click the down-arrow; the two table names should appear. Select *stores*, the parent table. This property specifies that this DataGridTableStyle maps to, or is connected to, the stores table.

STEP 4: Select the GridColumnStyles property, just above the MappingName. This is also a collection, so click the Build button to open the Data-GridColumnStyle Collection Editor. Click the *Add* button to add your first column style (Figure 4.17).

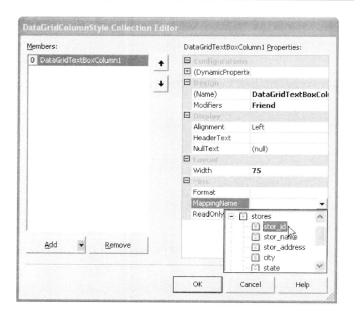

Figure 4.17

Add style properties for each column in the DataGridColumnStyle Collection Editor.

You need one DataGridColumStyle for each column that you want to appear in the stores table grid. Note that you can choose to not display some columns by not creating column styles for the fields.

STEP 5: First set the MappingName property, which sets the field name for the column. Click on the down arrow, expand the stores node, and select the *stor_id* field.

STEP 6: Set the HeaderText property to *Store ID*. Now you can have meaningful column headings instead of the cryptic field names.

STEP 7: Set the Width to *50*, which is the measurement in pixels. You may want to experiment with the column widths after you see the finished grid. Do not click *OK* on this dialog box until you finish all of the column styles. (Of course, you can always reopen the dialog box to add styles and make modifications.)

STEP 8: Click *Add* to add the second column style. Set the MappingName to *stor_name*. Set the HeaderText to *Store Name* and the Width to *200*.

STEP 9: Click *Add* to add the third column style. Set the MappingName to *stor_address*, the HeaderText to *Address*, and the Width to *175*.

STEP 10: Click *Add* to add the fourth column style. Set the MappingName to *city*, the HeaderText to *City*, and the Width to *100*.

STEP 11: Add the fifth column style for *state*. Set the HeaderText to *State* and the Width to *40*.

STEP 12: Add the sixth column style for *zip*. Set the Header Text to *ZIP* and the Width to *40*.

STEP 13: Click *OK* to close the DataGridColumnStyle Collection Editor, and *OK* again to close the DataGridTableStyle Collection Editor.

STEP 14: Resize the form and grid, if necessary, to show all of the columns.

STEP 15: Run the program. Make a note of any changes that you would like to make, stop the program, and modify the column styles.

TIP

When modifying column styles, move the TableStyle editor away from the grid before opening the ColumnStyle editor. Then you can move the ColumnStyle editor off the grid as well, and view the grid's column headings as you edit the styles. Any changes show up immediately, so you can view the widths and text as you work. ■

Create Table and Column Styles for the Sales Table

Now you will create column styles for the sales table.

STEP 1: Select the grid and select the Build button for TableStyle, which opens the DataGridTableStyle Collection Editor. Add a new style and set the MappingName to *sales*.

STEP 2: Open the DataGridColumnStyle Collection Editor (from the Grid-ColumnStyle property) and add new styles. You can use these values or choose your own:

MappingName	HeaderText	Width (Pixels)	Alignment
stor_id	Store ID	50	Left
ord_num	Order	50	Left
ord_date	Date	75	Left
qty	Quantity	50	Right
payterms	Terms	75	Left
title_id	Title ID	50	Left

STEP 3: Run the program and display child records. Make any needed changes and rerun. Note that you can rearrange the fields using the up and down arrows in the DataGridColumnStyle editor, and add and remove fields.

Feedback 4.2

1. Write the necessary Fill method statements for a form that contains a data grid control for Customers and Orders. Assume that the project contains two data adapters called daCustomers and daOrders as well as a dataset called DsCustomersOrders1 with the relationship Customers-Orders.
2. What steps are necessary to change the column headings and column widths on a DataGrid?
3. How can you delete some columns in a DataGrid? That is, make some of the fields in the dataset not display in the grid.

Master/Detail Records

In the preceding grid example, you displayed parent/child (or master/detail) data automatically in a grid. The next example expands on that application and displays the master records in one grid and the detail records in a second grid, so that both are visible at the same time. This example also allows the user to choose the master record from a drop-down list. Figure 4.18 shows the completed form.

Figure 4.18

A master/detail application. The user selects the store name from a list; the selected store record displays in the top grid, and the sales for that store display in the bottom grid.

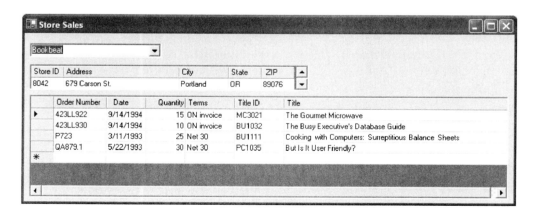

You may have noticed one more change in the sales grid from the earlier grid program. The sales table holds the title_id field for the sale, but the grid in Figure 4.18 displays the complete title, which was retrieved from a third table, the title table.

Setting Up the Objects for Selection

Writing the master/detail application is very similar to the first grid program. You still need the dataset that holds the stores and sales tables and the relationship between the tables (dsStoreSales). You also need a new dataset for the store names to populate the combo box (dsStoreNames). Figure 4.19 shows the connection, data adapters, and datasets for this application.

Figure   4.19

The data access objects for the master/detail application. The data adapter and dataset for store names have been added to the previous grid example.

Use the techniques you learned in Chapter 3 for setting the properties of the combo box and filling the list at Form_Load. Set the combo box properties:

DataSource	DsStoreNames1
DisplayMember	stores.stor_name
ValueMember	stores.stor_id

Filtering a Dataset

If you want to retrieve the records that match a specific value, you can use a parameterized query or a filter. A parameterized query creates a new dataset; a filter selects records from an existing dataset. When you already have the complete dataset, the best choice is to use a filter, rather than return to the original data source and create a new dataset.

To filter an existing dataset, you must create a data view, which is based on a table. Then you can apply a filter to the data view, using the RowFilter property.

```
'Filter the existing DsStoreSales1 dataset
Dim dvStore As New DataView()
With dvStore
    .Table = DsStoreSales1.stores
    .RowFilter = "stor_id = '" & cboStore.SelectedValue.ToString() & "'"
End With
```

Writing a Filter

The RowFilter in the preceding code looks quite cryptic, but is easy to create. The rules for creating a RowFilter are the same as for a WHERE clause of an SQL statement. Specify the field, a comparison operator (usually the equal sign), and the value to match. A string field value must be enclosed in quotes; numeric values are not enclosed.

```
"LastName = 'Jones'"
"SalesAmount = 1000"
"Quantity > 0"
```

The tricky part comes when you want to filter on variable data, rather than the constants in the preceding examples. You must concatenate the elements to create a filter string in the correct format. For string data, you must concatenate the single quotes around the data values:

```
"LastName = '" & strName & "'"
"LastName = '" & cboName.SelectedValue.ToString() & "'"
```

In the second statement, assume that cboName.SelectedValue = "Mills". After the concatenation, the entire string would be "LastName = 'Mills' ", which is exactly what is needed for the RowFilter property.

For numeric values, you create a filter string without the quotes:

```
"SalesAmount = " & decAmount.ToString()
"Quantity > " & txtQuantity.Text
```

Here is a list of the most useful operators. You can find a complete listing of operators on the "Comparison Operators" page in MSDN.

Operator	Meaning	Examples
=	equal to	`"Subject = 'Business'"` `"Subject = '" & txtSubject.Text & "'"`
>	greater than	`"Sales > 1000"` `"Sales > " & txtSales.Text`
<	less than	`"Sales < 1000"` `"Sales < " & txtSales.Text`

Like	pattern match	`"Subject Like ('B%')"`
		 (For SQL Server databases)
		 `"Subject Like 'B*'"`
		 (For Access databases)

Binding Controls to a Data View

You can bind the controls on a form to a field in a dataset or a dataview. For a dataview that you create in code at run time, you should set the control's DataSource property in code after creating the data view.

```
'Set up data view for the store and bind the grid
With dvStore
    .Table = DsStoreSales1.stores
    .RowFilter = "stor_id = '" & cboStore.SelectedValue.ToString() & "'"
End With
dgrStore.DataSource = dvStore
```

When you set the DataSource, the grid fills with the data in the data view. But what about the grid formatting? Unless you want to write statements to set up DataGridTableStyles and DataGridColumnStyles in code, use this technique: At design time, set the grid's DataSource and DataMember properties to the dataset and table in the designer, then set up the TableStyles property and the ColumnStyles property of the grid. At run time, you assign a new DataSource, but the formatting remains.

Matching Values in an SQL Select Statement

In the master/detail application, the sales grid displays one row for each sale, but the sales table holds the title_id, not the actual title. The title is found in the titles table. To retrieve the title as part of the dataset, we'll modify the SQL SELECT statement used by the daSales data adapter. In the Properties window for daSales, expand the SelectCommand node, select CommandText, and click on the Build (...) button, which opens the Query Builder.

Add the titles table to the query by right-clicking somewhere in the top panel and selecting *Add Table*. When you add the table, the designer already knows about the relationship between the tables. Select the title_id and title fields from the title table and watch the designer create the new SQL statement, which now contains an INNER JOIN clause (Figure 4.20). This joins the title from the title table that matches the title_id from the sales table.

Figure 4.20

The Query Builder generates an INNER JOIN *to retrieve the title from the title table.*

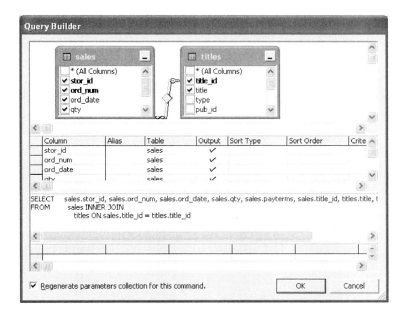

Controlling the Selection Timing

When you bind a combo box to a dataset, the SelectedIndexChanged event fires several times as the form and list are displayed. You don't want to search for any matching values until the list is finished loading and the user has made a selection. Use a module-level boolean variable to indicate that the list initialization is complete. In the complete program listing that follows, notice that the

Form_Load procedure sets the variable (mblnListInitialized) when complete, and the SelectedIndexChanged event procedure checks the variable.

The Completed Master/Detail Program

Refer to Figure 4.18 for the completed form and Figure 4.19 for the data components.

```
'Project:         Ch04StoreSales
'Programmer:      Bradley/Millspaugh
'Date:            January 2003
'Description:     Displays related stores and sales in a data grid.
'                 Includes the titles from the titles table.

Option Strict On

Public Class frmStoreSales
    Inherits System.Windows.Forms.Form

    [Windows Form Designer generated code]

    Dim mblnListLoaded As Boolean = False

    Private Sub frmStoreSales_Load(ByVal sender As System.Object, _
      ByVal e As System.EventArgs) Handles MyBase.Load
        'Fill the dataset for the store names combo box

        daStoreNames.Fill(DsStoreNames1)
        cboStore.SelectedIndex = -1
        mblnListLoaded = True
    End Sub

    Private Sub cboStore_SelectedIndexChanged(ByVal sender As System.Object, _
      ByVal e As System.EventArgs) Handles cboStore.SelectedIndexChanged
        'Select the data for the selected store
        Static blnFirstSelection As Boolean = True
        Dim dvStore As New DataView()
        Dim dvSales As New DataView()

        If mblnListLoaded Then
            'First time here, fill the dataset for the grids
            If blnFirstSelection Then
                daStores.Fill(DsStoreSales1)
                daSales.Fill(DsStoreSales1)
                blnFirstSelection = False
            End If
            'Set up data view for the store and bind the grid
            With dvStore
                .Table = DsStoreSales1.stores
                .RowFilter = "stor_id = '" & cboStore.SelectedValue.ToString() & "'"
            End With
            dgrStore.DataSource = dvStore
            'Set up data view for the sales and bind the grid
            With dvSales
                .Table = DsStoreSales1.sales
                .RowFilter = "stor_id = '" & cboStore.SelectedValue.ToString() & "'"
            End With
            dgrSales.DataSource = dvSales
        End If
    End Sub
End Class
```

Unbound Data Fields

Although it's easy and handy to bind data fields to controls, sometimes you need to work with data fields that are not bound to controls. You need to be able to retrieve rows of data and reference the individual records and fields. In this section you will create DataRelation objects that relate parent and child records, retrieve a selected parent row, retrieve an array of matching child rows, and refer to the individual fields in the selected rows.

The following examples use the employees and jobs tables of the pubs database, which are related by the job_id field.

Referring to Records and Fields

When you are working with data from a dataset, you often want to refer to an individual field from a selected record. The actual data values are held in DataRow objects. Each DataTable object in a dataset has a DataRows collection made up of DataRow objects (Figure 4.21).

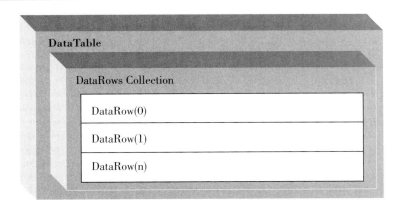

Figure 4.21

A DataTable object has a DataRows collection that consists of one DataRow object for each record in the table.

The data values are held in the DataRow.Items collection. You can refer to the individual fields either by index position (the first field is index 0) or by name, enclosed in quotes. For example, you can use either of these two statements to retrieve the fname field of this employee DataRow object:

```
strFirstName = drEmployee.Item(1)
```

or `strFirstName = drEmployee.Item("fname")`

Unless you want to look up the index position of each field in a record, you'll find that using field names is much preferred. The field names are specified in the dataset's XML schema file.

Retrieving a Related Parent Row

The following example allows the user to select an employee name and then displays the hire date from the employee table and the job description from the job table (Figure 4.22). The data fields are displayed in unbound text boxes;

that is, no data bindings exist. Each field is assigned to the Text property of a text box.

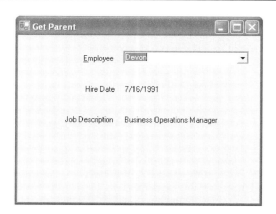

Figure   4.22

From the selected employee name, the program retrieves the correct employee DataRow and the matching jobs parent DataRow to display the job description.

When you allow the user to select a value from a list box, you write the code to retrieve the data in the SelectedIndexChanged method. There are basically three steps in the process: find the row in the employee table that matches the list box, use the **GetParentRow method** to retrieve the matching row from the jobs table, and retrieve the specific data item.

Find the Employee (Child) Row

Declare a DataRow object for the employee table and another one for the jobs table.

```
Dim drEmployee As DataRow
Dim drJob As DataRow
```

Use the SelectedValue from the combo box to find the record. Each table in the dataset contains a method to find records by the key field. Since the primary key in the employee table is emp_id, there is a FindByemp_id automatically generated for the table object.

The format for the find is

```
DataRow = DataSetName.TableName.FindMethod(PrimaryKeyValue)
```

If you set up the combo box ValueMember property as emp_id, then you can use this code to retrieve the correct employee record by its key field.

```
'Save the Employee ID for the selected employee
strEmployeeID = CStr(cboName.SelectedValue)
'Find the data row for this employee
drEmployee = DsEmployeeJobs1.employee.FindByemp_id(strEmployeeID)
```

Get the Parent Row

Now that you know the row in the employee (child) table that matches the combo box entry, you must get the parent row from the jobs table.

```
'Retrieve the parent row from the jobs table
drJob = drEmployee.GetParentRow("jobsemployee")
```

Note that "jobsemployee" in the GetParentRow method argument is the
name of the relation that we set up in Figure 4.9.

Retrieve a Specific Field

The final step is to get the field from the data row.

```
'Display the job_desc field from the row in the jobs table
lblJob.Text = CStr(drJob.Item("job_desc"))
```

The Complete Get Parent Program

```
'Project:        Ch04UnboundGetParent
'Programmer:     Bradley/Millspaugh
'Date:           January 2003
'Description:    Displays a list of employee last names;
'                retrieves and displays the hire date from the
'                employee record and the job description from the
'                parent jobs table.

Option Strict On

Public Class frmJobs
    Inherits System.Windows.Forms.Form

    Dim mblnListInitialized As Boolean = False

    Private Sub frmJobs_Load(ByVal sender As System.Object, _
      ByVal e As System.EventArgs) Handles MyBase.Load
        'Fill the datasets

        daNames.Fill(DsNames1)
        DsEmployeeJobs1.EnforceConstraints = False
        daEmployee.Fill(DsEmployeeJobs1)
        daJobs.Fill(DsEmployeeJobs1)

        cboName.SelectedIndex = -1
        mblnListInitialized = True

    End Sub

    Private Sub cboName_SelectedIndexChanged(ByVal sender As System.Object, _
      ByVal e As System.EventArgs) Handles cboName.SelectedIndexChanged
        'Find the selected record

        Dim strEmployeeID As String          'Hold emp_id of selected employee
        Dim drEmployee As DataRow             'Data row of selected employee
        Dim drJob As DataRow                  'Data row of job table

        If mblnListInitialized = True Then
            'Save the Employee ID for the selected employee
            strEmployeeID = CStr(cboName.SelectedValue)
            'Find the data row for this employee
            drEmployee = DsEmployeeJobs1.employee.FindByemp_id(strEmployeeID)
```

```
                    'Display the hire_date field from this data row
                    lblHireDate.Text = CStr(drEmployee.Item("hire_date"))
                    'Retrieve the parent row from the jobs table
                    drJob = drEmployee.GetParentRow("jobsemployee")
                    'Display the job_desc field from the row in the jobs table
                    lblJob.Text = CStr(drJob.Item("job_desc"))
            End If
        End Sub
End Class
```

Retrieving Related Child Rows

Retrieving related child rows is similar to retrieving a related parent row. The primary difference is that the **GetChildRows method** returns an array of rows rather than a single row. In this variation on the previous program, the user selects a job title from the combo box. The program retrieves the correct data row for the job and displays the array of matching employees in a list box (Figure 4.23). Note that the dataset and relationship in this program are exactly the same as in the preceding example.

Figure 4.23

When the user selects the job title (the parent), the program retrieves and displays an array of the matching employee (child) records.

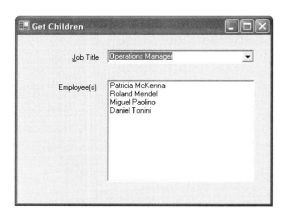

The Complete Get Child Program

```
'Project:       Ch04UnboundGetChild
'Programmer:    Bradley/Millspaugh
'Date:          January 2003
'Description:   Displays a list of job titles (the parent table);
'               retrieves and displays the list of employees with
'               that job title from the child table.

Option Strict On

Public Class frmJobs
    Inherits System.Windows.Forms.Form

    Dim mblnListInitialized As Boolean = False
```

```
      Private Sub frmJobs_Load(ByVal sender As System.Object, _
        ByVal e As System.EventArgs) Handles MyBase.Load
            'Load the datasets

          Try
              DsEmployeeJobs1.EnforceConstraints = False
              daJobNames.Fill(DsJobNames1)
              daEmployee.Fill(DsEmployeeJobs1)
              daJobs.Fill(DsEmployeeJobs1)
              mblnListInitialized = True

          Catch err As Exception
              MessageBox.Show(err.Message)
          End Try
      End Sub

      Private Sub cboJobs_SelectedIndexChanged(ByVal sender As System.Object, _
        ByVal e As System.EventArgs) Handles cboJobs.SelectedIndexChanged
            'Find the selected records
          Dim srtJobID As Short                    'Hold the job_id of the selected job
          Dim drJob As DataRow                     'Current row from job table
          Dim drsEmployee As DataRow()             'Array of matching data rows
          Dim drEmployee As DataRow                'One row from employee table
          Dim strEmployeeName As String            'Used to concatenate name from two fields

          Try
              If mblnListInitialized = True Then
                    'Get the job_id of the selected job
                    srtJobID = CShort(cboJobs.SelectedValue)
                    'Find the row from the job table that matches the job_id
                    drJob = DsEmployeeJobs1.jobs.FindByjob_id(srtJobID)
                    'Retrieve an array of employee (child) rows matching the job row
                    drsEmployee = drJob.GetChildRows("jobsemployee")
                    'Fill the list with the array of employee rows
                    lstEmployees.Items.Clear()
                    For Each drEmployee In drsEmployee
                        With drEmployee
                            strEmployeeName = CStr(.Item("fname")) & " " & _
                            CStr(.Item("lname"))
                        End With
                        lstEmployees.Items.Add(strEmployeeName)
                    Next
              End If

          Catch err As Exception
              MessageBox.Show(err.Message)
          End Try
      End Sub
End Class
```

Feedback 4.3

Use this data diagram to answer the following questions:

---

1. Assuming that a proper relationship has been set up, write the statements to retrieve the category name when the product name is selected from a list box.
2. Assuming the same proper relationship, write the statements to retrieve the products in a selected category.

Many-to-Many Relationships

Recall that a many-to-many relationship requires a third table, called a *junction table*. The following examples use the titles and authors tables of the pubs database, which are joined by the titleauthor table (Figure 4.24). Notice in the figure that au_id is the primary key in the authors table; a given au_id can appear only once. Similarly, title_id is the primary key of the titles table and any one title_id can appear only once. But in the junction table, titleauthor, any one au_id and any one title_id can appear any number of times. The combination of au_id and title_id makes up the primary key, so any one combination must be unique. As you set up the relationships, the junction table is the child table in the relationships with each of the parent tables.

Figure 4.24

In a M:N relationship, two 1:M relationships must be set up. The junction table is the child table in each of the two 1:M relationships. Each author can have multiple books and each title can have multiple authors.

Retrieving Matching Rows

It takes two steps to join the records from the titles and authors table: find the child records in the junction table and find the parent in the other table for each child record. For example, if you have the au_id of a selected author and want to find the titles written by that author, you must first get the child rows from the junction table, which produces an array of rows. Then you step through the array of rows and get the parent row of each from the titles table. You likely will store these parent rows in an array or display them in a list box. The example program that follows uses a two-tier approach, so the array of matching titles is passed back to the form and the form displays the titles in a list box (Figure 4.25).

Figure 4.25

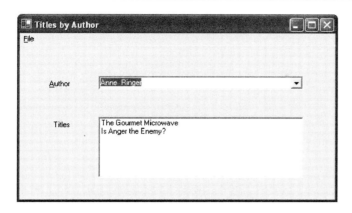

When the user selects an author from the list, the program finds the matching titles from the titles table.

Find the Child Rows

Assuming that you have the au_id of a selected author in strAuID, this code retrieves an array of child rows from the junction table. Note that the GetChildRows method uses the name of the relation between the authors and titleauthor tables (authorstitleauthor).

```
'Find the record for the selected author
drAuthor = DsTitlesAuthors1.authors.FindByau_id(strAuID)
'Retrieve the array of matching rows from the junction table
drsTitleAuthor = drAuthor.GetChildRows("authorstitleauthor")
```

Find the Parent Rows

Once you get the child rows from the junction table, you can iterate through the child rows to perform any needed processing. This example gets the title column from the parent row and adds it to a string array. If you were working in a single tier, you could just add the titles to a list box. This code resides in a data tier.

```
'Get each title and add to the array of titles
For Each drTitleAuthor In drsTitleAuthor
     'Retrieve the parent row and title field from the junction table row
     strTitle = drTitleAuthor.GetParentRow("titlestitleauthor").Item("title")
     'Add the title to the array
     strTitles(intRow) = strTitle
     'Increment index for next title
     intRow += 1
Next
```

You can see how this array is passed from the data tier to the presentation tier and the titles added to a list box in the complete program listing that follows.

The Titles by Author M:N Program

This M:N program is written as a multitier application. Figure 4.25 shows the
user interface, Figure 4.24 shows the data relationships, and Figure 4.26 shows
the data components in the data tier.

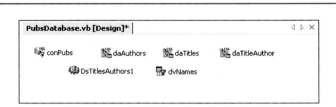

Figure 4.26

*The data tier component in
design mode.*

The Presentation Tier

```
'Project:        Ch04ManytoMany
'Module:         frmTitles
'Programmer:     Bradley/Millspaugh
'Date:           January 2003
'Description:    Displays titles for the selected author.
'                Uses a many-to-many relationship and a data tier component.

Option Strict On

Public Class frmTitles
    Inherits System.Windows.Forms.Form

    Dim mobjAuthors As PubsDatabase        'To hold instance of middle tier component
    Dim mblnListInitialized As Boolean = False

    Private Sub mnuFileExit_Click(ByVal sender As System.Object, _
      ByVal e As System.EventArgs) Handles mnuFileExit.Click
        'End the program

        Me.Close()
    End Sub

    Private Sub frmTitles_Load(ByVal sender As System.Object, _
      ByVal e As System.EventArgs) Handles MyBase.Load
        'Load the combo box
        Dim dvLastName As DataView
        Dim dsAuthorTitles As DataSet

        Try
            'Get the data from the data tier
            mobjAuthors = New PubsDatabase()
            dvLastName = mobjAuthors.getNames()

            'Bind the data view to the combo box
            With cboNames
                .DataSource = dvLastName
                .DisplayMember = "Name"
                .ValueMember = "au_id"
                .SelectedIndex = -1
            End With
```

```
                'Set flag to indicate that the list has been initialized
                mblnListInitialized = True

        Catch err As Exception
                MessageBox.Show(err.Message)
        End Try
    End Sub

    Private Sub cboNames_SelectedIndexChanged(ByVal sender As System.Object, _
        ByVal e As System.EventArgs) Handles cboNames.SelectedIndexChanged
            'Find the titles for the selected author
            Dim strAuthorID As String              'Hold the author ID of the selected author
            Dim strTitles(10) As String            'The array of matching titles
            Dim strTitle As String                 'Hold one title

        Try
            If mblnListInitialized = True Then
                'Save the au_id of the selected author
                strAuthorID = cboNames.SelectedValue.ToString()
                'Retrieve an array of matching records
                strTitles = mobjAuthors.getData(strAuthorID)
                'Fill the list with titles
                lstTitles.Items.Clear()
                'Iterate through the array
                For Each strTitle In strTitles
                    If strTitle <> Nothing Then
                        'Add the title to the list
                        lstTitles.Items.Add(strTitle)
                    End If
                Next
            End If

        Catch err As Exception
                MessageBox.Show(err.Message, "Titles")
        End Try

    End Sub
End Class
```

The Data Tier Component

```
'Project:        Ch04AuthorsTitles
'Module:         PubsDatabase
'Programmer:     Bradley/Millspaugh
'Date:           January 2003
'Description:    Data tier component for M:N Authors/Titles tables.

Public Class PubsDatabase
    Inherits System.ComponentModel.Component

    Public Function getData(ByVal strAuID As String) As String()
            'Find the titles for the selected author
            Dim drAuthor As DataRow                'Row for selected author
            Dim drsTitleAuthor As DataRow()        'Array of matching rows from junction table
            Dim drTitleAuthor As DataRow           'One row from junction table
            Dim intRow As Integer                  'Index for array
            Dim strTitle As String                 'Hold one title
            Dim strTitles(10) As String            'Array of titles for one author
```

```
            'Find the record for the selected author (the passed parameter)
            drAuthor = DsTitlesAuthors1.authors.FindByau_id(strAuID)
            'Retrieve the array of matching rows from the junction table
            drsTitleAuthor = drAuthor.GetChildRows("authorstitleauthor")
            'Get each title and add to the array of titles
            For Each drTitleAuthor In drsTitleAuthor
                'Retrieve the parent row and title field from the junction table row
                strTitle = drTitleAuthor.GetParentRow("titlestitleauthor").Item("title")
                'Add the title to the array
                strTitles(intRow) = strTitle
                'Increment index for next title
                intRow += 1
            Next
            Return strTitles  'Return the array of titles
        End Function

        Public Function getNames() As DataView
            'Fill the dataset with all 3 tables

            daAuthors.Fill(DsTitlesAuthors1)
            daTitles.Fill(DsTitlesAuthors1)
            daTitleAuthor.Fill(DsTitlesAuthors1)
            Return dvNames
        End Function
End Class
```

Feedback 4.4

Use this data diagram from the Northwind database to answer the following questions:

TIP

If you get a Null Exception error when accessing the data, make sure that you have filled all of the tables in the dataset. ∎

1. Name the parent table(s) and child table(s) and describe each of the relationships with the terms 1:1, 1:M, or M:N.
2. Assume that you have the OrderID for a selected order. Describe in words how to retrieve a list of the product names for that order.
3. Write the code to create an array of the product names in a selected order. The OrderID will be passed as a parameter to the data tier, and your code in the data tier should return the array.

Your Hands-On Programming Example

Create a program to display the sales for a selected store using a multitier application. Allow the user to select the store name from a drop-down list. Display the Store ID and City in bound labels and the sales for the store in a grid.

Note: For the grid column headings and column widths, you can create a dataset on the form to use at design time. Before writing the code to bind to the dataset from the data tier, delete the grid's DataSource property in the Properties window. The TableStyles and ColumnStyles will remain. Alternately, you can declare and assign TableStyles and ColumnStyles in code.

Multitier data binding note: When you bind controls at run time, you must reset the binding each time the data changes.

```
'Clear any previous bindings
lblStoreID.DataBindings.Clear()
lblCity.DataBindings.Clear()
'Filter and bind the store information
With dvStores
    .Table = dsStoreSales.Tables("Stores")
    .RowFilter = "stor_id = '" & cboStore.SelectedValue.ToString() & "'"
End With
lblStoreID.DataBindings.Add("text", dvStores, "stor_id")
lblCity.DataBindings.Add("text", dvStores, "city")
```

Planning the Project

Sketch a form (Figure 4.27) that your users sign off as meeting their needs.

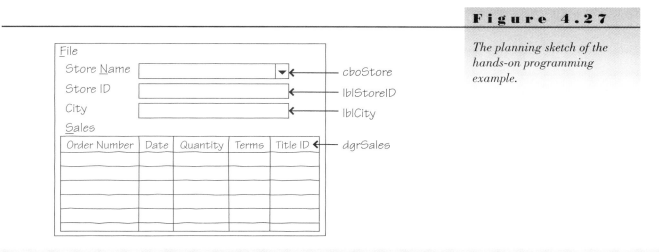

Figure 4.27

The planning sketch of the hands-on programming example.

Plan the Objects, Properties, and Methods

Plan the two tiers. Determine the objects and property settings for the form and its controls, and for the data tier component. Figure 4.28 shows the diagram of the program components.

Figure 4.28

The components for the hands-on programming example.

Presentation Tier	Data Tier
frmStoreNames	**PubsStoreSales**
cboStore	conPubs
lblStoreID	daStores
lblCity	daSales
dgrSales	dsStoreSales
mnuFileExit	DsStoreSales1
	daStoreNames
mnuFileExit_Click	dsNames
Form_Load	DsNames1
cboStore_SelectedIndexChanged	
BindControls	getDataset
	getNames

Presentation Tier

Object	Property	Setting
frmStoreNames	Name	frmStoreNames
	Text	Store Sales
Label1	Text	Store Name
Label2	Text	Store ID
Label3	Text	City
Label4	Text	Sales
cboStore	Name	cboStore
	Text	(blank)
lblStoreID	Text	(blank)
	BorderStyle	Fixed3D
lblCity	Text	(blank)
	BorderStyle	Fixed3D
dgrSales	Name	dgrSales
	CaptionVisible	False
	TableStyles	Add 1 TableStyle mapped to the sales table
	ColumnStyles	Add ColumnStyles mapped to each field
mnuFile	Text	&File
mnuFileExit	Text	E&xit

Event procedures/Methods	Actions—Pseudocode
mnuFileExit_Click	Exit the project.
Form_Load	Instantiate the data tier.
	Retrieve the dataset table to fill the combo box.
	Set the combo box properties.
	Set switch to show that the list has been loaded.
cboStore_SelectedIndexChanged	If the list has been loaded
	Clear any previous binding for the text boxes.
	Filter the stores table for the matching store.
	Bind the store data view to the text boxes.
	Filter the sales table for the matching store.
	Bind the sales data view to the grid.
BindControls	Bind the labels and the grid.

Data Tier

Object	Property	Setting
Class	Name	PubStoreSales
conPubs	Name	conPubs
daStores	Name	daStores
daSales	Name	daSales
DsStoreSales1	Name Tables	DsStoreSales1 stores and sales
daStoreNames	Name	daStoreNames
DsNames1	Name Table	DsNames1 stores

Methods	Actions—Pseudocode
getDataset	Create a dataset that holds the selected store and sales records. Return the dataset.
getNames	Fill the dataset holding the store names. Return the dataset.

Write the Project

Following the sketch in Figure 4.27, create the form. Figure 4.29 shows the completed form.

- Set the properties of each of the form objects, according to your plans.

- Create the data tier component, adding the objects from your plan.

- Write the methods for the data tier component, following the pseudocode.

- Write the code for the form. Working from the pseudocode, write each event procedure.

- When you complete the code, test the operation several times. Compare the screen output to the data tables to make sure that you are displaying the correct information.

Figure 4.29

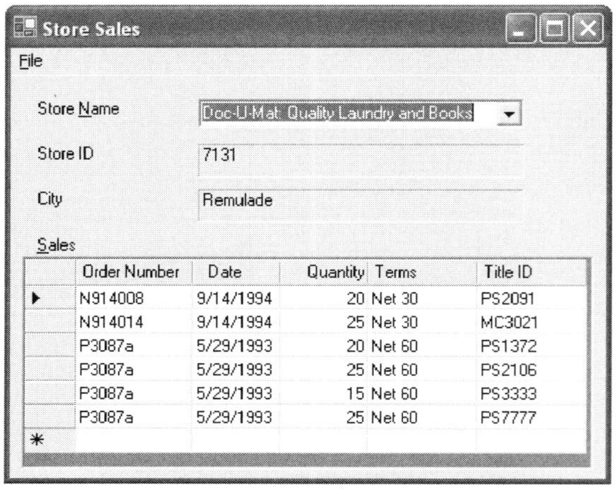

The completed form for the hands-on programming example.

The Project Coding Solution

The Form

```
'Project:        Ch04HandsOn
'Module:         frmStoreSales
'Programmer;     Bradley/Millspaugh
'Date:           January 2003
'Description:    Displays store information and sales for a
'                selected store. This is the presentation tier,
'                which uses the services of the data tier.

Option Strict On

Public Class frmStoreSales
    Inherits System.Windows.Forms.Form

    [Windows Form Designer generated code]

    Dim mobjData As PubsStoreSales      'Data tier component
    Dim mdsStoreSales As DataSet
    Dim mblnListLoaded As Boolean

    Private Sub frmStoreSales_Load(ByVal sender As System.Object, _
      ByVal e As System.EventArgs) Handles MyBase.Load
        'Instantiate the data component and fill the combo box
        Dim dsStoreNames As DataSet

        Try
            'Retrieve the dataset that holds the store names
            mobjData = New PubsStoreSales()
            dsStoreNames = mobjData.getNames()
            With cboStore
                'Bind to the stores table of the dataset
                .DataSource = dsStoreNames.Tables("stores")
                .DisplayMember = "stor_name"
                .ValueMember = "stor_id"
                .SelectedIndex = -1
            End With
```

```
                'Retrieve the store and sales dataset
                mdsStoreSales = mobjData.getDataset()
                'Set the flag to show that the list is loaded and program initialized
                mblnListLoaded = True

        Catch err As Exception
                MessageBox.Show(err.Message)
        End Try
    End Sub

    Private Sub cboStore_SelectedIndexChanged(ByVal sender As System.Object, _
      ByVal e As System.EventArgs) Handles cboStore.SelectedIndexChanged
        'Find the data to match the selected store
        Dim dvSales As New DataView()
        Dim dvStores As New DataView()

        If mblnListLoaded Then      'Do not come here until the list is initialized
            Try
                'Clear any previous bindings
                lblStoreID.DataBindings.Clear()
                lblCity.DataBindings.Clear()

                'Filter and bind the store information
                With dvStores
                    .Table = mdsStoreSales.Tables("Stores")
                    .RowFilter = "stor_id = '" & cboStore.SelectedValue.ToString() & "'"
                End With
                lblStoreID.DataBindings.Add("text", dvStores, "stor_id")
                lblCity.DataBindings.Add("text", dvStores, "city")

                'Filter and bind the sales information
                With dvSales
                    .Table = mdsStoreSales.Tables("Sales")
                    .RowFilter = "stor_id = '" & cboStore.SelectedValue.ToString() & "'"
                End With
                dgrSales.DataSource = dvSales

            Catch err As Exception
                MessageBox.Show(err.Message)
            End Try
        End If
    End Sub

    Private Sub mnuFileExit_Click(ByVal sender As System.Object, _
      ByVal e As System.EventArgs) Handles mnuFileExit.Click
        'End the application

        Me.Close()
    End Sub
End Class
```

The Data Tier

```
'Project:        Ch04HandsOn
'Module:         PubsStoreSales
'Programmer:     Bradley/Millspaugh
'Date:           January 2003
'Description:    Data tier for the store sales application.
'                Retrieves datasets for store names and store sales.

Option Strict On

Public Class PubsStoreSales
    Inherits System.ComponentModel.Component

    [Component Designer generated code]

    Public Function getDataset() As DataSet
        'Fill the dataset with both tables

        daStores.Fill(DsStoreSales1)
        daSales.Fill(DsStoreSales1)
        Return DsStoreSales1

    End Function

    Public Function getNames() As DataSet
        'Return the dataset with names for the combo box

        daStoreNames.Fill(DsStoreNames1)
        Return DsStoreNames1

    End Function

End Class
```

Summary

1. Relational databases are stored in multiple related tables. The primary table is the parent or master and the second table is referred to as the child or detail table.
2. The primary key of a table uniquely identifies each record. When the primary key of one table is included in a second table to link the tables together, the key included in the second table is called a *foreign key*.
3. Relationships may be one-to-many (1:M), many-to-many (M:N), or one-to-one (1:1). A M:N relationship requires a third table, called a *junction table*, to join the tables.
4. Constraints may be *unique constraints* or *foreign-key constraints*. Enforcing constraints is handled by the database management system to maintain referential integrity.
5. To create a dataset with related tables, you need one data adapter for each table. When you generate the dataset, you include both tables and set up the relationships in the .xsd file (the schema).

6. A DataGrid can display related records from multiple tables. You set the DataSource and DataMember for the parent table. The only code needed is to fill the dataset.

7. To format the columns of a grid, create one TableStyle for each table and add a ColumnStyle for each column.

8. In a 1:M relationship, the one is the parent table and the many is the child table.

9. To filter a dataset for specific values, create a new DataView object and set its Table property and its RowFilter property. A RowFilter is created with relational operators and resembles the WHERE clause in an SQL statement.

10. The actual data in a dataset are held in DataRow objects in the DataRows collection of the table. You can assign a record to a DataRow object and retrieve the data items from each field.

11. You can assign the value of a field to a control, which is referred to as an *unbound control*.

12. You can retrieve the parent row of a given child row by using the GetParentRow method, which returns a DataRow object. You can retrieve the child rows of a given parent by using the GetChildRows method, which returns an array of DataRow objects.

13. When working with a M:N relationship, each of the tables has a 1:M relationship with the junction table, which is considered a child to both of the other tables. To retrieve related records from the two master tables, get the child records for a row in one master and then get the parent rows from the second master table.

Key Terms

child table   *114*
DataRelation object   *117*
detail table   *114*
foreign key   *114*
foreign key constraint   *115*
GetChildRows method   *134*
GetParentRow method   *132*
junction table   *114*

many-to-many relationship   *114*
master table   *114*
one-to-many relationship   *114*
one-to-one relationship   *115*
parent table   *114*
referential integrity   *115*
unique constraint   *115*

Review Questions

1. Name the three types of table relationships and give an example of each.
2. What is a constraint? Give some examples.
3. Explain how to create a dataset that holds multiple tables.
4. Describe the steps necessary to establish a relationship in the IDE.
5. Can a relationship be edited or deleted? How?
6. Explain how to retrieve and display all matching child rows for a given parent row.
7. Explain the steps necessary to retrieve records from three tables.

Programming Exercises

For each of these exercises, create a multitier application with the database access in a separate component. Make sure to turn `Option Strict On`.

4.1   (Grid) Use the Northwind database to create a grid that displays Customers and Orders. Set up the relationship in the XML schema.

4.2   (Master/Detail) Use the Northwind database to display Customer and Order Information. Populate a combo box with the CompanyName sorted in alphabetic order. Display the customer information in bound labels and the order information in a grid. For customers, display the CustomerID, ContactName, ContactTitle, and Phone. For orders, display the OrderID, OrderDate, RequiredDate, and ShippedDate.

4.3   (Two grids) Use the Northwind database to display Customer and Order Information. Populate a list box with the CompanyName sorted in alphabetic order. Display customer information in the top grid and the order information in a second grid. For customers, display the CustomerID, Address, City, Region, PostalCode, and Country. For orders, display the OrderID, OrderDate, RequiredDate, and ShippingDate.

4.4   (Grid) Using the Orders table of the Northwind database, display the order ID, employee name, and order date for each order in the Orders table. Use the Employees table to find the employee names.

4.5   (M:N) Use the Employees, Territories, and EmployeeTerritories tables in the Northwind database to display related information. Populate a list box with the employee names (concatenated) in alphabetic order by last name. Use the EmployeeID as the ValueMember. Display a list of the territories for that employee, using the TerritoryDescription field from the Territories table.

4.6   (Challenge) Modify Exercise 4.2 to include the name of the employee for each order.

Case Studies

Claytor's Cottages

Modify your Claytor's Cottages case study project to display the room information. The *Edit/Rooms* menu item should display the Room form.

On the Room form include a list box that holds the room name. Use check boxes to indicate if the room has a Jacuzzi, Private access, and/or Fireplace. Display the Bed type and rates from the Beds table in labels.

The data are stored in the Cottages database. The Room table contains the following information:

Rooms

Room name	Bed code	Jacuzzi	Private access
Garden	K	Y	Y
Library	Q	N	Y
Sun room	D	N	N
Ocean	K	N	Y
Forest	Q	N	N

Beds

Bed code	Bed type	Weekend rate	Weekday rate
K	King	105.00	95.00
Q	Queen	95.00	85.00
D	Double	79.95	69.95

Christian's Car Rentals

Display the customer information in a data grid. Include the manufacturer name and model name of the related vehicle.

5

Windows Database Updates

1. Update a database table in a grid.

2. Use the form's binding context to navigate records.

3. Write an event handler and delegate for a component added in code.

4. Add, edit, and delete records in bound controls on a form.

5. Update a data source by returning the values from a dataset.

6. Sequence update statements to accurately update related tables.

In the preceding chapters you displayed data from datasets and related tables. In this chapter you will update the data, which includes adding records, deleting records, and making changes to existing records. You will use data adapters, datasets, and a binding manager.

Note that we have elected to use an Access database and the OleDb provider for most of the programs in this chapter. The concepts and statements for updating a SQLServer database are exactly the same as for an Access database. However, for testing update programs, it is very convenient to be able to copy over a fresh version of the database file. If you prefer to use SQLServer files, see Appendix C for instructions to reload the SQLServer sample databases.

The Data Objects

Remember that a dataset is a temporary set of data in memory, disconnected from the original data source. The user can make changes to the rows of data in the dataset, but those changes are not automatically sent back to the data source. The data adapter is the go-between for the data source and the dataset (Figure 5.1). You execute methods of the data adapter to send any changes back to the original data source.

Figure 5.1

The data adapter retrieves data from the data source to create the dataset and sends back changes from the dataset to the data source.

The DataSet Methods and Properties

Recall that a DataSet object can consist of multiple tables and each table can consist of multiple data rows, where the actual data *values* are stored (Figure 5.2). Each row of data has a **RowState property,** which indicates whether any changes have been made to the row. Table 5.1 shows the values of the DataRowState enumeration for the possible values of the RowState property.

Figure 5.2

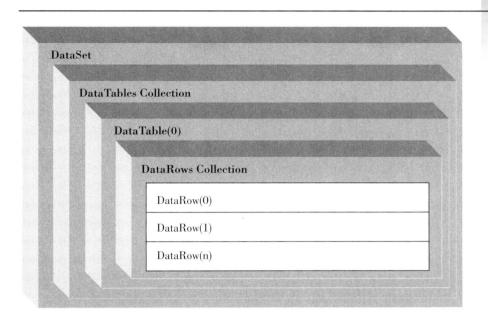

Each row of data belongs to a DataRows collection of a table.

Table 5.1

DataRowState Enumeration	Purpose
Added	Indicates that this is a new row.
Deleted	The row is marked for deletion.
Detached	The row is not a part of a collection. A row has the detached value before it is added or after it has been removed.
Modified	Changes have been made to the row.
Unchanged	No changes have been made to the row.

The DataRowState enumeration values that are used for the RowState property of a DataRow, which indicate whether any changes have been made to the row.

The HasChanges Method

You can determine if any changes have been made to a dataset by calling the **HasChanges method**, which returns a boolean value.

```
If DsEmployee1.HasChanges() Then
    'Query the user to save the changes
End If
```

One of the overloaded versions of the HasChanges method allows you to check for specific types of changes, using the values for DataRowState shown in Table 5.1.

```
If DsEmployee1.HasChanges(DataRowState.Deleted) Then
    'Code to handle the deletion(s)
End If
```

The GetChanges Method

You can use the **GetChanges method** of a dataset or a data table to retrieve the rows that have changes. Use an empty argument to retrieve all changed rows, or specify the type of changes that you want using the DataRowState enumeration values.

Create a new dataset that holds all changed rows:

```
Dim dsEmployeeChanges As DataSet
dsEmployeeChanges = DsEmployee1.GetChanges()
```

Create a dataset that holds all of the rows that are marked for deletion:

```
Dim dsEmployeeDeletes As DataSet
dsEmployeeDeletes = DsEmployee1.GetChanges(DataRowState.Deleted)
```

The Edit Methods

When the user modifies a row of data, the row must be in edit mode. However, if the data are displayed in bound controls, the edit methods are called automatically. When an edit begins, the **BeginEdit method** executes; when the edit terminates, the EndEdit method executes. Any time before the EndEdit method executes, you can call the CancelEdit method to return the field values to their original values.

DataRow Versions

The DataRow object maintains several versions of its column data: the Current, Original, and Default versions. If no changes have been made, the Current and Original versions are the same. While an edit is in progress—between the BeginEdit and EndEdit—one more version exists: the Proposed version. When EndEdit executes, the Current version is replaced by the Proposed version.

The EndEdit method confirms the changes, but the changes are not actually made in the dataset until the AcceptChanges method executes.

The AcceptChanges Method

The **AcceptChanges method** automatically

- Calls the EndEdit method of the data row.

- Removes all rows marked for deletion.

- Makes the adds and edits indicated for the table.

- Sets the Original version of each changed row to the Current version.

- Sets the RowState of each row to Unchanged.

The AcceptChanges method commits all of the changes to the dataset. The **RejectChanges method** rolls back all changes that have been made by replacing the Current versions with the Original versions. After either the AcceptChanges or RejectChanges method executes, all RowState properties are reset to Unchanged.

Remember that the dataset is disconnected, so the changes are made to the dataset, not to the original data source. To send the changes back to the data source, you must execute the data adapter's `Update` method before calling the `AcceptChanges` method.

The Data Adapter Update Method

Although the user can make changes to the dataset in memory, no changes are made to the original data source until you execute the **Update method** of the data adapter. You can choose to execute the `Update` method after every change, or once when the program terminates.

The `Update` method of the data adapter saves the changes from the dataset to the original data source.

The Update Method—General Form

```
DataAdapter.Update(DataSet)
DataAdapter.Update(DataSet, "Table")
```

If the dataset has only one table, you don't need to specify the table name.

The Update Method—Examples

```
daBook.Update(DsBooks1)
daBook.Update(DsBooks1, "Books")
```

You must decide when to execute the `Update` method. You can save the change every time an add, edit, or delete occurs, or you can wait until the program terminates. Or combine the two techniques by providing a *Save* option on a menu or button and then prompting for unsaved changes when the program terminates. This technique matches Office applications: You can save a document any time you want, but if you try to close without saving the changes, a dialog box displays.

The `Update` method causes communication from the data adapter to the data source. If the data are stored on the same system as the application, updating is no problem. However, if the data source is elsewhere, such as on an intranet or the Internet, saving each change may require substantial network traffic. You must consider where the application and data reside, how many users can make changes, and whether it's important that the data source be up-to-date at all times.

It may be best to wait and save all changes when the program terminates. (However, a loss of power could lose all changes.) To prompt for unsaved changes, place the `Update` method in the form's Closing event procedure. The Closing event occurs when `Me.Close` executes, which should happen when the user selects *Exit* from a menu or button, or when the user clicks the form's Close button or even exits Windows.

To ask the user whether to save the dataset when changes have been made, check the return value for the `HasChanges` method. If changes have been made, display the message "Do you want to save the changes?" The following code belongs in the form's Closing event procedure:

```
'Save the changes
Dim dgrResult As DialogResult

If DsBooks1.HasChanges() Then
    dgrResult = MessageBox.Show("Do you want to save the changes?", "Books", _
        MessageBoxButtons.YesNo, MessageBoxIcon.Question)
    If dgrResult = DialogResult.Yes Then
        Try
            'Save the changes to the original data source
            daBooks.Update(DsBooks1, "Books")
            'Reset the dataset to reflect the new data
            DsBooks1.AcceptChanges()
        Catch err As Exception
            MessageBox.Show(err.Message, "Books")
        End Try
    End If
End If
```

Feedback 5.1

Write the statements to save all of the changes to DsCustomer1 using the data
adapter daCustomer. Make sure to include the command to change all of the
RowState values for the dataset to Unchanged.

Updating Data in a Grid

You can allow updates to data in a bound Windows DataGrid control (Figure
5.3).

Figure 5.3

The user can update the dataset in a Windows DataGrid. The pencil icon indicates that the row is in edit mode.

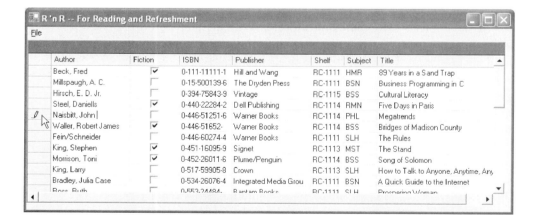

Modifying Data

When the user clicks in a row of data, the dataset enters edit mode. If you are
familiar with editing data in Access, you will recognize the little pencil icon

that appears for a row being edited. The user can make any desired changes to the data, within the bounds of any constraints, and move to another row; the pencil icon disappears and the `EndEdit` method executes. If the user presses the Esc key during an edit operation, the `CancelEdit` method executes and the row is replaced by the Original version.

Deleting Rows

To delete a row or record from the dataset, the user must select the entire row by clicking in the gray row-selector area at the beginning of the row and press the Delete key on the keyboard. This action automatically removes the row from the grid and marks the row for deletion from the dataset.

Adding Rows

To add a row, scroll to the row with a star (asterisk), beyond the last row in the table (Figure 5.4). Click in the first field and add the data for the new row. When you move off the row, the new row is added to the dataset (temporarily, until the `AcceptChanges` method executes).

Figure 5.4

Click in the row beyond the last record, indicated by a star, to add a new record to the table.

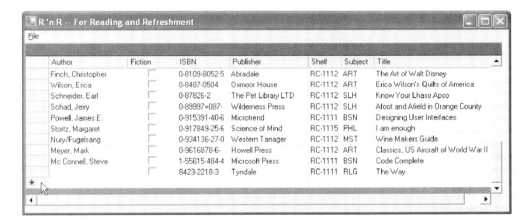

Constraints

When you add or modify records, you must be aware of any constraints for the data fields. For example, the emp_id field of the pubs employee table requires two or three alphabetic characters, then five numeric digits, then either "M" or "F". Any other values will cause a constraint-violation error. You can check the constraints for a SQL Server table using the Server Explorer. Select the table name, right-click, and select *Design Table*. In the table design, right-click and select *Check Constraints*. In the *Property Pages* dialog that appears (Figure 5.5), you can check the constraints, relationships, and indexes.

Figure   5.5

*Check the constraints for a
SQL Server table in the
Property Pages dialog box.*

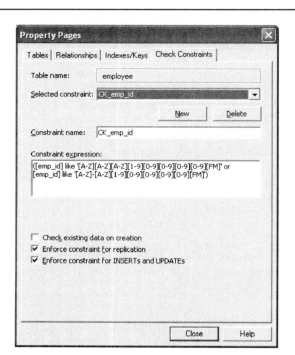

The Grid Update Program

Here is the code for the grid update program shown in Figures 5.3 and 5.4. This
update program uses an Access database for convenience, but the techniques
for updating a SQL Server database are exactly the same.

```
'File:          Ch05RnRGrid
'Programmer:    Bradley/Millspaugh
'Date:          January 2003
'Description:   Update book information in a grid

Public Class frmRnR
    Inherits System.Windows.Forms.Form

    Private Sub frmRnR_Load(ByVal sender As System.Object, _
      ByVal e As System.EventArgs) Handles MyBase.Load
        'Fill the dataset

        'Make the database file portable
        'Note that RnRBooks.mdb must be in the project's bin folder
        conRnR.ConnectionString = _
          "Provider=Microsoft.Jet.OLEDB.4.0;Data Source=RnRBooks.mdb"
        'Fill the dataset
        daBooks.Fill(DsBooks1)
    End Sub

    Private Sub mnuFileSave_Click(ByVal sender As System.Object, _
      ByVal e As System.EventArgs) Handles mnuFileSave.Click
        'Save any changes to the original data source
```

```
        Try
            'Save the changes to the original data source
            daBooks.Update(DsBooks1, "Books")
            'Reset the dataset to reflect the new data
            DsBooks1.AcceptChanges()
        Catch err As Exception
            MessageBox.Show(err.Message, "Books")
        End Try
    End Sub

    Private Sub mnuFileExit_Click(ByVal sender As System.Object, _
      ByVal e As System.EventArgs) Handles mnuFileExit.Click
        Terminate the project

        Me.Close()
    End Sub

    Private Sub frmRnR_Closing(ByVal sender As Object, _
      ByVal e As System.ComponentModel.CancelEventArgs) Handles MyBase.Closing
        'Save the changes
        Dim dgrResult As DialogResult

        If DsBooks1.HasChanges() Then
            dgrResult = MessageBox.Show("Do you want to save the changes?", "Books", _
                MessageBoxButtons.YesNo, MessageBoxIcon.Question)
            If dgrResult = DialogResult.Yes Then
                Try
                    'Save the changes to the original data source
                    daBooks.Update(DsBooks1, "Books")
                    'Reset the dataset to reflect the new data
                    DsBooks1.AcceptChanges()
                Catch err As Exception
                    MessageBox.Show(err.Message, "Books")
                End Try
            End If
        End If
    End Sub
End Class
```

Adding Menu Options

In the grid update program, it might be a good idea to help the user by providing menu items and/or context menu items for deleting and adding records. To do this, you must use the form's binding context, which is covered in the next section.

The BindingContext Object

When you are working with bound controls such as a grid, list, text box, or label, the bound table data are managed by the form's **BindingContext object.** Each form has a BindingContext object that contains a collection of **Binding-ManagerBase objects**—one object for each table (Figure 5.6). The Binding-ManagerBase objects may be instances of the CurrencyManager class (for grids and lists) or the PropertyManager class (for simple-bound controls such as labels and text boxes). Because the CurrencyManager and PropertyManager classes both inherit from the BindingManagerBase class and get most of their properties and methods from that class, you can refer to the manager for either type as a BindingManagerBase object.

Figure   5.6

Each form has a BindingContext, which contains a collection of BindingManagerBase objects, one for each table.

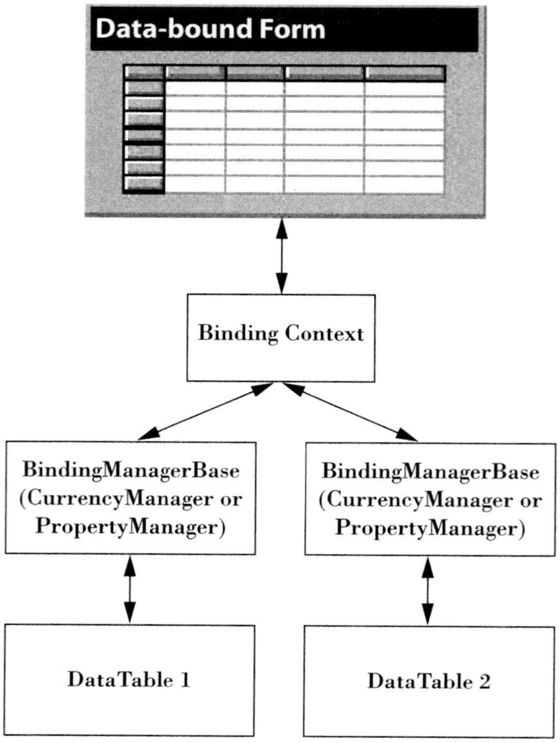

The binding manager controls the record position within a table and is responsible for assuring that all bound controls on a form display data from the same record. You use properties of the binding manager to determine the current record and to navigate from one record to the next.

Declaring a Binding Manager Object

You can refer to the binding manager for a table using this syntax:

```
Me.BindingContext.Item(DataSetName, "TableName")
```

or

```
Me.BindingContext(DataSetName, "TableName")
```

The second form is a shortcut for the first and is used most often. In a collection such as this, if you leave out the word "Item," it is assumed. Notice that the statement refers to the BindingContext of the current form, which is a collection of BindingManagerBase objects. By including the dataset name and the table name, you specify which object in the Tables collection you want.

Example

```
Me.BindingContext(DsBooks1, "books")
```

The easiest way to use a binding manager is to declare a variable at the module level and assign its value in the Form_Load event procedure. Then you can use the binding manager variable in all of the form's procedures.

```
'Module-level declarations
Dim bmBooks As BindingManagerBase 'Binding manager for the books table

'Inside the Form_Load event procedure:
'Fill the dataset
daBooks.Fill(DsBooks1, "books")
'Instantiate the binding manager for the Books table
bmBooks = Me.BindingContext(DsBooks1, "books")
```

Binding Manager Properties

The **Position property** of the binding manager holds the current row number (zero based) and the **Count property** indicates the number of records in a table.

```
Me.BindingContext(DsBooks1, "books").Position
Me.BindingContext(DsBooks1, "books").Count
```

If you have declared a variable for the binding manager as described in the preceding section, you can refer to that object:

```
bmBooks.Position        'Current record position
bmBooks.Count           'Number of records in the table
```

Using these properties, you can display the record number in a label or a status bar on the form: "Record 5 of 200".

Notice that you must add 1 to the Position property, since it is zero based.

```
With bmBooks
    lblRecordPosition.Text = "Record " & (.Position + 1).ToString() & _
        " of " & .Count.ToString()
End With
```

The **Current property** of the binding manager returns the current row. Notice that the object type must be DataRowView.

```
Dim CurrentRow As DataRowView
CurrentRow = CType(bmBooks.Current, DataRowView)
```

The binding manager also contains a Bindings collection, which is a collection of all of the objects bound to the data source.

Navigating Using the Position Property

You can use the Position property of the binding manager for record navigation. For example, you might have buttons for Next Record, Previous Record, First Record, and Last Record. Modifying the Position property changes the record position; and if you have bound fields or a grid, the new current record displays.

```
bmBooks.Position += 1                 'Navigate to the next record
bmBooks.Position -= 1                 'Navigate to the previous record
bmBooks.Position = 0                  'Navigate to the first record
bmBooks.Position = bmBooks.Count - 1  'Navigate to the last record
```

You should check to make sure that you don't try to go to a record beyond the last record or before the first record.

```
'Move to the next record
With bmBooks
    If .Position < .Count - 1 Then
        .Position += 1           'Next record
    Else
        .Position = 0            'First record
    End If
End With

'Move to the previous record
With bmBooks
    If .Position > 0 Then
        .Position -= 1           'Previous record
    Else
        .Position = .Count - 1 'Last record
    End If
End With
```

Binding Manager Methods

You can use the methods of the binding manager to maintain table data (Table 5.2). Use the **AddNew method** to begin the operation to add a new record to the dataset. When you execute the AddNew method for data displayed in a grid, the last line in the grid (the one with the asterisk) is activated so the user can enter a new row. If you execute AddNew for individually bound fields, the field contents are cleared so that the user can enter the new record. When the user moves off of the new record, the **EndCurrentEdit method** is executed automatically; or you can explicitly execute the method, perhaps in response to a button click. If the user wishes to cancel the add or edit, you can call the **CancelCurrentEdit method.** Remember that the dataset is disconnected, so any new records are added to the dataset in memory and not saved to the original data source until you execute the Update method.

Helpful methods of the BindingManagerBase object

Table 5.2

Method	Purpose	Example
AddNew	Clears bound fields to allow new data to be entered. Adds a new row to the table.	bmBooks.Addnew()
CancelCurrentEdit	Cancels the edit currently being processed.	bmBooks.CancelCurrentEdit()
EndCurrentEdit	Completes the current edit.	bmBooks.EndCurrentEdit()
RemoveAt	Deletes the current row from the table.	bmBooks.RemoveAt(bmBooks.Position)

Use the **RemoveAt method** to delete the current record:

```
With bmBooks
    .RemoveAt(.Position)
End With
```

Binding Manager Events

The two events for the BindingManagerBase class are the CurrentChanged event and the PositionChanged event. The **CurrentChanged event** occurs when a bound value is changed. When a user navigates to another record, the **PositionChanged event** occurs. The PositionChanged event procedure is a good place to display the current record number in a label or status bar.

Adding an Event Handler

An **event handler** (event procedure) should execute automatically when an event occurs. So far, all event handlers that you have used have been generated automatically for objects that you defined at design time. But the designer cannot automatically generate an event handler for an object that you declare in code, such as a binding manager.

Writing your own event handler requires two steps:

1. Write the procedure that you want to execute when the event occurs, including the *sender* and *EventArgs* arguments.
2. Add the handler, which is called a **delegate**. (You are delegating, or assigning, a particular event to a specific procedure.) Adding the handler, or delegate, turns the general procedure you wrote in step 1 into an event procedure.

In this example, the new event procedure is called `Position_Changed`. Notice that you assign the address of the procedure to the PositionChanged event of the binding manager.

```
'Get the BindingManagerBase for the Book table
Dim bmBooks as BindingManagerBase = Me.BindingContext(DsBooks1, "books")
'Add the delegate for the PositionChanged event
AddHandler bmBooks.PositionChanged, AddressOf Position_Changed
```

Once you have included the handler, the PositionChanged event occurs each time the current record changes, and your new event procedure executes automatically. This event procedure is a great place to display the current record number and record count.

Displaying the Record Number and Record Count

Use the binding manager that you declared earlier to supply the record number and record count. This procedure executes automatically every time the record number changes.

```
Private Sub Position_Changed(ByVal sender As Object, ByVal e As EventArgs)
    'Display the record number in the status bar panel

    With bmBooks
        sbpRecordNumber.Text = "Record " & (.Position + 1).ToString() & _
        " of " & .Count.ToString()
    End With
End Sub
```

Unfortunately, the PositionChanged event does not occur when the user deletes a record. For that situation, you can call the Position_Changed procedure yourself.

```
'Delete the current record
With bmBooks
    .RemoveAt(.Position)
End With
Position_Changed(sender, e)
```

Completing the Grid Update Program

Now that you can work with the binding manager, you can make the grid update program more user friendly. We will add menu items to add a new record and delete the current record, on both a main menu and a context menu. Also, a status bar panel displays the record number and record count. Following are the changes to the Ch05RnRGrid program shown earlier in the chapter:

```
'Module-level declaration
    Dim bmBooks As BindingManagerBase      'Binding manager for the books table

'New code added to the frmRnR_Load event procedure
    'Instantiate the binding manager for the Books table
    bmBooks = Me.BindingContext(DsBooks1, "books")
    'Add the delegate for the PositionChanged event of the binding manager
    AddHandler bmBooks.PositionChanged, AddressOf Position_Changed
    'Display the record number for the first row
    Position_Changed(sender, e)

'New procedures added

    Private Sub Position_Changed(ByVal sender As Object, _
      ByVal e As EventArgs)

        With bmBooks
            sbpRecordNumber.Text = "Record " & (.Position + 1).ToString() & _
                " of " & (.Count.ToString())
        End With
    End Sub
```

```
    Private Sub mnuEditDelete_Click(ByVal sender As System.Object, _
       ByVal e As System.EventArgs) Handles mnuEditDelete.Click, mnuContextDelete.Click
        'Delete the current record

        Try
            With bmBooks
                .RemoveAt(.Position)
            End With
            Position_Changed(sender, e)

        Catch err As Exception
            MessageBox.Show("Unable to delete the record." & ControlChars.NewLine & _
                err.Message, "Books", MessageBoxButtons.OK, MessageBoxIcon.Error)
        End Try
    End Sub

    Private Sub mnuEditAdd_Click(ByVal sender As System.Object, _
       ByVal e As System.EventArgs) Handles mnuEditAdd.Click, mnuContextAdd.Click
        'Add a new record

        bmBooks.AddNew()
    End Sub
End Class
```

> ## Feedback 5.2

For each of these questions, assume that the form's binding manager has been
assigned to bmCustomers.

1. Write the code to navigate to the previous record in the Customers table
   in DsCustomers1.
2. Write the statement(s) to delete the currently selected record from a
   dataset.
3. Write the statement(s) to begin an Add operation to add a new record to
   a dataset.

Dataset Updating

ADO.NET handles the complicated process of updating the original data
source based on the changes made to a disconnected dataset. Recall that each
row in a table has a RowState property that may be set to Unchanged, Modified,
Added, or Deleted. The Update method makes all of the indicated changes
from the dataset to the data source.

SQL Statements for Updates

When you configure a data adapter, several SQL statements are generated. In
addition to the SELECT statement that you are familiar with, an INSERT statement, DELETE statement, and UPDATE statement also are created. You can see

those SQL statements by examining the CommandText properties of the DeleteCommand, InsertCommand, and UpdateCommand properties of the data adapter. The syntax of the statements is affected by the concurrency setting (described in the next section).

When the Update method executes, ADO.NET sends the DELETE SQL command for each record with a RowState of Deleted, the INSERT SQL command for each record with a RowState of Added, and the UPDATE SQL command for all rows with a RowState of Modified.

Concurrency

If more than one user can update a file at the same time, **concurrency** problems can occur. **Concurrency control** is the process of handling conflicts in updates by multiple users. There are three types of concurrency control in ADO.NET:

1. Pessimistic concurrency control: A row is unavailable to other users from the time the record is retrieved until the update is complete.
2. Optimistic concurrency control: A row is unavailable only while an update is in progress. If an update has been made between the time a record is retrieved and an attempt is made to save changes, a currency violation occurs.
3. "Last in wins": A row is unavailable only when the update is being made. No checks are made for multiple changes to the same record.

Pessimistic concurrency control is not an option with a disconnected dataset. Using a DataReader, which you will learn about in Chapter 6, you can retrieve and update individual records; then you can specify pessimistic concurrency.

The default is optimistic concurrency. If you want to change the setting to "last in wins," run the data adapter configuration wizard and remove the check for concurrency. You might want to do this if you are making multiple changes to the same record during testing.

Testing Update Programs

You may encounter many types of errors when testing an Add or Update in an update program if you are not familiar with the database. First, you must have the proper rights to the database to allow you to write to the data source. Second, be aware of constraints—which fields can contain nulls, which are required fields, which must contain specific values. You should include exception handling for all statements that access the database. Display the exception message, which will help you determine the cause of the problem.

Updating a Dataset in Bound Controls

You can allow the user to update records using bound individual controls, which is more common than using a grid. You will need to display the dataset fields in bound text boxes, rather than labels, so that the user can type in changes. However, you will keep the text boxes locked unless an Add or Edit is in progress. Figure 5.7 shows the form for the update program, which updates the Books table in RnRBooks.mdb. Remember that all of the techniques for updating a dataset apply equally to an Access database and a SQL Server database.

Figure 5.7

The form for the update program.

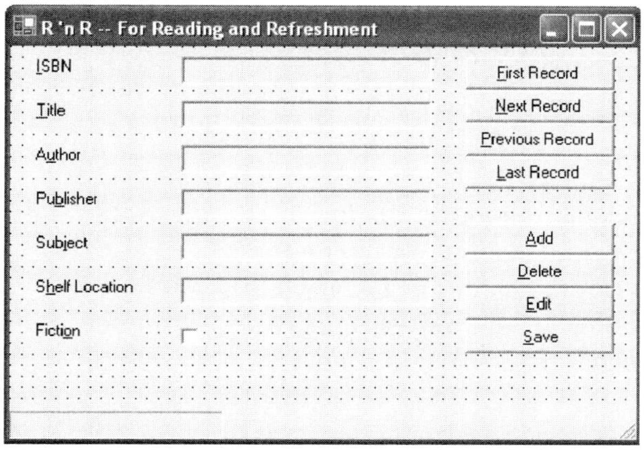

The Logic of an Update Program

An update program needs procedures to modify existing records (called *editing records*), delete records, and add new records. For this program, we will call the Update method after every change, so that the data source is up-to-date for every record.

Make sure to enclose all statements that access the dataset in Try/Catch blocks. You don't want to allow the program to cancel with an exception.

Deleting Records

Pseudocode for a Delete Operation

Confirm if record is to be deleted.
If yes,
    Mark the current record for deletion.
    Update the data source (actually delete the record).
    AcceptChanges to delete the record from the dataset.

Execute the RemoveAt method of the binding manager to delete a record.

```
Private Sub btnDelete_Click(ByVal sender As System.Object, _
  ByVal e As System.EventArgs) Handles btnDelete.Click
    'Delete the current record after confirming
    Dim dgrDelete As DialogResult

    Try
        dgrDelete = MessageBox.Show("Delete this record?", "Confirm Delete", _
        MessageBoxButtons.YesNo)
```

```
            If dgrDelete = DialogResult.Yes Then
                With bmBooks
                    .RemoveAt(.Position)        'Mark the record for deletion
                End With
                daBooks.Update(DsBooks1)        'Delete the record from the data source
                DsBooks1.AcceptChanges()        'Delete the record from the dataset
            End If
        Catch err As Exception
            MessageBox.Show(err.Message)
        End Try
    End Sub
End Sub
```

Adding Records

The logic of an Add operation is more complicated than editing or deleting. The user must click an *Add* button to begin an Add operation. The program must clear the text boxes, unlock them, and allow the user to enter the data for the new record. During the Add operation, the user should have only the choices *Save* and *Cancel*. The text on the *Add* button changes to *Cancel* during an Add operation.

All records are added to the end of the table.

The Add Button

The btnAdd_Click event procedure must perform the actions to begin an Add. And since we're changing the Text property of the Add button to *Cancel* during an Add or Edit, the procedure must also include the Cancel logic.

Pseudocode for the btnAdd_Click Event Procedure

If the button's Text is "Add" then
    Unlock the text boxes.
    Disable the navigation buttons.
    Set up the buttons for an Add:
        Change the Text of the Add button to "Cancel".
        Enable the Save button.
        Disable the Delete button.
        Disable the Edit button.
    Clear the text boxes.
    Set the focus to the first text box.

Else (the button's Text is "Cancel")
    Reject changes (replace the text boxes with their previous contents).
    Lock the text boxes.
    Enable the navigation buttons.
    Reset the buttons for normal operation:
        Disable the Save button.
        Set the Text of the Add button back to "Add".
        Enable the Delete button.
        Enable the Edit button.

The code for the btnAdd_Click event procedure:

```
Private Sub btnAdd_Click(ByVal sender As System.Object, _
  ByVal e As System.EventArgs) Handles btnAdd.Click
    'Begin an Add operation or cancel the current operation

    If btnAdd.Text = "&Add" Then
        UnlockTextBoxes()
        DisableNavigation()
        SetupButtonsForEdit()
        'Make sure current record is saved
        bmBooks.EndCurrentEdit()
        'Clear the fields
        bmBooks.AddNew()
        txtISBN.Focus()
    Else    'Cancel button clicked
        LockTextBoxes()
        EnableNavigation()
        ResetButtonsAfterEdit()
        bmBooks.CancelCurrentEdit()
    End If
End Sub
```

Saving an Added Record

After the user has entered the data for a new record and clicks the Save button, you must save the new data. The Save button is enabled for both Adds and Edits.

Pseudocode for the Save Button

'Save both Adds and Edits
End current edit
Update the data source.
Accept the changes to the dataset.
Lock the text fields.
Enable the navigation buttons.
Reset the buttons for normal operation:
 Disable the Save button.
 Set the Text of the Add button back to "Add".
 Enable the Delete button.
 Enable the Edit button.

The code for the btnSave_Click event procedure:

```
Private Sub btnSave_Click(ByVal sender As System.Object, _
  ByVal e As System.EventArgs) Handles btnSave.Click
    'Save updates to the dataset

    Try
        bmBooks.EndCurrentEdit()      'Complete the current edit
        daBooks.Update(DsBooks1)      'Update the data source
        DsBooks1.AcceptChanges()      'Reset the dataset
        LockTextBoxes()
        EnableNavigation()
        ResetButtonsAfterEdit()
    Catch err As Exception
        'Check for duplicate records and constraint violations
        MessageBox.Show(err.Message)
    End Try
End Sub
```

The Binding Bug

A big bug exists in the first release of ADO.NET: The `AddNew` method fails to clear all bound controls if a boolean field that is bound to a check box does not have a default value. This condition exists in the RnRBooks.mdb file and the pubs sample database that comes with SQL Server. For more information, see the Microsoft Knowledge Base article #Q321504. The article explains two ways to work around the bug: (1) change the field in the database to have a default value or (2) change the dataset schema in the application to assign a default value to the field. The following instructions demonstrate how to accomplish the second method, but you can modify the database if you prefer. (It's possible that this bug will be fixed in ADO.NET before you read this.)

The example update programs in this chapter update the RnRBooks.mdb database. Referring to Figure 5.7, you can see that the Fiction field is bound to a check box. To make the `AddNew` method clear the bound controls, we will modify the dataset schema to assign a default value of "false" to the Fiction field.

1. In the Solution Explorer, double-click on the dsBooks.xsd file to open the schema in the designer.
2. Click on the Fiction field to display the properties of the field in the Properties window.
3. For the Default property, enter "false" (without the quotes). *Caution:* This property is case-sensitive. Make sure to keep the entry in lower-case.
4. Close the design window for the schema, answering *Yes* to the *Save* question.

Editing Records

You display the data fields in bound text boxes. An easy way to allow changes to the data would be to just allow the user to type in changes in the text boxes. Any changes made to bound fields are automatically saved in the dataset. However, this is considered a dangerous practice. Instead, set the ReadOnly property of each text box to True, which locks the text box. For bound check boxes and lists, you can set the Enabled property to False; these controls don't have a ReadOnly property.

When the user clicks the Edit button, set the ReadOnly property of each text box to False. You also should disable the navigation buttons, so that the user cannot move off the record and automatically save any changes. The only choices the user should have during an edit should be Save or Cancel. Enable the *Save* button and change the Text property of the Add button to *Cancel*.

If the user clicks *Save*, all you have to do is reverse the actions taken for Edit: Set the ReadOnly property of the text boxes to True, enable the navigation buttons, disable the *Save* button, and set the Text property of the Add button back to *Add*.

Pseudocode to Begin an Edit

Disable the navigation buttons.
Unlock the text boxes.
Set up the buttons for an Edit:

Change the Text property of the Add button to "Cancel".
Enable the Save button.
Disable the Delete button.
Disable the Edit button.

The Complete Update Program

Here is the code for the complete update program. Remember that you should
include error trapping in every procedure that accesses the dataset. Figure 5.8
shows the form.

Figure 5.8

*The completed form for the
update program.*

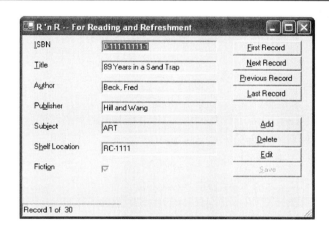

```
'Project:        Ch05UpdateRnR
'Programmer:     Bradley/Millspaugh
'Date:           January 2003
'Description:    Update the Books table from the RnRBooks.mdb database.

Option Strict On

Public Class frmRnR
    Inherits System.Windows.Forms.Form

    [Windows Form Designer generated code]

    Dim mblnListsInitialized As Boolean = False
    Dim bmBooks As BindingManagerBase

    Private Sub frmRnR_Load(ByVal sender As System.Object, _
      ByVal e As System.EventArgs) Handles MyBase.Load

        'Make the database file portable
        'Note that RnRBooks.mdb must be in the project's bin folder
        conRnR.ConnectionString = _
          "Provider=Microsoft.Jet.OLEDB.4.0;Data Source=RnRBooks.mdb"

        'Fill the datasets
        daBooks.Fill(DsBooks1)
        daSubjects.Fill(DsSubjects1)
        mblnListsInitialized = True
```

```
        'Get the BindingManagerBase for the books table.
        bmBooks = Me.BindingContext(DsBooks1, "books")

        'Add the delegate for the PositionChanged event.
        AddHandler bmBooks.PositionChanged, AddressOf Position_Changed

        'Display record number for first record
        Position_Changed(sender, e)
    End Sub

    Private Sub btnFirst_Click(ByVal sender As System.Object, _
      ByVal e As System.EventArgs) Handles btnFirst.Click
        'Move to the first record

        bmBooks.Position = 0
    End Sub

    Private Sub btnNext_Click(ByVal sender As System.Object, _
      ByVal e As System.EventArgs) Handles btnNext.Click
        'Move to the next record

        With bmBooks
            If .Position < .Count - 1 Then
                .Position += 1
            Else
                btnFirst_Click(sender, e)
            End If
        End With
    End Sub

    Private Sub btnPrevious_Click(ByVal sender As System.Object, _
      ByVal e As System.EventArgs) Handles btnPrevious.Click
        'Move to the previous record

        With bmBooks
            If .Position > 0 Then
                .Position -= 1
            Else
                btnLast_Click(sender, e)
            End If
        End With
    End Sub

    Private Sub btnLast_Click(ByVal sender As System.Object, _
      ByVal e As System.EventArgs) Handles btnLast.Click
        'Move to the last record

        With bmBooks
            .Position = .Count - 1
        End With
    End Sub

    Private Sub btnAdd_Click(ByVal sender As System.Object, _
      ByVal e As System.EventArgs) Handles btnAdd.Click
        'Begin an add operation or cancel the current operation

        If btnAdd.Text = "&Add" Then
            UnlockTextBoxes()
            DisableNavigation()
            SetButtonsForEdit()
```

```
                'Make sure current record is saved
                bmBooks.EndCurrentEdit()
                'Clear the fields
                bmBooks.AddNew()
                txtISBN.Focus()
        Else    'Cancel button clicked
            LockTextBoxes()
            EnableNavigation()
            ResetButtonsAfterEdit()
            bmBooks.CancelCurrentEdit()
        End If
End Sub

Private Sub btnDelete_Click(ByVal sender As System.Object, _
    ByVal e As System.EventArgs) Handles btnDelete.Click
    'Delete the current record after confirming
    Dim dgrDelete As DialogResult

    Try
        dgrDelete = MessageBox.Show("Delete this record?", _
          "Confirm Delete", MessageBoxButtons.YesNo)
        If dgrDelete = DialogResult.Yes Then
            With bmBooks
                .RemoveAt(.Position) 'Delete the record from the dataset
            End With
            daBooks.Update(DsBooks1) 'Update the data source
            DsBooks1.AcceptChanges() 'Reset the dataset
        End If
    Catch err As Exception
        MessageBox.Show(err.Message)
    End Try
End Sub

Private Sub btnEdit_Click(ByVal sender As System.Object, _
    ByVal e As System.EventArgs) Handles btnEdit.Click
    'Save edits to current record

    UnlockTextBoxes()
    DisableNavigation()
    SetButtonsForEdit()
End Sub

Private Sub btnSave_Click(ByVal sender As System.Object, _
    ByVal e As System.EventArgs) Handles btnSave.Click
    'Save updates to the dataset

    Try
        bmBooks.EndCurrentEdit()        'Complete the current edit
        daBooks.Update(DsBooks1)        'Update the data source
        DsBooks1.AcceptChanges()        'Reset the dataset
        LockTextBoxes()
        EnableNavigation()
        ResetButtonsAfterEdit()
    Catch err As Exception
        'Check for duplicate records and constraint violations
        MessageBox.Show(err.Message)
    End Try
End Sub
```

```
Private Sub DisableNavigation()
    'Disable the navigation buttons

    btnFirst.Enabled = False
    btnLast.Enabled = False
    btnPrevious.Enabled = False
    btnNext.Enabled = False
End Sub

Private Sub EnableNavigation()
    'Enable the navigation buttons

    btnFirst.Enabled = True
    btnLast.Enabled = True
    btnPrevious.Enabled = True
    btnNext.Enabled = True
End Sub

Private Sub LockTextBoxes()
    'Lock for Add or Edit

    txtISBN.ReadOnly = True
    txtTitle.ReadOnly = True
    txtAuthor.ReadOnly = True
    txtPublisher.ReadOnly = True
    txtSubjectCode.ReadOnly = True
    txtShelfLocation.ReadOnly = True
    chkFiction.Enabled = False
End Sub

Private Sub UnlockTextBoxes()
    'Unlock for Add or Edit

    txtISBN.ReadOnly = False
    txtTitle.ReadOnly = False
    txtAuthor.ReadOnly = False
    txtPublisher.ReadOnly = False
    txtSubjectCode.ReadOnly = False
    txtShelfLocation.ReadOnly = False
    chkFiction.Enabled = True
End Sub

Private Sub Position_Changed(ByVal sender As Object, _
  ByVal e As EventArgs)
    'Display the record position

    With bmBooks
        sbpRecordPosition.Text = "Record " & (.Position + 1).ToString() & _
          " of " & .Count.ToString()
    End With
End Sub

Private Sub ResetButtonsAfterEdit()
    'Reset the buttons after an Add or Edit operation

    btnAdd.Text = "&Add"
    btnSave.Enabled = False
    btnDelete.Enabled = True
    btnEdit.Enabled = True
End Sub
```

```
      Private Sub SetButtonsForEdit()
          'Set up the buttons for an Add or Edit operation

          btnAdd.Text = "&Cancel"
          btnSave.Enabled = True
          btnDelete.Enabled = False
          btnEdit.Enabled = False
      End Sub
End Class
```

Binding to Combo Boxes

When the user adds or modifies a field that requires only certain values, you can display the data in a drop-down list. Figure 5.9 shows a form for the preceding update program, modified to include combo boxes for the Subject and Shelf Locations. Notice that the complete subject name appears rather than the subject code; the subject is taken from the Subject table, rather than the Books table.

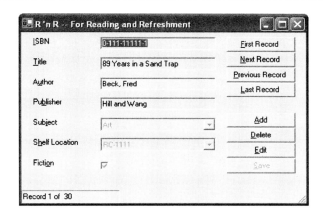

Figure 5.9

The update form with combo boxes in place of text boxes for fields that should present a list to the user.

Binding a Combo Box to a Database Field

You can bind a combo box to a field in a dataset, so that the correct value displays for each record. You also can fill the list with values from the same or a different table. Set the DisplayMember property to the field that you want to appear in the list; set the ValueMember to the field that should be transferred to the database field. If you want the user to select from the list but not add new values, set the DropDownStyle to DropDownList.

The Subject combo box displays the field values from the Subject table, even though we are updating the Books table, which holds the subject code rather than the subject. The program has two data adapters: daBooks and daSubjects; and two DataSet objects: DsBooks1 and DsSubjects1.

Settings for cboSubject

Property	Setting
DataBindings.SelectedValue	DsBooks1 - Books.Subject_Code
DataSource	DsSubjects1.Subject
DisplayMember	Subject
DropDownStyle	DropDownList
Enabled	False
ValueMember	SubjectCode

When the list drops down, all values from the Subject table appear (Figure 5.10). Note that if there are duplicate values in the table, they will appear in the list. The Subject table does not contain duplicate values, so each subject appears only once.

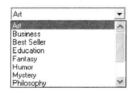

When the Subject combo box drops down, the field values from the Subject table appear, but the value passed to the bound field is the subject code.

You must make one other change to the update program to use combo boxes. In the Add procedure, the AddNew method clears all text boxes but does not clear the combo boxes. To make the combo boxes empty for a new record, set their SelectedIndex property to −1.

```
'Clear the fields
bmBooks.AddNew()
cboSubjectCode.SelectedIndex = −1
cboLocation.SelectedIndex = −1
```

The combo box for the Shelf Location is a little different. There isn't a second table that holds just one copy of each shelf number to fill the list. The easiest way to make the shelf locations fill the list is just to assign the possible values to the Items collection at design time. You can still bind the combo box to the database field, so the correct value always displays and is sent back to the dataset.

Settings for cboLocation

Property	Setting
DataBindings.Text	DsBooks1 - Books.Shelf_Location
DropDownStyle	DropDownList
Enabled	False
Items	RC-1111
	RC-1112
	RC-1113
	RC-1114
	RC-1115

Feedback 5.3

1. You want to delete a record from a dataset and the original data source. Place these statements in the correct order:

```
DsBooks1.AcceptChanges()
bmBooks.RemoveAt(bmBooks.Position)
daBooks.Update(DsBooks1)
```

2. What property of a check box should be bound to a boolean data field?
3. What properties of a combo box must you set to bind to a field in one table but display values from a second table?

Updating Related Tables

When you execute the Update method for a single table, you don't have to be concerned with how the records are updated. The Update method issues the proper INSERT, DELETE, and UPDATE SQL commands. But if you are updating multiple tables with parent and child relationships, you must take charge and issue the commands in the correct sequence.

Parent and Child Relationships

If you add a new child and a new parent record, you must add the parent first or there will be no relationship for the child record. However, if you are deleting a parent record, all of the child records must be deleted first. To maintain referential integrity, you must update in this order:

1. Delete any child records.
2. Insert, update, and delete the parent records.
3. Insert and update the child records.

You cannot delete a parent or master if there are still associated records. For example, you cannot eliminate a customer if there are still orders for the customer. First, all orders for the customer must be deleted, then the customer record can be deleted. Similarly, you cannot add child records for a parent record that has not yet been created. How could you add orders for a customer that is not on file?

Cascading Deletes and Updates

When you set up the relationship for related tables, you can specify **cascading deletes** and **cascading updates** (Figure 5.11). Cascading deletes and updates help to maintain referential integrity. When you delete a parent record, all child records for that parent are automatically deleted; and if you change the primary key field of a parent record, all child records that relate to that parent change to the new value. (However, allowing changes to the key field is not a good idea for most database applications.)

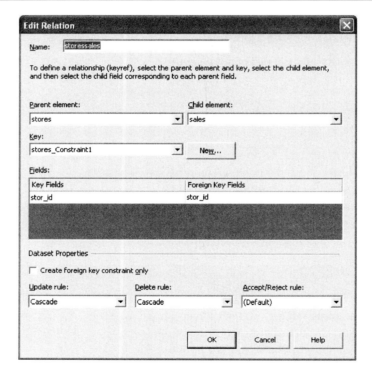

Figure 5.11

Set the relationship for cascading updates and deletes.

You set up the relationship between tables, including cascading deletes and updates, in the dataset's schema (Figure 5.12). These update and delete rules determine how records are deleted and updated in the disconnected dataset, not the original data source.

Figure 5.12

Create the relationship between parent and child tables in the dataset's schema.

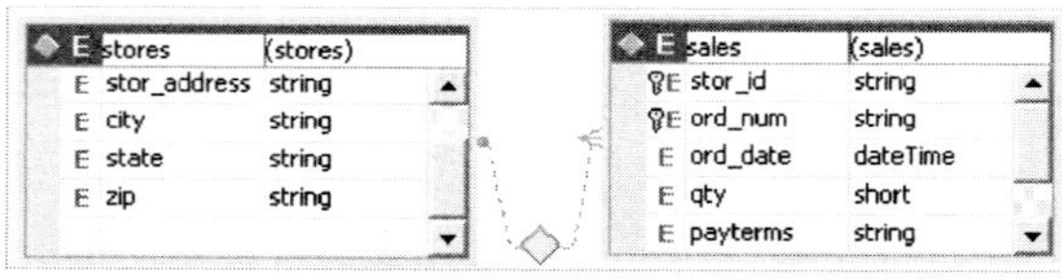

The Related-Table Update Program

This example program uses the stores and sales tables of the pubs SQLServer database, which you used in Chapter 4. The user can add, delete, and edit store records and add, delete, and edit sales records (Figure 5.13). This version of an update program demonstrates the alternate style of saving updates: The dataset is not updated for each change; instead, the user can select *File/Save* at any time, and in the form's Closing event procedure, if there are unsaved changes, a message box asks whether to save the changes.

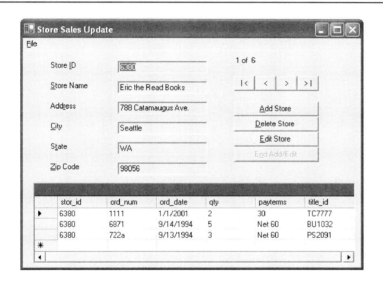

The store table is the parent and the sales table is the child. In a related-table update program, the user can make changes to records in both tables.

Filtering the Child Table

Notice in Figure 5.13 that the user can navigate from one store record to the next. In the Position_Changed event procedure, you must filter the sales table to display only the rows for the current store. Create a DataView object, set up the filter to match the current stor_id field, and bind the DataGrid to the DataView.

```
Private Sub Position_Changed(ByVal sender As Object, ByVal e As EventArgs)
    'Store changed. Get sales and display record number.
    Dim drvSalesView As New DataView()

    'Create a data view with the sales for this store
    With drvSalesView
        .Table = DsStoreSales1.sales
        .RowFilter = "Stor_id = '" & txtStoreID.Text & "'"
    End With

    'Bind the data view to the grid
    dgrSales.DataSource = drvSalesView

    'Display the record number
    With bmStores
        lblRecordNumber.Text = (.Position + 1).ToString() & " of " & _
            .Count.ToString()
    End With
End Sub
```

The Update Commands

Recall that the Update method belongs to the data adapter, and with related tables you have one data adapter for each table. If you allow changes to both tables, you must execute the Update method for both data adapters. You also must make sure to execute the updates in the correct sequence.

Save the Child Record Deletes

You must first save the deletes for child records. To execute the Update method for only the deleted records, you create a new table that holds only the rows marked for deletion. You can use the GetChanges method of a table or dataset to retrieve only the rows with a specific row state. Assign the retrieved rows to the new table and specify the table name as the argument of the Update method.

```
'Update child Deletes
If Not DsStoreSales1.sales.GetChanges(DataRowState.Deleted) Is Nothing Then
    'GetChanges for deleted child rows only
    Dim dtSalesDeletes As DataTable
    dtSalesDeletes = DsStoreSales1.sales.GetChanges(DataRowState.Deleted)
    daSales.Update(dtSalesDeletes)
End If
```

In the past we used the HasChanges method, but that method belongs to the dataset and now we must check each table separately. A table does not have a HasChanges method, but you can use the GetChanges method and test for Is Nothing to determine whether there are any changes.

Save All Parent Record Updates

After you save the deletes for the child table, you can save all updates for the parent table. Note that you must check first to determine that changes have been made.

```
'Update all parent row Adds, Deletes, and Changes
If Not DsStoreSales1.stores.GetChanges() Is Nothing Then
    daStores.Update(DsStoreSales1)
End If
```

Save the Child Adds and Edits

You must execute the Update method once for child record adds and once for edits. If you attempt to execute the Update method just once for all child updates, you generate an exception when it tries to delete a record that is already deleted.

```
'Update child Adds
If Not DsStoreSales1.sales.GetChanges(DataRowState.Added) Is Nothing Then
    'GetChanges for added rows only
    Dim dtSalesAdds As DataTable
    dtSalesAdds = DsStoreSales1.sales.GetChanges(DataRowState.Added)
    daSales.Update(dtSalesAdds)
End If
```

```
'Update child Edits
If Not DsStoreSales1.sales.GetChanges(DataRowState.Modified) Is Nothing Then
    'GetChanges for changed rows only
    Dim dtSalesChanges As DataTable
    dtSalesChanges = DsStoreSales1.sales.GetChanges(DataRowState.Modified)
    daSales.Update(dtSalesChanges)
End If
```

The Complete Program

The related-table update program needs a data adapter for each table. In the dataset schema, create a relationship between the tables and specify *cascade deletes*. This program is based on the stores and sales tables of the pubs SQL Server database.

```
'Project:           Ch05UpdateRelatedTables
'Programmer:        Bradley/Millspaugh
'Date:              January 2003
'Description:       Update related tables with store and sales information.
'                   Single tier application.

Option Strict On

Public Class frmUpdate
    Inherits System.Windows.Forms.Form

    [Windows Form Designer generated code]

    Dim bmStores As BindingManagerBase

    Private Sub frmUpdate_Load(ByVal sender As System.Object, _
      ByVal e As System.EventArgs) Handles MyBase.Load
        'Fill the dataset

        daStores.Fill(DsStoreSales1)
        daSales.Fill(DsStoreSales1, "sales")
        'Get the BindingManagerBase for the Employee table
        bmStores = Me.BindingContext(DsStoreSales1, "stores")
        'Add the delegate for the PositionChanged event
        AddHandler bmStores.PositionChanged, AddressOf Position_Changed
        'Initialize first record
        Position_Changed(sender, e)
    End Sub

    Private Sub frmUpdate_Closing(ByVal sender As Object, _
      ByVal e As System.ComponentModel.CancelEventArgs) Handles MyBase.Closing
        'Check for any unsaved updates
        Dim dgrResult As DialogResult

        If DsStoreSales1.HasChanges Then
            dgrResult = MessageBox.Show("Save the changes?", "Pubs Store Sales", _
              MessageBoxButtons.YesNoCancel, MessageBoxIcon.Question)
            Select Case dgrResult
                Case DialogResult.Yes
                    UpdateAll()
                Case DialogResult.Cancel
                    e.Cancel = True
            End Select
        End If
    End Sub
```

```vb
Private Sub btnFirst_Click(ByVal sender As System.Object, _
  ByVal e As System.EventArgs) Handles btnFirst.Click
    'Move to the first store record

    bmStores.Position = 0
End Sub

Private Sub btnLast_Click(ByVal sender As System.Object, _
  ByVal e As System.EventArgs) Handles btnLast.Click
    'Move to the last store record

    With bmStores
        .Position = .Count - 1
    End With
End Sub

Private Sub btnNext_Click(ByVal sender As System.Object, _
  ByVal e As System.EventArgs) Handles btnNext.Click
    'Move to the next store record

    Dim intRecordNumber As Integer = bmStores.Position + 1
    With bmStores
        If intRecordNumber < .Count Then
            .Position += 1
        Else
            btnFirst_Click(sender, e)
        End If
    End With
End Sub

Private Sub btnPrevious_Click(ByVal sender As System.Object,_
  ByVal e As System.EventArgs) Handles btnPrevious.Click
    'Move to the previous store record

    Dim intRecordNumber As Integer = bmStores.Position
    If intRecordNumber > 0 Then
        bmStores.Position -= 1
    Else
        btnLast_Click(sender, e)
    End If
End Sub

Private Sub btnAdd_Click(ByVal sender As System.Object, _
  ByVal e As System.EventArgs) Handles btnAdd.Click
    'Begin an Add operation or cancel the current operation

    If btnAdd.Text = "&Add Store" Then
        UnlockTextBoxes()
        DisableNavigation()
        SetButtonsForEdit()
        'Clear the fields
        bmStores.AddNew()
        With txtStoreID
            .ReadOnly = False    'Allow entry for an Add
            .Focus()
        End With
```

```vbnet
        Else           'Cancel button
            LockTextBoxes()
            EnableNavigation()
            ResetButtonsAfterEdit()
            bmStores.CancelCurrentEdit()
        End If
End Sub

Private Sub btnDelete_Click(ByVal sender As System.Object, _
  ByVal e As System.EventArgs) Handles btnDelete.Click
    'Delete the current record after confirming
    Dim dgrDelete As DialogResult

    dgrDelete = MessageBox.Show("Delete this store?", "Confirm Delete", _
      MessageBoxButtons.YesNo)
    Try
        If dgrDelete = DialogResult.Yes Then
            With bmStores
                .RemoveAt(.Position)      'Remove store from dataset
            End With
        End If
    Catch Err As Exception
        MessageBox.Show(Err.Message)
    End Try
End Sub

Private Sub btnEdit_Click(ByVal sender As System.Object, _
  ByVal e As System.EventArgs) Handles btnEdit.Click
    'Allow edits to current record

    UnlockTextBoxes()
    DisableNavigation()
    SetButtonsForEdit()
End Sub

Private Sub btnEndEdit_Click(ByVal sender As System.Object, _
  ByVal e As System.EventArgs) Handles btnEndEdit.Click
    'Complete Add or Edit operation

    bmStores.EndCurrentEdit()
    LockTextBoxes()
    EnableNavigation()
    ResetButtonsAfterEdit()
    Position_Changed(sender, e)
End Sub

Private Sub dgrSales_Enter(ByVal sender As Object, _
  ByVal e As System.EventArgs) Handles dgrSales.Enter
    'Grid entered. Make sure no Store edit in progress

    If btnEndEdit.Enabled = True Then
        MessageBox.Show( _
          "Complete the Store Add or Edit before entering sales.", _
          "Pubs Store Sales", MessageBoxButtons.OK)
        btnEndEdit.Focus()
    End If
End Sub
```

```vb
Private Sub mnuFileExit_Click(ByVal sender As System.Object, _
  ByVal e As System.EventArgs) Handles mnuFileExit.Click
    'Exit the application

    Me.Close()
End Sub

Private Sub mnuFileSave_Click(ByVal sender As System.Object, _
  ByVal e As System.EventArgs) Handles mnuFileSave.Click
    'Save all changes to the dataset

    UpdateAll()
End Sub

Private Sub DisableNavigation()
    'Disable the navigation buttons

    btnFirst.Enabled = False
    btnLast.Enabled = False
    btnPrevious.Enabled = False
    btnNext.Enabled = False
End Sub

Private Sub EnableNavigation()
    'Enable the navigation buttons

    btnFirst.Enabled = True
    btnLast.Enabled = True
    btnPrevious.Enabled = True
    btnNext.Enabled = True
End Sub

Private Sub LockTextBoxes()
    'Lock after Add or Edit

    txtStoreID.ReadOnly = True
    txtStoreName.ReadOnly = True
    txtAddress.ReadOnly = True
    txtCity.ReadOnly = True
    txtState.ReadOnly = True
    txtZipCode.ReadOnly = True
End Sub

Private Sub UnlockTextBoxes()
    'Unlock for Add or Edit

    txtStoreName.ReadOnly = False
    txtAddress.ReadOnly = False
    txtCity.ReadOnly = False
    txtState.ReadOnly = False
    txtZipCode.ReadOnly = False
End Sub

Private Sub ResetButtonsAfterEdit()
    'Reset buttons after an Add or Edit

    btnAdd.Text = "&Add Store"
    btnEndEdit.Enabled = False
    btnDelete.Enabled = True
```

```
            btnEdit.Enabled = True
        End Sub

        Private Sub SetButtonsForEdit()
            'Set up buttons for Add or Edit

            btnAdd.Text = "&Cancel"
            btnEndEdit.Enabled = True
            btnDelete.Enabled = False
            btnEdit.Enabled = False
        End Sub

        Private Sub Position_Changed(ByVal sender As Object, _
          ByVal e As EventArgs)
            'Store changed. Get sales and display record number.
            Dim drvSalesView As New DataView()

            'Create a data view with the sales for this store
            With drvSalesView
                .Table = DsStoreSales1.sales
                .RowFilter = "Stor_id = '" & txtStoreID.Text & "'"
            End With

            'Bind the data view to the grid
            dgrSales.DataSource = drvSalesView

            'Display the record number
            With bmStores
                lblRecordNumber.Text = (.Position + 1).ToString() & " of " & _
                    .Count.ToString()
            End With
        End Sub

        Private Sub UpdateAll()
            'Save updates to the dataset

            bmStores.EndCurrentEdit()
            If (DsStoreSales1.HasChanges()) Then
                Try
                    'First: Save child record deletes
                    'Second: Save all parent updates
                    'Third: Save rest of child changes

                    'Update child Deletes
                    If Not DsStoreSales1.sales.GetChanges(DataRowState.Deleted) _
                      Is Nothing Then
                        'GetChanges for deleted child rows only
                        Dim dtSalesDeletes As DataTable
                        dtSalesDeletes = _
                            DsStoreSales1.sales.GetChanges(DataRowState.Deleted)
                        daSales.Update(dtSalesDeletes)
                    End If
                    'Update all parent row Adds, Deletes, and Changes
                    If Not DsStoreSales1.stores.GetChanges() Is Nothing Then
                        daStores.Update(DsStoreSales1)
                    End If
```

```
                      'Update child Adds
                      If Not DsStoreSales1.sales.GetChanges(DataRowState.Added) Is Nothing Then
                          'GetChanges for added rows only
                          Dim dtSalesAdds As DataTable
                          dtSalesAdds = DsStoreSales1.sales.GetChanges(DataRowState.Added)
                          daSales.Update(dtSalesAdds)
                      End If
                      'Update child Edits
                      If Not DsStoreSales1.sales.GetChanges(DataRowState.Modified) _
                          Is Nothing Then
                          'GetChanges for changed rows only
                          Dim dtSalesChanges As DataTable
                          dtSalesChanges = _
                              DsStoreSales1.sales.GetChanges(DataRowState.Modified)
                          daSales.Update(dtSalesChanges)
                      End If

                      'Reset the dataset after update to indicate no unsaved changes
                      DsStoreSales1.AcceptChanges()

                  Catch err As Exception
                      MessageBox.Show(err.Message)
                  End Try
              End If
          End Sub
      End Class
```

Feedback 5.4

You are planning to update the customers and orders tables from Northwind
and allow adds, deletes, and edits to each table. In what sequence should the
updates be made to the database?

Your Hands-On Programming Example

Create a project to update the Books table in the RnRBooks.mdb database. This must be a multitier project, with the database access in a data tier
component.

Allow the user to add, edit, and delete book records. During an Add or
Edit, the only choices should be Cancel or Save; do not allow the user to click
a navigation button or any other button until the Add or Edit is complete. Keep
the text boxes locked (ReadOnly) and the check box and list boxes disabled unless an Add or Edit is in progress. Display a message box to confirm a Delete.

The user can select the Subject and Location from drop-down lists during
an Add or Edit. Make the Subject list display the actual subject name from the
Subject table, rather than the subject code.

Display the record number and record count in a status bar.

Planning the Project

Sketch a form (Figure 5.14) that your users sign off as meeting their needs.

Plan the Objects, Properties, and Methods

Plan the two tiers. Determine the objects and property settings for the form and
its controls and for the data tier component. Figure 5.15 shows the diagram of
the program components.

Figure 5.14

The planning sketch of the hands-on programming example.

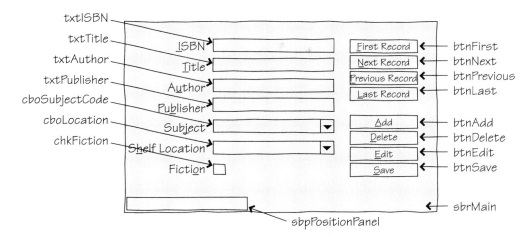

Figure 5.15

The components for the hands-on programming example.

Presentation Tier	Data Tier
frmRnR	**RnRData**
txtISBN	conRnR
txtTitle	daBooks
txtAuthor	daSubjects
txtPublisher	dsRnR
cboSubjectCode	DsRnR1
cboLocation	getData
chkFiction	update
btnFirst	
btnNext	
btnPrevious	
btnLast	
btnAdd	
btnDelete	
btnEdit	
btnSave	
sbrMain	
sbpPositionPanel	
Form_Load	
btnFirst_Click	
btnNext_Click	
btnPrevious_Click	
btnLast_Click	
btnAdd_Click	
btnDelete_Click	
btnEdit_Click	
btnSave_Click	
BindData	
DisableNavigation	
EnableNavigation	
Position_Changed	
ResetButtonsAfterEdit	
SetButtonsForEdit	
LockTextBoxes	
UnlockTextBoxes	

Presentation Tier

Object	Property	Setting
frmRnR	Name	frmRnR
	Text	R 'n R -- For Reading and Refreshment
Label1	Text	&ISBN
Label2	Text	&Title
Label3	Text	A&uthor
Label4	Text	Pu&blisher
Label5	Text	Sub&ject
Label6	Text	S&helf Location
Label7	Text	Ficti&on
txtISBN	Text	(blank)
	ReadOnly	True
txtTitle	Text	(blank)
	ReadOnly	True
txtAuthor	Text	(blank)
	ReadOnly	True
txtPublisher	Text	(blank)
	ReadOnly	True
cboSubjectCode	Text	(blank)
	DropDownStyle	DropDownList
	Enabled	False
cboLocation	Text	(blank)
	DropDownStyle	DropDownList
	Enabled	False
chkFiction	Text	(blank)
	Enabled	False
btnFirst	Text	&First Record
btnNext	Text	&Next Record
btnPrevious	Text	&Previous Record
btnLast	Text	&Last Record
btnAdd	Text	&Add
btnDelete	Text	&Delete
btnEdit	Text	&Edit
btnSave	Text	&Save
	Enabled	False
sbrMain	Text	(blank)
	ShowPanels	True
sbpPositionPanel	Text	(blank)

Event procedures/Methods	Actions—Pseudocode
Form_Load	Instantiate the data tier. Set the form's binding manager. Set the properties of cboSubject. Bind the data fields. Set the delegate for the Position_Changed event procedure. Display the record number for the first record.
btnFirst_Click	Move to the first record.

btnNext_Click	If not on the last record
	  Move to next record.
	Else
	  Move to the first record.

btnPrevious_Click	If not on the first record
	  Move to the previous record.
	Else
	  Move to the last record.

btnLast_Click	Move to the last record.

btnAdd_Click	If button's Text = "&Add"
	  Unlock text boxes.
	  Disable navigation buttons.
	  Set buttons for add or edit.
	  End any edit in progress.
	  Execute AddNew method to clear fields.
	  Set combo boxes' SelectedIndex = -1.
	  Unlock txtISBN.
	  Set the focus to txtISBN
	Else (button's Text = "&Cancel")
	  Cancel the edit.
	  Lock text boxes.
	  Enable navigation buttons.
	  Reset buttons for normal operation.

btnDelete_Click	Confirm delete in message box.
	If Yes
	  Delete the record from the dataset.
	  Update the data source.
	  Accept the changes to the dataset.

btnEdit_Click	Disable navigation buttons. Unlock text boxes. Set buttons for edit.

btnSave_Click	End the current edit.
	If the dataset has changes
	  Update the data source.
	  Accept the changes to the dataset.
	  Lock the text boxes.
	  Enable the navigation buttons.
	  Reset the buttons for normal operation.

BindData	Set the data bindings for the screen controls.
	  Text boxes: Text property
	  cboSubjectCode: SelectedValue
	  cboLocation: Text
	  chkFiction: Checked

DisableNavigation	Disable four navigation buttons.
EnableNavigation	Enable four navigation buttons.
Position_Changed	(Delegate for binding manager PositionChanged event) Display the record number in the status bar panel.
ResetButtonsAfterEdit	Change the Text property of btnAdd to "&Add". Disable btnSave. Enable btnDelete and btnEdit.
SetButtonsForEdit	Change the Text property of btnAdd to "&Cancel". Enable btnSave. Disable btnDelete and btnEdit.
LockTextBoxes	Set text boxes' ReadOnly property to True. Disable the combo boxes and check box.
UnlockTextBoxes	Set text boxes' ReadOnly property to False. Enable the combo boxes and check box.

Data Tier

Object	Property	Setting
Class	Name	RnRData
conRnR	Name	conRnR
daBooks	Name	daBooks
daSubjects	Name	daSubjects
dsRnR	Name	dsRnR
DsRnR1	Name	DsRnR1
	Tables	Books and Subjects

Methods	Actions—Pseudocode
getData	Create a dataset that holds the books and subjects tables. Return the dataset.
update(DataSet)	Update the data source.

Write the Project

Following the sketch in Figure 5.14, create the form. Figure 5.16 shows the completed form.

- Set the properties of each of the form objects, according to your plans.

- Create the data tier component, adding the objects from your plan.

- Modify the dataset schema to work around the binding bug (see page 170).

- Write the methods for the data tier component, following the pseudocode.

- Write the code for the form. Working from the pseudocode, write each event procedure.

- When you complete the code, test the operation several times. Compare the screen output to the data tables to make sure that you are displaying the correct information.

Figure 5.16

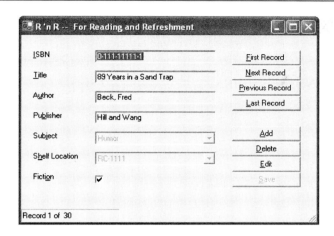

The form for the hands-on programming example.

The Project Coding Solution

The Form

```
'Project:        Ch05HandsOnRnRUpdate
'Programmer:     Bradley/Millspaugh
'Date:           January 2003
'Description:    Update the book table using multiple tiers.
'                This is the presentation tier, which uses the services
'                of the data tier.

Option Strict On

Public Class frmRnR
  Inherits System.Windows.Forms.Form

  [Windows Form Designer generated code]

    Dim objBooks As RnRData        'Instance of data tier component
    Dim dsRnRData As DataSet
    Dim bmBooks As BindingManagerBase

    Private Sub frmRnR_Load(ByVal sender As System.Object, _
      ByVal e As System.EventArgs) Handles MyBase.Load
        'Retrieve the dataset from the data tier component

      Try
          objBooks = New RnRData()                  'Instantiate data component
          dsRnRData = objBooks.getData()            'Retrieve dataset

          'Get the BindingManagerBase for the books table
          bmBooks = Me.BindingContext(dsRnRData, "Books")

          'Connect to the combo box
          '(This must be done before binding the combo box to display the
          ' first record correctly.)
          With cboSubjectCode
              .DataSource = dsRnRData.Tables("subjects")
              .DisplayMember = "Subject"
              .ValueMember = "SubjectCode"
              .Enabled = False
          End With
```

```vb
            'Bind the data fields
            BindData()

            'Add the delegate for the PositionChanged event
            AddHandler bmBooks.PositionChanged, AddressOf Position_Changed

            'Display the record number for the first record
            Position_Changed(sender, e)

        Catch err As Exception
            MessageBox.Show(err.Message, "Error")
        End Try
    End Sub

    Private Sub btnFirst_Click(ByVal sender As System.Object, _
      ByVal e As System.EventArgs) Handles btnFirst.Click
        'Move to the first record

        bmBooks.Position = 0
    End Sub

    Private Sub btnNext_Click(ByVal sender As System.Object, _
      ByVal e As System.EventArgs) Handles btnNext.Click
        'Move to the next record
        Dim intRecordNumber As Integer = bmBooks.Position

        If intRecordNumber < bmBooks.Count - 1 Then
            bmBooks.Position += 1
        Else
            btnFirst_Click(sender, e)
        End If
    End Sub

    Private Sub btnPrevious_Click(ByVal sender As System.Object, _
      ByVal e As System.EventArgs) Handles btnPrevious.Click
        'Move to the previous record
        Dim intRecordNumber As Integer = bmBooks.Position

        If intRecordNumber > 0 Then
            bmBooks.Position -= 1
        Else
            btnLast_Click(sender, e)
        End If
    End Sub

    Private Sub btnLast_Click(ByVal sender As System.Object, _
      ByVal e As System.EventArgs) Handles btnLast.Click
        'Move to the last record

        With bmBooks
            .Position = .Count - 1
        End With
    End Sub

    Private Sub btnAdd_Click(ByVal sender As System.Object, _
      ByVal e As System.EventArgs) Handles btnAdd.Click
        'Begin an Add operation or cancel the current operation
```

```
        If btnAdd.Text = "&Add" Then
            UnlockTextBoxes()
            DisableNavigation()
            SetButtonsForEdit()
            'Make sure current record is saved
            bmBooks.EndCurrentEdit()
            'Clear the fields
            bmBooks.AddNew()
            cboSubjectCode.SelectedIndex = -1
            cboLocation.SelectedIndex = -1
            With txtISBN
                .ReadOnly = False
                .Focus()
            End With
        Else        'Cancel button clicked
            bmBooks.CancelCurrentEdit()
            LockTextBoxes()
            EnableNavigation()
            ResetButtonsAfterEdit()
        End If
End Sub

Private Sub btnDelete_Click(ByVal sender As System.Object, _
    ByVal e As System.EventArgs) Handles btnDelete.Click
    'Delete the current record after confirming
    Dim dgrDelete As DialogResult

    Try
        dgrDelete = MessageBox.Show("Delete this record?", _
          "Confirm Delete", MessageBoxButtons.YesNo)
        If dgrDelete = DialogResult.Yes Then
            With bmBooks
                .RemoveAt(.Position)
            End With
            objBooks.update(dsRnRData)
            dsRnRData.AcceptChanges()
        End If
    Catch err As Exception
        MessageBox.Show(err.Message)
    End Try
End Sub

Private Sub btnEdit_Click(ByVal sender As System.Object, _
    ByVal e As System.EventArgs) Handles btnEdit.Click
    'Begin an Edit operation for the current record

    DisableNavigation()
    UnlockTextBoxes()
    SetButtonsForEdit()
End Sub

Private Sub btnSave_Click(ByVal sender As System.Object, _
    ByVal e As System.EventArgs) Handles btnSave.Click
    'Save updates to the dataset

    Try
        bmBooks.EndCurrentEdit()
        If (dsRnRData.HasChanges()) Then
            objBooks.update(dsRnRData)
            dsRnRData.AcceptChanges()
```

194 VISUAL BASIC *Windows Database Upates*

```vb
                LockTextBoxes()
                EnableNavigation()
                ResetButtonsAfterEdit()
            End If

        Catch err As Exception
            'Check for duplicate records and constraint violations
            MessageBox.Show(err.Message)
        End Try
    End Sub

    Private Sub BindData()
        'Bind the dataset to the controls

        txtISBN.DataBindings.Add("text", dsRnRData, "Books.ISBN")
        txtTitle.DataBindings.Add("text", dsRnRData, "Books.Title")
        txtPublisher.DataBindings.Add("text", dsRnRData, "Books.Publisher")
        txtAuthor.DataBindings.Add("text", dsRnRData, "Books.Author")
        cboSubjectCode.DataBindings.Add("SelectedValue", dsRnRData, "Books.Subject_Code")
        cboLocation.DataBindings.Add("text", dsRnRData, "Books.Shelf_Location")
        chkFiction.DataBindings.Add("checked", dsRnRData, "Books.Fiction")
    End Sub

    Private Sub DisableNavigation()
        'Disable the navigation buttons

        btnFirst.Enabled = False
        btnLast.Enabled = False
        btnPrevious.Enabled = False
        btnNext.Enabled = False
    End Sub

    Private Sub EnableNavigation()
        'Enable the navigation buttons

        btnFirst.Enabled = True
        btnLast.Enabled = True
        btnPrevious.Enabled = True
        btnNext.Enabled = True
    End Sub

    Private Sub Position_Changed(ByVal sender As Object, _
      ByVal e As EventArgs)
        'Display the record position

        With bmBooks
            sbpPositionPanel.Text = "Record " & (.Position + 1).ToString() & _
              " of " & .Count.ToString()
        End With
    End Sub

    Private Sub ResetButtonsAfterEdit()
        'Reset the buttons after an Add or Edit operation

        btnAdd.Text = "&Add"
        btnSave.Enabled = False
        btnDelete.Enabled = True
        btnEdit.Enabled = True
    End Sub
```

```
    Private Sub SetButtonsForEdit()
        'Set up the buttons for an Add or Edit operation

        btnAdd.Text = "&Cancel"
        btnSave.Enabled = True
        btnDelete.Enabled = False
        btnEdit.Enabled = False
    End Sub

    Private Sub LockTextBoxes()
        'Lock after Add or Edit is complete

        txtISBN.ReadOnly = True
        txtTitle.ReadOnly = True
        txtAuthor.ReadOnly = True
        txtPublisher.ReadOnly = True
        cboSubjectCode.Enabled = False
        cboLocation.Enabled = False
        chkFiction.Enabled = False
    End Sub

    Private Sub UnlockTextBoxes()
        'Unlock for Add or Edit

        txtTitle.ReadOnly = False
        txtAuthor.ReadOnly = False
        txtPublisher.ReadOnly = False
        cboSubjectCode.Enabled = True
        cboLocation.Enabled = True
        chkFiction.Enabled = True
    End Sub
End Class
```

The Data Tier (Make sure to modify the dataset schema to work around the binding bug.)

```
'Project:        Ch05HandsOn
'Module:         RnRData
'Programmer:     Bradley/Millspaugh
'Date:           January 2003
'Description:    Data tier for updating the books table in RnRBooks.mdb

Option Strict On

Public Class RnRData
  Inherits System.ComponentModel.Component

  [Component Designer generated code]

    Public Function getData() As DataSet
        'Fill the books dataset

        'Make the database file portable
        'Note that RnRBooks.mdb must be in the project's bin folder
        conRnR.ConnectionString = _
            "Provider=Microsoft.Jet.OLEDB.4.0;Data Source=RnRBooks.mdb"

        daBooks.Fill(DsRnR1, "books")
```

```
        daSubjects.Fill(DsRnR1, "subjects")
        Return DsRnR1
    End Function

    Public Sub update(ByVal dsRnR As DataSet)
        'Update the dataset

        Try
            daBooks.Update(dsRnR)
        Catch
            Throw 'Pass exceptions up to calling procedure
        End Try
    End Sub
End Class
```

Summary

1. A dataset remains disconnected from the data source. Any changes to the dataset must be sent back to the data source. The data adapter handles saving changes as well as creating the dataset.

2. The RowState property of each row in the dataset or table reflects any changes. The value can be Added, Deleted, Modified, or Unchanged.

3. The HasChanges method can be used to determine if there are any changes in the recordset since it was created or the AcceptChanges method has executed. You also can specify the type of changes to look for using the RowState as an argument.

4. The GetChanges method can return only the changes for a specific value in RowState.

5. The BeginEdit method starts an edit operation, which can be terminated with either EndEdit or CancelEdit.

6. Several versions of a DataRow are maintained: Current, Original, Default, and, during an edit, Proposed.

7. The AcceptChanges method commits the changes in the table. The Original version is set to the Current version and all RowState properties are set to Unchanged. The RejectChanges rolls back all of the changes.

8. The Update method of the data adapter calls SQL statements to make the changes in the dataset to the original data source. You can either execute the Update method for every change or hold the changes and update only when the user selects a *Save* option or when the program ends.

9. The form's BindingContext returns a BindingManagerBase object that tracks the position and count of rows in a table within a dataset. The binding manager makes sure that all bound controls display fields from the same record. Use the binding manager's Position property to view or change the current record number; the Count property returns the number of records in the table.

10. The AddNew, RemoveAt, CancelCurrentEdit, and EndCurrentEdit methods of the binding manager are used to update rows in a table.

11. The binding manager's PositionChanged event occurs each time the record number changes. To make a procedure execute automatically for the event,

you must write an event handler and a delegate for the procedure. The CurrentChanged event occurs when the dataset is updated.
12. To begin an Add, use the binding manager's `AddNew` method, which clears the bound fields for the new record.
13. Use the binding manager's `RemoveAt` method to remove a record.
14. When multiple users can update a database at the same time, the concurrency control settings determine how the changes are saved.
15. You can bind the SelectedValue property of a combo box to a database field and display data from a different table by setting the DataSource and DisplayMember properties.
16. When updating related tables, the sequence of the updates is important. First, save the deletes for child records; then save all changes to parent records; and then save the inserts and updates for child records.

Key Terms

`AcceptChanges` method *154*
`AddNew` method *162*
`BeginEdit` method *154*
BindingContext object *159*
BindingManagerBase object *159*
`CancelCurrentEdit` method *162*
cascading deletes *178*
cascading updates *178*
concurrency *166*
concurrency control *166*
Count property *161*
Current property *161*

CurrentChanged event *163*
delegate *163*
`EndCurrentEdit` method *163*
event handler *163*
`GetChanges` method *154*
`HasChanges` method *153*
Position property *161*
PositionChanged event *163*
RejectChanges method *154*
RemoveAt method *163*
RowState property *152*
Update method *155*

Review Questions

1. What is the purpose of the RowState property and what values can it hold?
2. Differentiate between the `GetChanges` method and the `HasChanges` method. Explain when each would be used.
3. List and explain each of the properties, methods, and events of the BindingManagerBase class.
4. How can you navigate from one record to the next using the binding manager?
5. Explain how you perform each of the following updates:
   a. Add a record.
   b. Delete a record.
   c. Modify a record.
   d. Save changes.
6. Explain how to prompt the user to save changes when the application closes.
7. Discuss the sequence of updates for related tables to ensure referential integrity.

Programming Exercises

Note: For each of these exercises, allow the user to add, edit, or delete a record. Do not allow the user to make changes to fields on the screen unless an add or edit is in progress. Make sure to query for any unsaved changes when the program closes.

5.1   Write a single-tier application to update the Subjects table from RnR-Books.mdb. Display the current record and number of records in a label or a status bar.

5.2   Modify Exercise 5.1 to use a separate data tier component.

5.3   Write a single-tier application that uses a DataGrid to update the publishers table from the pubs SQL Server database. Include an *Edit* menu with options to *Add* or *Delete* a record. Display the current record and number of records in a label or a status bar.

5.4   Modify Exercise 5.3 to use a separate data tier component.

5.5   Write a multitier application to update the authors table in the pubs SQL Server database. Use individual text boxes for display and data entry but make sure that the user can enter data only in Edit or Add modes.

   The project should include navigation buttons or menu items for navigation.

5.6   Write a single-tier application to update the stores table in the pubs SQL Server database. Use individual text boxes for display and data entry but make sure that the user can enter data only in Edit or Add modes.

   The project should include navigation buttons or menu items for navigation.

5.7   Modify Exercise 5.6 to use a separate data tier component.

Case Studies

Claytor's Cottages

Modify the Guest option to allow updates (add, delete, and edit) capability for the guest information. Replace the customer name drop-down list with text boxes.

Include buttons or menu options for navigation. Display the current record number and the number of records in the status bar.

Christian's Car Rentals

Code the *Customer* menu option to display and allow editing of customer information.

The fields are

First Name	Zip
Last Name	Vehicle ID
Street	Drivers License Number
City	Rental Date
State	

Use individual fields and make sure that all changes have been made before the Customer form closes. Include the current record number and number of records in the status bar. The form should display navigation buttons.

6

Using Web Forms— ASP.NET

1. Discuss concepts of Web-based applications.

2. Understand the types of files that make up a Web project.

3. Distinguish among the various types of button controls.

4. Understand the event structure used by Web applications.

5. Include hyperlinks and link buttons on a page.

6. Navigate from one Web page to another.

7. Validate Web input using the Validator controls.

8. Maintain state (data values) from one page to the next.

In the previous chapters you have worked with Windows Forms and created applications that run in a Windows environment. One of the most powerful features of .NET development is the ability to create applications that run on a variety of platforms. This chapter introduces you to the Web server controls and creating Web projects.

Note: To complete the exercises in this chapter, you must have IIS installed on your development machine or have available a remote Web server properly configured for .NET.

Web Applications

Developing an application for the Internet is considerably different from creating a Windows program. Visual Studio makes it as easy as possible for you to transition from one development environment to another. But to be an effective Web developer, you must understand the differences.

Windows Forms allow you to develop applications that can run on any system with Windows operating systems; Web Forms are your gateway to cross-platform development. The first key difference that you will note is that a Web form displays in a browser application such as Internet Explorer or Netscape Navigator rather than on your desktop. The most common type of access is through the Web.

What is the Internet? Many people use the Internet on a regular basis but do not actually understand the basics. The Internet is really just an extremely large network of computers and the World Wide Web (WWW) is the system of hyperlinked documents that reside on the Internet. No one owns or controls the network. To use the network, a computer must have some type of connection. Typically individuals get their connection from an Internet Service Provider (ISP), such as AOL, Earthlink, or MSN. Most phone companies and cable companies also provide service.

Client/Server Web Applications

Most Windows applications are stand-alone applications; Web applications require a server and a client. The Web **server** sends Web pages to the client, where the pages display inside a browser application.

Web Servers

To develop Web applications, you must either use a remote **Web server** or make your local machine a Web server. The most common practice is to make the development machine a server by installing Internet Information Services (IIS). IIS handles the Web server functions and the browser acts as the client.

Web Clients

Browsers display pages written in hypertext markup language (HTML). The pages also may contain programming logic in the form of script, such as JavaScript, VBScript, or JScript, or Java applets. The browser renders the page and displays it on the local system.

Likely you have seen Web pages that look different when displayed in different browsers or even in different versions of the same browser. Although many browser applications are available, the two most common are Internet Explorer and Netscape Navigator.

You may know which browser your users are using, such as when you are programming for a network within a company, called an **intranet**. Or you may develop applications that run on the Internet and might display in any browser. If your projects will run on different browsers, you should test and check the output on multiple browsers.

Browser Support

It's no secret that ASP.NET applications run best in Internet Explorer. However, you can run an application in any browser. Microsoft classifies browsers as *uplevel* and *downlevel*. Uplevel browsers are Internet Explorer 5.5 and above; downlevel are IE 5.05 and below, and all other browsers.

An ASP.NET application is aware of the browser in which it is running. The HTML that it sends to the client is customized for the capabilities of the browser. For example, if the browser is capable of handling cascading style sheets, the font style information is formatted using styles; otherwise the font formatting is sent in another way, such as a Font tag.

Web Pages

One characteristic of HTML Web pages is that they are stateless. That is, a page does not store any information about its contents from one invocation to the next. Several techniques have been developed to get around this limitation, including storing "cookies" on the local machine and sending state information to the server as part of the page's address, called the uniform resource locator (URL). The server can then send the state information back with the next version of the page, if necessary. For more information on managing state, see "State Management" later in this chapter.

When a user requests a Web page, the browser (client) sends a request to the server. The server may send a preformatted HTML file, or a program on the server may dynamically generate the necessary HTML to render the page. One Microsoft technology for dynamically generating HTML pages is dynamic HTML (DHTML); another more popular technique is active server pages (ASP).

ASP.NET

The latest Web programming technology from Microsoft is ASP.NET, which is their greatly improved and easier-to-use Web development tool that replaces ASP. ASP.NET provides libraries, controls, and programming support that allow you to write programs that interact with the user, maintain state, render controls, display data, and generate appropriate HTML. When you use Web Forms in Visual Basic .NET, you are using ASP.NET. Using VB and ASP.NET you can create object-oriented, event-driven programs. These programs can have multiple classes and use inheritance.

Visual Basic and ASP.NET

Each Web Form that you design has two distinct pieces: (1) the HTML and instructions needed to render the page and (2) the Visual Basic code. This separation is a big improvement over the older methods that mix the HTML and programming logic (script or applets). The Web Form designer generates a file with an .aspx extension for the HTML and another file with an .aspx.vb extension for the Visual Basic code.

Don't panic if you don't know HTML; the HTML is generated automatically by the Visual Studio IDE. This is similar to the automatically generated code in Windows Forms. You visually create the document using the IDE's designer, then you can view and modify the HTML tags in the Visual Studio editor.

The VB code contains the program logic to respond to events. This code module is called the "CodeBehind" file. The code looks just like the code you have been writing for Windows applications, but many of the events are different.

Files in Web Projects

The files that you find in a Web application differ greatly from those in a Windows application (Figure 6.1). Two files make up the form: the aspx file and the aspx.vb file. The aspx file holds the specifications for the user interface that are used by the server to render the page. The aspx.vb file holds the Visual Basic code that you write to respond to events. The aspx.vb file is the "code-behind" file for the aspx file. When you are designing the user interface, you select the FormName.aspx tab; when you are working on the code procedures, you select the FormName.aspx.vb tab.

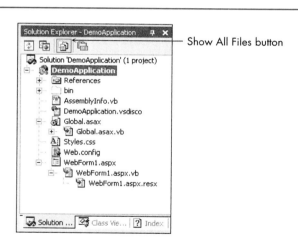

Show All Files button

Figure 6.1

*The Solution Explorer window for a Web application. Click on **Show All Files** and expand the collapsed nodes to see all files.*

Table 6.1 shows many of the file types in a Web project.

The ASP.NET Application File

The Global.asax file, also called the ASP.NET application file, is included in each Web project. You can use this file to write code for events of the Application and Session objects. This file is an improvement to ASP.NET and provides more security than the old ASP pages. Direct URL requests are automatically rejected and external users cannot view the code in the file.

Files in a Web project

File	File type	Purpose
FormName.aspx	ASP.NET	Dynamically generates a Web user interface allowing for server-side code.
FormName.aspx.vb	Visual Basic code	Supplies the code procedures for the form. The "code behind" the aspx file.
AssemblyInfo.vb	Project information	Holds information about the project such as assembly names and versions.
ProjectName.vsdisco	XML discovery file	Holds links (URLs) to help locate the necessary Web services.
Global.asax	ASP.NET application file	Supplies any code needed to respond to Application- and Session-level events.
Styles.css	Cascading style sheet	Formats and positions Web page elements.
Web.config	Configuration	Contains configuration information about each URL resource used in the project.

The default Global.asax file has empty event procedures for each of the events.

```
Imports System.Web
Imports System.Web.SessionState

Public Class Global
    Inherits System.Web.HttpApplication

    Sub Application_Start(ByVal sender As Object, ByVal e As EventArgs)
      ' Fires when the application is started
    End Sub

    Sub Session_Start(ByVal sender As Object, ByVal e As EventArgs)
      ' Fires when the session is started
    End Sub

    Sub Application_BeginRequest(ByVal sender As Object, ByVal e As EventArgs)
      ' Fires at the beginning of each request
    End Sub

    Sub Application_AuthenticateRequest(ByVal sender As Object, ByVal e As EventArgs)
      ' Fires upon attempting to authenticate the use
    End Sub

    Sub Application_Error(ByVal sender As Object, ByVal e As EventArgs)
      ' Fires when an error occurs
    End Sub
```

```
Sub Session_End(ByVal sender As Object, ByVal e As EventArgs)
    ' Fires when the session ends
End Sub

Sub Application_End(ByVal sender As Object, ByVal e As EventArgs)
    ' Fires when the application ends
End Sub

End Class
```

Cascading Style Sheets

The IDE generates a default cascading style sheet (CSS) file, **Styles.css**, for positioning and formatting text and elements on a Web page. See "Using Styles" later in this chapter for information on using the CSS file.

Web Configuration File

The **Web.config file** contains configuration settings for all of the files in its own directory as well as any child directories. If a child directory contains an additional Web.config, the child directory inherits all of the settings from the parent configuration file in addition to any settings that are included in the child directory.

The configuration information is an XML-based text file, which you can edit in the VS editor or any text editor. The information may include authorization, authentication, and session information; settings for debugging and globalization rules; file connection strings; and other application data needed by the program. Web security relies on the authorization and authentication settings. These topics are covered in more detail in Chapter 9.

A common use of the configuration file is to store a connection string for a database file. To do this, or add any custom application settings, add an `<appSettings>` section to the file. You then add key-value pairs, making up a name for the key and writing the value as a quoted string.

```
<configuration>
    <system.web>
        <customErrors mode="RemoteOnly" />
    </system.web>
    <appSettings>
        <add key="pubsConnection"
            value="server=(local)\NetSDK;Trusted_Connection=yes;database=pubs" />
    </appSettings>
</configuration>
```

You can write code in the program to retrieve the setting:

```
conPubs.ConnectionString = ConfigurationSettings.appSettings("pubsConnection")
daAuthors.Fill(DsAuthors1, "authors")
DataBind()
```

You also can set the connection's ConnectionString property to a dynamic property, which retrieves the connection string from Web.config at run time. (See page 240 and Appendix E.)

DLL Files

When you compile a Web project, the compiler generates **.dll** (dynamic link library) **files** that hold the compiled code. When a Web page is requested, the .dll file is loaded and run; it produces the HTML output for the page and sends it to the client; then the .dll in memory is destroyed. Each time a page is requested, the .dll is reloaded and destroyed.

Creating Web Forms

You begin a Web Forms project in much the same way as a Windows Forms project. In the *New Project* dialog box, select *ASP.NET Web Application* (Figure 6.2). Notice that the project location is set to *http://localhost*, which is the folder on your machine set up by IIS. Also notice that the *Name* box is disabled; you will find that you can name the project in the *Location* text box. Change the location to *http://localhost/ProjectName*; the ProjectName will become a new folder located in the Inetpub\wwwroot folder.

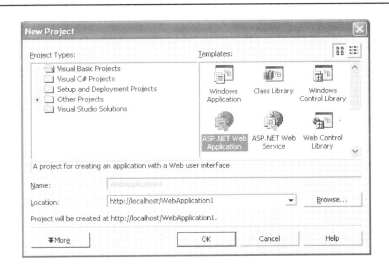

F i g u r e   6 . 2

Begin a new Web Forms project by selecting ASP.NET Web Application as the template from the New Project dialog box.

Note: You must have correct Web Permissions settings to create Web projects. If the security on your campus network does not allow the proper permissions, you cannot create Web applications.

Web Forms in the Visual Studio IDE

As soon as you open a Visual Basic Web application, you notice many differences from working on a Windows application. As the project opens, a connection to the Web server is established (Figure 6.3). Instead of a Windows form, you see a **Web document** (Figure 6.4), also called a **Web page** or a **Web form**. A message appears on the form indicating the layout type, by default a grid layout. The message also tells how to change the layout. As soon as you add a control to the form, the message disappears.

Figure 6.3

*The Create New Web dialog
box appears briefly to show the
Web connection for the new
project.*

Figure 6.4

The Visual Studio IDE with a new Web Form defined.

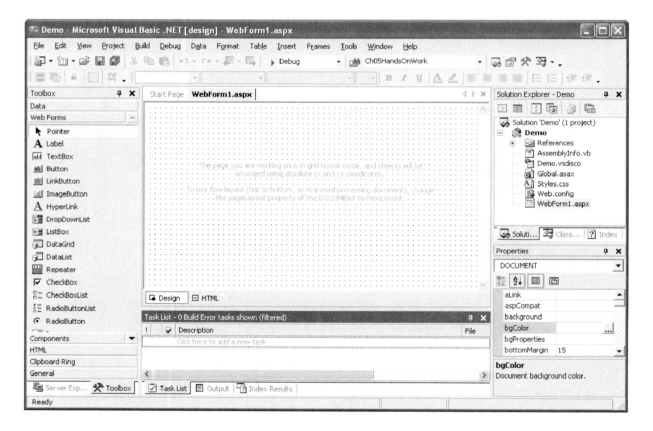

If you look closely at Figure 6.4, you will notice several other differences
from Windows Forms. The toolbar is different, as is the list of files in the Solution Explorer. The toolbox has different controls, and even those that look the
same, such as TextBoxes, Buttons, and Labels, are actually different from their
Windows counterparts and have some different properties and events. For example, Web controls have an ID property rather than a Name property.

When you look at the code for a Web form, you see that the form inherits
from System.Web.UI.Page, and a Button control inherits from System.Web.
UI.WebControls.Button.

Naming a Web Form

In a new Web project, the new Web Form is called WebForm1. To completely change the name requires three steps; you might find it easier to delete Web-Form1 and add a new form, which properly names all three locations.

Rename WebForm1

- In the editor, change the name of the class.

- In the Properties window for the form, change the Title property. This places a Title tag in the form's HTML, which determines the text that appears in the browser title bar when the program runs.

- In the Solution Explorer, change the name of the .aspx file, which also changes the name of the .aspx.vb file to match.

Begin with a new form

- In the Solution Explorer, delete WebForm1.

- Select *Project / Add Web Form* or use the shortcut menu from the Solution Explorer. Give your new form a name in the *Add New Item* dialog box.

- In the Solution Explorer, right-click the new form and select *Set As Start Page*.

  Although the form's Title property is not set (examine the Properties window), a Title tag is added to the HTML.

Controls

Several types of controls are available for Web Forms. You can mix the control types on a single form.

- *HTML controls.* These are the standard HTML elements that operate only on the client. You cannot write any server-side programming logic for HTML controls. As you submit forms to the server, any HTML controls pass to the server and back as static text. You might want to use HTML controls if you have existing HTML pages that are working and you want to convert to ASP.NET for additional capabilities. In this chapter we won't use any HTML controls.

- *HTML server controls.* These controls match HTML controls on a one-for-one basis. They have all of the attributes of HTML (client) controls plus the added capability of object-oriented, event-driven, server-side programming. However, HTML server controls do not provide many of the features of Web server controls, such as type checking for data and customized rendering of the control based on the browser.

  To change an HTML control to an HTML server control, right-click on the control and select *Run As Server Control.*

- *Web server controls, also called ASP.NET server controls.* These are the richest, most powerful controls provided by ASP.NET and the .NET Framework. Web server controls do not directly correspond to HTML controls, but are rendered differently for different browsers in order to achieve the desired look and feel. Some of the special-purpose Web server controls are validation controls, Calendar, DataGrid, CheckBoxList, and RadioButtonList.

In this chapter we will stick with Web server controls.

You can see the available controls in the toolbox when a Web Form is in Design view. Try clicking in the toolbox on *HTML*, *Web Forms*, and *Components*. The Web server controls on the *Components* list are nonvisual components that appear in the component tray of the Web Form. Keep your toolbox showing Web Forms controls.

In Design view, you can tell the difference between client-side HTML controls and server-side controls. The VS designer adds a small green arrow in the upper-left corner for all server controls (Figure 6.5), whether HTML server control or ASP.NET server control.

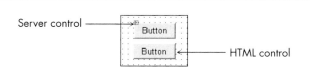

Figure 6.5

The small green arrow in the corner of a control indicates a server control.

Event Handling

You write VB code for events of Web controls in the same way that you write for Windows controls. The events may actually occur on either the client or the server, but the code is always executed on the server. The process of capturing an event, sending it to the server, and executing the required methods is all done for you automatically.

The events of Web Forms and controls are somewhat different from those of Windows Forms. For example, a Web Form has a Page_Load event rather than a Form_Load event. You can see the list of events of controls using the editor; drop down the Event list for a control such as a button. You will see that you still have a Click event, but the list of events is much shorter than it is for Windows Forms.

Some events may not occur and be handled as you would expect. All code executes on the server, but not all events are submitted to the server as they occur. A button click automatically triggers a postback to the server, but most other events do not. When an event is posted to the server, all events that have occurred since the last postback are processed. For example, the Change event of a text box and the SelectedIndexChanged event of a list box do not trigger a postback to the server. The next time a button is clicked and the page is submitted to the server, the event procedures for those events occur. If you need to change that behavior and submit the event to the server immediately, you can set the AutoPostBack property of most controls to True, which forces a postback.

Button Controls

The Web Forms toolbox holds three types of button controls (Figure 6.6): **Button**, **LinkButton**, and **ImageButton**. The three work the same but differ in appearance. As the names imply, a LinkButton looks like a hyperlink but functions like a button and fires a Click event. An ImageButton can display a graphic image.

Figure 6.6

Web server controls.

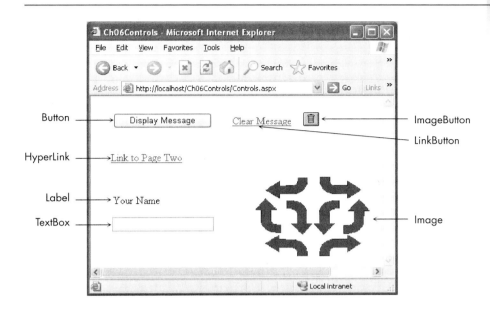

The code for the buttons is very similar to that in Windows Forms. Notice the event procedures for each type of button control.

```
'Project:        Ch06Controls
'Programmer:     Bradley/Millspaugh
'Date:           January 2003
'Description:    Use different types of buttons.

Option Strict On

Public Class Ch06Controls

    Inherits System.Web.UI.Page
    Protected WithEvents btnDisplay As System.Web.UI.WebControls.Button
    Protected WithEvents btnClear As System.Web.UI.WebControls.LinkButton
    Protected WithEvents HyperLink1 As System.Web.UI.WebControls.HyperLink
    Protected WithEvents btnTrash As System.Web.UI.WebControls.ImageButton
    Protected WithEvents Image1 As System.Web.UI.WebControls.Image
    Protected WithEvents txtName As System.Web.UI.WebControls.TextBox
    Protected WithEvents Label2 As System.Web.UI.WebControls.Label
    Protected WithEvents lblMessage As System.Web.UI.WebControls.Label

    [Web Form Designer Generated Code]

    Private Sub btnClear_Click(ByVal sender As System.Object, _
      ByVal e As System.EventArgs) Handles btnClear.Click
        'Clear the message using a link button

        lblMessage.Text = ""
    End Sub

    Private Sub btnTrash_Click(ByVal sender As System.Object, _
      ByVal e As System.Web.UI.ImageClickEventArgs) Handles btnTrash.Click
        'Clear the message using an image button
```

```
        lblMessage.Text = ""
    End Sub

    Private Sub btnDisplay_Click(ByVal sender As System.Object, _
        ByVal e As System.EventArgs) Handles btnDisplay.Click
        'Display a message using a button

        lblMessage.Text = "Welcome to Web Development"
    End Sub
End Class
```

The Hyperlink Control

The **HyperLink control** looks just like a LinkButton but is used to navigate to another Web page. A hyperlink does not have a Click event; it is intended strictly for navigation. When the user clicks the hyperlink, the browser navigates to the page indicated in the **NavigateUrl property**. The page can be any valid HTML page or another Web Form.

You have several options for setting the navigation path (URL). You can set the value at design time or at run time as well as using the data binding feature. You also can add parameters to be passed with the link.

To set the NavigateUrl property at design time, select the property and click on the Build button (the ellipsis). In the *Select URL* dialog box (Figure 6.7), you can browse to find the page you want. You can set the URL type to Document Relative, Root Relative, or Absolute. The Absolute setting stores the complete address of the page to which to navigate as the URL. For other Web pages in your application, use one of the relative settings (Document Relative or Root Relative); for links to other sites, use the absolute URL including "http://".

F i g u r e   6 . 7

Set the URL of the page to which to navigate in the **Select URL** *dialog box. It's best to set the URL Type to Document Relative or Root Relative for other pages in your application.*

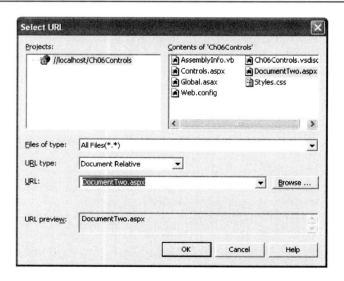

A hyperlink can appear as text or as an image, depending on the settings of the Text property and the ImageUrl property. If you set both properties, the image takes precedence and the text appears only when the image is not available.

It's easy to add a second Web Form to the Ch06Controls project shown earlier. You don't need any code to navigate to the second form, but it's a good idea to include a link on the second form to return to the first. Of course, the user can use the *Back* button of the browser to return to the first page. Figure 6.8 shows a hyperlink on a page.

Navigate to another page using a hyperlink.

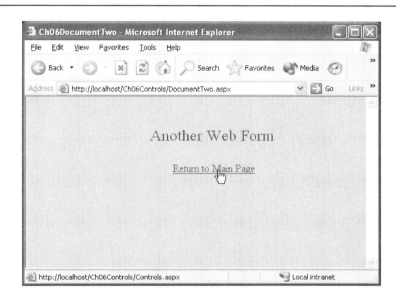

Choosing the Right Navigation Control

A hyperlink button and a link button look the same on the page. You can use either to navigate to another page. The hyperlink button has a NavigateUrl property, which holds the URL of the page to which to transfer. When the user clicks the button, a request is sent to the browser to retrieve the specified page.

If you need to perform any action before navigating to another page, use a link button. When the user clicks the link button, an event is fired and the page is submitted to the server. In the click event procedure, you can execute any necessary actions, such as saving the state of variables or controls, and then transfer to another page. Saving state is covered later in this chapter in the "State Management" section.

Linking to Another Page

To navigate to another Web page in code, you can use `Response.Redirect` or `Server.Transfer`. If you are transferring to another page on the same server (generally in the same application), use **Server.Transfer**. This method uses one less round trip to the server than does **Response.Redirect**.

In both of these methods you can specify the URL as absolute, with the complete path, or relative, which looks first in the current folder.

```
'Tells the browser (client) to request a new page
Response.Redirect("http://www.microsoft.com/")

'The server loads the new page and begins processing without a request from the browser
Server.Transfer("LoginPage.aspx")
```

The Calendar Control

A handy Web control is the Calendar control (Figure 6.9), which displays a monthly calendar and allows the user to scroll to future dates and back to previous ones and select a date. You may want this control on your Web page for selecting shipping dates, event dates, or any other instance where you want a date to appear. After you add the control to your Web page, you can right-click and select *AutoFormat* to change the design.

Figure 6.9

Use the Calendar control to display a calendar and allow the user to select a date.

The SelectedDate property holds the date selected on the calendar. You can set an initial value and/or retrieve the current setting. The control's SelectionChanged event fires when the user selects a new date.

```
'Project:        Ch06Calendar
'Programmer:     Bradley/Millspaugh
'Date:           January 2003
'Description:    Display and retrieve dates.

Option Strict On

Public Class Ch06Calendar
    Inherits System.Web.UI.Page
    Protected WithEvents calCurrent As System.Web.UI.WebControls.Calendar
    Protected WithEvents lblDate As System.Web.UI.WebControls.Label

    Private Sub Page_Load(ByVal sender As System.Object, _
      ByVal e As System.EventArgs) Handles MyBase.Load
        'Set Calendar to today's date

        calCurrent.SelectedDate = Now()
    End Sub

    Private Sub calCurrent_SelectionChanged(ByVal sender As System.Object, _
      ByVal e As System.EventArgs) Handles calCurrent.SelectionChanged
```

```
                  'Display date in the label

                  lblDate.Text = calCurrent.SelectedDate.ToString()
         End Sub
End Class
```

The Background Image

You can set a background image for the Web page using the property settings for DOCUMENT. Right-click on the page and select *Properties*, or select Background from the Properties list for the page. In the *DOCUMENT Property Pages* dialog box (Figure 6.10), browse to the file that you would like to use for the background. It is best to store the graphic file in the folder for your project.

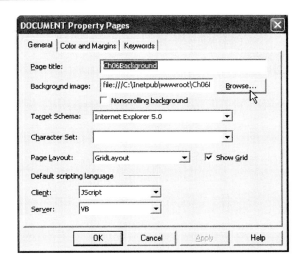

Figure 6.10

Select the file for the page's background image in the DOCUMENT Property Pages dialog box.

This example uses the Clipboard metafile (Clipbord.wmf) from the Visual Studio Graphics as a background image. Notice that the graphic repeats to fill the page (Figure 6.11).

Setting the Tab Order

Setting the tab order of controls is different for Web Forms than for Windows Forms. The *View / Order Tab* menu item is not available, and you must manually change the TabIndex property of each control. By default, each control that is capable of receiving the focus has its TabIndex property set to zero. When the user presses the Tab key, the focus moves from one control to the next in the order the controls were added to the page. Set the TabIndex property of each control, beginning with one for the first; zero means that the TabIndex is not set. If multiple controls have the same TabIndex, the tab moves in the order the controls were added to the page.

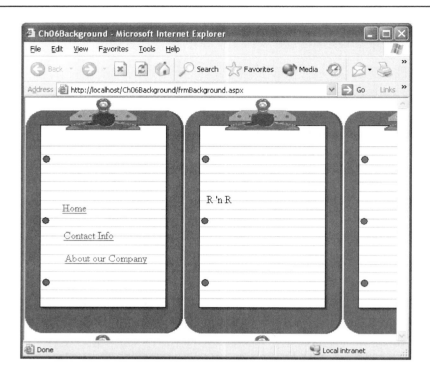

Setting Initial Focus

The Web controls do not have a `Focus` method, which makes it difficult to set the focus within a VB program. You must manually manipulate the HTML to set the focus. Although HTML coding is beyond the scope of this text, setting the initial focus is relatively easy. Add this code inside the `<body>` tag of the page:

```
onload="Form1.txtBoxName.focus()"
```

Example

```
<body MS_POSITIONING="GridLayout" onload="Form1.txtName.focus()" text="black">
```

The form name must be as it appears in the ID tag on the page and the text box name must be the ID of a text box.

Using Styles

If you have created Web pages using HTML, you have probably used styles to format the text. For example, the line

```
<H1>This is a Big Heading</H1>
```

formats the text with the specifications for H1. The H1 style can have font, color, style, size, and spacing specified, which you can apply to any text by using its tag. You can declare the formatting for the style in the Head section of an HTML page or in an external .css file that you link to the page.

A single .css file can be used to format multiple pages, which helps to keep the pages consistent.

The Default CSS File

A new Web project has a default CSS file, called Styles.css, which you can open, view, and edit. Here is a small section from the top of the default file:

```
/* Default CSS Stylesheet for a new Web Application project */

BODY
{
    BACKGROUND-COLOR: white;
    FONT-FAMILY: Verdana, Helvetica, sans-serif;
    FONT-SIZE: .8em;
    FONT-WEIGHT: normal;
    LETTER-SPACING: normal;
    TEXT-TRANSFORM: none;
    WORD-SPACING: normal
}

H1, H2, H3, H4, H5, TH, THEAD, TFOOT
{
    COLOR: #003366;
}
H1    {
    font-family: Verdana, Arial, Helvetica, sans-serif;
    font-size:        2em;
    font-weight:      700;
    font-style:       normal;
    text-decoration:  none;
    word-spacing:     normal;
    letter-spacing:   normal;
    text-transform:   none;
    }

H2    {
    font-family: Verdana, Arial, Helvetica, sans-serif;
    font-size:        1.75em;
    font-weight:      700;
    font-style:       normal;
    text-decoration:  none;
    word-spacing:     normal;
    letter-spacing:   normal;
    text-transform:   none;
    }
```

Linking a CSS File to a Web Page

If you are writing HTML manually, you write a Link tag in the Head section to attach a CSS file to a Web page. But the VS IDE provides two easy ways to automatically generate the Link tag.

1. Open the Web page in design view and switch to the HTML tab. Drag the Styles.css filename from the Solution Explorer to the Head section of the HTML. It's best to first insert a blank line in the Head section

TIP

Even though the Styles.css file is generated and automatically included in a Web application, the styles in the file are not used unless you link the file to a Web page. ∎

and drag the file to the new line. This is the Link tag that is added to your page:

```
<LINK href="http://localhost/ProjectFolder/Styles.css" type="text/css"
  rel="stylesheet">
```

2. Open the Web page in design view and select *Format / Document Styles*. In the *Document Styles* dialog box, click on the *Add Style Link* button; a *Select Style Sheet* dialog box appears, where you can browse and select the style-sheet file. Here is the Link tag generated by this action:

```
<LINK href="Styles.css" type="text/css" rel="stylesheet">
```

Notice that the Link tag generated by the first method has an absolute path to the .css file. The second method generates a relative path; that is, the file is expected to be in the same folder as the project. If you use the first (and easiest) method to generate the Link tag, you can edit the Link tag to remove the absolute path so that the project is more portable.

Modifying Styles

You can add your own styles to the style sheet or modify the existing styles. The IDE helps you immensely: Right-click within any style definition and select *Build Style*; the *Style Builder* dialog box appears (Figure 6.12) where you can make selections for the style elements. When you close the *Style Builder* dialog box, the correct style definitions appear in the .css file.

Select the style elements on the Style Builder *dialog box.*

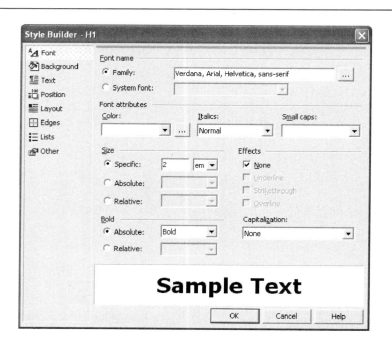

Applying the Styles

You can only apply the predefined style names to text using HTML:

```
<H2>What good is this?</H2>
```

But wait, you *can* apply styles to Web controls; it just takes one more step. Most Web controls have a CssClass property, to which you can assign a style name. The catch is that the style name must begin with a period. None of the styles in the default .css file have names that begin with a period, but you can fix that. You can add your own new styles (beginning the name with a period) or insert a period in front of an existing style name. For example, add a period in front of the H1 style name (.H1) and modify the style elements as desired. Then select a control on the Web page and set its CssClass property to H1 (without the period).

Testing Pages in Other Browsers

By default, your Web projects run in Internet Explorer. But you can test your project in other browsers, such as Netscape Navigator. First launch the browser and then type the URL of your page into the Address bar. (As a shortcut, you can copy and paste the URL from the Address bar of Internet Explorer.) For example, if your project and project folder are called Ch06Controls, the URL is `http://localhost/Ch06Controls/FormName.aspx`.
You also can select *File / Browse With* and select a different browser.

Feedback 6.1

1. Name some differences between a Windows Button control and a Web Forms Button control.
2. Compare a HyperLink control and a LinkButton control: How do their appearances compare? How do their behaviors compare?
3. Assume that you have a Calendar control on a Web page and the user has just selected a date. Write the code to assign the selected date to the variable datSelected.
4. In what order does the Tab key move the focus if you do not set the TabIndex property of any controls?
5. What steps must you take to create a named style and apply it to Web controls on a page? To apply it to more than one page?

Using the Validator Controls

ASP.NET provides several controls that can automatically validate input data. You add a **validator control**; attach it to an input control, such as a text box; and set the error message. At run time, if the user enters bad data, the error message displays. Table 6.2 shows the ASP.NET validator controls.

The timing of the validation varies depending on the browser. For an uplevel browser (IE 5.5 or above), the validation is performed on the client without a postback to the server, so the page is not submitted with bad data. On a downlevel browser (all other browsers), the validation is performed on the server when the page is submitted. In an uplevel browser, the error message appears after the user inputs data and moves to another control; on a downlevel browser, any error messages display after the user clicks a button.

The ASP.NET validator controls

Control	Purpose	Properties to set
RequiredFieldValidator	Requires that the user enter something into the field.	ControlToValidate ErrorMessage
CompareValidator	Compares the value in the field to the value in another control or to a constant value. You also can set the Type property to a numeric type and the CompareValidator will verify that the input value can be converted to the correct type.	ControlToValidate ControlToCompare *or* ValueToCompare Type (To force type checking) ErrorMessage
RangeValidator	Makes sure that the input value falls in the specified range.	ControlToValidate MinimumValue MaximumValue Type (To force type checking) ErrorMessage
RegularExpression Validator	Validates against a regular expression, such as a required number of digits, or a formatted value, such as a telephone number or Social Security number. Use the Regular Expression Editor to select or edit expressions; open by selecting the ellipses button on the ValidationExpression property.	ControlToValidate ValidationExpression ErrorMessage
ValidationSummary	Displays a summary of all of the messages from the other validation controls.	DisplayMode (Can be set to a bulleted list, list, or message box.)

Note that a blank entry passes the validation for each of the controls except the RequiredFieldValidator. If you want to ensure that the field is not blank *and* that it passes a range check, for example, attach both a RangeValidator and a RequiredFieldValidator control to a field.

The following example validates data entry using validator controls; Figure 6.13 shows the form for the project. The validator controls appear in design time, showing the text that you set for the ErrorMessage property. At run time the message does not appear unless the user violates the validation rule. Note that no code is required for the project to validate the data.

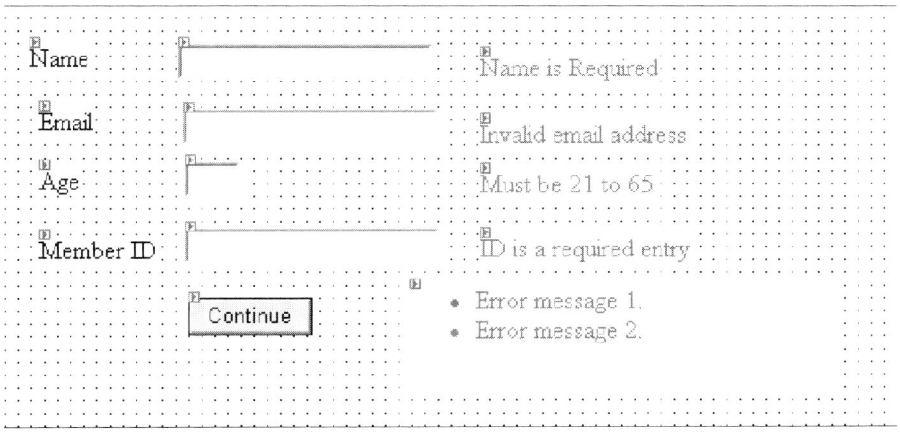

Figure 6.13

The Web Form for validator controls example program.

The form in Figure 6.13 uses these validator controls:

Control	Validator
txtName	RequiredFieldValidator
txtEmail	RegularExpressionValidator
txtAge	RangeValidator
txtMemberID	RequiredFieldValidator
(Form)	ValidationSummary

Displaying Asterisks

You can change the behavior of the validator controls to match a common technique used on many Web sites. If the user enters invalid data or omits a required entry, you can display an asterisk next to the field in error and make the actual message appear in another location, such as at the bottom of the page. Set the validator control's ErrorMessage property exactly as described above, but set its Text property to an asterisk (or any other character that you want to display). At run time, the control doesn't display anything unless the associated control fails the validation; but when it fails, the asterisk displays next to the field in error. The ValidationSummary control will display the entire message defined in the validator control's ErrorMessage property.

If you use this technique, make sure that your error messages are descriptive and identify the field in error. Figure 6.14 shows the previous validation example modified to display the error messages only in the ValidationSummary control.

Display an asterisk next to the field in error and the complete error message in the ValidationSummary control.

Testing for Validity

You don't need any code to check validity using the validator controls. But at times you may need to check whether a single control or all controls on the page have passed validation. Each of the validator controls has an IsValid property that returns True if the control assigned to the validator passes. Also, the Page object has an IsValid property that is set to True when all controls on the page pass their validation.

☑ TIP

To use a TextBox control for a password, set the TextMode property to Password. ∎

```
If RequiredFieldValidator1.IsValid Then
    'Perform some action
End If

If Page.IsValid Then
    lnkNavigate.Enabled = True
End If
```

► **Feedback 6.2**

Describe how to validate a text box called txtQuantity using validator controls. A numeric entry is required, in the range 1 to 100. The field must not be blank.

The IIS Application Objects

Your Web application has access to the IIS objects Request, Response, Session, Application, and Server. These are intrinsic objects that you can use without creating an instance. A Request passes from the client to the server; a Response goes from the server to the client.

The **Request object** holds information about the current user, data entered by the user, and arguments to an HTTP request. You use the Request object to create cookies and the **Response object** to retrieve them. You will learn to handle cookies in the "Cookies" section later in this chapter.

The Response object sends the HTML to render a page to the browser. This example inserts text directly into the HTML stream:

```
Private Sub Page_Load(ByVal sender As System.Object, _
  ByVal e As System.EventArgs) Handles MyBase.Load
    'Print Hello World on the page

    Response.Write("Hello World")
End Sub
```

The Session and Application objects are used to store state information in an ASP.NET application. These objects are covered in the "State Management" section that follows. You can use the `Transfer` method of the Server object to navigate to another Web page.

TIP

Include the trailing slash when linking to a directory ("http://www. mysite.com/mydirectory/"); it saves one extra round trip to the server. ■

State Management

As you know, traditional HTML pages are **stateless**, meaning that they do not retain values. Each time a Web page is rendered in a browser, all controls are recreated. Any values entered by the user, called the **state** of the page, are lost unless steps are taken to preserve the values. You may want to preserve state within a single page or to pass information from one page to another.

ASP.NET solves one of the problems of state management by maintaining the values in controls during a round trip to the server or navigation to another page and back again. The values in all controls that have their EnableView-State property set to True are encrypted and stored in a property of a hidden control. When the page is redisplayed, the ViewState data are decrypted and used to fill the controls. You can see the tag for the hidden control, which is called __VIEWSTATE, if you view the source of a page in the browser. The following is an example of the ViewState for a form that has been submitted to the server and redisplayed. The control names and their values are compressed and encrypted into the single string and assigned to the Value property.

```
<input type="hidden" name="__VIEWSTATE"
value="dDw5MTQ4NzEwMjE7Oz4tUQ/8e/xC31fa3oWMMe7CXP1EAg==" />
```

If you want to maintain other data, such as to keep the User ID, a dataset, the values of objects or properties, or variables to share among multiple forms, you will need to implement state management. The following sections discuss some of the techniques for maintaining state, including storing values on the server and keeping values on the client.

Overview of State Management Techniques

IIS and ASP.NET have several tools for storing state information. The choices for maintaining state in .NET Web applications include

1. Server side

   - *The Session and Application objects in IIS.* You can assign values to these objects, which are maintained on the server, and use them throughout an application. To use the Session object, the user must accept cookies or you must modify the web.config file to specify cookieless operation.

- *Database fields.* You can write data into database fields and read them back when appropriate.

2. Client side

- *Cookies.* You can create cookies in memory for temporary storage or on the user's hard drive for more permanent storage. This technique works only when the user's browser is set to accept cookies.

- *Hidden fields.* You can create a hidden field and assign it a value; the value is passed to the server when the page is submitted, and replaced into the field when the page is recreated.

- *A string appended to the URL.* State information can be appended to the URL of a page to which to navigate and retrieved by the new page. Example:

```
http://localhost/Ch06Controls/Form1.aspx?user=Robert
```

- *The Web Form's ViewState property.* You can declare key/value pairs and assign them to the ViewState of a form; the values are available for subsequent posting of the page, but not to other pages.

Application and Session Objects

The Application and Session objects are maintained on the server. You can use both to hold state information, but for applications with many users, this can be an inefficient technique.

The **Application object** stores information as long as the application is running. Only one copy exists for all users, so it is not a useful location to store information about users. The object is used sometimes to store information about the program, such as how many times the page has been hit or global values that are needed on multiple pages.

One instance of the **Session object** exists for each user, so you can use this object to store information about the user. Remember though that the information is stored on the server.

Each time the user accesses a site, the Session object is created and assigned a unique SessionID. The value is sent to the user through a dynamic cookie and is resent to the server in the HTTP header when the user navigates to another page.

Session values are maintained as long as the session exists. A Session object usually ceases to exist when the session times out, which is 20 minutes by default (but can be modified). Some sites have a logout option in which the code can call the `Session.Abandon` method. Also, if the IIS service terminates, the Session objects are lost.

Session objects are easy to use, but you must be aware of some drawbacks. Because the information is stored on the server, storing large amounts of data for multiple users could bog down the server. Also, many Web sites split the server load among several systems, referred to as a **Web farm**. It is not uncommon for the user to be routed to a different server in the Web farm for each postback. In this case, the state information might not be on the correct server. This problem is handled in .NET by specifying the name of the machine that stores the session values in the Web.config file.

You use the Contents collection of the Session object to store values in code. Each item in the collection has a name and a value; you make up the

☑TIP

If you know that you will not be using a Session object, set the document's enableSession property to False for improved efficiency. ∎

name and assign a value to it. For example, this code assigns the value in txtName to a session variable called "UserName".

```
Session("UserName") = txtName.Text
```

The session variable is available in all forms of the application. You can retrieve the data using the same session variable name or an index number for the position of the variable within the collection.

```
Private Sub btnDisplay_Click(ByVal sender As System.Object, _
  ByVal e As System.EventArgs) Handles btnDisplay.Click
    'Display a message

    Try
        lblMessage.Text = "Hello " & Session("UserName").ToString()
    Catch
        lblMessage.Text = "Welcome to Web Development"
    End Try
End Sub
```

If you want the name to appear automatically when a page displays (or redisplays), place the code in your Page_Load event procedure.

You can clear all session variables with the `Session.Clear()` method.

Cookieless Sessions

In normal operation, you cannot use the Session object if the user refuses to accept cookies or the browser cannot handle cookies. But ASP.NET includes a new feature to work around this limitation. You can declare a session to be cookieless in the Web.config file. In that case, an encrypted session ID is appended to the page's URL every time the page is posted to the server or the user navigates to another page.

Cookies

You can store state information as a cookie on the user's system. You can choose to store the value temporarily, for just the session, or store it on the user's hard drive for future trips to the Web site. You store the cookie using the Cookies property of the Response object and retrieve it using the Request object. The Expires property is used to make the value more permanent and set an expiration date. If you do not set the Expires property, the cookie expires when the current session ends. You cannot set either type of cookie if the user refuses to accept cookies.

A cookie is a string of text. Like session variables, you must assign a name and a value. This example stores the value from txtName into a cookie called UserName.

```
'Temporary cookie stored in RAM
Response.Cookies("UserName").Value = txtName.Text
```

or

```
Response.Cookies.Add(New System.Web.HttpCookie("UserName", txtName.Text))
```

✅ **TIP**

A text box TextChanged event does not cause a postback. The event is processed during the next postback that occurs when a button is clicked. You can force the event to occur when data are entered by changing the text box AutoPostBack property to True, but this would cause a Post-Back for every keystroke. ■

```
'Permanent Cookie stored on the hard drive
With Response.Cookies("UserName")
    .Value = txtName.Text
    .Expires = Today.AddYears(3)
End With

'Retrieve the cookie
lblMessage.Text = "Hello " & Request.Cookies("UserName").Value
```

The ViewState Property

The **ViewState property** is an ASP.NET server control feature for storing state with the Web page. Each control and the form itself have a ViewState property. As mentioned earlier, any control that has its EnableViewState property set to true is automatically saved and restored for each postback.

You can store text values in the ViewState of the form. You may want to do this to maintain settings, values entered by the user, values of variables, or even a dataset. The ViewState information is passed to the server on each postback and returned with the form, but the data values are not maintained on the server. The values are available only to the current form, not to the entire application as are session and cookie values.

The ViewState property uses System.Web.UI.StateBag, which is a dictionary collection that holds names and values. Similar to the session and cookie techniques, you make up a name and assign a value to it.

```
'Store a value in ViewState
ViewState("UserName") = txtName.Text

'Retrieve a value from ViewState
lblMessage.Text = "Hello " & ViewState("UserName").ToString()
```

Although you cannot access the ViewState information on a different page, you can retrieve it when you reload the same page on subsequent trips to the server. The data for a ViewState are actually stored in hidden controls on the Web Form. One disadvantage of using ViewState is that it increases the amount of information stored with a page, which can make the page take longer to load.

Note: If your application runs in a Web farm, you can assign one machine to handle all of the state management. To indicate this to the application, a change must be made to the <sessionState> element in the Web.config file by changing the mode from InProc to StateServer.

▶ Feedback 6.3

1. Write the statement to store the value in txtEmail to a Session object in a variable called *Email*.
2. What code is required to retrieve the value stored in the Session object Email and assign it to lblEmail?
3. Write the code to send the Email value to a cookie on the client machine. Give the cookie an expiration of 3 years.
4. What technique(s) for state management allow you to share the values with other Web pages in the same application or session?
5. What technique(s) for state management allow you to maintain values for the current page only?

Managing Web Projects

Managing the files for Web projects can be a challenge, especially if you need to move the project from one computer to another. Unless you are careful, your solution files (.sln and .suo) will be saved in a separate folder in a different location from the rest of your project.

Location of Files

The Visual Studio IDE saves solution files in the default folder that you select in *Tools / Options /Environment*. In the *Projects and Solutions* section, the entry for *Visual Studio projects location* determines the location of the .sln and .suo files. This location is the same for Windows projects and Web projects.

When you create a new Web project, all files *except the solution files* are stored in a new folder beneath Inetpub\wwwroot. For example, if you create a new Web project called *MyWebProject*, two folders called *MyWebProject* are created: one in your default project folder and one in wwwroot.

If you keep your project on a single development machine, the VS IDE can open either the project or solution file and keep track of the files. But if you need to move your project, the file arrangement can cause difficulties.

Recommendation: As soon as you open a new Web project, select the solution file in the Solution Explorer. Then select *File / Save SolutionName As*. Browse to find your folder name in Inetpub\wwwroot and save your solution file there. This will keep all of your files in the same folder.

Moving a Project

When you move a project folder from one computer to another, the project will not run until you take an extra step. To run a Web project from your local Web server (likely IIS), you must have a "virtual folder" defined. Fortunately, the VS IDE makes this happen when you create a new Web application. However, when you move the project to another computer, you must either create a virtual folder on that computer or declare the project folder to be Web-Shared.

To move a project, copy the project folder from Inetpub\wwwroot on the source computer to the same location on the target machine. Then either create a virtual directory or Web-share the folder.

Creating a Virtual Directory

After you move a project to a new computer, you must open the Internet Services Manager to create a virtual directory. Select *Start / Settings / Control Panel / Administrative Tools / Internet Information Services Manager* and expand the node for the computer and for the default Web site to view the folders. Notice that the icon for the new folder is different from the existing virtual directories. You can select the new folder and right-click to display its *Properties* dialog box. On the *Directory* tab, click *Create* and *OK*, which accepts the folder's name as the name of the new virtual directory.

Next you must set the project's startup page: open the project in the VS IDE, select the startup page in the Solution Explorer, right-click, and choose *Set as start page* from the shortcut menu.

Your project should run after these steps.

If you rename a folder for a Web project, you must edit the .sln file with a text editor, such as Notepad, to modify the hard-coded path of the project file. ∎

Web-Sharing the Project Folder

An alternative to creating an IIS virtual directory on the new computer is to declare the folder as Web-shared. This procedure is a little easier than creating a virtual directory but can cause security problems on a network. On the target computer, select the folder name using Explorer or My Computer, right-click, and choose *Properties*. On the *Web Sharing* tab, select the radio button for *Share this folder*. An *Edit Alias* dialog box appears; click OK and OK again on the *Properties* dialog box. This makes the folder Web-shared on the new machine.

Running the Relocated Project

After you create the virtual folder or Web-share your project folder and set the start page, you should be able to open and run your project in the VS IDE using the path Inetpub/wwwroot, or enter the URL of your page in a browser to run it. The URL should be something like this:

```
http://localhost/YourFolderName/YourFormName.aspx
```

Deleting a Web Project

You can delete a Web project; the procedure depends on how the project was created and whether its folder is an IIS virtual directory or a Web-shared folder. If the project is still in the location created by the VS IDE, it is in an IIS virtual directory. If you have moved or renamed the project, you may have created an IIS virtual directory or a Web-shared folder (see the previous section). You can easily delete an IIS virtual directory in Explorer or My Computer. When you try to delete a Web-shared folder, you receive a message telling you that the folder is in use.

To delete a Web-shared project folder, first unshare it: Right-click the folder name in My Computer or Explorer and select *Properties*. On the *Web Sharing* tab, select the button for *Do not share this folder* and answer *Yes* to the confirmation; then close the *Properties* dialog box. Although it seems like you should be able to delete the folder after this step, the folder is still marked as "In Use". You must either reboot or stop and restart IIS; then you can delete the folder.

Your Hands-On Programming Example

Write a project for R 'n R—For Reading and Refreshment. The Login page should prompt for the user name and account number. Validate that the account number is numeric and no more than four digits and that the name is not blank. Display an asterisk next to a field in error and display the error message in a validation summary.

Include a link to a second page. The second page should welcome the user by name and display contact information for R 'n R. It also should contain a link back to the previous page, which should redisplay the entries made by the user. The link to the second page should be disabled until the user has successfully signed in.

You can create a company logo or use the RnRLogo graphic file included in the StudentData folder.

Note: Do not validate the account number for specific values. Use a RangeValidator and accept numeric values from 0 to 9999.

Planning the Project

Sketch the forms (Figure 6.15*a* and *b*) that your users sign off as meeting their needs.

The planning sketches for the hands-on programming example: a. the Sign-in form; b. the Contact Information form.

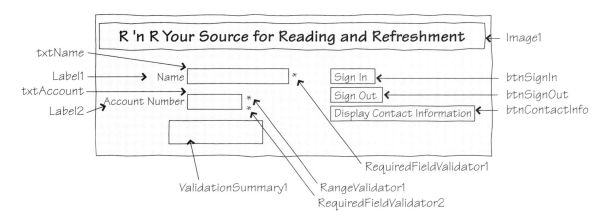

a.

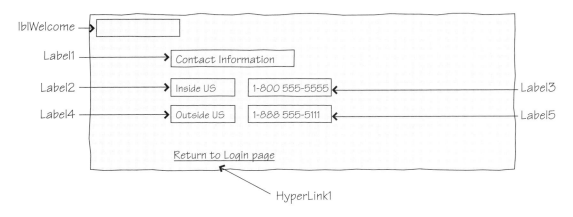

b.

Plan the Objects, Properties, and Methods

Plan the objects and property settings for the two forms and controls.

The Sign-in Form

Object	Property	Setting
Document	Name	RnR
	Title	R 'n R Sign-in
Image1	ImageUrl	RnRLogo.gif
Label1	Text	Name
Label2	Text	Account Number
txtName	Text	(blank)
txtAccount	Text	(blank)
btnSignIn	Text	Sign In
btnSignOut	Enabled	False
	Text	Sign Out
btnContactInfo	Enabled	False
	Text	Display Contact Information
RequiredFieldValidator1	ControlToValidate	txtName
	ErrorMessage	Name is required.
	Text	*
RequiredFieldValidator2	ControlToValidate	txtAccount
	ErrorMessage	Account number is required.
	Text	*
RangeValidator1	ControlToValidate	txtAccount
	ErrorMessage	Invalid account number.
	Text	*
ValidationSummary1		

Event procedures/Methods	Actions—Pseudocode

Page_Load	If session variables exist
	    Restore control contents.
	If sign-in was successful
	    Enable btnContactInfo & btnSignOut.
	    Disable btnSignIn.

btnSignIn_Click	If all fields passed validation
	Save name and account number in session variables.
	Save boolean IsValid session variable.
	Enable btnContactInfo and btnSignOut.
btnSignOut_Click	Clear text fields.
	Disable btnContactInfo and btnSignOut.
	Enable btnSignIn.
	Clear the session.
btnContactInfo_Click	Link to the ContactInfo page.

The Contact Information Form

Object	Property	Setting
Document	Title	R 'n R Contact Information
lblWelcome	Text	(blank)
Label1	Text	Contact Information
Label2	Text	Inside US
Label3	Text	1-800-555-5555
Label4	Text	Outside US
Label5	Text	1-888-555-5111

Methods	Actions—Pseudocode
Page_Load	Append name from session variable and display message.

Write the Project

Following the sketches in Figure 6.15, create the forms. Figure 6.16 shows the completed forms.

- Set the properties of each of the form objects, according to your plans.

- Write the code for the forms. Working from the pseudocode, write each event procedure.

- When you complete the code, test the operation several times. Test the validation routines and navigate back and forth between the forms. Sign out and make sure that you can sign in again and navigate correctly.

Figure 6.16

a.

b.

The forms for the hands-on programming example: a. the Sign-in form; b. the Contact Information form.

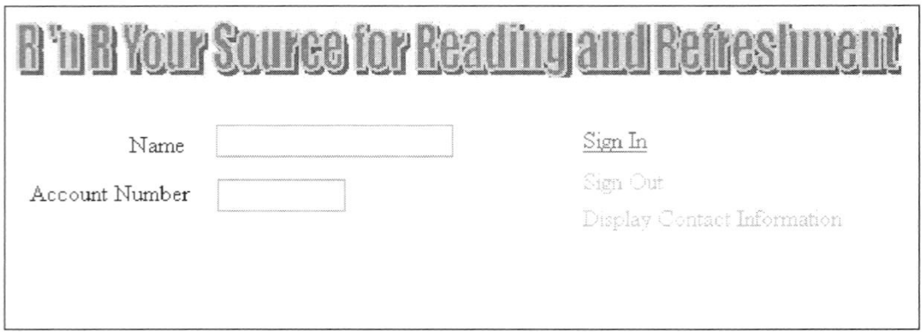

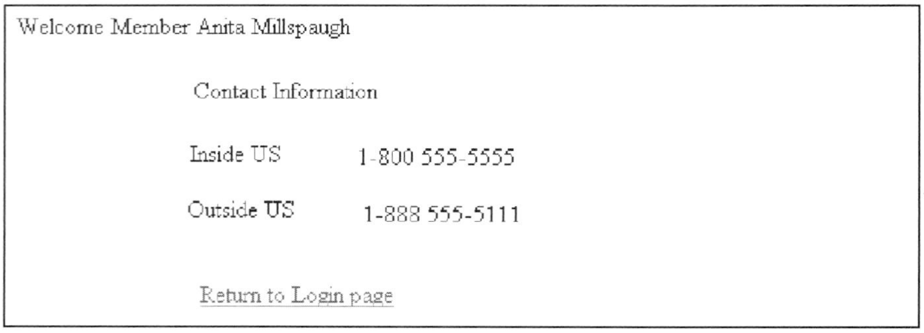

The Project Coding Solution

The Sign-In Form

```
'Project:        Ch06HandsOn
'Programmer:     Bradley/Millspaugh
'Date:           January 2003
'Description:    Enter and validate user information.
'                If valid, link to a second page.

Option Strict On

Public Class RnRLogin
    Inherits System.Web.UI.Page

    [Web Form Designer Generated Code]

    Private Sub Page_Load(ByVal sender As System.Object, _
      ByVal e As System.EventArgs) Handles MyBase.Load
        'Restore entered information for display after first load

        Try        'Skip if Session variables don't exist
            If txtName.Text = "" Then
                txtName.Text = Session("Member").ToString()
            End If
            If txtAccount.Text = "" Then
                txtAccount.Text = Session("MemberID").ToString()
            End If
```

```
            Dim blnValidLogin As Boolean = CType(Session("ValidLogin"), Boolean)
            If blnValidLogin Then
                btnContactInfo.Enabled = True
                btnSignOut.Enabled = True
                btnSignIn.Enabled = False
            End If
        Catch
        End Try
    End Sub

    Private Sub btnSignIn_Click(ByVal sender As System.Object, _
      ByVal e As System.EventArgs) Handles btnSignIn.Click
        'Sign in the user

        If Page.IsValid Then
            Session("Member") = txtName.Text
            Session("MemberID") = txtAccount.Text
            Session("ValidLogin") = True
            btnContactInfo.Enabled = True
            btnSignOut.Enabled = True
        End If
    End Sub

    Private Sub btnSignOut_Click(ByVal sender As System.Object, _
      ByVal e As System.EventArgs) Handles btnSignOut.Click
        'Log out the user and reset the page

        txtName.Text = ""
        txtAccount.Text = ""
        btnContactInfo.Enabled = False
        btnSignOut.Enabled = False
        btnSignIn.Enabled = True
        Session.Clear()
    End Sub

    Private Sub btnContactInfo_Click(ByVal sender As System.Object, _
      ByVal e As System.EventArgs) Handles btnContactInfo.Click
        'Link to the ContactInfo page

        Server.Transfer("ContactInfo.aspx")
    End Sub
End Class
```

The Contact Information Form

```
'Project:        Ch06HandsOn
'Form:           Contact Information
'Programmer:     Bradley/Millspaugh
'Date:           January 2003
'Description:    Display contact information for R 'n R

Option Strict On

Public Class ContactInfo
    Inherits System.Web.UI.Page

    [Web Form Designer Generated Code]
```

```
Private Sub Page_Load(ByVal sender As System.Object, _
   ByVal e As System.EventArgs) Handles MyBase.Load
      'Include user name in the welcome label

      lblWelcome.Text = "Welcome Member " & Session("Member").ToString()
End Sub
End Class
```

Summary

1. A Web application resides on a server and displays in the client's browser application.
2. A network within a company is called an intranet.
3. ASP.NET can send the correct code for any browser. Different code is sent for uplevel browsers and downlevel browsers.
4. HTML Web pages cannot store information from one access to the next.
5. ASP.NET is the newest Web programming technology from Microsoft. Web programming in Visual Studio .NET uses ASP.NET.
6. The aspx file contains the specifications for the user interface. The VB code is contained in the aspx.vb file, which is called the "code-behind" file.
7. The Global.asax file has events for the Application and Session.
8. You can use the Styles.css file to create formatting styles and apply those styles to Web page elements.
9. The settings for authentication, authorization, globalization, and cookies are stored in the Web.config file. There may be multiple configuration files making up a hierarchy of settings. The settings apply to all files within a directory and all of the child directories. Additional configuration files can add additional features. You can store application settings in Web.config, such as defining the connection string for a database connection.
10. The controls for Web Forms are not the same controls as for Windows Forms. Many of the controls are designed to work similarly to their Windows counterparts. Controls may be HTML controls, HTML server controls, or Web Form server controls.
11. Click events of buttons cause a postback to the server; most other events are not processed as they occur, but are held until the next postback.
12. The LinkButton acts like a button and looks like a hyperlink. Use a LinkButton rather than a Hyperlink control if you need to perform some action before navigating to the next page.
13. The `Response.Redirect` method can navigate to any other Web page. The `Server.Transfer` method can navigate to any other page on the same server and is more efficient than `Response.Redirect` because it requires one less round-trip to the server.
14. The Calendar control allows the user to enter or select a date that you can then display or use in the program.
15. You can set the background image for a form using the Background property of the DOCUMENT object.
16. Setting the tab order differs from a Windows application. By default, all controls have their TabIndex property set to zero, which means that it is

unset. You must manually set the TabIndex properties of controls that you want to appear in the tab sequence. To set the initial focus on the page, you must modify the HTML of a page.

17. To use styles in a .css file, you must modify the style names to begin with a period, attach the .css file to the Web page, and set the CssClass property of controls.

18. To test a project in another browser, open the browser and type the URL of your page into the Address bar.

19. The validator controls can validate input data on the client machine before being transmitted to the server when using an uplevel browser. The controls include the RequiredFieldValidator, CompareValidator, RangeValidator, RegularExpressionValidator, and the ValidationSummary.

20. An ASP.NET project can use the Request, Response, Session, Application, and Server IIS objects.

21. HTML pages do not maintain data values, called the state, from one access to another or from one page to another. Using the ViewState, ASP.NET can restore the contents of controls for a postback within a single page.

22. State management may be handled on the server side or the client side. Techniques include Application and Session objects, cookies, and the form's ViewState property.

23. Web projects are stored in a virtual directory. By default it is the Inetpub/wwwroot. You should save the solution file in the same location.

Key Terms

Review Questions

1. What are uplevel browsers and downlevel browsers? How are ASP.NET programs handled differently for the two levels of browsers?

2. Describe the purpose of these Web project files: aspx, aspx.vb, Global.asax, Styles.css, Web.config.

3. What are the three types of button controls available for Web Forms?

4. Explain the differences between a LinkButton and a HyperLink control.

5. What methods can you use to navigate to another page? How do they differ?
6. List the validator controls. Give an example for using each type.
7. What techniques are available for state management on the server side?
8. List four methods of state management and give the advantages and disadvantages of each.

Programming Exercises

6.1 Create a Web page for Tricia's Travels. Include an appropriate logo. The Sign-in screen should request the user name and account number; both fields are required. Include links for "Land" specials and "Cruise" deals of the week. Each link should display another page, each of which must include a link to the home page.

6.2 Create a personal Web page. The first page should include your name and a favorite image. Include links to pages describing your hobbies, education, and employment. Include links to other Web sites if you wish. Remember that you can navigate back to your Web page with the Back button on the browser application.

6.3 Create a Web project for your company (you may invent any products and/or company names that you wish). Include fields that require validation on the home page and links to at least three other pages.

Case Studies

Claytor's Cottages

Design and create a Web site for Claytor's Cottages. Your home Web page must include an image or a background picture along with a nicely formatted logo of the company name. Include a link to a second page that lists each of the room names as a link. The link for each room should describe the price and amenities for the room and/or show an image for the room (images of your choice).

Note: This is a Web page; make it attractive.

Christian's Car Rentals

Design and create a Web site for Christian's Car Rentals including a company logo and an image or background image. Allow the user to enter a name and account number (6 numeric characters). Name is a mandatory field. Include a link called *Contact Us* to a second page, which displays the following information:

By Mail   Christian's Car Rentals Customer Support
           1000 W. 14th Street
           Los Angeles, CA 92333
By Email   CustomerSupport@ChristiansCars.com
By Phone   1-800 555-1234

Allow the user to navigate back to the home page; their personal information should still be visible.

7

Web Forms Database

1. Display database fields on a Web form.

2. Determine when to use a data reader rather than a dataset.

3. Data bind controls to a Web Form.

4. Display data in a Web DataGrid.

5. Create pagination for a grid.

6. Set up a DataList control with data-bound template fields.

7. Use the CheckboxList and RadioButtonList controls.

8. Set up a multitier Web application.

9. Maintain state for list boxes.

The previous chapter introduced you to Web Forms. In this chapter you will expand your knowledge of Web applications by incorporating database access. You will also use components to create multitier Web projects.

Data Access in .NET

You can choose from two methods to access data using the .NET Framework: You can use a data adapter and its disconnected dataset or you can connect to the data directly using a data reader. Generally speaking, a data reader is faster but a dataset provides more flexibility.

Data Readers

A **DataReader object** provides a forward-only result set from a data source. You open the connection and transfer the data into the DataReader object. The connection stays open until you explicitly close it. The forward-only feature means that access is fast—sometimes called the "fire-hose" connection. However, it also means that a data reader is not suitable for doing file updates.

For a Web application, you don't want to stay connected to the database for a long period of time. But a data reader often provides the most expedient method for loading a list box or retrieving other small amounts of information that are not subject to change while the Web page displays. If you are displaying larger amounts of data or want to work with related tables, a dataset is the proper choice. Often a single application may contain both a data reader and a data adapter with a dataset.

Setting up a Connection and Command

A DataReader object requires a Connection object for the connection string and also a **Command object,** which holds the SQL statement or stored-procedure name. You can declare the connection and command in code or use the visual tools in the IDE. You can drag a connection from the Server Explorer or use the tools in the toolbox: the connection and command objects are both available in the Data tab of the toolbox. Currently you can find one set for SQL and another for OleDb. The type should match; that is, use an SqlConnection and SqlCommand, or an OleDbConnection and OleDbCommand.

For the Command object, you must set the CommandText property. Set the CommandType to Text and click on the CommandText property to open the Query Builder, where you can set up the SQL command.

Filling a List Box from a Data Reader

Assume that you want to populate a list box with the names of the stores in the stores table of the pubs database. First, add a connection to the pubs database, called conPubs. Then add a command object, name it cmdStores, set the Connection property to conPubs, and set the CommandText property to an SQL statement that selects the store names from the stores table:

```
SqlCommand       cmdStores
Connection       conPubs
CommandType      Text
CommandText      SELECT stor_name from stores
```

To declare a DataReader in code, you need an `Imports` statement at the top of the file, before the `Class` statement:

```
Imports System.Data
```

You generally fill a list in the Page_Load event procedure. Declare the DataReader using a prefix of "dr".

```
Dim drStores As SqlClient.SqlDataReader
```

The steps for filling a list box are

- Open the connection
- Assign the return from the connection's `ExecuteReader` method to the DataReader object.
- Set the DropDownList control's DataSource and DataTextField properties. The DataSource is the name of the DataReader and the DataTextField is the name of the field from the table, enclosed in quotes. You can also set the DataValue property if you are using the list selection to look up by a field other than the one displayed in the list.
- Bind the data.
- Close the DataReader.
- Close the connection.

To make sure that the list is not refilled every time the page is refreshed, include a check for postback.

```
Private Sub Page_Load(ByVal sender As System.Object, _
  ByVal e As System.EventArgs) Handles MyBase.Load
    'Load the list of store names using a data reader
    Dim drStores As SqlClient.SqlDataReader

    If Not IsPostBack Then
        conPubs.Open()
        drStores = cmdStores.ExecuteReader()
        ddlStores.DataSource = drStores
        ddlStores.DataTextField = "stor_name"
        ddlStores.DataBind()
        drStores.Close()
        conPubs.Close()
    End If
End Sub
```

Caution: If you declare a connection in code, you must make sure to close the connection before its variable goes out of scope. If you skip this step, the connection remains open with no way to refer to it and close it, which can fill the SQL Server connection pool.

DataSets

You create data adapters and datasets in the same manner in a Web Form as in a Windows Form. You can drag fields or a table from the Server Explorer to the form, which automatically creates a connection object and a DataAdapter object.

You can bind a database field to a control at design time or at run time, but the binding process is somewhat different for Web controls than for Windows controls. Figure 7.1 shows the dialog box that appears when you select the DataBindings property of a Web control. The first time you display the dialog box, you must expand the nodes under *Simple binding*.

Expand the nodes for the DataBindings property of a control to bind the control to a database field.

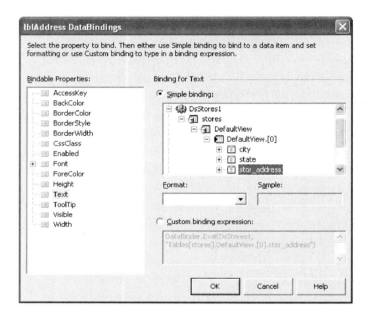

Setting the DataBindings property of a control is not enough to bind the data, as it is for a Windows control. For Web controls, you must execute the **DataBind method** in code to complete the binding process. You can use either the `DataBind` method of each control or the `DataBind` method of the form, which binds all controls on the page.

```
Me.DataBind()
```

or

```
lblAddress.DataBind()
lblCity.DataBind()
```

A DataReader and Dataset Example

This example allows the user to select the store name from a drop-down list and displays the data for the selected store in labels. The list is filled with a

DataReader and a dataset is used for the data in the labels. Note that you must set the drop-down list control's AutoPostBack property to True to trigger a post-back to the server when the user makes a selection. Figure 7.2 shows the completed Web page.

Figure 7.2

This example uses a DataReader to fill the list and a DataSet to bind to the individual fields.

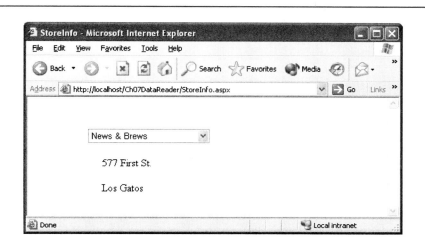

```
'Project:        Ch07DataReader
'Programmer:     Bradley/Millspaugh
'Date:           January 2003
'Description:    Display a list of store names; retrieve and display the
'                data for the selected record.
'                Uses a data reader to fill the list and a dataset for the
'                selected record.

Option Strict On

Imports System.Data

Public Class StoreInfo
    Inherits System.Web.UI.Page

    [Web Designer Generated Code]

    Private Sub Page_Load(ByVal sender As System.Object, _
      ByVal e As System.EventArgs) Handles MyBase.Load
        'Load the list of store names using a data reader
        Dim drStores As SqlClient.SqlDataReader

        If Not IsPostBack Then
            conPubs.Open()
            'Use a data reader to fill the list
            drStores = cmdStores.ExecuteReader()
            ddlStores.DataSource = drStores
            ddlStores.DataTextField = "stor_name"
            ddlStores.DataBind()
            drStores.Close()
```

```
            conPubs.Close()
        End If
    End Sub

    Private Sub ddlStores_SelectedIndexChanged(ByVal sender As System.Object, _
        ByVal e As System.EventArgs) Handles ddlStores.SelectedIndexChanged
        'Get the record to match the selection
        'Fill a dataset with the selected record

        DsStores1.Clear()
        daStores.SelectCommand.Parameters("@store").Value = ddlStores.SelectedItem.Text
        daStores.Fill(DsStores1)
        Me.DataBind()
    End Sub
End Class
```

Setting a Dynamic Connection String

If you plan to move your database project from one computer to another, perhaps to a classroom, lab, or home machine, you can save yourself some trouble by declaring a **dynamic connection string.** In the Properties window for the connection, expand the (*DynamicProperties*) node and click on the build button for ConnectionString (Figure 7.3). In the dialog box that appears, click in the check box for *Map property to a key in configuration file* (Figure 7.4). Note that the *Key* entry already appears when the dialog box displays.

In a Windows application, the config file is called *App.config*. See Appendix E for information for setting a dynamic connection string for both Windows and Web applications. ■

Figure   7.3

Define a dynamic connection string for a connection object by expanding the (DynamicProperties) node and clicking on the ConnectionString's build button.

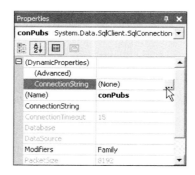

Figure   7.4

Select the option to map the ConnectionString property to a key in the configuration file.

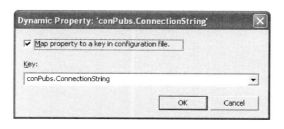

After you declare the dynamic ConnectionString property, open the Web.config file and scroll to the bottom. A new <appSettings> section appears. The settings are defined as key/value pairs, and a new key and value should appear for the ConnectionString.

```
<appSettings>
  <!- User application and configured property settings go here.->
  <!- Example: <add key="settingName" value="settingValue"/> ->
  <add key="conPubs.ConnectionString" value="data source=YourMachine\NetSDK;initial
catalog=pubs;integrated security=SSPI;persist security info=False;workstation id=Your
  Machine;packet
size=4096" />
</appSettings>
```

Modify the "value =" clause to a generic connection string that will run on any computer that has the .NET sample files installed:

```
value="server=(local)\NetSDK;Trusted_Connection=yes;database=pubs" />
```

When you move your Web application to another computer, you shouldn't have to modify the ConnectionString. *Note:* You can expand the designer-generated code in your form and see the statement that assigns the configuration value to the ConnectionString.

Warning: If the name of your server is *VSDotNet* or any value other than *NetSDK*, you are not using the SQL Server and sample files that came with the .NET Framework. You will likely have security problems running the programs in this text unless you install and use the correct server and sample files. See Appendix C for the installation instructions.

The dynamic connection string is supplied only at run time. If you need to view the data at design time, or modify the data adapter or dataset, you must also have the connection string set in the Properties window. You can keep the property set to a specific database in the Properties window for design time and allow it to use the dynamic property at run time.

Security Problems

If you have security problems accessing a database, first check to make sure that your server is named *NetSDK* (see Appendix C and "Making a Web Database Update Program Run" in Appendix E). If installing the correct server and data files does not solve the problem, check the Microsoft Knowledge Base article Q316989.

► **Feedback 7.1**

Write the code to fill a drop-down list of titles using a DataReader. Assume that cmdTitles and conPubs have been properly created.

Web Server DataGrid Controls

The **DataGrid control** for Web applications shares some similarities with its Windows counterpart, but mostly just in appearance. The Web DataGrid has some additional features, such as paging the grid and easier formatting of the grid.

Filling a DataGrid

The DataGrid control is often used to display information from a database. Using a grid is quick and provides for flexibility in formatting.

After you add a DataGrid control to your Web Form, connect it to a data source. Set the DataSource property to a data view, or set it to a dataset and set the DataMember property to a table within the dataset. The columns in the data grid are automatically set to the names of the fields in the data source. You can right-click the grid, select *Auto Format*, and choose one of many formatting styles.

You can easily select the columns that you want to appear in the grid by either limiting the number of fields in the dataset or by using the data grid's Property Builder. Display the *Property Builder* dialog box (Figure 7.5) from the grid's context menu.

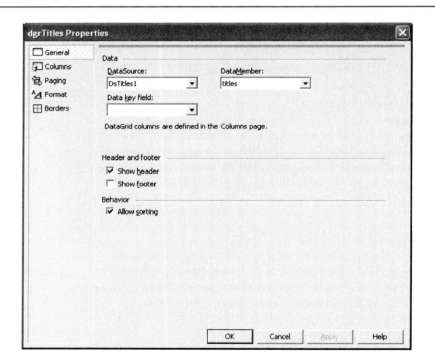

In the DataGrid's **Property Builder** *dialog box you can select the fields to display in the grid.*

This example displays selected fields from a dataset that holds the titles table from the pubs database. Select the *Columns* page (Figure 7.6), where you can select specific fields and set the Header text for the column. You also can set the Sort expression on this page, which chooses the sort order for the rows. The *Format* and *Borders* pages allow you to create your own formats or modify the format you select from the AutoFormat options.

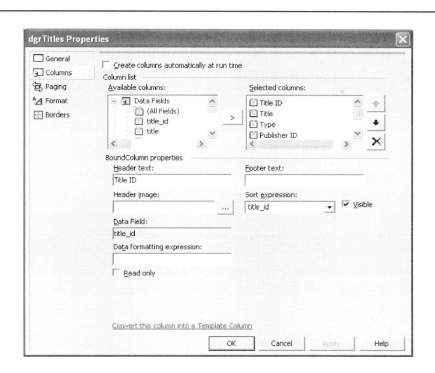

Figure 7.6

Select the fields that you want to display in the grid and enter custom column headings in the Header text box.

The only code needed is the `Fill` and `DataBind` methods in the Page_Load event procedure. Figure 7.7 shows the output.

Figure 7.7

The selected fields appear in the DataGrid with very little code.

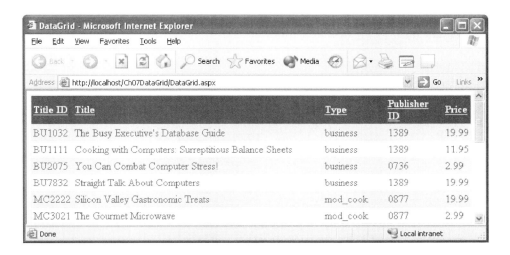

```
Private Sub Page_Load(ByVal sender As System.Object, _
  ByVal e As System.EventArgs) Handles MyBase.Load
    'Fill the dataset

    daTitles.Fill(DsTitles1)
    Me.DataBind()
End Sub
```

Sorting the Data in a Grid

You can allow the user to sort the data grid by clicking on a column heading, but you must set a property, set the data source to a DataView instead of a table, and write a little code to make it happen. Add a DataView component to the form and set its Table property to the table on which to base the view. Set the DataGrid's **AllowSorting property** to True, set the DataSource property to the DataView, and add code for the grid's **SortCommand event.**

When you set the grid's AllowSorting property to True, each column heading becomes a link. When the user clicks a column heading, the corresponding field name is passed to the SortCommand event procedure in the **e** argument. To write code for the SortCommand event, in the Editor window select the Data-Grid from the *Class* list and SortCommand from the *Event* list.

```
Private Sub dgrTitles_SortCommand(ByVal source As Object, _
  ByVal e As System.Web.UI.WebControls.DataGridSortCommandEventArgs) _
  Handles dgrTitles.SortCommand
    'Sort the data view by the selected field and rebind to the grid

    dvSort.Sort = e.SortExpression
    Me.DataBind()
End Sub
```

Paging a Data Grid

Very often the selected data produce more rows than fit on a screen. As you know, scroll bars appear automatically, but many users prefer to view just one page at a time. You can add pagination to a grid that displays a data view or a dataset by setting the **AllowPaging property** to True and adding a little code.

The code goes into the PageIndexChanged event procedure. To write the event procedure, select the DataGrid from the *Class* list in the Editor window and select PageIndexChanged from the *Event* list. In code set the **Current-PageIndex property** to the NewPageIndex value retrieved from the Data-GridPageChangedEventArgs parameter. Figure 7.8 shows the output.

Figure 7.8

Add paging to a DataGrid.

```
Private Sub dgrTitles_PageIndexChanged(ByVal source As Object, _
  ByVal e As System.Web.UI.WebControls.DataGridPageChangedEventArgs) _
  Handles dgrTitles.PageIndexChanged
    'Change to the selected page

    dgrTitles.CurrentPageIndex = e.NewPageIndex
    Me.DataBind()
End Sub
```

You can control how the paging appears on the Paging tab of the *Property Builder* dialog box (Figure 7.9). You can display page numbers or display Next and Previous buttons, which appear as < >. You can also specify the number of rows to display on a page; the default is 10 rows.

Select paging options on the Paging tab of the Property Builder dialog box.

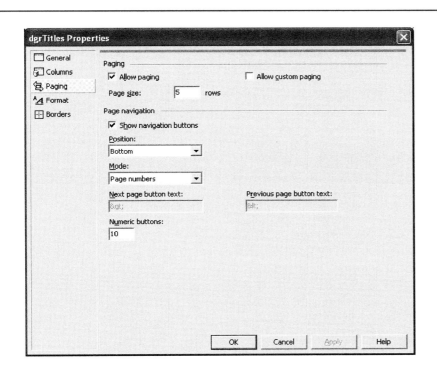

Web DataGrid Column Styles

You can set the column type for each column in a DataGrid Web Server control. The choices are BoundColumn, ButtonColumn, HyperlinkColumn, and TemplateColumn (see Table 7.1). Templates are covered later in this chapter under "DataList Controls." Set the column styles on the *Columns* page of the *Property Builder* dialog box (refer to Figure 7.6), which you can display by selecting *Property Builder* from the context menu or by clicking on the builder button (...) for the grid's Columns property. Notice in Figure 7.6 that you also can change the order of the columns.

The Column Types for a DataGrid Web Control

Type of column	Purpose
BoundColumn	Binds to a data source (default).
ButtonColumn	Displays Select, Edit, Update, Cancel, and Delete buttons for each row in the grid; can be set to display as push buttons or link buttons.
HyperlinkColumn	Contents of the cell display as a hyperlink and can be bound to a data source or contain text.
TemplateColumn	Follows a specified template allowing for custom controls in the grid.

▶ **Feedback 7.2**

1. Write the code to display data in dgrStudents from the dataset DsStudents1 and daStudents.
2. What properties must be set on the data grid?

The DataList Control

The **DataList control** provides an alternate way to display data from a data source. An advantage over the grid is that you have more control over the layout, which doesn't have to be just rows and columns. You can place other controls into a DataList, such as labels, hyperlinks, images, and buttons.

The DataList control requires an **ItemTemplate** that indicates how the data from each row should appear. You also can add templates for Headers and Footers and for Separators. Even though the control is called a DataList, you can arrange the output to appear in rows and columns like a table, or as a single list displayed either vertically or horizontally. You might like to display a list of links arranged horizontally at the top of your page or vertically at the left. You can have the elements "flow" or appear as a table (Figure 7.10).

Adding a Template

After you add a DataList control to a Web page, right-click and select *EditTemplate / Item Templates*. You can specify different templates for selected items from the list and for alternating items to aid in readability (Figure 7.11). The only required entry is the item template. You can add Web Server or HTML controls to the template.

You can provide a way for users to select items from the list by including a Hyperlink control or a LinkButton. For a LinkButton, either set the Text property yourself or bind it to a field in a database. Set the **CommandName property** for the LinkButton to a text string, such as "Select". Later you will use that CommandName to determine the action to take. The DataList sample program later in this chapter shows how to use the CommandName property.

Figure 7.10

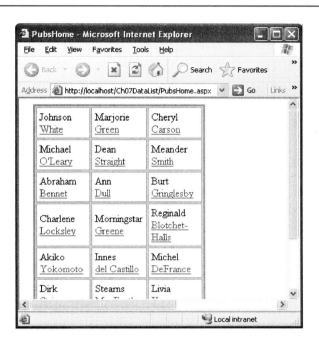

This DataList control displays with rows and columns. Each cell displays a bound label and a bound hyperlink.

Figure 7.11

Set up the item template for a DataList control by adding controls to the Item Template section.

Persisting a Dataset

When you create a dataset to display on a Web page, that dataset is "alive" for only one display of the page. Each time the user selects an item from a list or clicks a button, the page is posted back to the server and the dataset must be recreated. And if a user navigates to another page and back to your page, the dataset is no longer available.

You can save a dataset by storing it in a session variable or the form's View-State. As you recall from Chapter 6, ASP.NET passes the ViewState back to the server with the Request, and restores it on the Response. ViewState can maintain state within one page, but does not persist when the user navigates from one page to another. Using a session variable is preferable, since the Session object persists for as long as the user's session is alive and can be used by more than one Web page.

If you need to save a dataset, you should consider several factors, such as the size of the dataset and security. If a large dataset must be passed with every postback, the time to load a page can slow considerably. But for a small dataset, saving in a session variable can speed operations.

Here is the code to save a dataset in a session variable:

```
daAuthors.Fill(DsAuthors1)
'Store in a session variable
Session("DSAuthors") = DsAuthors1
```

Using the ItemCommand Event

The DataList and DataGrid controls are both considered containers, since both can hold additional controls such as buttons and links. When the user clicks any of the buttons or links inside the container control, the **ItemCommand event** of the container fires. In the ItemCommand event procedure, you can use the e argument in DataListCommandEventArgs to determine the action to take.

One of the elements of the DataListCommandEventArgs is Command-Name. You can use this property to retrieve the CommandName property of the selected LinkButton or Button control. (Setting the CommandName property of a LinkButton was introduced in the "Adding a Template" section.)

In this example, we set the LinkButton CommandName property to "Select". You can use an If statement or a Select Case to determine the action to take in the ItemCommand event procedure. It's more common to use a Select Case, because in most cases you will have more than one type of button and several possible values for CommandName.

```
Private Sub dlAuthors_ItemCommand(ByVal source As Object, _
   ByVal e As System.Web.UI.WebControls.DataListCommandEventArgs) _
   Handles dlAuthors.ItemCommand

If e.CommandName = "Select" Then
    'Perform the action for "Select"
'...
End If
```

or

```
Select Case e.CommandName
    Case "Select"
        'Perform the action for "Select"
    '...
End Select
```

Finding the Selected Item in the Dataset

In this example, the user selects an author name from a DataList and the program displays the phone number, address, and city for the selected person

(Figure 7.12). The fields in the DataList are bound to fields in a dataset, and the unbound phone number and address labels are assigned values from the selected row in the dataset. The dataset is saved in a session variable.

Figure 7.12

The DataList example program. The user selects a name from the list; the corresponding phone number and address are displayed in labels.

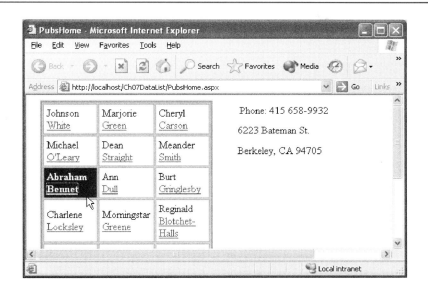

To find the match and display the data, we must

- Retrieve the dataset from the Session object.

- Find the currently selected row.

- Assign the correct elements of the row to the labels.

Retrieve the Dataset Declare a variable and retrieve the dataset. Because Option Strict is on, you must explicitly convert the object to a dataset.

```
Dim dsAuthorsSession As DataSet
dsAuthorsSession = CType(Session("DSAuthors"), DataSet)
```

Find the Selected Row The next step is to get the row for the currently selected item, once again using the e from the DataListCommandEventArgs.

```
Dim drwCurrentRow As DataRow
drwCurrentRow = dsAuthorsSession.Tables("authors").Rows(e.Item.ItemIndex)
```

Assign the Fields to the Labels

```
lblPhone.Text = "Phone:  " & drwCurrentRow("phone").ToString()
lblAddress.Text = drwCurrentRow("address").ToString()
lblCity.Text = drwCurrentRow("city").ToString() & ", " & _
  drwCurrentRow("state").ToString() & " " & _
  drwCurrentRow("zip").ToString()
```

The Complete Procedure Here is the complete procedure to respond to a click in the DataList and find and display the data for the selected name. Refer to Figure 7.12 for the completed Web page.

```
Private Sub dlAuthors_ItemCommand(ByVal source As Object, _
  ByVal e As System.Web.UI.WebControls.DataListCommandEventArgs) _
  Handles dlAuthors.ItemCommand
    'Display more author information
    Dim drwCurrentRow As DataRow
    Dim dsAuthorsSession As DataSet

    Select Case e.CommandName
        Case "Select"
            'Retrieve the dataset from the session variable
            dsAuthorsSession = CType(Session("DSAuthors"), DataSet)
            'Retrieve the row for the selected name
            drwCurrentRow = dsAuthorsSession.Tables("authors").Rows(e.Item.ItemIndex)
            'Assign the fields from the row to the labels
            lblPhone.Text = "Phone:   " & drwCurrentRow("phone").ToString()
            lblAddress.Text = drwCurrentRow("address").ToString()
            lblCity.Text = drwCurrentRow("city").ToString() & ", " & _
            drwCurrentRow("state").ToString() & " " & _
            drwCurrentRow("zip").ToString()
    End Select
End Sub
```

Creating a DataList Application—Step-by-Step

This step-by-step tutorial creates the DataList application described in the previous sections. The DataList displays a table of Author names. When the user clicks on a name link, the phone and address appear for the selected name. Notice in Figure 7.12 that the First Name is in a Label and the Last Name is a LinkButton within the Item Template.

Create the Project
STEP 1: Open a New Project called Ch07DataList using the ASP.NET Web Application template.
STEP 2: Save the solution file in the folder with the rest of the project. By default, that's Inetpub\wwwroot\Ch07DataList.

Add the Data Objects
STEP 1: Drag the pubs database authors table from the Server Explorer to the form.
STEP 2: Name the connection conPubs and the data adapter daAuthors.
STEP 3: Generate a dataset, naming it dsAuthors. The dataset component added to the designer will be DsAuthors1.
STEP 4: Select the conPubs component, in the Properties window expand the node for *(Dynamic Properties)*, and click on the build button (...) for ConnectionString. In the *Dynamic Property* dialog box, select *Map property to a key in configuration file* and click *OK*.

STEP 5: In the Solution Explorer, double-click on Web.config to open the file in the editor. Scroll to the bottom of the file to see the tag for the con-Pubs.ConnectionString.

STEP 6: Change the value to a generic string, so the project can run on another computer that has the sample database installed:

```
<add key="conPubs.ConnectionString"
     value="server=(local)\NetSDK;Trusted_Connection=yes;database=pubs" />
```

Add the DataList Control

STEP 1: Display the Web form and add a DataList control from the Web Forms toolbox.

STEP 2: Right-click on the control and select *Edit Template / Item Templates*.

STEP 3: Set the properties of the DataList Control.

ID	dlAuthors
DataKeyField	au_id
DataSource	DsAuthors1
RepeatColumns	3
RepeatDirection	Horizontal

Note: You may want to change the RepeatColumns and RepeatDirection after you view the page and determine the look you want.

STEP 4: Add a Label to the ItemTemplate area, widen it to hold a name, and set the properties:

ID	lblFirstName
Text	(blank)
DataBindings	Expand *Container* under *Simple Binding* and select au_fname.

STEP 5: Add a LinkButton control beside the label and set its properties.

ID	lnkLastName
Text	(blank)
DataBindings	au_lname
CommandName	Select

STEP 6: Right-click on the template and select *End Template Editing*.

STEP 7: Right-click on the DataList control, select *AutoFormat*, and pick a format.

Add Labels for Detail Information

STEP 1: Add labels for phone, address, and city-state-zip. Set the ID properties to lblPhone, lblAddress, and lblCity.

Add the Code

STEP 1: Code the Page_Load event procedure to fill the dataset, store it in a session variable, and bind the data fields.

```
Private Sub Page_Load(ByVal sender As System.Object, _
  ByVal e As System.EventArgs) Handles MyBase.Load
    'Obtain the data

    daAuthors.Fill(DsAuthors1)
    'Store in a session variable
    Session("DSAuthors") = DsAuthors1
    Me.DataBind()
End Sub
```

STEP 2: Select dlAuthors from the Class list and find ItemCommand in the Event list.

```
Private Sub dlAuthors_ItemCommand(ByVal source As Object, _
  ByVal e As System.Web.UI.WebControls.DataListCommandEventArgs) _
  Handles dlAuthors.ItemCommand
    'Display more author information
    Dim drwCurrentRow As DataRow
    Dim dsAuthorsSession As DataSet

    Select Case e.CommandName
        Case "Select"
            'Retrieve the dataset from the session variable
            dsAuthorsSession = CType(Session("DSAuthors"), DataSet)
            'Retrieve the row for the selected name
            drwCurrentRow = dsAuthorsSession.Tables("authors").Rows(e.Item.ItemIndex)
            'Assign the fields from the row to the labels
            lblPhone.Text = "Phone:  " & drwCurrentRow("phone").ToString()
            lblAddress.Text = drwCurrentRow("address").ToString()
            lblCity.Text = drwCurrentRow("city").ToString() & ", " & _
              drwCurrentRow("state").ToString() & " " & _
              drwCurrentRow("zip").ToString()
    End Select
End Sub
```

Execute the Project

STEP 1: Run the project. Test by clicking on various name links.

Formatting a Bound Template Control

You can perform a limited amount of formatting to bound data. In the example shown in Figure 7.13, a link button is bound to the Price numeric field in the titles table of the pubs database. The DataList control must first be bound to the DataSource so that the field names appear in the DataBindings for Container.

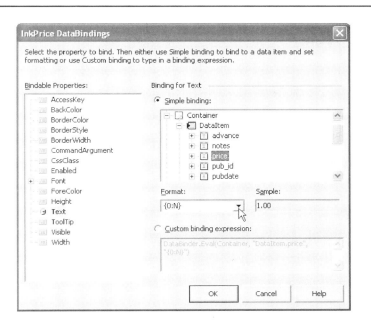

Figure 7.13

Select formatting for a numeric template column.

> ## Feedback 7.3
>
> 1. What controls should you place in the item template if you want to display the book title, price, and picture for each item?
> 2. Write the statement to retrieve the currently selected record in the Item-Command event procedure from the Employees table in a dataset called dsEmployees.

More Controls

Several specialized controls are available in the WebForms toolbox. These include the CheckBoxList, the RadioButtonList, the Literal, the PlaceHolder, and the AdRotator controls.

The CheckBoxList and RadioButtonList Controls

The **CheckBoxList** and **RadioButtonList** are handy controls available only for Web Forms. When you want to display a series of check boxes or a group of radio buttons on a Windows form, you must create multiple controls. But in Web applications, you can use these list controls as an easier way to present and access the choices. As with the corresponding single controls, only one item can be selected from a RadioButtonList but multiple selections may be made from a CheckBoxList.

The CheckBoxList and RadioButtonList are useful in many of the same situations as you would use a list box or combo box. The following program populates both a CheckBoxList and a RadioButtonList with the job descriptions

Figure 7.14

A CheckBoxList and RadioButtonList can present lists of choices to the user.

from the jobs table in the pubs database (Figure 7.14). For each control set the DataSource to the dataset and the DataTextField to the field to display.

The only code required is the typical `Fill` method and the `DataBind`. Include the test for postback, so that you don't reload the list for every page display.

```
'Project:       Ch07CheckBoxLists
'Programmer:    Bradley/Millspaugh
'Date:          January 2003
'Description:   Display a list of job descriptions.

Option Strict On

Public Class CheckBoxLists
    Inherits System.Web.UI.Page

    [Web Designer Generated Code]

    Private Sub Page_Load(ByVal sender As System.Object, _
      ByVal e As System.EventArgs) Handles MyBase.Load
        'Fill the dataset

        If Not IsPostBack Then
            daJobs.Fill(DsJobs1)
            Me.DataBind()
        End If
    End Sub
End Sub
```

Retrieving the Selection

You can retrieve the selection for a RadioButtonList using the SelectedIndex and SelectedItem properties. The following code generally appears in the Click event for a button:

```
'Get selected radio button
With rblJobs
    If .SelectedIndex > -1 Then
        lblStatus.Text = "You selected " & .SelectedItem.Text
    End If
End With
```

For a CheckBoxList, which can have multiple selections, check the Selected property of each item in the Items collection:

```
Dim intIndex As Integer

'Get selected check boxes
lblCheckBoxStatus.Text = ""
For intIndex = 0 To cblJobs.Items.Count - 1
    With cblJobs.Items(intIndex)
        If .Selected Then
            lblCheckBoxStatus.Text &= .Text & "; "
        End If
    End With
Next
```

Other Controls

Some of the other controls in the Toolbox require an understanding of coding in XML and HTML and are beyond the scope of this text. However, the purpose of each control may be of interest to you.

You have seen banner ads appear on Web Pages. The **AdRotator control** randomly selects from a collection of advertisements each time the page is displayed. The control uses an XML file that contains information about the ads. Using the **Literal control,** you can add HTML to a page at run time. And the **PlaceHolder control** allows you to add controls to the Web page at run time.

▶ Feedback 7.4

1. What code is required to load data into a CheckBoxList bound to DsEmployees1?
2. What code is needed to access the index of the selected radio button in a RadioButtonList?

Multiple Tiers

If it makes sense to separate a Windows application into multiple tiers, it makes twice as much sense for a Web application. In a Web application, you don't want to increase the amount of data that must be transferred to load and reload a page. It's best to include the data access components in a separate component class file or a Web Service component, which you will learn about in Chapter 9.

Using a DataGrid in a Multitier Application

The techniques for dividing a Web application into multiple tiers are similar to those for a Windows application. However, you must handle the DataGrid control a little differently in a Web app. If a dataset is declared in the form, the DataGrid can automatically set its own column properties. But with the dataset in a separate component, you must manually set the columns at design time using the *Property Builder* dialog box of the DataGrid control (Figure 7.15). Recall that you display the *Property Builder* from the context menu of the DataGrid.

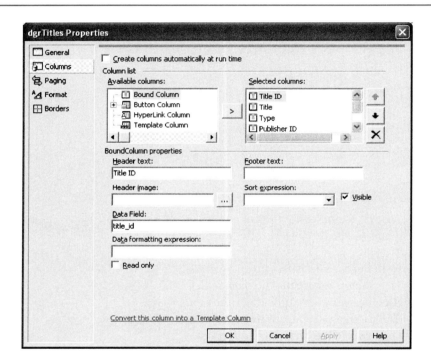

Figure   7.15

Manually set the columns and headers in the data grid's Properties dialog box.

The following multitier project passes a dataset from the data tier to a Web page, where it is stored in a session variable. The column properties of the DataGrid are set at design time and the dataset is bound to the grid in code. Figure 7.16 shows the completed form.

```
'Project:        Ch07Multitier
'Component:      Main page
'Programmer:     Bradley/Millspaugh
'Date:           January 2003
'Description:    Displays a grid of book titles. A multitier application
'                that performs the data access in a separate component.

Public Class Multitier
    Inherits System.Web.UI.Page
    Protected WithEvents dgrTitles As System.Web.UI.WebControls.DataGrid

    [Web Designer Generated Code]

    Dim dsDataset As DataSet                      'Variable to hold the dataset
```

Figure 7.16

The form for the multitier
project. The column properties
of the grid are set at design
time and the data are retrieved
from the data tier component
at run time.

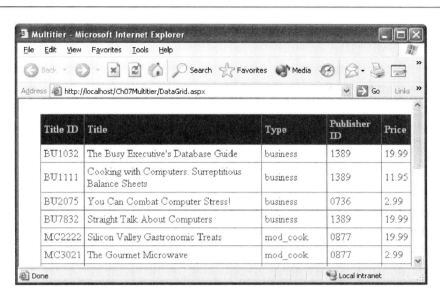

```vbnet
Private Sub Page_Load(ByVal sender As System.Object, _
    ByVal e As System.EventArgs) Handles MyBase.Load
      'Get the dataset from the data component
      Dim objData As New TitlesData()        'Instance of the data tier class

      If Not IsPostBack Then                 'Perform only the first time the page displays
          dsDataset = objData.getData()      'Retrieve the dataset
          dgrTitles.DataSource = dsDataset 'Set the grid's DataSource to the new dataset
          Session("Dataset") = dsDataset     'Save the dataset in a session variable
          Me.DataBind()                      'Bind the dataset to the grid
      Else
          dsDataset = Session("Dataset")     'Retrieve the dataset from the session variable
      End If
  End Sub

End Class

'Project:         Ch07Multitier
'Component:       TitlesData
'Programmer:      Bradley/Millspaugh
'Date:            January 2003
'Description:     The data tier for the project.

[Component Designer Generated Code]

Public Class TitlesData
    Inherits System.ComponentModel.Component

    Public Function getData() As DataSet
        'Return the dataset

        daTitles.Fill(DsTitles1)
        Return DsTitles1
    End Function
End Class
```

Using a DataList in a Multitier Application

Setting up the data binding for a DataList is a little tricky. The data binding code for each control appears in the form's HTML, so you cannot just add bindings at run time as in a Windows application. Here is the easiest and best way to set up data binding for the fields in an item template of a DataList:

- Write the data access in a separate data tier component, as you do for a Windows application. Include a GetData method that returns a dataset.

- Add the DataList control to the Web Form and name the control.

- From the *Data* tab in the toolbox, drag a DataSet component to the form. In the dialog box that opens, select the option to create a typed dataset based on the dataset .xsd file that already appears in the project. (You created a dataset in the first step, when you created the data tier component.) You are not actually going to use this DataSet component at run time, but only at design time to set up the data binding.

- Set the DataSource property of the DataList to the new DataSet component.

- Right-click the DataList and select *Edit Template*. Add the controls that you want to the ItemTemplate section.

- Set the DataBindings for each control, expanding the *Container* node as you did earlier in this chapter.

- When all of the template controls' bindings are complete, right-click the DataGrid and select *End Template Editing*.

- Delete the DataSource property of the DataList. Later, if the DataList does not fill with data, check to make sure that you remembered this step.

- In the form's Page_Load event procedure, retrieve the dataset from the data tier, set the DataGrid's DataSource property to the retrieved dataset, and bind the data.

```
Private Sub Page_Load(ByVal sender As System.Object, _
  ByVal e As System.EventArgs) Handles MyBase.Load
    'Get the data from the data tier for first-time loading

    If Not IsPostBack Then
        Dim dsBookTitles As DataSet
        Dim objData As New TitlesData()

        dsBookTitles = objData.GetData()
        Session("DataSet") = dsBookTitles
        dlTitles.DataSource = dsBookTitles
        Me.DataBind()
    End If
End Sub
```

Feedback 7.5

1. Write the code for the Component class to get the data from the Northwind Employees database.
2. What code would be needed for an Update method in the Component class?

Maintaining the State of List Boxes

As you know, the ViewState property can maintain the state of controls for multiple displays of a single page. But if the user navigates between pages, you must maintain the state, generally in a session variable. For labels and text boxes, the process is straightforward, but maintaining state of a list box is a little more complicated.

Maintaining the Selection of a Drop-Down List

If you want the form to "remember" which selection the user made from a drop-down list, you can save the SelectedIndex property in a session variable:

```
Session("CardType") = ddlCardType.SelectedIndex
```

Because you are saving the SelectedIndex, which is an integer, use this code to restore the selection:

```
ddlCardType.SelectedIndex = CType(Session("CardType"), Integer)
```

Maintaining the List in a Dynamic List Box

If you want to maintain state for a list box that has items added at run time, you must save the Items collection in a session variable:

```
Session("Titles") = lstTitles.Items
```

Saving the Items collection is easier than restoring it. You must declare a variable of type ListItemCollection and another variable to hold a single item as type ListItem. You loop through the collection and add each item to the list.

```
Dim lsiTitleItems As ListItemCollection
Dim liTitle As ListItem

lsiTitleItems = CType(Session("Titles"), ListItemCollection)
For Each liTitle In lsiTitleItems
    lstTitles.Items.Add(liTitle.ToString())
Next
```

Controlling Validation

You may need to turn validation on and off. For example, in the hands-on program that follows, the customer information is required only when the user wants to check out. Until that time, the user can display the form that shows the shopping cart multiple times without entering the personal information. You can turn off the validator controls by setting their Enabled property to False. Set the Enabled property to True to turn on the validation. After you set the property to True, use the Page.Validate method to force a validation.

```
'Validate the customer information
valCustomer.Enabled = True
valCity.Enabled = True
valAccountNumber.Enabled = True
valExpiration.Enabled = True
Page.Validate()              'Force a validation

If Page.IsValid Then
    Server.Transfer("Confirmation.aspx")
End If
```

Your Hands-On Programming Example

This project is considerably more involved than any done so far in this text. In it you will create a multitier and multipage application for R 'n R for purchasing books online. This is a shopping cart application, which allows the user to select book titles to add to the cart and to check out.

Include a separate data tier component for the database access, which produces the list of titles for purchase.

Home Page The Home page should include the company logo and a link to the Titles page.

Titles Page Display a list of book titles and prices from the pubs database. Allow the user to select an item from the list and add it to the "Shopping Cart". *Note:* At this point items can only be added to the cart (in the next chapter we'll discuss the delete process).

Shopping Cart Page (Purchase) The user should be able to display the purchase including the total purchase price, shipping charges, total amount due, and the number of items ordered. Prompt for personal information: name, street, city, state, and ZIP code; and credit card information: card type, card number, and expiration date.

The user should not have to enter the personal information until ready to complete the purchase. At that time, you must validate for missing fields. However, if the user *does* enter the personal information and return to select another title, the personal information must remain on the page.

In this example, a new style, called .NUMBER (with the period) is added to the .css file, the file is linked to the Purchase page, and the NUMBER style (without the period) is assigned to the CssClass property of the numeric fields, in order to right-align the numeric fields. Refer to "Using Styles" in Chapter 6 for a review of the technique.

Confirmation Page The *Complete Purchase* button should display a screen confirming the order and thanking the customer *by name* for the order.

Include a link back to the home page from all pages.

Planning the Project

Sketch the forms (Figure 7.17) that your users sign off as meeting their needs.

Figure 7.17

The planning sketches of the hands-on programming example: a. the Home page; b. the Titles page; c. the Purchase (shopping cart) page; d. the Confirmation page.

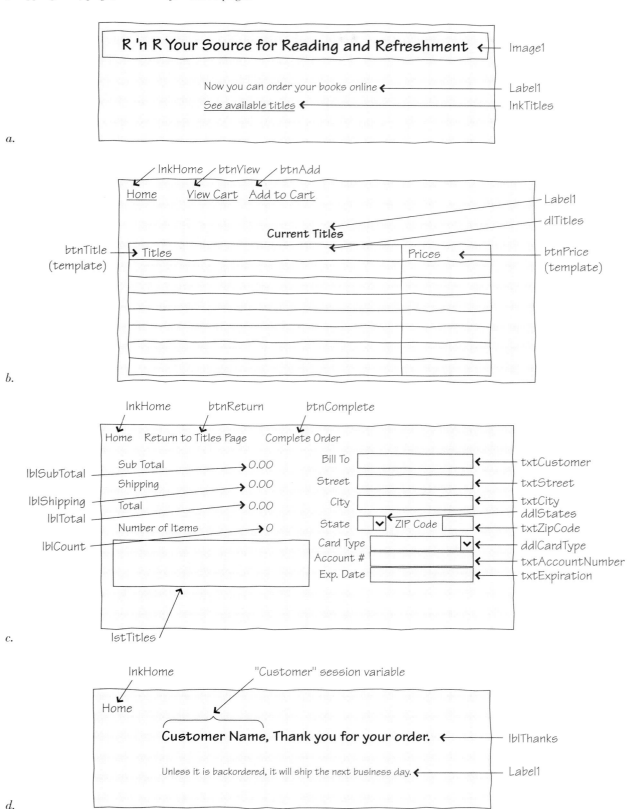

Plan the Objects, Properties, and Methods

Plan the two tiers. Determine the objects and property settings for the forms and their controls, and for the data tier component. Figure 7.18 shows the diagram of the program components.

Figure 7.18

The components for the hands-on programming example.

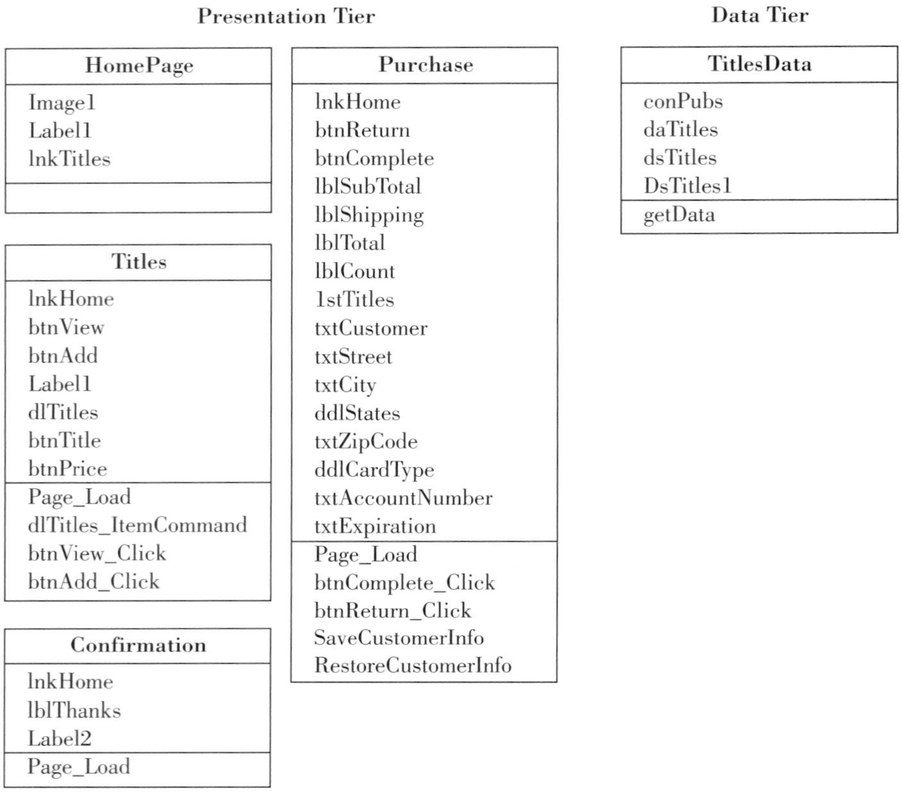

Presentation Tier

HomePage
Image1
Label1
lnkTitles

Titles
lnkHome
btnView
btnAdd
Label1
dlTitles
btnTitle
btnPrice
Page_Load
dlTitles_ItemCommand
btnView_Click
btnAdd_Click

Confirmation
lnkHome
lblThanks
Label2
Page_Load

Purchase
lnkHome
btnReturn
btnComplete
lblSubTotal
lblShipping
lblTotal
lblCount
1stTitles
txtCustomer
txtStreet
txtCity
ddlStates
txtZipCode
ddlCardType
txtAccountNumber
txtExpiration
Page_Load
btnComplete_Click
btnReturn_Click
SaveCustomerInfo
RestoreCustomerInfo

Data Tier

TitlesData
conPubs
daTitles
dsTitles
DsTitles1
getData

Presentation Tier

HomePage Page

Object	Property	Setting
Class	Name	HomePage
	Title	R 'n R Book Orders
Image1	ImageUrl	C:\Inetpub\wwwroot\Ch07HandsOn\RnRLogo.GIF
Label1	Text	Now you can order your books online.
lnkTitles	Text	See available titles.
	NavigateUrl	Titles.aspx

Event procedures/Methods	Actions—Pseudocode
(none)	

Titles Page

Object	Property	Setting
Class	Name	Titles
	Title	R 'n R Book Titles
lnkHome	NavigateUrl	HomePage.aspx
	Text	Home
btnView	Text	View Cart
btnAdd	Text	Add to Cart
	Enabled	False
dlTitles	ID	dlTitles
ItemTemplate		
btnTitle	CommandName	Select
btnPrice	CommandName	Select

Event procedures/Methods	Actions—Pseudocode

Page_Load	If not PostBack
	    Instantiate the data tier.
	    Retrieve the dataset.
	    Save the dataset in a session variable.
	    Set the data list's DataSource to the dataset.
	    Bind the form's controls.

dlTitles_ItemCommand	If CommandName = "Select"
	    Retrieve the dataset from the session variable.
	    Find the selected row.
	    Save the title and price from the selected row in
	       session variables.
	    Enable btnAdd.
	    Deselect the selected row.

btnView_Click	Set the Action session variable to "View". Navigate to the Purchase page.
btnAdd_Click	Set the Action session variable to "Add". Navigate to the Purchase page.

Purchase Page

Object	Property	Setting
Class	Name	Purchase
	Title	R 'n R Book Purchases
lnkHome	NavigateUrl	HomePage.aspx
	Text	Home
btnReturn	Text	Return to Titles Page
btnComplete	Text	Complete Order
Label1	Text	Sub Total
Label2	Text	Shipping
Label3	Text	Total
Label4	Text	Number of Items
lblSubTotal	Text	(blank)
	CssClass	NUMBER
lblShipping	Text	(blank)
	CssClass	NUMBER
lblTotal	Text	(blank)
	CssClass	NUMBER
lblCount	Text	(blank)
	CssClass	NUMBER
lstTitles	ID	lstTitles
Label5	Text	Bill To
Label6	Text	Street
Label7	Text	City
Label8	Text	State
Label9	Text	ZIP Code
Label10	Text	Card Type
Label11	Text	Account #
Label12	Text	Exp. Date
txtCustomer	Text	(blank)
txtStreet	Text	(blank)

Purchase Page—*continued*

Object	Property	Setting
txtCity	Text	(blank)
ddlStates	Items	"AL", "AZ", "CA","CO"
txtZipCode	Text	(blank)
ddlCardType	Items	"Visa", "MasterCard", "American Express", "Discover"
txtAccountNumber	Text	(blank)
txtExpiration	Text	(blank)
valCustomer	ControlToValidate Enabled ErrorMessage Text	txtCustomer False Name is required. *
valCity	ControlToValidate Enabled ErrorMessage Text	txtCity False City is required. *
valZip	ControlToValidate Enabled ErrorMessage Text	txtZipCode False ZIP code is required. *
valAccountNumber	ControlToValidate Enabled ErrorMessage Text	txtAccountNumber False Account # is required. *
valExpiration	ControlToValidate Enabled ErrorMessage Text	txtExpiration False Expiration date is required. *
ValidationSummary1		

Event procedures/Methods	Actions—Pseudocode

Page_Load	If not PostBack
	    Restore session variables.
	
	If Action = "Add" (not "View")
	    If price > 0
	        Add the title to the list.
	        Increment the count.
	        Add price to the subtotal.
	        Calculate the shipping charge.
	        Total = shipping charge + subtotal
	        Save variables in session variables.
	Display calculated values in labels.

btnComplete_Click	Enable the validator controls. Validate the page. If the page is valid Transfer to the confirmation page.
btnReturn_Click	Save the customer information in session variables. Navigate to the Titles page.
SaveCustomerInfo	Save all customer info in session variables. If validator controls are enabled Disable all validator controls.
RestoreCustomerInfo	Restore customer session variables to screen controls.

Confirmation Page

Object	Property	Setting
Class	Name Title	Confirmation R 'n R Order Confirmation
lnkHome	NavigateUrl Text	HomePage.aspx Home
lblThanks	Text	Thank You for Your Order.
Label2	Text	Unless it is backordered, it will ship the next business day.

Event procedures/Methods	Actions—Pseudocode
Page_Load	Concatenate name from session variable to "Thank You" label.

Data Tier

Object	Property	Setting
Class	Name	TitlesData
conPubs	Name	conPubs
daTitles	Name	daTitles
dsTitles	Name	dsTitles
DsTitles1	Name	DsTitles1

Methods	Actions—Pseudocode
getData	Create a dataset that holds the titles table. Return the dataset.

Write the Project

Following the sketches in Figure 7.17, create the forms. Figure 7.19 shows the completed forms.

- Create the data tier component, adding the objects from your plan. You need to create this first so that the dataset is available when you create the Titles page.

- Write the methods for the data tier component, following the pseudocode.

- Create each of the Web Forms, setting the properties according to your plans.

- Write the code for the forms. Working from the pseudocode, write each event procedure.

- When you complete the code, test the operation multiple times. Make sure that you can navigate back and forth between the pages without losing data. Try entering some of the customer information and then navigating back and selecting another title. Attempt to complete the transaction without completing the customer information. Make sure that all operations work correctly.

Figure 7.19

The forms for the hands-on programming example: a. the Home page; b. the Titles page; c. the Purchase (shopping cart) page; d. the Confirmation page.

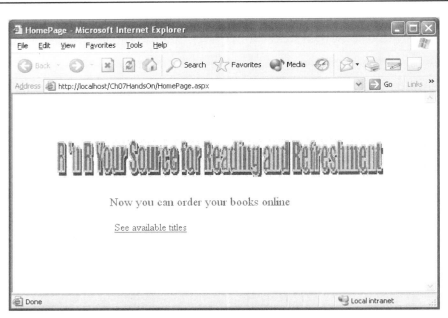

a.

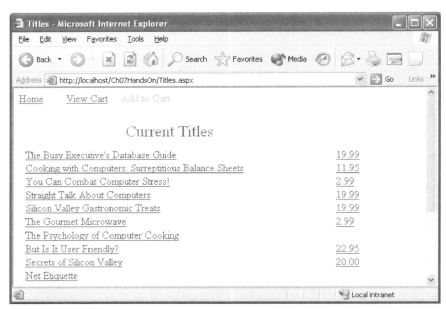

b.

Figure 7.19

Continued

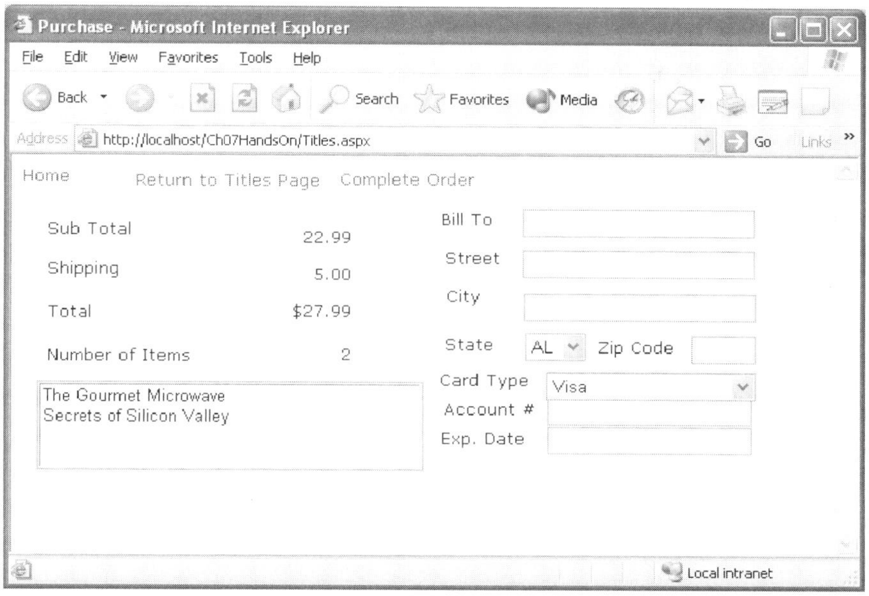

c.

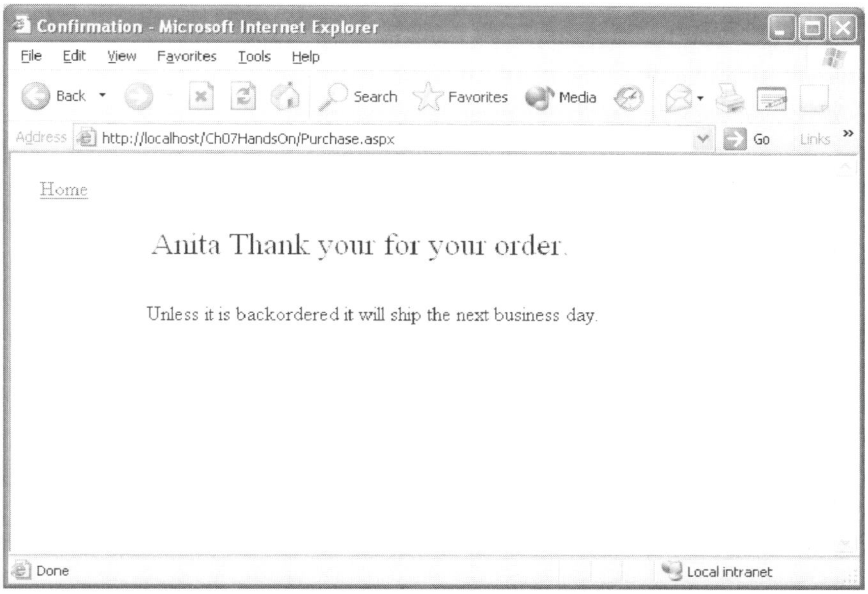

d.

The Project Coding Solution

Home Page

```
'Project:        Ch07HandsOn
'Page:           HomePage
'Programmer:     Bradley/Millspaugh
'Date:           January 2003
'Description:    Display the company information.

Option Strict On

Public Class HomePage
    Inherits System.Web.UI.Page
    Protected WithEvents Image1 As System.Web.UI.WebControls.Image
    Protected WithEvents lnkTitles As System.Web.UI.WebControls.HyperLink
    Protected WithEvents Label1 As System.Web.UI.WebControls.Label

    [Web Form Designer Generated Code]

End Class
```

Titles Page

```
'Project:        Ch07HandsOn
'Page:           Titles
'Programmer:     Bradley/Millspaugh
'Date:           January 2003
'Description:    Display book titles in a grid. Allow the user to select
'                titles and add to their shopping cart.

Option Strict On

Public Class Titles
    Inherits System.Web.UI.Page

    [Web Form Designer Generated Code]

    Private Sub Page_Load(ByVal sender As System.Object, _
      ByVal e As System.EventArgs) Handles MyBase.Load
        'Get the data from the data tier for first-time loading

        If Not IsPostBack Then
            Dim dsBookTitles As DataSet
            Dim objData As New TitlesData()

            dsBookTitles = objData.GetData()
            Session("DataSet") = dsBookTitles
            dlTitles.DataSource = dsBookTitles
            Me.DataBind()
        End If
    End Sub

    Private Sub dlTitles_ItemCommand(ByVal source As Object, _
      ByVal e As System.Web.UI.WebControls.DataListCommandEventArgs) _
      Handles dlTitles.ItemCommand
        'Find the current title and add the price to the total
        Dim drwCurrentTitle As DataRow
```

```
        Dim dsTitlesSession As DataSet

        'Check CommandName from link buttons
        If e.CommandName = "Select" Then
            'Retrieve the dataset
            dsTitlesSession = CType(Session("DataSet"), DataSet)
            'Find the selected row
            drwCurrentTitle = dsTitlesSession.Tables("titles").Rows(e.Item.ItemIndex)
            'Save the title and price from the selected row
            Session("Title") = drwCurrentTitle("title").ToString()
            Session("Price") = drwCurrentTitle("price").ToString()
            'Enable the link button for the Purchases page
            btnAdd.Enabled = True
            'Deselect the selected list item
            dlTitles.SelectedIndex = -1
        End If
    End Sub

    Private Sub btnView_Click(ByVal sender As System.Object, _
      ByVal e As System.EventArgs) Handles btnView.Click
        'Navigate to the Purchase page

        Session("Action") = "View"
        Server.Transfer("Purchase.aspx")
    End Sub

    Private Sub btnAdd_Click(ByVal sender As System.Object, _
      ByVal e As System.EventArgs) Handles btnAdd.Click
        'Navigate to the Purchase page

        Session("Action") = "Add"
        Server.Transfer("Purchase.aspx")
    End Sub
End Class
```

Purchase Page

```
'Project:        Ch07HandsOn
'Page:           Purchase
'Programmer:     Bradley/Millspaugh
'Date:           January 2003
'Description:    Shopping cart page. Displays a list of selected titles,
'                tax, and totals. Allows user to enter personal information
'                to complete the sale.

Option Strict On

Public Class Purchase
    Inherits System.Web.UI.Page

    [Web Form Designer Generated Code]

    Private Sub Page_Load(ByVal sender As System.Object, _
      ByVal e As System.EventArgs) Handles MyBase.Load
        'Build the page
        Dim decPrice As Decimal
        Dim decShipping As Decimal
        Dim decTotal As Decimal
```

```vb
        Dim decSubtotal As Decimal
        Dim intCount As Integer
        Dim liTitle As ListItem
        Dim licTitleItems As ListItemCollection
        Dim strAction As String

        'For postback of same page, all values should already be filled in
        If Not IsPostBack Then
            Try          'Skip if session variables have not yet been created

                'Restore all session variables
                intCount = CType(Session("Count"), Integer)
                decShipping = CType(Session("Shipping"), Decimal)
                decSubtotal = CType(Session("Subtotal"), Decimal)
                decTotal = CType(Session("Total"), Decimal)
                decPrice = CType(Session("Price"), Decimal)
                strAction = CType(Session("Action"), String)
                licTitleItems = CType(Session("Titles"), ListItemCollection)
                For Each liTitle In licTitleItems
                    lstTitles.Items.Add(liTitle.ToString())
                Next
                RestoreCustomerInfo()
            Catch
            End Try

            If strAction = "Add" Then
                If decPrice > 0 Then
                    'Add the title to the list
                    lstTitles.Items.Add(Session("Title").ToString())
                    'Add to the subtotal and calculate shipping
                    intCount += 1
                    decSubtotal += decPrice
                    Select Case decSubtotal
                        Case Is < 50D
                            decShipping = 5D
                        Case Is < 100D
                            decShipping = 9D
                        Case Else
                            decShipping = 15D
                    End Select
                    decTotal = decSubtotal + decShipping

                    'Save data for next page access
                    Session("Count") = intCount
                    Session("Shipping") = decShipping
                    Session("Subtotal") = decSubtotal
                    Session("Total") = decTotal
                    Session("Titles") = lstTitles.Items
                    SaveCustomerInfo()
                End If
            End If

            'Display calculated values on the page
            lblSubTotal.Text = FormatNumber(decSubtotal)
            lblShipping.Text = FormatNumber(decShipping)
            lblTotal.Text = FormatCurrency(decTotal)
            lblCount.Text = intCount.ToString()
        End If
    End Sub
```

```vb
    Private Sub btnComplete_Click(ByVal sender As System.Object, _
      ByVal e As System.EventArgs) Handles btnComplete.Click
        'Display the confirmation page

        'Validate the customer information
        valCustomer.Enabled = True
        valCity.Enabled = True
        valAccountNumber.Enabled = True
        valExpiration.Enabled = True
        Page.Validate()

        If Page.IsValid Then
            SaveCustomerInfo()
            Server.Transfer("Confirmation.aspx")
        End If
    End Sub

    Private Sub btnReturn_Click(ByVal sender As System.Object, _
      ByVal e As System.EventArgs) Handles btnReturn.Click
        'Return to the Titles page

        SaveCustomerInfo()
        Server.Transfer("Titles.aspx")
    End Sub

    Private Sub SaveCustomerInfo()
        'Save customer info for return to this page

        Session("Customer") = txtCustomer.Text
        Session("Street") = txtStreet.Text
        Session("City") = txtCity.Text
        Session("State") = ddlStates.SelectedIndex
        Session("ZIP") = txtZipCode.Text
        Session("CardType") = ddlCardType.SelectedIndex
        Session("AccountNumber") = txtAccountNumber.Text
        Session("Expiration") = txtExpiration.Text

        'Disable validation if enabled
        If valCustomer.Enabled Then
            valCustomer.Enabled = False
            valCity.EnableClientScript = False
            valAccountNumber.Enabled = False
            valExpiration.Enabled = False
        End If
    End Sub

    Private Sub RestoreCustomerInfo()
        'Restore any customer information that has been entered

        txtCustomer.Text = CType(Session("Customer"), String)
        txtStreet.Text = CType(Session("Street"), String)
        txtCity.Text = CType(Session("City"), String)
        ddlStates.SelectedIndex = CType(Session("State"), Integer)
        txtZipCode.Text = CType(Session("ZIP"), String)
        ddlCardType.SelectedIndex = CType(Session("CardType"), Integer)
        txtAccountNumber.Text = CType(Session("AccountNumber"), String)
        txtExpiration.Text = CType(Session("Expiration"), String)
    End Sub

End Class
```

Confirmation Page

```
'Project:        Ch07HandsOn
'Page:           Confirmation
'Programmer:     Bradley/Millspaugh
'Date:           January 2003
'Description:    Display a confirmation of the order.

Option Strict On

Public Class Confirmation
    Inherits System.Web.UI.Page

    [Web Form Designer Generated Code]

    Private Sub Page_Load(ByVal sender As System.Object, _
      ByVal e As System.EventArgs) Handles MyBase.Load
        'Personalize the thank you

        lblThanks.Text = Session("Customer").ToString() & ", Thank you for your order."
    End Sub

End Class
```

The Data Tier Component

```
'Project:        Ch07HandsOn
'Component:      TitlesData
'Programmer:     Bradley/Millspaugh
'Date:           January 2003
'Description:    Data tier

Option Strict On

Public Class TitlesData
    Inherits System.ComponentModel.Component

    [Component Designer Generated Code]

    Public Function GetData() As DataSet
        'Return the dataset

        daTitles.Fill(DsTitles1)
        Return DsTitles1
    End Function

End Class
```

Styles.css
Add this code to the file:

```
.NUMBER
{
    text-align: right;
}
```

Summary

1. A data reader provides a forward-only connection to a database for quick access of data. It is appropriate for small amounts of data that are not to be updated or for loading information into a control.

2. Web projects require a `DataBind` method to fill bound controls. All controls can be bound at once with a command to the form's method, `Me.DataBind()`.

3. A connection's ConnectionString can be set as a dynamic property, which uses a key/value pair in Web.config.

4. The Web Server DataGrid control has many features. It easily allows for pagination if there is a large number of rows. Data can easily be formatted and sorted.

5. The DataGrid's Property Builder offers an easy way to set the data source, column information, and paging styles, as well as setting formats and borders.

6. DataGrid and DataList controls have predefined actions for Command-Names. Naming a control "Select" causes the ItemCommand event to fire.

7. The DataGrid control provides several types of columns including Bound-Column, ButtonColumn, HyperlinkColumn, and TemplateColumn.

8. The DataList control allows great flexibility in laying out the elements from each record in a data source and can handle images and links as easily as text. DataList requires a template for at least the Items to indicate how the data are arranged. The appearance of the DataList may look like a table or flow like a list. You also have the option of displaying the information vertically or horizontally. Horizontal works well for a group of links at the top of a Web page.

9. The EventArgs argument of the ItemCommand event can indicate the selected row within a DataList, allowing for easy retrieval of detail information without the expense of a call to the server and without the use of a parameterized query.

10. The CheckBoxList and RadioButtonList provide alternate displays for the type of information that normally goes in a list box or combo box. They both work well with bound data. Additional controls are the Literal, the Place-holder, and the AdRotator.

11. With Web pages the use of multitier design is even more important than in Windows applications. Creating a data tier uses the same techniques as in a Windows application.

12. Using a DataGrid in a multitier application requires that you set up the columns manually and bind the grid at run time.

13. Setting up a DataList for a multitier application requires that you temporarily place a DataSet component on the form to set up the data bindings for the bound fields in the Item Template.

14. To maintain the state of a list box, you can store the SelectedIndex property in a session variable.

15. Maintaining the state for items that have been added to a list box requires that you save the Items collection in a session variable and restore the list by looping through the ListItemCollection to add each saved ListItem to the list.

16. To turn off the action of validator controls, set their Enabled property to False. After enabling the controls, force a validation with the `Page.Validate` method.

Key Terms

AdRotator control *255*

AllowPaging property *244*

AllowSorting property *244*

CheckBoxList control *253*

Command object *236*

CommandName property *246*

CurrentPageIndex property *244*

`DataBind` method *238*

DataGrid control *241*

DataList control *246*

DataReader object *236*

dynamic connection string *240*

ItemCommand event *248*

ItemTemplate *246*

Literal control *255*

PlaceHolder control *255*

RadioButtonList control *253*

SortCommand event *244*

Review Questions

1. Explain the differences between how a DataReader works versus a dataset.
2. What is a Command object and what would you expect to find in its CommandText property?
3. What is a dynamic property? Where is it stored? Why would you use one?
4. What extra steps must be taken to display data in a Web DataGrid server control compared to the Windows DataGrid control?
5. How is sorting accomplished for a DataGrid? Why is it necessary to use a DataView?
6. How do you set up paging on a DataGrid? What styles are available?
7. In what situation would you likely want to use a DataList control?
8. What is the purpose of the DataList's template? What steps are necessary to add the template?
9. What is the purpose of the CommandName property of a DataGrid and DataList?
10. To what object does the ItemCommand event belong? When does it fire? What action(s) would you likely code in its event procedure?
11. Give the purpose of each of the following controls:
    a. DataList
    b. AdRotator
    c. CheckBoxList
    d. RadioButtonList
    e. Literal
    f. PlaceHolder
12. What additional steps must you take to include a bound DataGrid control in a multitier application?
13. What additional steps must you take to include a bound DataList control in a multitier application?
14. Explain how to store and retrieve the state for a drop-down list in a multipage application.

15. Explain how to store and retrieve the state for a dynamic list, which holds items that have been added during the program run.

16. How can you force the validator controls to ignore the validation until you are ready to validate?

Programming Exercises

7.1 Write a project that uses a Web Form to display the Employee ID, Last Name, First Name, Hire Date, and Extension from the Employees table in the Northwind database. Use a data reader to load a drop-down list that holds the employee name. After the user selects a name, display the rest of the fields in labels.

7.2 Modify Exercise 7.1 to include a link to a second Web page. The link should say "Add this employee to the list." On the second page, display a list box with the names of the employees added to the list and a link back to the main page. Make sure that the user can navigate back and forth between the two pages and keep the data entered by the user on both pages.

7.3 Modify Exercise 7.2 to have a separate data tier component to supply the dataset.

7.4 Display the Suppliers table from the Northwind database in a data grid. Allow the grid to be sorted by Supplier ID, Company Name, or Region. Include pagination. Select a formatting style for the grid and use appropriate headers for the columns; that is, use Supplier ID with a space, not the default SupplierID.

7.5 Modify Exercise 7.4 to have a separate data tier component to supply the dataset.

7.6 Create a Web page that displays the Product ID and ProductName from the Northwind Products table in a DataList. Allow the user to display the Unit Price, the Units in Stock, and the Units on Order when a product is selected from the list. Use a separate data tier component.

Case Studies

Claytor's Cottages

1. Modify the Web application for the Chapter 6 case study. Add a page that displays the guest information in a data grid that allows for sorting by last name and by last visit date. Include pagination. Modify the room pages to include the information from the database.

(You created the page with static text in Chapter 6; now it's time to connect it to a data source.)

2. Modify the project to use a separate data tier component.

Christian's Car Rentals

1. Modify the Web application for the Chapter 6 Car Rental case study. Add a Web page that contains a list of the vehicles by manufacturer and model. When the user selects an item from the list, display the details for that car on a separate page. Include a Select button that transfers control to a Billing page. The Billing page should include the daily rate for the vehicle and rental terms. It also must collect customer information:

name, address, city, state, ZIP, credit card type (from a drop-down list), account number, and a phone number.

Allow navigation across all pages and maintain all values entered by the user.

2. Modify the project to use a separate data tier component.

8

Related Database Tables and Updates in Web Forms

1. Display data from related tables on Web Forms.

2. Edit, add, and delete records on Web Forms.

3. Determine whether to use bound or unbound fields to display database data.

4. Write and execute SQL statements directly to a database.

5. Alternately display a text box or a drop-down list, depending on the operation.

In the previous chapter, you displayed database data from a single table on Web Forms. In this chapter you will expand your knowledge to include displaying related tables and allowing updates to a database from a Web page.

Displaying Data from Related Tables

Many of the techniques for databases carry over from Windows to Web Forms. But due to the static nature of Web pages, you must adjust many of the techniques that you use. For example, navigating from one record to the next does not make any sense when every time the page displays, the dataset must be recreated and the page completely rerendered. The most common technique for Web database applications is to allow the user to enter or select a particular record and then display the details for that record.

Creating a Related Table Application

The following related-table example displays data from the stores and sales tables of the SQL Server pubs database. The user selects the store from a drop-down list; the program finds the record for the selected store in the stores table, displays additional fields for the store, finds the sales for that store in the sales table, and displays the sales in a grid. Figure 8.1 shows the completed form for this application. To refresh your memory about setting up the 1:M relationship between the stores and sales tables, refer to the hands-on example in Chapter 4 and Figures 4.2 (sample data showing the relationship), 4.6 (generating the dataset), 4.7 (setting up the relationship), 4.10 (the diagram of the dataset showing the relationship), 4.18 (output showing sales for a chosen store), and 4.19 (the components). The sections that follow illustrate the techniques that you use to create this Web application.

Always assign a dynamic ConnectionString property for the connection and modify the key value in Web.config to a generic connection string:

```
<add key="conPubs.Connec
tionString"value="server
=(local)\NetSDK;Trusted_
Connection=yes;database
=pubs"/>
```

Keep the ConnectionString property in the Properties window set to your specific machine, so that you can modify the dataset definition; the dynamic connection string is used at run time and will make the project portable. ■

Figure 8.1

The output of the related-table application. The user selects a store from the drop-down list and the program finds and displays the data from the stores and sales tables.

StoreSales - Microsoft Internet Explorer

File   Edit   View   Favorites   Tools   Help

Back   Search   Favorites   Media

Address   http://localhost/Ch08RelatedTables/StoreSales.aspx   Go   Links

Store Name	Eric the Read Books
Store ID	6380
Address	788 Catamaugus Ave.
City	Seattle
State	WA
Zip Code	98056

stor_id	ord_num	ord_date	qty	payterms	title_id
6380	1111	1/1/2001 12:00:00 AM	2	30	TC7777
6380	6871	9/14/1994 12:00:00 AM	5	Net 60	BU1032
6380	722a	9/13/1994 12:00:00 AM	3	Net 60	PS2091

Done   Local intranet

Filling and Saving the Dataset

You want to fill the dataset for the initial Page_Load. But remember that for every postback to the server, the application is completely reloaded and treated as a new application. The Page_Load procedure executes for every postback, which occurs at least once for every Click event procedure. For this reason, you should save the dataset, usually in a session variable, and only fill the dataset on the first execution (not a postback).

```
Private Sub Page_Load(ByVal sender As System.Object, _
  ByVal e As System.EventArgs) Handles MyBase.Load
    'Fill the dataset

  If Not IsPostBack Then
      'Fill the dataset
      daStores.Fill(DsStoreSales1)
      daSales.Fill(DsStoreSales1)
      'Save the dataset
      Session("Dataset") = DsStoreSales1
      ...
```

Determining Which Fields to Bind

Data binding is completely different for Web controls than for Windows controls. Web Forms do not have a binding manager, as in Windows Forms, so the concept of a "current record" does not exist. And binding is only one-way; that is, you can automatically display database fields in bound controls, but any changes to the data in the controls do not pass back automatically to the data source.

You will find data binding really helpful for filling drop-down lists and grids. But usually it's preferable to keep text boxes and labels unbound. You generally fill the text boxes and labels at run time; assigning values to the controls is easier and more efficient than the code to bind at run time. In the following example, we show both methods for filling the form's text boxes (refer to Figure 8.1).

Assume that you have created a data view that holds the selected record, the selected store in our example. Here is the code to bind the value of the Stor_id field to the text box and to directly assign the value of the Store_id field. You can choose from the two methods, since both fill the text box with data and neither automatically returns changes to the data source:

```
'Bind the data field to the text box
txtStoreID.Text = DataBinder.Eval(dvStoreView, "(0).Stor_id").ToString()

'Assign the data field to the text box
txtStoreID.Text = dvStoreView(0).Item("Stor_id").ToString()
```

Note that the second example above can be shortened, since the Item property is assumed if you leave it out. The examples in this chapter use the Item property for clarity.

```
txtStoreID.Text = dvStoreView(0)("Stor_id").ToString()
```

Each of these examples refers to the first (and only) row in the data view (dvStoreView(0)), and then to the named element of the row, which must be a field name from the database file.

The example program uses both bound and unbound controls. The drop-down list for store names is bound at design time and filled in the Page_Load event procedure. The text boxes for the store information are unbound and filled with data after a selection is made from the list (and initially, so that when the form displays, the text boxes match the store name that appears in the list). The data grid is bound at run time, so that the grid automatically fills with data after a selection is made.

Finding and Displaying Selected Data Items

When working with related tables you generally need to display fields from both the parent and the child records. You can filter the data using a data view to find the parent record and a second data view to filter for the matching child rows.

The steps are

- Filter the view for the parent.

- Assign the parent record fields to the text boxes.

- Filter the view for the matching child records.

- Bind the grid to the child data view.

The Complete Related-Table Program

Here is the complete program. The code to find and display the selected data is found in the ddlStoreNames_SelectedIndexChanged event procedure. Remember that you must set the drop-down list's AutoPostBack property to True so that this event fires a postback.

```
'Project:        Ch08RelatedTables
'Programmer:     Bradley/Millspaugh
'Date:           January 2003
'Description:    Display store and sales data for a selected store.
'                Uses related tables, bound and unbound controls,
'                in a single-tier application.

Option Strict On

Public Class StoreSales

[Web Form Designer Generated Code]

    Private Sub Page_Load(ByVal sender As System.Object, _
        ByVal e As System.EventArgs) Handles MyBase.Load
        'Fill the dataset

        If Not IsPostBack Then
            'Fill the dataset
            daStores.Fill(DsStoreSales1)
            daSales.Fill(DsStoreSales1)
            'Bind the drop-down list
            Me.DataBind()
```

```
                    Session("Dataset") = DsStoreSales1
                    'Display store data for the initial store
                    ddlStoreNames_SelectedIndexChanged(sender, e)
            End If
      End Sub

      Private Sub ddlStoreNames_SelectedIndexChanged( _
        ByVal sender As System.Object, ByVal e As System.EventArgs) _
        Handles ddlStoreNames.SelectedIndexChanged
            'Store changed. Get sales and store data.
            Dim dsData As DataSet
            Dim dvStoreView As New DataView()
            Dim dvSalesView As New DataView()

            'Retrieve the dataset from the session variable
            dsData = CType(Session("Dataset"), DataSet)

            'Find the store
            With dvStoreView
                .Table = dsData.Tables("Stores")
                .RowFilter = "Stor_id = '" & ddlStoreNames.SelectedItem.Value & "'"
            End With

            'Set the text boxes to the data values for the selected store
            txtStoreID.Text = dvStoreView(0).Item("Stor_id").ToString()
            txtCity.Text = dvStoreView(0).Item("City").ToString()
            txtAddress.Text = dvStoreView(0).Item("stor_Address").ToString()
            txtState.Text = dvStoreView(0).Item("State").ToString()
            txtZipCode.Text = dvStoreView(0).Item("Zip").ToString()

            'Alternate code: Bind the text boxes to the data values for the selected store
            'txtStoreID.Text = DataBinder.Eval(dvStoreView, "(0).Stor_id").ToString()
            'txtCity.Text = DataBinder.Eval(dvStoreView, "(0).City").ToString()
            'txtAddress.Text = DataBinder.Eval(dvStoreView, "(0).stor_Address").ToString()
            'txtState.Text = DataBinder.Eval(dvStoreView, "(0).State").ToString()
            'txtZipCode.Text = DataBinder.Eval(dvStoreView, "(0).Zip").ToString()
            'Create a data view with the sales for this store

            'Find the matching sales rows
            With dvSalesView
                .Table = dsData.Tables("sales")
                .RowFilter = "stor_id = '" & ddlStoreNames.SelectedItem.Value & "'"
            End With

            'Bind the data view to the grid
            With dgrSales
                .DataSource = dvSalesView
                .DataBind()
            End With
      End Sub
End Class
```

▶ **Feedback 8.1**

1. Write the statement(s) to set up a data view and filter for a book by the ISBN. The ISBN comes from a DataList called ddlISBN.
2. After completing the preceding step, you have a data view with book information for a specific ISBN and want the value of the Title field to

appear in txtTitle. Write both the statement to bind the Title field to txt-Title and to directly assign the field to the control.

Updating a Database

The logic steps for updating a database in a Web application are similar to those in a Windows application, but the implementation details vary considerably. Some of the changes are due to the differences between Web controls and Windows controls. For example, a Web drop-down list does not have an associated text box and cannot be bound to one table to fill the Items collection and to another table to determine the item to display. Other changes are necessary due to the different method of data binding, as discussed in the earlier section, and to the static nature of Web pages. It doesn't make sense to recreate a dataset for each postback and to issue a `DataSet.Update` method across the Internet, which transmits the entire dataset to update a single record.

In the following example, which updates the Books table in the Access file RnRBooks.mdb, you will learn to use Web controls and Web techniques to update a database. The program uses the OleDB data provider, but you could just as easily switch to the SQL data provider and update a SQL Server database.

This update program also introduces writing and executing the SQL statements `UPDATE`, `INSERT INTO`, and `DELETE FROM`, which update single records in the database. Figure 8.2 shows the completed Web page for reference as you work through the steps to create the program.

Note: Updating a database from a Web application presents security issues. Make sure to read through the section "Database Security for Web Applications" before attempting to run any of the following code.

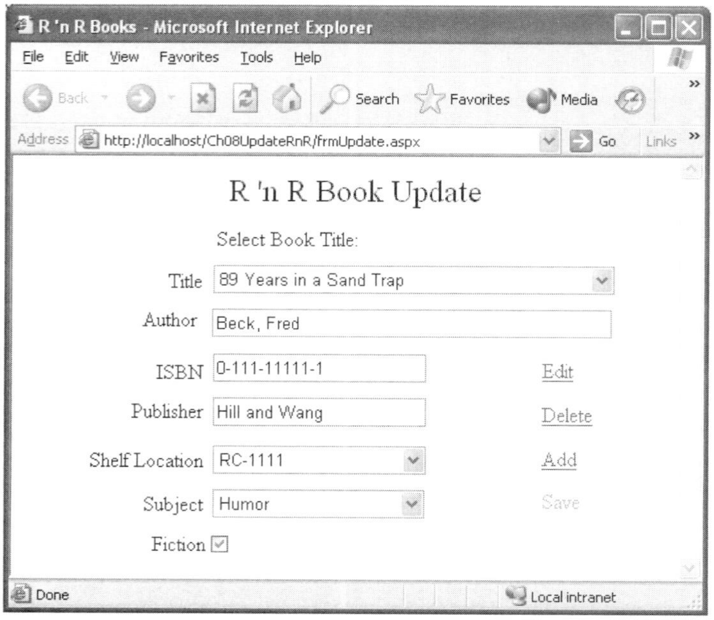

Figure 8.2

The completed Web update form. The user selects a book title from the drop-down list to display the record. The user can then choose to update or delete the selected record, or add a new record.

Managing State

As you know, Web pages do not maintain values from one invocation to the next. For a single-page postback to the server, the ViewState of server controls can maintain the values of the controls. However, if a user navigates to another page and back again, the ViewState data are lost; the state remains only for single-page server postbacks.

The static nature of Web pages also affects program variables. In Windows applications you are used to declaring module-level variables and/or static variables that maintain their values as long as the application runs. But in Web programs, the entire application file is reloaded for every postback to the server, which means that all variables are reinitialized. If you want to maintain any values for multiple event calls, you must manage the variables yourself, usually in session variables. For example, if you want to set a boolean variable indicating that an Add operation is in progress and check that value in another event procedure, or a later call to the same event procedure, you must create a session variable, rather than a module-level variable.

The following abbreviated event procedure shows the btnAdd_Click event procedure, which handles both an Add and a Cancel. This program, similar to the Windows program in Chapter 5, changes the text on the Add button to "Cancel" when either an Add or Edit is in progress.

```
Private Sub btnAdd_Click(...) Handles btnAdd.Click
    'Begin an Add operation or cancel the current operation
    Dim blnAddInProgress As Boolean

    If btnAdd.Text = "Add" Then    'Add button clicked
        '...Steps to begin an Add
        Session("AddInProgress") = True
    Else                           'Cancel button clicked
        '...Steps to cancel an Add or Edit
        blnAddInProgress = CType(Session("AddInProgress"), Boolean)
        If blnAddInProgress Then 'Cancel Add, display the first record
            'Set up the record to display
        End If
        Session("AddInProgress") = False
    End If
End Sub
```

Web Drop-Down Lists

The drop-down list controls for Web Forms have many capabilities, but they are completely different from Windows combo boxes and list boxes. The fact that drop-down lists do not have an associated text box greatly changes program logic if you want to allow the user to make new entries as well as select from the list. And the list binding properties will change your programming style considerably.

Filling and Accessing Web Drop-Down Lists

You cannot fill a drop-down list with the values from one table and bind the list to a single field in another data table. You must choose—either fill the list with values *or* bind to the database field to display. The sample program uses data binding to fill the list and assigns the value to display at run time. Notice in Figure 8.2 that there are two such lists: for Shelf Location and Subject.

The Location list and Subject list are filled differently and used differently, due to the nature of their values. The Location list must display each possible shelf location only once, and the value stored in the database field exactly matches the value shown in the list. The Subject list is filled from the Subject table (not the table being displayed or updated), and the value stored in the Books table is not the same as the text displayed in the list. The user sees and selects by complete subject name, but the value stored in the Books table is the subject code. For example, if the user drops down the Subjects list and selects "Business," then "BSN" is stored for that record.

The Location List In earlier chapters, the Location list was filled by hard-coding the Items collection at design time. But this example fills the list at run time from the database, which requires a special SELECT statement with a DISTINCT clause, since the values can (and do) appear multiple times.

Set up a separate data adapter for the locations and add the DISTINCT clause to the SQL statement in the Query Builder. (Also make sure to deselect the options to create the update SQL commands.)

```
SELECT DISTINCT Shelf_Location
FROM Books
ORDER BY Shelf_Location
```

Once you have created the data adapter, generate a dataset (in this example, the dataset is called DsLocations1). At design time, set the Location drop-down list properties:

DataSource: DsLocations1
DataTextField: Shelf_Location

When you are ready to display the data for a selected record, you must find the list item that matches the data field and set the index of the list to match its index. In this case, we use the **FindByText method** of the list's Items collection. This method searches the list items for a match of the supplied string and returns a **ListItem object.** Then we use the **IndexOf method** of the Items collection to find the index of the found ListItem. The IndexOf method returns the index, which we assign to the SelectedIndex property of the list. This step makes the item appear selected.

```
Dim liListItem As ListItem

'Set the value of the Location drop-down list
With ddlLocation                                    'Locate the text in the list
    liListItem = .Items.FindByText(dvBook(0).Item("Shelf_Location").ToString())
    .SelectedIndex = .Items.IndexOf(liListItem)    'Select the list item
End With
```

The Subject List The Subjects list displays the subject as its DataTextField and the subject code as the DataValueField, so that the user can select by name but return the code. You can use data binding to automatically fill the list and manually set its value for display, as for the Location list. Assuming that the main dataset (DsBooksSubjects) holds both the Books and Subjects tables, set the list's properties at design time:

DataSource: DsBooksSubjects1
DataTextField: Subject
DataValueField: SubjectCode

When the selected record changes and you need to display the correct value in the Subject list, you will use a similar technique as that used for the Location list. But in this case, you use the **FindByValue method** of the list's Items collection to search for a match by the subject code rather than the subject.

```
Dim liListItem As ListItem

'Set the value of the Subject drop-down list
With ddlSubjects                                   'Locate the value rather than the text
    liListItem = .Items.FindByValue(dvBook(0).Item("Subject_Code").ToString())
    .SelectedIndex = .Items.IndexOf(liListItem)    'Select the list item
End With
```

Adding a Blank Row to a List These two lists work well for most tasks. They both fill automatically and display the selected data value. The only other problem occurs during an Add operation. You can easily clear the text boxes for data entry, but to clear the drop-down lists, each must have a blank row that you can select. The lists are filled when the `DataBind` method executes, so you can insert a new blank row at the top of each list after they are bound.

```
'Bind the drop-down lists
Me.DataBind()

'Insert one blank row at the top of each list
ddlLocation.Items.Insert(0, "")
ddlSubjects.Items.Insert(0, "")
```

In the code to begin an Add operation, set the SelectedIndex property of each list to 0, the top element in the list.

```
'Show a blank selection
ddlLocation.SelectedIndex = 0
ddlSubjects.SelectedIndex = 0
```

Combining a Text Box and a Drop-Down List

When you want to allow the user to enter new values *or* select from a list, you start to really appreciate the Windows combo box. In Web applications, you must create both a drop-down list and a text box and manage what displays yourself. When the user can make a selection, you display the drop-down list; when an entry can be made, you display the text box. And if the user can make modifications to a selected list item, you must assign the selected list item to the text box before you display it and retrieve the value from the text box after the edit operation.

The first challenge in combining a text box and a drop-down list comes when you try to place them in the same spot on a Web form. The drop-down list must be on top of the text box, but you cannot directly create one on top of the other. The best plan is to first create the drop-down list control, then create a larger text box control and slide it under the list (Figure 8.3). Set the text box properties (ID and Text), then resize the control to be the same size as the (now covering) drop-down list. When you need to change the properties of either control, select its name from the *Objects* drop-down list in the Properties window.

Create a text box and slide it behind a drop-down list. Then resize the text box to match the list.

Switching between the Controls Use both controls' Visible properties to manage their display. Initially, the drop-down list should be visible and the text box should be invisible. When the user clicks on the Add button, you must switch the display:

```
'Switch from drop-down list to text box
ddlTitle.Visible = False
txtTitle.Visible = True
```

For an Edit operation, you must retrieve the selected item from the list and assign it to the text box before displaying the text box.

```
txtTitle.Text = ddlTitle.SelectedItem.ToString()
```

After both an Edit and Add operation, you use the value of the text box for the field value and switch the visibility back to the original state.

Executing SQL Statements

So far, you have used datasets and data readers to access data from a database. Now you will learn the remaining technique for communicating with a database: executing SQL commands directly. You have seen the INSERT, UPDATE, and DELETE commands that a data adapter generates automatically; these are used by the data adapter to send updates to the database when you execute the data adapter's Update method.

SQL statements come in two basic varieties: **selection queries** and **action queries.** Selection queries are the SELECT commands that you have created and modified using the Query Builder. These commands select data from a database and return the selected data to your program. Action queries actually perform some action on the data in the database: update or delete existing records or add new records (Table 8.1).

Note: This text uses the industry-standard for capitalization for SQL key words. SQL statements are not case-sensitive, so you can write "insert," "Insert," or "INSERT." However, the commands generated by the automatic tools

keep the key words in uppercase, and the capitalization can help in reading
and deciphering commands.

Table 8.1

Command	Purpose
INSERT INTO	Add a record.
DELETE FROM	Remove a record.
UPDATE	Change field values.

SQL action queries

Connections and Commands

To execute an SQL statement, you must have a **command object,** which can
be an OleDBCommand or a SQLCommand object and must match the provider
type of the connection. You assign properties to the command object, including
the Connection, the CommandType, and the CommandText, open the connection, and execute the command. In this example, the SQL statement is created
elsewhere and passed to this procedure. The individual statements are ex-
plained following the code:

```
Private Sub ExecuteDBCommand(ByVal strSQL As String)
    'Execute an action query to update the database
    Dim cmdBooks As OleDb.OleDbCommand
    Dim intRowCount As Integer

    Try
        'Set up and execute the command
        cmdBooks = New OleDb.OleDbCommand()
        With cmdBooks
            .Connection = conRnR
            .CommandType = CommandType.Text
            .CommandText = strSQL
            .Connection.Open()
            intRowCount = .ExecuteNonQuery()     'Execute the command
        End With

    Catch Err As Exception
        'For debugging help only
        lblErrorMessage.Text = Err.Message
    Finally
        With cmdBooks.Connection
            If .State = ConnectionState.Open Then
                .Close()
            End If
        End With
        'Debugging command, for development information only
        System.Diagnostics.Debug.WriteLine("Records affected = " & intRowCount.ToString())
    End Try
End Sub
```

Note: You can see an example of calling this procedure in the Ch08UpdateRnR
program later in this chapter.

Setting Up the Command Object The preceding example creates a command object using the empty constructor and assigns the properties to the new object. Note that in place of this code:

```
cmdBooks = New OleDb.OleDbCommand()
With cmdBooks
    .Connection = conRnR
    .CommandType = CommandType.Text
    .CommandText = strSQL
End With
```

You could supply the parameters when you instantiate the object:

```
Dim cmdBooks As New OleDb.OleDbCommand(strSQL, conRnR)
```

For the connection, you can use a connection object that was added and configured in the designer or create a new connection in code. This text sticks with the visual connection objects, but you may see examples in the MSDN documentation that create connections in code.

Opening and Closing the Connection When you use data adapters and datasets, you don't have to be concerned with opening and closing the connection. But when you execute commands, you must do both. It's very important that if you open a connection, you make sure to close it. Otherwise your connections remain open and hold system resources, even when the program goes out of scope.

This is a perfect location for the Finally clause of the Try block. Whether or not the command succeeds, you want to close the connection (but only if it was opened successfully).

```
Try
    'Code to open the connection and execute the command
Catch Err As Exception
    'For debugging help only
    lblErrorMessage.Text = Err.Message
Finally
    With cmdBooks.Connection
        If .State = ConnectionState.Open Then
            .Close()
        End If
    End With
    'Debugging command, for development information only
    System.Diagnostics.Debug.WriteLine("Records affected = " & intRowCount.ToString())
End Try
```

Notice two optional statements in this code, which are there only to help you with debugging. In the Catch block, you can display any error message in a label on the form. Of course, you don't expect any exceptions in a running application, but this technique can be a big help during development.

You have used Debug.WriteLine in Windows applications without specifying the namespace. In Windows applications, the designer automatically imports the System.Diagnostics namespace. In your Web applications, you can either write an Imports statement or specify the namespace on individual lines, as shown in the above example.

Executing the Command To actually execute an SQL command, you use the **ExecuteNonQuery method** of the command object. The `ExecuteNonQuery` method does not take any parameters but executes the SQL command stored in the CommandText property of the command object. The method returns an integer count of the number of records modified by the statement. Generally you expect a return of 1; a return of 0 means that no changes were made.

Writing SQL Statements

You can find entire books about writing SQL statements; this brief section covers the basics of the `INSERT INTO`, `UPDATE`, and `DELETE FROM` action queries.

In SQL statements, you write key words, table names, field names, and values.

- Key words: As mentioned earlier, key words appear in uppercase by convention.
  Examples: `UPDATE`, `DELETE FROM`, `INSERT INTO`.

- Table names and field names: Table and field names don't need quotes or brackets, unless the names contain spaces. To specify a two-word field name for Access files, enclose the name in square brackets.
  Examples: [First Name], [Last Name]

  For SQL Server files, enclose two-word names in double quotes.

- Field values: String values must be enclosed in single quotes. Numeric values and boolean values are not enclosed; date values must be enclosed with number signs (#) in Access files and single quotes for SQL Server.
  Examples: 'John', 100, #10/21/60#

  " ' " & txtName.Text & " ' " (This string inserts the contents of txtName into a quoted string.)

Warning: Do not include extra spaces in the SQL string. Extra spaces in the wrong spot will cause the statement to fail.

The SQL INSERT Statement—General Form

```
INSERT INTO TableName (Fieldlist) VALUES (ListOfValues)
```

In the `INSERT INTO` statement, name all of the fields, then all of the values, which must match in number, type, and sequence.

The SQL INSERT Statement—Examples

```
INSERT INTO Subjects(Subject, SubjectCode) VALUES ('Business', 'BSN')

INSERT INTO Subjects(Subject, SubjectCode) VALUES('" & txtSubject.Text & "', '" & _
      txtSubjectCode.Text & "'")

strSQL = "INSERT INTO Subjects(Subject, SubjectCode) VALUES('" & txtSubject.Text & _
      "', '" & txtSubjectCode.Text & "'")

INSERT INTO Patient ([Patient Number], [Last Name], [First Name])
      VALUES (500, 'Berry', 'Terry')
```

continued

The SQL INSERT Statement—Examples   *(continued)*

Examples

```
strSQL = "INSERT INTO Patient " _
        & "([Patient Number], [Last Name], [First Name], [Policy #]) " _
        & "VALUES(" & txtPatientNumber.Text & ", '" & txtLastName.Text _
        & "', '" & txtFirstName.Text & "', '" & txtPolicyNumber.Text & "')"
```

To help decipher the confusing mix of single and double quotes in the last example above, assume that

txtPatientNumber.Text = 125 (for a numeric field in the database)
txtLastName.Text = "Mills"
txtFirstName.Text = "Eric"
txtPolicyNumber.Text = "AB2578"

The result stored in strSQL will be

```
"INSERT INTO Patient ([Patient Number], [Last Name], [First Name], [Policy #]) " _
   "VALUES(125, 'Mills', 'Eric', 'AB2578')"
```

The SQL UPDATE Statement—General Form

General Form

```
UPDATE TableName
   SET FieldName = FieldValue, FieldName = FieldValue, ...
   WHERE Criteria
```

If you omit the WHERE clause, ADO.NET attempts to make the change to every record in the table.

The SQL UPDATE Statement—Examples

Examples

```
UPDATE Subjects SET Subject = 'Management' WHERE SubjectCode = 'MGM'

strSQL = "UPDATE Subjects SET Subject = '" & txtSubject.Text & _
         "' WHERE SubjectCode = '" & txtCode.Text & "'"

UPDATE Patient
   SET [Last Name] = 'Bowser'
   WHERE [Patient Number] = 500

UPDATE Visit
   SET Date = #1/1/2000#
   WHERE Date = #1/1/1900#

strSQL = "UPDATE Patient " & _
         "SET [Last Name] = '" & txtLastName.Text & "', " & _
           "[First Name] = '" & txtFirstName.Text & "', " & _
           "[Policy #] = '" & txtPolicyNumber & "' " & _
         "WHERE [Patient Number] = " & txtPatientNumber.Text
```

The SQL Delete Statement—General Form

General Form

```
DELETE FROM TableName
   WHERE Criteria
```

The SQL Delete Statement—Examples

Examples

```
DELETE FROM Subjects WHERE SubjectCode = 'BSN'

strSQL = "DELETE FROM Subjects WHERE SubjectCode = '" & txtSubjectCode.Text & "'"

DELETE FROM Patient
   WHERE [Patient Number] = 500

DELETE FROM Patient
   WHERE [Last Name] = 'Berry'

strSQL = "DELETE FROM Patient " _
           & "WHERE [Patient Number] = " & txtPatientNumber.Text
```

Writing Criteria The criteria specify which record(s) to modify or delete. Although most often the criteria for SQL statements use an equal sign, you also can write criteria to select multiple records. Note that the RowFilter property of data views uses these same symbols. In SQL statements, the criteria follow the WHERE clause; for the RowFilter property, you omit the WHERE keyword. You can find a complete listing of operators on the "Comparison Operators" page in MSDN.

Operator	Meaning	Examples
=	Equal to	`"Subject = 'Business' "` `"Subject = '" & txtSubject.Text & "'"`
>	Greater than	`"Sales > 1000"` `"Sales > " & txtSales.Text`
<	Less than	`"Sales < 1000"` `"Sales < " & txtSales.Text`

Like	Pattern match	`"Subject Like ('B%')"`
		 (For SQL Server databases)
		 `"Subject Like 'B*' "`
		 (For Access databases)

The SQL for the Update Program

The update program builds the SQL statements for each operation and calls the ExecuteSQLCommand procedure. This code appears in the btnSave_Click event procedure:

```
'Retrieve the session variable
blnAddInProgress = CType(Session("AddInProgress"), Boolean)

If blnAddInProgress Then                'Add in progress
    'Set up SQL statement
    strSQL = "INSERT INTO Books(Title, Author, ISBN, Publisher, " & _
        "Shelf_Location, Subject_Code, Fiction) " & _
        "VALUES('" & txtTitle.Text & "', '" & _
        txtAuthor.Text & "', '" & _
        txtISBN.Text & "', '" & _
```

```
                    txtPublisher.Text & "', '" & _
                    strShelf & "', '" & _
                    strSubject & "', " & _
                    blnFiction & ")"
Else                                    'Edit in progress
    'Set up SQL statement
    strSQL = "UPDATE Books SET " & _
        "Title = '" & txtTitle.Text & "', " & _
        "Author = '" & txtAuthor.Text & "', " & _
        "ISBN = '" & txtISBN.Text & "', " & _
        "Publisher = '" & txtPublisher.Text & "', " & _
        "Shelf_Location = '" & strShelf & "', " & _
        "Subject_Code = '" & strSubject & "', " & _
        "Fiction = " & blnFiction & _
        " WHERE ISBN = '" & txtISBN.Text & "'"
End If

'Execute the SQL statement
ExecuteDBCommand(strSQL)
```

This code appears in the btnDelete_Click event procedure, which also builds an SQL statement and calls an ExecuteDBCommand general procedure.

```
'Set up the SQL statement
strSQL = "Delete from Books " & _
    "Where ISBN = '" & txtISBN.Text & "'"

'Execute the SQL statement
ExecuteDBCommand(strSQL)
```

Database Security for Web Applications

As soon as you attempt to update a database from a Web application, you run into security problems. Whether you are updating an Access or SQL Server database, you will find that the system either requests a valid ID and password for login or cancels the program with an "Access Denied" message.

For both Access files and SQL Server files that are configured for Windows authentication, you should be able to open and update the files by following these two steps:

TIP

If a Web program refuses to run, try *Debug / Start without Debugging*, which often gives better messages about the cause of the problem. ∎

1. Remove Anonymous Access from the project's virtual folder: Open the IIS Manager with *Start/Control Panel/Administrative Tools/Internet Information Services.* Drill down on the local computer *Web Sites / Default Web Site* and select the folder for your project. Right-click and choose *Properties*; on the *Directory Security* tab, click *Edit.* Deselect the option for *Anonymous Access,* make sure that *Windows Authentication* is checked, and close the dialog box. *Note:* As a shortcut to display the IIS Manager, select *Start / Run* and type "inetmgr" into the *Open* box.

2. Modify the project's Web.config file: In your project, open the Web.config file. In the Authentication section, you should find this line:

```
<authentication mode="Windows" />
```

Add this line immediately following the preceding line:

```
<identity impersonate="true" />
```

Note: If your project does not contain the Web.config file, it should. The best way to add one is to set up the dynamic connection string for the connection object, which automatically adds the Web.config if it doesn't already exist. You also can add a Web.config file to a project by right-clicking the project and selecting *Add / Add New Item*. Choose the *Web Configuration File* template.

After taking these two steps, your database update programs should run without security problems. The exception is SQL Server files that have been configured with SECURITYMODE = SQL rather than Windows security. If this is the case, you must speak to your network administrator for access instructions.

The Update Program

Here is the complete update program. Refer to Figure 8.2 to see the form.

```
'Project:       Ch08UpdateRnR
'Programmer:    Bradley/Millspaugh
'Date:          January 2003
'Description:   Update the RnRBooks.mdb database file on a Web Form.
'               Uses bound drop-down lists and unbound screen controls.
'               Updates by executing SQL statements against the original
'               data source.

Option Strict On

Public Class frmUpdate
    Inherits System.Web.UI.Page

    [Web Form Designer Generated Code]

#Region " Event Procedures "

    Private Sub Page_Load(ByVal sender As System.Object, _
      ByVal e As System.EventArgs) Handles MyBase.Load
        'Initialize the page

        If Not IsPostBack Then
            InitializeFormFields()
            'Fill the controls for the first record
            ddlTitle_SelectedIndexChanged(sender, e)
        End If
    End Sub

    Private Sub ddlTitle_SelectedIndexChanged( _
      ByVal sender As System.Object, _
      ByVal e As System.EventArgs) _
      Handles ddlTitle.SelectedIndexChanged
        'Title changed. Get the record and fill the form controls.
        Dim dsBooks As DataSet
        Dim dvBook As New DataView()
        Dim liListItem As ListItem
```

```vb
        If ddlTitle.SelectedIndex <> -1 Then
            'Retrieve the dataset from the session variable
            dsBooks = CType(Session("Dataset"), dataset)

            'Filter for the selected record
            With dvBook
                .Table = dsBooks.Tables("Books")
                .RowFilter = "ISBN = '" & ddlTitle.SelectedItem.Value & "'"
            End With

            'Save the data view with selected record
            Session("CurrentRecord") = dvBook

            'Assign the data fields to the text boxes
            txtAuthor.Text = dvBook(0).Item("Author").ToString()
            txtPublisher.Text = dvBook(0).Item("Publisher").ToString()
            txtISBN.Text = dvBook(0).Item("ISBN").ToString()

            'Set the values of the drop-down lists
            With ddlLocation                      'Locate the text in the list
                liListItem = .Items.FindByText(dvBook(0).Item("Shelf_Location").ToString())
                .SelectedIndex = .Items.IndexOf(liListItem)      'Select the list item
            End With

            With ddlSubjects                  'Locate the value rather than the text
                liListItem = .Items.FindByValue(dvBook(0).Item("Subject_Code").ToString())
                .SelectedIndex = .Items.IndexOf(liListItem)      'Select the list item
            End With
            'Check box
            chkFiction.Checked = CType(dvBook(0).Item("Fiction"), Boolean)
        End If
End Sub

Private Sub btnAdd_Click(ByVal sender As System.Object, _
  ByVal e As System.EventArgs) Handles btnAdd.Click
    'Begin an Add operation or cancel the current operation
    Dim blnAddInProgress As Boolean

    If btnAdd.Text = "Add" Then               'Add button clicked
        UnlockTextBoxes()
        SetButtonsForEdit()
        ClearControls()
        Session("AddInProgress") = True
    Else                                       'Cancel button clicked
        LockTextBoxes()
        ResetButtonsAfterEdit()
        txtTitle.Visible = False
        With ddlTitle
            .Visible = True
            blnAddInProgress = CType(Session("AddInProgress"), Boolean)
            If blnAddInProgress Then       'Cancel Add, return to first record
                .SelectedIndex = 0
            End If
            ddlTitle_SelectedIndexChanged(sender, e)
        End With
        Session("AddInProgress") = False
    End If
End Sub
```

```vb
    Private Sub btnDelete_Click(ByVal sender As System.Object, _
      ByVal e As System.EventArgs) Handles btnDelete.Click
        'Delete the current record
        Dim strSQL As String

        'Set up the SQL statement
        strSQL = "Delete from Books " & _
          "Where ISBN = '" & txtISBN.Text & "'"
        'Execute the SQL statement
        ExecuteDBCommand(strSQL)

        'Delete the title from the list
        With ddlTitle
            .Items.RemoveAt(.SelectedIndex)
        End With
        'Make the form controls match the selected item in the list
        ddlTitle_SelectedIndexChanged(sender, e)
    End Sub

    Private Sub btnEdit_Click(ByVal sender As System.Object, _
      ByVal e As System.EventArgs) Handles btnEdit.Click
        'Edit button clicked. Enable editing

        UnlockTextBoxes()
        txtISBN.ReadOnly = True              'Do not allow changes to the key
        txtTitle.Text = ddlTitle.SelectedItem.ToString()
        SetButtonsForEdit()
        Session("AddInProgress") = False
    End Sub

    Private Sub btnSave_Click(ByVal sender As System.Object, _
      ByVal e As System.EventArgs) Handles btnSave.Click
        'Save an Edit or Add record
        Dim blnAddInProgress As Boolean
        Dim strSQL As String
        Dim strShelf As String
        Dim strSubject As String
        Dim blnFiction As Boolean
        Dim liListItem As ListItem

        'Set up the complicated fields
        With ddlLocation
            If .SelectedIndex > 0 Then    'Blank or no row selected
                strShelf = .SelectedItem.ToString()
            Else
                strShelf = ""
            End If
        End With
        With ddlSubjects
            If .SelectedIndex > 0 Then
                strSubject = .Items(.SelectedIndex).Value
            Else                             'Blank or no row selected
                strSubject = "BSS"        'Assign a default value (Cannot be blank)
            End If
        End With
        blnFiction = CType(chkFiction.Checked, Boolean)

        'Retrieve the session variable
        blnAddInProgress = CType(Session("AddInProgress"), Boolean)
```

```
    If blnAddInProgress Then              'Add in progress

        'Set up SQL statement
        strSQL = "INSERT INTO Books(Title, Author, ISBN, Publisher, " & _
            "Shelf_Location, Subject_Code, Fiction) " & _
            "VALUES('" & txtTitle.Text & "', '" & _
            txtAuthor.Text & "', '" & _
            txtISBN.Text & "', '" & _
            txtPublisher.Text & "', '" & _
            strShelf & "', '" & _
            strSubject & "', " & _
            blnFiction & ")"

    Else          'Edit in progress

        'Set up SQL statement
        strSQL = "UPDATE Books SET " & _
            "Title = '" & txtTitle.Text & "', " & _
            "Author = '" & txtAuthor.Text & "', " & _
            "ISBN = '" & txtISBN.Text & "', " & _
            "Publisher = '" & txtPublisher.Text & "', " & _
            "Shelf_Location = '" & strShelf & "', " & _
            "Subject_Code = '" & strSubject & "', " & _
            "Fiction = " & blnFiction & _
            " WHERE ISBN = '" & txtISBN.Text & "'"
    End If

    'Execute the SQL statement
    ExecuteDBCommand(strSQL)

    'Refill the dataset to retrieve the changes
    daBooks.Fill(DsBooksSubjects1)
    daSubjects.Fill(DsBooksSubjects1)
    Session("Dataset") = DsBooksSubjects1

    'Reset the list
    With ddlTitle
        .DataBind()
        liListItem = .Items.FindByText(txtTitle.Text)
        .SelectedIndex = .Items.IndexOf(liListItem)
    End With

    'Reset the form controls
    LockTextBoxes()
    ResetButtonsAfterEdit()
End Sub

#End Region

#Region " General Procedures "

Private Sub InitializeFormFields()
    'Fill the dataset and controls on initial page load

    'Fill the DsBooksSubjects1 dataset
    daBooks.Fill(DsBooksSubjects1)
    daSubjects.Fill(DsBooksSubjects1)
    Session("Dataset") = DsBooksSubjects1
```

```vb
        'Get the dataset for the Location list
        daLocations.Fill(DsLocations1)

        Me.DataBind()

        'Insert one blank row at the top of each list
        ddlLocation.Items.Insert(0, "")
        ddlSubjects.Items.Insert(0, "")
End Sub

Private Sub ClearControls()
    'Clear the screen controls for entry of a new record

        txtTitle.Text = ""
        txtAuthor.Text = ""
        txtISBN.Text = ""
        txtPublisher.Text = ""
        ddlLocation.SelectedIndex = 0
        ddlSubjects.SelectedIndex = 0
        chkFiction.Checked = False
End Sub

Private Sub ExecuteDBCommand(ByVal strSQL As String)
    'Execute an action query to update the database
    Dim cmdBooks As OleDb.OleDbCommand
    Dim intRowCount As Integer

    Try
        'Set up and execute the command
        cmdBooks = New OleDb.OleDbCommand()
        With cmdBooks
            .Connection = conRnR
            .CommandType = CommandType.Text
            .CommandText = strSQL
            .Connection.Open()
            intRowCount = .ExecuteNonQuery()                  'Execute the command
        End With

    Catch Err As Exception
        'For debugging help only
        lblErrorMessage.Text = Err.Message & Err.ToString()

    Finally
        With cmdBooks.Connection
            If .State = ConnectionState.Open Then
                .Close()
            End If
        End With
        'Debugging command, for development information only
        System.Diagnostics.Debug.WriteLine("Records affected = " & _
           intRowCount.ToString())
    End Try
End Sub

Private Sub LockTextBoxes()
    'Lock the text boxes and display the list

        ddlTitle.Visible = True              'Switch from text box to drop-down list
```

```
            txtTitle.Visible = False
            txtAuthor.ReadOnly = True
            txtISBN.ReadOnly = True
            txtPublisher.ReadOnly = True
        End Sub

        Private Sub UnlockTextBoxes()
            'Unlock the text boxes and hide the list

            ddlTitle.Visible = False          'Switch from drop-down list to text box
            txtTitle.Visible = True
            txtAuthor.ReadOnly = False
            txtISBN.ReadOnly = False
            txtPublisher.ReadOnly = False
        End Sub

        Private Sub ResetButtonsAfterEdit()
            'Reset buttons after an Add or Edit operation

            btnAdd.Text = "Add"
            btnSave.Enabled = False
            btnDelete.Enabled = True
            btnEdit.Enabled = True
        End Sub

        Private Sub SetButtonsForEdit()
            'Set up buttons for an Add or Edit operation

            btnAdd.Text = "Cancel"
            btnSave.Enabled = True
            btnDelete.Enabled = False
            btnEdit.Enabled = False
        End Sub
#End Region

End Class
```

> ## Feedback 8.2

1. Write the statements to save the boolean variable blnAddPending in a session variable and to later retrieve the value.
2. Write the statement to add a blank row to the top of a drop-down list called ddlName. Then write the statement to select that blank row.
3. Write the statements to set up a command object and execute an SQL statement.
4. Write an SQL statement to delete the record from the Employee table with the EmpID field of 1234 (a string field).
5. Write an SQL statement to delete the record from the Employee table with the EmpID field that matches the text in txtEmpID.

Multitier Considerations

Writing an update program as a multitier application is similar to the multitier database applications you have already written. Create all connections, data adapters, datasets, and commands in the data tier component. For the RnR-

Books update program in the previous sections, you will need one connection and data adapters for the Books table, the Subjects table, and another one for the Location field from the Books table, since it needs a DISTINCT SQL statement to fill the Location list.

The function to execute an SQL statement, ExecuteDBCommand, also should appear in the data tier component, since it performs actions against the database. It makes sense to execute database commands in the data tier, since that's where your connection is declared. The code in the form builds the SQL statement and passes it as a parameter to the ExecuteDBCommand method, which must be declared as a Public Function.

It's a good idea to handle exceptions in the data tier component by passing them back up to the calling program. You can easily do that with a **Throw statement**, which "throws" any caught exceptions back up a level.

Data Tier Component

```
Public Sub ExecuteDBCommand(ByVal strSQL As String)
    'Execute an action query to update the database
    Dim cmdBooks As OleDb.OleDbCommand
    Dim intRowCount As Integer

    Try
        'Set up and execute the command
        cmdBooks = New OleDb.OleDbCommand()
        With cmdBooks
            .Connection = conRnR
            .CommandType = CommandType.Text
            .CommandText = strSQL
            .Connection.Open()
            intRowCount = .ExecuteNonQuery()    'Execute the command
        End With
    Catch
        Throw                    'Pass the exception back to the caller
    Finally
        With cmdBooks.Connection
            If .State = ConnectionState.Open Then
                .Close()
            End If
        End With
    End Try
End Sub
```

User Interface (Form) Class

```
Try
    objDataHandler = New DataHandler() 'Instantiate data tier component

    'Execute the SQL statement
    objDataHandler.ExecuteDBCommand(strSQL)
Catch Err As Exception
    lblErrorMessage.Text = Err.Message
End Try
```

You must make some changes to the code in the form, since you cannot bind any controls at design time. In fact, you should make sure to remove the field bindings or you will receive error messages. To set up binding for the

drop-down lists (the only bound controls in this program), set their properties
when the page is loaded.

```
Private Sub InitializeFormFields()
    'Fill the dataset and controls on initial page load
    objDataHandler = New DataHandler() 'Instantiate data tier component

    'Fill the DsBooksSubjects1 dataset
    dsData = objDataHandler.getBooksSubjectsDataset()
    Session("Dataset") = dsData
    'Set up binding for the Titles list
    With ddlTitle
        .DataSource = dsData
        .DataMember = "Books"
        .DataTextField = "Title"
        .DataValueField = "ISBN"
    End With

    'Get the dataset for the Location list
    dsLocation = objDataHandler.getLocationDataset()

    'Set up binding for the drop-down lists
    With ddlLocation
        .DataSource = dsLocation
        .DataTextField = "Shelf_Location"
    End With
    With ddlSubjects
        .DataSource = dsData
        .DataMember = "Subjects"
        .DataTextField = "Subject"
        .DataValueField = "SubjectCode"
    End With

    Me.DataBind()

    'Insert one blank row at the top of each list
    ddlLocation.Items.Insert(0, "")
    ddlSubjects.Items.Insert(0, "")
End Sub
```

One word of warning is in order: The drop-down lists don't "remember"
their binding settings from one postback to the next. The lists retain their values due to the ViewState settings, but if you need to rebind a list during program execution, you must reset the field properties. This differs from properties
that you set at design time, which *do* retain their settings for every postback.

```
Private Sub btnSave_Click . . .
    'Code to save an Add or Update goes here.
    'Note that both can modify a title, and the list must be updated for the changes.
    . . .
    'Reset the Titles list
    With ddlTitle
        .DataSource = dsData
        .DataMember = "Books"
        .DataTextField = "Title"
```

```
                .DataValueField = "ISBN"
                .DataBind()
                'Select the list item that matches the text box
                liListItem = .Items.FindByText(txtTitle.Text)
                .SelectedIndex = .Items.IndexOf(liListItem)
            End With
            'More code goes here ...
```

Access versus SQL Server Commands

Although the update programs in this chapter use Access files for ease of porta-
bility and replacement, it's easy to switch to SQL Server files. In this example,
the RnRBooks.mdb file has been converted to a SQL Server file, called *upsizing* from Access to SQL Server. The only changes to the program are the connection, data adapters, and command object. Using the SQL data provider, you
add an SqlConnection object and SqlDataAdapter objects. In code, specify the
SQL version of the command object:

```
Public Sub ExecuteDBCommand(ByVal strSQL As String)
    'Execute an action query to update the database
    Dim cmdBooks As SqlClient.SqlCommand
    Dim intRowCount As Integer

    Try
        'Set up and execute the command
        cmdBooks = New SqlClient.SqlCommand()

        With cmdBooks
            .Connection = conRnRSQL
            .CommandType = CommandType.Text
            .CommandText = strSQL
            .Connection.Open()
            intRowCount = .ExecuteNonQuery()              'Execute the command
        End With
    Catch
        Throw                   'Pass the exception back to the caller
    Finally
        With cmdBooks.Connection
            If .State = ConnectionState.Open Then
                .Close()
            End If
        End With
    End Try
End Sub
```

In converting this program from an Access file to a SQL Server file, the
only other change was to change the connection key and value in the Web.con-
fig file:

```
<add key="conRnRSQL.ConnectionString"
    value="server=(local)\NetSDK;Trusted_Connection=yes;database=RnrBooksSQL" />
```

Feedback 8.3

1. Write the statement(s) to pass an exception that occurs in a component back up to the calling procedure.
2. When would you have to set a drop-down list's binding properties more than once in the code of a multitier application?

Your Hands-On Programming Example

Create a multitier Web application that allows the user to update the Books table of the RnRBooks.mdb database file. The user should be able to modify or delete existing records or add new records. Do not allow changes unless the user first clicks an *Edit* button. During an Add or Edit operation, the only choices the user should be allowed to make are Save or Cancel.

The three drop-down lists (Title, Location, and Subject) should fill automatically with data from the database. Make sure that no duplicates appear in the Location list.

For an Edit operation, the user must be allowed to change the book title but not its ISBN (the primary key).

This program is similar to the update program earlier in this chapter. However, that is a single-tier application and this must be multitier, with all data access in a data tier component.

Planning the Project

Sketch a Web page (Figure 8.4) that your users sign off as meeting their needs.

Figure 8.4

The planning sketch of the hands-on programming example.

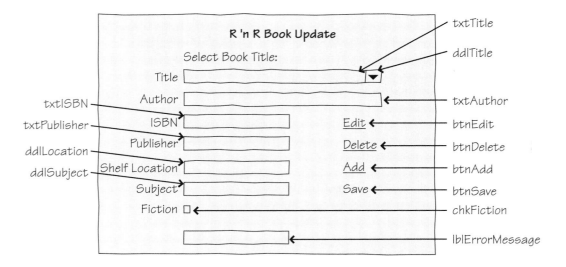

Plan the Objects, Properties, and Methods

Plan the two tiers. Determine the objects and property settings for the form and its controls, and for the data tier component. Figure 8.5 shows the diagram of the program components.

Figure 8.5

The components for the hands-on programming example.

Presentation Tier	Data Tier
frmUpdate	**DataHandler**
ddlTitle	conRnR
txtTitle	daBooks
txtAuthor	daSubjects
txtISBN	dsBooksSubjects
txtPublisher	DsBooksSubjects1
ddlLocation	daLocations
ddlSubject	dsLocations
chkFiction	DsLocations1
btnAdd	getBooksSubjectsDataset
btnDelete	getLocationDataset
btnEdit	executeDBCommand
btnSave	
lblErrorMessage	
Page_Load	
ddlTitle_SelectedIndexChanged	
btnAdd_Click	
btnDelete_Click	
btnEdit_Click	
btnSave_Click	
InitializeFormFields	
ClearControls	
LockTextBoxes	
UnlockTextBoxes	
ResetButtonsAfterEdit	
SetButtonsForEdit	

Presentation Tier

Object	Property	Setting
frmUpdate	Name	frmUpdate
	Title	R 'n R Books
Label1	Text	R 'n R Book Update
	Font	(Select a larger font)
Label2	Text	Select a Book Title
Label3	Text	Title
Label4	Text	Author
Label5	Text	ISBN
Label6	Text	Publisher

continued

Object	Property	Setting
Label7	Text	Shelf Location
Label8	Text	Subject
Label9	Text	Fiction
ddlTitle	AutoPostBack (unbound)	True
txtTitle	Text Visible	(blank) (Appears behind ddlTitle) False
txtAuthor	Text ReadOnly	(blank) True
txtISBN	Text ReadOnly	(blank) True
txtPublisher	Text ReadOnly	(blank) True
ddlLocation	(unbound)	
ddlSubject	(unbound)	
chkFiction	Text	(blank)
btnAdd	Text	Add
btnDelete	Text	Delete
btnEdit	Text	Edit
btnSave	Text Enabled	Save False
lblErrorMessage	Text	(blank)

Event procedures/Methods	Actions—Pseudocode

Page_Load	If not postback
	    Initialize form fields.
	    Find and display data for the first title.

ddlTitle_SelectedIndexChanged	If a list item is selected
	    Filter for the selected title.
	    Assign the data fields to the text boxes.
	    Make selections from Location and Subject lists.
	    Set the Fiction check box.

btnAdd_Click	If button's Text = "Add"
	    Unlock text boxes.
	    Set buttons for edit.
	    Clear the screen controls.
	    Set AddInProgress = True

continued

Event procedures/Methods	Actions—Pseudocode

	Else (button's Text = "Cancel")
	    Lock text boxes.
	    Reset buttons for normal operation.
	    Hide the Title text box.
	    Show the Title drop-down list.
	    If AddInProgress
	        Select first title in list.
	    Display data for selected title.
	    Set AddInProgress = False.

`btnDelete_Click`	Build the `DELETE` SQL statement for the selected record. Execute the SQL statement. Delete the title from the list. Display data for the selected title.
`btnEdit_Click`	Unlock text boxes. Lock txtISBN. Set txtTitle to selected list item. Set buttons for edit. Set AddInProgress = False.

`btnSave_Click`	Set up fields for drop-down lists and check box.
	If AddInProgress
	    Build the `INSERT` SQL statement.
	Else
	    Build the `UPDATE` SQL statement.
	Execute the SQL statement.
	If exception
	    Display message in txtErrorMessage.
	Refill the dataset to retrieve all changes.
	Rebind the Titles list.
	Select the item in the Titles list that matches txtTitle.
	Lock text boxes.
	Reset buttons for normal operation.

`InitializeFormFields`	Declare an instance of the data tier component. Retrieve the dataset. Save the dataset in a session variable. Bind the Titles list. Retrieve the Locations dataset. Bind the Location list. Bind the Subject list. Insert a blank row at the top of the Location and Subject lists.
`ClearControls`	Clear each text box. Select the blank row for Location and Subject lists. Uncheck the check box.
`LockTextBoxes`	Switch from Title text box to drop-down list. Set text boxes' ReadOnly property to True.
`UnlockTextBoxes`	Switch from Title drop-down list to text box. Set text boxes' ReadOnly property to False.
`ResetButtonsAfterEdit`	Change the Text property of btnAdd to "Add". Disable btnSave. Enable btnDelete and btnEdit.
`SetButtonsForEdit`	Change the Text property of btnAdd to "Cancel". Enable btnSave. Disable btnDelete and btnEdit.

Data Tier

Object	Property	Setting
Class	Name	DataHandler
conRnR	Name	conRnR
daBooks	Name	daBooks
daSubjects	Name	daSubjects
dsBooksSubjects	Name	dsBooksSubjects
DsBooksSubjects1	Name Tables	DsBooksSubjects1 Books and Subjects
daLocations	Name Command text	daLocations `SELECT DISTINCT` Location from Books `ORDER BY` Location
dsLocations	Name	dsLocations
DsLocations1	Name	DsLocations1

Methods	Actions—Pseudocode
`getBooksSubjectsDataset`	Fill a dataset that holds the Books and Subjects tables. Return the dataset.
`getLocationDataset`	Fill the Locations dataset. Return the dataset.
`executeDBCommand(strSQL)`	Try Open the connection. Set up the command. Execute the strSQL command. Catch Throw exception back to caller. Finally If the connection is open Close the connection.

Write the Project

Following the sketch in Figure 8.4, create the form. Figure 8.6 shows the completed form.

- Create the data tier component, adding the objects from your plan.

- Write the methods for the data tier component, following the pseudocode.

- Set the properties of each of the form objects, according to your plans.

- Write the code for the form. Working from the pseudocode, write each event procedure.

- When you complete the code, test the operation several times. Compare the screen output to the data tables, to make sure that the table is correctly updated.

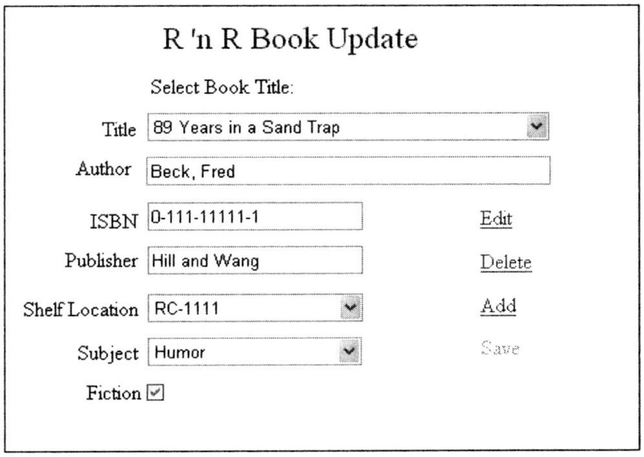

Figure 8.6

The form for the hands-on programming example.

R 'n R Book Update

Select Book Title:

Title [89 Years in a Sand Trap ▼]

Author [Beck, Fred]

ISBN [0-111-11111-1]   Edit

Publisher [Hill and Wang]   Delete

Shelf Location [RC-1111 ▼]   Add

Subject [Humor ▼]   Save

Fiction ☑

The Project Coding Solution

The Form

```
'Project:      Ch08HandsOn
'Programmer:   Bradley/Millspaugh
'Class:        frmUpdate
'Date:         January 2003
'Description:  Update the RnRBooks.mdb database file on a Web Form
'                 using a separate data tier component.
'                 Uses bound drop-down lists and unbound screen controls.
'                 Updates by executing SQL statements against the original
'                 data source.

Option Strict On

Public Class frmUpdate
    Inherits System.Web.UI.Page

    [Web Form Designer Generated Code]

    Dim objDataHandler As DataHandler 'Data tier component
    Dim dsData As DataSet
    Dim dsLocation As DataSet

#Region " Event Procedures "

    Private Sub Page_Load(ByVal sender As System.Object, _
      ByVal e As System.EventArgs) Handles MyBase.Load
        'Initialize the page

        If Not IsPostBack Then
            InitializeFormFields()
            'Fill the controls for the first record
            ddlTitle_SelectedIndexChanged(sender, e)
        End If
    End Sub
```

```vb
    Private Sub ddlTitle_SelectedIndexChanged( _
      ByVal sender As System.Object, _
      ByVal e As System.EventArgs) _
      Handles ddlTitle.SelectedIndexChanged
          'Title changed. Get the record and fill the form controls.
          Dim dsBooks As DataSet
          Dim dvBook As New DataView()
          Dim liListItem As ListItem

          If ddlTitle.SelectedIndex <> -1 Then
              'Retrieve the dataset from the session variable
              dsBooks = CType(Session("Dataset"), DataSet)

              'Filter for the selected record
              With dvBook
                  .Table = dsBooks.Tables("Books")
                  .RowFilter = "ISBN = '" & ddlTitle.SelectedItem.Value & "'"
              End With

              'Save the data view with selected record
              Session("CurrentRecord") = dvBook

              'Assign the data fields to the text boxes
              txtAuthor.Text = dvBook(0).Item("Author").ToString()
              txtPublisher.Text = dvBook(0).Item("Publisher").ToString()
              txtISBN.Text = dvBook(0).Item("ISBN").ToString()

              'Set the values of the drop-down lists
              With ddlLocation                          'Locate the text in the list
                  liListItem = .Items.FindByText(dvBook(0).Item("Shelf_Location").ToString())
                  .SelectedIndex = .Items.IndexOf(liListItem)    'Select the list item
              End With

              With ddlSubjects                    'Locate the value rather than the text
                  liListItem = .Items.FindByValue(dvBook(0).Item("Subject_Code").ToString())
                  .SelectedIndex = .Items.IndexOf(liListItem)    'Select the list item
              End With
              'Check box
              chkFiction.Checked = CType(dvBook(0).Item("Fiction"), Boolean)
          End If
    End Sub

    Private Sub btnAdd_Click(ByVal sender As System.Object, _
      ByVal e As System.EventArgs) Handles btnAdd.Click
          'Begin an Add operation or cancel the current operation
          Dim blnAddInProgress As Boolean

          If btnAdd.Text = "Add" Then                        'Add button clicked
              UnlockTextBoxes()
              SetButtonsForEdit()
              ClearControls()
              Session("AddInProgress") = True
          Else        'Cancel button clicked
              LockTextBoxes()
              ResetButtonsAfterEdit()
              txtTitle.Visible = False
```

```vb
                With ddlTitle
                    .Visible = True
                    blnAddInProgress = CType(Session("AddInProgress"), Boolean)
                    If blnAddInProgress Then          'Cancel Add, return to first record
                        .SelectedIndex = 0
                    End If
                    ddlTitle_SelectedIndexChanged(sender, e)
                End With
                Session("AddInProgress") = False
            End If
    End Sub

    Private Sub btnDelete_Click(ByVal sender As System.Object, _
      ByVal e As System.EventArgs) Handles btnDelete.Click
        'Delete the current record
        Dim strSQL As String

        objDataHandler = New DataHandler() 'Instantiate data tier component

        'Set up the SQL statement
        strSQL = "Delete from Books " & _
          "Where ISBN = '" & txtISBN.Text & "'"
        Try
            'Execute the SQL statement
            objDataHandler.ExecuteDBCommand(strSQL)
        Catch err As Exception
            lblErrorMessage.Text = err.Message
        End Try

        'Delete the title from the list
        With ddlTitle
            .Items.RemoveAt(.SelectedIndex)
        End With

        'Make the form controls match the selected item in the list
        ddlTitle_SelectedIndexChanged(sender, e)
    End Sub

    Private Sub btnEdit_Click(ByVal sender As System.Object, _
      ByVal e As System.EventArgs) Handles btnEdit.Click
        'Edit button clicked. Enable editing

        UnlockTextBoxes()
        txtISBN.ReadOnly = True                      'Do not allow changes to the key
        txtTitle.Text = ddlTitle.SelectedItem.ToString()
        SetButtonsForEdit()
        Session("AddInProgress") = False
    End Sub

    Private Sub btnSave_Click(ByVal sender As System.Object, _
      ByVal e As System.EventArgs) Handles btnSave.Click
        'Save an Edit or Add record
        Dim blnAddInProgress As Boolean
        Dim strSQL As String
        Dim strShelf As String
        Dim strSubject As String
        Dim blnFiction As Boolean
        Dim liListItem As ListItem
```

```
'Set up the complicated fields
With ddlLocation
    If .SelectedIndex > 0 Then        'Blank or no row selected
        strShelf = .SelectedItem.ToString()
    Else
        strShelf = ""
    End If
End With
With ddlSubjects
    If .SelectedIndex > 0 Then
        strSubject = .Items(.SelectedIndex).Value
    Else                              'Blank or no row selected
        strSubject = "BSS"            'Assign a default value (Cannot be blank)
    End If
End With
blnFiction = CType(chkFiction.Checked, Boolean)

'Retrieve the session variable
blnAddInProgress = CType(Session("AddInProgress"), Boolean)

If blnAddInProgress Then              'Add in progress

    'Set up SQL statement
    strSQL = "INSERT INTO Books(Title, Author, ISBN, Publisher, " & _
        "Shelf_Location, Subject_Code, Fiction) " & _
        "VALUES('" & txtTitle.Text & "', '" & _
        txtAuthor.Text & "', '" & _
        txtISBN.Text & "', '" & _
        txtPublisher.Text & "', '" & _
        strShelf & "', '" & _
        strSubject & "', " & _
        blnFiction & ")"

Else            'Edit in progress
    'Set up SQL statement
    strSQL = "UPDATE Books SET " & _
        "Title = '" & txtTitle.Text & "', " & _
        "Author = '" & txtAuthor.Text & "', " & _
        "ISBN = '" & txtISBN.Text & "', " & _
        "Publisher = '" & txtPublisher.Text & "', " & _
        "Shelf_Location = '" & strShelf & "', " & _
        "Subject_Code = '" & strSubject & "', " & _
        "Fiction = " & blnFiction & _
        " WHERE ISBN = '" & txtISBN.Text & "'"
End If

Try
    objDataHandler = New DataHandler() 'Instantiate data tier component

    'Execute the SQL statement
    objDataHandler.ExecuteDBCommand(strSQL)
Catch Err As Exception
    lblErrorMessage.Text = Err.Message
End Try

'Refill the dataset to get changes
dsData = objDataHandler.getBooksSubjectsDataset()
Session("Dataset") = dsData
```

```
            'Reset the Titles list
            With ddlTitle
                .DataSource = dsData
                .DataMember = "Books"
                .DataTextField = "Title"
                .DataValueField = "ISBN"
                .DataBind()
                'Select the list item that matches the text box
                liListItem = .Items.FindByText(txtTitle.Text)
                .SelectedIndex = .Items.IndexOf(liListItem)
            End With

            'Reset the form controls
            LockTextBoxes()
            ResetButtonsAfterEdit()
        End Sub

    #End Region

#Region " General Procedures "

    Private Sub InitializeFormFields()
        'Fill the dataset and controls on initial page load
        objDataHandler = New DataHandler()
        'Fill the DsBooksSubjects1 dataset
        dsData = objDataHandler.getBooksSubjectsDataset()
        Session("Dataset") = dsData

        'Set up binding for the Titles list
        With ddlTitle
            .DataSource = dsData
            .DataMember = "Books"
            .DataTextField = "Title"
            .DataValueField = "ISBN"
        End With

        'Get the dataset for the Location list
        dsLocation = objDataHandler.getLocationDataset()

        'Set up binding for the drop-down lists
        With ddlLocation
            .DataSource = dsLocation
            .DataTextField = "Shelf_Location"
        End With
        With ddlSubjects
            .DataSource = dsData
            .DataMember = "Subjects"
            .DataTextField = "Subject"
            .DataValueField = "SubjectCode"
        End With

        Me.DataBind()

        'Insert one blank row at the top of each list
        ddlLocation.Items.Insert(0, "")
        ddlSubjects.Items.Insert(0, "")
    End Sub

    Private Sub ClearControls()
        'Clear the screen controls for entry of a new record
```

```
            txtTitle.Text = ""
            txtAuthor.Text = ""
            txtISBN.Text = ""
            txtPublisher.Text = ""
            ddlLocation.SelectedIndex = 0
            ddlSubjects.SelectedIndex = 0
            chkFiction.Checked = False
        End Sub

        Private Sub LockTextBoxes()
            'Lock the text boxes and display the list

            ddlTitle.Visible = True                    'Switch from text box to drop-down list
            txtTitle.Visible = False
            txtAuthor.ReadOnly = True
            txtISBN.ReadOnly = True
            txtPublisher.ReadOnly = True
        End Sub

        Private Sub UnlockTextBoxes()
            'Unlock the text boxes and hide the list

            ddlTitle.Visible = False                   'Switch from drop-down list to text box
            txtTitle.Visible = True
            txtAuthor.ReadOnly = False
            txtISBN.ReadOnly = False
            txtPublisher.ReadOnly = False
        End Sub

        Private Sub ResetButtonsAfterEdit()
            'Reset buttons after an Add or Edit operation

            btnAdd.Text = "Add"
            btnSave.Enabled = False
            btnDelete.Enabled = True
            btnEdit.Enabled = True
        End Sub

        Private Sub SetButtonsForEdit()
            'Set up buttons for an Add or Edit operation

            btnAdd.Text = "Cancel"
            btnSave.Enabled = True
            btnDelete.Enabled = False
            btnEdit.Enabled = False
        End Sub
#End Region

End Class
```

The Data Tier Component

```
'Project:        Ch08HandsOn
'Programmer:     Bradley/Millspaugh
'Class:          DataHandler
'Date:           January 2003
'Description:    Provides the data services for the two-tier project.
```

```
Option Strict On

Public Class DataHandler
    Inherits System.ComponentModel.Component

    [Component Designer Generated Code]

    Public Function getBooksSubjectsDataset() As DataSet
        'Fill and return the BooksSubjects dataset

        Try
            daBooks.Fill(DsBooksSubjects1)
            daSubjects.Fill(DsBooksSubjects1)
            Return DsBooksSubjects1
        Catch
            Throw                                   'Pass the exception to the caller
        End Try
    End Function

    Public Function getLocationDataset() As DataSet
        'Fill and return the Locations dataset

        Try
            daLocations.Fill(DsLocations1)
            Return DsLocations1
        Catch
            Throw                                   'Pass the exception back up to the caller
        End Try
    End Function

    Public Sub ExecuteDBCommand(ByVal strSQL As String)
        'Execute an action query to update the database
        Dim cmdBooks As OleDb.OleDbCommand
        Dim intRowCount As Integer

        Try
            'Set up and execute the command
            cmdBooks = New OleDb.OleDbCommand()
            With cmdBooks
                .Connection = conRnR
                .CommandType = CommandType.Text
                .CommandText = strSQL
                .Connection.Open()
                intRowCount = .ExecuteNonQuery()        'Execute the command
            End With
        Catch
            Throw       'Pass the exception back to the caller
        Finally
            With cmdBooks.Connection
                If .State = ConnectionState.Open Then
                    .Close()
                End If
            End With
        End Try
    End Sub

End Class
```

Summary

1. The static nature of Web pages requires changes in the logic of applications. For example, record navigation is seldom done in a Web page. Generally the user enters or selects a record and the program displays the details for that record.

2. Small datasets can be stored in a session variable, so that the dataset does not have to be recreated for every postback.

3. Data binding in Web Forms differs greatly from that in Windows Forms. Drop-down lists cannot be set to display data from one table and bind to a field in a different table. Binding is one way, for display only. Changes in controls are not passed back to the dataset. For labels and text boxes, it's usually best to use unbound controls.

4. The logic of a related-table Web program is similar to that of a Windows program, but the syntax is different due to the differences between Web controls and Windows controls.

5. The logic of an update Web program differs from that of a Windows program due to the static nature of Web pages and the differences in data binding.

6. Any program variables that you must maintain between procedure calls must be stored in session variables rather than module-level or static variables.

7. To create a dataset with no duplicates for filling a list, use the DISTINCT keyword in the SQL SELECT statement.

8. To display a selected item in a list to match the contents of a database field, use the List Items collection FindByText or FindByValue method.

9. After a bound drop-down list is filled with data, you can add a blank item to the list using the Items Collection Insert method.

10. A drop-down list does not have an associated text box. To allow selection from a list and entry of new data, you must create both a list and a text box and manage their display in program logic.

11. Execute the SQL action queries INSERT INTO, DELETE FROM, and UPDATE to update a database directly, without using a dataset.

12. To execute an SQL statement, you create a Command object and set its CommandText property to the statement. You must open the connection, execute the command, and close the connection.

13. The operators that you use to write the criteria for an SQL statement are the same as those used in a filter for a data view.

14. Updating a database from a Web application requires extra steps to satisfy security requirements.

15. Use a Throw statement in a component to pass an exception back to the calling procedure.

16. If you set the binding properties of a control at run time, such as DataSource and DataMember, those properties do not persist for multiple page loads. You must reset the properties each time you rebind the control.

Key Terms

action queries *288*
command object *289*
DELETE FROM *291*
ExecuteNonQuery method *291*
FindByText method *286*
FindByValue method *287*

IndexOf method *286*
INSERT INTO *291*
ListItem object *286*
selection queries *288*
Throw statement *301*
UPDATE *291*

Review Questions

1. What differences between Web Forms and Windows Forms require logic changes in programs?
2. Explain how a data-bound drop-down list can display one value (such as Subject) and return a different value (such as SubjectCode). What steps are necessary to make the list show the selected data for a database field?
3. Explain how data binding works for text boxes and labels on Web pages. Why or why not would data binding be useful?
4. Explain why you cannot store values in module-level variables in a Web application.
5. How can you combine a text box and a drop-down list for data entry or selection?
6. Why would one want to add a blank item to a drop-down list? Why must you wait until after filling the list to do so?
7. What are the differences between SQL select queries and action queries? Give some examples of action queries.
8. Explain the procedure for executing an SQL action query.
9. Discuss database security for Web applications. How and why does it differ from that of Windows applications?

Programming Exercises

8.1 Write a Web application to display data from the related tables in the VBVideo.mdb database file from your CD. Display the studio names in a drop-down list to allow the user to select. When the user selects a studio, display the Studio ID, Contact Person, and Phone in labels and a list of the videos for that studio in a grid.

The VBVideo.mdb database

Studio	Video
Studio ID (key)	Movie Number (key)
Studio Name	Studio ID
Contact Person	Title
Phone	Category
	Length

8.2   Write a Web application to display Patient and Visit data from related tables in the AVB.mdb database file. Display the patient name in a drop-down list, in the form: "LastName, FirstName." When the user selects a name from the list, display the Patient Number and Phone fields in labels, and the Visit information for that patient in a data grid.

Patient	Visit
Patient Number (key)	Patient Number
Last Name	Date
First Name	Diagnosis
Street	Duration
City	Exam Type
State	Contact Lens
Zip Code	Pathology/Ocular
Phone	
Insurance Company	
Policy #	

Hint: You must concatenate the last name and first name to display in the drop-down list. The best way to do this is to modify the SQL statement to concatenate the fields, producing a new field that you can use for binding:

```
SELECT [Last Name], [First Name], [Patient Number] , Phone,
   [Last Name] + ', ' + [First Name] AS Name
   FROM Patient
   ORDER BY [Patient Number]
```

8.3   Write a Web application to display the orders for a selected employee in the Northwind Employees table. Allow the user to select the employee name from a drop-down list. When a name is selected, display the employee's Title and Extension fields in labels and the orders for that employee. The last name and first name are stored in separate fields; you must concatenate the fields to display "LastName, FirstName" in the drop-down list. *Hint*: See the hint for concatenating the fields in Exercise 8.2.

```
SELECT EmployeeID, LastName, FirstName, Title, Extension,
   LastName + ', ' + FirstName AS Name
   FROM Employees
   ORDER BY LastName
```

8.4   Write a Web application to update the publishers table of the pubs database. Display the pub_name field in a drop-down list. When the user selects a publisher, display the data for the record and allow the user to Add, Edit, or Delete. For an Add or Edit, the only two available options should be Save or Cancel.

8.5   Write a Web application to update the employee table of the pubs data-base. Display the name as "LastName, FirstName, MiddleInitial", con-catenated in the SQL statement (see the hint in Exercise 8.2). For the job_id field, display the job_desc field from the jobs table in a drop-down list. For the pub_id field, display the pub_name field from the publishers table in a drop-down list. Allow the user to Add, Edit, and Delete em-ployee records. For an Add or Edit, the only two available options should be Save or Cancel.

   Additional challenge: Help the user select a valid job_level for the job_id selected. You can display a label with the minimum and maximum values when the user selects the job_id, or create entries in the job de-scription list that show the range of acceptable values.

8.6   Write a Web application to update the Video table of the VBVideo.mdb database (see Exercise 8.1 for the file layout). Display the video titles in a drop-down list for the user to select. When the user selects a video, dis-play the Movie Number (the primary key), Studio, Category, and Length fields. The Studio names, provided by the Studio table, should appear in a drop-down list. Provide options to Edit, Delete, and Add, plus Save and Cancel for the Edit and Add operations.

Case Studies

Claytor's Cottages

Create a Web application that allows users to make a reservation. The page should allow the users to enter their name, address, and phone number. The credit card type (use a drop-down list or radio buttons), the card number, and the expiration date are required fields. Test that the card number and expiration date contain valid data.

Use a calendar control for the arrival and depar-ture dates. Allow room selection from a drop-down list.

Verify that the dates are available for that room. If available, add the reservation to the reservation table in the database. If not, display a message requesting other dates or another room.

Christian's Car Rentals

Create a Web project that allows users to reserve a car. Allow entry of the name, the pick-up date, the driver's license number, and the state the license is from (op-tionally, use a drop-down list containing the state abbreviations). Provide radio buttons or a drop-down list specifying the car size: economy, midsize, or full-size. Save the record in the Reservations table of the database.

Web Services

1. Discuss the concepts of Web services and understand the terminology.

2. Create a Web service.

3. Add a Web reference to a Windows project.

4. Consume a Web service from a Windows project.

5. Consume a Web service from a Web project.

6. Perform calculations in a Web service.

7. Access data through a Web service.

One of the most important features of the .NET Framework is **XML Web Services**. Web services are classes that are compiled and stored on the Web, which you can instantiate and use in both Windows and Web applications. You can think of Web services as the components that you have created for multi-tier applications, but stored and made available on the Web.

It takes very little code changes to turn a middle-tier or data-tier component into a Web Service. A Web application or Windows application can then "consume" the service, which involves instantiating an object of the Web Service class and calling its available methods. This chapter discusses the requirements and technologies for creating a Web Service and demonstrates how to access the Web Service after it is created.

Concepts and Terminology

When you create a Windows component and use it in a Windows application, each element of the project conforms to Windows specifications. But when you create a component as a Web Service, many other services and technologies are required. These services include XML, SOAP, WSDL, and UDDI. Although this may look like alphabet soup or appear rather intimidating, .NET handles most of the details so you don't need to study each of these technologies. However, you should understand the purpose of each.

You can think of each of the following technologies as protocols, or "rules" that both sides understand, to store, locate, and use Web services.

Note: Web services can be created and consumed using many languages and platforms. Not all Web services use XML. Web services created with .NET should more accurately be referred to as *XML Web Services*.

XML

As you already know, XML is a standard method for storing data that can be transferred easily from one machine or platform to another. One of the key advantages of using XML for Web services is that data are transmitted in a text format rather than in binary format. This feature allows data to pass through many firewalls that binary data cannot penetrate. You have been using XML since your first days of creating Visual Basic applications. You don't need to learn any more concepts about XML for Web services, because the .NET Framework takes care of the details.

SOAP

Once data are in a format that can be sent (XML), you need a protocol for sending the data. **Simple Object Access Protocol (SOAP)** is the emerging standard. SOAP establishes a protocol for handling requests and responses including class names, method names, and parameters. SOAP works with XML but does not include a specific protocol for transporting the response and request packets. The transport protocol is most frequently HTTP.

WSDL

The format of the calls to the methods in Web services are controlled by a description specified in **Web Services Description Language (WSDL)**. WSDL contains information about the names of the methods, the parameters that can be passed, and the values that are returned from the functions. You will find an automatically generated .wsdl file in the Web References folder of a project that consumes a Web service.

UDDI

A big part of working with Web services is some way to let others know that the service is available and find those that you need. Of course, if you wrote the Web service and the consumer application, you know what is available and what the capabilities are. But if you want to search for available Web services and determine their functionality, you need the services of **Universal Description, Discovery, and Integration (UDDI)**. The industry-standard UDDI is often called a *directory service* for Web services. You can learn more about UDDI at http://uddi.org *or* http://uddi.microsoft.com.

You can register your service or search for an existing service on the *XML Web Services* tab of the Visual Studio IDE's Start Page (Figure 9.1).

Figure 9.1

Search for existing Web services or register your own on the XML Web Services tab of the Start Page.

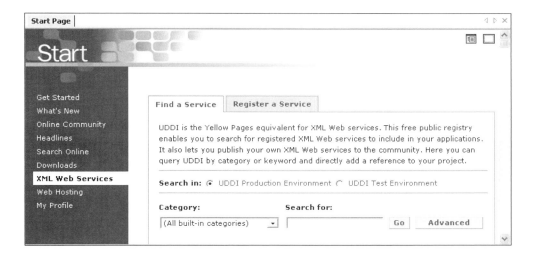

More Acronyms

You should know a few additional acronyms before beginning a Web service example. A **Universal Resource Identifier (URI)** uniquely identifies a resource on the Web and is somewhat more generic than the older term, *URL*. For technical specifications, the industry-standard term *URI* is preferred to *URL*. For more information on URIs and URLs, see

http://www.w3.org/Addressing/

Each Web project must have a target namespace, which defaults to "http://tempuri.org/." For development, you can accept the default, but for production Web services, you should substitute a URI for a site that you control. You will see an example of changing the default target namespace in the example project that follows.

TIP

Always end your URI (or URL) with a backslash such as "http:/MySite/" to avoid an extra trip to the server to determine that it is a site rather than a directory. ■

Feedback 9.1

Match the following:

1. WSDL	a. Address that identifies a specific resource on the Web.
2. UDDI	b. Rules for accessing objects from Web services.
3. XML	c. Specifications for registering and locating available Web services.
4. SOAP	d. Describes the behavior of a Web service.
5. URI	e. Text strings that both describe and hold the data to transmit.

Creating a Web Service

We are going to use the sample code supplied in a Web Service file to see the basic parts of a Web Service project. Although the project doesn't do much, it gives you an opportunity to associate names to some of the parts of the project.

Create a Web Service Project

To start this first example, create a new project called *Ch09FirstWebService* using the ASP.NET Web Services template. Notice that there is no user interface (Figure 9.2), but a design surface for adding components; this is similar to the component classes that you created in the past for multitier applications. A Web service may hold server connections, data components, other components from the toolbox, as well as the methods that you write to perform some type of action.

Notice in Figure 9.2 that the Web service file is named *Service1.asmx* by default. Change yours to *Ch09FirstWebService.asmx*. Always make sure to maintain the .asmx file extension for Web services.

Examine the default code and notice the commented lines:

```
Imports System.Web.Services
<WebService(Namespace := "http://tempuri.org/")> _
Public Class Service1
    Inherits System.Web.Services.WebService

    [Web Service Designer Generated Code]

    'WEB SERVICE EXAMPLE
    'The HelloWorld() example service returns the string Hello World.
```

```
'To build, uncomment the following lines then save and build the project.
'To test this Web service, ensure that the .asmx file is the start page
'and press F5.
'
'<WebMethod()> Public Function HelloWorld() As String
'    HelloWorld = "Hello World"
'End Function

End Class
```

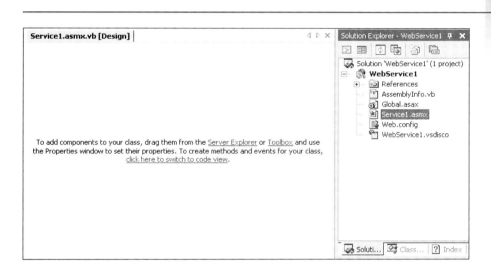

Figure 9.2

A new Web service has a design surface for adding components.

Attribute Tags

Notice the two **attribute tags** in the code: `<WebService(Namespace :=`
`"http://tempuri.org/")>` as an attribute of the class and `<WebMethod()>`
as an attribute of the `HelloWorld` method. These attributes are used to generate the metadata for the Web service and identify the method as available from
a consumer application.

The WebService attribute includes the default URI, *http://tempuri.org/*,
which is the default target namespace for the service. You can use this default
for development projects or change it to some other value (the recommended
practice). For development, the namespace can be any value you choose; for
production projects you should change this URI to a location on your server.
It's best to change the value, otherwise several warnings are generated when
you compile and run the Web service.

Change

```
<WebService(Namespace := "http://tempuri.org/")>
```

to

```
<WebService(Namespace := "http://MyService.org/")>
```

or other value of your choosing.

You should change the name of the class; this name appears on the sample test page.

```
Public Class MyFirstWebService
```

The function header is preceded by an attribute tag. This makes the method available to consumers of the Web service.

```
<WebMethod()> Public Function HelloWorld() As String
```

You don't need to make any changes to this code, but remember to add the `<WebMethod()>` attribute to each method when you create your own methods in a Web service. The consumer application is able to execute **Web methods** as easily as local methods.

This particular method returns the value "Hello World". Recall that assigning the value to the name of the function is equivalent to using the statement

```
Return "Hello World"
```

Testing a Web Service

It's time to test this Web service. Uncomment the function by removing the apostrophes from the method and add a descriptive comment:

```
<WebMethod()> Public Function HelloWorld() As String
    'Return the phrase "Hello World"

    HelloWorld = "Hello World"
End Function
```

Right-click the .asmx filename (Ch09FirstWebService.asmx) in the Solution Explorer and select *Set as Start Page*. Then click the *Run* button or press F5 to test the Web service. The VS IDE compiles the code and runs it in a sample test page in the browser (Figure 9.3). The test page displays the name of your class and a link to the method. Note that if your Web service had several methods, each would be listed on this page.

You can test the `HelloWorld` method by clicking on its name. A new test page appears for the `HelloWorld` method (Figure 9.4). Click on the *Invoke* button to run the method and the "Hello World" text string displays.

Notice the link for *Service Description* in Figure 9.3. Click on the link and note the address line; you are now looking at the code for WSDL (Figure 9.5).

When you create a Web service, you normally do not run it in a browser except to test it. You are creating the service to be used, or "consumed," by other applications.

Attribute Properties

The values inside the parentheses for an attribute are properties of the attribute. For example, in the Web service's attribute, `<WebService(Namespace := "http://tempuri.org/")>`, we set the URI for the WebService attribute

Figure 9.3

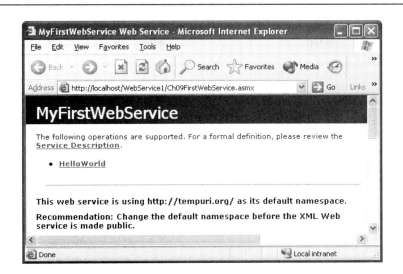

A sample test page appears to help you test a Web service.

Figure 9.4

Run the HelloWorld method by clicking the Invoke button.

Figure 9.5

Display the WSDL for the Web service by clicking on the Service Description link.

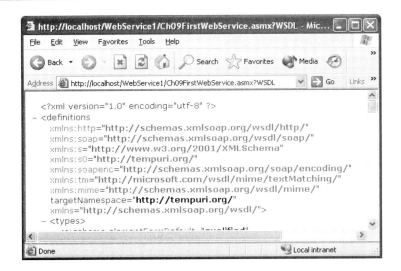

using the Namespace property. You also can set some optional properties for the WebMethod attribute. Set the Description property to give a description of the method that will be included in the WSDL information and appear on the sample test page to describe the method.

```
<WebMethod(Description := "Return a 'Hello World' string")> _
    Public Function HelloWorld() As String
```

Notice that you use a colon and an equal sign to assign a value to the property.

Feedback 9.2

Assume that you want to create a Web service to extend the price times quantity.
1. What should appear in the Web service attribute tag?
2. Where should the tag be placed?
3. What other attribute tag is required?

Consuming a Web Service

Next we are going to create a Windows application to consume (use) the HelloWorld method from the Web Service.

Create a Project with a Web Reference

Create a new Windows project called *Ch09ConsumeHelloWorld*.

To access the Web service you must add a **Web reference**. Right-click on the project name in the Solution Explorer and select *Add Web Reference*. If you have a live Internet connection, you can search UDDI for registered Web services (Figure 9.6). For your own Web services, enter the address of the service in the format:

```
http://localhost/ProjectFolder/ServiceName.asmx.
```

After you enter the address of your Web service and press Enter, the description that you provided appears below the method along with links to *View Contract* and *View Documentation* (Figure 9.7). Viewing the contract displays the WSDL code that you previously saw for *Service Description*. Click the *Add Reference* button at the bottom of the page and you should see a new Web References folder in the Solution Explorer (Figure 9.8).

TIP

If you get an error when adding a Web reference, make sure that the full path and file names are typed correctly and that there is no closing slash. ■

Call the Web Service Method

Once you have added a reference to a Web service, you can instantiate an object of the class and call its methods, in the same way that you access methods of any other class. The data type of the object variable should be localhost.WebServiceClassName. Notice that IntelliSense pops up with *localhost* and the class name (Figure 9.9).

```
Dim wsHello As New localhost.MyFirstWebService()
```

Figure 9.6

Enter the address of your Web service in the **Add Web Reference** *dialog box. You also can search for available Web services registered in UDDI.*

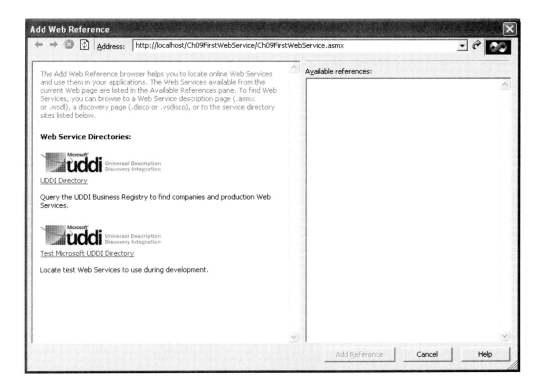

Figure 9.7

View the documentation for the Web service before adding its reference to your project.

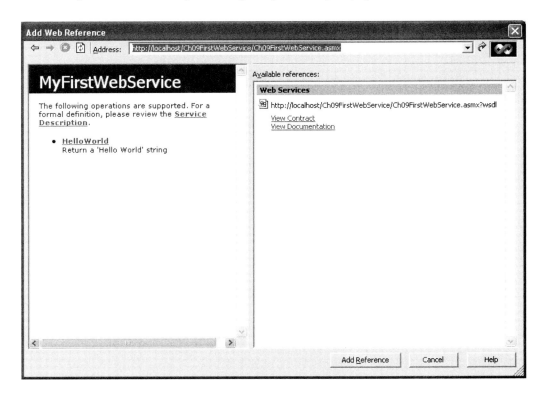

Figure 9.8

Figure 9.9

```
Private Sub frmMain_Load(ByVal sender As System.Object, _
  ByVal e As System.EventArgs) Handles MyBase.Load
    'Call a method from a Web service
    Dim wsHello As New localhost.
                                    [MyFirstWebService]
```

Use the object name to call the `HelloWorld` method. Remember that the method returns a string, which you can assign to a label.

```
lblHello.Text = wsHello.HelloWorld()
```

☑**TIP**

If you modify a Web service component while working on a consumer application, right-click the *localhost* node under *Web References* and select *Update Web Reference*, which retrieves the current version. ▪

The Windows Consumer Application

It's time to show the complete Hello World application. Figure 9.10 shows the form.

Figure 9.10

```
'File:            Ch09ConsumeHelloWorld
'Programmer:      Bradley/Millspaugh
'Date:            January 2003
'Description:     Call the HelloWorld Web service

Option Strict On

Public Class frmMain
    Inherits System.Windows.Forms.Form

    [Windows Form Designer Generated Code]

    Private Sub frmMain_Load(ByVal sender As System.Object, _
      ByVal e As System.EventArgs) Handles MyBase.Load
        'Call a method from a Web service
        Dim wsHello As New localhost.MyFirstWebService()

        lblHello.Text = wsHello.HelloWorld()
    End Sub
End Class
```

> ## Feedback 9.3

Write the code to instantiate a Web service object called *Inventory* from localhost.

Performing Calculations in a Web Service

This next example Web service performs a calculation. We will pass the ExtendedPrice method two arguments (price and quantity) and the method will calculate and return the extended price.

```
<WebMethod()> Public Function ExtendedPrice(ByVal decPrice As Decimal, _
  ByVal intQuantity As Integer) As Decimal
    'Calculate the extended price

    Return decPrice * intQuantity
End Function
```

When you test the Web service on the sample test page, it prompts you for the two arguments (Figure 9.11).

Test the Web service by typing "12" for the price and "2" for the quantity before clicking *Invoke*. You should see the result shown in Figure 9.12.

The next step is to create a client or consumer application. This example uses a Web application rather than a Windows application, but the techniques are just the same. Add a Web reference to the project and add controls to the Web Form. You will want text boxes to enter the price and the quantity, a label to display the result, and a button to calculate the result. Figure 9.13 shows the completed Web Form.

Figure 9.11

When you test a Web service method that requires arguments, the sample test page requests the arguments.

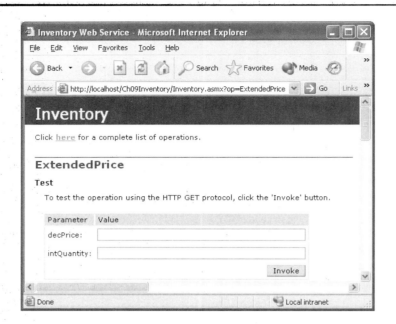

Figure 9.12

The result of the ExtendedPrice *method.*

Figure 9.13

The completed form that uses the Web service.

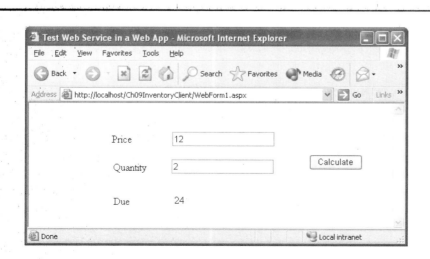

```
Private Sub btnCalculate_Click(ByVal sender As System.Object, _
  ByVal e As System.EventArgs) Handles btnCalculate.Click
    'Call the Web service to calculate the result
    Dim wsInventory As New localhost.Inventory()

    lblDue.Text = wsInventory.ExtendedPrice(CDec(txtPrice.Text), _
      CInt(txtQuantity.Text)).ToString()
End Sub
```

Accessing Data through a Web Service

You can easily create a Web service that returns a dataset. Use the techniques that you learned for creating a data-tier component: Add a connection, data adapter, and dataset to the Web service design surface and write a method to return the dataset. Make sure to set a generic connection string in Web.config so that your users can access the data. (Refer to "Setting a Dynamic Connection String" in Chapter 7 for more information.)

The Web Service Method

```
<WebMethod()> Public Function TitlesData() As DataSet
    'Fill the dataset and return it

    daTitles.Fill(DsTitles1)
    Return DsTitles1
End Function
```

When you test the Web service in the sample test page, the method returns the XML schema and the actual data in XML format (Figure 9.14).

Figure 9.14

The Web service TitlesData *method returns a dataset, which you can view in the sample test page.*

The Consumer Application

The consumer application can be a Windows or Web application. After you add a Web reference to the project for the Web service, you can instantiate the object and execute the method to fill a DataSet object. This example Web application fills a grid with the dataset returned by the Web service. Figure 9.15 shows the Web Form for the completed consumer application.

```
Private Sub Page_Load(ByVal sender As System.Object, _
  ByVal e As System.EventArgs) Handles MyBase.Load
    'Set the data source for the grid from the Web Service
    Dim wsTitles As New localhost.TitlesData()

    dgrTitles.DataSource = wsTitles.TitlesData
    Me.DataBind()
End Sub
```

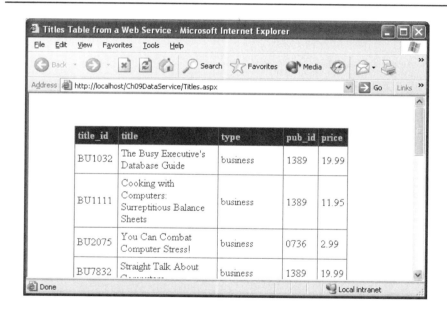

Figure 9.15

This Web application fills the grid with the dataset returned from a Web service.

Moving a Web Service Project

You may want to move a Web Service project from one computer to another while developing your application. Or you may want to run one of the Web services from the student CD. Follow these steps to make a Web Service project portable:

1. Copy the folder for the Web service into Inetpub/wwwroot.
2. Open the IIS Manager and expand the node for the default Web site.
3. Locate your new folder, right-click, and choose *Properties*.
4. In the *Directory* tab, click on *Create*. Then on the *Directory Security* tab, click *Edit* and make sure that *Anonymous Access* is selected. Click *OK* to save the virtual directory settings.

Caution: If you create the virtual directory by selecting *Web Sharing* in the Windows Explorer, *Anonymous Access* is not selected by default and your Web Service will not run on the new computer.

5. Open the Web service project in Visual Studio, right-click on the .asmx file name in the Solution Explorer, and select *Set As Start Page*.
6. Build and run the project. The Web service should run in the sample test page.

If you also are moving the consumer application, rather than writing a new one, you also must update the Web service reference. If the consumer application is a Web app, move the folder, create a virtual folder, open the project, and set the start page. Then for either a Web or Windows application

1. Expand the *Web References* node in the Solution Explorer.
2. Right-click on *localhost* and select *Update Web Reference*.

After these steps your consumer application should be able to access the Web service and run.

Your Hands-On Programming Example

Write a project to display store and sales information from the pubs database. The data should be supplied by a Web service. The form can be a Windows Form or a Web Form. (This example uses a Web Form.)

This project is similar to Ch08RelatedTables, but does not update the database. Display the store names in a drop-down list. When the user selects a store, display information about the store in text boxes or labels and the sales for that store in a data grid.

You must bind the drop-down list and the data grid to database fields. For the store information, you can choose to use either bound or unbound text boxes or labels. You will not allow changes to the data, so if you choose to use text boxes, make them ReadOnly.

Planning the Project
Sketch a form (Figure 9.16) that your users sign off as meeting their needs.

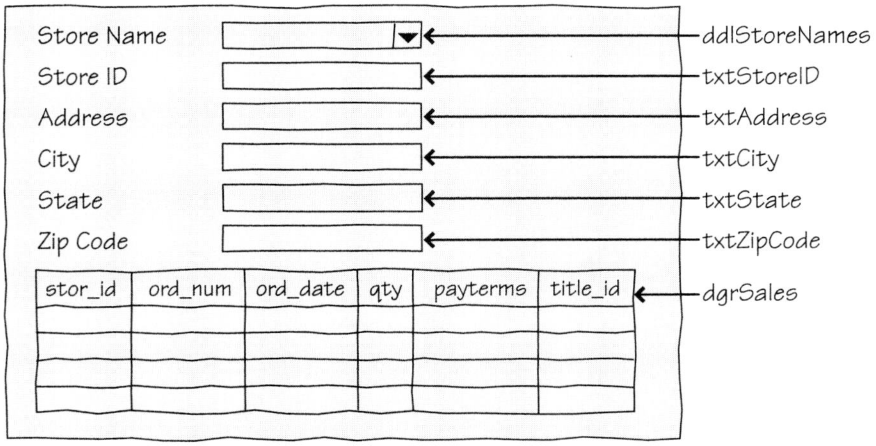

Figure 9.16

The planning sketch of the hands-on programming example.

Plan the Objects, Properties, and Methods

First plan the Web service for the data-tier component; then plan the objects
and property settings for the form and its controls. Figure 9.17 shows the diagram of the program components. Remember that the data tier is a Web service
and will be created in a separate solution.

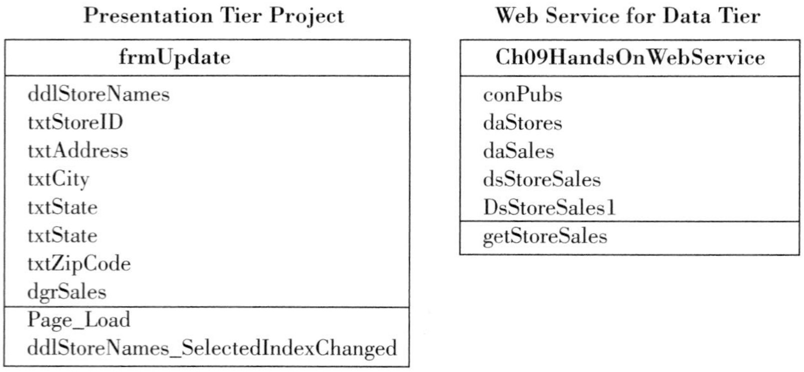

Figure 9.17

*The components for the hands-
on programming example.*

Presentation Tier Project

frmUpdate
ddlStoreNames
txtStoreID
txtAddress
txtCity
txtState
txtState
txtZipCode
dgrSales
Page_Load
ddlStoreNames_SelectedIndexChanged

Web Service for Data Tier

Ch09HandsOnWebService
conPubs
daStores
daSales
dsStoreSales
DsStoreSales1
getStoreSales

Web Service for the Data Tier

Object	Property	Setting
Class	Name	Ch09HandsOnWebService
conPubs	Name	conPubs
daStores	Name	daStores
daSales	Name	daSales
dsStoreSales	Name	dsStoreSales
DsStoreSales1	Name	DsStoreSales1
	Tables	Stores and Sales

Methods	Actions—Pseudocode
getStoreSales	Create a dataset that holds the stores and sales tables. Return the dataset.

Presentation Tier

Object	Property	Setting
frmStoreSales	Name	frmStoreSales
	Title	Display Store Sales
Label1	Text	Store Name
Label2	Text	Store ID
Label3	Text	Address
Label4	Text	City

continued

Object	Property	Setting
Label5	Text	State
Label6	Text	ZIP Code
ddlStoreNames	Name AutoPostBack	ddlStoreNames True
txtStoreID	Text ReadOnly	(blank) True
txtAddress	Text ReadOnly	(blank) True
txtCity	Text ReadOnly	(blank) True
txtState	Text ReadOnly	(blank) True
txtZipCode	Text ReadOnly	(blank) True
dgrSales	Name	dgrSales

Event procedures/Methods	Actions—Pseudocode

Page_Load	Instantiate the data tier Web service.
	If not IsPostBack
	   Retrieve the dataset from the Web service.
	   Bind the list box to the store information.
	   Save the dataset in a session variable.
	   Display the store and sales data for the first
	     store.

ddlStoreNames_SelectedIndexChanged	Retrieve the dataset from the session variable.
	Create a data view that holds the row for the
	   selected store.
	Fill the text boxes for the selected store.
	Create a data view that holds the sales for the
	   selected store.
	Bind the data grid to the sales data view.

Write the Project

First create the Web service for the data tier, following the plan that you created.

* Create the Web service component in its own project and solution.

* Add and name the objects to the Web service, according to your plan.

* Write the methods for the Web service, following the pseudocode.

* Test the Web service to make sure that it works before beginning the consumer application.

Create the consumer application following the sketch in Figure 9.16. Figure 9.18 shows the completed Web Form.

- Create the Web application as a separate project and solution.

- Set the properties of each of the form objects, according to your plans.

- Write the code for the form. Working from the pseudocode, write each event procedure.

- When you complete the code, test the operation several times. Compare the screen output to the data tables, to make sure that you are displaying the correct information.

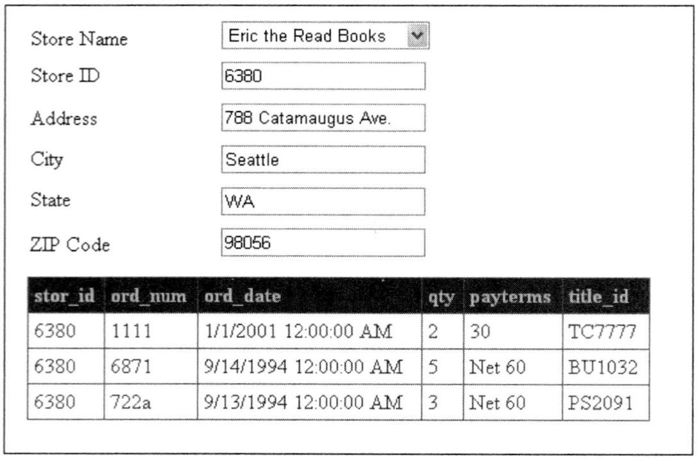

Figure 9.18

The form for the hands-on programming example.

Store Name	Eric the Read Books ▾
Store ID	6380
Address	788 Catamaugus Ave.
City	Seattle
State	WA
ZIP Code	98056

stor_id	ord_num	ord_date	qty	payterms	title_id
6380	1111	1/1/2001 12:00:00 AM	2	30	TC7777
6380	6871	9/14/1994 12:00:00 AM	5	Net 60	BU1032
6380	722a	9/13/1994 12:00:00 AM	3	Net 60	PS2091

The Project Coding Solution

The Web Service for the Data Tier

```
'Project:          Ch09HandsOnDataService
'Programmer:       Bradley/Millspaugh
'Date:             January 2003
'Description:      Provides relational store/sales data.

Option Strict On

Imports System.Web.Services

<WebService(Namespace:="http://Ch09HandsOnDataService/")> _
Public Class Ch09HandsOnWebService
    Inherits System.Web.Services.WebService

    [Web Services Designer Generated Code]

    <WebMethod(Description:="Return a dataset from the titles table")> _
    Public Function getStoreSales() As DataSet
        'Fill the dataset and return it

        daStores.Fill(DsStoreSales1)
```

```
            daSales.Fill(DsStoreSales1)
            Return DsStoreSales1
        End Function
    End Class
End Class
```

The Form

```
'Project:        Ch09HandsOn
'Programmer:     Bradley/Millspaugh
'Date:           January 2003
'Description:    Display store and sales data for a selected store.
'                Uses a Web service.

Option Strict On

Public Class StoreSales
    Inherits System.Web.UI.Page

    [Web Form Designer Generated Code]

    Dim objData As New localhost.Ch09HandsOnWebService()

    Private Sub Page_Load(ByVal sender As System.Object, _
      ByVal e As System.EventArgs) Handles MyBase.Load
        'Get the dataset from the Web service and bind the list
        Dim dsStoreSales As DataSet

        If Not IsPostBack Then
            'Get dataset
            dsStoreSales = objData.getStoreSales()
            'Bind the list box
            With ddlStoreNames
                .DataSource = dsStoreSales
                .DataMember = "stores"
                .DataTextField = "stor_name"
                .DataValueField = "stor_id"
            End With
            Me.DataBind()
            Session("DataSet") = dsStoreSales
            'Display store data for the initial store
            ddlStoreNames_SelectedIndexChanged(sender, e)
        End If
    End Sub

    Private Sub ddlStoreNames_SelectedIndexChanged( _
      ByVal sender As System.Object, ByVal e As System.EventArgs) _
      Handles ddlStoreNames.SelectedIndexChanged
        'Store changed. Get sales and store data.
        Dim dsStoreSales As DataSet
        Dim dvStoreView As New DataView()
        Dim dvSalesView As New DataView()

        'Retrieve the dataset from the session variable
        dsStoreSales = CType(Session("Dataset"), DataSet)
```

```
'Find the store
With dvStoreView
    .Table = dsStoreSales.Tables("Stores")
    .RowFilter = "Stor_id = '" & ddlStoreNames.SelectedItem.Value & "'"
End With

'Fill the text boxes for the store
txtStoreID.Text = dvStoreView(0).Item("Stor_id").ToString()
txtCity.Text = dvStoreView(0).Item("City").ToString()
txtAddress.Text = dvStoreView(0).Item("stor_Address").ToString()
txtState.Text = dvStoreView(0).Item("State").ToString()
txtZipCode.Text = dvStoreView(0).Item("Zip").ToString()

'Create a data view with the sales for this store
With dvSalesView
    .Table = dsStoreSales.Tables("sales")
    .RowFilter = "stor_id = '" & ddlStoreNames.SelectedItem.Value & "'"
End With

'Bind the data view to the grid
With dgrSales
    .DataSource = dvSalesView
    .DataBind()
End With
    End Sub
End Class
```

Summary

1. A Web service is a code component stored on the Web that can be used by other applications. Web services require standard protocols for data, message formats, and transmissions. The .NET Framework accomplishes these with XML, SOAP, WSDL, and UDDI.
2. A URI uniquely identifies a resource on the Web.
3. A Web service needs a `WebService` attribute before the class header and a `WebMethod` attribute before each method header.
4. Web services can be tested in the IDE before attempting to connect them to another application.
5. To make use of a Web service in another application, called the *consumer* or *client* application, you must add a Web reference to the project in the Solution Explorer. Then you can declare and instantiate an object of the Web service class and call its methods.
6. A Web method returns a value to the client or consumer application when the Web service method is called. The return value can be an object such as a dataset or a specific value such as a String or the Decimal result of a calculation.

Key Terms

attribute tags   *325*
Simple Object Access Protocol
  (SOAP)   *322*
Universal Description, Discovery,
  and Integration (UDDI)   *323*
Universal Resource Identifier
  (URI)   *323*

Web method   *326*
Web reference   *328*
Web Services Description Language
  (WSDL)   *323*
XML Web Services   *322*

Review Questions

1. Describe the purpose of each of the following:
     a. XML
     b. WSDL
     c. UDDI
     d. SOAP
2. Explain the steps required to create a Web service.
3. What attribute tags are required to allow exposure of the Web service and its methods?
4. What types of applications have access to the services provided by a Web service?
5. What code is needed in a consumer application to access a Web method?

Programming Exercises

9.1 Modify any multiple-tier project to use a Web service instead of a component.
9.2 Use a Web service for accessing the data in the titles table in the pubs database. Write a Windows application that consumes the Web service and displays the data in a grid.
9.3 Rewrite the hands-on programming example from Chapter 3, which returns a dataset and a data view. Place the data tier in a Web service and convert the data view to a dataset. Display the full name in the combo box, concatenated as LastName, FirstName MiddleInitial. When the user selects a name from the list, find the corresponding record by primary key (emp_id). Display the Employee ID, Hire Date, First Name, Middle Initial, and Last Name in labels for the selected record.
9.4 A local recording studio rents its facilities for $200 per hour. Management charges only for the number of minutes used. Create a Windows project or a Web project in which the input is the name of the group and the number of minutes it used the studio. Use a Web service to calculate the appropriate charges.
     Form: Use labeled text boxes for the name of the group and the number of minutes used. The charges for the current group should be displayed formatted in a label. Include buttons for Calculate and Clear.
     Code: Do not allow bad input data to cancel the program.

9.5   Create a Windows project or a Web project that determines the future value of an investment at a given interest rate for a given number of years. Use a Web service for the calculations. The formula for the calculation is

Future value = Investment amount * (1 + Interest rate) ^ Years

Form: Use labeled text boxes for the amount of investment, the interest rate (as a decimal fraction), and the number of years the investment will be held. Display the future value in a label formatted as currency.

Include buttons for Calculate and Clear. Do not allow bad data to cancel the program.

Case Studies

Claytor's Cottages

Modify the Rooms option of the Claytor's Cottages case study project from Chapter 2 to use a Web service for the calculations.

Presentation Tier

The form should have a drop-down list or radio buttons for King, Queen, or Double. Include text boxes for entering the customer's name, phone number, the number of nights stayed, credit card type (use a list box for Visa, Mastercard, and American Express), and credit card number. Name, nights stayed, and credit card number are required fields. Use a check box for weekend or weekday rate and a check box for AARP or AAA members. Display the price in a label.

Web Service Business Tier

Calculate the price using the table shown in the Chapter 2 case study. Add a room tax of 7 percent. AAA and AARP customers receive a 10 percent discount rate.

Christian's Car Rentals

Modify your Christian's Car Rentals project from Chapter 2. Code the Rentals form using a Web Service for the calculations.

Web Service Presentation Tier

The presentation tier should include data entry for the size of car: Economy, Mid-size, or Luxury. Include text boxes for entering the renter's name, phone number, driver's license, credit card type, and credit card number. Use a drop-down list to select the credit card type. A group box should include the number of days rented, the beginning odometer reading, and the ending odometer reading.

Validate that the ending odometer reading is greater than the beginning odometer reading before allowing the data to be sent to the Web service component. Make sure that an entry has been made for driver's license and number of days rented.

Web Service

Validate that the number of days rented is greater than 0. There is no mileage charge if the number of miles does not exceed an average of 100 miles per day rented.

Use the rate table that appears in the Chapter 2 case study.

10

Writing Database Reports Using Crystal Reports

1. Create a Crystal Reports template and display the report from a Windows Form or a Web Form.

2. Use advanced reporting features, such as numeric functions, grouping, sorting, and special fields.

3. Base a report on a data file or a dataset.

4. Display a report at run time based on a user request.

Using Crystal Reports

One of the powerful features of Visual Studio .NET is the report designer by Crystal Decisions called **Crystal Reports.** The Crystal Report Gallery contains "experts" to guide you in creating standard reports, forms, and even mailing labels, or you can use an existing report or generate a new one. You can display a report from a Windows Form or a Web Form.

It takes two steps to create and display a simple report:

1. Add a **Report Designer** and design the report template. The template includes the settings for connection to the database and the layout of the report.
2. Add a **CrystalReportViewer** control to a form and connect it to the report template.

Once you have added the report to a project and run the project, you can view the report and send the report to the printer, if you wish.

When you create a report template, you are setting up the format of the report. The data are not included in the report layout; instead, each time you run the report, you view the current data.

Creating and Displaying a Report

Adding a Report Designer

You can add a new Report Designer to a project by selecting *Add New Item* from the *Project* menu and choosing the *Crystal Report* icon. In the *Add New Item* dialog box, give the report a name (Figure 10.1). You can either enter the .rpt extension or leave it off; the extension is added by default.

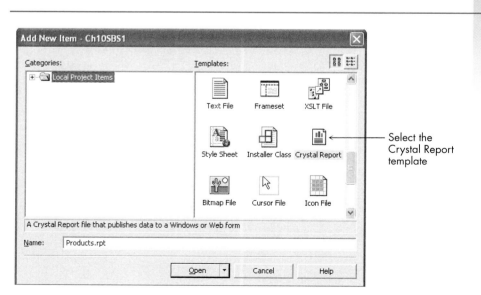

Figure 10.1

Select the Crystal Report icon and give the new report a name in the Add New Item dialog box.

Select the Crystal Report template

Next you are given a choice of the type of report to create (Figure 10.2). You can choose *Using the Report Expert* to open a wizard that steps you through the report creation process. Or you can choose *As a Blank Report* to create your own report from scratch. The third choice, *From an Existing Report*, allows you to create a modification of a report you have already created. The following example uses the wizard.

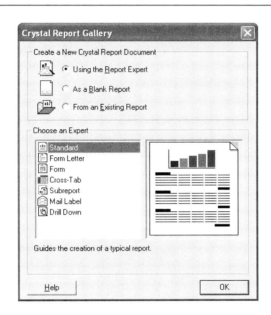

Figure 10.2

Select the Report Expert (the wizard) and the type of report.

Note: The report design is compiled into the project's .exe file. If you modify the report design, you must recompile the project to see the changes.

Creating a Grouped Report—Step-by-Step

This tutorial walks you through the steps for creating a Crystal Report template in a Windows Form application. Figure 10.3 shows the completed report, which is based on the Products and Categories tables of the Northwind SQLServer database.

Create the Project

STEP 1: Create a new Windows Application project called Ch10SBS.
STEP 2: Change the form's Text property to "Northwind Product Report".
STEP 3: Change the form's Name property to frmReport, display the project properties, and set the project's startup object to frmReport.
STEP 4: Rename Form1.vb to frmReport.vb in the Solution Explorer.

Design the Report

STEP 1: In the Solution Explorer, right-click on the project name and select *Add / Add New Item* from the shortcut menu. Click on the *Crystal Report* icon.

Figure   10.3

The completed report for the step-by-step tutorial.

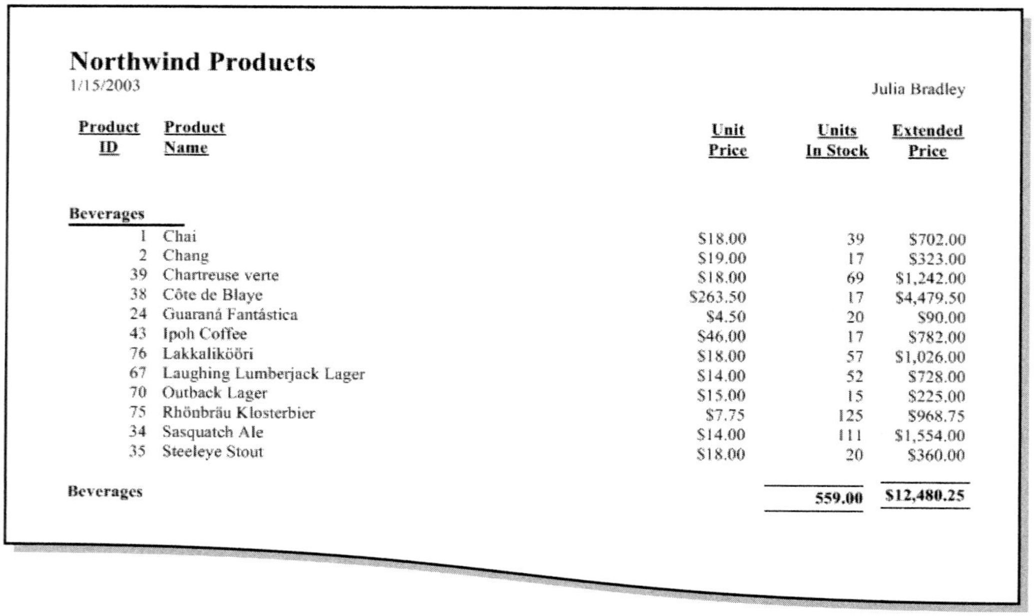

Northwind Products
1/15/2003   Julia Bradley

Product ID	Product Name	Unit Price	Units In Stock	Extended Price
Beverages				
1	Chai	$18.00	39	$702.00
2	Chang	$19.00	17	$323.00
39	Chartreuse verte	$18.00	69	$1,242.00
38	Côte de Blaye	$263.50	17	$4,479.50
24	Guaraná Fantástica	$4.50	20	$90.00
43	Ipoh Coffee	$46.00	17	$782.00
76	Lakkalikööri	$18.00	57	$1,026.00
67	Laughing Lumberjack Lager	$14.00	52	$728.00
70	Outback Lager	$15.00	15	$225.00
75	Rhönbräu Klosterbier	$7.75	125	$968.75
34	Sasquatch Ale	$14.00	111	$1,554.00
35	Steeleye Stout	$18.00	20	$360.00
Beverages			**559.00**	**$12,480.25**

STEP 2: Type the name "Products" and click *Open* (refer to Figure 10.1). The Registration Wizard may appear; you can click "Register Later" or stop to register the product.

STEP 3: Make sure the option for *Using the Report Expert* and the standard report type are selected (refer to Figure 10.2). Click *OK*.

STEP 4: On the first screen of the Standard Report Expert (the wizard), click on the plus sign for *OLE DB (ADO)*; an *OLE DB (ADO)* dialog box appears. Select the provider; *Microsoft OLE DB Provider for SQL Server*, and click *Next*. Drop down the *Server* list and select your local server (Server/NetSDK) (see the note below if your server name does not appear), select the check box for *Integrated Security*, drop down the *Database* list, and select *Northwind*. (On some systems you may need to enter an ID and password rather than select Integrated Security.) Click *Next* and *Finish* on the last screen.

Note: If the *Server* drop-down list does not show your server, you should be able to type in the name. You can see the name of any running server by hovering your mouse pointer over the SQL Server icon in the task bar's tray area.

Northwind should appear as a node under your server in the Standard Report Expert's *Data* tab. Expand the *Northwind* node, the *dbo* node, and the *Tables* node (Figure 10.4).

STEP 5: Select the Products table and click *Insert Table* (or double-click the Products table) to add the table name to the *Tables in report* list. Then add the Categories table to the *Tables in report* list (Figure 10.5).

You can use the *Next* button to click through every tabbed page of the wizard, or use the tabs to go directly to the pages that you want to use.

Figure 10.4

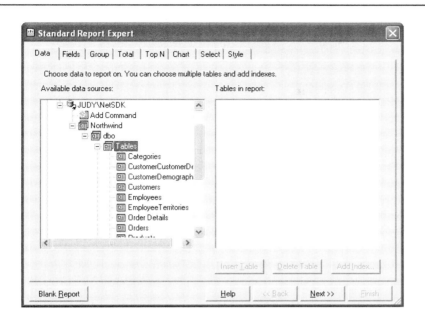

Click on the plus signs to display the table names in the Northwind database.

Figure 10.5

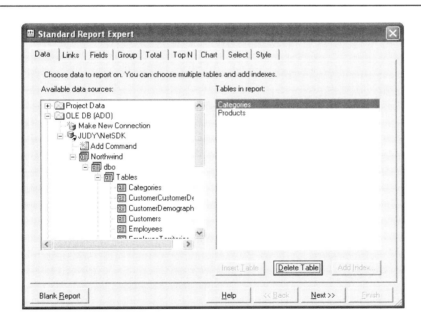

Add the Products and Categories tables to the report.

STEP 6: Click *Next*, which takes you to the *Links* page of the wizard. On this page, the wizard attempts to determine the fields that link the related tables. When the fields have identical names, as do the CategoryID fields in these tables, the wizard has no problem determining the links (Figure 10.6). When key fields are not identically named, you must manually connect the fields on this screen to show the links. (The procedure for connecting the fields is demonstrated in Figure 10.24.)

Figure 10.6

The Links page shows how the two tables are linked.

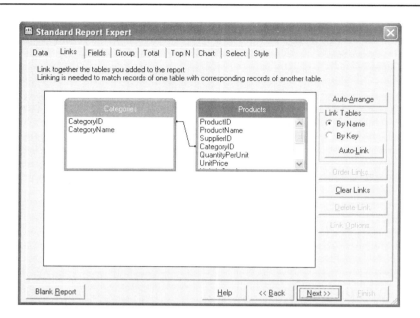

STEP 7: Click *Next* to display the *Fields* page. On this page you select the fields that you want to display on the detail lines of the report. Select the field names from the list on the left and add them to the list on the right. You can either click the field name and click *Add* or double-click the field name.

STEP 8: From the Products table, add these fields: ProductID, ProductName, UnitPrice, and UnitsInStock (Figure 10.7).

✓ TIP

Click on a field in the *Available Fields* list and select *Browse Data* to see the actual data in the table. ∎

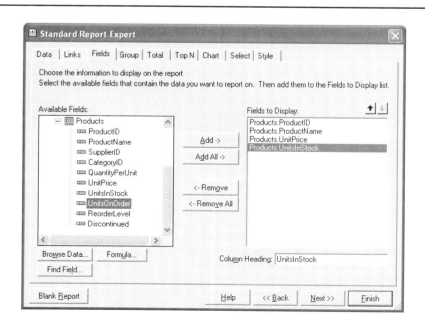

STEP 9: Click *Next* to view the *Group* page. You use this tab to choose the field on which to sort the report. You must sort on any field that you want to use for group breaks (subtotals). Click *Categories.CategoryName* and *Add* to add the CategoryName field to the *Group By* box. Notice the *Sort Order* at the bottom of the page (Figure 10.8).

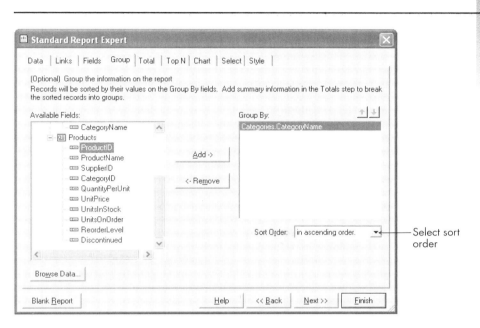

STEP 10: Click *Next* to display the *Total* page. On this page you select the fields that you want to subtotal and total. The wizard automatically includes all fields defined as numeric. But it doesn't make sense to calculate totals on some numeric fields, such as the ProductID and UnitPrice fields.

Remove the ProductID and UnitPrice fields from the *Summarized Fields* list. Also, drop down the *Summary Type* list to see all the choices. Make sure to leave *sum* selected (Figure 10.9).

STEP 11: Click on the *Style* tab at the top of the wizard. (If you want to view the other tabs, you can click *Next* through each page. For this report, you only need the *Style* tab.)

STEP 12: For *Title*, type "Northwind Products". Click on each of the entries in the *Style* box to see the possibilities. Then click on *Standard* and click *Finish.* The report designer appears with the entries that you selected (Figure 10.10).

At this point, the report template is complete. However, you will make lots of adjustments and changes to the content and format. The various parts of the report layout screen are covered in the section "Modifying a Report Design."

Figure 10.9

Allow the wizard to summarize only the UnitsInStock field.

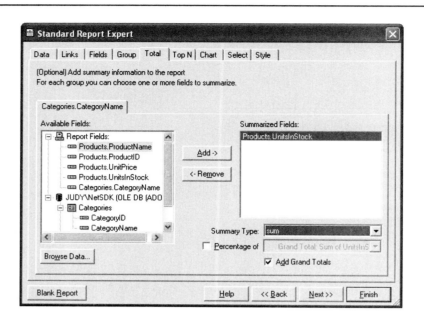

Figure 10.10

The Crystal Reports report designer with the selected options.

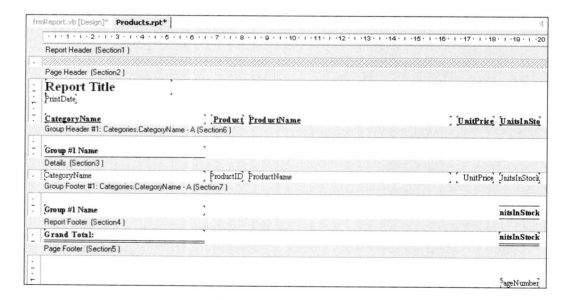

Displaying a Report from a Windows Form—Step-by-Step

To see how the report looks and decide if you want to make modifications, you need to display the report from a form.

Display the Report

STEP 1: Return to the Form Designer window.

STEP 2: Drag a CrystalReportViewer control to the form. It's the last tool in the list if your toolbox isn't sorted.

STEP 3: Increase the size of the form and of the viewer.

STEP 4: Change the Name property of the viewer to crvProducts.

STEP 5: Set the ReportSource property to Products.rpt by using the *Browse* option and finding the file in the Ch10SBS folder.

Note that you can set the ReportSource property in code to make one report form display different reports.

STEP 6: Change the DisplayGroupTree property to False.

STEP 7: Set the Anchor property of the control to anchor to all four edges (top, bottom, left, and right). This will make the control resize when the user resizes the form. Figure 10.11 shows the form at this point.

Figure 10.11

Enlarge the form and the CrystalReportViewer control.

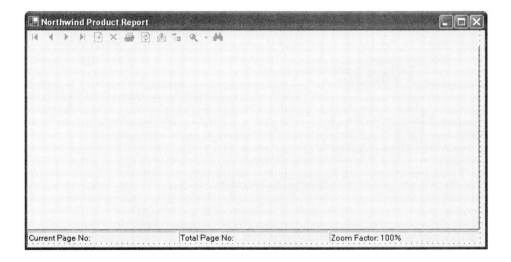

Run the Project

STEP 1: Run the project. The report should appear with the data you selected. Maximize the form to see the entire report.

Notice that the wizard automatically included the category name on the detail lines, which we will remedy soon. Take note of the spacing and formatting to see if there is anything else you'd like to change.

STEP 2: Close the form to return to design mode. You will make some adjustments to the report layout in the section "Modifying a Report Design."

You can switch to the report designer at any time by double-clicking on the .rpt file in the Solution Explorer or by clicking on the .rpt tab in the main document window.

Using the Report Designer

When the Crystal Reports report designer displays, you have many options. You can see two new toolbars, a separate section in the toolbox (Figure 10.12),

and a **Field Explorer** window (Figure 10.13), which appears as a separate tab in the Toolbox window. You can use the Field Explorer to add new fields to your report. Use the items in the toolbox to add elements such as lines, boxes, or additional text that is not bound to a data field, such as explanations or additional title lines.

Note: If the Field Explorer window does not appear, select *View / Other Windows / Document Outline.*

The report template contains several bands for information. Refer to Figure 10.10.

- The **Report Header** appears one time at the beginning of the report. You can place any item in this section that you want to appear on only the first page of a multipage report.

- The **Page Header** appears at the top of each page. Generally the Page Header section holds the report title and column headings.

- The **Group Header** band appears when you select grouping for your report. This band appears in the report each time the field contents change in the field that you selected for grouping.

- The **Details** section holds the data for the body of the report. Here you place the fields that you want to appear on each line of the report. Generally, these are the data from each record.

- The **Group Footer** band appears when you select grouping for your report. This band appears at the end of each group and generally displays subtotals.

- The **Page Footer** appears at the bottom of each page. By default, page numbers appear in this band.

- The **Report Footer** appears once at the end of the report. If your report has totals, they appear in this band.

Modifying a Report Design

You can move, resize, and reformat the fields in the designer. Click on any field and resize using the sizing handles, or drag the control to move it. To reformat a field, right-click and select *Format* from the shortcut menu.

If you want to recall the Report Expert (the wizard) or change the style of the report, right-click on any white area of the report design. On the shortcut menu, select *Report* (Figure 10.14). From the popup menu, you can choose *Report Expert* to open the wizard or *Style Expert* to select a new report style.

Right-click on the report design to view the shortcut menu. Select Report / Report Expert to return to the wizard.

Modifying the Products Report—Step-by-Step

The default settings for the Product report need some modifications.

Remove the Extra Field

STEP 1: Right-click somewhere on one of the white sections of the report, not on a gray divider. From the shortcut menu, select *Report / Report Expert* to return to the wizard. On the warning screen, click *Yes.*

When you return to the wizard, you can step through all of the pages and modify your choices. However, if you have already customized the report manually, you will lose those changes. In this case, you haven't made any custom modifications, so it is safe to return to the wizard.

STEP 2: Click on the *Fields* tab and notice that the wizard automatically included the Categories.CategoryName field. You don't want to display the category name on every detail line, so remove that field from the list.

STEP 3: Click *Finish* to return to the report designer. Notice that the Category-Name field no longer appears in the Details band and that the remaining fields have been rearranged somewhat.

Note: If you clicked on the *Group* tab in the wizard after removing the CategoryName field, the wizard put the field back on the list. You must remove the field and click *Finish*, without clicking on the *Group* tab, to permanently remove the field. Or you can delete the field from the report design by selecting it and pressing the Delete key.

Set the Page Margins

STEP 1: In the report designer, display the shortcut menu and choose *Designer / Page Setup*.

STEP 2: Increase the top margin to 0.5 inch. You also can increase the left and right margins if your printer is one of those that cannot print closer than 1/3 inch from the edge of the page. Click *OK*.

Sort the Report

STEP 1: Right-click on the report to display the shortcut menu. Select *Report / Sort Records*.

STEP 2: Add Product.ProductName to the list. This will sort by product name within each category group. Notice the *Sort Direction* defaults to *Ascending*. Click *OK*.

STEP 3: Run the project again. This time the report should be sorted by product name within categories, with a larger top margin.

Look carefully at the column headings and data in the fields. Many are cut off and should be fixed. Stop execution so you can further modify and beautify the report.

Add a Calculated Field

STEP 1: Display and examine the Field Explorer (Figure 10.15). Notice that you can expand the nodes for the database fields to see which fields

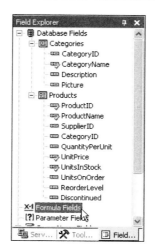

Figure 10.15

The Field Explorer shows the fields that are included in the report and can be used to add new fields.

are included in the report. The selected fields appear with a red checkmark.

STEP 2: Right-click on *Formula Fields* and select *New* from the shortcut menu.

STEP 3: Enter ExtendedPrice for the formula name and click *OK*. The Formula Wizard opens to help you create a new formula (see Figure 10.16.)

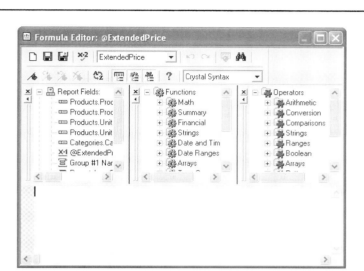

Figure 10.16

Use the Formula Wizard to create or edit formulas.

STEP 4: Before creating the new formula, examine the Formula Wizard. Expand the nodes to see the functions and operations that you can select. You will use the wizard to create a very simple formula.

STEP 5: Make sure that ExtendedPrice is still showing in the box at the top of the wizard. Then in the list on the left, select *Products.UnitPrice* from *Report Fields.* Double-click on the field name and see that it is added to the large box at the bottom of the wizard.

STEP 6: In the list on the right side, expand the *Arithmetic Operators* node and double-click on *Multiply.* An asterisk is added to the formula you are building.

STEP 7: Double-click on *Products.UnitsInStock* in the leftmost list; your formula should be complete (see Figure 10.17).

STEP 8: Click on the wizard's *Save and Close* button.

STEP 9: In the Field Explorer, expand the *Formula Fields* node to see your new ExtendedPrice field. Now you will add the new ExtendedPrice field to the Details section of your report.

STEP 10: You must be able to see the right side of the report design; you can either scroll the Designer window or close your Solution Explorer and Properties window to view the right end of the lines.

STEP 11: Drag the ExtendedPrice field from the Field Explorer and drop it at the right end of the Details section of the report (Figure 10.18). You may have to adjust field size and/or spacing to allow room for the new field.

When you drop the outline of the field, you will see the new field appear in the Details section and the new column heading appear in the Page Header section of the report.

Save and Close button

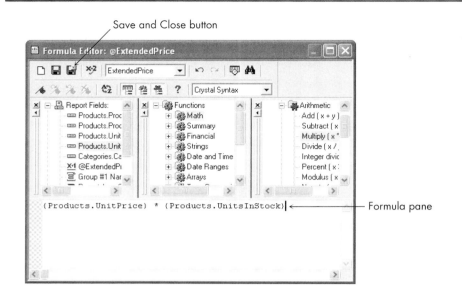

Formula pane

Figure 10.18

Drag the new field to the right end of the Details line.

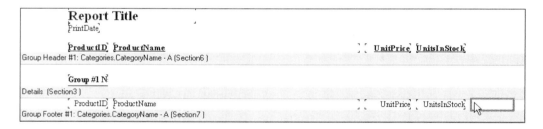

STEP 12: Right-click the new ExtendedPrice field in the Details section and choose *Insert Subtotal*. In the *Insert Subtotal* dialog box (Figure 10.19), you can specify where the subtotal should appear, as well as define the grand total field. Select the two check boxes: *Insert summary fields for all groups* and *Insert grand total field*. Click *OK* to see the new fields in the Group Footer section and the Report Footer section (Figure 10.20).

Notice that the formatting and alignment of the new fields do not match the existing fields. Soon you will modify the formatting, alignment, and spacing of the fields on the report.

Add a Special Field

STEP 1: In the Field Explorer, expand the *Special Fields* node and notice all of the predefined fields that you can add to a report.

STEP 2: Drag the *Page N of M* field to the Page Footer section. Delete the existing Page field, resize the new field, and move it to the bottom-right corner of the section.

You can create highly intelligent reports by programming nearly every element of a report. See the Crystal Decisions Web site for many examples. ∎

Figure 10.19

Specify that the subtotal should appear for each group and that you want grand totals on the report.

Figure 10.20

The ExtendedPrice field has a subtotal in the Group Footer section and a grand total in the Report Footer section.

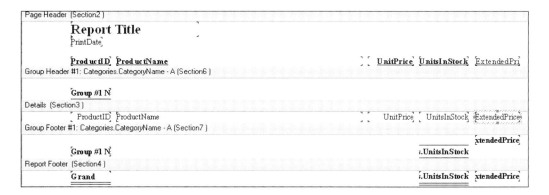

STEP 3: Add the File Author field to the Page Header section, to the right of the PrintDate field. You will likely want to resize and adjust the File Author field after you view the report.

STEP 4: Right-click in any white area of the report design and select *Report / Summary Info.* Enter your name into the Author text box, so that your name will appear in the File Author special field. Notice that you can enter other properties of the report, which you also can display using special fields. Check out the *Statistics* tab while you're here, then click *OK*.

Fix the Field Spacing, Alignment, and Column Headings

As you make the following changes, you can rerun the project as often as you like to view the result of your modifications and see what else must be done. You may want to set the form's WindowState property to Maximized to more easily view the entire report. Refer back to Figure 10.3 for help as you work through the following steps.

STEP 1: Run the project and look at the report. It needs lots of formatting changes. Notice that the report date may be cut off, that the left margin is much larger than the right margin (due to the new field that you added), that the headings should be reformatted and aligned, that the group totals should be formatted alike and aligned, and that the report totals should be formatted alike and aligned.

Also check the placement of the two special fields that you added: Author and Page N of M. Do you need to make any changes to those?

STEP 2: In the Page Header section, locate and select the field that displays the PrintDate (just below the ReportTitle). Drag its right sizing handle to widen the field, so that the date won't be cut off when the report displays.

STEP 3: Select all of the column headings, the fields in the Details section, the subtotals, and the grand totals. You can do this with Shift-click or Ctrl-click or by dragging a selection box around the fields using the mouse pointer. When all of the fields are selected, drag left about 1/2 or 3/4 inch. Your goal is to make the left and right margins approximately equal. If you don't like the result, you can Undo, or make individual adjustments.

STEP 4: In the Group Footer section, select both subtotal fields (you may have to deselect the rest of the report fields first). With the two fields selected, right-click to see the *Multiple Object Selection* context menu. Select *Format Multiple Objects* and set the top and bottom border style of both objects to be the same. Click *OK* in the dialog box and display the context menu again. This time select *Align / Tops*.

STEP 5: Format and align both grand total fields in the Report Footer section.

Next you will modify the column headings. You don't have to keep the field names as column headings—you can write headings that are more meaningful and friendlier to a user. You also can make the headings appear on multiple lines.

STEP 6: Point to the dividing line between the Page Header and Group Header sections. Drag downward to increase the size of the Page Header section.

STEP 7: Select the ProductID header and drag a bottom handle downward to allow for two lines of text.

STEP 8: Double-click on the ProductID header to begin edit mode; the selection handles will disappear and the border will change. When the border resembles that in Figure 10.21, you can click in the text and make modifications. Click between the two words and press the Enter key to make the heading appear on two lines.

ProductID

F i g u r e   1 0 . 2 1

Double-click on a field to change the border into the style that allows text editing of the field.

STEP 9: If you are still in edit mode, click on a white area of the report design to return to design mode. Right-click on the ProductID heading and select *Format*. Examine your many choices for formatting. Then on the *Paragraph* tab select *Centered Alignment*. You also can select the alignment from the toolbar.

STEP 10: Modify each of the other column headings to have multiple words appearing on two lines and bold the Extended Price heading.

STEP 11: Run your program again and examine the alignment and spacing. Make note of any fields that should be moved or realigned or have data cut off. Then return to design mode and finish up the report layout. The report should now look like Figure 10.3.

Displaying a Report from a Web Form

You can display reports from Web Forms, but there are a few differences from Windows Forms. Just as with all controls, you use a different CrystalReportViewer control on your form. You will find the correct control in the Web Forms section of the toolbox. The Web version of the report viewer does not have a printer option; you can only display the report in the browser. To print the report, you must use the browser's *Print* menu option.

It is easy to display the report that you designed in the previous step-by-step tutorial from a Web Form. Begin a new Web Forms project and copy the two files for the report, Products.rpt and Products.vb, into the project's virtual folder. For example, for a project called DisplayProductReport, copy the report files to Inetpub\wwwroot\DisplayProductReport.

You must set the viewer's ReportSource property in code, rather than the Properties window. Add this code to the Web Form's Page_Load event procedure, substituting the path and report designer name for the actual name on your system.

```
Private Sub Page_Load(ByVal sender As System.Object, _
   ByVal e As System.EventArgs) Handles MyBase.Load
    'Put user code to initialize the page here

    crvReport.ReportSource = _
      "C:\inetpub\wwwroot\DisplayProductReport\Products.rpt"
End Sub
```

Note: To make this code run, it sometimes is necessary to add the .rpt file to the project. If so, right-click the project name in the Solution Explorer and select *Add / Add Existing Item* from the shortcut menu.

Moving a Crystal Reports Project

When you move a project that has a Crystal Report, you must make two changes:

1. Change the data source for the report template. In the Field Explorer, right-click on the *Database Fields* icon and choose *Set Location* from the shortcut menu. In the *Set Location* dialog box you can browse to find the current location of the database file.

2. Change the ReportSource property of the CrystalReportViewer control on the form. You can browse to locate the project's current folder.

Setting the Report at Run Time

Sometimes it makes sense to select the report to print at run time, as well as base a report on an ADO.NET dataset. The following step-by-step example shows how to base a report on a dataset, sets the report at run time, and illustrates some more features of Crystal Reports. Also, the report is based on RnRBooks.mdb, an Access database file.

Begin a New Project

STEP 1: Begin a new Windows Form project called Ch10SBSDataset.

STEP 2: Name the form frmDisplayReport in both the Properties window and the Solution Explorer, and change the form's Text property to *Display Report*. Set the project's startup object to frmDisplayReport.

STEP 3: Add a CrystalReportViewer control to the form, name the control *crvDisplay,* and set its Anchor property to *top, bottom, left, right.*

STEP 4: Select *Build / Build Solution.* The purpose of this step is to create the bin folder.

Set up the Dataset

STEP 1: Copy RnRBooks.mdb from the StudentData folder on your CD to the project's bin folder. You are going to base the report on this file and make the project portable.

STEP 2: In the Server Explorer, add a new connection to the RnRBooks.mdb file, using Microsoft Jet OLE DB 4.0 Provider. Select the new copy of the file that is in the project's bin folder.

STEP 3: In the Server Explorer, expand the node for the new connection. In the *Tables* node, select the Books and Subjects tables and drag them to the form. This should create a connection object and two data adapter objects. Name the connection *conRnR,* the first adapter *daBooks,* and the second adapter *daSubjects* (Figure 10.22).

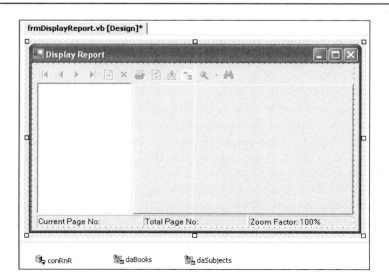

F i g u r e   1 0 . 2 2

Add and rename the connection and two data adapters for the two tables.

STEP 4: Select conRnR and in the Properties window, expand *DynamicProper-ties* and click the build button for ConnectionString. Select *Map property to a key in configuration file* and click *OK*. Notice that a new file, app.config, was added to the Solution Explorer.

STEP 5: Open app.config and locate the line that begins

```
<add key="conRnR.ConnectionString" value= …
```

STEP 6: Change the connection string value to read

```
<add key="conRnR.ConnectionString" value="Provider=Microsoft.Jet.OLEDB.4.0;Data
Source=RnrBooks.mdb;Mode=Share Deny None" />
```

This minimal connection string will force the connection to look in the bin folder for the database file.

STEP 7: Switch back to design view for the form, right-click one of the data adapters, and select *Generate Dataset*. Call the new dataset *dsBooksAndSubjects*, select both the Books and Subjects tables, and choose the option to add the dataset to the designer. You should have a new dataset object called DsBooksAndSubjects1.

Create the Report Based on Two Tables in the Dataset

STEP 1: In the Solution Explorer, right-click on the project name, select *Add / Add New Item*, and select the Crystal Report template. Name the report *rptBooksAndSubjects*.

STEP 2: Select the options to use the Report Expert and standard style.

STEP 3: On the *Data* tab of the Report Expert, expand the nodes for Project Data, ADO.NET DataSets, and the new dataset. Add both the Books and Subjects tables to the report (Figure 10.23).

Figure 10.23

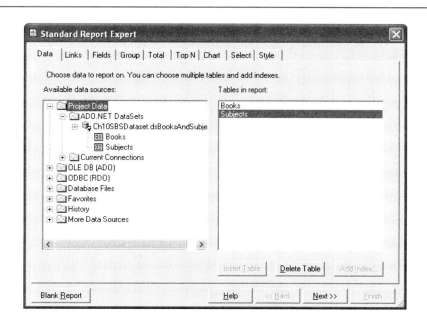

Select both the Books and Subjects tables from the project's ADO.NET dataset.

STEP 4: Click *Next* (or the *Links* tab) to display the table links. Generally the Report Expert can automatically determine the links when the field names are the same in both tables. In this case, you must manually create the link because the field names are not the same.

STEP 5: Click on SubjectCode in the Subjects table. Then drag to the Subject_Code field in the Books table. This creates a link between the two fields. Click on *Auto-Arrange* to improve the view (Figure 10.24).

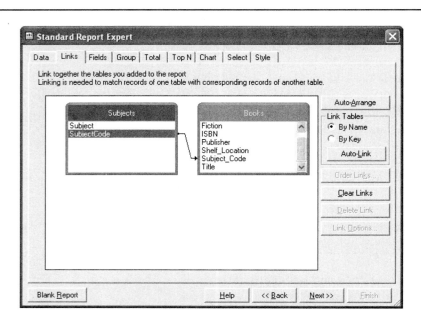

Figure 10.24

Create the link between the two fields by dragging the SubjectCode field to the Subject_Code field.

STEP 6: Click on *Next* (or the *Fields* tab). Add ISBN, Title, and Author to the report fields.

STEP 7: Click on *Next* (or the *Group* tab). Group by Subjects.Subject. This selects the subject name, rather than the subject code.

STEP 8: Click on the *Style* tab and enter "Books by Subject" for the report title. Click *Finish*.

STEP 9: Notice that the report designer added the Subject field to the Details section. To remove that field, select the field in the Details section and press Delete. Then select the Subject column heading in the Page Header section and delete that.

STEP 10: Right-click the designer and select *Designer / Page Setup*. Change the top margin to 0.5 in.

STEP 11: Widen the PrintDate field in the ReportHeader. For some reason, Crystal Reports usually makes that field too narrow to display the date.

Write the Code to Display the Report

STEP 1: Switch to the form's Editor window, add the remarks at the top of the form, and add the Imports statement.

```
'Project:        Ch10SBSDataset
'Programmer:     Bradley/Millspaugh
'Date:           January 2003
'Description:    Display a report at run time. The report is based
'                on a dataset

Imports System.Data.OleDb
```

STEP 2: Inside the form's class, declare a variable to use to refer to the report in code:

```
Public rptPrintReport As rptBooksAndSubjects
```

STEP 3: In the Form_Load procedure, write this code to fill the dataset, set the report's data source to the dataset, and assign the report to the report viewer control. Note that this code could appear in any other procedure based on the logic of the program. For example, if the user selects a menu item or a button, this code could go in the appropriate event procedure.

```
'Instantiate a report object
rptPrintReport = New rptBooksAndSubjects()
'Fill the dataset
daBooks.Fill(DsBooksAndSubjects1, "Books")
daSubjects.Fill(DsBooksAndSubjects1, "Subjects")
'Set the report's data source to the dataset
rptPrintReport.SetDataSource(DsBooksAndSubjects1)
'Set the report viewer's report source to the report
crvDisplay.ReportSource = rptPrintReport
```

STEP 4: Run the project. If all goes well, the form and report should display (Figure 10.25). (If it doesn't go well, check to make sure that the database file is in the project's bin folder.)

Figure 10.25

The Books by Subject report appears at run time.

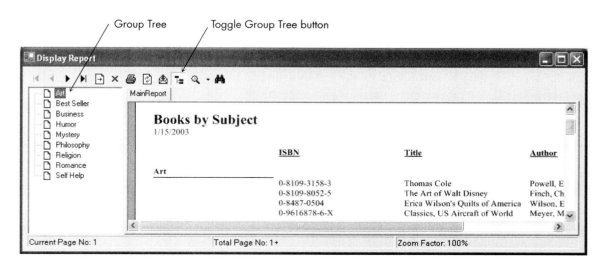

Investigate and Modify the Report

STEP 1: In this report, we did not turn off the group tree. Try clicking on each of the subjects in the group tree. You can hide the group tree by clicking on the *Toggle Group Tree* button.

STEP 2: Notice that each group on the report has a group header and a group footer, which repeats the subject. Next we will hide that footer.

STEP 3: Stop program execution and display the report design. Right-click on the shaded divider labeled "Group Footer #1" and select *Suppress(No Drill-Down)* from the shortcut menu. That section should appear shaded by diagonal lines.

STEP 4: Run the program again. The report should appear without the group footers.

Using a Dataset for a Report on a Web Form

You can easily display a report based on a dataset from a Web Form. All of the procedures described in the previous section work for a Web Form as well as a Windows Form. The only problem you will encounter is the same security issue for data files that you have encountered in the past. Make sure that the project virtual folder's Directory Security is not set for anonymous access and include these two lines in the authentication section of the project's Web.config file:

```
<authentication mode="Windows" />
<identity impersonate="true" />
```

You must also include an absolute path to the data file for the connection string.

Selecting from Multiple Reports

In this section, you will allow the user to select the desired report and display the report on a second form. In order to pass the selection to the second form, you will set up a property of the form and set up an enum to assist in the selection. The example has a frmMain, with menu selections to print one of two reports. The menu commands must pass the selection to the second form, frmReports. On frmReports, a single CrystalReportViewer control can display the selected report.

Creating a Property of the Form

The frmMain menu commands must pass data to frmReports indicating the report to display. The best way to do this is to add a property to frmReports.

```
'Module-level property declaration
Private mintSelectedReport As Integer        'SelectedReport property of form

WriteOnly Property SelectedReport() As Integer
    'Set SelectedReport property using the ReportType enum

    Set(ByVal Value As Integer)
        mintSelectedReport = Value
    End Set
End Property
```

Notice that the SelectedReport property is declared as integer. Although you could set up the property as string or boolean, there is a real advantage in using integer—you can create an enumeration for the available choices. In frmReports, in addition to creating the SelectedReport property, we'll create an Enum to indicate the possible choices.

```
'Selection for report type
Enum ReportType
    BooksBySubject
    BooksByAuthor
End Enum
```

To refer to one of the elements of the enum, use Name.Element: `Report-Type.BookBySubject` or `ReportType.BookByAuthor`. If you are referring to an enum in a different class, include the class name: `frmReports.ReportType.BooksByAuthor`.

In frmMain, the user can select a particular report from a menu choice. The menu item's event procedure can set frmReport's property using the enum values.

```
'frmMain
Private Sub mnuFileReportsAuthor_Click(ByVal sender As System.Object, _
  ByVal e As System.EventArgs) Handles mnuFileReportsAuthor.Click
    Dim frmReports As New frmReports()

    frmReports.SelectedReport = frmReports.ReportType.BooksByAuthor
    frmReports.Show()
End Sub
```

In frmReports, the code can check the value of the property by using the enum values:

```
'frmReports
If mintSelectedReport = ReportType.BooksBySubject Then
    'Print the Books by Subject report
ElseIf mintSelectedReport = ReportType.BooksByAuthor Then
    'Print the Books by Author report
End If
```

Your Hands-On Programming Example

Write a project to display one of two reports. On the main form the user can select the report from menu choices. When a selection is made, display the report on a second form.

Main form menu

File

  Reports

    Books by Subject

    Books by Author

  Exit

Reports form menu

File

  Close

Note that you should display the reports in the Report form's Form_Activated procedure, rather than the Form_Load procedure. The Form_Load event occurs only the first time a form is loaded; the Form_Activated occurs every time a form displays.

The two reports should be based on the RnRBooks.mdb Access datafile. Create datasets on the Reports form and base the reports on the datasets.

Planning the Project

Sketch the forms (Figure 10.26) that your users sign off as meeting their needs. Also sketch the two reports (Figure 10.27), which the users must sign off.

Figure 10.26

The planning sketches for the hands-on programming example: a. the Main form; b. the Reports form.

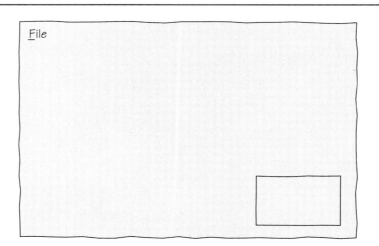

a.

Figure 10.26

Continued

← crvViewReport

b.

Figure 10.27

The two reports to display: a. the Books by Subject report; b. the Books by Author report.

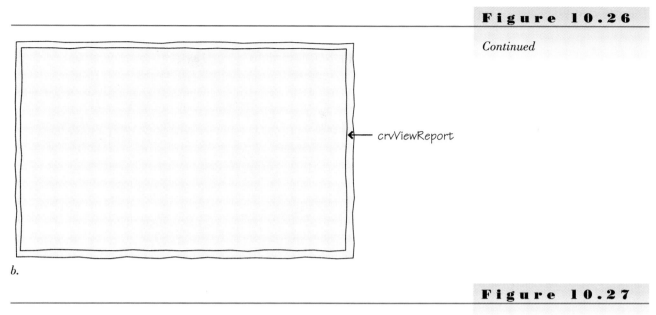

R 'n R Books by Subject
1/15/2003

ISBN	Title	Author
Art		
0-8109-3158-3	Thomas Cole	Powell, Earl A.
0-8109-8052-5	The Art of Walt Disney	Finch, Christopher
0-8487-0504	Erica Wilson's Quilts of America	Wilson, Erica
0-9616878-6-X	Classics, US Aircraft of World War II	Meyer, Mark
Best Seller		
0-394-75843-9	Cultural Literacy	Hirsch, E. D. Jr.
0-446-51652-X	Bridges of Madison County	Waller, Robert James
0-452-26011-6	Song of Solomon	Morrison, Toni
0-8041-0753-X	The Kitchen God's Wife	Tan, Amy

a.

R 'n R Books by Author
1/15/2003

	ISBN	Title
	8423-2218-3	The Way
Beck, Fred		
	0-111-11111-1	89 Years in a Sand Trap
Bradley, Julia Case		
	0-534-26076-4	A Quick Guide to the Internet
	0-697-12897-0	QuickBasic and QBasic Using Modular Structure
	0-697-21361-7	Desktop Publishing Using PageMaker 5.0

b.

Plan the Objects, Properties, and Methods

Plan the objects and property settings for the two forms and their controls. Figure 10.28 shows the diagram of the program components.

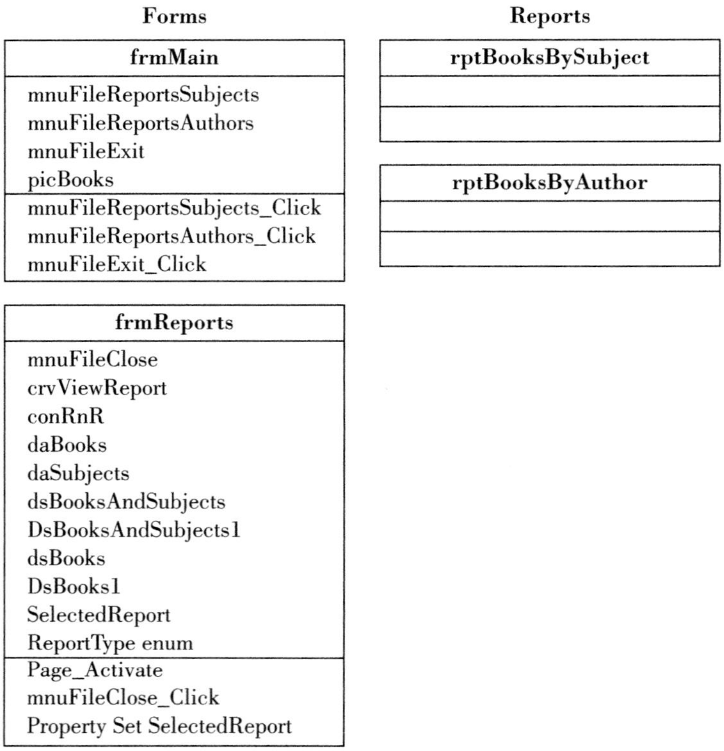

Figure 10.28

The components for the hands-on programming example.

Forms

frmMain
mnuFileReportsSubjects
mnuFileReportsAuthors
mnuFileExit
picBooks
mnuFileReportsSubjects_Click
mnuFileReportsAuthors_Click
mnuFileExit_Click

frmReports
mnuFileClose
crvViewReport
conRnR
daBooks
daSubjects
dsBooksAndSubjects
DsBooksAndSubjects1
dsBooks
DsBooks1
SelectedReport
ReportType enum
Page_Activate
mnuFileClose_Click
Property Set SelectedReport

Reports

rptBooksBySubject

rptBooksByAuthor

Main Form

Object	Property	Setting
frmMain	Name	frmMain
	Icon	Graphics\icons\writing\Books04.ico
	Title	Report Selection
mnuFile	Text	&File
mnuFileReports	Text	&Reports
mnuFileReportsSubjects	Text	Books by &Subject
mnuFileReportsAuthors	Text	Books by &Author
mnuFileExit	Text	E&xit
picBooks	Image	Graphics\icons\writing\Books04.ico
	SizeMode	StretchImage

Event procedures/Methods	Actions—Pseudocode
mnuFileReportsSubjects_Click	Set frmReports.SelectedReport to ReportBySubject. Display frmReports.
mnuFileReportsAuthors_Click	Set frmReports.SelectedReport to ReportByAuthor. Display frmReports.
mnuFileExit_Click	Close the form.

Reports Form

Object	Property	Setting
frmReports	Name	frmReports
	Icon	Graphics\icons\writing\Books04.ico
	Title	Reports
mnuFileClose	Text	&Close
crvViewReport	Anchor	top,bottom,left,right
conRnR	DynamicProperty	Map to conRnR.ConnectionString in App.config
daBooks		
daSubjects		
dsBooksAndSubjects		Tables: Books and Subjects
DsBooksAndSubjects1		
dsBooks		Table: Books
DsBooks1		
Property	SelectedReport	Integer
Enum	ReportType	BooksBySubject
		BooksByAuthor

Event procedures/Methods	Actions—Pseudocode
Page_Activate	If SelectedReport = BooksBySubject 　Instantiate correct report object. 　Fill the dataset. 　Assign the dataset to the report source. 　Assign the report to the viewer control. ElseIf SelectedReport = BooksByAuthor 　Instantiate correct report object. 　Fill the dataset. 　Assign the dataset to the report source. 　Assign the report to the viewer control.
mnuFileClose_Click	Close the form.
Property Set SelectedReport	Set the value of the property.

Write the Project

Create the application following the sketches in Figure 10.26 and 10.27. Figure 10.29 shows the completed Windows forms.

- Create a project with the two forms.

- Set the properties of each of the form objects, according to your plans.

- Set up the connection, data adapters, and datasets on frmReports.

- Add the two Crystal Reports components, basing the reports on the datasets.

- Write the code for the forms. Working from the pseudocode, write each event procedure.

- When you complete the code, test the operation multiple times. The program should be able to display either report, multiple times, in any sequence.

Figure 10.29

The forms for the hands-on programming example: a. the Main form; b. the Reports form.

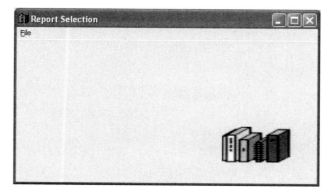

a.

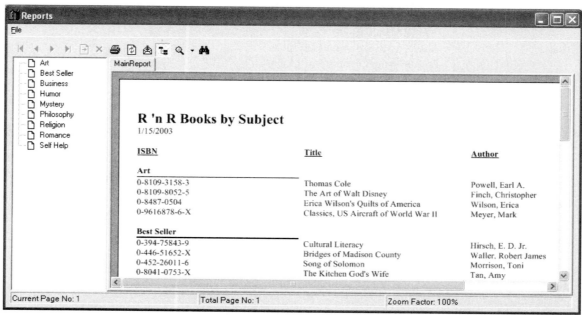

b.

The Project Coding Solution

frmMain

```
'Project:        Ch10MultipleReports
'Class:          frmMain
'Programmer:     Bradley/Millspaugh
'Date:           January 2003
'Description:    Display the selected report.

Public Class frmMain
    Inherits System.Windows.Forms.Form

    [Windows Form Designer generated code]

    Private Sub mnuFileReportsSubject_Click( _
      ByVal sender As System.Object, _
      ByVal e As System.EventArgs) _
      Handles mnuFileReportsSubject.Click
        'Display the Books by Subject report
        Dim frmReports As New frmReports()

        frmReports.SelectedReport = frmReports.ReportType.BooksBySubject
        frmReports.Show()
    End Sub

    Private Sub mnuFileReportsAuthor_Click(ByVal sender As System.Object, _
      ByVal e As System.EventArgs) Handles mnuFileReportsAuthor.Click
        'Display the Books by Author report
        Dim frmReports As New frmReports()

        frmReports.SelectedReport = frmReports.ReportType.BooksByAuthor
        frmReports.Show()
    End Sub

    Private Sub mnuFileExit_Click(ByVal sender As System.Object, _
      ByVal e As System.EventArgs) Handles mnuFileExit.Click
        'Exit the project

        Me.Close()
    End Sub
End Class
```

frmReports

```
'Project:        Ch10MultipleReports
'Class:          frmReports
'Programmer:     Bradley/Millspaugh
'Date:           January 2003
'Description:    Display the selected report.
'                Reports are based on datasets.

'This statement required to declare report objects
Imports System.Data.OleDb

Public Class frmReports
    Inherits System.Windows.Forms.Form

    [Windows Form Designer generated code]
```

```vb
        Private mintSelectedReport As Integer     'SelectedReport property of form

        'Selection for report type
        Enum ReportType
            BooksBySubject
            BooksByAuthor
        End Enum

        'Report objects
        Public rptPrintReport1 As rptBooksBySubject
        Public rptPrintReport2 As rptBooksByAuthor

        Private Sub frmReports_Activated(ByVal sender As Object, _
          ByVal e As System.EventArgs) Handles MyBase.Activated
            'Display the selected report

            If mintSelectedReport = ReportType.BooksBySubject Then
                rptPrintReport1 = New rptBooksBySubject()
                daBooks.Fill(DsBooksAndSubjects1, "Books")
                daSubjects.Fill(DsBooksAndSubjects1, "Subjects")
                rptPrintReport1.SetDataSource(DsBooksAndSubjects1)
                crvViewReport.ReportSource = rptPrintReport1
            ElseIf mintSelectedReport = ReportType.BooksByAuthor Then
                rptPrintReport2 = New rptBooksByAuthor()
                daBooks.Fill(DsBooks1)
                rptPrintReport2.SetDataSource(DsBooks1)
                crvViewReport.ReportSource = rptPrintReport2
            End If
        End Sub

        Private Sub mnuFileClose_Click(ByVal sender As System.Object, _
          ByVal e As System.EventArgs) Handles mnuFileClose.Click
            'Close this form

            Me.Close()
        End Sub

        WriteOnly Property SelectedReport() As Integer
            'Set SelectedReport property using the ReportType enum

            Set(ByVal Value As Integer)
                mintSelectedReport = Value
            End Set
        End Property
    End Class
```

App.config

Make sure that RnRBooks.mdb is in the project's bin folder.

```xml
<?xml version="1.0" encoding="Windows-1252"?>
<configuration>
  <appSettings>
    <!- User application and configured property settings go here.->
    <add key="conRnR.ConnectionString" value="Provider=Microsoft.Jet.OLEDB.4.0;Data
Source=RnrBooks.mdb;Mode=Share Deny None" />
  </appSettings>
</configuration>
```

Summary

1. Crystal Reports is a tool for producing reports from database files.
2. You add a Crystal Reports report designer to a project, use the Report Expert (a wizard) to design the report, add a CrystalReportViewer control to a form, and assign the viewer's ReportSource property to the report.
3. You can select the data for a report from the Server Explorer or from a dataset defined in the project.
4. The Field Explorer holds elements that can be added to a report.
5. The report designer is organized into bands, called the Report Header, Page Header, Group Header, Details, Group Footer, Page Footer, and Report Footer.
6. The *Special Fields* node in the Field Explorer holds many predefined fields that can be added to a report.
7. You can write code to instantiate a report and display it at run time.

Key Terms

Crystal Reports *344*
CrystalReportViewer *344*
Details *352*
Field Explorer *352*
Group Footer *352*
Group Header *352*

Page Footer *353*
Page Header *352*
Report Designer *344*
Report Footer *353*
Report Header *352*

Review Questions

1. Why use Crystal Reports instead of the printing feature of VB?
2. What is the function of the .rpt file? The CrystalReportViewer control?
3. Explain the concept of bands in report design. What bands are available for a report?
4. Explain where these bands appear in a finished report: Report Header, Page Header, Details.
5. Name some examples of Special Fields that can be added to a report.

Programming Exercises

10.1 Add a report to one of your previous projects. Make the report show data related to the application.
10.2 Create an application to display a report of the authors in the pubs database. Include the last name, first name, city, and phone fields. The project can be a Web Form or a Windows Form.
10.3 Write a Windows application to display a report based on the Northwind database. The report should show employees by territory. Use the Employees, EmployeeTerritories, and Territories tables and group by territory. Make sure to display the territory name rather than the ID.

10.4 Write a Windows or a Web application to display a selected report. Include two reports and allow the user to select during program execution. Make one report display the store name and address information from the pubs database. Make the second report show sales by store, with group totals by store.

Case Studies

Claytor's Cottages

Modify the Guests page of the Claytor's Cottages case study project. Add a button or a menu item to display a report that shows the guest information.

Christian's Car Rentals

Modify the Customers page of your Christian's Car Rentals project. Add a button or a menu item to display a report that shows the customer information.

11

Using Collections

1. Declare and reference collections.

2. Determine the proper collection type for a specific situation.

3. Understand various data structures.

4. Create a collection of objects and add and remove items in the collection.

5. Add objects to the Items collection of a list box, control the display, and retrieve selected objects.

Throughout your programming you have used a series of Collections. List boxes have a collection of items. Tables have a collection of rows and of columns and datasets have collections of tables. In this chapter you will examine various types of collections such as stacks, queues, dictionaries, hash tables, sorted lists, and array lists. A collection may consist of a group of individual data items or a collection of objects (remember that a data item is an object).

You will find that programmers and programming documentation often use the words *collection, list,* and *data structure* interchangeably. For most of the references in this chapter, you can substitute one term for another.

Referencing Collection Items

You have been referencing some of the built-in collections of VB all along. You can refer to the individual elements of most collections by either a key (a string value) or an index (the numeric position). For example, to reference an individual table in the Tables collection of a DataSet object:

```
DsStoreSales1.Tables("Stores")      'The Stores table
```

or

```
DsStoreSales1.Tables(0)            'Also refers to the Stores table, assuming that it
                                    is the first table
```

In fact, assuming that DsStoreSales1 is a dataset based on an .xsd file, called a *strongly typed dataset,* you can also refer to the Stores table as

```
DsStoreSales1.Stores
```

System.Collections Namespace

A collection is a group of objects. The **System.Collections namespace** provides classes for several different types of collections. When you need to create a collection, you should be aware of the different types available and the strengths and weaknesses of each type. You may need to inherit from a list class or simply select the type of collection best for a specific situation. An understanding of the types of collections can make the task easier and the program more efficient.

Some types of collections are based on the way the items are handled. For example, a **queue** is like a line: the first item in should be the first one out (**FIFO**—first in, first out). Compare this to a **stack**: the last one in is the first one out (**LIFO**—last in, first out). We often use these terms in conversation; for example, when you refer to a stack of dishes at the end of the buffet line, it is a collection of dishes in which the last one in the stack should be the first one removed. And hopefully the first person in the queue is the first one served.

Several types of collections are of the dictionary type. A **dictionary** consists of a key and value pair, similar to a word and its corresponding definition in a language dictionary. Two types of dictionary lists are the Hashtable and the SortedList.

Collection class	Purpose
ArrayList	A collection that is similar to an array. The size of the list is dynamically increased to accommodate the elements added. Provides some useful methods, such as `Contains`, `Insert`, `RemoveAt`, and `Sort`.
BitArray	A collection that holds Boolean values.
CollectionBase	The parent class for creating strongly typed collections. An abstract class used only for inheritance.
DictionaryBase	The parent class for creating dictionary-type collections with pairs of keys and values. An abstract class, used only for inheritance.
Hashtable	A dictionary-type collection of keys and values. Sorted by the keys, which are hash codes of the values.
Queue	An unsorted collection in which the first element in is the first out (FIFO).
SortedList	A dictionary-type collection of keys and values sorted by the keys. Keys may be based on hash codes.
Stack	An unsorted collection in which the last element in is the first element out (LIFO).

Because all of the collection classes inherit from the same base, they share many properties and methods. A good example is the Count property, which contains the number of elements in the list.

The following examples are based on a program in which an array of strings is used to add and remove items from the different types of collections. Figure 11.1 shows the program with the original list, which is loaded from the mstrLanguage array with this definition:

```
Dim mstrLanguage As String() = {"English", "Spanish", "Chinese", "Italian", _
    "German", "French", "Tagalog"}
```

Each of the collections is declared at the module level:

```
Dim mstrList As SortedList
Dim mhshTable As Hashtable
Dim mstkList As Stack
Dim mqueList As Queue
```

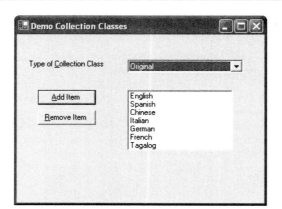

Figure   11.1

The form used for the collection examples. The user can choose to create a stack, queue, sorted list, or hash table and add and remove items in the collections.

Using Stacks

The Stack class provides an unsorted list in which the last item added is the first one removed. The terms *push* and *pop* are used to refer to adding and deleting from a stack. Use the **Push method** to add an item to the list and a **Pop method** to remove an item.

```
'Add an item to the stack
mstkList.Push(strItem)
```

The Pop method removes the last item from the list. If you want to look at the last item without removing it, use the **Peek method**.

```
'View the last item without removing it
strItem = mstkList.Peek()

'Remove the last item from the list
mstkList.Pop()
```

Because stacks are unsorted, they are not the best type of list if you must perform searches. Items in a stack appear in the reverse order of entry. Figure 11.2 shows the example program with the elements added to a stack.

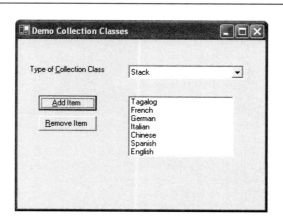

Figure   11.2

The elements in a stack appear in reverse order from original entry.

Using Queues

The Queue class provides an unsorted list of items in which the first item added to the list is the first one to be removed. You use the **Enqueue method** to add items to the queue and the **Dequeue method** to remove items.

```
'Add an item to the queue
mqueList.Enqueue(strItem)
```

A queue, like a stack, provides a Peek method for viewing the next item to be removed without actually removing it.

```
'View the next item to be removed without removing it
strItem = mqueList.Peek()

'Remove the first item from the list
mqueList.Dequeue()
```

Queues share several characteristics with stacks: both are unsorted and slow for searching. Do not use either a stack or queue if you will be performing many searches on your list.

A queue appears in the same order as the original data. Figure 11.3 shows the example program with the elements added to a queue.

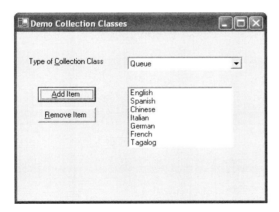

Figure 11.3

The elements in a queue appear in the same order as the original entry.

Using Hash Tables

The HashTable class provides a dictionary-type collection that is based on key/value pairs. **Hash tables** are the fastest type of list for searching. The keys of a hash table are calculated using an algorithm, which must produce a unique key for each entry and produce the same key every time the calculation is made. You can write your own code for creating hash codes, or use the GetHashCode method to calculate the key. Add items to a hash table using the Add method and remove an item using the Remove method.

```
'Calculate the hash code for the key
strKey = strItem.GetHashCode.ToString()
```

```
'Add an item to the hash table
mhshTable.Add(strKey, strItem)

'Calculate the hash code of a selected item
strItem = lstLanguages.SelectedItem.ToString()
strKey = strItem.GetHashCode.ToString()
'Remove the selected item by key
mhshTable.Remove(strKey)
```

A hash table is not a good choice when you need the data in a specific order or when you need to add elements at a specific position. You do not control where the hash table inserts new elements. Hash tables require that each key be unique, so it's not a good choice if there could be duplicate keys.

When you refer to the collection of items in a hash table, you must specify the Values property.

```
'Reload the list from the hash table collection
lstLanguages.Items.Clear()
For Each strItem In mhshTable.Values
    lstLanguages.Items.Add(strItem)
Next
```

Sorted Lists

As the name implies, a SortedList is a collection that is arranged in sorted order. The list consists of key and value pairs and is automatically sorted by the keys. New items are placed in the proper sequence based on the key. Sorted lists use the Add, Remove, and RemoveAt methods. The example program uses the first three letters of the item as the key.

Sorted lists combine many of the features of a hash table and an array list. You can access an element of a sorted list by key, by value, or by index. The keys that you assign must be unique and may be created from a hash code calculation.

```
'Create the key
strKey = strItem.Substring(0, 3)
'Add the key and item to the sorted list
msrtList.Add(strKey, strItem)
```

Sorted lists work well when you need to search for items or remove items from the middle of the list.

```
'Retrieve the selected item to be removed
strItem = lstLanguages.SelectedItem.ToString()
'Set the key as the first three characters of the item
strKey = strItem.Substring(0, 3)
'Remove the item by key
msrtList.Remove(strKey)
```

You also can remove an item from a sorted list by its index. But you must be careful, because the indexes of items change as elements are added or removed from the list.

```
'Remove the item by index
msrtList.RemoveAt(intIndex)
```

When you refer to the collection of items in a sorted list, you must specify the Values property.

```
'Reload the list box from the sorted list collection
lstLanguages.Items.Clear()
For Each strItem In msrtList.Values
    lstLanguages.Items.Add(strItem)
Next
```

The values of a sorted list appear in sorted order. Figure 11.4 shows the example program with the elements added to a sorted list.

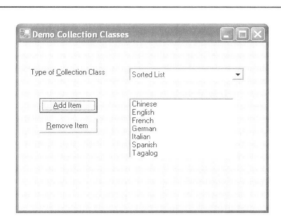

Figure   11.4

The elements in a sorted list appear in alphabetic order.

Using the Example Program

The example program loads a string array with languages and allows the user to select the collection type. The user can then add an element to the collection or remove an element. Each time the collection changes, the Items property of the list box is cleared and reloaded with the contents of the collection. Refer to Figures 11.2, 11.3, and 11.4 for the completed form.

```
'Project:        Ch11Lists
'Programmer:     Bradley/Millspaugh
'Date:           January 2003
'Description:    Store an array of strings in various collection types.

Option Strict On

Public Class frmLists
    Inherits System.Windows.Forms.Form

    [Windows Form Designer generated code]

    Dim mstrLanguage As String() = {"English", "Spanish", "Chinese", "Italian", _
        "German", "French", "Tagalog"}
    Dim mstrListType As String
    Dim mintIndex As Integer
```

```
Dim mstrList As SortedList
Dim mhshTable As Hashtable
Dim mstkList As Stack
Dim mqueList As Queue

Private Sub cboStyle_SelectedIndexChanged( _
  ByVal sender As System.Object, ByVal e As System.EventArgs) _
  Handles cboStyle.SelectedIndexChanged
     'Create a new collection based on the selected collection type

    mintIndex = 0
    lstLanguages.Items.Clear()
    Select Case cboStyle.SelectedItem
        Case "Hashtable"
            mhshTable = New Hashtable()
            mstrListType = "HashTable"
        Case "Original"
            DisplayOriginal()
            mstrListType = "Original"
        Case "Queue"
            mqueList = New Queue()
            mstrListType = "Queue"
        Case "Sorted List"
            mstrList = New SortedList()
            mstrListType = "SortedList"
        Case "Stack"
            mstkList = New Stack()
            mstrListType = "Stack"
    End Select
End Sub

Private Sub DisplayOriginal()
    'Display the array in its original order
    Dim strItem As String

    lstLanguages.Items.Clear()
    For Each strItem In mstrLanguage
        lstLanguages.Items.Add(strItem)
    Next
End Sub

Private Sub btnAdd_Click(ByVal sender As System.Object, _
  ByVal e As System.EventArgs) Handles btnAdd.Click
    'Add the next element to the selected collection
    Dim strKey As String
    Dim strItem As String

    If mintIndex <= mstrLanguage.GetUpperBound(0) Then          'Array finished
        strItem = mstrLanguage(mintIndex)
        Select Case mstrListType
            Case "SortedList"
                strKey = strItem.Substring(0, 3)
                mstrList.Add(strKey, strItem)
                'Reload the list from the sorted list collection
                lstLanguages.Items.Clear()
                For Each strItem In mstrList.Values
                    lstLanguages.Items.Add(strItem)
                Next
            Case "HashTable"
                strKey = strItem.GetHashCode.ToString()
                mhshTable.Add(strKey, strItem)
```

```
                    'Reload the list from the hash table collection
                    lstLanguages.Items.Clear()
                    For Each strItem In mhshTable.Values
                        lstLanguages.Items.Add(strItem)
                    Next
                Case "Stack"
                    mstkList.Push(strItem)
                    'Reload the list from the stack
                    lstLanguages.Items.Clear()
                    For Each strItem In mstkList
                        lstLanguages.Items.Add(strItem)
                    Next
                Case "Queue"
                    mqueList.Enqueue(strItem)
                    'Reload the list from the queue
                    lstLanguages.Items.Clear()
                    For Each strItem In mqueList
                        lstLanguages.Items.Add(strItem)
                    Next
                Case "Original"
                    MessageBox.Show("Cannot add to the original list")
            End Select
            mintIndex += 1                 'Move to the next array element
        Else
            MessageBox.Show("No more items for the list")
        End If
End Sub

Private Sub btnRemove_Click(ByVal sender As System.Object, _
    ByVal e As System.EventArgs) Handles btnRemove.Click
        'Remove an item from the collection
        Dim strKey As String
        Dim strItem As String

        Select Case mstrListType
            Case "SortedList"
                If lstLanguages.SelectedIndex <> -1 Then
                    strItem = lstLanguages.SelectedItem.ToString()
                    strKey = strItem.Substring(0, 3)
                    mstrList.Remove(strKey)
                    'Reload the list from the sorted list collection
                    lstLanguages.Items.Clear()
                    For Each strItem In mstrList.Values
                        lstLanguages.Items.Add(strItem)
                    Next
                Else
                    MessageBox.Show("Select the item to remove")
                End If
            Case "HashTable"
                If lstLanguages.SelectedIndex <> -1 Then
                    strItem = lstLanguages.SelectedItem.ToString()
                    strKey = strItem.GetHashCode.ToString()
                    mhshTable.Remove(strKey)
                    'Reload the list from the hash table collection
                    lstLanguages.Items.Clear()
                    For Each strItem In mhshTable.Values
                        lstLanguages.Items.Add(strItem)
                    Next
                Else
                    MessageBox.Show("Select the item to remove")
                End If
```

```
        Case "Stack"
            mstkList.Pop()
            'Reload the list from the stack
            lstLanguages.Items.Clear()
            For Each strItem In mstkList
                lstLanguages.Items.Add(strItem)
            Next
        Case "Queue"
            mqueList.Dequeue()
            'Reload the list from the stack
            lstLanguages.Items.Clear()
            For Each strItem In mqueList
                lstLanguages.Items.Add(strItem)
            Next
        Case "Original"
            MessageBox.Show("Cannot remove from the original list")
    End Select
    End Sub
End Class
```

Using Array Lists

An ArrayList can dynamically increase in size as new elements are added. You can use the **Capacity property** to set the size of the list. However, if additional elements are added, the capacity is automatically increased in chunks. You can use the **TrimToSize method** to reduce the size of the collection.

An array list is similar to an array in many respects, but provides more properties and methods to make array programming much easier. Here is a list of some of the most useful properties and methods of an array list:

Array list properties and methods	Purpose
Capacity	Holds the number of elements that the collection can contain.
Count	Holds the actual number of elements in the collection.
IsFixedSize	Determines whether the collection is a fixed size.
IsReadOnly	Determines whether the collection is read only.
Item	The value stored at the specified index.
Add	Add an element to the end of the collection.
AddRange	Add the contents of a collection to the end of the collection.
Clear	Remove all elements from the collection.
Contains	Searches for a specific value in the collection.
CopyTo	Copy elements into an existing array.
RemoveAt	Remove the element at the specified location.
RemoveRange	Remove a series of elements.
ToArray	Copy the elements to a new array.
TrimToSize	Set the capacity to the actual number of elements.

> ## Feedback 11.1

Write the code to add strElement to the following:

Class	Object name
1. Hashtable	mhshTable
2. SortedList	msrtList
3. Stack	mstkList
4. Queue	mqueList

Creating a Collection of Objects

When you create your own business class, such as Product, Book, Person, or Employee, you usually need more than one of each object type. One Product or Book object is not very useful—you likely need to define multiple items. You can accomplish this by creating a collection class and adding objects to the collection. You can choose from the various types of collection classes, depending on your needs for speed, sorting, retrieval by value, index, or key.

You can refer to the members of a collection in two different ways depending on the type of collection. Like an array, you can specify an index number, which is the object's position in the collection. This method is convenient only if the order of the members does not change. Alternately, you can give each object a string key that uniquely identifies the object, and can store and retrieve the objects in the collection by their keys. Sometimes objects already have a field that is unique and can be used as a key, such as a personal identification number (PIN), a customer number, or an account number. Or you can use a hashing algorithm to create a unique key based on the name or some other unique value. When you remove objects from a collection, the indexes for the remaining objects change to reflect their new position, but the key fields never change.

A Collection of Student Objects

The following examples create and access a collection of Student objects. The project has a Student class with properties for Name and GPA. In the form (Figure 11.5), the user can enter a student's name and GPA and add to the collection, remove a selected student from the collection, or display the GPA for a selected student. A list box on the form displays the current contents of the collection after each addition or deletion, and a label on the form displays the Count property of the collection.

Declaring a Collection

You can declare and instantiate the collection at the module level. Select the best collection type for your application. This example uses a sorted list and a hash code of the name as the key.

```
Dim mcolStudents As New SortedList()
```

Figure 11.5

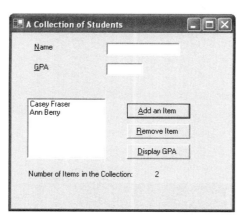

*Add or remove students from a
collection, or display the GPA
for a selected student.*

Adding Objects to a Collection

After the user enters the name and GPA and clicks the Add button, create the
key using the GetHashCode method, which performs a calculation on the name
and produces an integer. Because the key must be string, convert the hashed
key to a string.

```
'Declare and instantiate a new Student.
Dim objStudent As New Student(txtName.Text, CDec(txtGPA.Text))
'Calculate a key
strKey = objStudent.Name.GetHashCode.ToString()
'Add to the collection
mcolStudents.Add(strKey, objStudent)
```

Removing an Element from a Collection

Many collection types have both a Remove and RemoveAt method. The Remove
method generally deletes an element by key and the RemoveAt method removes
by index. For a keyless collection, such as an ArrayList, the Remove method
removes the specified object from the collection and the RemoveAt deletes by
index.

   The example program uses the Remove method. It retrieves the selected
name from the list box, calculates the key using GetHashCode, and removes the
element by key.

```
With lstStudents
    If .SelectedIndex <> -1 Then
        'Get the key from the selected student name
        Dim strKey As String = .SelectedItem.GetHashCode.ToString()
        mcolStudents.Remove(strKey)
        DisplayList()
    Else
        MessageBox.Show("Select a student from the list.", _
          "A Collection of Students")
    End If
End With
```

Retrieving an Element from a Collection

You can retrieve an object that has been placed in a collection using the Item property. Dictionary-type collections, such as sorted lists and hash tables, return an object of **DictionaryEntry data type**. Therefore, you must cast the element to the object type that you need.

```
Dim objStudent As Student

'Get the key for the selected name
Dim strKey As String = .SelectedItem.GetHashCode.ToString()
objStudent = CType(mcolStudents.Item(strKey), Student)
```

For most collection types, the Item property is defined as the default property of the collection. You can leave out the word "Item" from statements:

```
objStudent = CType(mcolStudents(strKey), Student)
```

Using For Each / Next

When you want to access each object in a collection, you can use a For Each/Next structure. Because the data type of each element is DictionaryEntry, declare a variable of that type and cast its Value property to the object type that you need.

```
'Loop through the collection and display the items in a list box
Dim objStudent As Student
Dim deStudent As DictionaryEntry

lstStudents.Items.Clear()
For Each deStudent In mcolStudents
    objStudent = CType(deStudent.Value, Student)
    lstStudents.Items.Add(objStudent.Name)
Next
```

The Completed Program

Here is the complete Student collection application. It has a Student class and a form, which appears in Figure 11.5.

The Student Class

```
'Project:        Ch11StudentCollection
'Module:         Student
'Programmer:     Bradley/Millspaugh
'Date:           January 2003
'Description:    Create a Student class.

Option Strict On

Public Class Student

    'Private property variables
    Private strName As String
```

```
        Private decGPA As Decimal

        'Property procedures
        Public Property Name() As String
            Get
                Return strName
            End Get
            Set(ByVal Value As String)
                strName = Value
            End Set
        End Property

        Public Property GPA() As Decimal
            Get
                Return decGPA
            End Get
            Set(ByVal Value As Decimal)
                decGPA = Value
            End Set
        End Property

        'Class constructor
        Public Sub New(ByVal strName As String, ByVal decGPA As Decimal)
            'Create a Student object

            Me.Name = strName
            Me.GPA = decGPA
        End Sub
End Class
```

The Form Class

```
'Project:         Ch11StudentCollection
'Module:          frmCollections
'Programmer:      Bradley/Millspaugh
'Date:            January 2003
'Description:     A form for entering and viewing student objects
'                 in a Students collection. Uses a SortedList collection.

Option Strict On

Public Class frmCollection
    Inherits System.Windows.Forms.Form

    [Windows Form Designer generated code]

    Dim mcolStudents As New SortedList()

    Private Sub btnAdd_Click(ByVal sender As System.Object, _
        ByVal e As System.EventArgs) Handles btnAdd.Click
        'Create a Student object and add it to the collection
        Dim strKey As String

        If txtName.Text <> "" Then
            Try
                'Declare and instantiate a new Student.
                Dim objStudent As New Student(txtName.Text, CDec(txtGPA.Text))
                'Calculate a key
```

```vbnet
            strKey = objStudent.Name.GetHashCode.ToString()
            'Add to the collection
            mcolStudents.Add(strKey, objStudent)
            DisplayList()
            'Clear the text boxes
            With txtName
                .Clear()
                .Focus()
            End With
            txtGPA.Clear()
        Catch err As InvalidCastException
            With txtGPA
                .SelectAll()
                .Focus()
            End With
            MessageBox.Show("Numeric GPA required." & ControlChars.NewLine & _
                txtName.Text & " Not Added.", "A Collection of Students")
        Catch err As Exception
            With txtName
                .SelectAll()
                .Focus()
            End With
            MessageBox.Show("Duplicate student name." & ControlChars.NewLine & _
                txtName.Text & " Not Added." & Err.message, "A Collection of Students")
        End Try
    Else
        With txtName
            .SelectAll()
            .Focus()
        End With
        MessageBox.Show("Please enter a name.", "A Collection of Students")
    End If
End Sub

Private Sub btnDisplay_Click(ByVal sender As System.Object, _
  ByVal e As System.EventArgs) Handles btnDisplay.Click
    'Display the GPA for the selected student
    Dim objStudent As Student

    With lstStudents
        If .SelectedIndex <> -1 Then
            'Get the key for the selected name
            Dim strKey As String = .SelectedItem.GetHashCode.ToString()
            'Get the selected student item from the collection
            objStudent = CType(mcolStudents.Item(strKey), Student)
            MessageBox.Show("The GPA for " & objStudent.Name & " is " _
                & objStudent.GPA, "A Collection of Students")
        Else
            MessageBox.Show("Select a student from the list.", _
                "A Collection of Students")
        End If
    End With
End Sub

Private Sub btnRemove_Click(ByVal sender As System.Object, _
  ByVal e As System.EventArgs) Handles btnRemove.Click
    'Remove selected item from the collection

    With lstStudents
        If .SelectedIndex <> -1 Then
```

```
            'Get the key from the selected student name
            Dim strKey As String = .SelectedItem.GetHashCode.ToString()
            mcolStudents.Remove(strKey)
            DisplayList()
        Else
            MessageBox.Show("Select a student from the list.", _
              "A Collection of Students")
        End If
    End With
End Sub

Private Sub DisplayList()
    'Loop through the collection and display the items in a list box
    Dim objStudent As Student
    Dim deStudent As DictionaryEntry

    lstStudents.Items.Clear()
    For Each deStudent In mcolStudents
        objStudent = CType(deStudent.Value, Student)
        lstStudents.Items.Add(objStudent.Name)
    Next
    'Display the count
    lblCount.Text = mcolStudents.Count.ToString()
End Sub
End Class
```

Feedback 11.2

1. Write the code to refer to a single item in a collection of the Persons class. The collection is a hash table with hash codes of the person's name as the key.
2. Which property of a collection class is usually the default property?
3. Write the code to remove an object from the Persons collection.
4. Write the code to retrieve a Person object from the collection.

Using an Items Collection

The **Items collection** of a text box or combo box is actually a collection of objects, not just strings. You can add objects to the Items collection and retrieve the complete object in the Item property.

When you add an object to the Items collection, what displays in the list? The answer is whatever is returned by the object's ToString method. You can write your own ToString method in the object's class, which must override the base class ToString method.

```
'Procedure in the Client class
Public Overrides Function ToString() As String
    'Return the Name property for this object's ToString method

    Return mstrName
End Function
```

In the form, add an object to a list box Items collection:

```
lstClients.Items.Add(objClient)
```

When you request a selected Item property, its data type is DictionaryEntry, so you must convert the object to the correct type:

```
objClient = CType(lstClients.Items(lstClients.SelectedIndex), Client)
```

You can retrieve the Item property from the list, convert to the correct type, and reference the individual properties of the object.

```
objClient = CType(lstClients.Items(lstClients.SelectedIndex), Client)
MessageBox.Show("The phone number for " & objClient.Name & " is " & _
   objClient.PhoneNumber)
```

Feedback 11.3

1. If you add an object to the Items collection of a list box or combo box, what displays in the list?
2. How can you specify which property of your object should appear in the list?

Your Hands-On Programming Example

Create a program that maintains a collection of Client objects. The Client class should have properties for Name, PhoneNumber, and AccountNumber. Use a sorted list collection and use the account number as the key. (Do not use a hash code, but use the actual account number.)

On the form, allow the user to add new clients using text boxes for Name, Account Number (the key field), and Phone Number. The list box should show the client names from the collection. Allow the user to add new clients, remove clients, and display the information (name, account number, and phone number) for a selected client. Display the current count of the number of clients in the collection.

The program must create a Client object, add it to the collection, and add it to the list box, which must display the client names. Do not allow missing data or a missing selection to cancel the program.

Planning the Project

Sketch the form (Figure 11.6) that your users sign off as meeting their needs.

Plan the Objects, Properties, and Methods

Plan the objects and properties for the Client class and for the form and its controls. Figure 11.7 shows the diagram of the program components.

Figure 11.6

The planning sketch for the hands-on programming example.

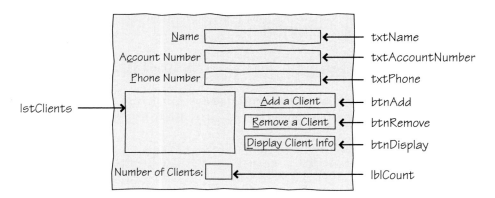

Figure 11.7

The components for the hands-on programming example.

Presentation Tier
frmClients
txtName
txtAccountNumber
txtPhone
lstClients
btnAdd
btnRemove
btnDisplay
lblCount
btnAdd_Click
btnDisplay_Click
btnRemove_Click
DisplayCollection

Business Tier
Client
Name
PhoneNumber
AccountNumber
New(strName, strPhoneNumber, strAccountNumber)
ToString

The Form

Object	Property	Setting
frmClients	Name	frmClients
	AcceptButton	btnAdd
	Title	A Collection of Clients
Label1	Text	&Name
Label2	Text	A&ccount Number
Label3	Text	&Phone Number
Label4	Text	Number of Clients:
txtName	Text	(blank)
txtAccountNumber	Text	(blank)

continued

Object	Property	Setting
txtPhone	Text	(blank)
lstClients	Name	lstClients
btnAdd	Text	&Add a Client
btnRemove	Text	&Remove a Client
btnDisplay	Text	&Display Client Info
lblCount	Text	(blank)

Event procedures/Methods	Actions—Pseudocode
btnAdd_Click	If Name is present If AccountNumber is present Set up the key. Create a new Client object. Add the Client to the collection. Add the Client to the list box. Display the collection count. Clear the text boxes and set the focus. Else Display error message for missing AccountNumber. Else Display error message for missing Name.
btnDisplay_Click	If a selection is made from the list Retrieve the selected Client object. Set up the string with all client information. Display the information in a message box. Else Display error message for missing selection.
btnRemove_Click	If a selection is made from the list Retrieve the selected Client object. Set up the key of the object. Remove the selected Client from the collection by key. Display the collection in the list box. Display the collection count. Else Display error message for missing selection.
DisplayCollection	Clear the list. Loop through the collection. Add each object to the list.

Client Class

Properties	Private property variables
Name	mstrName
PhoneNumber	mstrPhoneNumber
AccountNumber	mstrAccountNumber

Procedures/Methods	Actions—Pseudocode
New	Instantiate a Client object.
ToString	Return mstrName.
Property Get and Set	Name.
Property Get and Set	AccountNumber.
Property Get and Set	PhoneNumber.

Write the Project

Create the application following the sketch in Figure 11.6. Figure 11.8 shows the completed Windows Form.

- Create a project with a Windows Form.
- Create and code the Client class, following your plans.
- Set the properties of each of the form objects, according to your plans.
- Write the code for the forms. Working from the pseudocode, write each event procedure.
- When you complete the code, test the operation multiple times. The program should be able to add, remove, and display client information in any order, and keep the count current at all times.

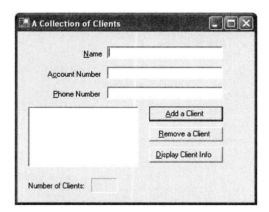

Figure 11.8

The form for the hands-on programming example.

The Project Coding Solution

frmClients

```
'Project:       Ch11HandsOn
'Class:         frmClients
'Programmer:    Bradley/Millspaugh
'Date:          January 2003
'Description:   Collect and display client information.
'               Uses Client objects in a Client collection and
'               stores Client objects in the Items collection of
'               a list box.

Option Strict On
```

```
Public Class frmClients
    Inherits System.Windows.Forms.Form

    [Windows Form Designer generated code]

    Dim mcolClients As New SortedList()

    Private Sub btnAdd_Click(ByVal sender As System.Object, _
      ByVal e As System.EventArgs) Handles btnAdd.Click
        'Create a Client object and add it to the collection
        Dim strKey As String

        If txtName.Text <> "" Then
            If txtAccountNumber.Text <> "" Then
                strKey = txtAccountNumber.Text
                'Declare and instantiate a new Client
                Dim objClient As New Client(txtName.Text, txtPhone.Text, _
                  strKey)
                'Add to the collection
                mcolClients.Add(strKey, objClient)
                'Add the client to the list box
                lstClients.Items.Add(objClient)
                'Display the count
                lblCount.Text = mcolClients.Count.ToString()
                'Clear the text boxes
                With txtName
                    .Clear()
                    .Focus()
                End With
                txtPhone.Clear()
                txtAccountNumber.Clear()
            Else
                'Missing account number
                MessageBox.Show("Please enter the account number.", "Clients")
                txtAccountNumber.Focus()
            End If
        Else
            'Missing name
            MessageBox.Show("Please enter a name.", "Clients")
            txtName.Focus()
        End If
    End Sub

    Private Sub btnDisplay_Click(ByVal sender As System.Object, _
      ByVal e As System.EventArgs) Handles btnDisplay.Click
        'Display the information for one client
        Dim objClient As Client
        Dim strInfoString As String

        With lstClients
            If .SelectedIndex <> -1 Then
                'Retrieve the selected Client object from the list
                objClient = CType(.Items(.SelectedIndex), Client)
                strInfoString = "Client: " & objClient.Name & _
                  ControlChars.NewLine & _
                  "Account Number: " & objClient.AccountNumber & _
                  ControlChars.NewLine & _
                  "Phone Number: " & objClient.PhoneNumber
                MessageBox.Show(strInfoString, "Selected Client Information", _
                  MessageBoxButtons.OK, MessageBoxIcon.Information)
```

```
                Else
                    'No selection made from the list
                    MessageBox.Show("Select a client name from the list", "Clients")
                End If
            End With
        End Sub

        Private Sub btnRemove_Click(ByVal sender As System.Object, _
          ByVal e As System.EventArgs) Handles btnRemove.Click
            'Remove the selected client from the collection
            Dim objClient As Client
            Dim strKey As String

            With lstClients
                If .SelectedIndex <> -1 Then
                    'Retrieve the selected Client object from the list
                    objClient = CType(.Items(.SelectedIndex), Client)
                    strKey = objClient.AccountNumber
                    'Remove the Client object from the collection by key
                    mcolClients.Remove(strKey)
                    'Display the objects in the collection
                    DisplayCollection()
                    lblCount.Text = mcolClients.Count.ToString()
                Else
                    'No selection made from the list
                    MessageBox.Show("Select an item from the list", "Clients")
                End If
            End With
        End Sub

        Private Sub DisplayCollection()
            'Display the complete collection in the list box
            Dim deClient As DictionaryEntry
            Dim objClient As Client

            lstClients.Items.Clear()
            For Each deClient In mcolClients
                objClient = CType(deClient.Value, Client)
                lstClients.Items.Add(objClient)
            Next
        End Sub
    End Class
```

Client Class

```
'Project:        Ch11HandsOn
'Class:          Client
'Programmer:     Bradley/Millspaugh
'Date:           January 2003
'Description:    Create a client object.

Option Strict On

Public Class Client
    Private mstrName As String
    Private mstrPhoneNumber As String
    Private mstrAccountNumber As String
```

```
     Public Property Name() As String
         Get
             Return mstrName
         End Get
         Set(ByVal Value As String)
             mstrName = Value
         End Set
     End Property

     Public Property PhoneNumber() As String
         Get
             Return mstrPhoneNumber
         End Get
         Set(ByVal Value As String)
             mstrPhoneNumber = Value
         End Set
     End Property

     Public Property AccountNumber() As String
         Get
             Return mstrAccountNumber
         End Get
         Set(ByVal Value As String)
             mstrAccountNumber = Value
         End Set
     End Property

     Public Sub New(ByVal strName As String, _
       ByVal strPhoneNumber As String, _
       ByVal strAccountNumber As String)
         'Instantiate a Client object

         Me.Name = strName
         Me.PhoneNumber = strPhoneNumber
         Me.AccountNumber = strAccountNumber
     End Sub

     Public Overrides Function ToString() As String
         'Return the Name property for this object's ToString method

         Return mstrName
     End Function
End Class
```

Summary

1. Items in a collection may be referenced by their key, their value, or their index, depending on the type of collection.
2. The .NET System.Collections namespace contains several types of collection classes with differing characteristics, advantages, and disadvantages.
3. A queue is first-in, first-out (FIFO); stacks are last-in, first-out (LIFO).
4. A dictionary style of list contains key and value pairs; examples include the hash table and the sorted list.

5. Stacks use `Push` and `Pop` for adding to and removing from a collection; queues use `Enqueue` and `Dequeue` for adding and removing. Both have a `Peek` method to allow you to view the next element without removing it.

6. A hash table is a dictionary-type collection and is the quickest list type for searching. The keys of hash tables may be based on a hash code of some unique value. Use the `Add` and `Remove` methods for hash tables.

7. A sorted list is a dictionary-type collection that you can access by key, value, or index. Use the `Add`, `Remove`, and `RemoveAt` methods for adding and removing items. The keys must be unique and may be based on hash codes.

8. An ArrayList can be resized at run time. This collection type has many useful methods that can simplify array handling.

9. An element of the Items collection of a dictionary-type collection has a data type of DictionaryEntry.

10. `For Each/Next` loops are used to iterate through a collection.

11. You can add objects to the Items collection of a list box or combo box; the list box displays the value returned by the object's `ToString` method. You can retrieve a selected object from the list and access the individual properties of the object by casting the Item property from a DictionaryEntry to an object of the correct type.

Key Terms

Capacity property   *384*
collection   *376*
data structure   *376*
Dequeue method   *379*
dictionary   *377*
DictionaryEntry data type   *387*
Enqueue method   *379*
FIFO   *376*
hash table   *379*
Items collection   *390*

LIFO   *376*
list   *376*
Peek method   *378*
Pop method   *378*
Push method   *378*
queue   *376*
stack   *376*
System.Collections namespace   *376*
TrimToSize method   *384*

Review Questions

1. Describe each of the following collection styles:
   a. Dictionary
   b. Hash table
   c. Stack
   d. Queue
   e. Sorted list
2. What is an ArrayList?
3. What are the advantages of using a collection instead of an array?
4. What are the advantages of using a hash table over a sorted list? The disadvantages?
5. What is the data type of an item from the Items collection of a dictionary-type collection?
6. What displays in a list box or combo box if you add an object to the list?

Programming Exercises

11.1 Modify the chapter hands-on exercise to use a hash table instead of a sorted list.

11.2 Create a project that maintains a collection of vendors. Each vendor should have properties for company name, phone, contact person, and email. Allow the user to add a vendor, display the list of vendors, display a single vendor, or remove a vendor. Display the vendor names in a list box. As each vendor is added to the collection, add the name to the list; when a vendor is removed from the collection, remove the name from the list. Allow the user to select a vendor from the list and display the vendor's properties in a message box. Use a hash code of the company name for the key.

11.3 Write an application that maintains a collection of customers. Each Customer object should have properties for Last Name, First Name, PIN (the key), Phone Number, Cell Phone Number, and FAX Number. The user can add customers, remove customers, and display the complete information for a selected customer. Store the concatenated first and last names in a list box, to show the current contents of the collection and allow the user to select a customer to remove or display.

Display the customer information in a message box, or consider using a second form. If you use a second form, you will need to create a property of the form that holds a Customer object, so you can pass the selected object to the form.

Case Studies

Claytor's Cottages

Create a project that maintains a collection of customers. Each customer object should contain Customer Name, Customer Number (key for collection), and Phone Number. Allow options for adding and removing objects. Use a list box to display the Customer Names, giving the user the option to display a selected customer.

Christian's Car Rentals

Create a project that maintains a collection of advertisers. Each advertiser object should contain Company Name, Number (key for collection), and Account Representative's Name. Allow options for adding and removing advertiser objects. Use a list box to display the Company Name, giving the user the option to display a selected advertiser.

12

User Controls

1. Create a Windows user control using inheritance from an existing control.

2. Add a new user control to a form.

3. Add properties to a user control.

4. Raise an event in a control class and write code to handle the event in a form.

5. Create a new composite control by combining preexisting controls.

6. Create a Web control and add it to a Web page.

7. Create a control that provides for database access.

You can create your own controls to use on Windows Forms or Web Forms. You may want to modify or combine existing controls, called ***user controls***, or write your own controls from scratch, called *custom controls*. Because of the object-oriented nature of .NET, you can inherit from existing controls and modify their behavior, such as creating a text box with validation or a self-loading list box.

This chapter shows you how to create user controls for both Windows and the Web. Just as for built-in controls, Windows controls are completely different from Web controls, so they are covered in separate sections of the chapter.

Windows User Controls

When you want to modify the behavior of an existing control or combine controls to use in multiple situations, you can create your own user control. Sometimes you find yourself using a certain set of controls in many situations, such as text boxes for name and address, or maybe a combination of text and graphics for a company logo. You can create your own user control that is made up of the individual controls. The new user control is called a ***composite control***, and the controls that you combine are called ***constituent controls***. You can add the new user control to the toolbox and use it in other Windows projects.

New to VB .NET, you can inherit a new control from an existing control. The first example in this chapter uses inheritance to create a new control, and later you will create a composite control.

The Control Author versus the Developer

The distinction between a control's author and the **developer** who uses the control is much more important with user controls than any of the other project types. The **author** creates the control (and tests and compiles it) and the control appears in the toolbox. When you author a control, you must plan for the design-time behavior of your control as well as its run-time behavior.

Creating a New Control

Generally you create a new control by beginning a new project based on the Windows Control Library project type. The controls that you create in this type of project can be used in multiple Windows projects. You also can choose to add a new UserControl to an existing project, which is the technique that you use if you want to use the control in only the current project. In both techniques, the new UserControl object appears as a design surface, similar to a form, in a Designer window (Figure 12.1).

> *Note:* The Windows Control Library template is not available in the Standard Edition of Visual Basic. Use the Empty Project template instead.

You design the visual interface for a composite control in the Designer window by dragging the constituent controls to the design surface. For an inherited control, you do not see the visual representation of your control in the designer; instead you use the designer to add nonvisual components, similar to the Component classes you have used in the past.

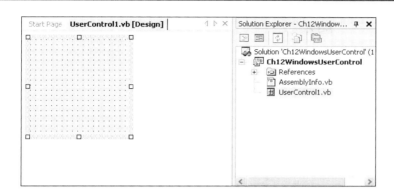

Figure 12.1

Use the design surface of a UserControl to create a new user control.

In the Code Editor window, you can view and modify the class that is created for the control. The class automatically inherits from the UserControl class.

```
Public Class UserControl1
    Inherits System.Windows.Forms.UserControl
```

Inheriting from an Existing Control

The newest and easiest way to create a user control is to inherit from an existing control. You can inherit from most of the Windows Forms controls except the Progress Bar. For example, you can create your own Label control that has the font, size, color, and text alignment set as you want it; or create a new TextBox control that validates in a certain way, that only accepts numeric keystrokes, or always selects the entry when it gets the focus, or has a particular font or alignment. Your new control will have all of the properties, methods, and events of the base class, unless you write code to override the behaviors. And you can add new properties, methods, and events for your derived control.

To create your customized control, follow these general steps. The step-by-step exercise that follows gives the detailed instructions.

- Create a project based on the Windows Control Library template.

- Modify the class name and the `Inherits` clause to inherit from the base class that you want to use, such as TextBox, Label, or Button.

- Add any additional functionality that you want.

- Build the DLL. After you create the DLL, you will need to create a Windows project to test the new control.

Creating an Inherited User Control—Step-by-Step

In this step-by-step exercise, you will create a new UserControl that inherits from a TextBox control. The new control, called ValidDate, will look exactly like all other text boxes, but it will validate the entry for a valid date in the control's Validating event procedure. If the entry is not a valid date, it will appear highlighted (selected) and the Cancel argument is set to True, so that the focus remains in the control. This essentially forces the user to fix the entry be-fore moving to the next control. Later you will learn to raise an event for invalid entries, for which you can write code in the form. You should *not* display a mes-sage box to the user from the control; that task should be left to the form's code.

Create a New Project

STEP 1: Begin a new project called *Ch12ValidDate* using the Windows Control Library template (Figure 12.2).

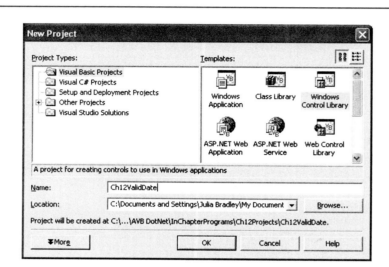

Figure   1 2 . 2

Create a new project using the Windows Control Library template.

STEP 2: This next step may seem foolish, but can save you lots of trouble later. You will delete the UserControl file in the project and add a new one, with the control's name set correctly: Right-click the UserControl1.vb file and select *Delete*. Then right-click the project name and select *Add / Add New Item*. Select UserControl and type the name of the new con-trol as *ValidDate.vb* (Figure 12.3).

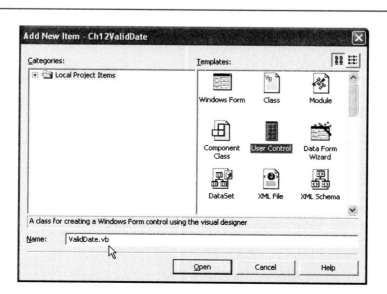

Figure   1 2 . 3

Add a new UserControl called ValidDate.vb.

The actual name of the control, which is used in the toolbox, is taken from the class name. You'll save yourself some complications later if you always make sure that the class is correctly named before making any changes to the control or compiling the code. By adding the correctly named control to the project, the class is automatically named correctly.

STEP 3: Close the Designer window and open the Code Editor window. Check the class name and modify the `Inherits` clause to inherit from TextBox instead of UserControl:

> **✓ TIP**
>
> **K**eep the control's Designer window closed at all times unless you need to add a component, and then close it again. Having the Designer window open when you compile can cause the control to not compile correctly and may remove it from the toolbox. ■

```
Public Class ValidDate
    Inherits System.Windows.Forms.TextBox
```

STEP 4: At the top of the code, before the `Class` statement, add the remarks and `Option Strict On`.

```
'Project:        Ch12ValidDate
'Programmer:     Your Name
'Date:           Today's date
'Description:    A new user control to extend the function of a text box.
'                Validates for a valid date entry.

Option Strict On
```

Add an Event Procedure

STEP 1: Drop down the *Class* list and select *(Base Class Events)*. This step gives you access to all of the events for the TextBox class.

STEP 2: From the *Events* list select *Validating*.

STEP 3: Type the code to test for a valid date. The code tests for an invalid date; if the date is invalid, it highlights the text and keeps the focus in the field. Notice that you use the Me keyword to refer to the current class, or this control itself.

```
Private Sub ValidDate_Validating(ByVal sender As Object, _
    ByVal e As System.ComponentModel.CancelEventArgs) _
    Handles MyBase.Validating
    'Test for a valid date

    If Not IsDate(Me.Text) Then
        Me.SelectAll()
        e.Cancel = True
    End If
End Sub
```

Build the Project

STEP 1: Select *Build / Build Ch12ValidDate*. This step should place .dll and .pdb files in the project's bin folder. You can choose *Show All Files* to see these files. The .dll file holds the new control; the .pdb file holds debugging information. For production jobs, when debugging is complete, you no longer create or need debugging files.

Test the User Control in a Form

To test the control, you need a form. Although you can create a new solution, the easiest method is to add another project to this solution.

STEP 1: From the *File* menu select *Add Project / New Project* and select *Windows Application*. (Alternative: Right-click the solution in the Solution Explorer and select *Add / New Project*.) Name the new project *Ch12TestUserControl*.

        The new project is created in a new folder but in the same solution. The solution file remains in the folder with the control.

STEP 2: Name the form's class *frmTestDate* and the file *frmTestDate.vb*.

STEP 3: Display the project properties and change the startup object to frmTest-Date.

STEP 4: Right-click on the form's project in the Solution Explorer and set it as the startup project.

STEP 5: Set the Text property of the form to *Test ValidDate Control*.

        The form's project must have a reference set to the control's project before it can use the control.

STEP 6: In the Solution Explorer, right-click on the form's project (Ch12Test-UserControl) and choose *Add Reference*, or select *Add Reference* from the Project menu.

STEP 7: In the *Add Reference* dialog box (Figure 12.4), click on the *Projects* tab, select your project, and click *Select* and then *OK*. Scroll down to the bottom of the toolbox; your new ValidDate control should appear there.

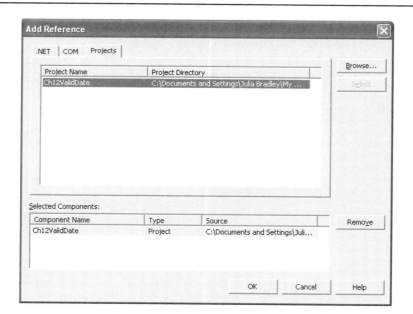

Figure 12.4

Add a reference to the control's project to the form's project in the **Add Reference** *dialog box.*

Add Controls to the Form

STEP 1: Add two labels, a ValidDate control, and a text box to the form, changing these properties (Figure 12.5).

Control	Property	Setting
Label1	Text	Date:
Label2	Text	Name:
ValidDate1	Name	valDate
	Text	(blank)
TextBox1	Name	txtName
	Text	(blank)

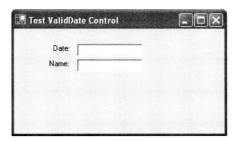

Figure 12.5

The completed form to test the ValidDate control.

Run the Project

STEP 1: Run the project. Your form should appear.

STEP 2: Type in 11 or other bad data in the Date text box and press the Tab key. The text should appear highlighted and the focus should remain in the control. Try various good and bad data and tab to the next control.

STEP 3: Close the form. *Note:* If the control contains bad data, you won't be able to close the form using the Close box. Enter good data in the text box or return to the VS IDE and click the *Stop Debugging* button.

If you change the name of your user control, you must rebuild the project, close the solution, and reopen to update the toolbox. ■

Adding Properties to a Control

You can set up new properties of a control class, just as you do for other classes. Declare a module-level private variable to hold the property and write Property procedures.

```
Private mdatMinimumDate As Date = Now.Date
Private mdatMaximumDate As Date

Public Property MaximumDate() As Date
    Get
        Return mdatMaximumDate
    End Get
    Set(ByVal Value As Date)
        mdatMaximumDate = Value
    End Set
End Property
```

```
Public ReadOnly Property MinimumDate() As Date
    Get
        Return mdatMinimumDate
    End Get
End Property
```

After you rebuild the project, the new properties are automatically exposed to the developer in the Properties window. Read-only properties appear grayed and are available only at run time (in code).

Adding Events to a Control

Most objects can generate events, also called *raising events* or *firing events*. The controls on the user interface raise events, such as Click, DoubleClick, MouseUp, and Move. The form (the container of the control) can respond to each event with code, or ignore an event. Events are often caused by user action, such as a click or mouse move, but some events are generated by the system, such as a timer firing or events such as Form_Load.

The objects that you create from your classes or user controls can generate events, which the form can respond to (or ignore). For example, if a condition exists in an object and the user should be notified, your object *should not* display a message to the user; the user interface must display the message. Your object must either raise an event or throw an exception, to which the form module can respond.

First we need a little terminology: An object that generates or raises an event is called the **event source** or the **event provider**. The object that responds to an event is called an **event sink** or an **event consumer**. For example, when the user clicks a command button and the form's btnOK_Click event procedure executes, the command button is the event source and the form is the event sink.

Raising Events

Two things are needed for your control class to generate events:

1. Declare the event in the Declaration section of the class, including any arguments that you intend to pass.

```
Public Event InvalidDate(ByVal Message As String)
```

2. Raise the event in code. When a condition occurs that should trigger the event, use the RaiseEvent statement.

```
If Not IsDate(Me.Text) Then
    RaiseEvent InvalidDate("Invalid date.")
End If
```

The Event and RaiseEvent Statements—General Form

```
[Public] Event EventName([Arguments])
RaiseEvent EventName [(Arguments)]
```

An **Event statement** must appear at the module level and is public by default.

The Event and RaiseEvent Statements—Examples

```
'Module-level
Event QuantityBelowReorderPoint(intQuantity As Integer)
'In program logic
RaiseEvent QuantityBelowReorderPoint(mintQuantity)

Event TaskComplete()              'Declared at the module level
RaiseEvent TaskComplete           'In a code procedure
```

The **RaiseEvent statement** must appear in the same module as the Event declaration.

Responding to Events

Any class can be an event sink and respond to the events raised by your event source. You, as the application developer, can write code to respond to the control's events. After you add a user control to a form, the new event will be available. Drop down the *Methods* list in the Editor window and your event will appear on the list. You can select the event to create the code template (Sub and End Sub statements) for the event procedure and write the code that you want to execute when the event fires.

```
Private Sub valDate_InvalidDate(ByVal Message As String) _
   Handles valDate.InvalidDate
     'Display the validation error message

     MessageBox.Show(Message)
End Sub
```

The form will respond to the event by displaying a message to the user. Remember, the user interface should handle all interaction with the user—the control should never display messages.

Putting It All Together

Now that you have seen the individual elements of creating properties and generating events, it's time to put it all together. This code shows the completed control that you began in the step-by-step exercise. The control tests for a valid date as well as a date within the selected range: between the MinimumDate and MaximumDate properties. If the Text property fails either test, an event is raised, with an appropriate error message.

Notice the extra code in the `Property Get` procedure to handle a missing MaximumDate property. Even though the property has a default value, the application developer can delete the value in the Properties window. The default value is just an initial value that appears when the control is added to a form.

The User Control

```
'Project:        Ch12ValidDate
'Programmer:     Bradley/Millspaugh
'Date:           January 2003
'Description:    A new user control to extend the function of a text box.
'                Validates for a valid date entry within a given range.

Option Strict On

Public Class ValidDate
    Inherits System.Windows.Forms.TextBox

    [Windows Form Designer generated code]

    'Declare the event
    Event InvalidDate(ByVal Message As String)

    'Property variables
    Private mdatMinimumDate As Date = Now.Date
    Private mdatMaximumDate As Date = Now.Date.AddYears(1)     'Set default value

    Public Property MaximumDate() As Date
        Get
            Try          'Check for empty property
                Dim datTest As Date = CDate(mdatMaximumDate)
            Catch
                mdatMaximumDate = Now.Date.AddYears(1)
            End Try
            Return mdatMaximumDate
        End Get
        Set(ByVal Value As Date)
            mdatMaximumDate = Value
        End Set
    End Property

    Public ReadOnly Property MinimumDate() As Date
        Get
            Return mdatMinimumDate
        End Get
    End Property

    Private Sub ValidDate_Validating(ByVal sender As Object, _
      ByVal e As System.ComponentModel.CancelEventArgs) _
      Handles MyBase.Validating
        'Test for a valid date

        If Not IsDate(Me.Text) Then
            'Invalid date format, raise an event
            RaiseEvent InvalidDate("Invalid date.")
            Me.SelectAll()
            e.Cancel = True
        Else
            'Check the date range
```

```
                     Dim datText As Date = CType(Me.Text, Date)
                     If datText < mdatMinimumDate Or datText > mdatMaximumDate Then
                          RaiseEvent InvalidDate("Date out of range.")
                          Me.SelectAll()
                          e.Cancel = True
                     End If
               End If
        End Sub
End Class
```

The Form for Testing the User Control

```
'Project:        Ch12TestUserControl
'Programmer:     Bradley/Millspaugh
'Date:           January 2003
'Description:    Test the ValidDate user control, which extends the function
'                of a text box to validate for a valid date entry within
'                a given range.

Public Class frmTestClass
    Inherits System.Windows.Forms.Form

    [Windows Form Designer generated code]

    Private Sub valDate_InvalidDate(ByVal Message As String) _
      Handles valDate.InvalidDate
        'Display the validation error message

        With valDate
            MessageBox.Show(Message & " Range: " & .MinimumDate.ToShortDateString() _
                & " to " & .MaximumDate.ToShortDateString())
        End With
    End Sub
End Class
```

Creating a Composite User Control

Another common reason for creating a user control is to combine multiple controls into a single user control. You may want to do this to avoid adding the same type of labels and text boxes repeatedly or perhaps you have a consistent combination of company logo and sign-in boxes for multiple forms.

This example creates a new composite control that combines the ValidDate control with a label. The label will have a default Text property that can be modified by the application developer. The steps for creating the control are similar to those already covered except that you leave the inheritance as a UserControl. Treat the UserControl Design area just like a form. It is a container that can contain as many controls as you need. You can name the constituent controls and refer to them as you would in any application.

Adding a Control to the Toolbox

Controls that have already been developed are not automatically added to the toolbox, but it's easy to add them yourself. In this case, we are beginning a new project to create a new user control that has our ValidDate control as one of the constituent controls, so ValidDate must be added to the toolbox. Right-click on the toolbox and choose *Customize Toolbox*. In the *Customize Toolbox* dialog box, click on the *.NET Framework Components* tab and the *Browse* button. Browse to find your control's .dll file in its bin folder and select it; the control will then appear selected on the *.NET Framework Components* tab. When you close the dialog box, the control appears in the toolbox with a different icon than you saw during development (Figure 12.6).

Figure 12.6

Customize the toolbox to display your own user control.

```
ValidDate
```

You can use the *Customize Toolbox* dialog box to add many other controls, as well as to remove tools from the toolbox. Any controls that you add will appear on the toolbox tab that is active at the time of the addition.

Adding Constituent Controls

You can add any controls or components from the toolbox to the design surface of your composite control. Figure 12.7 shows adding a label and a ValidDate control. Notice also that the label's Text property has been set to a default value and the text alignment has been changed from the default.

Figure 12.7

Add constituent controls to the design surface of the composite user control.

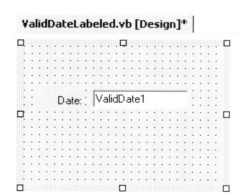

ValidDateLabeled.vb [Design]*

Date: ValidDate1

Usually it's best to resize the composite control to not have extra space around the edges (Figure 12.8). Also, if you set the constituent controls to anchor to all four edges of the user control, the interior controls will resize when the developer resizes the user control. Otherwise, the sizes of the interior controls will remain fixed when the composite control is resized in the final application.

Exposing Properties of Constituent Controls

The properties of the constituent controls are available inside the composite control, but not to the application developer. You, as the control author,

Figure 12.8

Resize the composite control to remove the extra space around the edge and anchor the constituent controls to all four edges of the control.

determine which properties of the constituent controls to expose to the application developer.

In the example shown in Figures 12.7 and 12.8, you want to allow the developer to modify the Text property of the label and the Text property of the ValidDate control. So, in this case, we'll create new properties called TextLabel and TextDate that will be tied to the Text properties of the constituent controls.

```
'Composite user control properties
Private strTextDate As String
Private strTextLabel As String = "Date: "      'Default value

Property TextDate() As String
    Get
        Return strTextDate
    End Get
    Set(ByVal Value As String)
        strTextDate = Value
        valDate.Text = strTextDate
    End Set
End Property

Property TextLabel() As String
    Get
        Return strTextLabel
    End Get
    Set(ByVal Value As String)
        strTextLabel = Value
        lblDate.Text = strTextLabel
    End Set
End Property
```

Notice in the preceding code that the TextLabel property is assigned a beginning (default) value of "Date: ", but the TextDate property does not have a default value. We want to assign a default value, but it should be the automatically generated name of the control, such as ValidDateLabeled1. The location to assign this default value is in the control class's constructor, which appears in the designer-generated code.

```
#Region " Windows Form Designer generated code "

    Public Sub New()
        MyBase.New()

        'This call is required by the Windows Form Designer.
        InitializeComponent()
```

```
'Add any initialization after the InitializeComponent() call
Me.TextDate = Me.Name

End Sub
```

Using the Composite Control

After you create the composite control, you can test it in a form, in the same way that you tested the inherited control. Add a new project for the test form, add a reference to the project that holds the composite control, and add the control to the form. If the new control does not appear in the toolbox, use the *Customize Toolbox* command, as described earlier.

As you test the new control, you may decide to make modifications to the user control. Make sure to close the user control's designer before rebuilding. The first release of VS .NET has problems with sometimes losing the control's definition for the toolbox, which hopefully will be corrected before the second release.

Troubleshooting User Control Development

The process of creating and modifying a user control does not always work as advertised. Hopefully the next release of Visual Studio will improve some of the details. You may have problems making the user control appear in the toolbox or having it disappear after making modifications. Here are some suggestions to help you work around any problems:

- Keep the user control's designer closed at all times, except when making modifications. Close it again before building the project.

- If changes don't show up in the control in the toolbox, try closing the solution and reopening it.

- Try closing the solution and in Windows Explorer delete the bin folder and the solution's .suo file. Reopen and rebuild the solution.

- You can always add the control to the toolbox using *Customize Toolbox*. See "Adding a Control to the Toolbox" in the preceding section. If you make changes to a control after adding it to the toolbox, you may need to remove it and re-add it to use the updated version.

▶ Feedback 12.1

1. Write the statements necessary to raise an event called Will-SoundAlarm in a class module. Where will each statement appear?
2. What statements are necessary to respond to the WillSoundAlarm event in a form. Where will each statement appear?

Web User Controls

Web user controls work differently from Windows user controls. You can think of a Web user control as a "mini-page" that you can display on many other pages. You can create reusable pieces of your interface that contain HTML controls, server controls, and any needed code in a code-behind module. You create the user control and drag it to one or more Web pages. Create Web user controls by creating a project using the ASP.NET Web Application template and then adding a WebUserControl to the project.

Note: The Web Control Library template is used to create new custom controls from scratch and does not provide a design surface. Creating custom controls is beyond the scope of this text.

In the past you have created many applications that use a DataGrid filled with the data from a table in the pubs database. Each time you added a grid to a project, you set the properties, added the data source, and formatted the columns. Setting the headings and some of the details may take a bit of time. Another alternative is to create a user control to display the data in the grid. The following step-by-step exercise creates a Web user control that displays the stores table from the pubs database.

Creating a Web User Control—Step-by-Step

In this step-by-step exercise you will create a Web user control that holds a bound DataGrid that automatically fills with data. You can then add the user control to one or more Web pages.

Create the Project

STEP 1: Open a new project using the *ASP.NET Web Application* template and name it *Ch12WebControlApp*.

STEP 2: Delete the WebForm1.aspx file. (We will add a form later after the user control is built.)

STEP 3: From the project menu add a *Web User Control* and name it *StoresDataGrid.ascx*. The new user control appears in a designer window.

Design the User Interface

Notice that the user control is in flow layout, rather than grid layout. Usually flow layout is best for a user control, so that the destination page can better manage the page formatting. However, if your user control must have aligned columns of controls, you can switch to grid layout.

STEP 1: Add a DataGrid control and name it *dgrTitles*.

STEP 2: From the Server Explorer drag the stores table from the pubs database to the design surface.

STEP 3: Name your connection *conPubs* and the data adapter *daStores*.

STEP 4: Generate the dataset, calling it *dsStores*.

STEP 5: Right-click on the DataGrid and select *PropertyBuilder*.

STEP 6: Set the DataSource to *DsStores1*, the DataMember to *stores*, and the Data key field to *stor_id*.

STEP 7: On the *Columns* tab deselect the checkbox for *Create columns automatically at run time*.

STEP 8: Move each field shown in the following table to the *Selected Columns* list and set the header text for each field. Then click *OK*.

Column	Header
stor_id	ID
stor_name	Name
stor_address	Address
city	City
state	State
zip	ZIP Code

STEP 9: Right-click on the DataGrid and choose *AutoFormat*. Select a style. Figure 12.9 shows the user control at this point.

Figure 12.9

Set up the Web user control in its designer.

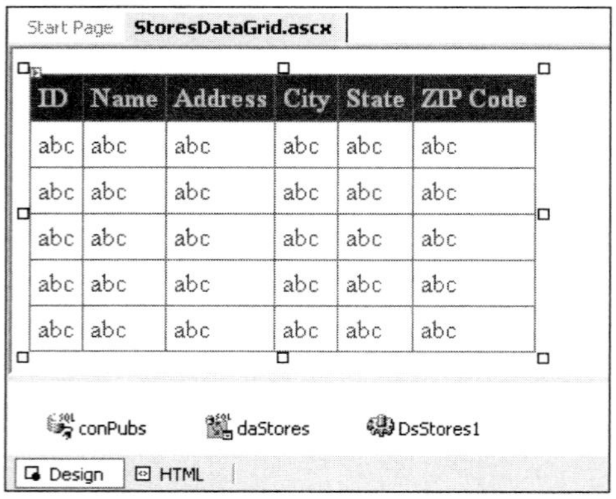

STEP 10: Switch to the Editor window and add code to fill the dataset and bind the grid.

```
Private Sub Page_Load(ByVal sender As System.Object, _
  ByVal e As System.EventArgs) Handles MyBase.Load
    'Put user code to initialize the page here

    'Fill the dataset and bind the grid
    daStores.Fill(DsStores1)
    Me.DataBind()
End Sub
```

STEP 11: Build the solution.

Test the Control

STEP 1: Add a Web Form to the project. Name the form *TestControl.aspx*, which should also set the form's Title property.
STEP 2: Right-click on the form file in the Solution Explorer and set it as the start page.

STEP 3: Drag the user control file, StoresDataGrid.ascx, from the Solution Explorer to the form's design surface (Figure 12.10).

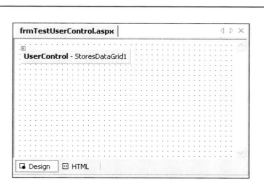

Figure 12.10

Drag the user control to the Web page.

STEP 4: Run the project. The grid should fill with data (Figure 12.11).

Figure 12.11

The user control displays a grid filled with data.

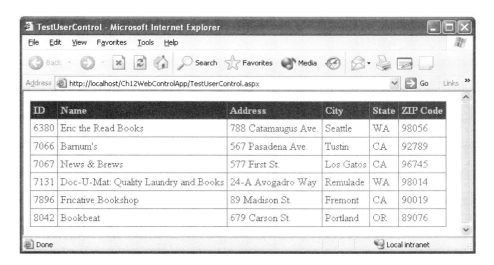

This example has demonstrated the ease of adding data access to a user control as well as how to create a Web user control. Although this control may be useful in some instances, you will likely want your data in a separate tier.

Feedback 12.2

How do you add a Web user control to a form?

Your Hands-On Programming Example

Create a Windows user control that contains the labels and text boxes for data entry of ID, Name, Address, City, State, and ZIP Code. Add a project to test the control; for testing purposes, display the values from the controls in a MessageBox.

This control must make the data entered available to the form, which means that properties must be exposed. The control could either expose each text box as a separate property or create one property that returns a data structure holding all of the values. In this program, we will expose a PersonText property, which is based on a Person structure.

To share a Person structure between the control and the form, each project must be declared in the same namespace. By default, each project is created in its own **root namespace**. The easiest and best way to change this is to display the *Project Properties* dialog box and change the root namespace before building the project. Figure 12.12 shows changing the root namespace of the user control's project to Ch12HandsOn.

Figure 12.12

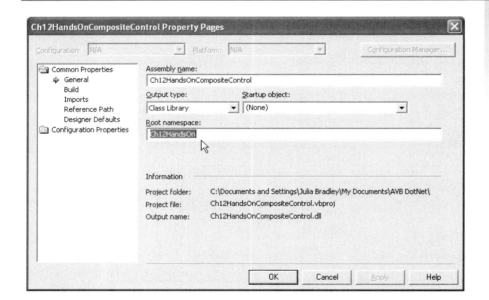

By default, the project name is also the root namespace name. Change the root namespace to that of the form so that both projects can share a Person data structure.

You will declare the Person structure in the user control's module and expose a property based on the structure. The form can declare a variable of type Person to retrieve the property of the control.

Planning the Project

Sketch the control (Figure 12.13) and a form (Figure 12.14) that your users sign off as meeting their needs.

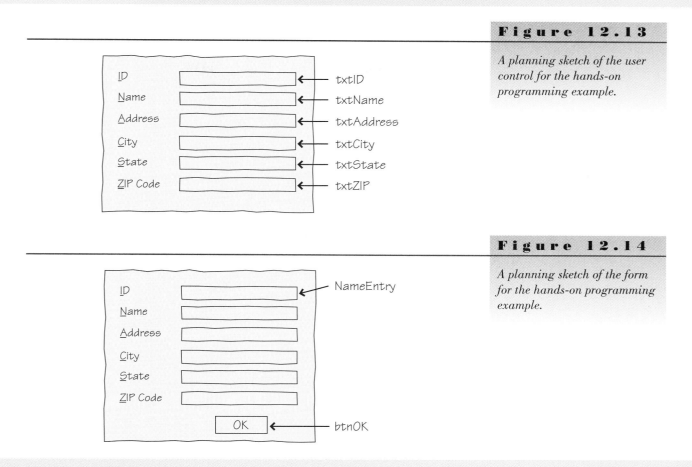

Figure 12.13

A planning sketch of the user control for the hands-on programming example.

Figure 12.14

A planning sketch of the form for the hands-on programming example.

Plan the Objects, Properties, and Methods

Plan the objects and properties for the user control and for the form and its controls. Figure 12.15 shows the diagram of the program components.

Figure 12.15

The components for the hands-on programming example.

Form
frmDataEntry
NameEntry
btnOK
btnOK_Click

The User Control

Object	Property	Setting
UserControl	Name	NameAddress
Label1	Text	&ID
	TabOrder	0
Label2	Text	&Name
	TabOrder	2

continued

Object	Property	Setting
Label3	Text	&Address
	TabOrder	4
Label4	Text	&City
	TabOrder	6
Label5	Text	&State
	TabOrder	8
Label6	Text	&ZIP Code
	Tab Order	10
txtID	Text	(blank)
	Tab Order	1
txtName	Text	(blank)
	TabOrder	3
txtAddress	Text	(blank)
	TabOrder	5
txtCity	Text	(blank)
	TabOrder	7
txtState	Text	(blank)
	TabOrder	9
txtZIP	Text	(blank)
	TabOrder	11

Event procedures/Methods	Actions—Pseudocode
`ReadOnly Property Get PersonText`	Set up the Person structure. Return the Person structure.

The Person Structure

Name	Elements
Person	ID As String
	Name As String
	Address As String
	City As String
	State As String
	ZIP As String

The Form

Object	Property	Setting
frmDataEntry	Name	frmDataEntry
	Text	Consume the User Control
	AcceptButton	btnOK
UserControl	Name	NameEntry
btnOK	Name	btnOK
	Text	OK

Event procedures/Methods	Actions—Pseudocode
btnOK_Click	Retrieve the PersonText property from the control.
	Display the fields in a message box.

Write the Project

Create the application following the sketches in Figures 12.13 and 12.14. Figure 12.16 shows the completed Windows Form.

* Create a project based on the Windows Control Library or an empty project. Set the project's root namespace to *Ch12HandsOn*.

* Create and code the control, following your plans.

* Add a project for the form, calling the project Ch12HandsOn. Both this project and the control's project should have Ch12HandsOn as the root namespace.

* Set the properties of each of the form objects, according to your plans.

* Write the code for the form. Working from the pseudocode, write each event procedure.

* When you complete the code, test the operation.

Figure 12.16

The completed form for the hands-on programming example.

The Project Coding Solution

The NameAddress User Control (Root namespace Ch12HandsOn)

```
'Project:        Ch12HandsOnCompositeControl
'Programmer:     Bradley/Millspaugh
'Date:           January 2003
'Description:    A user control for entering name and address information.

Option Strict On

Public Class NameAddress
    Inherits System.Windows.Forms.UserControl

    [Windows Form Designer generated code]

    Private mPerson As Person

    ReadOnly Property PersonText() As Person
        Get
            mPerson.ID = txtID.Text
            mPerson.Name = txtName.Text
            mPerson.Address = txtAddress.Text
            mPerson.City = txtCity.Text
            mPerson.State = txtState.Text
            mPerson.ZIP = txtZip.Text
            Return mPerson
        End Get
    End Property
End Class

Public Structure Person
    Dim ID As String
    Dim Name As String
    Dim Address As String
    Dim City As String
    Dim State As String
    Dim ZIP As String
End Structure
```

The Form (Root namespace Ch12HandsOn)

```
'Project:        Ch12HandsOn
'Programmer:     Bradley/Millspaugh
'Date:           January 2003
'Description:    Consume a control for name and address entry.

Option Strict On

Public Class frmDataEntry
    Inherits System.Windows.Forms.Form

    [Windows Form Designer generated code]

    Private Sub btnOK_Click(ByVal sender As System.Object, _
      ByVal e As System.EventArgs) Handles btnOK.Click
        'Retrieve the entered information
        Dim perPerson As Person
```

```
        perPerson = NameEntry.PersonText
        MessageBox.Show( _
          perPerson.ID & ControlChars.NewLine & _
          perPerson.Name & ControlChars.NewLine & _
          perPerson.Address & ControlChars.NewLine & _
          perPerson.City & ", " & perPerson.State & _
          " " & perPerson.ZIP, "Display Entered Information")
    End Sub
End Class
```

Summary

1. A user control provides the ability to create a composite control consisting of other constituent controls or to inherit and modify the functionality of an existing control.
2. Windows user controls are created with the Windows Control Library template.
3. Properties are added to user controls in the same fashion as in other classes. The public properties are automatically exposed in the properties window. Properties may have default values set.
4. It takes two steps to raise events from a user control: (1) Declare the event using the Event statement in the Declarations section of the class; (2) fire the event in the program logic using the RaiseEvent method.
5. The application developer writes event procedures for the events of user controls in the same fashion as for other control events.
6. Web user controls are created by adding a Web User Control object to an ASP.NET Web Application. Create the user control using a Web User Control template. Drag the completed control to the design surface of a Web page.
7. To declare and use a structure or a class in more than one project, each must have the same root namespace. You can change the root namespace for a project in the *Project Properties* dialog box.

Key Terms

author *402*
composite control *402*
constituent control *402*
developer *402*
event consumer *408*
event provider *408*

event sink *408*
event source *408*
Event statement *409*
RaiseEvent statement *409*
root namespace *418*
user control *402*

Review Questions

1. Discuss the differences in the inheritance when creating a composite control compared to expanding the functionality of an existing control.

2. Differentiate between the terms *developer* and *author* when discussing user controls. What different tasks must be done by each?

3. What project type is used when creating a Windows user control?

4. Explain how to expose properties for a user control.

5. What is an event? How is one added to a user control? How is the event accessed and used by the developer?

6. How can a user control be added to a form?

7. How can a Web user control be added to a Web Form?

Programming Exercises

12.1 Create a user control that has text boxes and labels for
>   First Name
>   Last Name
>   Address
>   City
>   State
>   ZIP Code
>   Email

Expose the fields as properties, either as individual properties or as a single property based on a structure or a class.

Add a project to test the user control. Display the entered data in the format of your choice, in a message box, in a second form, or on the printer.

12.2 Create a Windows user control that consists of a text box that only accepts a range of numeric values. Allow properties to set the minimum and the maximum values. Test the control for the range of 0 to 100. Create a form to test the control.

12.3 Create a Web user control for the fields listed in Exercise 12.1.

12.4 Create a Windows user control to display the data from the titles table in pubs.

Case Studies

Claytor's Cottages

Create a control that holds a graphic and text for a company logo. Place the control on your About form and at least one other form.

Christian's Car Rentals

Create a control that holds a graphic and text for a company logo. Place the control on your About form and at least one other form.

13

Creating Help Files

1. Create the necessary files to set up HTML Help.

2. Use the HTML Help Workshop to create a Help file with a table of contents, index, and display pages.

3. Connect the Help file to a VB application.

4. Set up and display F1 context-sensitive Help.

5. Display and activate the title bar Help button.

Windows applications support the use of HTML Help files. HTML Help files have a browser look-and-feel. Using HTML Help you can display Help to your user in several different formats, including a Help facility with topics, an index, and table of contents. You also can implement context-sensitive Help (F1) and Pop-up Help.

HTML Help Workshop

HTML Help Workshop is a separate application from Visual Studio. You use the program to organize and assemble your pages and then compile the various files into one compiled Help file with an extension of .chm. HTML Help Workshop also includes the Microsoft **HTML Help Image Editor** for creating screen shots and working with images, an HTML editor, and an **HTML Help ActiveX control** that you can use to add navigation to an HTML page. The **Help Viewer** provides a three-paned window for displaying online Help topics, many Help screens, and an extensive reference to HTML tags, attributes, character sets, and style sheets.

You should check to see if you have the HTML Help Workshop installed on your system. If not, you can download it from Microsoft at http://www. microsoft.com/downloads/release.asp?releaseid=33071. Download the html help.exe and the HelpDoc.Zip files. Do not download the update files (hhupd.exe) for Windows 2000 and Windows XP systems.

One great feature of HTML Help is that the size of the files is not limited. The Workshop condenses the files as it compiles, reducing storage requirements. It also includes a feature that can convert the older WinHelp files from earlier applications to HTML Help. VB .NET does not support WinHelp files.

Setting up Help

The first step in setting up a Help system is to plan its organization. Decide on the main subject headers and the topics beneath each header. Each page that you display is a separate HTML file, which you organize and connect together using HTML Help Workshop.

A Help Facility

Figure 13.1 shows a Help screen for HTML Help Workshop, which illustrates how your Help pages will appear. The left pane holds tabs for *Contents* and *Index* (also *Search* and *Favorites* tabs, which this chapter doesn't cover). Each of the book icons represents a heading, and each page icon represents an HTML page.

To get a better idea of the look and feel of Help, take a closer look at the *Contents* tab of Visual Studio Help (MSDN) (Figure 13.2), which is just a very large application of HTML Help. Each header (book icon) can display open or closed. Beneath each header are topics (page icons) and/or additional headers, creating a hierarchy of headers and topics. Notice too that if you select a header and display it in the Contents window, a screen appears that usually has some introductory information and links to the topics beneath the header.

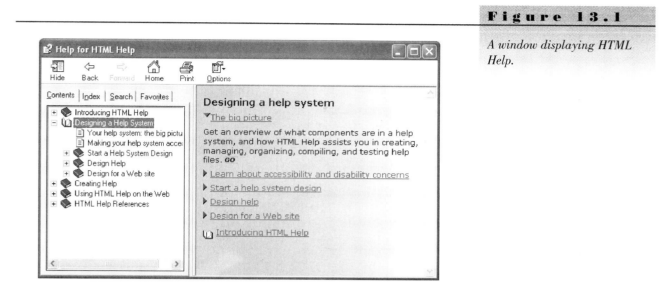

Figure 13.1

A window displaying HTML Help.

Figure 13.2

A screen from Visual Studio Help, which is HTML Help.

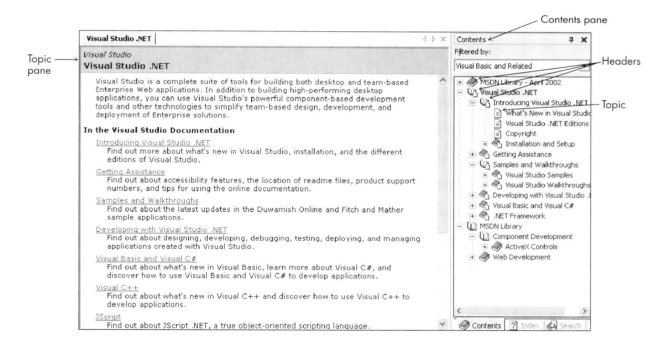

Every screen that displays in the Contents pane is a called a ***Help topic*** and is a separate HTML file. So your first step is to design the header pages, topic pages, and any extra pages that you want to display from links. You also may think of Help topics that you want to display only from context-sensitive Help. Plan the links that you want to include on each page before you begin creating the pages. Although you can add links later, you'll save yourself considerable time by entering the links when you create the pages. You must create all of the pages as HTML documents (file extension .htm). You can use Word,

FrontPage, or any HTML editor to create the pages. (The HTML files for this chapter were created in Microsoft Word.)

Save yourself some trouble and first create a folder for the htm files. Place any graphics, sounds, and multimedia files that you want to use in the folder. When you create links to any files or other documents, link to the file in the folder, but do not include a path as part of the link. For example, if a PageA.htm requires a link to PageB.htm, do not allow the editor to specify "a:\MyProjectFolder\HTMLHelpFiles\PageB.htm". Instead make the link say simply "PageB.htm" (no backslashes). Later you will be able to move or rename the folder without changing the links. And if no path is provided, the current folder is searched first.

This text is not intended to be a tutorial on creating HTML pages. The chapter illustrations assume that you already have created the HTML files.

File Types

An HTML Help project consists of several files. Some you create yourself, using a text editor; others are created as you work in HTML Help Workshop.

File type	File extension	Purpose
Project Header file	.hhp	Holds references to the rest of the files in the project. Similar to the project file in a VB project. The Workshop creates this file when you begin a new project.
Topic files	.htm	Holds the pages to display in the Help Contents pane, one file for each screen. These are in HTML (Web page) format. You create these files using an HTML editor or text editor.
Graphic and multimedia files	.jpeg, .gif, .png, wav, .midi, .avi, and others	Images, sounds, and videos for which you supply links on HTML pages. You supply these files.
Table of Contents file	.hhc	Stores the headings and organization for the *Contents* tab. Created by the Workshop when you define the table of contents.
Index file	.hhk	Holds the entries for the searchable index. Created by the Workshop when you define the index.
Compiled Help file	.chm	Holds the compiled Help project. The Workshop creates this file when you compile the project.

Creating the Files

Before you begin using HTML Help Workshop, you should first plan your Help system and create the HTML files. Here are the general steps for creating help files; detailed instructions follow in the step-by-step exercise.

1. Plan the topics to include.
2. Create html pages for each topic.
3. Using HTML Help Workshop:
   - Add the html files.
   - Create the Table of Contents.
   - Create the Index.
   - Compile the Help file.
4. Connect the compiled Help file to the application.

Creating a Help Facility

The following step-by-step exercise creates a Help facility using HTML pages that are already created. For this tutorial, you can design and create your own HTML pages or use the ones supplied on your text CD in the folder *Ch13SBS/HTML*.

Before you begin the tutorial, make sure that you have HTML Help Workshop on your system. If not, refer to "HTML Help Workshop" earlier in this chapter.

Creating a Help Facility—Step-by-Step

Figure 13.3 shows the completed Help facility, and Figure 13.4 shows the Hours of Operation topic page with two additional links.

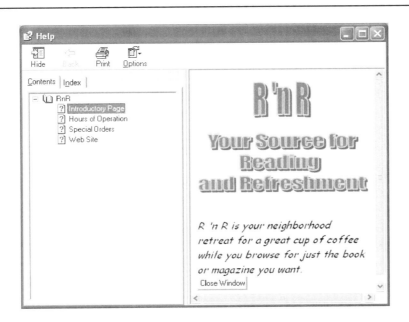

Figure 13.3

The completed Help facility for the step-by-step exercise.

Figure 13.4

A topic page that has links to two additional pages. These linked pages are included in the Help project but do not appear in the Contents.

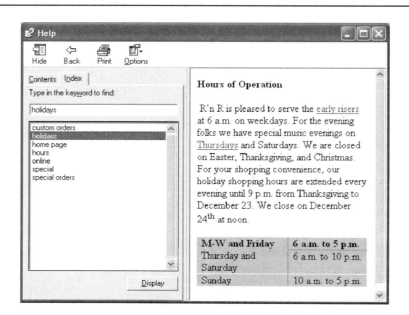

Begin the Exercise

STEP 1: Locate the Ch13SBS folder on your text CD; copy it to a diskette or the hard drive. Examine the files. You should have a folder with VB solution, project, and form files, and an HTML folder holding six .htm files and a subfolder called RnR_files. You will use the HTML files to create the Help facility and later connect it to the VB project.

Begin a Project in the Workshop

STEP 1: Open *HTML Help Workshop*.

STEP 2: Select *New* from the *File* menu. Notice that several components are listed; choose *Project*. Click *OK*.

STEP 3: On the first Wizard screen click *Next*.

STEP 4: On the *New Project Destination* page, use the *Browse* button to locate and open the HTML folder beneath your project folder and name the file *RnRHelp*. (The wizard will add the extension .hhp.) Click *Open*, then click *Next*.

STEP 5: On the *Existing Files* page, select *HTML files (.htm)*. Click *Next*.
   Note: We are going to add the files now, with the Wizard. You also can add files later.

STEP 6: On the *HTML Files* page, click *Add*. You can add all of the .htm files at once: Click on the first file name, shift-click on the last one (to select them all), and click *Open*. Back on the *HTML Files* page, you should see all six files. Click *Next*.

STEP 7: On the final Wizard screen click *Finish*. You will see a listing of the beginnings of your project file.

STEP 8: Take a look at the menus and buttons (Figure 13.5). The buttons down the left edge of the window change, depending on which tab is displayed. You will see this later as we create *Contents* and *Index* tabs.

Figure 13.5

The HTML Help Workshop window, showing the entries in the project file.

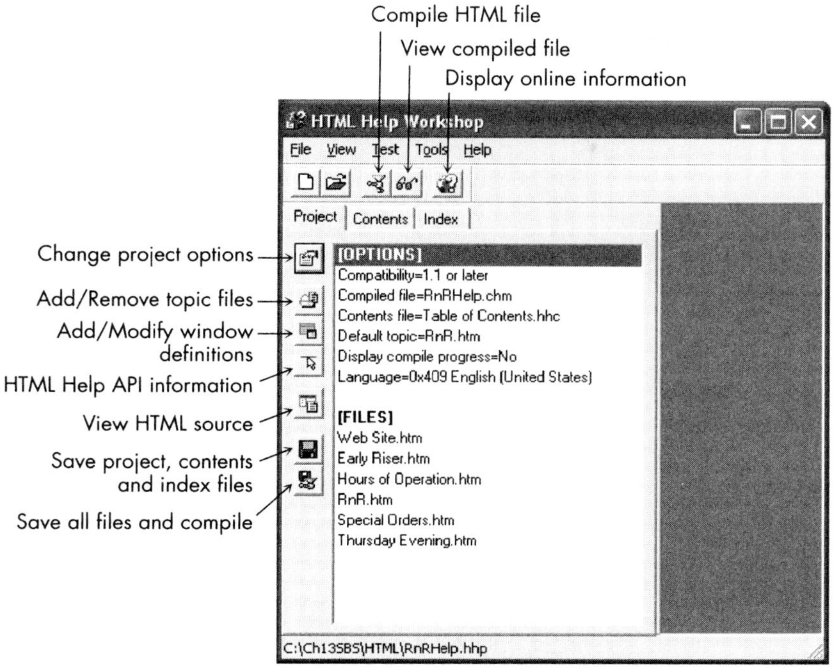

Compile HTML file
View compiled file
Display online information

Change project options
Add/Remove topic files
Add/Modify window definitions
HTML Help API information
View HTML source
Save project, contents and index files
Save all files and compile

HTML Help Workshop

File View Test Tools Help

Project | Contents | Index

[OPTIONS]
Compatibility=1.1 or later
Compiled file=RnRHelp.chm
Contents file=Table of Contents.hhc
Default topic=RnR.htm
Display compile progress=No
Language=0x409 English (United States)

[FILES]
Web Site.htm
Early Riser.htm
Hours of Operation.htm
RnR.htm
Special Orders.htm
Thursday Evening.htm

C:\Ch13SBS\HTML\RnRHelp.hhp

Change Project Options

STEP 1: Click on the *Change Project Options* button to display the *Options* dialog box.

STEP 2: On the *General* tab, drop down the list for *Default File* and select RnR.htm. Click *OK*.

STEP 3: On the *Files* tab, change the compiled file to *RnRHelp.chm*.

Create the Table of Contents

STEP 1: Switch to the *Contents* tab. On the next dialog, select the option to create a new contents file and accept the default name: *Table of Contents.hhc*. Click *Save*.

STEP 2: Notice that a different set of buttons displays. Figure 13.6 shows the completed *Contents* tab.

STEP 3: Click on *Contents properties* and view the *General* tab.

STEP 4: Deselect the option to *Use folders instead of books* (if it is selected). Notice also that you can supply your own images—one for the closed state and one for the open state. Click *OK*.

STEP 5: Click on *Insert a heading* and enter the title that you want to display for the first heading icon: *RnR*. Click on *Add* and select the topic "R 'n R – –For Reading and Refreshment," which is the RnR.htm file. Click *OK* and *OK* again to return to the *Contents* tab.

In the next few steps, if you get the dialog box asking if you want this entry at the beginning, answer No.

STEP 6: Click on *Insert a page*. Enter *Introductory Page* and add the *RnR.htm* topic.

Figure 13.6

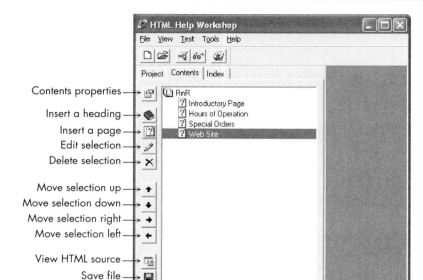

Contents properties

Insert a heading

Insert a page

Edit selection

Delete selection

Move selection up

Move selection down

Move selection right

Move selection left

View HTML source

Save file

STEP 7: Add an entry for *Hours of Operation,* selecting the *Hours of Operation* topic.

STEP 8: Add an entry for *Special Orders,* selecting the *Special Orders* topic.

STEP 9: Add an entry for *Web Site,* selecting the *Web Site* topic.

The Table of Contents should be complete.

Create the Index

The index takes some planning. You should select words that a person would be apt to search for. Since our minds don't all work the same way, it sometimes takes a little creativity to think of topics that people might enter. However, you don't want to clutter the index by including every word in the Help file. Certainly one page may have multiple entries in the index.

STEP 1: Click on the *Index* tab and select the option to create a new index file. Accept the default name *Index.hhk.* Notice that the buttons have changed for the *Index* tab.

STEP 2: Click on *Insert a keyword* and enter the word *hours,* which will display in the index. Click on the *Add* button and select the *Hours of Operation* topic file. Click *OK* and *OK* again to get back to the *Index* tab.

STEP 3: The *Hours* topic could use some more keywords in the index: Add *holidays* referring to *Hours of Operation.*

　　Note that the order of entry is not important. The Workshop knows how to sort. You will sort the index when it is complete.

STEP 4: Add the keyword *custom orders* that refers to the *Special Orders* topic.

STEP 5: Add the keyword *special orders* that refers to the *Special Orders* topic.

STEP 6: Add the keyword *special.* On the *Path or URL* dialog box, add three file names: *Special Orders.htm, Thursday Evening.htm,* and *Early Riser.htm.*

STEP 7: Add the keyword *online* that refers to the *Web Site* topic.

STEP 8: Add the keyword *home page* that refers to the *Web Site* topic.

STEP 9: Examine the buttons and notice that you can edit or delete an entry, as well as move an entry up, down, left, or right (Figure 13.7), which you can use to create hierarchical relationships.

STEP 10: Click the *Sort* button to sort in alphabetic order.

The Index should be finished now. You can always add more entries later.

Figure 13.7

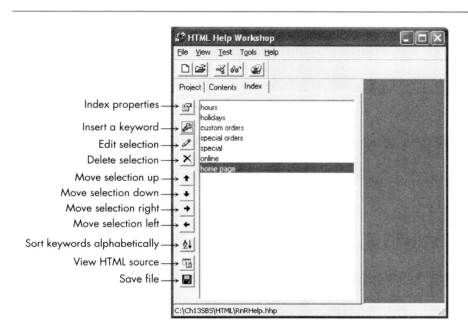

The index keywords in the Index *tab.*

Compile the Help Project

STEP 1: Switch back to the *Project* tab and click the *Save all files and compile button* at the bottom left. The Workshop compiles the file and displays statistics in the right pane (Figure 13.8). You may want to widen the pane a little to view the results. If the compiler detects any problems with missing or misspelled files or links, it displays error diagnostics in the right pane. No error diagnostics means a clean compile and we are ready to connect this file to the VB project.

If you have any error diagnostic messages, you must locate them, fix them, and recompile. When you do, you will be prompted to save the Log file. Accept the defaults.

View and Test the Help File

STEP 1: Click on the *View compiled file* toolbar button (the glasses) or select *View / Compiled Help File*. You may have to browse for your file, called *RnRHelp.chm*. Open the file to display your Help file in a new window.

STEP 2: Test the entries in the *Contents* tab and the *Index* tab. Test the two links on the Hours of Operation page to make sure that they work.

If a link doesn't work, you may have to return to the HTML editor and correct a page. Any time you change a page or any entry, *you must recompile the Help project.*

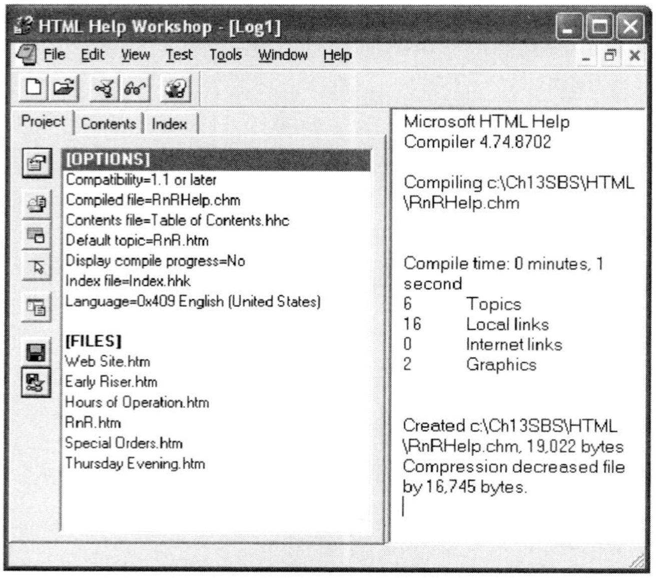

Figure 13.8

The compiler displays any error diagnostic messages and statistics.

When you are finished, close the viewer window and return to the main window with the *Project* tab displayed.

Add Navigation Using the ActiveX Control

The HTML Help Workshop comes with a control, called the *HTML Help ActiveX control,* which you can add to Web pages.

STEP 1: In the [Files] section on the *Project* tab, double-click on RnR.htm, which opens the page in the HTML editor.

STEP 2: Look at the tags and text and scroll down to the bottom of the file.

STEP 3: Click just before the closing `</body>` tag and verify that you have an insertion point rather than selected text.

STEP 4: Click on the *HTML Help ActiveX Control* button on the toolbar (the wizard's cap), which starts a wizard. Drop down the list for commands and notice that there are many choices. Select *Close Window* and click *Next.*

STEP 5: Select *As a button* and click *Next.*

STEP 6: On the *Button Options* page, choose to display text on the button and enter *Close Window* for the text. Click *Next,* then *Finish.*

STEP 7: Notice in the HTML editor window that code has been added for an object. Save and compile again. (Any time you change *anything,* you must recompile.)

STEP 8: View your compiled Help file again. After you are sure that everything else works, test the new button on the introductory page.

STEP 9: Close the HTML Help Workshop.

Connecting the HTML Help File to an Application

To add Help to your VB project, all you have to do is drag a **HelpProvider component** to your form and set the **HelpNamespace property** to the Help's .chm file. Adding a HelpProvider component has some similarities with adding a ToolTip component—new properties are added to the other controls on the form. For example, if you add a HelpProvider component named Help-Provider1, the form and each button will have new properties for HelpKeyword on HelpProvider1, HelpNavigator on HelpProvider1, and HelpString on Help-Provider1.

Property	Purpose
HelpKeyword	Used to specify the exact topic to display. Use the html file name. The HelpNavigator property must be set to *Topic* for this to work. *Example:* Hours of Operation.htm
HelpNavigator	Determines the page to display, such as Table of Contents, Index, or Topic.
HelpString	An actual string of text to display for pop-up Help.

Continuing the Step-by-Step Exercise

It's time to add the compiled Help file to a VB project.

Open the Project
STEP 1: Open the solution file in the Ch13SBS/Ch13SBSHelp folder.
STEP 2: Display the form in the designer.

Connect the Help File for F1 Help
STEP 1: Add a HelpProvider component to the form. Name the component *hlpFile*.
STEP 2: Set the HelpNamespace property of hlpFile to your Help file (RnRHelp.chm). You can browse to select the file.
STEP 3: Set the form's ShowHelp on hlpFile property to True.
STEP 4: Set the form's HelpNavigator on hlpFile property to TableOfContents.
STEP 5: Run the program and press F1. Your Help screen should pop up with the Table of Contents displayed.

Adding Help to a Menu

You can use two methods of the Help object to display Help in code: the **ShowHelp method** and the **ShowHelpIndex method**.

ShowHelp Method—General Forms

General Forms

```
Help.ShowHelp(control, helpfile)
Help.ShowHelp(control, helpfile, HelpNavigatorSetting)
Help.ShowHelp(control, helpfile, string for keyword to display)
Help.ShowHelp(control, helpfile, HelpNavigatorSetting, TopicID)
```

The various options allow you to specify whether the Index, Table of Contents, or a specific topic should display.

ShowHelp Method—Examples

Examples

```
Help.ShowHelp(Me, "RnRHelp.chm")
Help.ShowHelp(Me, "c:\My Documents\RnRHelp.chm")
```

Notice that you can use the full path for the Help file, but for development it works best to place a copy of the .chm file in the bin folder for the project and specify the filename as a string without the path.

The ShowHelpIndex method is similar to the ShowHelp, but always displays the *Index* tab of the Help file.

ShowHelpIndex Method—Example

Example

```
Help.ShowHelpIndex(Me, "RnRHelp.chm")
```

Display the Help File from Menu Items

STEP 1: Move a copy of RnRHelp.chm to the project's bin folder.

STEP 2: Modify the hlpFile component's HelpNamespace property to remove the path. Without the path, the program will search in the bin folder for the file.

STEP 3: Write the code for the two *Help* menu items: mnuHelpContents and mnuHelpIndex.

```
'Project:       Ch13SBSHelp
'Programmer:    Bradley/Millspaugh
'Date:          January 2003
'Description:   Incorporates F1 help, help from a menu, _
'               and a Help button

Option Strict On

Public Class frmMain
    Inherits System.Windows.Forms.Form

    [Windows Form Designer generated code]

    Private Sub mnuFileExit_Click(ByVal sender As System.Object, _
      ByVal e As System.EventArgs) Handles mnuFileExit.Click
        'Close the program

        Me.Close()
    End Sub
```

```
    Private Sub mnuHelpContents_Click(ByVal sender As System.Object, _
       ByVal e As System.EventArgs) Handles mnuHelpContents.Click
          'Display the Help Contents

          Help.ShowHelp(Me, "RnRHelp.chm")
    End Sub

    Private Sub mnuHelpIndex_Click(ByVal sender As Object, _
       ByVal e As System.EventArgs) Handles mnuHelpIndex.Click
          'Display the Help Index

          Help.ShowHelpIndex(Me, "RnRHelp.chm")
    End Sub
End Class
```

STEP 4: Test it all!

Modifying Help Files

You can modify the Help Web pages, add pages to Help, and change the organization of the Help project. You must always remember to recompile after any change. The compiled Help .chm file holds all of the HTML pages in compressed form. When Help displays, it uses only those compressed pages, not the individual HTML pages. When you distribute an application, only the .chm file is needed, not the many files that make up the Help project.

Connecting Context-Sensitive Help Topics to Controls

If you have gotten this far in developing applications, you have probably used **context-sensitive Help**. You place the cursor on an element, press F1, and a Help topic (hopefully about the element you selected) pops up.

    You can implement context-sensitive Help in your VB applications by setting the HelpKeyword and HelpNavigator for each element. The control must be able to receive the focus, so although labels and picture boxes have the appropriate properties, they cannot respond to F1 Help. Set the control's HelpNavigator property to *Topic* and the HelpKeyword property to the name of an html file.

TIP

Close the Help project in HTML Help Workshop when you are working on a VB project and close the VB project when you are working in the Workshop. One application cannot work on the file if the other is using it. ■

Continue the Example Program?

You can test context-sensitive Help: open the Ch13SBSHelp project and add two or three buttons. For each control, set the HelpNavigator property to *Topic* and HelpKeyword property to one of these values: *RnR.htm, Hours of Operation.htm, Special Orders.htm, Web Site.htm, Early Riser.htm, Thursday Evening.htm.*

The Help Button

A Windows application that has a Help button on the title bar can provide pop-up Help while the user is working. When the user clicks the Help button, the pointer changes into the question mark (Figure 13.9). Then the user can click on an element and a Help topic pops up (Figure 13.10). Unlike F1 Help, you

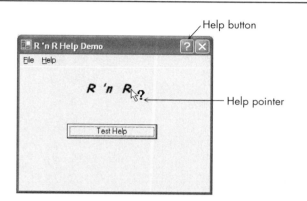

Help button

Help pointer

Figure 13.9

When the user clicks the Help button on the title bar, the pointer changes to the question mark icon. Clicking on an object pops up Help text.

This is an application to give lots of help to RnR users.

Figure 13.10

A pop-up Help topic pops up on top of the selected element.

can assign pop-up Help to controls that cannot receive the focus, such as labels and picture boxes.

You can create pop-up Help by setting the form's HelpButton property to True and both the MaximizeBox and MinimizeBox properties to False. For each control that should display pop-up Help, you set the HelpString property to the text to show in a ToolTip-style box.

Other Forms of User Assistance

Good programs provide assistance to the user. In this chapter you learned about providing Help, context-sensitive Help, and pop-up Help. You also can provide helpful information using ToolTips and status bars. You might consider showing the formula for a calculation in a ToolTip as well as instructions for data entry. Instructions in status bars can be very useful and unobtrusive. It's a good idea to use the MouseOver event of controls to change the message in a status bar, then use the MouseOver event of the form to reset the status-bar text.

▶ Feedback 13.1

1. Give the file type and purpose of each of the following file extensions.
   a. .hhk
   b. .hhc
   c. .chm
   d. .jpeg
   e. .avi
   f. .htm

2. List five types of user assistance that can be added to an application.

S u m m a r y

1. Windows supports Help files in HTML Help.
2. The HTML Help Workshop is a separate application that combines topic files (HTML pages), graphics and multimedia files, contents files, and index files into a Help project. The compiled file has the extension .chm.
3. The HelpFile can be assigned to the VB project at design time or run time. At run time, use the ShowHelp or ShowHelpIndex method.
4. Adding a HelpProvider component to a form adds properties to the other controls on the form. Set the HelpKeyword, HelpNavigator, and HelpString properties to determine how Help is displayed for each control.
5. For context-sensitive Help, set the HelpNavigator property of a control to *Topic* and the HelpKeyword property to the name of an html file.
6. To display the Help button on the title bar of a form, set the form's Help-Button property to True and the MaximizeBox and MinimizeBox properties to False. For each control, set the HelpText property to the text that you want to display.
7. ToolTips and status bars also can be considered a part of the Help supplied by an application.

K e y   T e r m s

context-sensitive Help   *437*
Help topic   *427*
Help Viewer   *426*
HelpKeyword property   *435*
HelpNamespace property   *435*
HelpNavigator property   *435*
HelpProvider component   *435*

HelpString property   *435*
HTML Help ActiveX
    control   *426*
HTML Help Image Editor   *426*
HTML Help Workshop   *426*
ShowHelp method   *435*
ShowHelpIndex method   *435*

R e v i e w   Q u e s t i o n s

1. How is each Help topic defined in HTML Help?
2. How is the Help file connected to a VB project for F1 Help?
3. How do you connect individual forms and controls to specific Help topics?
4. What Help file(s) must be distributed with a VB application?
5. How do you display Help in code from a menu item?
6. What is pop-up Help?

P r o g r a m m i n g   E x e r c i s e s

13.1 Use Word or any HTML editor to create Web pages about your favorite hobbies or sports. Include at least one image.
       Assemble and compile the file using HTML Help Workshop.
       Add the Help to a small VB project.
13.2 Add Help to any of your VB projects.

CHAPTER

14

Looking Ahead

1. Install and use the Microsoft Mobile Internet Toolkit.

2. Display database information on a mobile device.

3. Use multiple forms on a mobile device.

4. Understand and apply the concepts of localization.

5. Use threading in an application.

This final chapter introduces you to some of the features of programming for the future. As more mobile devices appear on the market, it becomes more important to have a scalable development environment. Visual Studio .NET fills the bill; you can program for these devices using the same tools that you already know.

Another topic in this chapter, localization, also deals with the increased worldwide use of communication devices. When you are creating Web pages that can be viewed in many countries, you should consider the needs of the users in each country.

Microsoft Mobile Internet Toolkit

Creating output for PDAs, cell phones, and pagers requires different protocols and languages, but Visual Studio can make the work easier for you by allowing you to develop in Visual Basic. The **Microsoft Mobile Internet Toolkit (MMIT)** allows you to easily create applications for mobile devices. Typically, mobile devices use **Wireless Markup Language (WML)** instead of HTML. Rather than HTTP, most current cell phones use **Wireless Application Protocol (WAP)** for transmissions. Emulators are available for a large number of devices to allow you to easily test the appearance of program output.

Installing the Toolkit

You can download the MMIT for free from Microsoft. When you install the toolkit, it is added to your Visual Studio development environment. See http://msdn.microsoft.com/downloads/default.asp?url=/downloads/sample.asp?url=/msdn-files/027/001/817/msdncompositedoc.xml (making sure to include the entire URL on one line).

After you download and install the toolkit, your *New Project* dialog box contains a new Mobile Web Application template (Figure 14.1).

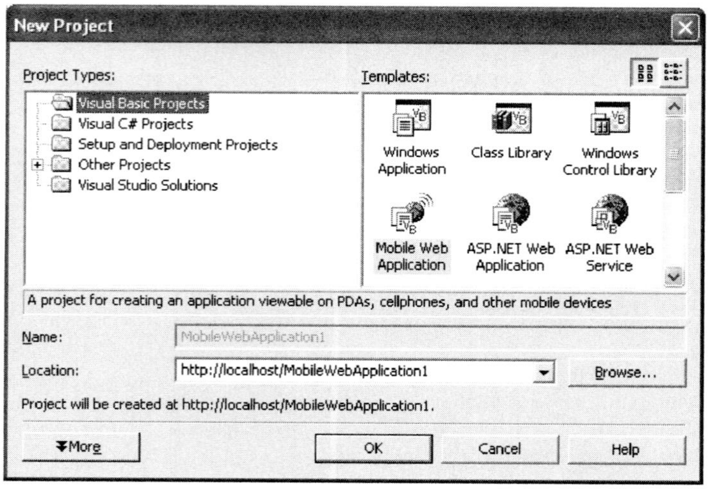

Figure 14.1

The Mobile Web Application template appears in the New Project dialog box after you install the Mobile Internet Toolkit.

Notice that the new mobile application is stored in Localhost, as for a Web application. Name the project on the *Location* line, as you do for a Web app. A small form appears in the Document window (Figure 14.2).

You can see in Figure 14.2 that the toolbox is open to a new set of controls for Mobile Web Forms. You also can use the Data and Web Forms controls on Mobile Web Forms.

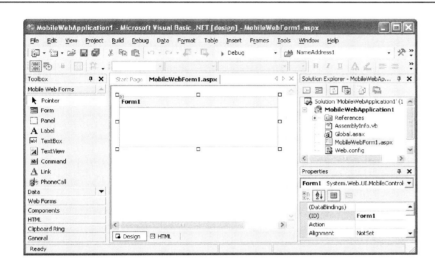

F i g u r e   1 4 . 2

A new MobileWebForm appears in the VS IDE Document window.

Using Emulators

When you run your application from the VS IDE, the program output displays in a browser. If you want a better feel for how it will actually appear on a device, you can use an emulator. An image of the device appears on the computer monitor giving a better visual concept of the final output. As you can imagine, the screen appears much different on a phone device than it does on a device like the Pocket PC.

At the time of this writing, the Mobile Internet Toolkit download 1.0 works with more than 80 different devices. You can find a listing of the devices at http://msdn.microsoft.com/vstudio/device/mitdevices.asp.

Not all of the devices that work with the toolkit have an emulator, but you will find a list of emulators at the same site.

For each emulator you must download it from the manufacturer's site and install it according to their directions. To view using an emulator, select the device you want from *File/Browse With*. The browser appears with a skin: a form in the shape of the specific device (see Figure 14.3).

You can find Nokia emulators at http://forum.nokia.com. Other useful links are http://www.gotdotnet.com/team/mit/, http://msdn.microsoft.com/theshow/Episode023/default.asp, and http://msdn.microsoft.com/vstudio/techinfo/articles/clients/mobilewebforms.asp.

Writing a Simple Hello Program

It's time for another Hello World application: Begin a new Mobile Web Application called *Ch14MobileHelloWorld* (change the name on the *Location* line). The project will be created in Localhost. Add a text box, a label, and a button (called a *Command* control) to the form (Figure 14.4). Note that if you simply double-click on the toolbox item, the control may appear on the document outside of the form. You will see an error message (Figure 14.5); simply drag the control onto the form.

Figure 14.3

Program output in an emulator.

Figure 14.4

Add a text box, a label, and a button to the Mobile Web Form.

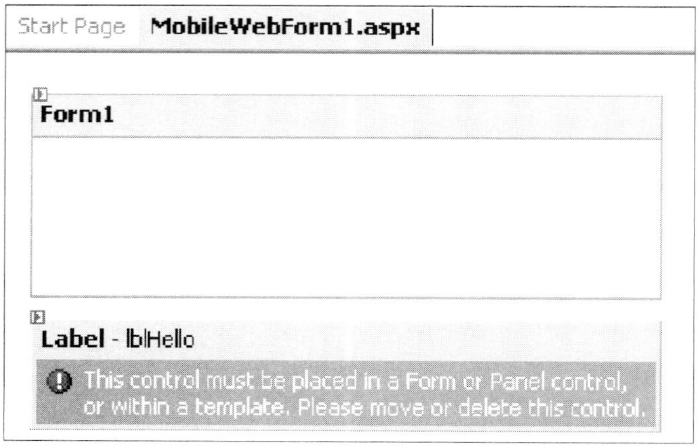

Figure 14.5

If the control is added outside the form area, you can drag the control onto the form.

Set the properties of the controls, but do not change the name of the form.

Control		Setting
TextBox	ID	txtName
	Text	(blank) — No change required
Label	ID	lblHello
	Text	(blank)
Command	ID	btnDisplay
	Text	Display

Code the btnDisplay_Click event procedure (and add remarks). This code looks just like every other program that you have written. Figure 14.6 shows the program output.

```
'Project:        Ch14MobileInternetToolkit
'Programmer:     Bradley/Millspaugh
'Date:           January 2003
'Description:    A mobile Hello World

Option Strict On

Public Class MobileWebForm1

    Private Sub btnDisplay_Click(ByVal sender As System.Object, _
        ByVal e As System.EventArgs) Handles btnDisplay.Click
        'Display the Hello message

        lblHello.Text = "Hello " & txtName.Text
    End Sub
End Class
```

Figure 14.6

The completed Hello World Mobile Web Application.

 TIP

If you receive a parser error when attempting to run your program, the compiler cannot find the file. If you have changed the name of the class, change it back to Mobile WebForm1. ∎

Web Controls versus Mobile Controls

The mobile Web Forms toolset allows you to create interfaces for a large selection of devices. The mobile controls are designed to adapt to different devices.

Web Forms control	Mobile control	Note
Button, ImageButton, LinkButton	Command	The mobile control combines the functionality of all three button types.
Calendar	Calendar	The mobile control exposes an underlying Web Forms calendar through the WebCalendar property.
n/a	PhoneCall	Initiates calls on dial-capable devices.
DataList, Repeater	List	The mobile control can have different templates for different devices.
DataGrid	ObjectList	The ObjectList provides multiple views.
n/a	DeviceSpecific	Used to override properties and templates for specific devices.
n/a	Form	Multiple screens for the same Web page (covered later in the chapter).
HyperLink	Link	Mobile control cannot render images; an Image control must be used for an image link.
CheckBox, CheckBoxList, DropDown, DropDownList, ListBox, RadioButton, RadioButtonList	SelectionList	The SelectType property indicates the look and functionality for the mobile control.
n/a	StyleSheet	Mobile controls use the StyleSheet control instead of a cascading style sheet.
n/a	TextView	Can display a large amount of text.

Displaying Database Data

You can display database data on a mobile form. The mobile toolset provides an **ObjectList control** instead of a DataGrid. When you add the control to a form, you see only a single column (Figure 14.7), but you can change that. Right-click the control to display its Property Builder, where you can set the data source and the data member, as well as the columns. Working with the ObjectList's Property Builder is similar to working with the Property Builder for a Web Forms DataGrid.

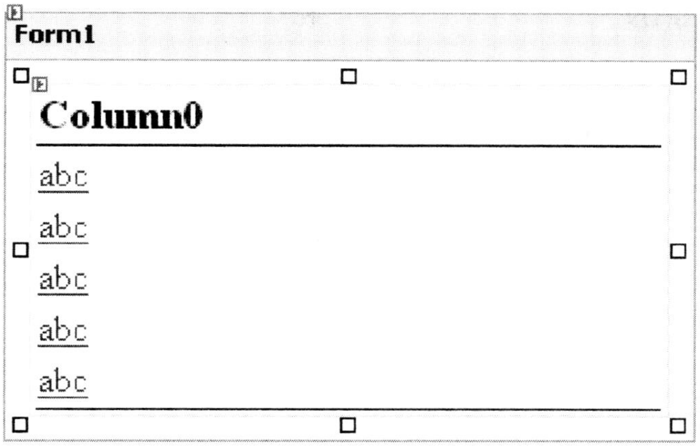

Figure 14.7

The ObjectList control has a single column by default, but you can change that in the Property Builder.

Setting up a Database Application

To write a mobile database application, you can add connections, data adapters, and datasets in the same way as for a Windows or Web application (Figure 14.8). The following example displays three fields from the titles table of the pubs database. The SQL SELECT statement selects the title, price, and title_id fields.

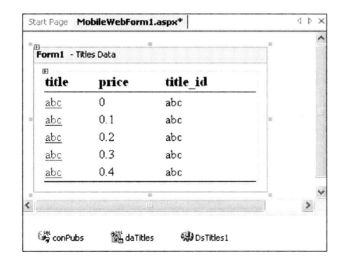

Figure 14.8

Add a database connection, data adapter, dataset, and ObjectList control. You can set the data source and data member properties of the ObjectList in the Property Builder.

The only code that you need is the familiar Fill and Databind methods. Figure 14.9 shows the completed mobile application in a browser.

```
Private Sub Page_Load(ByVal sender As System.Object, _
  ByVal e As System.EventArgs) Handles MyBase.Load
    'Fill the dataset

    daTitles.Fill(DsTitles1)
    Me.DataBind()
End Sub
```

Figure 14.9

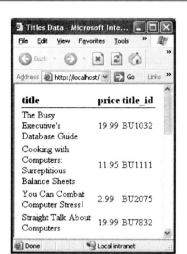

Displaying Details Using the ObjectList Control

You can display data in several different formats using the ObjectList control. In the preceding example, the data were displayed as a table. Another option for the object list is to display a single field as a link, so that the user can choose to display details. In the Property Builder for the object list, if you select the fields to display, the data display as a table. If you leave the *Selected Fields* list empty, only one field displays. By default, the first field from the data source displays, but you can choose a different field in the LabelField list (Figure 14.10). Figure 14.11 shows the application with the title_id field selected as the LabelField, and Figure 14.12 shows the screen after a selection is made.

Figure 14.10

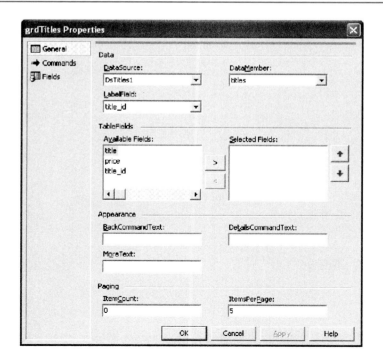

Figure 14.11

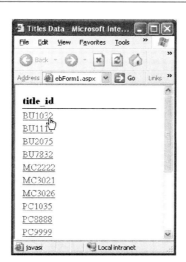

A single field displays as links, so the user can select which record to display.

Figure 14.12

The selected record displays.

Using Multiple Forms

One of the major challenges in working with mobile devices is the size of the screen. Unlike an ASP.NET Web application, in a mobile application you can place multiple forms on the same document. Actually, a form is one of the controls in the Mobile Web Forms toolbox. A form is a container that can hold other controls, and one document can hold multiple forms. You can easily navigate from one form to another. Since you are actually displaying the same Web page, your data exist for all of the forms, but only one form displays on the screen of the mobile device at any one time.

This example creates two forms, frmMain and frmDetail. In frmMain, a List control displays the title field from the titles table. When the user selects a title from the list, the program displays a second form with the details for the selected title displayed in labels. Figure 14.13 shows the two forms in the Document window and Figure 14.14 shows the Property Builder for lstTitles, the List control on frmMain.

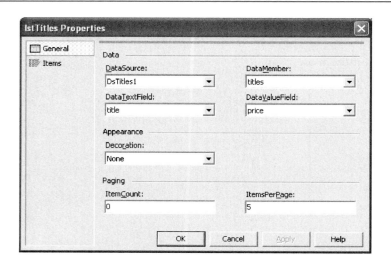

Figure 14.14

The Property Builder for the List control on frmMain. Set the DataSource, DataMember, DataTextField, and DataValueField properties here.

On frmMain, the user can click on a title to display the details for that book on the second form. When the user clicks an item, the list's ItemCommand event fires. You can find the values for the chosen item from the event procedure's EventArgs argument.

```
Private Sub lstTitles_ItemCommand(ByVal sender As System.Object, _
  ByVal e As System.Web.UI.MobileControls.ListCommandEventArgs) _
  Handles lstTitles.ItemCommand
    'Display selected information in controls on frmDetail

    lblPrice.Text = e.ListItem.Value
    lblTitle.Text = e.ListItem.Text
    ActiveForm = frmDetail                'Display the second form
End Sub
```

Figure 14.15*a* and *b* shows the two forms for the running application.

a.   b.

Figure 14.15

The running multiform application: a. *frmMain;* b. *frmDetail.*

One more element of the multiform program needs some explanation. On frmDetails, the *Back* link is created with a Link control. Set the Link control's NavigateUrl to *#frmMain*, which refers to another form on the same document. Here is the complete code for the mobile multiform program:

```
'Project:        Ch14MMITMultiForms
'Programmer:     Bradley/Millspaugh
'Date:           January 2003
'Description:    Display titles and prices from the pubs
'                database on two forms.

Option Strict On

Public Class MobileWebForm1
    Inherits System.Web.UI.MobileControls.MobilePage

    Private Sub Page_Load(ByVal sender As System.Object, _
      ByVal e As System.EventArgs) Handles MyBase.Load
        'Fill the dataset

        daTitles.Fill(DsTitles1)
        Me.DataBind()
    End Sub

    Private Sub lstTitles_ItemCommand(ByVal sender As System.Object, _
      ByVal e As System.Web.UI.MobileControls.ListCommandEventArgs) _
      Handles lstTitles.ItemCommand
        'Display selected information in controls on frmDetail

        lblPrice.Text = e.ListItem.Value
        lblTitle.Text = e.ListItem.Text
        ActiveForm = frmDetail                'Display the second form
    End Sub
End Class
```

Feedback 14.1

Write the statements to display the product ID and description on a second page from lstProducts, a list of products.

World-Ready Programs

There was a time when the term *localization* meant that you had to create a separate version of an application for each specific language or country. This was an after-the-fact approach. Today's approach is the opposite. The planning of applications that will be used in different countries, languages, and cultures should be part of the design and original development stages.

Globalization, Localizability, and Localization

Making your programs "world-ready" is a three-part process: globalization, localizability, and localization. **Globalization** is the process of designing your program for multiple cultures and locations. The user interface as well as the output should allow for multiple languages. This is implemented through a set of rules and data for a specific language called a ***culture/locale***. A culture/locale contains information about character sets, formatting, currency and measurement rules, and methods of sorting.

Localizability determines whether an object can be localized. The resources that must change are separated from the rest of the code, resulting in one set of code that can change and another set that does not change.

The final step is **localization,** the actual process of translating the interface for a culture/locale. By setting the form's Localizable property to True, you can set different Text values for each control for each language. The form has a Language property that is set to *(Default)*, the current language set by the operating system. You can select a different language by dropping down the list for the Language property (Figure 14.16). When you change the form's Language property to a different language, you can enter the Text property of each control in the current language. A separate resource file is created for each language that you select (Figure 14.17).

Drop down the list for the form's Language property to select a language for development.

```
(Default)
Afrikaans
Afrikaans (South Africa)
Albanian
Albanian (Albania)
Arabic
Arabic (Algeria)
Arabic (Bahrain)
Arabic (Egypt)
Arabic (Iraq)
Arabic (Jordan)
Arabic (Kuwait)
Arabic (Lebanon)
```

Figure 14.17

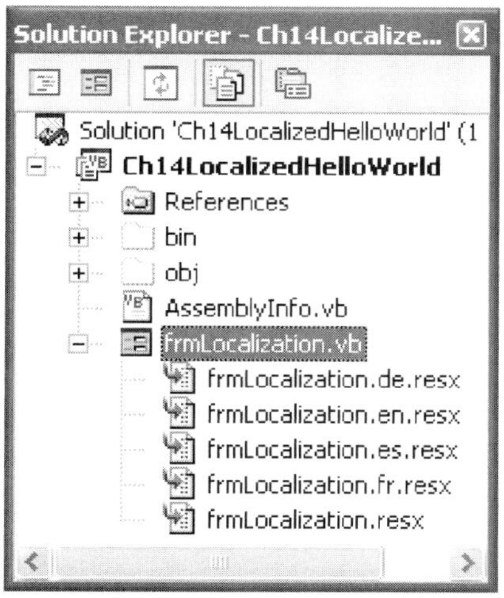

A resource file is created for each language. The .resx file holds the text strings for the Text properties of each control.

The **CultureInfo class** contains an associated language, sublanguage, calendar, and access to cultural conventions for number formatting, date formatting, and comparisons of strings. Table 14.1 shows a partial list of the choices; see the Help files for *CultureInfo Class* for a complete listing of all of the culture/locale values. To use the CultureInfo class in a program, you must import the System.Globalization namespace.

A Partial Listing of the Values for the CultureInfo Class — **Table 14.1**

CultureInfo value	Language—Country/region
af	Afrikaans
af-ZA	Afrikaans—South Africa
ca	Catalan
zh-HK	Chinese—Hong Kong SAR
zh-CHS	Chinese (Simplified)
en-CA	English—Canada
en-GB	English—United Kingdom
en-US	English—United States
fr-FR	French—France
es-ES	Spanish—Spain
de-DE	German—Germany

Normally, the language set in the operating system is the language that displays on the user interface. You also can set the language for testing purposes by modifying the `New` procedure within the designer-generated code section.

Set the culture in the New procedure; the argument for CultureInfo specifies the language and region that you want to test.

```
Public Sub New()
    MyBase.New()
    ' Set the UI culture to German (Germany)
    Thread.CurrentThread.CurrentUICulture = New CultureInfo("de-DE")

    'This call is required by the Windows Form Designer.
    InitializeComponent()

End Sub
```

Writing a Localized Hello World—Step-by-Step

STEP 1: Create a new Windows Application project called *Ch14Localized-HelloWorld*.

STEP 2: Name the form and change or delete the Text property.

STEP 3: Set the form's Localizable property to True.

STEP 4: Add a Label and change its Font property to a larger size, such as 14 or 16 point.

Note that if you change the font before you change languages, the font change applies to all languages unless you specifically override the font for a given language.

STEP 5: Set the Text property of the label to *Hello World*. You may need to enlarge the label, depending on the font size.

STEP 6: Change the Form's Language property to French.

STEP 7: Set the Text property of the label to *Bonjour*.

STEP 8: Change the Form's Language property to Spanish.

STEP 9: Set the Text property of the label to *Hola*.

STEP 10: Change the Form's Language property to German.

STEP 11: Set the Text property of the label to *Hallo*.

STEP 12: Switch to the Code Editor and add these two lines before the Class statement:

```
Imports System.Globalization
Imports System.Threading
```

STEP 13: Modify the New procedure by adding the following lines before the InitializeComponent() call.

```
' Set the UI culture to German (Germany)
Thread.CurrentThread.CurrentUICulture = New CultureInfo("de-DE")
```

STEP 14: Test the program. Try changing the CultureInfo argument to see the French and Spanish text.

Feedback 14.2

1. Write the statement to test the Hello World application for French.
2. Where should the statement be placed?

Threading

The localization process required a thread in the `New` procedure. You may be wondering "what is a thread?" A **thread** is a separate execution path that allows a program to do more than one thing at a time. To make your application access data or process information while doing some other task at the same time, you can set up a separate thread. A program may have several threads running at once. What actually happens is that a thread runs for a short time and suspends operation (goes to sleep) so the program can switch to another thread. Each thread has its own code to execute the desired operations, and the computer switches rapidly from one to the next, so it appears that all are executing simultaneously.

You should be aware of the differences between the terms *multitasking* and *multithreading.* Multitasking allows your computer to appear as though it is running several programs at once. Actually, each program, called a *process,* gets a share of the processor time. Each process executes in a separate area of memory and requires substantial computer resources. A process requires a complete copy of a program's code and data. However, within a single program, you may have multiple tasks to perform. Each of the tasks in the one program can be set up as a thread. A thread uses fewer resources than a process because the thread does not require its own copy of the code and all data. However, the programmer must be very careful about what each thread is doing and with which data items.

You may want to have multiple threads for several reasons. If you want your application to display animation and also have the user enter information and perform other processing, you can place each task in a separate thread. You also can use a thread to display a splash screen while an application is loading. Splash screens are covered in the section "Using a Thread to Display a Splash Screen" later in this chapter. Some methods, such as connecting to a network or a database, may have to wait for a response. Methods that wait for a response are called *blocking methods.* Often a blocking method is placed in a separate thread so that if a problem occurs with the connection, you can interrupt just the thread rather than the entire application.

The localization process merely changes the action of the current thread:

```
' Set the UI culture to German(Germany)
Thread.CurrentThread.CurrentUICulture = New CultureInfo("de-DE")
```

You can instantiate a separate Thread object to create multiple threads in an application. There is an example using complex calculations in your Help files titled "Walkthrough: Authoring a Simple Multithreaded Component with Visual Basic."

Threading is a great new feature for Visual Basic. Several books are devoted entirely to this single subject. For a brief preview, check out http://www.microsoft.com/mspress/developer/feature/060502.asp.

To use threading, import the System.Threading and System.Threading. Thread namespaces. Create a new thread by declaring a Thread object and supplying the constructor with `AddressOf` and the name of the procedure that you want to execute on the thread.

```
Dim MyThread As New System.Threading.Thread(AddressOf Calculations)
```

Methods for threads include Start, Abort, Sleep, and Suspend.

```
'Project:        Ch14Threads
'Programmer:     Bradley/Millspaugh
'Date:           January 2003
'Description:    Demonstrate using multiple threads.

Option Strict On

Imports System.Threading
Imports System.Threading.Thread

Public Class frmThreads
    Inherits System.Windows.Forms.Form

    [Windows Form Designer generated code]

    Private Sub frmThreads_Load(ByVal sender As System.Object, _
      ByVal e As System.EventArgs) Handles MyBase.Load
        Dim threadOne As New Thread(AddressOf Hello)
        Dim threadTwo As New Thread(AddressOf Hello)

        'Put the current thread to sleep to delay the next two threads
        MessageBox.Show("Current Thread is " & _
          CurrentThread.GetHashCode())

        threadOne.Start()
        threadTwo.Start()
    End Sub

    Private Sub Hello()
        'Display a message

        MessageBox.Show("Hello " & CurrentThread.GetHashCode())
    End Sub
End Class
```

Using a Thread to Display a Splash Screen

Another good use of threading is to display a **splash screen**, such as the one displayed in Figure 14.18. Professional applications often use splash screens, also called splash forms, to tell the user that the application is loading and starting. It can make a large application appear to load and run faster, since something appears on the screen while the rest of the application loads.

Displaying a splash form brings up several new issues. When the startup form closes, the application quits, even if several other forms are still open. Therefore, the splash form cannot be the startup object. Instead, you must write a Sub Main procedure, which should appear in a separate code module. You then set the startup object (in the *Project Properties* dialog box) to Sub Main. In Sub Main you must start a thread for the splash form and then run the application. You will see how to accomplish this in the example that follows, which adds the splash screen shown in Figure 14.18 to a database application written earlier (Ch05RnRGrid).

Figure   14.18

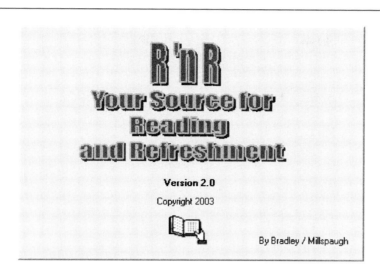

A splash screen can display while the rest of the application loads, which makes the application appear to load faster.

Create a Splash Screen

To create a splash screen, add a new Windows Form to an existing project. Set the properties to remove the title bar, to make the form nonresizable, and to remain on top of any other forms. Notice that you must set four properties to hide the form's title bar: ControlBox, MaximizeBox, MinimizeBox, and Text.

Property	Setting	Description
Name	SplashForm	Name the file SplashForm.vb and the class SplashForm.
ControlBox	False	Hide the Close button and Control menu icon; needed to hide the title bar.
FormBorderStyle	FixedDialog	Select a nonresizable style; also can be FixedSingle or Fixed3D.
MaximizeBox	False	Hide the maximize box; needed to hide the title bar.
MinimizeBox	False	Hide the minimize box; needed to hide the title bar.
StartPosition	CenterScreen	Center the splash form on the screen.
Text	(blank)	Needed to hide the title bar.
TopMost	True	Make the splash form remain on top of the main form until it closes.

Create a Sub Main Procedure

The Sub Main procedure belongs inside a module, not inside any classes in your program. Generally Sub Main is stored in a separate code module. However, just as you can place more than one class inside a single file, you can also code a module in the same file as one or more classes. This example uses the more standard approach of using a separate file.

Add a new **module** to your application by selecting *Project / Add Module* (or right-clicking on the project name and selecting *Add / Add Module*). Select the Module template and give the module a name, which will have a .vb extension. The new file will have these statements at the beginning and end:

```
Module YourModuleName

End Module
```

You can write sub procedures and functions inside the module. Just as with classes, any public variables and procedures are available to the entire application; private variables and procedures are available only inside the module.

You must write a public Sub Main procedure and set the project's startup object to Sub Main. This module displays the splash form, begins a new thread, and calls the Application.Run method, which loads and runs the main form. Notice that the thread sleeps for a short time, which you can adjust, to give the main form time to load. When the splash form closes, its thread ends.

```
'Project:       Ch14Splash
'Module:        StartupModule
'Programmer:    Bradley/Millspaugh
'Date:          January 2003
'Description:   Display a splash screen using a thread.

Option Strict On

Imports System.Threading

Module StartupModule

    Dim threadSplash As Thread
    Dim frmSplash As SplashForm

    Public Sub Main()
        'Display the splash screen and start a new thread

        frmSplash = New SplashForm()
        With frmSplash
            .Show()
            .Refresh()                  'Force a repaint
        End With
        threadSplash = New Thread(AddressOf hideSplash)
        threadSplash.Start()

        'Run the application's main form
        Dim frmMain As New MainForm()
        Application.Run(frmMain)        'Begin the application
    End Sub

    Private Sub hideSplash()
        'Hide the splash screen after the thread sleeps

        threadSplash.Sleep(1000)        'Pause 1 second
        frmSplash.Close()
    End Sub
End Module
```

One more statement in the preceding code needs explanation: The `frmSplash.Refresh` method forces the system to completely draw the splash form. When a thread sleeps, all form painting stops. Without the `Refresh`, the form does not completely paint before the thread goes to sleep.

Feedback 14.3

1. Write the statement to create a thread to run the DisplayImage procedure.
2. Write the code to start execution of your thread.

Your Hands-On Programming Example

Create a multitier mobile Internet application to display the store information from the stores table in the pubs database. Use an ObjectList to display the Store IDs. When the user selects a Store ID, the information for that store will appear.

Create a data tier component using a Web Service, which returns a dataset based on the stores table.

Planning the Project

This project should have only one form. The ObjectList changes configuration when the user makes a selection from the list. Figure 14.19*a* and *b* shows the form layout, which your users sign off as meeting their needs.

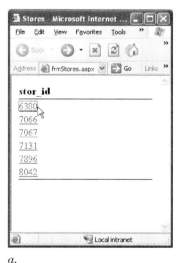

a.

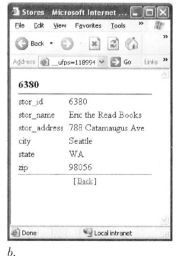

b.

Figure 14.19

The design of the form for the hands-on programming example: a. the original display; b. the display after the user makes a selection from the list.

Plan the Objects, Properties, and Methods

First plan the Web service for the data tier component; then plan the objects and property settings for the mobile form and its controls. Figure 14.20 shows the diagram of the program components. Remember that the data tier is a Web service and will be created in a separate solution.

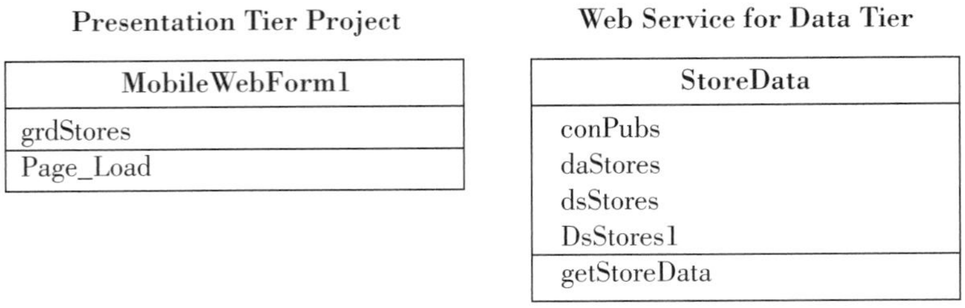

Figure 14.20

The components for the hands-on programming example.

Presentation Tier Project	Web Service for Data Tier
MobileWebForm1	**StoreData**
grdStores	conPubs
Page_Load	daStores
	dsStores
	DsStores1
	getStoreData

Web Service for the Data Tier

Object	Property	Setting
Class	Name	StoreData
conPubs	Name	conPubs
daStores	Name	daStores
dsStores	Name	dsStores
DsStores1	Name	DsStores1
	Table	Stores

Methods	Actions—Pseudocode
getStoreData	Create a dataset that holds the stores table.
	Return the dataset.

Presentation Tier

Object	Property	Setting
MobileWebForm1	Name	MobileWebForm1
	Title	Stores
ObjectList	ID	grdStores (All other properties are set in code.)

Event procedures/Methods	Actions—Pseudocode
Page_Load	Instantiate the data tier Web service.
	Retrieve the dataset from the Web service.
	Bind the object list to the store information.

Write the Project

First create the Web service for the data tier, following the plan that you created.

- Create the Web service component in its own project and solution.

- Add and name the objects to the Web service, according to your plan.

- Write the method for the Web service, following the pseudocode.

- Test the Web service to make sure that it works before beginning the consumer application.

Create the consumer application following the output shown in Figure 14.19.

- Create the mobile Web application as a separate project and solution.

- Set the properties of the form objects, according to your plans.

- Write the code for the form. Working from the pseudocode, write the event procedure.

- When you complete the code, test the operation several times.

The Project Coding Solution

The Web Service for the Data Tier

```
'File:           Ch14StoreData
'Programmer:     Bradley/Millspaugh
'Date:           January 2003
'Description:    The StoreData Web Service for Ch14HandsOn.

Option Strict On

Imports System.Web.Services

<WebService(Namespace:="http://StoreData")> _
Public Class StoreData
    Inherits System.Web.Services.WebService

    [Web Services Designer Generated Code]

    <WebMethod()> Public Function getStoreData() As DataSet
        'Fill the dataset and return it

        daStores.Fill(DsStores1)
        Return DsStores1
    End Function

End Class
```

The Mobile Web Form for the Presentation Tier

```
'Project:        Ch14HandsOn
'Programmer:     Bradley/Millspaugh
'Date:           January 2003
'Description:    Display store information on a mobile device.

Option Strict On

Public Class MobileWebForm1
    Inherits System.Web.UI.MobileControls.MobilePage
    Protected WithEvents grdStores As System.Web.UI.MobileControls.ObjectList
    Protected WithEvents frmStores As System.Web.UI.MobileControls.Form

    [Web Form Designer Generated Code]

    Private Sub Page_Load(ByVal sender As System.Object, _
      ByVal e As System.EventArgs) Handles MyBase.Load
        'Get the data from the Web service
```

```
        Dim wsStoreData As New localhost.StoreData()
        grdStores.DataSource = wsStoreData.getStoreData()
        grdStores.DataBind()
    End Sub
End Class
```

S u m m a r y

1. The Microsoft Mobile Internet Toolkit (MMIT) makes it possible to develop applications for mobile devices using Visual Studio.
2. Mobile devices use WML and WAP in place of HTML and HTTP.
3. Emulators allow testing for output to many specific devices.
4. The Visual Basic code for mobile applications is the same as for Web Forms and Windows Forms.
5. Controls are available for mobile devices with similar functionality as for Web Form controls but provide rendering for specific devices.
6. Data can be accessed on a mobile device using data adapters and datasets.
7. An ObjectList control can display as a table or as a list linked to the detail information for all fields in the record.
8. Multiple Form controls on the same Web page provide an easy way to divide the data displayed into smaller portions.
9. Applications can be world-ready through globalization, localizability, and localization.
10. The CultureInfo class contains many language/region combinations for localization of applications.
11. Localization applies formatting and language modifications to applications to customize them for a specific country or region.
12. Threading allows multiple actions to occur simultaneously, sharing the processing time for an application.

K e y   T e r m s

culture/locale   *452*
CultureInfo Class   *453*
globalization   *452*
localizability   *452*
localization   *452*
Microsoft Mobile Internet Toolkit
  (MMIT)   *442*
module   *458*

ObjectList control   *446*
splash screen   *456*
thread   *455*
Wireless Application Protocol
  (WAP)   *442*
Wireless Markup Language
  (WML)   *442*

R e v i e w   Q u e s t i o n s

1. What transmission protocol and markup language are used for mobile devices?
2. What steps must be taken for Visual Studio to provide a template for Mobile Applications?
3. List three generic devices and emulators available for mobile application development.
4. Discuss accessing data for display on a mobile device.
5. Explain the advantages of using multiple forms on a single Web page.
6. Define each of the following:
    a. Globalization
    b. Localizability
    c. Localization
    d. Culture/locale
7. Using Help files, list three countries or locales for each of the following languages:
    a. English
    b. Spanish
    c. Arabic
8. List the steps to create a Button control with different Text properties for multiple languages.
9. Explain the purpose and significance of multithreading in applications.

P r o g r a m m i n g   E x e r c i s e s

14.1 Write a mobile application that displays the company name, address, and hours of operation. Use your own information or use the following:
    Tricia's Travels
    1101 Main Place
    Tustin Hills, AZ
    Open M–F 9–5 and Saturdays 10–2
14.2 Create a mobile application for converting miles into kilometers. Use a text box to enter the miles and display the result in kilometers. Include a button labeled *Calculate*.
14.3 Use localization to modify your miles to kilometers conversion application (Exercise 14.2) for at least one more language.
14.4 Create a mobile application that uses a Web service that you have already created for another project, perhaps from Chapter 9.
14.5 Create a mobile application and a Web service to display the data from the publishers table in the pubs database.
14.6 Add a splash screen to any of your previous projects.

Case Studies

Claytor's Cottages

Create a Web page for mobile devices for Claytor's Cottages. Include a "link" to a second form for each month of the year with the average daytime and evening temperatures for each month.

Christian's Car Rentals

Create a mobile application that displays the information in the vehicle table.

Answers to Feedback Questions

► Feedback 1.1

1. A set of classes for developing and running Windows applications, Web applications, and XML Web services written in multiple languages on multiple platforms.
2. What is the meaning and function of each of these terms?
    a. CLR: Common Language Runtime. An environment that manages the execution of code during run time, including security and memory management.
    b. CLS: Common Language Specification. Standards that specify how a language that interacts with the CLR should behave.
    c. MSIL: Microsoft Intermediate Language, the result of a compile of a .NET source language.
    d. PE: Portable executable file, combines the MSIL with metadata.

► Feedback 1.2

```
asmInfo = [Assembly].Load("Attributes")
objAttributes = asmInfo.GetCustomAttributes(False)
Dim objItem as Object
For Each objItem In objAttributes
    If objItem.GetType.ToString() = "System.Reflection.AssemblyCopyrightAttribute" Then
        atrCopyright = CType(objItem, AssemblyCopyrightAttribute)
        lblCopyright.Text = atrCopyright.Copyright.ToString()
    End If
Next
```

► Feedback 2.1

1. Validation, calculations, business logic, and enforcing business rules.
2. Data entry using visual controls such as radio buttons, check boxes, and list boxes.
   User event handling with buttons and menu selections.
   Sending user input to the business tier.
   Doing form level validation such as checking for null values.
   Displaying the forms requested by the user.

► Feedback 2.2

1. Property procedures allow the private properties in your class to be accessed through Gets and Sets
2. Each class needs to be in charge of its own data. If the properties are not declared as private, the objects of that class have access to those variables.
3.
```
Sub New(ByVal strLastName As String, ByVal strFirstName As String, _
    ByVal dteBirthDate As Date)
End Sub
```

4. `Dim mStudent As New Student(txtFirstName.Text, txtLastName.Text, CDate(txtDate.Text))`
5. An exception should be thrown in the business tier and a message should appear in the presentation tier, telling the user what error has occurred and what they can do to fix it.

▶ Feedback 2.3

1. Module-level, can be used by all procedures in that file, module, or class.
2. When the project ends, the variable is destroyed.
3. Private.
4. No.

▶ Feedback 3.1

1. A *row* contains all of the fields that make up a record about one friend.
   A *column* contains one piece of information, such as a name or phone number.
   A *record* contains all of the information about a single friend.
   A *field* contains one piece of information, such as a name or a phone number.
   A *primary key field* contains a piece of information that uniquely identifies each friend. In this case, it's likely the name.
2. XML data are stored as text, which will allow them to pass through firewalls and over the Internet.

▶ Feedback 3.2

1. Find and expand the DataBindings node in the properties of the label.
   Click on the drop-down box next to the Text property of the DataBindings section.
   Expand the node of the DataSet that you want to use.
   Expand the node of the table that you want to use.
   Click on the field from which you want to display information.
2. Set the criteria of the ZIP code field to @Zipcode.
3. Using the XML schema design window, add a new row, setting the type as *E* for element.
   In the Properties window for that row, set the Expression field to contain the concatenated fields.

▶ Feedback 3.3

1. The data connection and data adapter are placed in the data tier.
2. The return type must be DataSet.
3. `lblFirstName.DataBindings.Add("Text", dsCustomers.Tables("Customer"), "FirstName")`

▶ Feedback 4.1

1. 1:1: Each user has one id and each id is associated with only one user.
   1:M: Each customer may have many orders. Each order can only belong to one customer.
   M:N An ingredient may be in many recipes and a recipe may have many ingredients.
2. The Categories table is the one-table and the Products table is the many-table.
   The primary key field is CategoryID from the Categories table and the foreign key field is CategoryID in the Products table.
3. The Categories table is the parent table and the Products table is the child table.

▶ Feedback 4.2

1. ```
   daCustomers.Fill(DsCustomersOrders1)
   daOrders.Fill(DsCustomersOrders1)
   ```
2. Open the DataGridTableStyle Collection Editor in the TableStyles property of the DataGrid.
   Click on the *Add* button to add your first table style.
   Select the MappingName property (under *Misc*) and click the down-arrow; select the parent table.
   Select the GridColumnStyles property.
   Open the DataGridColumnStyle Collection Editor.
   Click the *Add* button to add your first column style.
   First set the MappingName property, which sets the field name for the column.
   Set the HeaderText property to the heading of your choice.
   Set the Width to the size that you desire.
3. You can choose to not display columns by not creating column styles for the fields.

▶ Feedback 4.3

1. ```
   'Retrieve the product name
   strProductName = CStr(lstProductName.SelectedValue)
   'Create a datarow based on the selected product name
   drProduct = DsProductCategories.Product.FindByprod_name(strProductName)
   drCategory = DrProduct.GetParentRow("CategoriesProducts")
   'Display the category name in a label
   lblCategory.Text = CStr(drCategegory.Item("Category_name"))
   ```
2. ```
   'Get the category_id of the selected category
   strCategoryID = lstCategories.SelectedValue
   'Find the row from the categories table that matches the category_id
   drCategory = DsCategoriesProducts1.categories.FindBycategory_id(strCategoryID)
   'Retrieve an array of products (child) rows matching the category row
   ```
   ```

```
drsProducts = drCategory.GetChildRows("CategoriesProducts")
'Fill the list with the array of product rows
lstProducts.Items.Clear()
For Each drProduct In drsProducts
    strProductName = CStr(drProduct.Item("ProductName"))
    lstProducts.Items.Add(strProductName)
Next
```

➤ Feedback 4.4

1. This represents a M:N relationship between the Orders table and the Products table. The OrderDetails table is the junction table, which creates two 1:M relationships, joining the two tables. The Orders-to-OrderDetails relationship is a 1:M with the Orders table as the parent and the OrderDetails table as the child. The Products-to-OrderDetails relationship is a 1:M with the Products table as the parent and the OrderDetails table as the child.
2. You would first retrieve all of the ProductIDs from the OrderDetails table based on the OrderID. Then you would retrieve the ProductName for each of those ProductIDs from the Products table.
3.
```
    'Code for the presentation tier
    Dim dataProducts As OrdersDatabase
    Dim strProducts() as String
    strProducts = dataProducts.getProducts(strOrderID)

'Code for the data tier
Public Function getData(ByVal strAuID As String) As String()
    'Find the titles for the selected author
    Dim drProduct As DataRow                 'Row for selected product
    Dim drsOrderProduct As DataRow()         'Array of matching rows from junction table
    Dim drOrderProduct As DataRow            'One row from junction table
    Dim intRow As Integer                    'Index for array
    Dim strProduct As String                 'Hold one product name
    Dim strProducts(10) As String            'Array of products for one order

    'Find the record for the selected OrderID (the passed parameter)
    drProduct = DsProducts1.products.FindByorder_id(strOrderID)
    'Retrieve the array of matching rows from the junction table
    drsOrderProduct = drProduct.GetChildRows("ordersorderdetails")
    'Get each title and add to the array of titles
    For Each drOrderProduct In drsOrderProduct
        'Retrieve the parent row and title field from the junction table row
        strProduct = _
          drOrderProduct.GetParentRow("productsorderdetails").Item ("ProductNam")
        'Add the title to the array
        strProducts(intRow) = strProduct
        'Increment index for next title
        intRow += 1
    Next
    Return strProducts                 'Return the array of products
End Function
```

➤ Feedback 5.1

```
daCustomer.Update(DsCustomer1)
DsCustomer1.AcceptChanges()
```

➤ Feedback 5.2

```
1.  With bmCustomers
        If .Position > 0 Then
            .Position -= 1 'Previous record
        Else
            .Position = .Count -1 'Last record
        End If
    End With
2.  With bmCustomers
        .RemoveAt(.Position)
    End With
3.  bmCustomers.AddNew()
```

➤ Feedback 5.3

```
1.  bmBooks.RemoveAt(bmBooks.Position)
    dabooks.Update(DsBooks1)
    DsBooks1.AcceptChanges()
```
2. Checked
3. DataBindings.SelectedValue
    DataSource
    DisplayMember
    ValueMember

➤ Feedback 5.4

First you must update any deletes for the orders table. Next, update any changes that were made to the customers table. Finally, update all other changes made to the orders table.

➤ Feedback 6.1

1. A Windows Button has a Name property and a Web Forms Button has an ID property. A Windows Button has a BackgroundImage property. A Web Forms Button has a BorderColor property.

2. The HyperLink control and the LinkButton control look the same. However, the LinkButton has a click event and the HyperLink has a Navigate-Url property.
3. `datSelected = calDate.SelectedDate`
4. The order in which the controls were placed on the document.
5. Create a new style in the Styles.css file, making sure to begin the style name with a period.
   Link the Web document to the Styles.css file.
   Assign the style name to controls using the CssStyle property.
   You can link other Web pages to the same Styles.css file and assign the styles to controls.

Feedback 6.2

Add a RequiredFieldValidator, a RangeValidator, and a CompareValidator to your document.
Set the ControlToValidate property for all three validators to txtQuantity.
Set the RequiredFieldValidator Enabled property to True.
Set the RangeValidator's MinimumValue property to 1 and its MaximumValue to 100.
Finally, set the CompareValidator's Type property to a numeric type (Integer or Double).

Feedback 6.3

1. `Session("Email") = txtEmail.Text`
2. `lblEmail.Text = Session("Email").ToString()`
3. ```
   With Response.Cookies("Email")
        .Value = Session("Email").ToString()
        .Expires = Today.AddYears(3)
   End With
   ```
4. Use the Session object or store the state values in a cookie on the client machine.
5. Using the ViewState property allows you to maintain values only for the current page.

Feedback 7.1

```
If Not IsPostBack Then
    conPubs.Open()
    drStores = cmdTitles.ExecuteReader()
    ddlTitles.DataSource = drStores
    ddlTitles.DataTextField = "Title"
    ddlTitles.DataBind()
    drStores.Close()
    conPubs.Close()
End If
```
```

Feedback 7.2

1. ```
   daStudents.Fill(DsStudents1)
   Me.DataBind()
   ```
2. You must set the DataSource property to a data view or to a dataset and set the DataMember property to a table within the dataset.

Feedback 7.3

1. You should place two labels and a PictureBox in the item template.
2. ```
   Dim dsEmployeesSession As DataSet
   Dim drwCurrentRow As DataRow
   dsEmployeeSession = CType(Session("dsEmployees"), DataSet)
   drwCurrentRow = dsEmployeeSession.Tables("Employees").Rows(e.Item.ItemIndex)
   ```

Feedback 7.4

1. ```
   If Not IsPostBack Then
       daEmployees.Fill(DsEmployees1)
       Me.DataBind()
   End If
   ```
2. `rblList.SelectedIndex`

Feedback 7.5

1. ```
   Public Function getData() As DataSet
       'Return the dataset

       daEmployees.Fill(DsEmployees1)
       Return DsEmployees1
   End Function
   ```
2. `daEmployees.Update(dsPassedDataSet)`

Feedback 8.1

1. ```
   With dvISBN
       .Table = dsData.Tables("Books")
       .RowFilter = "ISBN = '" & ddlISBN.SelectedItem.Value & "'"
   End With
   ```
2. ```
   txtTitle.Text = dvISBN(0).Item("Title").ToString()
   txtTitle.Text = DataBinder.Eval(dvISBN, "(0).Title").ToString()
   ```

Feedback 8.2

1.  ```
    'Save
    Session("AddPending") = blnAddPending

    'Retrieve
    blnAddPending = CType(Session("AddPending"), Boolean)
    ```
2.  ```
    ddlName.Items.Insert(0, "")
    ddlName.SelectedIndex = 0
    ```
3.  ```
    cmdObject = New OleDb.OleDbCommand()
    With cmdObject
        .Connection = conObject
        .CommandType = CommandType.Text
        .CommandText = strSQL
        .Connection.Open()
        .ExecuteNonQuery
    End With
    ```
4.  ```
    "DELETE FROM Employee WHERE EmpID = '1234'"
    ```
5.  ```
    "DELETE FROM Employee WHERE EmpID = '" & txtEmpID.Text & "'"
    ```

Feedback 8.3

1. Throw
2. If the list changes. If updates occur, you must refill the list. Binding properties that are set at run time do not persist and must be reset if you want to rebind the control. In a single-tier application, the binding properties are set at design time, so all it takes is Me.Databind to rebind the list.

Feedback 9.1

1. d
2. c
3. e
4. b
5. a

Feedback 9.2

1. The Namespace clause containing the URI of the Web service.
2. Before the Class header.
3. The <WebMethod()>
    ```

▶ Feedback 9.3

```
Dim wsInventory As New localhost.Inventory()
```

▶ Feedback 11.1

1. ```
   strKey = strElement.GetHashCode.ToString()
   mhshTable.Add(strKey, strElement)
   ```
2. `msrtList.Add(strKey, strElement)`
3. `mstkList.Push(strElement)`
4. `mqueList.Enqueue(strElement)`

▶ Feedback 11.2

1. `objPerson = CType(colPersons.Item(strKey), Persons)`
2. The Item property of a collection is usually the default property.
3. `colPersons.RemoveAt(strKey)`
4. `objPerson = CType(colPersons.Item(strKey), Persons)`

▶ Feedback 11.3

1. Whatever is returned by that object's `ToString` method.
2. You can write your own `ToString` method, which must override the base class `ToString` method.

▶ Feedback 12.1

1. Event `WillSoundAlarm()` must appear at the module level.
   `RaiseEvent WillSoundAlarm()` will be placed in the program logic.
2. The Events list in the Editor window will contain an event for the control when it is added to the form.

▶ Feedback 12.2

Add a WebUserControl to the project; create your control; then drag the control file onto a Web Form.
   ```

► Feedback 13.1

1. a. .hhk is an index file that holds entries for the searchable index.
   b. .hhc is the Table of Contents file, which stores the headings and organization for the Contents tab.
   c. .chm is a compiled help file, which holds the compiled Help project.
   d. .jpeg is a graphic file used to hold images.
   e. .avi is a multimedia file used to store movies.
   f. .htm is a topic file that holds the screens to display in the Help Contents pane.
2. Context-sensitive help
   Pop-up help
   ToolTips
   Status bars
   Help menu

► Feedback 14.1

```
lblProdID.Text = e.ListItem.Value
lblProdDesc.Text = e.ListItem.Text
ActiveForm = frmDetail
```

► Feedback 14.2

1. `Thread.CurrentThread.CurrentUICulture = New CultureInfo("fr-FR")`
2. The statement should be placed in the `Sub New()` procedure before the call to `InitializeComponent`.

► Feedback 14.3

1. `Dim threadImage as New Thread(AddressOf DisplayImage)`
2. `threadImage.Start()`

B

Review of Introductory VB .NET Concepts

This appendix is intended as a review of VB topics generally covered in an introductory course. You should always treat the MSDN Help files as your primary reference and look there when you need more explanation about any of these topics.

Microsoft's Visual Studio .NET

The latest version of Microsoft's Visual Studio, called Visual Studio .NET, includes Visual Basic, Visual C++, the new language C# (C sharp), and the .NET Framework. Visual Studio .NET, sometimes referred to as Version 7, is a total rewrite from Version 6.

The .NET Framework

The programming languages in Visual Studio .NET run in the new .NET Framework. The Framework provides for easier development of Web-based and Windows-based applications, allows objects from different languages to operate together, and standardizes how the languages refer to data and objects. Many third-party vendors have announced versions of other languages to run in the .NET Framework, including FORTRAN, COBOL, and Java.

The .NET languages all compile to a common machine language, called Microsoft Intermediate Language (MSIL). The MSIL code, called *managed code*, runs in the Common Language Runtime (CLR), which is part of the .NET Framework.

Microsoft includes the .NET Framework as part of the Windows operating system. When a person installs any available updates for the operating system, the .NET Framework is included.

Visual Studio .NET

Visual Studio (VS) is a collection of products from Microsoft. The package comes with the Visual Studio integrated development environment (IDE) and Visual Basic, C++, and C# programming languages. All of the languages share the same IDE, so it should be relatively easy for a programmer to switch from one language to another. Visual Studio comes in several versions with varying capabilities and prices. In Help you can see a matrix showing the features of the Standard Edition, Academic Edition, Professional Edition, Enterprise Developer Edition, and Enterprise Architect Edition. You also can purchase VB .NET by itself (without the other languages but *with* the .NET Framework and the VS IDE).

Visual Studio runs on Windows 2000 and Windows XP. Although you can write applications using VS that run on Windows 98, the development environment won't run there.

Namespaces

Namespaces are used to organize and reference groups of classes in the .NET Framework. No two classes can have the same name within a namespace. The classes in the Framework are organized into namespaces, such as

System
System.Data
System.Drawing
System.Windows.Forms

Multiple files can be in the same namespace, and one file can hold more than one namespace. Some businesses use namespaces to organize their classes by application area.

By default, a new VB project includes references for certain namespaces. If you want to use the classes in other namespaces, you can add an `Imports` statement. For example, to write data in a StreamWriter (which replaces a sequential file for VB .NET), you must declare an object of the StreamWriter data type, which is in the System.IO namespace (not included in the default references). You can use either of the following two approaches:

1. Use an `Imports` statement:

```
'This statement appears at the top of the file, before the Class statement:
Imports System.IO
—
'This statement appears inside the class, either at the module-level
  'or inside a procedure
Dim dtaBooks As StreamWriter
```

2. Do not use an `Imports` statement, but qualify every reference by including the namespace:

```
'This statement appears inside the class, either at the module-level
  'or inside a procedure.
Dim dtaBooks As System.IO.StreamWriter
```

If you examine the code automatically generated by the designers, you will see that every reference is completely qualified.

Visual Basic Solutions and Projects

A VB solution consists of one or more projects and a project consists of several files. The Visual Studio IDE automatically creates a folder for a new solution; all files in the solution should be stored in that folder.

The Solution File

The VB solution file is a text file that stores the names of the projects and configuration information for the solution. The file can be edited with a text editor and has an extension of .sln. The companion .suo file stores information about the screen layout of the environment and is *not* a text file, so it cannot be edited. However, you can delete the .suo file; the next time you open the solution, the .suo file is rebuilt.

For Windows solutions, the .sln file holds the project names without a folder or path. But for Web applications, the solution file holds the complete path. If you decide to move or rename a Web application, you may have to edit the solution file. See "Rename a Copied Web Project" in Appendix E.

Project Files

VB project files, which have the extension .vbproj and .vbproj.user, are text files that store configuration settings, the names of the files needed for the project, and references to library routines needed by the project. You can examine and modify the project file with a text editor (very carefully).

VB Files

All VB code, including general classes, Windows form classes, and code modules, are stored in files with a .vb extension. A .vb file is sometimes referred to as a *module,* although, technically speaking, a module in VB .NET is defined by `Module / End Module` statements.

A single .vb file can hold one or more classes. Or a file can consist only of sub procedures and functions to be called by classes defined in other files.

A .vb file that is used to define a Windows form has a companion resource file with an extension of .resx. The resource file holds strings of text and any graphics or other resources needed to render the form on the screen.

For a Web application, the form files have the extension .aspx. The .aspx file is used to create the form and controls, which will be rendered with HTML. The companion file, the .aspx.vb file, holds the VB code for the form. This code file is called the *code-behind* file.

By default, some of the files in a solution are not shown in the Solution Explorer. You can display all files by selecting the project name and clicking on the *Show All Files* button at the top of the Solution Explorer window.

Data Types, Variables, and Constants

The data values that you use in a VB project may be variables or constants. They may be stored and manipulated as one of the intrinsic data types, a structure, or an object based on one of the built-in classes or classes that you write. The intrinsic data types in VB .NET are based on classes and have properties and methods. You can see these by typing a variable name and a period—IntelliSense will pop up with the list of properties and methods.

Data Types

Data type	Use for		Storage size in bytes
Boolean	True or False values		2
Byte	0 to 255, binary data		1
Char	Single Unicode character		2
Date	1/1/0001 through 12/31/9999		8

continued

Data type	Use for	Storage size in bytes
Decimal	Decimal fractions, such as dollars and cents	16
Single	Single-precision floating-point numbers with six digits of accuracy	4
Double	Double-precision floating-point numbers with 14 digits of accuracy	8
Short	Small integer in the range −32,768 to 32,767	2
Integer	Whole numbers in the range −2,147,483,648 to +2,147,483,647	4
Long	Larger whole numbers	8
String	Alphanumeric data: letters, digits, and other characters	Varies
Object	Any type of data	4

Selecting the Data Type

Use String data type for text characters; also, for numbers that are used for identification, such as part numbers, social security numbers, and ID numbers. As a general rule, do not use numeric data types for numbers unless you plan to calculate with the numbers. In VB .NET, strings are immutable, which means that once created, they cannot be changed. Each time that your code makes changes to a string, behind the scenes a new string is created for the new value. You also can use Char for single-character text fields.

When dealing with whole numbers, use Integer for any values that you don't expect to surpass the range limit (see table above). For example, make counters and ages Integer. Use Long for whole numbers that may be larger than the limit. Use Byte only for compatibility with routines that require it, such as reading byte data from a file.

For fractional values, you can choose Single, Double, or Decimal. Single and Double are stored as floating-point numbers, which can have some rounding errors when working with decimal fractions, such as dollars and cents. Use Decimal for dollar amounts as well as other values stored in tenths and hundredths, such as interest rates or temperatures.

Variables

You declare variables using the Dim statement (for dimension), or one of the other declaration statements that define the accessibility of the variable, such a Public, Private, Friend, or Static. A variable name (identifier) can be as long as you like (up to 16,383 characters); may consist of letters, digits, and underscores; cannot contain any spaces or periods; cannot be a VB keyword; and must begin with a letter or underscore.

```
{Dim|Public|Private|Friend|Static} VariableName As DataType
```

New to VB .NET, you can assign an initial value to a variable as you declare it, and you can declare multiple variables on one statement and all will have the assigned data type.

Examples

```
Dim strName As String
Public decTotal As Decimal
Private mintObjectCount As Integer = 1
Dim frmMyForm As Form
Static intEventCount As Integer
Dim intCount, intIndex, intNumber As Integer 'Three Integer variables
Dim strCompanyName As String = "Amalgamated Programming, Inc."
```

Naming Conventions

Good programming practice dictates that variable names should always be meaningful. The prefixes you see are not required by VB but are recommended to indicate the data type and scope. The prefixes for data type used in this text are shown below. Use the lowercase prefix and capitalize each word of the name. Always use mixed case for variable names.

Examples

blnAllDone
decSalesAmount
strFirstName

Data type	Prefix
Boolean	bln
Byte	byt
Char	chr
Date	dat
Decimal	dec
Double	dbl
Integer	int
Long	lng
Object	obj
Single	sng
String	str

Constants

Declare a constant for a value that will not change during program execution. The naming rules for constants are the same as for variables. However, this text uses the widely used naming convention of all uppercase names with underscores to separate words. Use a three-character prefix to indicate the data type.

```
Const strCOMPANY_NAME As String = "R 'n R -- For Reading and Refreshment"
Const intTYPE_ONE As Integer = 1
```

Declaring Numeric Constants

VB .NET is a strongly typed programming language. Although you can choose to ignore the typing (see "Option Explicit and Option Strict" later in this appendix), you should always be aware of the data type. When you declare a numeric constant, such as 100 or 125.59, VB assigns a data type. By default, any whole number is created as Integer and any fractional value is created as Double. If you want the constant to be another data type, add a type-definition character to the right end of the number; for example, 125.5D for Decimal data type or 125.5F for Single (the *F* stands for floating-point). The type-declaration characters:

Decimal	D
Double	R
Integer	I
Long	L
Short	S
Single	F

Intrinsic Constants

Intrinsic constants are system-defined constants that reside in the .NET class library. You must specify the class or group name to use the constants. Some examples of helpful constants: Color.Red, Color.Blue, Color.Orange (and dozens more); ControlChars.NewLine, ControlChars.LineFeed; MessageBoxButtons.YesNoCancel; and MessageBoxIcons.Question. IntelliSense is a great help; just type the group name and a period, and all of the available choices pop up for your selection.

Scope and Lifetime

See Chapter 2 for a review of scope and lifetime. The scope of variables and constants has changed from VB 6.

VB .NET scope: block-level, local (procedure-level), module-level, and namespace-level.

Public, Private, and Static Variables

The form for a Dim statement is

```
{Dim|Public|Private|Friend|Protected|Static} VariableName As DataType
```

The default is Private, so if you use either the Dim or Private keyword, the variable is Private. Public variables are available to any other object and can violate encapsulation rules. Private variables are available only to the class in which they are declared; Protected variables are available to the current class and any classes that inherit from the current class. Friend variables are available to any classes in the current application.

Static variables are local variables with a lifetime that matches the class rather than the procedure. If you declare a variable as Static, it is not destroyed each time the procedure exits. Instead, the variable is created once the first time the procedure executes and retains its value for the life of the module. You can use a static variable to maintain a running count or total, as well as keep track of whether a procedure has executed previously.

```
Static blnDoneOnce As Boolean     'Boolean variables are initialized as False
If blnDoneOnce Then
    Exit Sub       'Already been here before
Else
    'Coding that you want to do one time only
    blnDoneOnce = True
End If
```

Option Explicit and Option Strict

Option Explicit and Option Strict can significantly change the behavior of the editor and compiler. Turning the options off can make coding somewhat easier but provide opportunities for hard-to-find errors and very sloppy programming.

Option Explicit

When Option Explicit is turned off, you can use any variable name without first declaring it. The first time you use a variable name, VB allocates a new variable of Object data type. This is a throwback to very old versions of Basic that did not require variable declaration and caused countless hours of debugging programs that had only a small misspelling or typo in a variable name.

You should always program with Option Explicit turned on. In VB .NET, the option is turned on by default for all new projects.

Option Strict

Option Strict is a new option introduced in VB .NET. This option makes VB more like other strongly typed languages, such as C++, Java, and C#. Option Strict does not allow any implicit (automatic) conversions from a wider data type to a narrower one, or between String and numeric data types.

With Option Strict turned on, you must use the conversion functions, such as CInt and CDec to convert to the desired data type from String or from a wider data type to a narrower type, such as from Decimal to Integer.

The best practice is to always turn on Option Strict, which can save you from developing poor programming habits and likely save hours of debugging time. By default, Option Strict is turned off. You can turn it on either in code or in the *Project Properties* dialog box. Place the line

```
Option Strict On
```

before the first line of code, after the general remarks at the top of a file.

To turn on `Option Strict` or `Option Explicit` for the entire project, open the *Project Properties* dialog box and select *Common Properties / Build*. There you will find settings for both `Option Explicit` and `Option Strict`. By default, `Option Explicit` is turned on and `Option Strict` is turned off. Setting *Option Strict On* in the project properties has one additional effect—any new files that you add to the project will have the option turned on automatically.

Note: `Option Strict` includes all of the requirements of `Option Explicit`. If `Option Strict` is turned on, variables must be declared, regardless of the setting of `Option Explicit`.

Conversion between Data Types

With `Option Strict` turned on, you must explicitly convert data to the correct type. Each of the following functions converts an expression to the named data type.

Function	Return type	Example
`CBool(`*Expression*`)`	Boolean	`blnResult = CBool(intResult)`
`CDate(`*Expression*`)`	Date	`datResult = CDate(txtDate.Text)`
`CDbl(`*Expression*`)`	Double	`dblAnswer = CDbl(decNumber)`
`CDec(`*Expression*`)`	Decimal	`decNumber = CDec(txtNumber.Text)`
`CInt(`*Expression*`)`	Integer	`intNumber = CInt(txtNumber.Text)`
`CLng(`*Expression*`)`	Long	`lngNumber = CLng(txtNumber.Text)`
`CObj(`*Expression*`)`	Object	`objObject = CObj(txtNumber.Text)`
`CShort(`*Expression*`)`	Short	`srtNumber = CShort(txtNumber.Text)`
`CSng(`*Expression*`)`	Single	`sngNumber = CSng(txtNumber.Text)`
`CStr(`*Expression*`)`	String	`strIDNumber = CStr(intIDNumber)`
`CType(`*Object, Type*`)`	Specific type	`dsDataSet = CType(DataInput, DataSet)`
		`intNumber = CType(txtNumber.Text, Integer)`

Calculations

Calculations are performed according to the hierarchy of operations:

1. All operations within parentheses. Multiple operations within the parentheses are performed according to the rules of precedence.
2. All exponentiation, using the ∧ operator. Multiple exponentiation operations are performed from left to right.
3. All multiplication and division (∗ /). Multiple operations are performed from left to right.
4. All addition and subtraction (+ −) are performed from left to right.

There are no implied operations in VB. For example, the algebra expression 2Y must be written as $2 * Y$ in VB.

Arrays

Use the `Dim` statement to declare arrays. You declare the array name and data type, and you can choose to either specify the upper bound of the array *or* assign initial values to the array. The upper bound of the array is the highest subscript allowed and is 1 less than the number of elements in the array, since all arrays are zero based. For example, the statement

```
Dim strNames(10) As String
```

declares an array of 11 elements, with subscripts from 0 to 10.

Alternately, you can assign initial values to the array, in which case you do not specify the upper bound but you use empty parentheses to indicate that it is an array. Use brackets around the initial values. For example, the statement

```
Dim strNames() As String = {"Sue", "Lee", "Tony", "Ann", "Leslie", "Sammy", "Terry", _
    "Laura", "Theresa", "Richard", "Dennis"}
```

also declares an array of 11 elements with subscripts from 0 to 10.

All of the array elements are the same data type. If you omit the data type, just as with single variables, the type defaults to Object, unless Option Strict is turned on, in which case an error message is generated.

Example Array Declarations

```
Dim decBalance(10) As Decimal
Dim mstrProduct(99) As String
Dim mintValue() As Integer = {1, 5, 12, 18, 20}
Dim mstrDepartments() As String = {"Accounting", "Marketing", "Human Relations"}
Private mstrCategory(10) As String
Public mstrIDNumbers(5) As String
Private mintQuestion(5, 100) As Integer 'Two-dimensional array
Static strAnswer(100, 25, 5) As String  'Three-dimensional array
```

Collections

A collection is similar to an array, but much more powerful. Collections have an Items property, which contains the references to all elements of the collection. You can add elements using the `Items.Add` method, remove elements using the `Items.Remove` or `Items.RemoveAt` method, and access the `Count` property.

Retrieve a single element of the collection by using the Item property. You can specify the element using an index, as in an array, or by a key, which is a unique string.

VB has many built-in collections, such as the DataTable collection of a DataSet and a DataRow collection of a DataTable. The preferred method of traversing all elements of a collection is to use the `For Each` loop. See the topic "For Each . . . Next" for further information.

Chapter 11 covers creating and using collections of various types.

Structures

You can use the `Structure` and `End Structure` statements to combine multiple fields of related data. For example, an Employee structure may contain last name, first name, Social Security number, street, city, state, ZIP code, date of hire, and pay code. A Product structure might contain a description, product number, quantity, and price.

```
[Public | Private] Structure NameOfStructure
    Dim FirstField As Datatype
    Dim SecondField As Datatype
    . . .
End Structure
```

The `Structure` declaration cannot go inside a procedure. You generally place the `Structure` statement at the top of a file with the module-level declarations. You also can place a `Structure` in a separate file.

```
Structure Employee
      Dim strLastName As String
      Dim strFirstName As String
      Dim strSSN As String
      Dim strStreet As String
      Dim strCity As String
      Dim strState As String
      Dim datHireDate As Date
      Dim intPayCode As Integer
End Structure

Public Structure Product
      Dim strDescription As String
      Dim strID As String
      Dim intQuantity As Integer
      Dim decPrice As Decimal
End Structure

Structure SalesDetail
      Dim decSale() As Decimal
End Structure
```

By default, a structure is Public. If you include an array inside a structure, you cannot specify the number of elements. You must use a `ReDim` statement in your code to declare the number of elements.

In many ways, a structure is similar to defining a new data type.

Declaring Variables Based on a Structure

Once you have created a structure, you can declare variables of the structure, just as if it were another data type. Make up a prefix for the variable that helps to identify the structure, such as *prd* for Product or *sls* for Sales.

Example

```
Dim empOffice As Employee
Dim empWarehouse As Employee
Dim prdWidget As Product
Dim prdInventory(100) As Product
Dim sdtHousewares As SalesDetail
Dim sdtHomeFurnishings As SalesDetail
```

Accessing the Elements in a Structure Variable

Each field of data in a variable declared as a structure is referred to as an *element* of the structure. To access elements, use the dot notation similar to that used for objects: Specify *Variable.Element*.

```
empOffice.strLastName
empOffice.datHireDate
empWarehouse.strLastName
prdWidget.strDescription
prdWidget.intQuantity
prdWidget.decPrice
prdInventory(intIndex).strDescription
prdInventory(intIndex).intQuantity
prdInventory(intIndex).decPrice
```

Notice the use of indexes in the preceding examples. Each example was taken from the preceding Structure and Dim statements. A variable that is not an array, such as prdWidget, does not need an index. However, for prdInventory, which was dimensioned as an array of 101 elements, you must specify not only the prdInventory item but also the element within the structure.

Including an Array in a Structure

To declare an array in a structure, use the ReDim statement inside a procedure to give the array a size.

```
'Module-level declarations
Structure SalesDetail
    Dim decSale() As Decimal
End Structure

Dim sdtHousewares As SalesDetail

'Inside a procedure:
ReDim sdtHousewares.decSale(6)      'Establish the number of elements in the array

'In processing
sdtHousewares.decSale(intDayIndex) = decTodaysSales
```

Exception Handling

Run-time errors are called exceptions. Exceptions can occur when you try to use a conversion function, such as CInt or CDec, and the user has entered nonnumeric data or left a text box blank. When an operation fails, the CLR throws an exception, which you can trap and handle using .NET's new structured exception handling.

Try / Catch Blocks

To trap or catch exceptions, enclose any statement(s) that might cause an error in a Try / Catch block. If an exception occurs while the statements in the

`Try` block are executing, program control transfers to the `Catch` block; if a `Finally` statement is included, the code in that section executes last, whether or not an exception occurred.

```
Try
    'statements that may cause error
Catch [VariableName As ExceptionType]
    'statements for action when exception occurs
[Finally
    'statements that always execute before exit of Try block]
End Try

Try
    intQuantity = CInt(txtQuantity.Text)
    lblQuantity.Text = CStr(intQuantity)
Catch
    lblMessage.Text = "Error in input data."
End Try
```

The `Catch` as it appears in the preceding example will catch any exception. You can also specify the type of exception that you want to catch, and even have several `Catch` statements, each to catch a different type of exception. To specify a particular type of exception to catch, you use one of the predefined exception classes, which are all based on, or derived from, the SystemException class. View a complete list of system exception classes by selecting *Debug / Exceptions*.

To catch bad input data that cannot be converted to numeric, write this `Catch` statement:

```
Catch MyErr As InvalidCastException
    lblMessage.Text = "Error in input data."
```

The Exception Class

Each exception is an instance of the Exception class. The properties of this class allow you to determine the code source of the error, the type of error, and the cause. The Message property contains a text message about the error and the Source property contains the name of the object causing the error.

You can include the text message associated with the type of exception by specifying the Message property of the Exception object, as declared by the variable you named on the `Catch` statement.

```
Catch MyErr As InvalidCastException
    lblMessage.Text = "Error in input data: " & MyErr.Message
```

Handling Multiple Exceptions

Include multiple `Catch` blocks (handlers) to trap for different kinds of errors. When an exception occurs, the `Catch` statements are checked in sequence. The first one with a matching exception type is used.

```
Catch MyErr As InvalidCastException
    'statements for nonnumeric data
```

```
Catch MyErr As ArithmeticException
    'statements for calculation problem
Catch MyErr As Exception
    'statements for any other exception
```

The last `Catch` will handle any exceptions that do not match the first two exception types. Note that it is acceptable to use the same variable name for multiple `Catch` statements.

Control Structures

You use control structures to modify the sequence of the logic flow in a program. Each of the control structures tests conditions to determine the path to take.

Conditions

You test a condition for True or False. A condition may be based on the value of a Boolean variable or on the relationship of two or more values. You can form a condition using the six relational operators and the logical operators.

Relational operators		Logical operators
>	(greater than)	And
<	(less than)	Or
=	(equal to)	Not
>=	(greater than or equal to)	
<=	(less than or equal to)	
<>	(not equal to)	

Comparisons must be on like types, and may compare strings and/or numeric values.

If ... Then ... Else

Although you will see examples of the single-line `If` statement, the block `If` statement is the recommended form.

The Single-Line If Statement

```
If Condition Then ActionToTakeWhenTrue Else ActionToTakeWhenFalse
```

Example

```
If intCount > 0 Then DisplayTheCount()
```

The Block If Statement

```
If Condition Then
    Action(s)ToTakeWhenTrue
[ElseIf Condition Then
    Action(s)ToTake]
[Else
    Action(s)ToTake]
End If

If blnFirstTime Then
    InitializeVariables()
    blnFirstTime = False
End If

If txtName.Text <> "Smith" Then
    'Take some action
Else
    MessageBox.Show("Hello Ms. Smith")
End If
```

Select Case

The Select Case structure can test for several values and is easier to read and debug than a deeply nested If statement. The data type of the expression to test must match the type of the constants. For the constants, you can use a combination of relational operators, constant ranges, and multiple constants.

- When using a relational operator (e.g., Is >= 100) the word Is must be used.

- To indicate a range of constants, use the word To (e.g., 80 To 99).

- Multiple constants should be separated by commas.

The elements used for the constant list may have any of these forms:

```
constant [, constant…]           Case 2, 5, 9
constant To constant             Case 25 To 50
Is relational-operator constant  Case Is < 10
```

When you want to test for a string value, you must include quotation marks around the literals.

```
Select Case Expression
    Case ConstantList
        Statement(s)ToExecute
    [Case ConstantList
        Statement(s)ToExecute]
    …
```

```
        [Case Else]
            [Statement(s)ToExecute]
End Select

Select Case intListIndex
    Case 0
        HandleItemZero()
    Case 1, 2, 3
        HandleItems()
    Case Else
        HandleNoSelection()
End Select

Select Case txtTeamName.Text.ToUpper()
    Case "TIGERS"
        '(Code for Tigers)
    Case "LEOPARDS"
        '(Code for Leopards)
    Case "COUGARS", "PANTHERS"
        '(Code for Cougars and Panthers)
    Case Else
        '(Code for any nonmatch)
End Select
```

If the `Case Else` clause is omitted and none of the `Case` conditions is True, the program continues execution at the statement following the `End Select`. If more than one `Case` value is matched by the expression, only the statements in the *first* `Case` clause execute.

Loops

A loop repeats program statements and checks a condition to determine when to exit the loop. VB has several constructs for forming loops, including the `For ... Next`, `Do ... Loop`, and `For Each ... Next`. Each time execution passes through a loop is called one *iteration*.

For ... Next

A `For ... Next` is the preferred looping construct when you know ahead of time how many iterations you need. You must declare a variable to use as the loop index, which can be any of the numeric data types. The initial value, test value, and step may be constants, variables, numeric property values, or expressions.

```
For LoopIndex = InitialValue To TestValue [Step Increment]
    'Statement(s) to execute inside the loop
Next [LoopIndex]
```

When `Step` is omitted, the increment defaults to 1.

```
For intIndex = 1 To 10
    Debug.WriteLine(intIndex)
Next intIndex
```

The loop index is compared to the test value. If the loop index is *greater than* the test value, control passes to the statement following the `Next` statement.

Otherwise, the statement(s) inside the loop are executed. At the `Next` statement, the loop index is incremented and tested again.

You can use a negative increment. In this case, the test is made for *less than* the test value.

```
For intIndex = 10 To 1 Step - 1
    Debug.WriteLine(intIndex)
Next intIndex
```

Do Loops

Do Loops begin with the `Do` keyword and end with the `Loop` keyword. You can test a condition at the top of the loop (called a *pretest*), which might prevent the statements within the loop from executing even once, or at the bottom of the loop (called a *posttest*). You can form the condition for ending the loop with either the `While` or `Until` keywords. The `While` continues execution of the loop as long as a condition is True; the `Until` continues execution until the condition becomes True.

```
Do {While | Until} Condition
    'Statement(s) to execute inside the loop
Loop
```

or

```
Do
    'Statement(s) to execute inside the loop
Loop {While | Until} Condition

Do While intCountDown > 0
    'Statements inside the loop
    intCountDown -= 1
Loop

Do
    'Statements to check for a match
    If txtInput.Text = strSearchValue Then
        blnFound = True
    End If
    'More statements here, including a statement that modifies strSearchValue
Loop Until blnFound
```

For Each ... Next

The `For Each ... Next` loop is the preferred construct for stepping through all elements of an array or a collection. When `Option Strict` is on, you must declare a single variable of the same type as the array elements or the members of the collection. Inside the loop, the variable holds the current object or array element. One great advantage of using the `For Each ... Next` is that you don't have to manipulate indexes or test for the number of elements.

```
For Each VariableName In {ArrayName | CollectionName}
    'Statements to execute inside the loop
Next
```

```
Dim strItem As String
For Each strItem In strStringArray
    Debug.WriteLine(strItem)
Next

Dim drsEmployee As DataRow()            'Array of data rows
Dim drEmployee As DataRow               'A single data row
'Code here to fill the drsEmployee array with rows (found in Chapter 4)
For Each drEmployee In drsEmployee
    Debug.WriteLine("Employee First Name = " & drEmployee.Item("fname"))
    Debug.WriteLine("Employee Last Name = " & drEmployee.Item("lname"))
Next
```

See Chapter 11 for many examples of using `For Each` with various types of collections, including the Items collection of a list box.

Early Exit

In each of the loop constructs you can exit early, before the test condition is True. Although many structured-programming purists advise against this practice, it is widely used in programming.

Use the `Exit For` or `Exit Do`, depending on the type of loop you are using.

```
Do
    If txtInput.Text = "END" Then
        Exit Do
    Else
        If txtInput.Text = strSearchValue Then
            blnFound = True
        EndIf
    EndIf
    'More statements here, including a statement that modifies strSearchValue
Loop Until blnFound

For intIndex = 1 To 10
    Debug.WriteLine(intIndex)
    If intIndex = intMatchValue Then
        Exit For
    End If
Next intIndex
```

Message Boxes

You can display a message to the user in a message box, which is a predefined instance of the MessageBox class. The overloaded `Show` method of the MessageBox object allows you to specify the message, title bar text, button(s), and an icon.

```
MessageBox.Show(TextMessage)
MessageBox.Show(TextMessage, TitlebarText)
MessageBox.Show(TextMessage, TitlebarText, MessageBoxButtons)
MessageBox.Show(TextMessage, TitlebarText, MessageBoxButtons, MessageBoxIcon)

MessageBox.Show("Enter numeric data.")
```

```
MessageBox.Show("Try again.", "Data Entry Error")

MessageBox.Show("This is a message.", "This is a title bar", MessageBoxButtons.OK)

Try
    intQuantity = CInt(txtQuantity.Text)
    lblQuantity.Text = intQuantity
Catch err As InvalidCastException
    MessageBox.Show("Nonnumeric Data.", "Error", MessageBoxButtons.OK, _
       MessageBoxIcon.Exclamation)
End Try
```

The message string you display may be a string literal enclosed in quotes or it may be a string variable. If the message is too long for one line, Visual Basic wraps it to the next line. You can control the line breaks by concatenating `ControlChars.NewLine` characters into the string.

The string that you specify for TitlebarText will appear in the title bar of the message box. If you choose the first form of the `Show` method, without the TitlebarText, the title bar will appear empty.

You specify the buttons to display using the MessageBoxButtons constants from the MessageBox class. The choices are OK, OKCancel, RetryCancel, YesNo, YesNoCancel, and AbortRetryIgnore. The default for the `Show` method is OK, so unless you specify otherwise, you will get only the OK button. The `Show` method returns a DialogResult object that you can check to see which button the user clicked.

The easy way to select the icon to display is to select from IntelliSense, which pops up with the complete list. The actual appearance of the icons varies from one operating system to another. You can see a description of the icons in Help under the "MessageBoxIcon Enumeration" topic.

Declaring an Object Variable for the Method Return

To capture the information about the outcome of the `Show` method, declare a variable to hold an instance of the DialogResult type.

```
Dim dgrResult As DialogResult

dgrResult = MessageBox.Show("Clear the current order figures?", "Clear Order", _
    MessageBoxButtons.YesNo, MessageBoxIcon.Question)
```

The next step is to check the value of the return, comparing to the DialogResult constants such as Yes, No, OK, Retry, Abort, and Cancel.

```
If dgrResult = DialogResult.Yes Then
    'Code to clear the order
End If
```

Specifying a Default Button and Options

Two additional signatures for the `MessageBox.Show` method are

```
MessageBox.Show(TextMessage, TitlebarText, MessageBoxButtons, MessageBoxIcons, _
    MessageBoxDefaultButton)
MessageBox.Show(TextMessage, TitlebarText, MessageBoxButtons, MessageBoxIcons, _
    MessageBoxDefaultButton, MessageBoxOptions)
```

To make the second button (the *No* button) the default, use this statement:

```
dgrResult = MessageBox.Show("Clear the current order figures?", "Clear Order", _
    MessageBoxButtons.YesNo, MessageBoxIcon.Question, MessageBoxDefaultButton.Button2)
```

You can make the message appear right-aligned in the message box by setting the MessageBoxOptions argument:

```
dgrResult = MessageBox.Show("Clear the current order figures?", "Clear Order", _
    MessageBoxButtons.YesNo, MessageBoxIcon.Question, MessageBoxDefaultButton.Button2, _
    MessageBoxOptions.RightAlign)
```

Sub and Function Procedures

Programs are made up of a series of procedures, which are the building blocks of programming. In VB, you *must* write event procedures to respond to the events caused by the user. You can also create *general* procedures, which are not associated with any event but are called from other procedures.

You can write sub procedures, function procedures, and property procedures. A sub procedure is a block of code that does not return a value. A function procedure (or just *function*) is a block of code that returns a value. Property procedures are used to get or set the values of properties in class modules and form modules.

Calling Procedures

You can call a sub procedure with or without the optional word `Call`. Assuming that you have written a sub procedure named PrintHeadings that requires an ending date as an argument, you call it with either of these statements:

```
Call PrintHeadings(datEndingDate)
```

or

```
PrintHeadings(datEndingDate)
```

To call a sub procedure that does not require arguments, use empty parentheses:

```
Call DisplayTheDate()
```

or

```
DisplayTheDate()
```

You call a function procedure by using it in an expression, just like calling one of VB's built-in functions. Assuming that you have written a function called *AverageCost* that requires three Decimal arguments and returns a Decimal result, call the function like this:

```
decAverage = AverageCost(decCostOne, decCostTwo, decCostThree)
```

Passing Arguments

The values that you pass to procedures are called *arguments*. You absolutely *must* supply the arguments in the correct order and in the correct data type. The names of the variables are not passed to the called procedure, only a copy of the data (ByVal) or the address of the data value (ByRef). (Refer to the "ByRef and ByVal" topic.)

When you write sub procedures and functions, you must specify the values to be passed. Inside the procedures, those values are referred to as *parameters*. (The calling code passes *arguments;* the called procedure receives those values and calls them *parameters.*)

Writing Sub Procedures

To write a new procedure, place the insertion point on a blank line between procedures and type the procedure header (without the parentheses). For example, you can type `Private Sub PrintHeading` and press Enter. VB adds the parentheses and the `End Sub` (or `End Function`) statement.

```
Private Sub PrintHeadings()
End Sub
```

Of course, you can also type the parameter list and the parentheses, if you wish.

```
Private Sub PrintHeadings(ByVal datEndingDate As Date)
```

The parameter passed to the PrintHeadings sub procedure is a local variable inside the procedure. Call the PrintHeadings sub procedure in any of these ways:

```
PrintHeadings(Today) 'Pass today's date
PrintHeadings(datMyFavoriteDate)
PrintHeadings(#2/2/2002#)
```

The PrintHeadings sub procedure uses the datEndingDate parameter inside the procedure to reference the value passed for the parameter.

```
Private Sub PrintHeadings(ByVal datEndingDate As Date)
 'Print the date

 Debug.WriteLine(FormatDateTime(datEndingDate, vbShortDate))
End Sub
```

Writing Function Procedures

Functions return a value, so a function procedure must have a data type for the return value. The procedure header for a function looks like this:

```
[{Public|Private|Protected|Friend}] Function FunctionName(ParameterList) As DataType
```

Somewhere inside the function procedure, before exiting, you must return a value. You can use the `Return` statement (the preferred technique) or assign a value to the function name. That value is returned to the calling statement.

```
Private Function AverageCost(ByVal decCost1 As Decimal, _
   ByVal decCost2 As Decimal, ByVal decCost3 As Decimal) As Decimal
      'Calculate the average of three numbers

      'Preferred statement:
      Return (decCost1 + decCost2 + decCost3) / 3D
      'Alternate statement:
      AverageCost = (decCost1 + decCost2 + decCost3) / 3D
End Function
```

ByRef and ByVal

By default, arguments are passed `ByVal` (by value), which is a change since VB 6. `ByVal` forces VB to make a copy of the data and pass the copy. If the called procedure makes any changes to the argument, it has no effect on the original variable that you passed. By contrast, passing an argument `ByRef` (by reference) means that the address of your program variable is passed to the procedure. Therefore, if the called procedure makes any changes to the argument's value, the change will be made to the original variable. To protect your variables and provide better separation of program tasks, you should specify that an argument be passed `ByVal`, unless you have a very good reason for allowing the called procedure to modify the original variable.

Public, Private, Protected, or Friend

Just as for variable declarations, you can declare sub procedures and functions to be Public, Private, Protected, or Friend. The accessibility of procedures matches that of similarly declared variables. If you omit the accessibility keyword when writing a procedure, the default is Private.

VB Functions

VB provides many intrinsic functions and methods for math operations, financial calculations, string manipulation, and date/time processing.

IntelliSense helps you type the arguments of functions and methods. When you type the parentheses, the arguments pop up, showing the correct order. The argument to enter is shown in bold. The order of the arguments is important because the function uses the values based on their position in the argument list. If the arguments are supplied in the incorrect order, the result is wrong. And if the data types are incorrect, an exception occurs.

Methods may have overloaded argument lists, which means that there is more than one way to call the method. When you enter the arguments, you must match one of the argument lists exactly.

Formatting Numeric Data

Use the formatting functions to set up numeric data for display or printing. Each of the functions returns a formatted string. You can use each function with a single numeric argument, which returns the default format, such as the number of decimal positions, whether to enclose negative values in parentheses, whether to include leading zeros, and whether to include commas. If you want to specify any of these items, IntelliSense and Help will show you how. The default settings are based on the regional settings in the operating system and can be changed.

Function	Returns by default
`FormatCurrency(NumericExpression)`	Dollar sign, commas, two digits to the right of the decimal point.
`FormatNumber(NumericExpression)`	Commas and two digits to the right of the decimal point.
`FormatPercent(NumericExpression)`	Argument multiplied by 100, with a percent sign and two digits to the right of the decimal point.

Working with Dates

You can use the date functions and the methods of the DateTime structure to retrieve the system date, break down a date into component parts, test whether the contents of a field are compatible with the Date data type, and convert other data types to a Date.

The DateTime Structure

When you declare a variable of Date data type in VB, the .NET Common Language Runtime uses the DateTime structure, which has an extensive list of properties and methods. You can use the shared members of the DateTime structure (identified by a yellow "S" in the MSDN Help lists) without declaring an instance of Date or DateTime. For example, to use the Now property:

```
datToday = Now
```

To use the nonshared members, you must reference an instance of a DateTime structure, such as a variable of Date type. Example:

```
lblTime.Text = datToday.ToShortTimeString()
```

Here is a partial list of some useful properties and methods of the Date-Time structure:

Property or method	Purpose
Date	Date component
Day	Integer day of month; 1–31
DayOfWeek	Integer day; 0 = Sunday
DayOfYear	Integer day; 1–366
Hour	Integer hour; 0–23
Minute	Integer minutes; 0–59
Second	Integer seconds; 0–59
Month	Integer month; 1 = January
Now (Shared)	Retrieve system date and time
Today (Shared)	Retrieve system date
Year	Year component
`ToLongDateString`	Date formatted as long date
`ToLongTimeString`	Date formatted as long time
`ToShortDateString`	Date formatted as short date
`ToShortTimeString`	Date formatted as short time

Retrieving the System Date and Time

You can retrieve the system date and time from your computer's clock using the Now property or the Today property. Now retrieves both the date and time; Today retrieves only the date.

```
Dim datDateAndTime As Date
datDateAndTime = Now

Dim datDate As Date
datDate = Today
```

To display the values formatted:

```
lblDateAndTime.Text = datDateAndTime.ToLongDateString()
lblDate.Text = datDate.ToShortDateString()
```

Date Variables

The Date data type may hold values of many forms that represent a date. Examples could be May 22, 2002, or 5/22/02 or 5-22-2002. When you assign a literal value to a Date variable, enclose it in # signs:

```
Dim datMyDate as Date
datMyDate = #5-22-02#
```

You can also use the `FormatDateTime` function to format dates and times.

Converting Values to a Date Format

If you want to store values in a Date data type, you need to convert the value to a Date type. The `CDate` function converts a value to Date type, but throws an exception if unable to create a valid date from the argument. Use the `IsDate` function first to make sure you have a valid date value, or catch the exception.

```
If IsDate(txtDate.Text) Then          Try
    datMyDate = CDate(txtDate.Text)       datMyDate = CDate(txtDate.Text)
Else                                  Catch
    MessageBox.Show("Invalid date")       MessageBox.Show("Invalid date")
End If                                End Try
```

Financial Functions

Visual Basic provides functions for many types of financial and accounting calculations, such as payment amount, depreciation, future value, and present value. When you use these functions, you eliminate the need to know and code the actual formulas yourself. Each financial function returns a value that you can assign to a variable, or to a property of a control.

Category	Purpose	Function
Depreciation	Double-declining balance	DDB
	Straight line	SLN
	Sum-of-the-years digits	SYD
Payments	Payment	Pmt
	Interest payment	IPmt
	Principal payment	PPmt
Return	Internal rate of return	IRR
	Rate of return when payments and receipts are at different rates	MIRR
Rate	Interest rate	Rate
Future value	Future value of an annuity	FV
Present value	Present value	PV
	Present value when values are not constant	NPV
Number of periods	Number of periods for an annuity (Number of payments)	NPer

You must supply each function with the necessary arguments in the correct sequence and data type. For example, the following `Pmt` function has three arguments: the interest rate, number of periods, and amount of loan. If you supply the values in a different order, the `Pmt` function will calculate incorrectly.

The PMT Function

You can use the `Pmt` function to find the amount of each payment on a loan if the interest rate, the number of periods, and the amount borrowed are known.

```
Pmt(dblInterestRatePerPeriod, dblNumberOfPeriods, dblAmountOfLoan)
```

The interest rate must be specified as Double and adjusted to the interest rate per period. For example, if the loan is made with an annual rate of 12 percent and monthly payments, the interest rate must be converted to the monthly rate of 1 percent. Convert the annual rate to the monthly rate by dividing by the number of months in a year (`AnnualPercentageRate / 12`).

The number of periods for the loan is the total number of payments. If you want to know the monthly payment for a five-year loan, you must convert the number of years to the number of months. Multiply the number of years by 12 months per year (`NumberOfYears * 12`).

The `Pmt` function requires Double arguments and returns a Double value.

```
Try
    dblMonthlyRate = CDbl(txtRate.Text) / 12
    dblMonths = CDbl(txtYears.Text) * 12
    dblAmount = CDbl(txtAmount.Text)
    dblMonthlyPayment = -Pmt(dblMonthlyRate, dblMonths, dblAmount)
    lblMonthlyPayment.Text = FormatCurrency(dblMonthlyPayment)
Catch
    MessageBox.Show("Invalid data")
End Try
```

Notice the minus sign when using the `Pmt` function. When an amount is borrowed or payments made, that is considered a negative amount. You need the minus sign to reverse the sign and make a positive answer.

The Rate Function

You can use the `Rate` function to determine the interest rate per period when the number of periods, the payment per period, and the original amount of the loan are known.

```
Rate(dblNumberOfPeriods, dblPaymentPerPeriod, dblLoanAmount)
```

The `Rate` function requires Double arguments and returns a Double value.

```
Try
    dblMonths = CDbl(txtYears.Text) * 12
    dblPayment = CDbl(txtPayment.Text)
    dblAmount = CDbl(txtLoanAmt.Text)
    dblPeriodicRate = Rate(dblMonths, -dblPayment, dblAmount)
    dblAnnualRate = dblPeriodicRate * 12
    lblYearlyRate.Text = FormatPercent(dblAnnualRate)
```

```
Catch
    MessageBox.Show("Invalid data")
End Try
```

Notice that the `Rate` function, like the `Pmt` function, needs a minus sign to produce a positive result.

Functions to Calculate Depreciation

If you need to calculate the depreciation of an asset in a business, Visual Basic provides three functions: the double-declining-balance method, the straight-line method, and the sum-of-the-years'-digits method.

The `DDB` function calculates the depreciation for a specific period within the life of the asset, using the double-declining-balance method formula. Once again, you do not need to know the formula but only the order in which to enter the arguments.

```
DDB(dblOriginalCost, dblSalvageValue, dblLifeOfTheAsset, dblPeriod)
```

The `DDB` function returns a Double value and requires Double arguments.

```
dblCost = CDbl(txtCost.Text)
dblSalvage = CDbl(txtSalvage.Text)
dblYears = CDbl(txtYears.Text)
dblPeriod = CDbl(txtPeriod.Text)
lblDepreciation.Text = FormatCurrency(DDB(dblCost, dblSalvage, dblYears, dblPeriod))
```

The other financial functions work in a similar manner. You can use Help to find the argument list, an explanation, and an example.

Mathematical Functions

In Visual Basic .NET, the mathematical functions are included as methods in the System.Math class. To use the methods, you must either import System.Math or refer to each method with the Math namespace. For example, to use the `Abs` (absolute value) method, you can use either of these techniques:

```
dblAnswer = Math.Abs(dblArgument)
```

or

```
Imports System.Math        'At the top of the file
dblAnswer = Abs(dblArgument)    'Inside a procedure
```

A few functions are not methods of the Math class but are Visual Basic functions. These functions, such as `Fix`, `Int`, and `Rnd`, cannot specify the Math namespace.

A good way to see the list of math functions is to type "Math." in the Editor; IntelliSense will pop up with the complete list. The following is a partial list of the Math methods:

Method	Returns	Argument data type	Return data type
Abs(x)	The absolute value of x $\lvert x \rvert = x$ if $x \geq 0$ $\lvert x \rvert = -x$ if $x \leq 0$	Overloaded: All types allowed	Return matches argument type
Atan(x)	The angle in radians whose tangent is x	Double	Double
Cos(x)	The cosine of x where x is in radians	Double	Double
Exp(x)	The value of e raised to the power of x	Double	Double
Log(x)	The natural logarithm of x, where $x \geq 0$	Double	Double
Max(x1, x2)	The larger of the two arguments	Overloaded: All types allowed; both arguments must be the same type	Return matches argument type
Min(x1, x2)	The smaller of the two arguments	Overloaded: All types allowed; both arguments must be the same type	Return matches argument type
Round(x) Round(x, DecimalPlaces)	The rounded value of x, rounded to the specified number of decimal positions. Note: .5 rounds to the nearest even number.	Overloaded: Double or Decimal; Integer DecimalPlaces	Return matches argument type
Sign(x)	The sign of x -1 if $x < 0$ 0 if $x = 0$ 1 if $x > 0$	Overloaded: All types allowed	Return matches argument type
Sin(x)	The sine of x where x is in radians	Double	Double
Sqrt(x)	The square root of x where x must be ≥ 0	Double	Double
Tan(x)	The tangent of x where x is in radians	Double	Double

Here are some useful VB functions:

Function	Returns	Argument data type	Return data type
Fix(x)	The integer portion of x (truncated)	Any numeric expression	Integer
Int(x)	The largest integer $\leq x$	Any numeric expression	Integer
Rnd( )	A random number in the range 0–1 (exclusive)		Single

Working with Strings

Visual Basic provides many methods for working with text strings. Strings in Visual Studio are immutable, which means that once a string is created, it cannot be changed. Although many programs in this text seem to modify a string, actually a new string is created and the old string is discarded.

For string handling, you can use any of the many methods of the String class. You also can use the StringBuilder class, which is more efficient if you are building or modifying strings, since the string can be changed in memory. In other words, a StringBuilder is *mutable* (changeable) and a String is *immutable*.

Here is a partial list of the methods in the String class. For shared methods, you don't need to specify a String instance; for nonshared methods, you must attach the method to the String instance. For example:

Shared method

```
If Compare(strA, strB) > 0 Then
    '…
```

Nonshared method

```
If strMyString.EndsWith("ed") Then
    '…
```

Method	Returns

Compare(*strA, strB*)
(Shared)
	Integer:
	    Negative if *strA* < *strB*
	    Zero if *strA* = *strB*
	    Positive if *strA* > *strB*

Compare(*strA, strB,*
blnIgnoreCase)
(Shared)
	Case insensitive if blnIgnoreCase is True.
	Integer:
	    Negative if *strA* < *strB*
	    Zero if *strA* = *strB*
	    Positive if *strA* > *strB*

Compare(*strA, intStartA, strB,*
intStartB, intLength)
(Shared)
	Compare substrings, start position indicates beginning character to compare for a length of intLength.
	Integer:
	    Negative if *strA* < *strB*
	    Zero if *strA* = *strB*
	    Positive if *strA* > *strB*

continued

Method	Returns

Compare(*strA, intStartA, strB, intStartB, intLength, blnIgnoreCase*)
(Shared)
	Case insensitive if blnIgnoreCase is True.
	Compare substrings, start position indicates beginning character to compare for a length of intLength.
	Integer:
	    Negative if $strA < strB$
	    Zero if $strA = strB$
	    Positive if $strA > strB$

EndsWith(*strA*)	Boolean. True if the String instance ends with strA. Case sensitive.
Equals(*strA*)	Boolean. True if the String instance has the same value as strA. Case sensitive.

IndexOf(*strA*)	Integer. Index position in String instance that strA is found.
	    Positive: String found at this position.
	    Negative: String not found.

IndexOf(*strA, intStartPosition*)	Integer. Index position in String instance that strA is found, starting at intStartPosition.
	    Positive: String found at this position.
	    Negative: String not found.

IndexOf(*strA, intStartPosition, intNumberCharacters*)	Integer. Index position in String instance that strA is found, starting at intStartPosition, for a length of intNumberCharacters.
	    Positive: String found at this position.
	    Negative: String not found.

Insert(*intStartIndex, strA*)	New string with strA inserted in the String instance, beginning at intStartIndex.
LastIndexOf(*strA*)	Integer: Index position of strA within String instance, searching from the right end.
LastIndexOf(*strA, intStartPosition*)	Integer: Index position of strA within String instance, searching leftward, beginning at intStartPosition.
LastIndexOf(*strA, intStartPosition, intNumberCharacters*)	Integer: Index position of strA within String instance, searching leftward, beginning at intStartPosition, for a length of intNumberCharacters.
PadLeft(*intTotalLength*)	New String with String instance right justified; padded on left with spaces for a total length of intTotalLength.
PadLeft(*intTotalLength, chrPad*)	New String with String instance right justified; padded on left with the specified character for a total length of intTotalLength.
PadRight(*intTotalLength*)	New String with String instance left justified; padded on right with spaces for a total length of intTotalLength.
PadRight(*intTotalLength, chrPad*)	New String with String instance left justified; padded on right with the specified character for a total length of intTotalLength.

continued

Method	Returns
Remove(*intStartPosition, intNumberCharacters*)	New String with characters removed from String instance, beginning with intStartPosition for a length of intNumberCharacters.
Replace(*strOldValue, strNewValue*)	New String with all occurrences of the old value replaced by the new value.
StartsWith(*strA*)	Boolean. True if the String instance starts with strA. Case sensitive.
Substring(*intStartPosition*)	New String that is a substring of String instance; beginning at intStartPosition, including all characters to the right.
Substring(*intStartPosition, intNumberCharacters*)	New String; a substring of String instance, beginning at intStartPosition for a length of intNumber characters.
ToLower()	New String; the String instance converted to lowercase.
ToUpper()	New String; the String instance converted to uppercase.
Trim()	New String; the String instance with all white-space characters removed from the left and right ends.
TrimEnd()	New String; the String instance with all white-space characters removed from the right end.
TrimStart()	New String; the String instance with all white-space characters removed from the left end.

Functions for Determining the Data Type

At times you may need to determine the data type of a value, as in the earlier example for checking a date.

Function	Return / purpose
IsArray(*VariableName*)	True or False, depending on whether the variable is an array.
IsDate(*Expression*)	True or False, depending on whether the expression is a valid date or time value.
IsNumeric(*Expression*)	True or False, depending on whether the expression evaluates to a numeric value.
IsObject(*VariableName*)	True or False, depending on whether the variable represents an object.
Is Nothing	True or False, depending on whether an object variable is set to Nothing. Example: `If objMyObject Is Nothing Then`
TypeOf	Checks the type of an object variable. This special syntax can only be used in a logical expression: `If TypeOf `*ObjectVariable*` Is `*ObjectType*` Then` Example: `If TypeOf MyControl Is TextBox Then`
TypeName(*VariableName*)	Returns the data type of a nonobject variable. Example: `Debug.WriteLine(TypeName(varMyValue))`

Windows Forms

A Windows project can have one or more forms. Each form is a separate class that has a visible user interface plus code. Because a form is a class, you can add properties to the form by declaring a module-level variable and Property Get/Let procedures.

The Startup Object

When a project begins execution, the startup object is loaded into memory. The startup object can be a form or a Public procedure called `Sub Main`. Set the startup object in *Project / Properties*.

Declaring and Showing Forms

To show a form, you must instantiate an object of the form's class and show it.

```
Dim frmProgramSummary As New frmSummary
frmProgramSummary.Show()
```

or

```
frmProgramSummary.ShowDialog()
```

The `Show` method shows the form as a regular window, called a *modeless* window. The `ShowDialog` method displays the form as a modal window (dialog box), which means that the user must respond to the dialog box before switching to another window in the application.

Closing Forms

Use `Me.Close` to close the current form, or `frmName.Close` to close any other form. The keyword `Me` refers to the current class, and is assumed if omitted, so you can close the current form with just `Close`.

Form Properties

The two properties of a form that you always set are the Name and Text. You also can choose whether to display minimize and maximize buttons, a close button, and a control box (the system menu that pops up at the left end of the title bar). If you want to display a form with no title bar, you must set Control-Box to False and Text to an empty string.

Size and Location Properties

When a form is first displayed, it uses several properties to determine the location and size. Set the StartPosition to set its position on the screen. Window-State determines whether the form displays in the size you created it or maximized or minimized.

The Location property determines the form's placement in its container, and the Size property sets the size in pixels.

Set the IsMDIContainer property to True for a parent form that will hold child forms. To create a child form, you cannot set a property at design time; instead you must set the parent in code:

```
Dim frmChildOne As New frmChildOne()
frmChildOne.MdiParent = Me
frmChildOne.Show()
```

Accept and Cancel Buttons

One of the buttons on a form should be the *accept button* and one should be the *cancel button*. When a user types information on a form, generally he or she wants to press the Enter key when finished, rather than pick up the mouse and click a button. Set the form's AcceptButton to the button that should activate when the user presses Enter; set the CancelButton to the button to activate when the user presses the Escape key. Good programmers make sure to set an accept button on every form and a cancel button when appropriate.

Form Events

These events occur in this order when a form first loads into memory:

New	The constructor. Occurs once when the form is instantiated.
Load	Occurs once before the first time the form is displayed. The controls on a form are not available during the Load event; therefore, you cannot set the focus in this event procedure. This procedure is the location most programmers use for initialization tasks.
Activated	Occurs when a form becomes the active window. During a project with multiple forms, the Activate event occurs each time the user switches from one form to another. The Deactivate event occurs for the form losing active status.

These events occur as a form's life ends.

Deactivate	Occurs when the form loses focus to another form in the project. It does not occur if the user switches to another application, the application closes, or the form closes.
Closing	Occurs just before the Closed event. This gives the programmer a chance to cancel the Close process if necessary.
Closed	Occurs after the form is closed. Most programmers place cleanup code in this event procedure.

Using Multiple Forms

A project can show and hide multiple forms. Each form is a class and can have Public and Private members. You can access the Public members (variables and procedures) of one form from another. However, this is considered poor form as it violates rules of encapsulation.

You can share data between forms by setting properties of the form. If you need to pass data between forms, create a property of the form, write Property Get/Set procedures, and set the properties as needed.

Controls

The VB intrinsic (built-in) controls appear in the toolbox, and you can add more controls to the toolbox by right-clicking on the toolbox and selecting *Customize Toolbox.*

Create an instance of a control class on a form by clicking on the control's icon and drawing the control on the form or by double-clicking the control's icon, which creates a control of default size. You can create multiple controls of one class by Ctrl-clicking on the icon—the pointer remains a crossbar and you can create as many controls of that type as you wish. Press the Esc key or click on the toolbox Pointer when you are finished drawing that control type.

You can select multiple controls using Ctrl-click or Shift-click. The selected controls are treated as a group and you can move them, delete them, or change their properties.

Common VB Controls

The majority of VB programming is performed using just a few controls: Label, TextBox, CheckBox, RadioButton, ListBox, ComboBox, and Button.

The Label Control

Use a Label control for the words and instructions on the form as well as program output that you don't want the user to be able to modify. Set the Text property for the words that you want to appear. You also can set the font and size and change its style with the BorderStyle and BackColor properties. A Label cannot receive the focus.

The TextBox Control

Use a TextBox for user input. The Text property holds the contents of the TextBox. You can enable/disable a TextBox.

The CheckBox Control

Use a CheckBox for options the user can select or deselect. Each CheckBox operates independently, so any number of check boxes may be selected.

The Checked property of a CheckBox holds its current state, and may be True or False. You can test and set the Checked property in code.

```
If chkMyCheckOption.Checked Then
    'Take some action
    chkMyCheckOption.Checked = False
End If
```

The Radio Button Control

Radio buttons, formerly called *option buttons,* appear in groups. Only one radio button in a group can be selected at one time. A group is defined as all of the buttons that belong to one container. A container can be a form or a GroupBox.

The Checked property of a radio button holds its state and can be True or False. The Text property determines the words next to the button. You can test or change the Checked property in code.

```
If radMyRadioButton.Checked Then
    'Take action for the selected button
    radMyRadioButton.Checked = False
End If
```

List Boxes and Combo Boxes

ListBoxes and ComboBoxes are very similar. A ListBox appears on the form in the size that you create it; a ComboBox can be made to appear small and drop down when the user clicks on the down arrow. You can set the DropDownStyle property of a ComboBox control to Simple, Dropdown, or Dropdown List. A Simple and Dropdown both have a text box, which allows the user to make an entry as well as select from the list. A Dropdown List does not have a text box, so the user can make a selection from the list but cannot add any entries.

List controls have an Items property that holds the elements that appear in the list. You can set the Items property at design time or add elements at run time using the `Items.Add` method.

```
cboNames.Items.Add("John")
```

You can remove items from the list using the `Items.Remove` method to remove a particular value and `Items.RemoveAt` to remove an element by index. Clear the list using the `Items.Clear` method.

Each item in the list can be referenced by an index (zero-based). The SelectedIndex property holds the index of the currently selected list element and is −1 if nothing is selected. The Items.Count property holds a count of the number of elements in the list. Setting the list's Sorted property to True causes VB to keep the list sorted in alphabetic order.

The elements in the Items collection are actually objects that can have multiple properties. See "Using the Items Collection of a List Box" in Chapter 11 to store and use objects.

The Button Control

Buttons typically carry out the actions of a program. Set the button's Name property before writing any code for its Click event and set its Text property for the words that you want to appear on the button.

Buttons should be accessible from the keyboard, so set their Text properties with a keyboard access key. Place an ampersand in front of the letter that you want to be the access key. For example, set the Text to *&Print* in order to display *Print*. To actually display an ampersand, use two ampersands: *Name && Address* to display *Name & Address.*

Setting the Tab Order

When the user presses the Tab key, the focus should move from one control to the next, in sequence. Each of the controls on the form has a TabIndex property and most have a TabStop property. The TabIndexes determine the order that the focus moves using the Tab key.

Labels do not have a TabStop property, since they cannot receive the focus. But labels *do* have a TabIndex property. This allows you to use a label to set up keyboard access keys for the text boxes that accompany the labels. For example, set a label's Text to &Name and its TabIndex property to 1. Then set the corresponding text box's TabIndex to 2 (one higher than the TabIndex for its label). When the user enters the access key (Alt + N in this case), the focus attempts to go to the label and instead goes to the next higher TabIndex for a control that *can* receive the focus.

You can manually set the TabIndex property of each control or use the slick feature of VB .NET: With the form designer window active, select *View / Tab Order*. Click the crosshair mouse pointer on each control, in sequence, to set the tab order. Note that a TabIndex of zero means that the TabIndex is not set; use 1 for the first control in the tab sequence.

Using the Validating Event and CausesValidation Property

Use the Validating event and CausesValidation property for field-level validation on a form. You can check the validity of each field in its Validating event procedure.

Each control on the form has a CausesValidation property that is set to True by default. When the user finishes an entry and presses Tab or clicks on another control, the Validating event occurs for the control just left. That is, the event occurs if the CausesValidation property of the *new* control is set to True. You can leave the CausesValidation property of most controls set to True, so that validation occurs. Set CausesValidation to False on a control such as Cancel or Exit to give the user a way to bypass the validation if he doesn't want to complete the transaction.

The Timer Component

Programmers often use a Timer component to animate an image or keep the current time displayed on the screen. A Timer can fire events at a predetermined interval. Add a Timer component to a form, where it appears in the component tray. Set the Interval property to the length of time to wait before firing a Tick event. The interval is measured in milliseconds, so set it to 1000 for a 1-second delay. The Enabled property turns the Timer on or off; much like turning on or off an alarm clock. You can set the Enabled property at design time or run time.

Write code in the Timer's Click event procedure, such as moving an image or displaying the current time.

Menus

It's easy to create menus using the new VS menu editor. Add a MainMenu control from the toolbox, which appears in the component tray below the form. The words *Type Here* appear at the top of the form, so that you can enter the text for your first menu. After you type the text for the first menu name, the words *Type Here* appear both below the menu name and to the right of the menu name. You can choose to next enter menu items for the first menu, or type the words for the second menu. As you type the words for menu names and menu items, you are entering the Text property of individual controls. You can select each menu item and set its Name property in the Properties window, or right-click anywhere on the menu and select *Edit Names*. The control names will appear in the menu editor, where you can modify each one. To toggle off the names, select *Edit Names* a second time.

Recommended naming conventions:

Text	Name	Description
&File	mnuFile	File menu
&Print	mnuFilePrint	Print menu command
-		Separator bar
E&xit	mnuFileExit	Exit menu command
&Edit	mnuEdit	Edit menu
&Sort	mnuEditSort	Sort menu command
By &Name	mnuEditSortName	Pop-up submenu item below Sort
By &City	mnuEditSortCity	Pop-up submenu item below Sort
&Help	mnuHelp	Help menu
&About	mnuHelpAbout	About menu command

Notice the separator bar entry under the *File* menu. To create a separator, set the Text to a single hyphen.

Printing

VB is designed to create programs with a graphical user interface. It is not designed to create nicely formatted reports. Crystal Reports is a nice feature if you want to print a report from a database, but doesn't help much for program output. Many third-party vendors sell products that can create reports from a VB program.

That said, you *can* print from VB, but printing is not easy to format well. Use the new VB .NET PrintDocument and PrintPreviewDialog classes to produce output for the printer and also preview on the screen.

Note: You can see a complete print/print preview program in the ApxBPrinting folder in the InChapterPrograms folder on your CD.

The PrintDocument Control

You set up output for the printer using the methods and events of the new PrintDocument control. Add a PrintDocument control to a form; the control appears in the component tray.

To start printing output, you execute the `Print` method of the PrintDocument control. This code belongs in the Click event procedure for the Print button or menu item that the user selects to begin printing.

```
Private Sub btnPrint_Click(ByVal sender As System.Object, _
  ByVal e As System.EventArgs) Handles btnPrint.Click
    'Print output on the printer

    prtDocument.Print()           'Start the print process
End Sub
```

The logic for the actual printing belongs in the PrintDocument's PrintPage event procedure. The PrintPage event is fired once for each page to be printed. This technique is referred to as a *callback,* in which the object notifies the program that it needs to do something or that a situation exists that the program needs to handle. The object notifies the program of the situation by firing an event.

The PrintDocument object is activated when you issue its `Print` method. It then fires a PrintPage event for each page to print. It also fires events for BeginPrint and EndPrint, for which you can write code if you wish.

```
Private Sub prtDocument_PrintPage(ByVal sender As Object, _
  ByVal e As System.Drawing.Printing.PrintPageEventArgs) _
  Handles prtDocument.PrintPage
    'Set up actual output to print

End Sub
```

Notice the argument:
`e As System.Drawing.Printing.PrintPageEventArgs`.
You can use some of the properties and methods of the PrintPageEventArgs argument for such things as determining the page margins and sending a string of text to the page.

The Graphics Page

You set up a graphics page in memory and then the page is sent to the printer. The graphics page can contain strings of text as well as graphic elements.

You must specify the exact location on the graphics page for each element that you want to print. You can specify the upper-left corner of any element by giving its X and Y coordinates, or by using a Point structure or a Rectangle structure.

Using the DrawString Method

You use the `DrawString` method to send a line of text to the graphics page. The `DrawString` method belongs to the Graphics object of the Print-PageEventArgs argument (refer back to the procedure header for the PrintPage event).

The `DrawString` method is overloaded. The format presented here is the least complicated and requires that page coordinates be given in X and Y format.

```
DrawString(StringToPrint, Font, Brush, Xcoordinate, Ycoordinate)

e.Graphics.DrawString(strPrintLine, fntPrintFont, Brushes.Black, sngPrintX, sngPrintY)
e.Graphics.DrawString("My text string", fntMyFont, Brushes.Black, 100.0, 100.0)
e.Graphics.DrawString(txtName.Text, New Font("Arial", 10), Brushes.Red, sngLeftMargin, _
    sngCurrentLine)
```

Before you execute the `DrawString` method, you should set up the font that you want to use and the X and Y coordinates.

Setting the X and Y Coordinates

For each line that you want to print, you must specify the X and Y coordinates. It is helpful to set up some variables for setting these values, which should be declared as Single data type.

```
Dim sngPrintX As Single
Dim sngPrintY As Single
```

The PrintPageEventArgs argument has several useful properties, such as MarginBounds, PageBounds, and PageSettings. You can use these properties to determine present settings. For example, you may want to set the X coordinate to the current left margin and the Y coordinate to the top margin.

```
sngPrintX = e.MarginBounds.Left
sngPrintY = e.MarginBounds.Top
```

To send multiple lines to the print page, you must increment the Y coordinate. You can add the height of a line to the previous Y coordinate to calculate the next line's Y coordinate.

```
'Declarations at the top of the procedure
Dim fntPrintFont As New Font("Arial", 12)
'Make the line 2 pixels higher than the font
Dim sngLineHeight As Single = fntPrintFont.GetHeight + 2
' … more declarations here

'Print a line
e.Graphics.DrawString(strPrintLine, fntPrintFont, Brushes.Black, sngPrintX, sngPrintY)
'Increment the Y position for the next line
sngPrintY += sngLineHeight
```

Aligning Decimal Columns

Alignment of the decimal points in numeric output can be tricky with proportional fonts, where the width of each character varies. The best approach is to format each number as you want it to print and then measure the length of the formatted string. You need an object declared as a SizeF structure, which has a Width property, and you need to use the `MeasureString` method of the Graphics class. Both the SizeF structure and `MeasureString` method work with pixels, which is the same unit of measure used for the X and Y coordinates of the `DrawString` method.

The following example prints a left-aligned literal at position 200 on the line and right-aligns a formatted number at position 500. (Assume that all variables are properly declared.)

```
Dim stzStringSize As New SizeF()                'SizeF structure for font size info.

'Set X for left-aligned column
sngPrintX = 200
'Set ending position for right-aligned column
sngColumnEnd = 500

'Format the number
strFormattedOutput = FormatCurrency(decAmount)

'Calculate the X position of the amount
'Measure string in this font
stzStringSize = e.Graphics.MeasureString(strFormattedOutput, fntPrintFont)
'Subtract width of string from the column position
sngColumnX = sngColumnEnd - stzStringSize.Width

'Set up the line--each element separately
e.Graphics.DrawString("The Amount = ", fntPrintFont, Brushes.Black, sngPrintX, _
  sngPrintY)
e.Graphics.DrawString(strFormattedOutput, fntPrintFont, Brushes.Black, sngColumnX, _
  sngPrintY)
sngPrintY += sngLineHeight                'Increment line for next line
```

Note: To see a program that creates right-aligned output, see ApxB-SomePrintingExtras on your CD. The sample program also shows how to create multiple-page output.

Displaying a Print Preview

A really great feature of the new VB .NET printing model is *print preview.* You can view the printer's output on the screen and then choose to print or cancel, thus saving paper while testing your programs.

Add a PrintPreviewDialog control to your form's component tray and name it; then write two lines of code in the event procedure for the button or menu item where the user selects the print preview option. The PrintPreviewDialog class uses the same PrintDocument control that you declared for printer output. You assign the PrintDocument to the Document property of the PrintPreviewDialog and execute the `ShowDialog` method. The same PrintPage event procedure executes as for the PrintDocument. The example program on your CD, ApxBPrinting, demonstrates using a PrintPreviewDialog.

Web Applications

Chapter 6 of this text reviews all of the elementary topics for creating Web applications.

Data Files

Visual Studio handles data files using streams, which are objects designed to transfer a series of bytes from one location to another. The various stream objects are found in the System.IO namespace, which you should import at the top of the file.

The simplest way to read and write small amounts of data is to use the StreamReader and StreamWriter objects. Generally, you write the StreamWriter code first, to create the data file. Then you can write the StreamReader code to read the file that you just created.

Writing Data

To write data to a file, you first have the user input the data into text boxes and then write the data to the disk. The steps for writing data are

- **Declare a new StreamWriter object**, which also declares the name of the data file. Instantiating a new StreamWriter object opens the file. The file must be open before you can write in the file. If the file does not already exist, a new one is created. The default location for the file is the bin folder beneath the folder for the current project. You also can specify the complete path of the file. Set the BooleanAppend argument to True to specify that you want to append data at the end of an existing file.

- **Use the StreamWriter's WriteLine method** to copy the data to a buffer in memory. (A buffer is just a temporary storage location.)

- **Call the StreamWriter's Close method**, which transfers the data from the buffer to the file and releases the system resources used by the stream. After you write a file, you can view it using a text editor or the VS IDE.

Instantiating a StreamWriter Object

```
Dim ObjectName As New StreamWriter("FileName")
Dim ObjectName As New StreamWriter("FileName", BooleanAppend)

Dim dtaPhone As New StreamWriter("Phone.txt")
Dim dtaNames As New StreamWriter("C:\MyFiles\Names.txt")
Dim dtaLogFile As New StreamWriter("C:\MyFiles\LogFile.txt", True)
```

The StreamWriter object has both a `Write` and a `WriteLine` method. The difference between the two is that the `WriteLine` method places a carriage-return character between the elements.

The WriteLine Method

```
ObjectName.WriteLine(DataToWrite)
```

The DataToWrite argument may be string or numeric. The WriteLine method converts any numeric data to string and actually writes string data in the file.

```
dtaPhone.WriteLine(txtName.Text)
dtaPhone.WriteLine(txtPhone.Text)

dtaNames.WriteLine("Sammy")

dtaBankBalance.WriteLine(decBalance.ToString())
```

Closing a File

Use the StreamWriter's Close method when finished writing the data.

Reading Files

Use the StreamReader class to read the data from a file that you created with a StreamWriter.

The steps for reading the data from a file are

- **Declare an object of the StreamReader class**. The constructor declares the filename and optional path. Instantiating the object opens the file so that you can read from it. However, if no such file exists, an exception occurs. For this reason, you must declare the StreamReader object in a procedure, so that you can enclose it in a Try/Catch block.

- **Use the ReadLine method to read the data**. You may need to use a loop to retrieve multiple records.

- When finished, **close the stream using the StreamReader's Close method**.

Instantiating a StreamReader Object

```
Dim ObjectName As New StreamReader("FileName")

Try
    Dim datNames As New StreamReader("C:\MyFiles\Names.txt")
Catch
    MessageBox.Show("File does not exist")
End Try

'In declarations section, to create a module-level variable name
Dim dtaPhone As StreamReader
…
'In a procedure, to catch an exception for a missing file
Try
    dtaPhone = New StreamReader("Phone.txt")
Catch
    MessageBox.Show("File does not exist")
End Try
```

The ReadLine Method

The StreamReader's ReadLine method, which has no arguments, reads the next line from the file. Assign the data read to the desired location, such as a label, a text box, or a string variable.

```
lblName.Text = dtaPhone.ReadLine()
```

Checking for the End of the File

The StreamReader's Peek method looks at the next element without really reading it. The value returned when you peek beyond the last element is negative 1 (−1).

```
If datPhone.Peek <> -1 Then
    lblName.Text = dtaPhone.ReadLine()
    lblPhone.Text = dtaPhone.ReadLine()
End If
```

The ReadLine method does not throw an exception when you attempt to read past the end of the file.

C

MSDE: SQL Server Desktop Version

Microsoft Data Engine (MSDE) is the desktop or personal version of SQL Server, which is included with the .NET Framework. You can consider MSDE a "stripped-down" version of SQL Server. It provides access to SQL Server database files and uses the same version of SQL as SQL Server. What MSDE is missing is the management and design tools of SQL Server.

You can install MSDE and the sample databases, so that your machine runs the MSDE server. After installation, the SQL Server Service Manager can run automatically when you start the computer.

Installing MSDE

STEP 1: Use Windows Explorer or My Computer to open the `C:\Program Files\Microsoft Visual Studio .NET\FrameworkSDK\Samples \Setup\msde` folder.

STEP 2: Double-click on the instmsde.exe application to install MSDE.

Load the Sample Databases

STEP 1: Navigate up one folder level to the `C:\Program Files\Microsoft Visual Studio .NET\FrameworkSDK\Samples\Setup` folder.

STEP 2: Double-click on ConfigSamples.exe file to install the sample databases.

STEP 3: Reboot your system.

Start or Stop the SQL Server Service Manager

STEP 1: Double-click on the MSSQL Server icon in the tray on the task bar.

STEP 2: Click on the *Stop* button to stop the server.

STEP 3: Examine the icon.

STEP 4: Restart the server.

STEP 5: Check out the icon when the server is running.

STEP 6: Also look at the name assigned to the Server. After installing, the default name assigned is your system name plus NetSDK.

Deleting the Sample Files

If you find that you want to replace the sample databases, you cannot simply run the ConfigSamples application a second time. You must first remove the old files. Delete both the .mdf and the .ldf files from `C:\Program Files\ Microsoft SQL Server\MSSQL$NetSDK\Data` directory. You can then rerun the samples configuration utility.

Security

If your machine is running Internet Information Services (IIS) 6.0, you may get a "Login failed for user nnnnn\NetSDK". The default account for IIS does not have access to SQL Server. You can correct this by turning on impersonation. This requires an identity tag in the authorization section of the web.config file.

```
<identity impersonate = "true"/>
```

In addition, anonymous access must be turned off for the virtual directory. For more information, see "Database Security for Web Applications" in Chapter 8, page 294, and http://localhost/iishelp.

Upsizing Access Database Files

You can convert your Access .mdb files to SQL Server databases. From within Access, use the Upsizing Wizard from the *Tools / Database Utilities* menu. Select the option for creating a new database file.

D

SQL Primer

Using .NET you can write your own SQL statements and execute them in a variety of ways. SQL SELECT statements select data from a database and return the results to the program. You can specify which fields from which table or tables, and select only certain records based on criteria.

You also can write SQL statements that perform actions on the database rather than just select data. The actions that you can perform include inserting records, deleting and updating records, as well as modifying the structure of a database, such as adding tables and fields.

In SQL statements, you write key words, table names, field names, and values.

- Key words appear in uppercase by convention.

  Examples: SELECT, WHERE, JOIN, UPDATE, DELETE FROM, INSERT INTO.

- Table names and field names don't need quotes or brackets, unless the names contain spaces. To specify a two-word field name for Access databases, enclose the name in square brackets.

  Examples: [First Name], [Last Name]

  For SQL Server files, enclose two-word names with single quotes.

  Examples: 'First Name', 'Last Name'

- Field values: String values must be enclosed in single quotes. Numeric values and boolean values are not enclosed; date values must be enclosed with number signs (#) for Access databases and single quotes for SQL Server databases.

  Examples: 'John', 100, #10/21/60#

  "'" & txtName.Text & "'" (This string inserts the contents of txtName into a quoted string.)

  Warning: Do not include extra spaces in the SQL string. Extra spaces in the wrong spot will cause the statement to fail.

  This next section provides a brief tutorial on writing SELECT statements. Later in the appendix you will learn to write SQL statements that perform an action.

Writing SQL SELECT Statements

This section shows the syntax that you need to write your own SQL SELECT statements. But remember, you can always use the Query Builder. When the Query Builder is open, you can write and test your own queries.

The SQL Select Statement—General Form

```
SELECT [DISTINCT] Field(s) FROM Table(s) [IN Database]
   [WHERE Criteria]
   [GROUP BY Field(s)]
   [HAVING GroupCriteria]
   [ORDER BY Field(s)]
```

For the field(s), you can list the field names or use an asterisk to indicate all fields from the named table(s). Multiple-word field names must be enclosed in square brackets or accent grave marks. The optional DISTINCT drops out duplicates so that no two records are alike.

The SQL SELECT Statement—Examples

```
SELECT [Last Name], [First Name], Phone FROM Customer
    ORDER BY [Last Name], [First Name]
SELECT DISTINCT 'Last Name' FROM Customer
    ORDER BY 'Last Name'
SELECT * FROM Patient
    WHERE [Last Name] = "'" & txtSearch.Text & "'"
SELECT * FROM Patient, InsuranceCompany
    WHERE Patient.[Insurance Company Code] = InsuranceCompany.Code
```

Note that the last example retrieves data from the Patient and InsuranceCompany tables so that the actual name of the company, not just the Insurance Company Code, is included in the results. The preferable approach for combining data from two tables is to use the JOIN clause of the SQL SELECT statement. See "Joins" later in this appendix.

The WHERE Clause

The syntax of a WHERE clause is the same as the syntax for a Filter method. You can use a WHERE clause to specify the criteria for selecting records and retrieve data from more than one table:

```
"WHERE Patient.[Insurance Company Code] = InsuranceCompany.Code"
"WHERE Patient.[Insurance Company Code] = 'ABC'"
"WHERE Patient.[Insurance Company Code] = '" & strSelectedCompany & "'"
```

You can include multiple conditions in a WHERE clause:

```
"WHERE Patient.[Insurance Company Code] = InsuranceCompany.Code " & _
 "AND Patient.[Insurance Company Code] = '" & strSelectedCompany & "'"
```

Comparing Database Fields to Visual Basic Fields

String fields must be compared only to string data; numeric fields must be compared only to numeric data.

```
'Compare a string field to a string variable
"WHERE [Last Name] = '" & strName & "'"

'Compare a string field to a string property
"WHERE [Last Name] LIKE '" & txtSearchName.Text & "*'"

'Compare a string field to a string constant
"WHERE [Last Name] = 'Jones'"

'Compare a numeric field to a numeric variable
"WHERE [Duration] = " & intSearchMinutes.ToString()
```

```
'Compare an Integer numeric field to a property
"WHERE [Duration] = " & txtSearchString.Text

'Compare a numeric field to a numeric constant
"WHERE [Duration] = 15"
```

The ORDER BY Clause

It is incredibly easy to sort your data in SQL—just use the ORDER BY clause. You can order by one or more fields, in ascending or descending sequence. If you don't specify the direction, ascending is assumed.

```
"ORDER BY [Last Name], [First Name]"
"ORDER BY InsuranceCompany.Name ASC"
"ORDER BY DateDue DESC"
```

Joins

One of the primary characteristics of relational databases is that data are stored in multiple tables that are related to each other by common fields. Data can be stored once and used in many places by using the relationships between tables. You often will want to select some fields from one table and other fields from another related table, maybe even fields from several related tables. You have already seen examples of this relationship using a WHERE clause to join the Patient and InsuranceCompany tables. Joining the tables allows you to display the name of the company from the InsuranceCompany table rather than just the code stored in the Patient table.

Joins are of three types: **inner join**, **left join**, and **right join**. The table below shows the three types of joins. *Note:* The left join and right join are often called *left outer join* and *right outer join*.

Join type	Selects
INNER JOIN	Only records that have matching records in both tables.
LEFT JOIN	All records from the first table and only the matching records from the second table.
RIGHT JOIN	All records from the second table and only the matching records from the first table.

The examples are based on the following related tables.

Patient Table

Patient Number	Last Name	First Name	Insurance Company Code	Policy #
150	Raster	Ken	ABC	234567
151	Raster	Viola	ABC	234567
160	Mills	Tricia		
162	Mills	Eric	VS	10034-0
163	Mills	Kenna	VS	10034-0
170	Westley	Henry	Medicaid	
171	Westley	Irene		
175	Crow	Paul	ABC	456789
176	Crow	Margaret	ABC	456789

InsuranceCompany Table

Code	Name
ABC	ABC Inc.
DIA	Diamond, Inc.
INT	International
OCS	Optical C
VS	Vision Services

The tables show data in the Patient table and the InsuranceCompany table. Notice that two patients have no entry for Insurance Company Code and one has "Medicaid," which doesn't match any entry in the InsuranceCompany table.

Inner Join

For an inner join, those three unmatched patients do not appear in the dataset.

Last Name	First Name	Insurance Company Code	Name
Raster	Ken	ABC	ABC Inc.
Raster	Viola	ABC	ABC Inc.
Mills	Eric	VS	Vision Services
Mills	Kenna	VS	Vision Services
Crow	Paul	ABC	ABC Inc.
Crow	Margaret	ABC	ABC Inc.

The SQL statement that created the table is

```
SELECT Patient.[Last Name], Patient.[First Name], Patient.[Insurance Company Code],
   InsuranceCompany.Name
      FROM InsuranceCompany
      INNER JOIN Patient ON InsuranceCompany.Code = Patient.[Insurance Company Code];
```

Note: Using a `WHERE` clause to join the tables produces this same result.

Left Join

To code a `LEFT JOIN` clause, name only the first table in the `FROM` clause (this becomes the left table). Then specify the join type and the second table name; then write the relationship for the join using the `ON`. With a left join, all records appear and if the record has an entry in the second table that matches an entry in the left table, those data display.

```
SELECT [Last Name], [First Name], [Insurance Company Code], Name
      FROM Patient
      LEFT JOIN InsuranceCompany
         ON Patient.[Insurance Company Code] = InsuranceCompany.Code
```

Result of Left Join

Last Name	First Name	Insurance Company Code	Name
Raster	Ken	ABC	ABC Inc.
Raster	Viola	ABC	ABC Inc.
Mills	Tricia		
Mills	Eric	VS	Vision
Mills	Kenna	VS	Vision
Westley	Henry	Medicaid	
Westley	Irene		
Crow	Paul	ABC	ABC Inc.
Crow	Margaret	ABC	ABC Inc.

Right Join

If you use the same SQL statement but change the join to a right join, you will get all records from the InsuranceCompany table and only those patients that have matching records.

```
SELECT Patient.[Last Name], Patient.[First Name], Patient.[Insurance Company Code],
   InsuranceCompany.Name
FROM InsuranceCompany
   RIGHT JOIN Patient ON InsuranceCompany.Code = Patient.[Insurance Company Code];
```

Result of Right Join

Last Name	First Name	Insurance Company Code	Name
Crow	Margaret	ABC	ABC Inc.
Crow	Paul	ABC	ABC Inc.
Raster	Viola	ABC	ABC Inc.
Raster	Ken	ABC	ABC Inc.
Mills	Kenna	VS	Vision Services
Mills	Eric	VS	Vision Services
			Optical C
			Diamond, Inc.
			International

Joining Multiple Tables

To join multiple tables, the joins must be nested using parentheses. The join inside the parentheses is performed first. The following SELECT statement selects all records from the Prescription table, only matching records from the FrameStyle table, and only matching records from the Patient table. For good measure, we included WHERE and ORDER BY clauses.

Big hint: Create complicated queries in the Query Builder, then copy and paste the query into your VB code.

```
SELECT Patient.[Last Name], Patient.[First Name],
  Prescription.[Frame Size], FrameStyle.[Frame Style] FROM Patient
  RIGHT JOIN (FrameStyle RIGHT JOIN Prescription
  ON FrameStyle.ID = Prescription.[Frame Style])
  ON Patient.[Patient Number] = Prescription.[Patient Number]
  WHERE (Prescription.Date>#1/1/99#)
  ORDER BY Prescription.Date
```

SQL Action Queries

The SQL SELECT statements in the preceding section retrieve data from a database. The statements in this section are called *action queries*; they perform some action on the data in the database.

The SQL INSERT Statement—General Form

```
INSERT INTO TableName (Fieldlist) VALUES (ListOfValues)
```

The SQL INSERT Statement—Examples

```
INSERT INTO Subjects(Subject, SubjectCode) VALUES ('Business', 'BSN')

INSERT INTO Subjects(Subject, SubjectCode) VALUES("'" & txtSubject.Text & "'" , "'"
    & txtCode.Text & "'")

strSQL = "INSERT INTO Subjects(Subject, SubjectCode) " & _
    "VALUES('" & txtSubject.Text & "', '" & txtCode.Text & "')"

INSERT INTO Patient ([Patient Number], [Last Name], [First Name])
    Values (500, 'Berry', 'Terry')

strSQL = "INSERT INTO Patient " _
        & "([Patient Number], [Last Name], [First Name]) " _
        & "VALUES (" & txtPatientNumber.Text & ", '" & txtLastName.Text _
        & "', '" & txtFirstName.Text & "')"
```

In the `INSERT INTO` statement, name all of the fields, then all of the values, which must match in number, type, and sequence. All string values must be enclosed in single quotes.

The SQL UPDATE Statement—General Form

```
UPDATE TableName
  SET FieldName = FieldValue, FieldName = FieldValue, ...
  WHERE Criteria
```

The SQL UPDATE Statement—Examples

```
UPDATE Subjects SET Subject = 'Management' WHERE SubjectCode = 'MGM'

strSQL = "UPDATE Subjects SET Subject = '" & txtSubject.Text & _
         "' WHERE SubjectCode = '" & txtCode.Text & "'"

UPDATE Patient
  SET [Last Name] = 'Bowser'
  WHERE [Patient Number] = 500

UPDATE Visit
  SET Date = #1/1/2000#
  WHERE Date = #1/1/1900#

strSQL = "UPDATE Patient " & _
         "SET [Last Name] = '" & txtLastName.Text & "', " & _
         "[First Name] = '" & txtFirstName.Text & "', " & _
         "[Policy #] = '" & txtPolicyNumber.Text & "' " & _
         "WHERE [Patient Number] = " & txtPatientNumber.Text
```

If you omit the `WHERE` clause, ADO.NET attempts to make the change to every record in the table.

The SQL Delete Statement—General Form

```
DELETE FROM TableName
   WHERE Criteria
```

The SQL Delete Statement—Examples

```
DELETE FROM Subjects WHERE SubjectCode = 'BSN'

strSQL = "DELETE FROM Subjects WHERE SubjectCode = '" & txtSubjectCode.Text & "'"

DELETE FROM Patient
   WHERE [Patient Number] = 500

DELETE FROM Patient
   WHERE [Last Name] = 'Berry'

strSQL = "DELETE FROM Patient " _
         & "WHERE [Patient Number] = " & txtPatientNumber.Text
```

Writing Criteria

The criteria specify which record(s) to modify or delete. Although most often the criteria for SQL statements use an equal sign, you also can write criteria to select multiple records. Note that the RowFilter property of data views uses these same symbols. In SQL statements, the criteria follow the WHERE clause; for the RowFilter property, you omit the WHERE keyword. You can find a complete listing of operators on the "Comparison Operators" page in MSDN.

Operator	Meaning	Examples
=	equal to	"Subject = 'Business' " "Subject = '" & txtSubject.Text & "'"
>	greater than	"Sales > 1000" "Sales > " & txtSales.Text
<	less than	"Sales < 1000" "Sales < " & txtSales.Text
Like	pattern match	"Subject Like ('B%')" (For SQL Server databases) "Subject Like 'B*' " (For Access databases)

Tips and Shortcuts for Mastering the Environment

Set Up the Screen for Your Convenience

As you work in the Visual Studio integrated development environment (IDE), you will find many ways to save time. Here are some tips and shortcuts that you can use to become more proficient in using the IDE to design, code, and run your projects.

Close or Hide Extra Windows

Arrange your screen for best advantage. While you are entering and editing code in the Editor window, you don't need the toolbox, the Solution Explorer window, the Properties window, or any other extra windows. You can hide or close the extra windows and quickly and easily redisplay each window when you need it.

Hiding and Displaying Windows

You can use AutoHide on each of the windows in the IDE. Each window except the Document window in the center of the screen has a push-pin icon that you can use to AutoHide the window or "tack" it into place.

You can AutoHide each window separately, or select *Window / Auto Hide All*. In this screen, all extra windows are hidden.

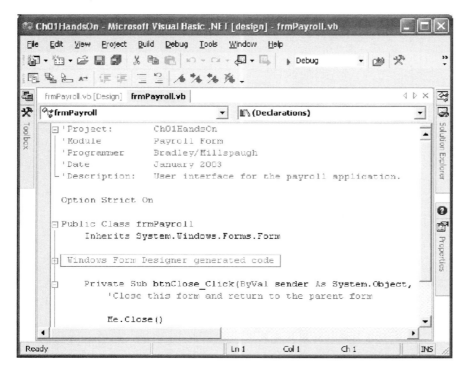

Point to the icon for one of the hidden windows to display it. Notice the mouse pointer on the Solution Explorer icon, which opens the Solution

Explorer window temporarily. When you move the mouse pointer out of the window, it hides again.

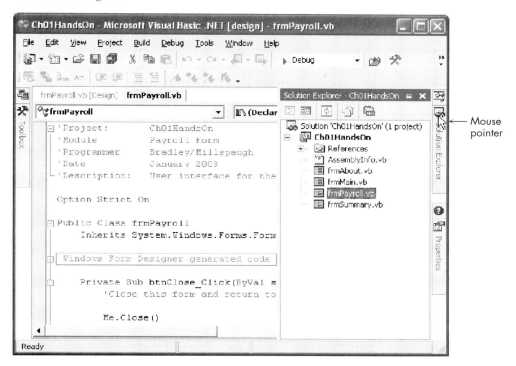

To undo the AutoHide feature, display a window and click its push-pin icon.

Closing Windows

You can close any window by clicking its Close button. You also can close any extra tabs in the Document window; each document has its own close button.

Displaying Windows

You can quickly and easily open each window when you need it. Each window is listed on the *View* menu, or use the buttons on the standard toolbar.

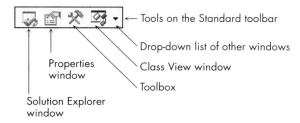

Display Windows Using Keyboard Shortcuts

Solution Explorer window	Ctrl + Alt + L
Properties window	F4
Toolbox	Ctrl + Alt + X

Switch between Documents

When you have several tabs open in the Document window, you can switch by clicking on their tabs or use keyboard shortcuts.

Editor window for form's code	F7
Form Designer	Shift + F7
Cycle through open document tabs	Ctrl + Tab *or* Ctrl + F6
Navigate backward (to previous Help page)	Backspace key or Ctrl + − (minus sign)
Navigate forward (after navigating backward)	Ctrl + Shift + − (minus sign)

Use the Full Screen

When you are designing a form or editing code, you can work in full-screen mode. This gives you maximum screen space by getting rid of all extra windows. Unfortunately, it also hides all toolbars (the Edit toolbar can be a great timesaver while editing code). Select *View / Full Screen* to display in full-screen mode. A small *Full Screen* button appears, which you can use to switch back to regular display. You also can press Shift + Alt + Enter or select *View / Full Screen* a second time to toggle back.

Modify the Screen Layout

For most operations, the new Visual Studio tabbed Document window layout is an improvement over the VB 6 environment. However, if you prefer, you can switch to MDI (multiple document interface), which is similar to the style used in VB 6. Set this option in the *Tools / Options / Environment / General* settings.

Each of the windows in the IDE is considered either a Tool window or a Document window. The Document windows generally display in the center of the screen with tabs. The rest of the windows—Solution Explorer, Properties window, Task List, Output, Server Explorer, and others—are Tool windows and share many characteristics. You can float each of the windows, tab-dock them in groups, and move and resize individual windows or groups of windows. For example, you can point to a window's title bar and drag it on top of another window to tab-dock them together. Drag on a tab to separate a window from its tabbed group. The following floating window has the Properties window, Toolbox, Solution Explorer, Server Explorer, Class View, Help Contents, and Help Index all docked together. The window was also resized to make the tabs more readable.

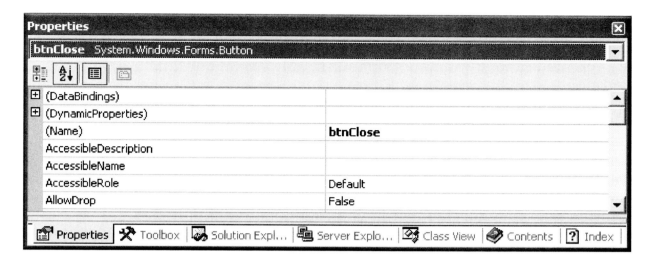

    This combined window is *not* a recommended layout. It is intended only to show the possibilities. You may want to experiment with moving and resizing windows for your own convenience. You also can float a window, which makes it appear on top of the other windows, or dock the window along the top, bottom, left, or right. Experiment!

    If you want to return to the default layout, choose *Tools / Options / Environment / General / Reset Window Layout.*

Set Options for Your Work

You can change many options in the VS IDE. Choose *Tools / Options* to display the *Options* dialog box. You may want to click on each of the categories to see the options that you can select.

    Note: If you are working in a shared lab, check with the instructor or lab technician before changing options.

Environment

General: If it isn't already set, you may want to set the *At startup* option to *Show Start Page.*

Dynamic Help: Set categories and topic types to limit the help available. See the note on the next page.

Projects and Solutions: Set the default folder for your projects. It's best to leave the *Build* and *Run* options to automatically save changes, but you may prefer to have a prompt or save them yourself.

Text Editor You can set options for all languages or for Basic, which is Visual Basic. The following presume that you first select Basic.

General: Make sure that *Auto list members* is selected and *Hide advanced members* is deselected. You may want to turn on *Word wrap*, so that long lines wrap to the next line instead of extending off the right edge of the screen.

Tabs: Choose *Smart* indenting; *Tab size* and *Indent size* should both be 4.

VB Specific: All three options should be selected.

Windows Forms Designer

Grid Settings: Notice that you can change the spacing of the grid dots, turn the grid on or off, and set the snap-to-grid option.

Turn Off Dynamic Help

Dynamic Help can be very useful; it displays a series of links that relate to the current operation. However, unless you have a very fast computer with lots of memory, the option can slow the IDE response time considerably. Try creating a project with Dynamic Help turned on and with it turned off to see what works best for you.

   Turn off Dynamic Help by closing its window; display it again by selecting *Help / Dynamic Help*. You also can adjust the number and types of links displayed in *Tools / Options / Environment / Dynamic Help*.

Use Shortcuts in the Form Designer

You can save time while creating the user interface in the Form Designer by using shortcuts.

Create Multiple Controls of the Same Type

When you want to create several controls of the same class, you must select the toolbox tool each time you draw a new control; that is, unless you use this method: When you select the toolbox tool for the first control, hold down the Ctrl key as you click. After you create the first new control, the tool stays selected so that you can create as many more controls of that class as you wish.

   When you are finished, click on the Pointer to deselect the tool, or click on another toolbox tool.

Use the Layout Toolbar

The Layout toolbar is great for working with multiple controls. You must have more than one control selected to enable many of the buttons. The same options are available from the *Format* menu.

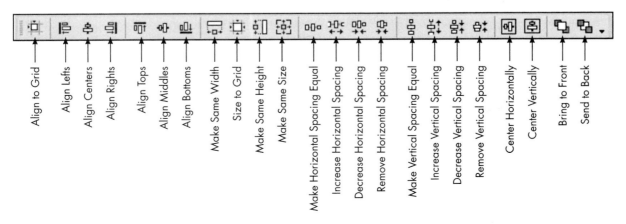

Nudge Controls into Place

Sometimes it is difficult to place controls exactly where you want them. Of course, you can use the alignment options of the *Format* menu or the Layout toolbar. You also can nudge controls in any direction by holding down the Ctrl key and pressing one of the arrow keys. Nudging moves a control one pixel in the direction you specify. For example: Ctrl + right arrow moves a selected control one pixel to the right.

Use Shortcuts in the Editor

Several features of the Editor can save you time while editing code.

Use the Text Editor Toolbar

By default the Text Editor toolbar displays when the Editor window is open.

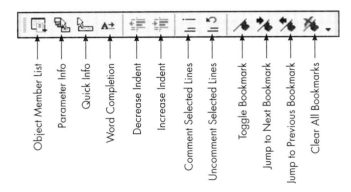

You can save yourself considerable time and trouble if you become familiar with and use some of these shortcuts.

Comment Selected Lines: Use this command when you want to convert some code to comments, especially while you are testing and debugging projects. You can remove some lines from execution to test the effect, without actually removing them. Select the lines and click the *Comment Selected Lines* button; each line will have an apostrophe appended at the left end.

Uncomment Selected Lines: This command undoes the *Comment Selected Lines* command. Select some comment lines and click the button; the apostrophes at the beginning of the lines are deleted.

Increase Indent and *Decrease Indent:* You can use these buttons to indent or outdent single lines or blocks of code. The buttons work the same as the Tab and Shift + Tab keys.

Toggle Bookmark: This button sets and unsets individual bookmarks. Bookmarks are useful when you are jumping around in the Editor window. Set a bookmark on any line by clicking in the line and clicking the *Toggle Bookmark* button; you will see a mark in the gray margin area to the left of the marked line. You may want to set bookmarks in several procedures where you are editing and testing code.

Jump to Next Bookmark and *Jump to Previous Bookmark:* Use these buttons to quickly jump to the next or previous bookmark in the code.

Clear All Bookmarks: You can clear individual bookmarks with the *Toggle Bookmark* button or clear all bookmarks using this button.

Object Member List, *Parameter Info*, and *Quick Info:* Generally these IntelliSense options are turned on and the information pops up automatically. You might prefer to keep these options turned off (*Tools / Options / Text Editor*) and click the buttons when you actually want the lists to appear.

Word Completion: This is a good one! Try clicking the *Word Completion* button as you are typing the name of an object or a variable. If you have typed enough for the editor to identify the word, it will automatically fill in the rest when you press Enter or another character such as a space bar or equal sign. Or better yet, use one of the keyboard shortcuts: Ctrl + Spacebar or Alt + right arrow.

Use Keyboard Shortcuts When Editing Code

While you are editing code, save yourself time by using keyboard shortcuts.

Task	Shortcut
Delete the current line (insertion point anywhere in the line).	Ctrl + L
Delete from the insertion point left to the beginning of the word.	Ctrl + Backspace
Delete from the insertion point right to the end of the word.	Ctrl + Delete
Complete the word.	Ctrl + Spacebar *or* Alt + right arrow
Jump to a procedure (insertion point on procedure name). Use this shortcut while working on the sub procedures and functions that you write. For example, when writing a call to a function, you might want to check the coding in the function. Point to the procedure name in the `Call` and press F12. If you want to return to the original position, set a bookmark before the jump.	F12
Jump to the top of the current code module.	Ctrl + Home
Jump to the bottom of the current module.	Ctrl + End
Indent a block of code.	Select the lines and use the Tab key or the *Increase Indent* toolbar button
Outdent (decrease indent) a block of code.	Select the lines and use the Shift + Tab keys or the *Decrease Indent* toolbar button
View the form's Designer window.	Shift + F7
Return to the Editor window.	F7

You will find that most of the editing and selecting keyboard shortcuts for Microsoft Word also work in the Editor window.

Split the Editor Window

You can view more than one section of code at a time by splitting the Editor window. Point to the Split bar at the top of the vertical scroll bar and drag the bar down to the desired location. To remove the split, you can either drag the split bar back to the top or double-click the split bar.

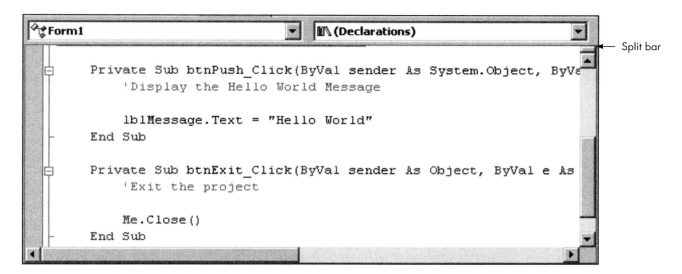

Split bar

Use Drag-and-Drop Editing

You can use drag-and-drop to move or copy text to another location in the Editor window or to another project. To move code, select the text, point to the selection, and drag it to a new location. You can copy text (rather than move it) by holding down the Ctrl key as you drag.

Use the Task List

The Task List displays error messages after your program is compiled. This makes sense—your tasks are to fix each of the errors. You also can add items to the task list as a reminder to yourself, so that you don't forget to do something. A very easy way to add items to the Task List is to write a comment in your code with the TODO keyword.

```
'TODO Come back here and write this code.
'TODO Check on this.
```

You also can add tasks to the Task List by clicking at the top of the list; this creates a new line where you can enter text. If the Task List is filtered, as shown in its title bar, select *View / Show Tasks* and choose *All*.

Use the Class View Window

The Class View window shows your project in a hierarchical tree view. You can view the classes, objects, event procedures, general procedures, and variables in your projects. You can view the declaration of the various symbols and jump directly to locations in your code.

Each type of object displays with a different symbol. In addition, the symbols may display signal icons that indicate the object's accessibility, such as Public, Private, Protected, or Friend.

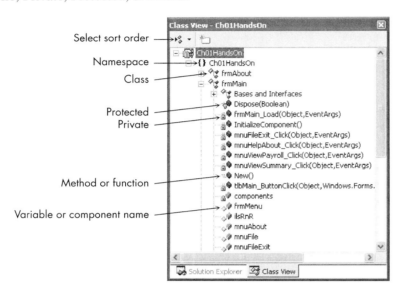

You can jump to the definition of any symbol in the Editor window. This is especially helpful for jumping to procedures in a large project. Point to the name of an event procedure, such as btnCalculate_Click; then double-click, or right-click and select *Go To Definition* from the shortcut menu. If you choose to go to a definition that is in your code, the Editor window opens (if necessary) and the insertion point appears on the selected line. If you choose to go to a definition that is in another class, the Object Browser opens with that symbol selected.

Use the Object Browser

The Visual Studio Object Browser can be a valuable source of information. You can use the Object Browser to examine namespaces, objects, properties, methods, events, and constants for your project and for all Visual Studio namespaces. Use the *Find Symbol* button to look up any symbol that you want to examine.

The Object Browser and the Class View window use the same symbols and signal icons.

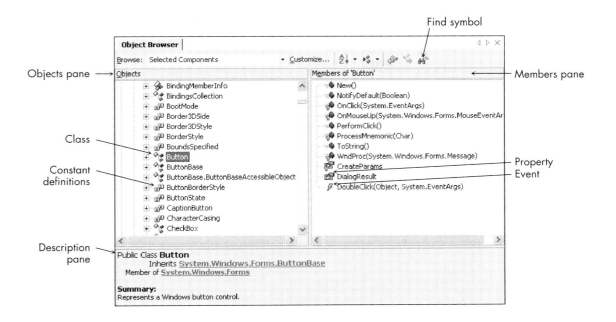

Use Context-Sensitive Help

The quickest way to get Help is to use context-sensitive Help. Click on a control or a line of code and press F1; Help displays the closest matching item it can locate. You also can get help on the IDE elements: Click in any area of the IDE and press Shift + F1; the Help explanation will be about using the current window or IDE element, rather than about the objects and language.

Use the Debugging Tools

The VS IDE provides many tools to help you debug programs. The most helpful techniques are to examine the values of variables during program execution and to single-step through the program and watch what happens.

The Debug Toolbar and Menu

You can use the *Debug* menu or the tools on the Debug toolbar for debugging. The Debug toolbar appears automatically during run time, or you can display the toolbar by right-clicking any toolbar and selecting *Debug*. The most useful items for debugging your programs are shown in the following table.

Menu command or Toolbar button	Purpose	Keyboard shortcut
Start	Begin debug execution.	F5
Continue	Continue execution. (Available at break time only.)	F5
Start Without Debugging	Begin execution without invoking the debugger. This option can make a program run sometimes when it won't run with *Start*.	Ctrl + F5
Stop Debugging	Stop execution of a program.	Shift + F5
Step Into	Execute the next statement; steps into any called sub procedures or functions. (Available at break time only.)	F11
Step Over	Execute the next statement; rapidly executes any calls to sub procedures or functions without stepping. (Available at break time only.)	F10
Step Out	Rapidly finish the current procedure; reenter break time when the procedure finishes.	Shift + F11

Set Breakpoints

You can set breakpoints in code, which cause execution to halt on the marked statement. After setting a breakpoint, begin execution as usual. When the breakpoint line becomes current, the program halts, enters break time, and displays the code with the current line highlighted (as the *next* statement to execute).

To set a breakpoint, use the *Debug* menu, the Debug toolbar, a keyboard shortcut (Ctrl + B), or the easiest way: Place the mouse pointer in the gray margin indicator area at the left edge of the Editor window and click; the line will be highlighted in red and a large red dot will display in the margin indicator.

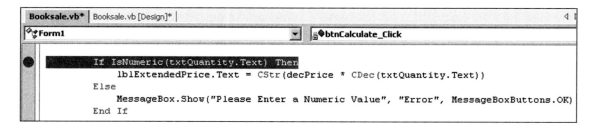

View the Contents of Expressions

At break time you can view the current values of expressions in several ways. The three most useful techniques are

1. Display the value in a ToolTip-like popup in the Editor window. Point to the variable or expression that you want to view and pause; the current value pops up in a label. If you want to view the contents of an expression of more than one word, such as a condition or arithmetic expression,

highlight the entire expression and point to the highlighted area; the current value will display.

```
'Calculate summary values
mintQuantitySum += intQuantity
mdecDiscountSum += decDisc intQuantity = 10
mdecDiscountedPriceSum += decDiscountedPrice
mintSaleCount += 1
decAverageDiscount = mdecDiscountSum / mintSaleCount
```

2. Use the Locals window, which displays all objects and variables that are within scope at break time. You also can expand the Me entry to see the state of the form's controls.

Locals			⊡ ×
Name	Value	Type	
⊞ Me	{Project1.frmBookSale}	Project1.frmBookSale	
⊞ eventSender	{System.Windows.Forms.Button}	Object	
⊞ eventArgs	{System.EventArgs}	System.EventArgs	
decAverageDiscount	0D	Decimal	
decDiscount	19.425D	Decimal	
decDiscountedPrice	110.075D	Decimal	
decExtendedPrice	129.5D	Decimal	
decPrice	12.95D	Decimal	
intQuantity	10	Integer	

Autos | Locals | Watch 1

3. Use the Autos window, which "automatically" displays all variables and control contents that are referenced in the current statement and three statements on either side of the current one.

```
'Calculate summary values
mintQuantitySum += intQuantity
mdecDiscountSum += decDiscount
mdecDiscountedPriceSum += decDiscountedPrice
mintSaleCount += 1
decAverageDiscount = mdecDiscountSum / mintSaleCount
```

Autos			⊡ ×
Name	Value	Type	
decAverageDiscount	0D	Decimal	
decDiscount	19.425D	Decimal	
decDiscountedPrice	110.075D	Decimal	
decExtendedPrice	129.5D	Decimal	
intQuantity	10	Integer	
mdecDiscountSum	0D	Decimal	
mdecDiscountedPriceSum	0D	Decimal	
mintQuantitySum	10	Integer	
mintSaleCount	0	Integer	

Autos | Locals | Watch 1

Single-Step through Code

The best way to debug a project is to thoroughly understand what the project is doing every step of the way. Use the Visual Studio stepping tools to trace program execution line by line and see the progression of the program as it executes through your code.

You step through code at break time. Set a breakpoint or choose one of the stepping commands at design time; the program will begin running and immediately transfer to break time.

The three stepping commands are *Step Into*, *Step Over*, and *Step Out*. These commands force the project to execute a single line at a time and to display the Editor window with the current statement highlighted. As you execute the project, by pressing a command button, for example, the Click event occurs. Execution transfers to the click procedure, the Editor window for that procedure appears on the screen, and you can follow line-by-line execution.

Most likely you will use the *Step Into* command more than the other two stepping commands. When you choose *Step Into*, the next line of code executes and the program pauses again in break time. If the line of code is a call to another procedure, the first line of code of the other procedure displays.

To continue stepping through your program execution, continue choosing the *Step Into* command. When a procedure is completed, your form will display again, awaiting an event. You can click on one of the form's buttons to continue stepping through code in an event procedure. If you want to continue execution without stepping, choose the *Continue* command.

The *Step Over* command also executes one line of code at a time. But when your code calls another procedure, *Step Over* displays only the lines of code in the current procedure being analyzed; it does not display lines of code in the called procedures.

You use the *Step Out* command when you are stepping through a called procedure. It continues rapid execution until the called procedure completes, and then returns to break mode at the statement following the Call. When you have seen what you want to see, continue rapid execution by choosing the *Continue* command (F5). If you want to restart execution from the beginning, choose the *Restart* command (Shift + F5).

Write to the Output Window

You can place a Debug.WriteLine method in your code. In the argument you can specify a message to write or an object that you want tracked.

```
Debug.WriteLine(TextString)
Debug.WriteLine(Object)

Debug.WriteLine("btnCalculate procedure entered.")
Debug.WriteLine(txtQuantity.Text)
```

When the Debug.WriteLine method executes, its output appears in the Output window. New to the VS IDE, you can clear the Output window. Right-click in the window and choose *Clear All*.

An advantage of using WriteLine, rather than the other debugging techniques, is that you do not have to break program execution.

Copy and Move Projects

In a programming class, you often must move projects from one computer to another, and must base one project on another one. To create a new project based on a previous one, you should copy the project. Then you can move it as necessary.

Windows projects that do not connect to a database file are very easy to copy and move. The problems occur for Web projects and database projects.

Copy and Move a Windows Project

You can copy an entire Windows project folder from one location to another using Windows Explorer or My Computer. Make sure that the project is not open in Visual Studio and copy the entire folder.

To base one project on a previous project:

* Make sure the project is not open.

* Copy the folder to a new location using Windows Explorer or My Computer.

* Rename the new folder for the new project name, still using Windows Explorer or My Computer.

* Open the new project (the copy) in the Visual Studio IDE.

* In the IDE's Solution Explorer, rename the solution and the project. The best way to do this is to right-click on the name and choose the *Rename* command from the shortcut menu.

* Rename the forms, if desired. If you rename the startup form, you must open the *Project Properties* dialog box and set the Startup Object.

Warning: Do not try to copy a project that is open using the *Save As* command, attempting to place a copy in a new location. The original solution and project files are modified and you won't be able to open the original project.

Copy and Move a Web Project

If you plan to copy and/or move a Web project, it's best to explicitly save the solution file in the same folder as the project. By default, VB creates two folders for your Web projects: one in Inetpub\wwwroot and one in your default location for project files. If you save the solution file in the same folder as the rest of the project (in Inetpub\wwwroot), then you can delete or ignore the second project folder.

You can copy a Web project and make it run on another computer, but it takes a few steps to make it happen:

1. Copy the entire folder using Windows Explorer or My Computer and store it in Inetpub\wwwroot on the destination machine.
2. Create a virtual directory for the project folder:
   a. Open Internet Information Services Manager. The procedure can vary a little depending on your operating system and settings, but these steps should be close: Select *Start / Settings / Control Panel / Administrative Tools / Internet Information Services.*
   b. Expand the node for the computer and the default Web site to view the folders. Notice that the icon for the new folder is different from the existing virtual directories.
   c. Right-click the new folder and choose *Properties.*
   d. In the *Directory* tab of the *Properties* dialog box, click on the *Create* button. By default your folder name is used for the *Application Name* entry. Accept the defaults and click *OK.*

3. Open the project in the VS IDE and select the startup page: In the Solution Explorer, right-click on the file for the Web form (.aspx extension) and choose *Set as start page* from the shortcut menu.

After these steps, your relocated project should run. If you attempt to run and receive a message saying that it cannot debug your project, it means that you didn't create the virtual directory (step 2).

Rename a Copied Web Project

Renaming a Web project is a bit tricky because the complete path name is stored in the solution file (.sln) and the vbproj.webinfo file. If your project folder *does* contain a solution file, you must edit that file; if you don't have a solution file, you must edit the vbproj.webinfo file.

If you are copying and renaming a folder for a Web project, first copy and rename the folder. Then create the virtual directory (see step 2 in the preceding section). Next you must edit the solution or webinfo file before you can open the project in the VS IDE.

Both the solution file and webinfo file are text files that you can edit in any text editor, such as Notepad. Open the solution file and edit the line that holds the complete path name, changing the folder name to your new folder name. Do not attempt to rename the project in this file—that's easily done in the Solution Explorer after you open the project in the IDE.

For example, here are the first few lines of a solution file:

```
Microsoft Visual Studio Solution File, Format Version 7.00
Project("{F184B08F-C81C-45F6-A57F-5ABD9991F28F}") = "ch09webhello",
"http://localhost/mywebhello/ch09webhello.vbproj",
"{E6383E11-9A84-4BCC-A6A3-988277DD146F}"
EndProject
```

Change only the folder name, taking care to not change anything else:

```
"http://localhost/myNewwebhello/ch09webhello.vbproj"
```

Save the file. It must be a text file; do not save as a Word document, or it will save lots of formatting codes, which will keep the project from running.

If your project folder does not contain a solution file, open and edit the vbproj.webinfo file. You will find a similar line with the complete path that you can modify.

Note: It isn't necessary to modify both the solution and webinfo file. If you have both, edit only the solution file.

Delete a Web Project

You can delete a Web project, but it takes a few steps. You must first remove the virtual directory using IIS Manager. (Follow the earlier instructions for creating a virtual directory, but click *Remove* on the *Virtual Directory* tab of the *Properties* dialog box.) After you remove the virtual directory, you still cannot delete the folder using Windows Explorer or My Computer until after you re-boot the computer or stop and restart IIS.

Move a Database Project

The problem with moving a database project is that the Connection object is tied to a physical file that includes the file's path. There are several ways that you can make the project portable, however. These instructions are for the sample SQL Server files, such as pubs and Northwind, that exist on the destination computer as well as the source computer. (Instructions for installing the sample files are in Appendix C.)

You can use any one of the following techniques; the recommended choice is to use a dynamic property for the connection string.

1. **Reset the ConnectionString property of the Connection object**: In the Properties window for the Connection object, click on the value for ConnectionString; a drop-down arrow will appear. Drop down the list and choose the connection for the desired database. If no connection exists, choose the *New Connection* option. Once you reset the ConnectionString for the Connection object, the data adapters and datasets should work without any modification.

2. **Change the ConnectionString to a generic connection**: After you have the Connection, Data Adapter, and Dataset objects working correctly, but before you move the project, you can modify the connection string to work on any computer. Use this statement for the pubs database (or modify it for Northwind):

```
server=(local)\NetSDK;Trusted_Connection=yes;database=pubs
```

This connection string should work on any computer that has the pubs sample database installed. However, if you need to reconfigure the data adapter, you will have to reset the connection string to use a connection that is set up for your specific machine.

3. **Use a dynamic property for the connection string**: After you have set up the Connection, Data Adapter, and Dataset objects, select the Connection object, scroll to the top of the Properties window, and expand the node for *(Dynamic Properties)*. Click on ConnectionString and its build button (...). Select the box to map the property to a key in the configuration file. This step creates a new entry in App.config for Windows projects or in Web.config for Web projects.

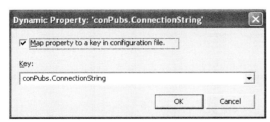

Open App.config or Web.config, scroll to the AppSettings tag, and modify the connection string to contain the generic connection string:

```
<appSettings>
  <!- User application and configured property settings go here.->
  <!- Example: <add key="settingName" value="settingValue"/> ->
  <add key="conPubs.ConnectionString"
    value="server=(local)\NetSDK;Trusted_Connection=yes;database=pubs"/>
</appSettings>
```

Using this technique can be the best solution. The dynamic connection string is used at run time. If you need to modify the data adapter and dataset, you can easily use technique 1 above to point to the local connection, but the program should run on any computer that you move it to without modification.

Make a Web Database Update Program Run

Web applications that display database data can usually run just fine, but Web applications that update the data can have problems with security and permissions. Many options exist for setting up networks, Windows, SQLServer, and IIS. See "Database Security for Web Applications" in Chapter 8, page 294, for a technique that should work on most systems.

Glossary

A

abstract class Used only to create derived classes; cannot have an object instantiated from the class.

abstraction A model of an object, for the purpose of determining the characteristics (properties) and the behaviors (methods) of the object.

AcceptChanges method Resets a dataset to indicate that no changes have been made. Usually used after an Update method, which commits the changes to the original data source.

accessibility (classes, variables, and procedures) Used to determine which classes can use the element. Examples: Public, Private, Protected, Friend, and Protected Friend.

accessibility (software) Program design that allows a disabled person to use your application.

action queries SQL statement that performs an action on the data in the database, such as updating, deleting, or adding records.

Active Server Pages (ASP) A platform for developing server-based Web applications.

ActiveX Data Objects (ADO) .NET A standard set of objects that Visual Studio programmers can use to retrieve and modify data from any source.

AddNew method Used to begin the Add operation for adding a new record to the dataset.

AdRotator control A Web control that randomly selects from a collection of advertisements each time the page is displayed.

AllowPaging property Adds pagination to a DataGrid Web control.

AllowSorting property Allows the user to sort the data grid by clicking on a column heading.

Application object Stores state information as long as the application is running.

assembly A basic unit of code that may be a single PE file or multiple files; built and deployed as a single implementation unit.

assembly manifest A file that contains metadata about the version, a table describing all of the files needed by the assembly, and a reference list that specifies all of the external files needed, such as DLLs created by someone else.

Assembly object Instantiated in an application; used to retrieve assembly attributes.

attribute tags Predefined words that appear in angle brackets (<Word>) to specify metadata. Examples: <WebService> and <WebMethod()>.

attributes See *attribute tags*.

author The programmer that creates the control used by the developer.

B

base class The parent class of the current class, from which the current class is inherited.

BindingContext class object Manages the collection of BindingManagerBase objects.

BindingManagerBase object Responsible for assuring that all bound controls on a form display data from the same row. Keeps track of the current row of the dataset.

block-level scope A variable that is visible and accessible only within the block of code in which it is declared.

business rules The logic performed by an application, including validation, calculations, and updating rules.

business tier One segment of a multitier application; the class or classes that perform the business rules.

Button A control that the user can click to perform an action. Windows Button control: fires a Click event; Web Button control: fires a Click event and causes a Postback to occur.

C

CancelCurrentEdit method Cancels the current edit or add and returns to the original version of the data.

Capacity property   Sets or retrieves the size of an ArrayList.

cascading deletes   When you delete a parent record, all child records for that parent are automatically deleted.

cascading updates   Updates all related child records when the primary key field of the parent is modified.

CheckBoxList control   A Web control that displays a group of check boxes in a list box.

child class   An inherited class. Also called a *subclass* or *derived class.*

child table   The "many" table in a 1:M relationship in a relational database.

collection   An object used to hold and manage the references to a group of related objects.

column   Used to store a single element of a row in a table. Also called a *field.*

Command object   Holds an SQL statement or stored-procedure name that will be used to retrieve or modify the data in the data source.

CommandName property Holds a text string that determines the procedure to execute when that Web control is clicked.

common language runtime (CLR)   Manages the execution of managed code developed for the .NET Framework.

Common Language Specification (CLS)   Standards that specify how a language that interacts with the CLR should be formed and should behave.

composite control   New user control created by combining individual controls.

concurrency   An issue that arises when more than one user can update the same file.

concurrency control   The process of handling conflicts in updates by multiple users.

Connection object   A link to a data source.

constituent control   The individual controls that are used to create a composite control.

constructor   A method that automatically executes when an object is instantiated; the New method.

context-sensitive Help Displays the Help topic that concerns the current element; triggered by placing the pointer on or clicking in an element and pressing F1.

Count property   Retrieves the number of elements in a table or collection.

criteria   The condition used in the WHERE clause of an SQL statement to specify which rows should be retrieved or modified; also used for the RowFilter property of a DataView.

Crystal Reports   A feature included in VS .NET that allows you to easily generate database reports.

CrystalReportViewer   A control that is added to a form to display a report.

culture/locale   A set of rules that contains information about a specific language and culture; includes specifications for numeric formatting. Used for localization.

CultureInfo class   Provides access to culture-specific information.

Current property   A property of the BindingManagerBase that returns the current row.

CurrentChanged event   An event of the BindingManagerBase; fires when a bound value is changed.

CurrentPageIndex property Holds the index of the current page being displayed in a Web DataGrid.

D

data structure   A grouping of related variables; declared with Structure / End Structure statements.

data tier   One segment of a multitier application; the class or classes that retrieve and store the data in a database.

DataAdapter object   Handles the retrieving and updating of the data in a DataSet object.

DataBind method   Required by Web projects to fill bound controls.

DataBindings object   The property of a control that will bind that control to a single data field.

DataGrid control   A Windows or Web control that displays data in rows and columns. The Web version allows for features such as pagination.

DataList control   A Web control used to display data using a template for the rows; the row template may contain controls such as labels, images, and hyperlinks.

DataReader object   Provides a forward-only result set from a data source.

DataRelation object　An object that describes the relationship between the tables in a relational database.

DataSet object　Holds a copy of the data in memory, disconnected from the data source. May contain multiple tables, relationships, and constraints.

DataSource property　Used for binding to connect a control to a dataset.

DataTable object　A single table that holds data in rows and columns; may be a member of the DataTables collection of a DataSet object.

delegate　Assigns the procedure to run when the specified event occurs.

DELETE FROM　SQL statement used to delete records from a data source.

Dequeue method　Used to remove an item from a Queue list.

derived class　An inherited class. Also called a *subclass* or *child class.*

destructor　A method that automatically executes when an object is destroyed. In .NET, the `Dispose` method is the destructor, which executes at an indeterminate time, whenever garbage collection occurs.

detail table　The child table in a master/detail or parent/child relationship in a relational database.

Details　The section of a Crystal Reports object that holds the data for the individual lines in the body of the report.

developer　The programmer who writes an application that incorporates controls; as opposed to the author that creates the controls.

Dictionary　A type of collection that consists of key and value pairs.

DictionaryEntry data type　The type of a single entry in a dictionary collection.

DisplayMember property　For the various list controls, determines the field name for the data to display in the list.

.dll file　Dynamic link library file, which holds executable code; used for Web projects.

dynamic connection string　The ConnectionString property is determined at run time, based on a key in the config file (App.config or Web.config).

E

encapsulation　The combination of characteristics of an object along with its behaviors.

EndCurrentEdit method　Ends the current edit for a grid control.

Enqueue method　Used to add items to a Queue list.

enum　The key word used to create an enumeration.

enumeration　A list of constant values, which must be one of the integer data types.

event consumer　The object that responds to a raised event. Also called *event sink.*

event handler　A procedure that executes automatically when an event occurs.

event provider　An object that generates or raises an event. Also called *event source.*

event sink　The object that responds to a raised event. Also called *event consumer.*

event source　An object that generates or raises an event. Also called *event provider.*

Event statement　Must appear at the module level in order for your class to raise an event.

ExecuteNonQuery method　Executes an action SQL command.

F

Field Explorer　A section of the toolbox that displays while Crystal Reports is active; holds elements that can be added to a report.

fields　The elements represented in columns of a table; also used to refer to variables.

FIFO　First-in, first-out. The organization used to store items in a Queue.

FindByText method　Finds a specific text string in the Items collection of a DataList control.

FindByValue method　Finds a specific entry in a DataList based on the Value property rather than the text being displayed.

foreign key　The field in a child table that links a record to the corresponding record in the parent table.

foreign key constraints　Ensures that if the primary key in the parent table is modified or deleted that the corresponding record(s) in the child table are modified to match.

G

garbage collection　The process in which the .NET Framework destroys unused objects and reclaims memory.

GetChanges method   Used to retrieve only the rows with the specified row state.

GetChildRows method   Retrieves an array of rows that are linked to the parent row.

GetParentRow method   Retrieves the parent row of a child row.

globalization   Designing your application for multiple languages, cultures, and locations.

Group Footer   A section of a Crystal Reports object that appears at the end of each group and generally displays subtotals.

Group Header   A section of a Crystal Reports object that appears in the report at the top of a new group, based on the field that you selected for grouping.

H

HasChanges method   Used to determine if any changes have been made to a DataSet.

hash table   The fastest type of collection for searching. Based on a key/value pair where the key is calculated using an algorithm.

Help topic   A single HTML page in HTML Help; each screen that displays in the Contents pane.

Help Viewer   Part of the HTML Help Workshop that provides a way to view Help topics, screens, and HTML references.

HelpKeyword property   A property of a control that appears when a HelpProvider is added to the form; used to specify the exact topic to display.

HelpNamespace property   A property of a HelpProvider control; specifies the path and name of the Help file.

HelpNavigator property   A property of a control that appears when a HelpProvider is added to the form; used to specify the page to display, such as Table of Contents, Index, or Topic.

HelpProvider component   Used to display Help files in your application. Adding the component to a form adds new Help properties to the controls on the form.

HelpString property   An actual string of text to display for popup Help.

HTML Help ActiveX control   Used for adding navigation to an HTML page. Add the control to a page in the HTML Help Workshop.

HTML Help Image Editor   A separate application used for creating screen shots and working with images.

HTML Help Workshop   A separate application used to create Help files for an application.

Hyperlink   A Web control used to navigate to another Web page.

I

identifier   The name for a variable, field, object, or procedure; supplied by the programmer.

ImageButton   A Web button control that can display a graphic.

IndexOf method   Used to find the index of a specific ListItem.

inheritance   Derive a new class from an existing class. The new class has all of the public and protected properties and methods of the existing class.

INSERT INTO   An SQL statement used to insert a new record into a data source.

intranet   A network within a company.

ItemCommand event   Fires when a control in a Web DataList or DataGrid is clicked.

Items collection   The collection of related objects in a single object or control such as a ListBox.

ItemTemplate   Determines how the data for each row should appear in a DataList.

J

junction table   A third table used to link two tables in a many-to-many relationship.

L

lifetime   The length of time that a variable exists.

LIFO   Last-in, first-out; the technique used to store items in a stack.

LinkButton   A Web control that looks like a hyperlink but functions like a button and fires a click event.

list   A collection of related objects.

ListItem object   A single object from the Items collection of a Web list box control.

Literal control   A Web control that allows you to add HTML to a page at run time.

localizability   A setting of a form that allows an application to be localized; the resources that must be localized are separated from the code that does not change.

localization   The actual process of translating the interface for a culture/locale.

M

managed code   Code that is compiled to run in the CLR.

managed data Data that are managed by the CLR during run time.

many-to-many relationships A relationship between tables in a relational database in which multiple records in one table can be related to multiple records in the second table.

master table The primary table in a relational database. The "one side" of a one-to-many relationship. Also called the *parent table*.

metadata Data that describe data. For example, attributes that describe an application, such as <WebService> or <WebMethod>.

Microsoft Data Engine (MSDE) The personal desktop version of SQL Server, which is included with the .NET Framework.

Microsoft intermediate language (MSIL) A platform-independent set of compiled instructions that is combined with the metadata to form a file called a portable executable (PE) file.

Microsoft Mobile Internet Toolkit (MMIT) A set of classes that you can download and add to VS .NET; allows you to easily create applications for mobile devices.

module A section of code defined by Module / End Module statements. Also used to refer to a single .vb file.

module-level scope A Private variable that is declared inside any class, structure, or module, but outside of any sub procedure or function. Can be used in any procedure of the current class or module.

multitier application An application that separates the functions of an application into multiple classes; separating the user interface from the business logic from the database access.

N

namespace A way of organizing classes, interfaces, and structures into groups. Any Public class or identifier in any one namespace must be unique. To qualify the name of an item, include the complete namespace designation, such as System.Web.UI.WebControls.

namespace scope A variable, constant, class, or structure declared with the Public modifier. The identifier can be used in any procedure within the namespace, usually the entire application.

NavigateUrl property A property of a Web control that determines the address of the page to navigate to when the user clicks on the control.

.NET Framework A set of class library files that provides for developing and running Windows applications, Web applications, and XML Web Services written in multiple languages on multiple platforms.

.NET Framework class library The files that hold the classes and interfaces that form the .NET Framework.

O

ObjectList control Used to display database information on a mobile Web form.

OLEDB Microsoft's technology designed to implement the concept of Universal Data Access (UDA).

OleDbClient The .NET Framework managed provider that is to be used with any database format.

one-to-many relationship In a relational database, one record in the parent table may be related to many records in a child table.

one-to-one relationship In a relational database, one record in the parent table relates to only one record in the child table.

overloading When two methods have the same name but a different argument list.

Overridable The keyword used in the base class to allow a method in a derived class to override (replace) the method from the superclass.

override A method in a derived class that is used instead of the method in the base class that has the same name. An overriding method must have the same argument list as the method in the base class.

P

Page Footer A section of a Crystal Reports object that will appear at the bottom of each page of a report and generally contains the page number.

Page Header A section of a Crystal Reports object that will appear at the top of each page and generally holds the report title and column headings.

parameterized constructor A constructor (New method) that requires arguments.

parameterized query A query in which a wild card is used in place of hard-coded criteria so that the value can be specified at run time.

parent class The original class that can be inherited to create a

child class. Also called a *superclass* or *base class.*

parent table The primary table in a relational database. The "one side" of a one-to-many relationship. Also called a *master table.*

Peek method Used to look at the last item in a stack or queue without removing it.

PlaceHolder control A Web control that allows you to add controls to the page at run time.

polymorphism Refers to method names having identical names but different implementations depending on the current object or the arguments supplied.

Pop method Used to remove an item from a stack list.

populate Fill a DataSet object with data from a data source.

Position property A property of the binding manager of a form that holds the current row number.

PositionChanged event An event of the binding manager of a form; fires when a user navigates to another record.

presentation tier The segment of a multitier application that provides the user interface.

primary key field The field (or combination of fields) that uniquely identifies each record.

procedure-level scope The scope of any variable that you declare inside a procedure or function, but not within a block. The variable can be used only inside that procedure.

property procedure Procedures that expose the private properties of a class.

Push method Used to add an item to a stack list.

Q

queue An unsorted collection in which the first element in is the first out (FIFO).

R

RadioButtonList control A Web control that can display a group of RadioButtons in a list box.

RaiseEvent statement Raises (or fires) an event; must appear in the same module as the Event declaration in order for your control class to raise an event.

ReadOnly The modifier used in a property procedure to create a property that can be returned but not changed.

record The data for one item, person, or transaction. Also known as a *row.*

reference object An object used to connect a Visual Basic project to external components. Found in the References node of the Solution Explorer.

reference type An identifier that refers to an object, such as a form. The identifier holds the address of the object; as opposed to a value type, which holds the actual value, such as a numeric variable.

referential integrity In a relational database, a constraint that requires that the keys of the records in a child table match keys in the parent table. If a record in the parent table is modified or deleted, the changes also must apply to the corresponding record(s) in the child table.

RejectChanges method Rolls back all changes that have been made to a dataset since it was created or the last `AcceptChanges` method executed.

RemoveAt method Deletes an item from a collection by index number.

Report Designer The design window in Crystal Reports; used to create and modify report templates.

Report Footer In Crystal Reports, the section of the report that appears once at the end of the report.

Report Header In Crystal Reports, the section of the report that appears one time at the beginning of the report.

Request object An object sent by the browser to the server; holds information about the current user, data entered by the user, and arguments for an HTTP request.

Response object An object returned by the server to the browser in an HTML page. Can be used to retrieve the cookies being held in the Request object.

Response.Redirect The method used to navigate to another Web page in code.

reusabillity The ability to reuse or obtain the functionality from one class when you have another similar situation; writing applications in components that can be used in more than one situation.

root namespace The primary namespace used by an application. By default, named the same as the application, but can be overridden with `Namespace` directives.

row The data for one item, person, or transaction. Also known as a *record.*

RowState property A property of a DataRow; indicates whether any changes have been made to the row.

S

scalability The ability of an application to handle an increase or decrease in the number of users and the number of servers.

scope The area of the program that can "see" and reference a variable, constant, or method. May be namespace-level, module-level, procedure-level, or block-level.

SELECT An SQL statement that selects and returns database data.

selection queries Queries that select data from a database and return the selected data to your program.

server Web applications: formats and sends Web pages to the client system.

Server.Transfer The method used to transfer to another Web page that is located on the same server.

Session object An object used for managing state in a Web application; holds data for the current user.

shadow Replaces the base-class method in the derived class, but not in any new classes derived from that class. A shadowing method need not have the same argument list as the base-class method.

shared property A property of a class that exists once for all instances of the class.

shared variable A variable of a class that exists once for all instances of the class; often used to accumulate totals.

ShowHelp method The method used to display a Help topic page from code.

ShowHelpIndex method Displays the Help files with the *Index* tab selected.

Simple Object Access Protocol (SOAP) Establishes a protocol for handling requests and responses including class names, method names, and parameters. Used to standardize object creation and calling sequences across platforms.

SortCommand event The event that fires when the user clicks the column header of a sortable data grid; the event procedure in which you place the code to sort and rebind to the data grid.

splash screen A form that displays first, while the rest of the application loads.

SQLClient The .NET Framework managed provider for use with SQL Server.

stack An unsorted collection in which the last element in is the first element out (LIFO).

state The current values of all variables and controls in a Web page.

stateless The state of the page is not saved. By default, HTML pages are stateless and techniques must be used to save the state.

Styles.css A cascading style sheet file; holds style information for formatting and positioning elements on a Web page.

subclass An inherited class. Also called a *child class* or *derived class*.

superclass May be inherited to create a subclass. Also called a *base class* or *parent class*.

System.Collections namespace Provides classes for several different types of collections.

T

table Data stored in rows and columns or records and fields.

thread A separate path of execution that allows a program to do more than one thing at a time.

throw an exception Generate an exception object to indicate that an error has occurred.

Throw statement Sends or "throws" an exception. A `Throw` statement in a `Catch` block sends any caught exceptions up a level.

Timer A Windows control that can fire an event at a specified interval.

TrimToSize method Used to reduce the size of an ArrayList to the number of elements that actually hold data.

U

unique constraint In a relational database, a constraint that specifies that a specific column cannot contain duplicate entries.

Universal Description, Discovery, and Integration (UDDI) Industry-standard dictionary service used to search for available Web services.

Universal Resource Identifier (URI) Uniquely identifies a resource on the Web.

UPDATE An SQL action query used to send updates for an individual record or a set of records to the data source.

Update method A method of a data adapter to transfer all changes in the dataset to the data source.

user control A new control developed by combining or inheriting existing controls.

V

validator control Controls for Web applications that can validate user input on the client side.

Value keyword In a `Property Set` procedure, used to refer to the incoming value for the property.

value type An identifier that holds the actual value of the object; as opposed to a reference type, which holds the address of an object.

ValueMember property A property of a bound Windows ListBox or ComboBox control; holds the field name of the data to return for a selected item. For example, the DisplayMember holds the data that display in the list (such as a string of text) and the ValueMember holds the record key that corresponds to the DisplayMember.

ViewState property An ASP.NET server control feature for storing state with the Web page.

W

Web document See *Web form.*

Web farm Many servers sharing the load to host Web sites.

Web form Used to create the user interface for a Web application. Also called a *Web document.*

Web method A Public procedure written in a Web service.

Web page An HTML representation of a display page for Web applications; used to create the user interface for a Web application.

Web reference A reference set in the Solution Explorer to allow the application to access a Web service.

Web server The computer/software needed to format and send HTML pages to a browser.

Web Services Description Language (WSDL) Specifications for describing Web services, including information about the names of the methods, the parameters that can be passed, and the values that are returned from the functions.

Web.config file Contains configuration settings for a Web application. Can be used to set security and permissions as well as dynamic properties such as connection strings.

Wireless Application Protocol (WAP) Used for transmissions on most cell phones instead of HTTP.

Wireless Markup Language (WML) Used by mobile devices to describe the display of information from the Web; replaces HTML for mobile devices.

WriteOnly The modifier used in a property procedure to create a property that can be set but not returned.

X

XML Extensible markup language. An industry-standard format for storing and transferring data in text using identifying tags.

XML Web Services Classes that are compiled and stored on the Web for use by other applications.

Index